THE JOURNALS AND
LETTERS OF
FANNY BURNEY

ALEXANDRE PIOCHARD D'ARBLAY

at the age of sixty

THE JOURNALS AND LETTERS OF
FANNY BURNEY
(MADAME D'ARBLAY)

VOLUME VIII

1815

LETTERS 835–934

Edited by

PETER HUGHES

with

JOYCE HEMLOW, ALTHEA DOUGLAS

and

PATRICIA HAWKINS

OXFORD

AT THE CLARENDON PRESS

1980

Oxford University Press, Walton Street, Oxford OX2 6DP

OXFORD   LONDON   GLASGOW
NEW YORK   TORONTO   MELBOURNE   WELLINGTON
KUALA LUMPUR   SINGAPORE   HONG KONG   TOKYO
DELHI   BOMBAY   CALCUTTA   MADRAS   KARACHI
NAIROBI   DAR ES SALAAM   CAPE TOWN

Published in the United States by
Oxford University Press, New York

© *Oxford University Press 1980*

British Library Cataloguing in Publication Data
Burney, Fanny
    The journals and letters of Fanny Burney
    (Madame d'Arblay)
    Vol. 8: 1815
    1. Burney, Fanny – Correspondence
    2. Burney, Fanny – Diaries
    I. Hughes, Peter
    823'.6   PR3316.A4Z/   78–40643
    ISBN 0–19–812507–0

Printed in Great Britain
at the University Press, Oxford
by Eric Buckley
Printer to the University

ACKNOWLEDGEMENTS

In addition to the many individuals and institutions whose help has made this edition possible, the following are those to whom I and this volume are especially indebted. For help in the various stages of reading and checking I am grateful to Lesley Abrams and Vicki Owen in Toronto and Martha Linke in Ithaca, where much of this work was done during a year spent as a Fellow of the Cornell Society for the Humanities at the generous invitation of the Society and of its Director, Professor Henry Guerlac. The staff of the Society and of the splendid Cornell library were unfailingly helpful. In the preparation of the notes I have been greatly helped by Stefanie Meier of the English Seminar at the University of Zürich.

The archival and textual research done for this volume would not have been possible without the resources and learned advice of the Berg Collection of the New York Public Library and of its Curator, Dr. Lola Szladits; the Archives de France, the Bibliothèque Nationale, and Bibliothèque Historique, all in Paris; the Service Historique de l'Armée at the Chateau de Vincennes; the Stadtarchiv in Trier and its Director, Dr. Laufner; the Algemeen Rijksarchief in The Hague and its Deputy Keeper, Mr. J. Fox; the Archives de la Ville de Bruxelles and the Archivist, Mlle Dr. Mina Martens; the Archives Générales du Royaume in Brussels and the General Archivist of the Kingdom, Dr. Carlos Wyffels; the Stadtarchiv-und-Wissenschaftliche Stadtbibliothek in Bonn and Stadtarchivinspektor Herr Körschner; the Zentralbibliothek in Zurich; the Berio Library in Genoa; the Beinecke Library at Yale and the Widener Library at Harvard; the Barrett Collection and staff of the Manuscripts Room of the British Museum, and the staff of the National Portrait Gallery.

Those to whom I am indebted in matters of identification and in particular problems of research include Cynthia and John Comyn, Olwen Hedley, Jean-Claude and Béatrice Bonne, John Baird, Robert Hume, George Falle, E. H. Buckle and the vicar of the parish church of St. Peter and St. Paul in Bromley, Kent, E. J. Davis, Archivist for the County of Buckingham, W. H.

Chaloner, Jill Bourdais de Charbonnière, Warren Derry, Lillian and Edward Bloom.

Other editors will know, and the reader should be told of the learning and zeal of the staff of the Burney Project at McGill University. I am especially grateful to Althea Douglas, Patricia Hawkins, and Gary Bowers. Through it all I have been encouraged, informed, and prodded by Joyce Hemlow, who has been my guide through the labyrinth of the Burney Papers she has done so much to gather, restore, and publish.

CONTENTS

LIST OF ILLUSTRATIONS

INTRODUCTION

ALTHOUGH the letters and journals in this volume cover the greater part of 1815, they chiefly concern the Hundred Days and their aftermath. Since this period was filled with false reports of real catastrophes, the modern reader of these letters, which both reflect and intensify the confusions of the time, will often need the explanations offered in the notes that follow. But the modern reader may want something else explained: the constant concealments and disguised meanings in the letters of Fanny Burney and her husband. On a practical level, the letters reflect the fact that the d'Arblays wrote under the well-founded fear that their letters might be intercepted and that they might themselves fall into the hands of Napoleon's troops or the Prussians. This helps to account for otherwise puzzling aspects. Most of the many veiled references and obliterations (though some of these were intended to remove merely drab or trivial material concerning the d'Arblays' recurrent complaints about money or health or their son Alexander's shortcomings) were meant to conceal dangerous revelations from prying and possibly accusing eyes.

This practice of camouflage became especially important after M. d'Arblay had taken up his thankless and hopeless task at Trèves. His attempts to recruit deserters to serve against Napoleon could by themselves have led to his execution in the event of capture. But he had in addition issued and signed a manifesto urging the overthrow of the new regime, an act that identified him to all the enemies of Louis XVIII. These in-included not only Napoleon and his followers but also the Prussians, many of whom considered France and the entire French people to be their enemy. An influential faction in Prussian military and political circles, a faction that dominated their vociferous propaganda service, even advocated the dismemberment of France and its extinction as a European power. These attitudes were restrained by the more moderate policies of England, Austria, and Russia. But they were shared by many of the Prussians that d'Arblay had to deal with at Trèves; their commander von Kleist was a pleasant exception to a rule of neglect and even hostility. We know from letters exchanged between the Prussians with whom his mission brought him into contact that many considered him to be more an enemy agent than an ally (L. 871 n. 5). The attitudes that d'Arblay had to contend with have in fact a disturbingly modern ring to them, a foreshadowing of the policies of total war, unconditional surrender, and racial hatred that have marked conflicts in the twentieth century. Their influence and menace were a further source of inhibition and strain in the letters of the late spring and summer months.

By 1815 this need to write in parables and prudent evasions had become second nature to the d'Arblays and helps to explain some relations between private and public life, letters and literature that have hitherto gone unnoticed or neglected. Mme de Staël, their old acquaintance from the *émigré* days in England, was the first to perceive that all aspects of literary expression had become historical through the intrusion of history into everyday life and thought during the period of the French Revolution and the Napoleonic Wars. As René Girard has put it: 'Mme de Staël did not simply add to the discourse on literature the *theme* of history. She was the first to grasp *all* themes historically.'[1] Fanny Burney never developed a theory comparable to those of her old acquaintance from Juniper Hall. But her letters from this period and her novel *The Wanderer* offer striking evidence for this new sense of history's pervasion of even the workings of the imagination and the structures of fiction. Even though the dedicatory preface to her last novel *The Wanderer* defines the novel as 'a picture of supposed, but natural and probable human existence',[2] the work itself suggests that historical upheaval meant a picture had to be cast in the form of an allegory or parable. The wanderings of its heroine Juliet can be understood as an allegory of M. d'Arblay's exile in England. There can be little doubt that prudence and fear of reprisal occasioned Fanny Burney's discreet near-silence about her life under Napoleon. Although she asserted in this same preface 'during the ten eventful years, from 1802 to 1812, that I

---

[1] 'Critical Reflections on Literary Studies' in *Velocities of Change*, ed. Richard Macksey (Baltimore, 1974), pp. 72–88.
[2] *The Wanderer; or, Female Difficulties*. By the author of *Evelina*; *Cecilia*; and *Camilla* (5 vols., 1814), i, p. xvi.

resided in the capital of France, I was neither startled by any species of investigation, nor distressed through any difficulties of conduct',[1] a revealing letter in the present volume makes it plain that this security was bought at the price of self-denial and self-censorship. Writing to her old friend Georgiana Mary Ann Port Waddington, then still an admirer of Napoleon, Fanny, perhaps heartened by the recent and decisive events of the Waterloo campaign, for once wrote openly:

How is it that my ever dear Mary can thus on one side be fascinated by the very thing that, on the other, revolts her? how be a professed & ardent detester of Tyranny; yet an open & intrepid admirer of a Tyrant? O had you spent, like me, 10 years within the control of his unlimited power, & under the iron rod of its dread, how would you change your language! by a total reverse of sentiment! yet was I, because always, innoffensive, never molested: as safe There, *another* would say, as in London; but *you* will not say so; the safety of deliberate prudence, or of retiring timidity, is not such as would satisfy a mind glowing for freedom like your's: it satisfies, indeed, NO *mind*, it merely suffices for *bodily* security. It was the choice of my Companion, not of my Taste that drew ME to such a residence. (L. 908)

The only alternative to this stifled withdrawal and inner exile after Napoleon's return was the further exile and flight of the Hundred Days. In living through and bearing witness to this predicament, the d'Arblays and their letters offer a touching and important 'picture of . . . human existence', a picture of a human condition that we have since come to recognize as part of the nightmare of history. Later in the letter just quoted this condition of exile and rootless ambition is described with bleak and final authority: '. . . I am tranquil in nothing during this wandering, houseless, homeless, Emigrant life. This is no siecle for those who love their home, or who have a home to love. 'Tis a siecle for the Adventurous, to whom Ambition always opens resources; or for the New, who guess not at the Catastrophes that hang on the rear, while the phantom Expectation allures them to the front.'

[1] *The Wanderer*, p. xiv.

A LIST OF COMMANDERS

THE following list gives short biographical sketches of some generals and commanders who figure in the background of the events that effected the d'Arblays during the Hundred Days: each one is indicated by an asterisk in the notes to this volume.

LEOPOLD HERMANN LUDWIG VON BOYEN (1771–1848), a well-educated East Prussian Junker who early showed himself to be a capable staff officer and military theorist. In 1808 he began the important work in the reorganization of the Prussian army after its disastrous defeat at Jena that led to his appointment as war minister in 1814. It was in this position that he corresponded with Kleist concerning M. d'A's presence in Trier, and it was as minister that he published the decree on compulsory military service ('Ueber die allgemeine Verpflichtung zum Kriegdienst') that provided the basis of Prussian military power and militarist policies throughout the nineteenth century.

EMMANUEL DE GROUCHY (1766–1847), marquis de, one of the few officers of aristocratic birth and court connections to support the French Revolution and Republic from the start. He distinguished himself as a cavalry officer in many of Napoleon's campaigns, and the Emperor made him a marshal and pair des Cent Jours after the return from Elba. But his entire earlier career and later life were obliterated by his failure to prevent the juncture of Blücher and Wellington at Waterloo. He was thereafter scorned by the royalists as a traitor to his class, by his former comrades as a traitor to Napoleon. His military rank and honours were restored to him only by Louis-Philippe in 1830.

ROWLAND HILL (1772–1842), Baron (1814) and Viscount (1842) Hill; perhaps the most trusted of the generals who served with Wellington in the Peninsular War. When Napoleon's escape from Elba became known in England, Hill was sent to advise the Prince of Orange, under whom he was given command of an army corps in Belgium. He fought at Waterloo and later became second-in-command of the army of occupation in France from 1815 until 1818.

MIKHAIL LARIONOVICH GOLENISHCHEV-KUTUSOV (1745–1813), Prince of Smolensk (1813). Perhaps most famous for his Fabian defence and pursuit during Napoleon's Russian invasion and retreat in 1812–13, Kutusov rallied the Russian and Prussian armies against the French, but died early in 1813 before their joint campaign could begin.

JOACHIM MURAT (1767–1815), King of Naples. Although famous as the most brilliant cavalry leader of his age, Murat gained further importance through his attempts to preserve and aggrandize the kingdom of Naples, which Napoleon conferred on him in 1808, through complex dealings and double-dealings with the Allies and Napoleon between 1813 and 1815. Once a fervent revolutionary, Murat attached himself to Napoleon's career and dynasty, which he married into in 1800, then repeatedly tried to establish himself as a sovereign in his own right. His last pathetic attempt ended before a firing-squad in Calabria in October of 1815.

GEORGE DUBISLAW LUDWIG VON PIRCH (1763–1838), called 'Pirch I' to distinguish him from his brother, had risen by 1813 to command a brigade under Zieten. He fought at Dresden, Kulm, and Leipzig. At the outbreak of hostilities in 1815 he commanded a brigade in the 2nd Army Corps, then the Corps itself at Ligny and Waterloo.

OTTO KARL LORENZ VON PIRCH (1765–1824), known as 'Pirch II', became in 1809 governor of Prince Wilhelm, later Kaiser Wilhelm I, and served with him in the campaigns of 1813, attached to Blücher's headquarters. He commanded a brigade in France during the campaign of 1814, and after April 1815 the 2nd Brigade in Zieten's 1st Army Corps at Waterloo and during the invasion of France.

KARL PHILIPP, Prince (Fürst) zu Schwarzenberg (1771–1820), Austrian field-marshal, had shown his abilities in campaigns both against and with the French. Although the senior general in the allied invasion of France in 1813–14, he played only a minor role in the 1815 campaign. After concerting policy with Wellington at the Congress of Vienna, he led the Austrian armies to Heilbronn and then across the Rhine, entering Paris after the Prussians and English on 17 July.

KARL ERNST JOB VON WITZLEBEN (1783–1837), a distinguished Prussian officer, military theorist, cabinet minister, and musician who began his career when he entered the Corps of Pages at Potsdam in 1799. He fought at Auerstadt (1806) and rose through the campaigns of the Prussian army to become a Colonel (Oberst) and

xvi

Chief of Staff to the *Norddeutschen Bundesarmeecorps* at the start of the 1815 campaign. He had attracted Rossini's attention in Paris in 1814 for his musical talents. He later won royal favour in Berlin for his statesmanlike abilities, becoming *Chef des militärcabinets* in 1817, *General leutnant* in 1831, and War Minister during 1833–4.

DOMINIQUE-RENÉ VANDAMME (1770–1830), count (1808), one of Napoleon's most able and loyal generals and the one most hated by the royalists and Prussians for his rough and republican behaviour. After many campaigns he was forced to surrender at Kulm and was harshly treated in captivity. When he returned to France after the First Restoration in 1814, Louis XVIII forbade him to live in Paris. Vandamme rejoined Napoleon during the Hundred Days and was given command of the 3rd Corps in the Waterloo campaign. Imprisoned under the Second Restoration, then exiled, he was never again re-employed.

KARL PHILIPP FÜRST VON WREDE (1767–1838) gave up his wild student's life at Heidelberg to become a civil servant. He gave up this dull life to raise his own volunteer corps of recruits in the Palatinate during the early campaigns against the armies of revolutionary France. After reorganizing the Bavarian army, he led it as an ally of France until both he and his kingdom went over to the anti-Napoleonic side in 1813. Wrede supported Blücher in the invasion of France in 1814. Although they took the field, his Bavarian troops were not actively engaged in the Waterloo campaign. Wrede later became the chief minister of Bavaria in 1817 and the head of a council of regency in 1835.

HANS ERNST KARL GRAF VON ZIETEN (1770–1848), one of the most able Prussian commanders during the Napoleonic wars, served with Kleist in 1813. The outbreak of war in 1815 found him commanding Blücher's 1st Corps, which he led at Ligny and Waterloo. During the Hundred Days Mazancourt emphasized his connection with Zieten and mentioned in his requests to be employed that he had been on Zieten's staff during his earlier *émigré* days in Prussian service. Zieten later became a general in 1825 and a field-marshal on his retirement in 1839.

ABBREVIATIONS

SHORT TITLES

Standard encyclopaedias, biographical dictionaries (both national and professional), peerages, armorials, baronetages, knightages, school and university lists, medical registers, lists of clergy, town and city directories, road guides, almanacs, and ephemerides of all kinds have been used but will not be cited unless for a particular reason. Also consulted were annual

Abbreviations

Navy, Army, and Law Lists, *Royal Kalendar,* and the many editions of Edmund Lodge's *The Peerage of the British Empire as at Present Existing* and of Sir John Bernard Burke's *A Genealogical and Heraldic History of the Peerage and Baronetage* and *A Genealogical and Heraldic History of the Landed Gentry of Great Britain and Ireland.* In all such dated series, though the wording of titles varies somewhat, citation will be to the commonly used short title with the date of the volume or edition.

SHORT TITLES

of books referred to in this volume

AR	*The Annual Register, or a View of the History, Politics, and Literature* . . ., 1758– .
Bertier de Sauvigny	Guillaume de Bertier de Sauvigny, *La Restauration,* 1955.
Beugnot	Jacques-Claude, comte Beugnot, *Mémoires du comte Beugnot, ancien ministre (1783–1815),* 2 vols., 1866.
Boigne	Charlotte-Louise-Éléonore-Adélaïde, comtesse de Boigne, *Mémoires de la comtesse de Boigne née d'Osmond* . . ., ed. Jean-Claude Berchet, 2 vols., 1971.
Bouchary	Jean Bouchary, *Les Manieurs d'argent à Paris à la fin du XVIIIᵉ siècle,* 3 vols., 1939–43.
Broughton	John Cam Hobhouse, Lord Broughton, *Recollections of a Long Life,* ed. Lady Dorchester, 6 vols., 1909–11.
Capel	Lady Caroline Capel, *The Capel Letters . . . 1814–1817,* ed. the Marquess of Anglesey, 1955.
Castries	René de la Croix, duc de Castries, *Louis XVIII, portrait d'un roi,* 1969.
Catalogue	*A Catalogue of the Burney Family Correspondence 1749–1878,* compiled by Joyce Hemlow with Jeanne M. M. Burgess and Althea Douglas, New York, 1971.
CCR	*The Court and City Register.*
[Chateaubriand]	François-René, vicomte de Chateaubriand, *Mémoires d'outre-tombe,* ed. M. Levaillant and G. Moulinier, Pléiade edition, 2 vols., 1951.
Creevey Papers	Thomas Creevey, *The Creevey Papers; a selection from the correspondence and diaries of the late Thomas Creevey,* ed. Sir Herbert Maxwell, 2 vols., 1904.
Dalton	Charles Dalton, *The Waterloo Roll Call,* 2nd edn., 1904.
Dard	Émile Dard, *Un Confident de l'Empereur, le comte de Narbonne,* 1943.

Abbreviations

Dean	Capt. G. G. T. Dean, *The Royal Hospital, Chelsea*, 1950.
de Ros	Blanche A. G. Swinton, *A Sketch of the Life of Georgiana, Lady de Ros, with some reminiscences of her family and friends*, 1893.
Disp.	Arthur Wellesley, 1st Duke of Wellington, *The Dispatches of Field Marshal the duke of Wellington . . . from 1799 to 1818*, comp. by Lt.-Col. John Gurwood, 13 vols. in 12, 1834–9.
DL	*Diary and Letters of Madame d'Arblay (1778–1840)*, ed. Austin Dobson, 6 vols., 1904–5.
FB & the Burneys	*Fanny Burney and the Burneys*, ed. R. Brimley Johnson, 1926.
Fleischman	Théo Fleischman and Winand Aerts, *Bruxelles pendant la bataille de Waterloo*, Brussels, 1956.
Fortescue	The Hon. J. W. Fortescue, *A History of the British Army*, 13 vols. in 20, 1899–1930.
Galesloot	Louis Galesloot, *Chronique des évènements les plus remarquables arrivés à Bruxelles de 1780–1827*, 2 vols., 1858.
Gazley	John G. Gazley, *The Life of Arthur Young, 1741–1820*, 1973.
GM	*The Gentleman's Magazine*, 1731–1880.
Hall	Sir John Richard Hall, *The Bourbon Restoration*, 1909.
HFB	Joyce Hemlow, *The History of Fanny Burney*, Oxford, 1958.
Houssaye, *1815*	Henri Houssaye, *1815*, 3 vols., 1907.
Jaucourt	Arnail-François, marquis de Jaucourt, *Correspondance . . . avec le prince Talleyrand pendant le Congrès de Vienne . . .*, 1905.
Later Corr. Geo. III	*The Later Correspondence of George III*, ed. A. Aspinall, Cambridge, 7 vols., 1963– .
[La Tour du Pin, *Memoirs*]	Henriette-Lucie, marchionesse de La Tour du Pin de Gouvernet, *Memoirs of Madame de La Tour du Pin*, ed. and trans. Felice Harcourt, 1970.
Lewis	Michael Lewis, *Napoleon and his British Captives*, 1962.
Liederkerke Beaufort	Christian de Liedekerke Beaufort, *Le Comte Hilarion, souvenirs et biographie du premier comte de Liedekerke Beaufort*, 2 vols., Brussels, 1968.
Manwaring	G. E. Manwaring, *My Friend the Admiral, the Life, Letters, and Journals of Rear-Admiral James Burney, F.R.S.*, 1931.

Abbreviations

Müffling	Friedrich Carl Ferdinand, Baron von Müffling, *Passages from my Life, 1813–1814*, trans. and ed. Philip Yorke, 1853.
Müffling, *History*	*History of the Campaign of the British, Dutch, Hanoverian and Brunswick armies . . . in 1815 . . .*, 1816.
Pasquier	Étienne-Denis Pasquier, *Mémoires du chancelier Pasquier*, 6 vols., 1893–5.
Pflugk-Harttung	Julius von Pflugk-Harttung, *Das preussische Heer und die norddeutschen Bundestruppen unter General v. Kleist, 1815*, Gotha, 1911.
Plotho	Carl von Plotho, *Der Krieg des verbündeten Europa gegen Frankreich im Jahre 1815*, Berlin, 1818.
Reiset	Marie-*Antoine*, vicomte de Reiset, *Souvenirs du lieutenant général, vicomte de Reiset*, 3 vols., 1899.
Robiquet	Jean Robiquet, *La Vie quotidienne au temps de Napoléon*, 1942.
Rochechouart	Louis-Victor-Léon, comte de Rochechouart, *Souvenirs sur la révolution, l'empire, et la restauration*, 1933.
Romberg	J. B. Romberg, *A New Picture of Brussels and its Environs*, Brussels, 1820.
Romberg and Malet	Édouard Romberg and Albert Malet, *Louis XVIII et les Cent-jours à Gand*, 2 vols., 1898.
Scholes	Percy A. Scholes, *The Great Dr. Burney*, 2 vols., 1948.
Serre	Pierre-François-Hercule, comte de Serre, *Correspondance du Cte de Serre (1776–1824), annotée et publiée par son fils*, 6 vols., 1876–7.
Six	Georges Six, *Dictionnaire biographique des généraux et amiraux français de la révolution et de l'empire (1792–1814)*, 2 vols., 1934.
Stenger	Gilbert Stenger, *The Return of Louis XVIII*, trans. Mrs. R. Stawell, 1909.
Supp. Desp.	Arthur Wellesley, 1st Duke of Wellington, *Supplementary Despatches, Correspondence, and Memoranda of Field Marshal Arthur Duke of Wellington*, ed. Arthur, 2nd Duke of Wellington, 15 vols., 1858–72.
Talleyrand	Charles-Maurice, duc de Talleyrand-Périgord, *Correspondance inédite du prince Talleyrand et du roi Louis XVIII . . .*, ed. M. G. Pallain, 1881.
Teignmouth	Charles John Shore, 2nd Baron Teignmouth, *Reminiscences of Many Years*, 2 vols., Edinburgh, 1878.
Thiry	Jean Thiry, *Les Cent Jours*, 1943.
Villemain	Abel-François Villemain, *Souvenirs contemporains d'histoire et de littérature . . .*, 2 vols., 1854–5.
Vincennes	Archives du Service historique de l'armée, Château de Vincennes.

[8, rue de Miroménil,
Paris, *pre* 15 December 1814]

To H.R.H. the Princess Elizabeth

L.S., copy in hand of M. d'A (Barrett, Eg. 3699A, ff. 2–6), *n.d.*
Nine pages (8·3 × 6·6″) in a Letter Book bound in boards, covered with
pink marble, unpaged, *entitled*: MSS. Lettres Pars 3 / Letters to / & from /
RFʸ
p. 1, *annotated in pencil*: 2 / From F. B d'A, / to HRH.

Madam
    The high honour conferred upon me by the so condescin-
dingly writen commission¹ of your Royal Highness would have
impelled my immediate & most devoted acknowledgements,
had I dared listen to the first impulse of gratitude & delight
excited by your Royal highnesses gratious & partial goodness:
but I have restrained my intrusive wishes till I could give some
account of my commission, which, alas! was executed only—
Yesterday! ᴵ
    A delay so singular, & which unexplained, must appear so
unpardonable, forces me to assume courage for entering into
a little narrative of the *pourquoi.* & though it must be long &
personal, I venture to trust in, the hereditary urbanity, which

835. ¹ The commission is extant in a letter (Berg) of 6 Nov. 1814 from the Princess:
'My dear Madame d Arblais I trouble you with this note to enclose one to my dear
Lady Melville. what I wish to beg of you is to send it to the Bankers at Toulouse,
. . . as I know neither the house or Street where my friend lives. . . . The next thing
is to say Adieu to You, & say in an old-fashioned way God bless you, which is the
best & surest way of ensuring you all that is good. . . . I heartily pray that you may
regain your health in a better & milder climate than dear Old England.—I shall
look forward with delight to your return in June—when I hope the Sun will shine,
& that you will be able to stay some days with your old friends, where you are truly
valued & loved, & by none more than
                                                          Your sincere friend
Nov: *6ᵗʰ*   Eliza'

    Lady Melville, formerly Lady Jane Hope (1766–1829), had married in 1793 as
his second wife Henry Dundas (1742–1811), 1st Viscount Melville (1802), and
secondly on 16 Feb. 1814 Thomas Wallace (1768–1844), M.P. (1790–1828), a lord
of the admiralty (1797–1800), cr. Baron Wallace (1828). She continued to be known
as Lady Melville.
    The Dowager Viscountess Melville was a Lady of the Bedchamber to Queen
Charlotte at £500 a year from 1 June 1813 [BL, Add. MSS. 17891 (2)] until the
Queen's death in 1818, after which she received a pension of £500 a year until her
own death on 9 June 1829 (Queen Charlotte's Pensions, PRO, E 404/579–83).

I

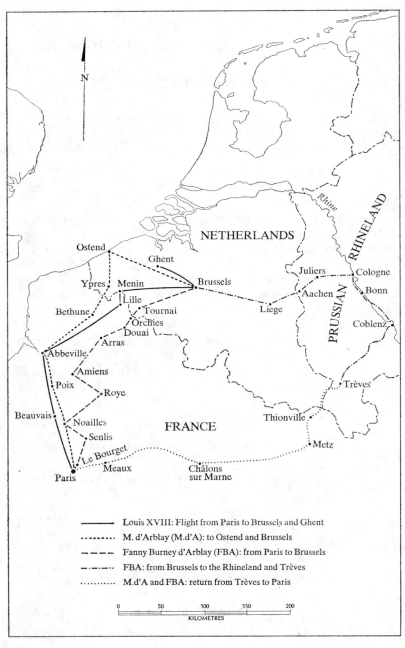

I. Map showing travel routes, Paris to Brussels, Brussels to Trèves, etc.,
by Geoffrey J. Matthews

Louis XVIII: Flight from Paris to Brussels and Ghent
M. d'Arblay (M.d'A): to Ostend and Brussels
Fanny Burney d'Arblay (FBA): from Paris to Brussels
FBA: from Brussels to the Rhineland and Trèves
M.d'A and FBA: return from Trèves to Paris

0   50   100   150   200
KILOMETRES

never judges unheard, of your Royal Highness, to forgive my egotism.

For 10 days after my happiest honours at Windsor, I was confined to my apartment at Richmond by my inveterate cold,[2] which, even then, required a week's slow travelling to bring me to Dover. From thence to Calais, our passage, though short, was so stormy, that it appeared to me an Hurricane, occasioned me such violent and unremitting sufferings,[3] that when arrived, I was unable to walk on shore, & M^r d'Arblay hired ⎮ me an escort, not a very military one!—of Fishermen, to carry me, by relays, on an arm chair to Dessein's Hotel.[4] In our way, a Gentleman, touched by the almost lifeless state which I appeared to be in, stopt M^r d'Arblay, who walked by my side, to offer him some cordial medecine for me. M^r d'Ay turned round to thank ⎮ him; but while yet speaking, a female voice crying 'Gare!' he hastily turned back, & perceived, but too late to save himself, a man, a monster, I had almost said! standing upright in a cart, which he drove rapidly upon him. M^r d'A.y was not only renversé, the brancards[5] striking him upon his breast, but flung to some distance by the force of the blow. The wretch, who, no doubt, is one of the still existing Jacobins of the worst of times, had neither cried *Gare*, nor attempted to stop his cart; ⎮ & neither M^r d'A.y nor the gentleman whose unfortunate humanity caused this dreadful mischief; had heard or heeded it's approach. The man could have no personal enmity to M^r d'A: whom he had never seen: his action must have been merely the effect of general brutality; & of a nature instinctively at war with whatever appeared less gross & less vile than itself. He was loaded with execrations by the populace; but he escaped his merited punishment, as M^r d'A:, who was judged to be fatally wounded! ⎮ occupied all the attention of the better part.

---

[2] FBA's last visit to the Royal Family at the beginning of November 1814 was cut short by 'a Furious cold', as she explained in a letter to CB Jr. of 8 Nov. 1814 (vii, L. 834).
[3] The misfortunes of the d'Arblays following their departure from England in November 1814, feelingly retold in the following letters, were the sad continuation of earlier illness and misfortune (see vii *passim*).
[4] Dessein's Hotel (v, L. 508 n. 7) was known by several names to thousands of English travellers in France during the eighteenth and early nineteenth centuries. It had changed hands in 1814, but John Barnes, author of *A Tour throughout the whole of France* ... (1815), still considered it in that year 'the best inn in France' (p. 111).
[5] The cart's shaft.

M^r d'A: soon, however raised himself, for his head, I praise God! was uninjured; but his breast felt bent double, and he could not stand upright—I, still half dead with convulsive sickness knew nothing of this cruel accident, till sometime after we got to dessein's, where M^r d'A.y was put to bed, blooded, & attended by the military surgaon of Calais[6] for several days. We then slowly reached Paris where I had at least the solace to see him under the care of the Prince of Surgeons Dr Larrey.[6]

The commission with which I was honoured, & | with which I had been so delighted, I am grieved to say lay all this time dormant. All the inquiries I could make relative to a banker at Toulouse were fruitless, as I had no means to discover the house employed by Lady Melville.[1] I was forced therefore to wait till M^r d'A: could see the Viscomte d'Agoult[7] his old intimate & faithful friend now first Equerry to S.A.R. M^{de} la Duchesse d'Angoulême & high in confidence & favour. The Viscomte immediately sent me an inclosure for the Cte de Ferrand,[8] Post Master General, with an injuction that the letter should be safely delivered into Lady Melville's own hands.

May I, Madam, hope that your Royal Highness. | will gratiously pardon this long history? May I venture to even lengthen it by adding that M^r d'A—is now nearly recovered? But that this succession of retarding events has brought us into so bad a season, that Dr Larrey is of opinion it is too late for me to travel further; & that therefore, I shall spend this Winter at Paris? I have been & still am, too disordered to dare think, as yet, of my presentation to Mad^e la D^{esse} d'An-goulême,[9] which will, nevertheless take place as soon as I am

---

[6] As a general officer returning to active service, M. d'A had every right to be attended by a military surgeon. The Napoleonic wars had led to great advances in surgery, many of them introduced by the d'Arblays' friend Baron Larrey (vi, L. 595 n. 9).

[7] Antoine-Jean d'Agoult (vii, L. 793 n. 8), vicomte d'Agoult, had been promoted to the rank of lieutenant-general on 9 Nov. 1814. He had also held at court the high office of 'premier écuyer de Mme la Dauphine'.

[8] Antoine-François-Claude Ferrand (1751–1825), comte (1814), whose re-actionary zeal gained him the nickname le 'Marat blanc' and caused him to be remembered for his opinion that 'Si la clémence est un plaisir, la justice est un devoir' (Houssaye, *1815*, i. 41).

[9] Presentation at court and other matters of monarchal etiquette were as important to the d'Arblays as they had been to members of their class before the Revolution. Although Louis XVIII had to temporize and yield prerogatives through the *Charte* that accompanied his restoration, he kept all the rigid ceremony of the old court—except the *lever* and *coucher royals* that the King 'trouvait peu compatibles avec ses disgrâces physiques' (Castries, p. 219).

well enough to equip myself rather less like one of the Witches in Macbeth. I am almost surprised at the courage with which the sweetness and condescension of Your Royal Highness has inspired me; [|] & I am half frightened lest it should appear like presumption. But no. The ties that so long have bound me, with an attachement as ardent as it is dutiful, to my beloved Royal Mistress, & to all your Royal Highnesses, must be my guarantee, that an even fresh devotion is excited by this fresh mark of extream goodness with which your Royal Highness has deigned to distinguish her who has the honour to subscribe herself with the deepest respect

Madame

Your Royal Highnesses

Most faithful, most grateful

and most obedient humble

Servant

Signed FB. d'Arblay [|]

836

8, rue de [Miroménil,
Paris], 15 December [1814]

To H.R.H. the Princess Elizabeth

L.S., copy in hand of M. d'A (Barrett, Eg. 3699A, ff. 6b–7), 15 Dec.
Three pages (8·3 × 6·6″) in the Letter Book *entitled*: MSS. Lettres Pars 3 / Letters to / & from / RF^y
p. 1, *annotated in pencil*: *3* / FB d'A to HRH

Madam

With equal humility, but with much lessened fear, I venture to again adress your Royal Highness, since it is no more of my little self but of Mad^e la D^{sse} d'Angoulême I have to speak. I earnestly hope I have not done wrong in desiring M^r d'Arblay to mention to the Vte d'Agoult the doubts which your Royal Highness entertained relative to a letter sent by M. de la Châtre¹ to S.A.R. M^{de} la D^{esse} d'Angoulême. Le Viscomte

836. ¹ Claude-Louis de la Châtre (ii, p. xvi) was to be raised to the title of duc héréditaire on 24 Nov. 1815. Long residence in England among the *émigrés* and his appointment as French ambassador in London had made him a suitable person to

said that it would be a matter of such moment to the D^ss
that he would name it directly; & the next day S.A.R. in
deigning to express to M. d'A.y her satisfaction that I was
arrived in France, told him that she had never received the
letter in question! & she said it with such an air of regret,
that both the ˡ Viscomte & M^r d'A.y encourage me to make the
circumstance known to your Royal Highness. Again therefore,
I presume upon the goodness of your Royal Highness for forgiveness, and for permitting me the high honour of signing
myself with profound respect

Madam

Your Royal Highnesses

Most humble

most faithful

and most obedient

Servant

Signed FB d'Arblay

Mad^e d'Angoulême has still no establishment! She receives
her Court, M. d'A. tells me with no other attendment than
the Vte d'Agoult who stands on her left side, to name all who
approach. She has ladies only occasionaly,[2] i.e. when she
appears in public.
Paris, Lundi Miromenil F^bg St Honoré
⟨X^be⟩ 15.

I take the liberty to reopen my letter to add that M^r d'A.
has this moment ˡ told me that the ladies of M^de la D^esse
d'Angoulême are just named, and le Vte d'Agoult says, are
now in the portefeuille de S.A.R. but that they will not be
anounced till the opening of the new year. She will still however have no separate establishment from that of her Beau
pere M^r le Cte d'Artois.[3] The Roi is astonishingly better, &
bears his exertions, dangers, & difficulties,[4] with an heroic

deliver to the duchesse d'Angoulême (vii, L. 768 n. 1) the letter in which the Queen
requested the favour of presentation for FBA.

[2] Some of the ladies-in-waiting of the duchesse d'Angoulême are named in the
account that FBA was to write of her presentation (L. 845 nn. 7, 13).

[3] Together with her brother, the comte d'Artois (vii, L. 767 n. 1), the duchesse
d'Angoulême formed the centre of the Pavillon de Marsan, the separate court
(within the Tuileries) noted for reactionary views.

[4] The difficulties in following a moderate policy, attacked and subverted by both
extreme reactionaries of the Pavillon de Marsan and the active supporters of
Napoleon, who were still opposed to the restoration of the Bourbons.

equanimity, that gains ground upon all hearts & all descriptions of people daily. The affair of Lord Oxford[5] has made much bruit, & raises endless reports. He is, however, so weak a man, that he is supposed to be not only a MERE, but even an unconscious instrument in what he was undertaking—be it what it might. ¦

837   [8, rue de Miroménil,
                        Paris], 30 January 1815

To H.R.H. the Princess Elizabeth

L., copy in hand of M. d'A (Barrett, Eg. 3699A, ff. 10–13b.), 30 Jan. 1815
Eight pages (8·3 × 6·6″) in the Letter Book *entitled*: MSS. Lettres Pars 3 / Letters to / & from / RF[y]
p. 1, *annotated in pencil*: 5

Nobody can conceive the joy of my mind, & the thankfulness of my heart at a proposition[1] so many wais framed to give me

5 On 26 Nov. 1814, soon after leaving Paris for Naples, Edward Harley (1773–1848), 5th Earl of Oxford and Mortimer, was stopped at Villejuif by the French police. Louis XVIII's advisers gained Wellington's permission to arrest him for the offence of carrying private correspondence in violation of the postal laws. His real crime, however, was conspiracy with dangerous Bonapartist sympathizers. See Hubert Cole, *The Betrayers Joachim and Caroline Murat* (1972), pp. 217–18. Lord Oxford and his wife, Jane Elizabeth *née* Scott (1773–1824), were both Whigs and fervent supporters of Napoleon. They were also intimately involved in the promiscuous society of Regency radicals—Lady Oxford so much so that her children, attributed to a variety of fathers, were known as 'the Harleian Miscellany'. If Lady Oxford was notorious, Lord Oxford was despised; a man, according to Castlereagh, deserving no 'sort of respect'.

837. 1 In a letter (Berg) of 28 Dec. 1814 the Princess, in acknowledging FBA's 'delightful' L. 835, went on to suggest a continued correspondence. 'I shall unceasingly trouble you with an uninteresting *scrawl* in hopes of having a few delightful lines from dear Madame d'Arblay, my mother was quite pleased knowing what pleasure it gave & is very happy that I will write. . . . You . . . may be sure I shall say nothing that may not be read in the *High Street* both here & Where you are; I look upon myself as *Nobody*, & as *Nobody* shall I write—tho when you come to consider my *fat figure* you may be inclined to say I think there is *some BODY* mais n'importe take me as you will, & whatever defects there may be in my stumpy figure, I humbly hope that my heart is in the right place & that I am able to enter into all the anxieties of my friends.'
    The correspondence thus initated continued for nineteen years. Of the fifty extant letters (Berg) from the Princess to FBA, four sent in 1815 to Brussels were unsigned, the letter above concluding with the exhortation, 'think of *Nobody*—but recollect that *Somebody* is sincerely attached to You—
Dec: 28th
1814'

the most exquisite delight—But alas! how always because fresh though for the same reason, always trite, is every remark that has been, or that can be made upon the imperfection of our enjoyments! Could I have believed that a letter of which the playful sweetness, even while it made me laugh, filled my eyes with tender gratitude should prove to me a source of difficulty embarassment, & affright? & involve me in a labyrinth of doubt how to act, from which, after ruminating with all my might, in wastful suspence, I can devize one only attempt of extrication, namely that of frankly relating my perplexity to somebody whose sagacity can comprehend, & whose instructions can relieve it? and whose indulgence will, I trust, deign to pardon an anxious appeal excited by an indescribable solicitude to avoid any errour or mistake.

About a week after I had written the only letter ¹ except to my son, which the Shattered state of my nerves has, as yet, let me dispatch from my fireside, I was suddenly seized with a high fever, the effect of long concentrated apprehensions, which confined me to my bed for a week & to my chamber for a month. During this latter interval, I was told that a gentleman had brought me a letter which he must deliver into my own hands. Still as unhabituated to visits in my sanctuary as if I had never crossed the little ditch,[2] as lady K[eith][3] stills[4] it, I declined receiving him, & he was forced, malgré lui, to leave the letter with my maid: but when it reached me, & I recognised the handwriting, how reviving was it to all my sensations! Like a charm, it acted upon them, in the pleasing[4] it excited, & the delightful expectations it admitted: but oh! here came the poize so ever cruelly at hand to balance joy with pain! The ¹ delicious plan that doubles the devotion of my heart in setting aside the formalities that must else fill or rather empty my [purse][5] announces & includes the intention of a nameless correspondence; wat therfore was my consternation when I learnt that this gentleman had publicly told the domestics that he

---

[2] It was quite usual in France—but emphatically not so in England—for ladies to receive visitors in their bedrooms.

[3] Hester Maria *née* Thrale (1764–1857), the wife of George Keith Elphinstone (1746–1823), Viscount Keith (1814), Commander-in-chief of the Channel Fleet (vii, L. 684 n. 3).

[4] Conjecturally M. d'A copies 'stills' in error for *styles* and 'pleasing' for *pleasure*.

[5] M. d'A, probably unable to read the original, left a blank. See L. 845 n. 4 for the cost of court dress.

was commissioned to give me a direction by which I might adress my answer to—I will not write to whom, but by no means to Nobody!! how widely different!

The evident meaning of my dear precious letter so little corroborates with the procedure, that I could only, as soon as I was well enough to be *visible* resolve, to consult with the messenger. but I found him, which I think right to confess to nobody, so little satisfactory, that I could only try to give him a practical lesson of discretion, by my ¹ own dryness & reserve, & determine to cast myself upon the mercy of my benevolent judge, in supplicating fresh documents for the Future, with gentle amnisty for the Past.

But alas! a third attack again, & immediately confined me to my bed, & it is only to day that I quit it, to again take my pen, & to indulge the solacing belief that the rigorous laws of compensation which so severely have checked my first happiness may at length be satisfied, & permit the brighter side to again prevail.

Amen encore Amen!

The very morning after I had the honour of sending my last, the Vᵉ d'A.[6] with great glee, announced to Mʳ d'A. that the expected & wished for letter was arrived.[7] Intrusted as I have now the happiness to be with a ¹ commission so truly delightful to me, I long to hasten my intended presentation, but the cold at present, is as ungenial, for such an effort, as my precarious health.

The lady Toulouse[8] has favoured me with a very polite acknowlegment of the reception of the letter from her 'dearest P[rincess]'. She had just been made extremely happy, also, by one from H. M.[9] & two other letters, she adds, from 'that dearest P.' had already reached her.

The greatest satisfaction has been given here to all thinking people for even here some people of that class are to be found, by the postponing our B[irth] D[ay] Fête[10] to a week of less

---

⁶ The vicomte d'Agoult (L. 835 n. 7).

⁷ Apparently a letter from Queen Charlotte (cf. vii. 295–317).

⁸ The 'Lady Toulouse' is emended in pencil: 'The lady at Toulouse.' This is Lady Melville (L. 835 n. 1).

⁹ Queen Charlotte and the Princess Elizabeth.

¹⁰ The postponed birthday fête was that given later by the Duke of Wellington for Queen Charlotte (*Morning Chronicle,* 19 May), whose birthday was celebrated on

melancholy reminiscence. To me the delay was peculiarly soothing from my internal conviction that the ¦ revered object of the festival would be foremost approve so feeling an attention.

In the only visit I made during the short interval of my two first illnesses, I met with a General who had been 6 years absent from the 'tight little Island';[11] & I had some interesting conversation with him upon various circumstances of the miraculous event of the visit made through the Pyrennees. I should have conversed with him with yet greater eagerness had I known, at the time, he was a son of the late Lord & Lady Courtown.[12]

M^r d'A. brought me the good intelligence, yesterday morning, from the *white Ruband Corps*[13] that the estimable & exemplary niece received du monde with a great encrease of attention in her manner of addressing them. The late solemn rites,[14] so religiously performed, have ¦ probably relieved the Sorrows of her filial piety. She was so good as to mention with approbation to M. d'.A. that she was reading a certain recent

13 January, three days before the commemoration of Louis XVI's execution of 21 Jan. 1793.

[11] A phrase taken from a song 'Snug Little Island' in the patriotic play *The British Raft* (1797) by Thomas John Dibdin (1771–1841). For its earlier use and popularity, see v, L. 543 n. 5.

[12] Sir Edward Stopford (1766–1837), G.C.B. and K.T.S., second son of James Stopford (1731–1810), 2nd Earl of Courtown, 1st Baron Saltersford, and his wife Mary *née* Powys (*c.* 1737–1810), lady-in-waiting to Queen Charlotte (iv, L. 269 n. 18). General Stopford's Peninsular experience went back as far as the Battle of Bussaco in 1810 when he first commanded the Brigade of the First (later Guards) Division, which he subsequently led throughout the campaigns in Spain, the battles of the Pyrenees, and the invasion of south-western France. His most notable exploit in the previous year's entry into France was the skilful transfer of troops from his brigade across to the French-held north bank of Adour on 23 Feb. 1814, a manœuvre that helped bring about the encirclement of the fortress of Bayonne (Fortescue, ix. 500–2).

[13] M. d'A had been received at court by the duchesse d'Angoulême, niece of Louis XVIII, on Sunday 29 January (see Diary Entries). The Bourbon royal family had been styled 'the *white Rubband Corp*' by Princess Elizabeth in her letter of 28 December (n 1). 'White rubbands', worn like the white cockades of the royal army as token of loyalty to the Bourbons, had overtones of reactionary defiance. See La Tour du Pin, p. 125, for the reported frivolous distribution of white ribbons at Versailles the day before the march of the people of Paris on 5 Oct. 1789. The rumour of Louis XVIII's return in 1814 had provoked a cry for white cockades, but it was, apparently, a demand made by people who were hedging their political bets (La Tour du Pin, p. 415).

[14] This refers to the devout and, to many, the sinister display of dynastic grief staged by the Bourbon family on 21 Jan. 1815 to commemorate the regicide of the duchesse's father Louis XVI. See FBA's Diary Entry, 21 Jan. 1815; and for a full account of the ceremonies, see *Moniteur*, 23 and 24 Jan. 1815.

ouvrage[15] in which she had reason to imagine he took no little interest: but I am mortified to find it is in French she reads it, as the translation, I am told, is really abominable. She was attended, by 4 ladies, & her Chev^r d'honneur le Ve de M[ontmorency] & her 1st Ec[uyer] le Ve d'A[goult].[16]

Embarassing as it was to me, thus situated, to begin, Nobody, I am sure, can imagine how unwillingly I leave off without daring to allow myself one small little tiny syllable upon the sentiments of gratitude and Hope, that 'comes to call' will not be denied breathing a fluttering prognostic that neither the relapsing illnesses, nor the pondering ¦ perplexities that so long have enchained my pen, will harden the kind heart of my gentle judge from blessing my present, & I hope more permanent recovery with permission still to sail in this channel or with a few hints towards discovering some other

How thankful I feel for the flourishing state of the revered Magnolia,[17] how full of awful veneration for the favourite Trident Tree![18] & how grateful for the sweet odours thus benignly wafted to me from the lovely plants I so warmly admire! Long may they purify the ambient air! & enhale themselves some of the blessings they expand around them!

Jany 30th 1815

[15] A translation of FBA's *The Wanderer* had appeared within months of its first publication in London in March 1814: *La Femme errante, ou les embarras d'une femme, par Miss Burney . . . Traduit de l'anglais* par J.-B.-J. Breton de la Martinière et A.-J. Lemierre d'Argy (5 vols., 1814).

[16] Mathieu-Jean-Félicité de Montmorency-Laval (1767–1826), vicomte de Laval et de Montmorency (1809), duc (1824), had earlier associated with the circle of Mme de Staël and the moderate monarchist *émigrés* of Juniper Hall, where he stayed briefly in November 1792 (see ii, p. xv, and vii, L. 736 n. 12); but he returned soon after to France, and during the intervening years had become one of the most fanatical of the reactionary royalists, the *purs* (Bertier de Sauvigny, pp. 18–19, 24, 32–4).

The four ladies who served the duchesse d'Angoulême on this occasion were probably from the group that had accompanied her on 21 January at the funeral ceremonies for her father. This group included the comtesse de Damas-Crux (vii, L. 818 n. 12), *dame d'honneur en survivance*, and the comtesse de Choisy (vii, L. 818 n. 11), *dame d'atours*. A complete list appeared in contemporary accounts of the ceremonies (*Moniteur*, 24 Jan. 1815).

[17] Queen Charlotte. For FBA's botanical code names to be used for the Royal Family, see v. 360–1.

[18] The trident tree would seem to be an alternative code name for George III, otherwise the oak. FBA may have chosen this curious name because he was the third of his name or because the trident was the emblem of Britannia.

To Esther (Burney) Burney

A.L.S. (rejected Diary MSS. 6032–[5], Berg), 11 Jan.–8 Feb. 1815
    Double sheet large 4to   4 pp.   *pmks*   FOREIGN / ⟨   ⟩ 18[15]
PORTPAYE   17 FE 1815   17 FE 1815   black seal
    Addressed: ANGLETERRE / À Madame / Madame Burney, / Turnham
Green, / near / LONDON.
    Endorsed by EBB: answered / March 9ᵗʰ
    Edited by FBA, CFBt, *and the* Press. *See* Textual Notes.

Janʸ 11ᵗʰ 1815
Rue de Miromenil, N⁰ 8—
Fauxbourg Sᵗ Honoré, à Paris.
   Ah my dearest Esther! what pain—suffering—& alarm
have fallen to my lot since our separation! You must have
wondered not to have heard from me—so must my dear Charlotte & my Brothers,[1] & my dear Mrs. Lock[2]—but I have
been ill,—frightened,—& incapacitated;—& 2 Letters to my
Alexander, & 2 of *indispensable* necessity[3] make This sheet
merely the 5ᵗʰ Epistle I have been able to take in hand since
my arrival. I have not been negligent, my dear Hetty, but
silent, FIRST from not having a moment for my pen, 2ᵈˡʸ from
unwillingness to make you—uselessly, participate in my apprehensions & uneasiness, & 3ᵈˡʸ from physical difficulty to write.
As I much doubt whether you have any communication with
Alexander, whose epistolary diligence is not amongst his most
prominent virtues, I must relate our doleful adventures, to
avoid the risk of being unintelligible.—
   Our passage was rough & stormy; I had resolved upon
remaining upon the Deck, to try if that might save me from the
deadly sea malady by which I had been twice assaulted; but
alas, I was seized with it again, & so cruelly, that I could not

838.   [1] FBA's sister Charlotte Ann (CBFB) and her two brothers James (JB) and
Charles (CB Jr.). See i, pp. lxix–lxxiii. As this hurried and elliptical letter suggests,
FBA had lost touch with her family and friends in England through the injury
suffered by M. d'A at Calais and her own continuing bad health.
   [2] FBA's old friend Frederica Augusta Locke *née* Schaub (1750–1832) of Norbury
Park, the widow of William Locke (1732–1810). See i, L. 1 n. 3 and *passim*.
   [3] Only one of the letters to AA, L. 839, is extant; the two of '*indispensable* necessity' are the two preceding letters to Princess Elizabeth.

descend to the Cabin, though I earnestly wished it. My prop &
Guardian held me on my seat the whole voyage, or I must have
fallen a thousand times from the unremitting violence of my
sufferings; & when we arrived at Calais, I was more dead than
alive; & he himself, for the first time, was totally disordered.
As I could neither walk nor stand, he desired I might be carried
in a great Chair to the Inn; (Dessein's;) bespeaking me a set
of fishing Boys, who were to change hands in conveying me. I
was so nearly insensible, except to still continued & convulsive
sickness, that to keep my seat was all of attention of which
I was capable. I knew nothing, therefore, of the Scene that
soon unhappily, was acted almost by my side. A gentleman—
a Portuguese by birth, perceiving with compassion my almost
lifeless state, stopt M. ¹ d'Arblay, to offer him a viol
containing a cordial, which he said was precious & would
instantly revive me. M. d'A turned round to thank him, &
while holding a brief discourse, heard a woman's voice cry
'Gare!' he turned hastily back—& in one & the same moment
saw a man standing upright in a cart, & felt its beam strike
full upon his breast. He was thrown down, & with a force so
violent as to be flung to some distance by the blow. The
inhuman wretch who, without crying *Gare* himself, or making
any effort to stop his Cart, drove thus barbarously upon an
unheeding passenger, was now stopt himself by the justly en-
raged spectators—but he escaped the punishment he merited,
from the attention of all present being called off to M: d'A—
who, though he soon raised himself, had received so dreadful a
hurt, that he could not stand upright! he felt, & looked, bent
double!—& held his hands folded upon his breast, which he
thought crushed!—Providentially for me, I knew nothing of
what was passing. I was carried on to the Inn, & to a great
kitchen Fire, for the fury of the waves had wetted me through
all my thick equipment; & there, Madᵉ Dessein⁴ recovered
me by drops, & heaven knows what, & I began, by degrees,
for I was in a state nearly torpid, to comprehend the dreadful
accident that had happenned. We were both conveyed to a
large Chamber on the Ground floor,—a surgeon was sent for,
& an old one of eminence, belonging to the Military hospital,⁵

⁴ Probably the wife of the new proprietor (see L. 835 n. 4).
⁵ A consequence of Napoleon's far-flung campaigns had been the creation

was fortunately at hand—My generous partner, in the midst of his pain, & a terrible belief that the blow he had received would be fatal!—ordered me a Bed, & with a voice that could scarcely be heard, gave me in charge to all round— Oh my dear Hetty! what a tragical moment!—my stupor, I thank God! was not sufficiently over to permit me still the full consciousness of the misery with which it seemed big; & I only learnt the danger I had run by hearing it had been escaped, for the first words that were perfectly intelligible to me, were that the least higher, upon the *breast,* or the least lower, upon the *stomach,* the blow must have been mortal! My poor Patient was put to bed—he was copiously blooded—in a sallad bowl!— & ordered to be kept wholly without food. He took only de l'Eau Vulneraire⁶—& was continually rubbed upon the bruised bone with some medicament. We hired a Nurse—& 4 days here we remained—I, in that period, never taking off my cloaths, though forced to hide myself, in the middle of every night, from my anxious Patient. The 5ᵗʰ day, slowly, we set out on our Journey to Paris—I thought no more of Tours,⁷ nor of any thing but my admirable Dr. Larrey,⁸ who cupped M. d'A: but assured me solemnly *THERE WAS NO DANGER,* though care, temperance, & every sort of attention to health, would be necessary all winter. He is now, I thank God! & so I am sure will my dear Hetty, & ALL my dear Family & Friends,

within the French army of field ambulances (Baron Larrey's invention), surgeries, and military hospitals superior to any other medical facilities in Europe.

⁶ This was powerful spirit made by infusing a wide variety of herbs in alcohol: 'C'est un excitant, un stimulant, c'est un remède populaire contre les contusions, les coups à la tête, les chutes. Il est bon de dire en passant qu'on ne peut pas l'employer plus mal à propos' (*Larousse XIXᵉ*).

⁷ The d'Arblays apparently planned to winter in Tours (see L. 841), a city which appealed to the new wave of English travellers and residents that reached the Continent after Napoleon's first abdication in 1814. 'Tours has a gay, brisk and clean appearance. . . . Provisions, house-rent, fuel &c. are very cheap; the former very plentiful, and the latter must be considered as an exception to the general high price of it in France. . . . In many years there is no such thing as snow, and frosts are not frequent, and never severe; . . . there are no fogs and vapours as in the nothern parts of the kingdom' (Barnes, pp. 67–8). A part of Tours handsomely rebuilt after a fire during the reign of Louis XVI was even thought to bear a 'perfect resemblance to Bath'. Arthur Young had admired the long avenue of new stone houses that were a-building in 1787 and clearly shared the English delight in the climate of Touraine. See *Travels in France & Italy during the Years 1787, 1788 & 1789,* ed. Constantia Maxwell (Cambridge, 1929), p. 65.

⁸ Dominique-Jean, Baron Larrey (vi, L. 595 n. 9), Napoleon's surgeon-general, who had operated on FBA on 30 Sept. 1811, thereby probably saving her life (see **vi,** L. 595).

nearly well—though not yet re-instated in his looks nor strength. You cannot wonder to hear that I should have remained unwell ever since, thus dreadfully shaken, after such a suffering Voyage: nor yet, to learn that, after long struggling against general indisposition, I finished by a very serious illness. About 3 weeks ago, I was suddenly seized with a high fever, attended by every symptom of a grave malady; M. d'A. forced upon me a physician: but I attribute my recovery to James's Powders.[9] I am now so well, that I hope to-morrow to be able to take the air.

What a second melancholy ditty is this I write to my dear Esther![10] I am afraid she will never like the sight of a long Letter from me again! Don't take your revenge! but send me as chearful a contrast as circumstances will admit. My Alex has made me very happy by saying that Mr. Burney is MUCH BETTER, & *dear Aunt Hetty* quite well. He had seen, too, his Uncle Charles[11]—& his poor harrassed but ever kind Aunt Charlotte.[11] How I grieve for her new distress about poor Clement![12] I long to hear from you All—I found here an old Letter from you, & though all its contents were familiar to me, I read it with eagerness.—Let me entreat you to remember your promise of enlightening an old Letter of mine! Pray let me know how the little blind Boy, Cupidon, goes on. And our money matters? Have you received the *moitié* from Mr. White?[13] Has the Museum come to a decision?[14] If you are paid, may I hope you will do me the kindness to beg of Charles; with my kind love, to pay the *ditto* for me to Messrs Hoare, Fleet Street,[15]

[9] A remedy FBA used and mentioned repeatedly (see i, L. 7 n. 2 and *passim*).

[10] The first was vi, L. 595, an account of her mastectomy.

[11] CB Jr. and CBFB (i, pp. lxxi–lxxiii).

[12] The health of CBFB's son Clement Robert Francis (1792–1829), the studious brother of a studious sister (MF), had begun to collapse at Cambridge, perhaps through the strain of overwork (see MF's comments, vii, L. 798 n. 3, and M. d'A's remarks below, L. 840). Although he was to stand eighth wrangler in 1817 and to be elected a fellow of Caius, he spent much of the remainder of his short life a semi-invalid (*HFB*, pp. 417–18; and Teignmouth, ii. 221–4).

[13] John White (vii, L. 782 n. 11), auctioneer, who was to dispose of some of CB's effects (vii *passim*).

[14] The British Museum had purchased the printed books for £253 (Scholes, ii. 273–4). For details of the auction and sales of CB's 'Musical Library', see vii, L. 782 nn. 10–12; L. 792 n. 1.

[15] Messrs. Hoare of Fleet Street were FBA's bankers in London and remained so throughout her life. See *DL*, vi. 429.

who will give us notice of its receipt, & who have our Letter of Attorney for ¦ placing it. And will you forgive me if I entreat you, also, to enquire whether Mr. White has sold the few Chattels M. d'A delivered to him from our Cottage?[16] &, if so, to desire that he will be so good as to pay the result into the hands of Messʳˢ Hoare, in our name, after he has paid himself. Mr. Hoare will give him a receipt for us. Beckey,[17] too, must have her money for the sofa. Will my dearest Hetty take it, in my name, from Mr. White, & pay it, in the same name, with every kind wish, to good Beckey? Have you heard any thing of the large old Screen left in the apartments at Chelsea? Messʳˢ Leigh[18] have sent you, I hope, the Books selected for Mʳ Tow⟨nshend⟩,[19] Mr. Graham,[20] Charlotte Barrett, Marianne Francis, & Clement?[21] I feel very anxious to know how that sweet Charlotte & her Infant go on. For the latter I have much fear. My southern expedition was necessarily relinquished, from these cruel accidents: but we have carpetted, & put *poëles*[22] into our rooms here, & made ourselves as warm as we can. I wish much for news from yourself, to confirm the good tidings of my Alex. I beg you to remember me most kindly to both my Brothers, to Charlotte, for whom I feel much ⌐anxiety;⌐ to Mrs. J. Burney;[23] to Edward,[24] with my sincere regret at not seeing him, & to Maria with kindest love— as well as to Sophy, Fanny, Cecilia, & Amelia[25]—Martin,

---

[16] See vii, L. 829 n. 2.

[17] CB's servant Rebecca More (*fl.* 1794–1819), the cook who had served him with 'probity and diligence' for twenty years (v, L. 505 n. 1).

[18] The firm of Leigh and Sotheby, booksellers and auctioneers, 145 Strand, who sold Dr. Burney's miscellaneous library (vii, L. 787 nn. 2, 3; L. 808 n. 14).

[19] Probably the Hon. John Townshend (1757–1833), Lord of the Admiralty (1782–3), one of CB's pallbearers (vii, L. 787 n. 6).

[20] Richard Robert Graham (vii, L. 649 n. 2), apothecary at Chelsea Hospital (Dean, p. 221).

[21] These are the three children (see i, pp. lxxii–lxxiii) of CB's daughter Charlotte Ann (CBFB) by her first husband Clement Francis (*c.* 1744–92).

Charlotte Barrett (1786–1870) had given birth on 11 Oct. 1814 to her fourth child and second son Henry John Richard, who survived his infancy but who was to die in early adolescence in 1829.

[22] *Poëles* were small stoves introduced from Germany but still a rarity in Paris. FBA was not alone in finding them and the carpets mentioned here necessary. The drafty chill of French houses, heated only by meagre wood fires, was notorious among those from northern countries accustomed to their metal or porcelain *poëles* (Robiquet, p. 109).

[23] Sarah *née* Payne (1758–1832), the wife of FBA's brother James (i, p. lxix).

[24] Edward Francesco Burney (1760–1848), one of the Worcester Burneys and FBA's cousin, who in 1782 had painted her well-known portrait.

[25] EBB's eldest daughter, the widowed Maria Bourdois. Known in her girlhood

Sally,[26]—& all else as occasion occurs, but ⟨most⟩ chiefly to my dear Mrs. Lock & sweet Mrs. Angerstein,[27] to whom I hope now to write very soon. But I am still amazingly weak, & writing fatigues me greatly. Lastly, say every thing that is kindest to my dear good Mr. Burney,[28] & receive for him & yourself the best love of M. d'A. with that of your truly affec^te.

F B d'A.

With kind love also to Sarah,[29] who I hope is well, entreat her to tell Mr. R[aper][30] that poor Me. de Maureville[30] is à *l'agonies* for a favourable reply to her petition. Forgive, my dearest Esther, all this worry, & take your own *Time* & *Opportunity.*

Alex assures me, also, that Brother James, Mr. B. Martin & Sally are all well—but how sorry I am for poor Charles & poor Rosette![31]

If I had not been so unwell & so harrassed, in my last days, I should certainly have written to dear Blue[32]—& thanked kind Mrs. Sandford—& said adieu to dear Maria & Mrs. Hawkens & my engaging Cecilia.[32] |

This Letter, written at different periods, is closed This *8th Feb^y* when I can faithfully assu[re] my dearest Esther that we are *BOTH* considerably better—nearly well. I had been promised an opportunity for sending this, but it fails, & I will wait no longer. Heaven bless you! |

as 'Marianne' though christened *Hannah* Maria, as she discovered in the baptismal registers in the year of her marriage (1800), she decided henceforth to use the name Maria (see iv, L. 394 n. 3 and *passim*). For Maria and her four unmarried sisters, see i, p. lxix.
26 JB's two surviving children, Martin Charles (1788–1852) and Sarah (1796–*post* December 1868).
27 For Mrs. Locke (L. 838 n. 2), her daughter Amelia Angerstein (1776–1848), and the Locke family, see v, L. 472 n. 2.
28 EBB's husband Charles Rousseau Burney (1747–1819), a music teacher.
29 FBA's half-sister Sarah Harriet Burney (i, p. lxxiv), novelist.
30 Charles Chamier Raper (*c.* 1777–1842) of the Foreign Office, who had married in 1807 FBA's niece Fanny Phillips (i, p. lxxi). He had had to deal with a petition for a pension (see vii, L. 809 n. 1) presented by Henriette-Marguerite Guignot de Soulignac (iii, L. 237 n. 9), widow of Jean-Louis-Bernard-Bidé de Maurville (d. 1796).
31 FBA's brother Charles, the Greek scholar, and his wife Sarah *née* Rose (i, p. lxxi), who was subject to fits of depression (vii *passim*).
32 These were the Worcester Burneys (i, pp. lxxiv–lxxv), EBB's cousins and sisters-in-law: Elizabeth Warren Burney (1755–1832); Rebecca (1758–1835), wife of the surgeon William Sandford (1759–1823); and Ann, widow of the Revd. John Hawkins (d. 1804), who had adopted EBB's daughter Cecilia (1788–1821).

Paris,
[9–10 February 1815]

To M. d'Arblay

A.L. (Berg), jeudi, vendredi
Double sheet 8vo   3 pp.   wafer
Addressed: À / M. le Chevalier d'Arblay, / officier du garde du Corps /
Compagnie de Luxembourg / à Senlis
Edited by FBA, p. 1, *annotated and redated*: 10 Fev^r (1815)   (I)   From
Paris to *Senlis*, where M. d'Arblay was *de* service.
Edited also by CFBt. *See* Textual Notes.

Ce Jeudi soir—
Rue de Miurominil—

How am I rejoiced to open the shortest—I hope!—of all
correspondences, by the good news that Bazille[1] is safely
lodged again at the Lycee! I had hardly breathed a sigh that
no efforts could suppress at your departure—hardly lost the
shadow of the carriage which my Eye followed till it turned the
corner, when a Letter was delivered to me, ⌜requiring, they
said, an immediate answer; as it was for you, &⌝ from *La
Lycee*, ⌜I concluded it was from some angry professor, but
opened it without hesitation, certain you would wish me to
judge whether or not to forward it to la Madre; but I found it
was from⌝ the Fugitive himself, ⌜dated *La Lycee*, underwriting
his conduct, naming his Mother, & enclosing a Letter from his
grandfather, which was surprisingly confidential.⌝

I found he was safely lodged, I sent word that you were at
Senlis till Monday, & should then have the Letter: but as the
Master at the Lycee had engaged to let the Madre[1] know
when they heard of the runaway, I have sent her no message
& do not mean to publish that I know the contents of this
packet. But I heartily rejoice the youth is restored to his proper
dwelling & seems to have received great provocation & his
Grandfather is his fond friend & supporter. Poor Boy! he

839.   [1] This was one of the surviving sons of Jean-Baptiste-*Gabriel*-Edmé Bazille
(1767–1804) and his wife the 'Madre', Marie-Julie *née* Ragon (1772–1840), perhaps the eldest, Edmé-Charles (1796–1825), whose education M. d'A had helped
to make provision for on his father's death (vi, L. 561 nn. 1, 2). The boy's 'Grandfather' was M. d'A's uncle Gabriel Bazille (see vi, genealogical table, *facing* p. 476).

certainly knows—or is eager that he will soon discover the whole disgraceful history that ought to be hidden from him, forever.⌐2

I must now ⌐put up my paper, to make it,⌐ as you desire, an annal of *Gourmandise*—

Jeudi au soir. Eh bien! I can assure you my Partridge, 2 *oeufs frais et très frais*, with a double portion of excellent semouille,3 & baked Pears, have nourished me just as your kind anxious heart could wish. And I was solaced with 2 full hours of the society of my dear tenderly attached Mᵉ de Maisoneuve.4

I have spent the day chiefly in preparations for my presentation. All is in good train; & Mᵐᵉ de Segur5 has sent me word I may wear a shawl. Bon soir, mon Ami!—que n'entends-je pas cet Echo qui m'est si cher?—*Bon soir!*— |

⌐Vendredi matin—Une Lettre est just arrivée de Mᵐᵉ Bazille par laquelle je vois que on l'a averti que son fils est en toute sûreté—et aux ecrits—⌐

soyez ainsi tranquil jus'qu'à votre retour—et soyez gai et bien pourtant—pour me consoler de votre absence. L'air peut vous faire du bien—Je l'éspere!—,

adio—mio *ben!*—

adio ben mio?—

I am well.

2 The death of the younger Bazille's father in 1804 uncovered rash, perhaps even dishonest, financial dealings that impoverished his family (vi, L. 554; L. 560 n.1).
3 'Semouille'—semolina—is of course an easily digested food.
4 Marie-Françoise-Élisabeth de Fay de Latour-Maubourg (1770–1850), divorced since 1800 from her adventurous husband Gérard-Joseph Bidault de Maisonneuve, had visited FBA in November and several times in January (Diary Entries, November and 10, 12, 27 January). Her husband's wide-ranging career as a diplomat and soldier under several flags (see v, L. 515 n. 10) from 1770 to 1800 was a paradigm of the lives of those who spanned both *ancien régime* and revolution.
5 Marie-Félicité-Henriette d'Aguesseau (1778–1847) had married on 13 Mar. 1797 Octave-Gabriel-Henri de Ségur (1779–1818), comte de Ségur (vi, L. 580 n. 13). As a former lady-in-waiting to the Empress Joséphine she may have been able to give FBA advice on court etiquette, though both dress and protocol under the restored Bourbons were more rigid than they had been in the Napoleonic court she knew.

Conjointly with M. d'Arblay
To Alexander d'Arblay

A.L. & A.L.S. (Berg), 3 Jan.–10 Feb. 1815
Double sheet 4to   4 pp.   *pmks*   PORT PAYE   FOREIGN / 17 FE
181⟨5⟩   17 FE 1815   black seal
Addressed: Angleterre. / Alexander d'Arblay Junr Esqr / Caius College, /
Cambridge.
Edited by CFBt. *See* Textual Notes.

Reçois mon cher Alex, mes bien tendres remerciemens pour
les excellentes etrennes[1] que tu nous as données par ta lettre
du 23 decembre qui ne nous est parvenue qu'aujourdhui
3 Janvier au moment où nous venions de nous mettre à table.
C'est pour nous une bien douce satisfaction sans doute que
d'apprendre que tu as remporté un prix dans ton College,[2]
mais une plus vive encore est celle que nous avons eprouvée en
lisant que Mr Chapman[3] est content de toi et que tu te portes
bien. J'espere, mon ami, que tu pourras bientot nous en dire
autant de Clement[4] que je plains de toute mon ame d'être
obligé de s'imposer la loi si severe de moderer pendant quelque
tems le gout si vif qu'il a pour l'application, de peur de se
trouver bientôt dans la necessité absolue d'y renoncer entière-
ment par l'impossibilité de s'y livrer avec fruit. Dis lui bien
que ce sacrifice momentané est non seulement necessaire
mais indispensable; et tu peus lui ajouter d'aprés ma propre
experience que s'il a la force de s'y soumettre il en sera payé
trés amplement et avec usure par la nouvelle vigueur avec

840.   [1] M. d'A uses this particular term for a New Year's Day gift because AA's
letter (now lost) reached him so soon after that date. The return of the custom of
gifts and visits on *le Jour de l'An* was one of the first signs of the return under the
Consulate of traditional observances abolished by the Revolution (Robiquet,
pp. 26–7).
   [2] The 2nd Mathematical Prize, 1814. Five weeks before the examinations AA in
a letter (Berg) of 1 November to his mother had expressed doubt that he would win
even this. FBA had clearly hoped for more (see L. 869 n. 9).
   [3] The Revd. Benedict Chapman (vii, L. 740 n. 1) was one of AA's relentless
critics (vii, p. 465; ix *passim*).
   [4] Clement Francis (L. 838 n. 12). From his vantage point at Caius he could
inform FBA's confidants (CBFB and CFBt) concerning AA's chequered career.

la quelle il pourra suivre ensuite son penchant dominant. Tu ne peus, mon cher Alex, exprimer en termes trop forts à ton ami Jones[5] combien je suis reconnoissant des marques d'interest tendre qu'il t'a données, et à quel point je suis sensible à celles qu'il me fait ecrire d'un souvenir au quel j'attache reellement beaucoup de prix. Ce serait pour moi bien veritablement un beau jour que celui où je pourrais être de quelqu' utilité à tes amis de Cambridge. Avec quelle gratitude, mon cher Alex, je trouve que le respectable archidiacre[6] de ce nom a surpassé tout ce que son noble caractère m'avait fait presumer d'attendre de lui. Continue mon ami à te conduire de maniere à prouver que tu es digne d'avoir un protecteur si eclairé, et jouissant si justement d'une reputation dont l'honnorable influence peut tellement seconder tes efforts, et ᶦ non seulement preparer leur sucçes, par la confiance que te donnera cet encouragement, mais encore ajouter au plaisir que tu en recevras. Je te le repete mon ami, tu ne pouvais nous donner de meilleures ètrennes et je t'en renouvelle mès remerciemens, en te priant de me faire savoir ce que nous pourrions t'envoyer pour les tiennes. Ma santé est de jour en jour meilleure, mais n'est pas encore tout à fait bonne. Puisse la tienne continuer à l'être longtems, et fasse le Ciel que sans lui nuire comme l'a fait ce cher Clement tu puisses continuer ton travail et la satisfaction de tes dignes maitres et camarades, au souvenir des quels je te prie de me rappeller.

[By Madame d'Arblay]

Feby 10th 1815. Your kindest Father, my Alex, took the pen the moment your most welcome Letter was read, to express our delight at the satisfaction of Mr. Chapman, & at your Prize, & at the goodness of my excellent Friend Mr. Cam-

---

[5] Richard Jones (1790–1855) was admitted pensioner at Caius on 28 Feb. 1812, B.A. (1816), M.A. (1819), admitted to the Inner Temple (1818). He took Holy Orders and was curate successively of various places in Sussex, curate at Brasted, Kent (1822–33), professor of political economy and history at the East India College, Haileybury (1835–55). He published among other works *An Essay on the distribution of Wealth and on the sources of Taxation* . . . (1831) and *Text Book of Lectures on the Political Economy of Nations* . . . (Hertford, 1852); and he was well known as a historical economist and critic of Ricardo.

[6] This was the Revd. George Owen Cambridge (vi, L. 631 n. 32), Archdeacon of Middlesex, who was generously acting as AA's guardian during this difficult period. On his early and abandoned courtship of FBA, see i, L. 8 n. 7 and *HFB*, pp. 187–93.

bridge,[7] & at the *proof* of the Ensemble alltogether that you are firm in your new system of regularity in your devoirs. Continual indispositions, none alarming, but all weakening, have kept me from finishing this Letter, which, nevertheless, I could not suffer to set off for the *Tight little Island*[8] without some sign of life from myself: &, in fact, as I know another Letter from us must have reached you, long, long since, I have daily expected another from yourself. Has my Boy forgotten he was to give two for one? our impatience for news is so much more urgent than it is possible yours can be, that you must not struggle against so just a condition. Your Second Letter, upon trust, shall always, I promise you, have an immediate answer. The truth is, I had purposed with holding this, till your second arrived: but I am wearied of waiting, & too infinitely eager for fresh intelligence to persevere in my plan. Write, therefore, at once; & never neglect to give me a few *sister's lines*, either at the beginning or end I of every Letter, to tell me if there is any thing in which a *sister's help*, or *advice*, or *influence* may shew my dearest Alex that he has not more certainly a Mother to be his admonisher & his support, than a Sister to be his Friend & his Confident. Do not, then, forget my double quality. I know well you will give me no distress you can avoid; but always remember, if any evil must be known, the sooner the better; & that all I can hear from yourself is paliated by the very communication. In that case, only recollect to *direct* to *Mad^e d'A*, chez M. le Chev^r9 &c. Your best of Fathers gives me full & free permission to aid your inexperience, or help your embarrassments after my own fashion: well aware, from the very nature of things that you must have more courage for any little *unpleasant* confessions with me than with him; & equally sensible that whatever is made known in time, is already nearly remedied. Speak to me, therefore, of your *rising, Chapel, Lectures, Mr. Chapman, Dr Davy*,[10] & your *expences*; with the result of the X^mas *examination*: in which I am prepared for your having no

---

[7] In later years the Archdeacon was to be AA's most solicitous 'protecteur', advisor, and friend (see vols. xi, xii *passim*).

[8] See L. 837 n. 11.

[9] That is, the chevalier d'Arblay, his title until he was created comte d'Arblay by Louis XVIII at Ghent during the Hundred Days.

[10] Martin Davy (vii, L. 659 n. 4) was Master of Caius College from 1803 to 1839.

prize by my having no Letter! *What* was the 3 G^d prize? classical or Mathematical?[11] Pray do not forget to tell me. How did you get on in the X^{mas} vacation? *really* studying? or only *nominally?* be sincere. *We* always rise by Candle-light, for the benefit of our faculties in longevity; all researches on that subject uniting to make early rising the best patron of intellectual life. You were very considerate to name so many of the family. Alas! they must think us lost! it was only yesterday I wrote my *first* Letter that is not to yourself,[12] two of indispens-able *necessity* excepted![13] I have been so perpetually unwell, or frightened, for your dearest Padre, that I could not bear to take a pen in hand, lest I should spread my alarm where it would be useless, & therefore cruel. I hope, now, for happier days. I shall now soon, I hope, write to every body. I have begun with your dear Aunt Hetty—but how shall I thank your other dear Aunt[14] for her infinite kindness & attention to you? I have had a ǀ most precious Letter from her, & a few sweet lines from her sweet Name-sake. My Brothers I hope are well? My kindest love to them all, & not forgeting la *petite tante*,[15] & all the nieces & nephews in the World: & if you have opportunity, my ever dear Mrs. Locke & her loved Amelia.[16]

I have lost my companion for a few days; he is ordered to *Senlis*,[17] 'Tis the 1st time since his return he has been able to attempt any service. & it is too cold for me at present, after

[11] FBA's question may reflect her hope that Alexander might give up the rigours of mathematics for literary studies.
[12] L. 838 to EBB (actually completed two days earlier).
[13] Letters 836 and 837.
[14] For FBA's sister Charlotte Ann (1761–1838) and her daughter by her first husband Clement Francis (*c.* 1744–92), Charlotte Barrett (1786–1870), see i, pp. lxxii–lxxiii. Although this letter is not extant, others show that CBFB and CFBt were FBA's most dependable source of reports on AA's behaviour and progress at Cambridge.
[15] Sarah Harriet Burney (L. 838 n. 29).
[16] Frederica Augusta Locke and her daughter Amelia Angerstein (L. 838 nn. 2, 27).
[17] M. d'A had been posted to an artillery company of the Garde du Corps, whose barracks were at Senlis, roughly twenty-five miles north-east of Paris. In the French Army of this time the household troops of the monarch included a wider selection and variety of units and arms of service. Although the artillery company was disbanded in the reorganization of the Garde du Corps that followed the King's return from Ghent in 1815, its presence in the Maison du Roi at the start of the Hundred Days shows the continuance of a pattern established under the *ancien régime* and revived by Napoleon, namely, the growth of the military household into a small but formidable army.

so much illness, to accompany him, though how I miss him no words can express. Made de Maisonneuve[18] is my sheet anchor: she gives me the solace of her charming society, with always augmenting confidence & affection, almost daily. Charles de Beauvau is preparing to marry Mlle de Praslin, sister to the Duke of that name;[19] & Edmond is now swallowed up by Balls![20] The *dansomanie* is in such vogue, that scarcely a young man or young maid retires to rest till the Elders are nearly ready for Breakfast. Maxime[21] is ordered to Metz. Edmond has at present a *congée*, for the marriage of his Brother. Florimond has been returned some time from Turkey.[22] He has visited me with all the amiability of constant attachment, & enquires after you with cordial friendship. He *admires* your decision to finish your Education at the celebrated University of Cambridge, & expects you to make a brilliant figure in life as a man of science. Amen! Dear General victor comes to me frequently.[23] M. Le Noir[24] sends you 1000 Loves. I have not

[18] For Mme de Maisonneuve, see above L. 839 n. 4 and v, L. 518 n. 10.

[19] On 9 June 1815 François-Victurnien-*Charles*-Just de Beauvau (1793–1864), the eldest son of Marc-Étienne-Gabriel, prince de Beavau-Craon (v, L. 513 n. 2), had married Lucie-Virginie de Choiseul de Praslin (1795–1834), younger sister of Claude-Raynald-Laure-Félix de Choiseul (1778–1841), duc de Praslin and comte de l'Empire (vii, L. 808 n. 11).

[20] The brother of the bridegroom-to-be was Edmond-Henri-Étienne-Victurnien (v, L. 513 n. 2), and the dancing madness he delighted in—together with the balls that marked the first season of the Restoration—figure in several accounts of these confident weeks. See Boigne, i. 358–61, La Tour du Pin, *Memoirs*, pp. 426–8, and Stenger, pp. 300–1.

[21] Only son of Mme de Maisonneuve (n. 18), 'Maxime' or Frédéric-Gérard-Bénoni-César Bidault de Maisonneuve (1797–1869) was a schoolmate of AA in Passy (vi *passim*). He had been ordered to the important garrison town of Metz as a youthful officer in the royal army. For his early military career see vii, L. 736 n. 2.

[22] Just-Pons-*Florimond* de Fay (1781–1837), marquis de Latour-Maubourg and baron de l'Empire, the eldest surviving son of Mme de Maisonneuve's brother César (ii, p. xvii), had returned from a diplomatic posting to Turkey and had with his aunt visited FBA on 12 and 14 January (Diary Entries). See vii, L. 736 n. 3.

[23] Marie-*Victor*-Nicolas de Fay de Latour-Maubourg (1768–1850), baron (1808), comte (1814), called on the d'Arblays on 16 and 20 Jan. 1815 (Diary Entries). For an account of this cavalry general's career, see v, L. 456 n. 9. Victor's friendship and political connection with M. d'A go back to 1792, when with his brother César he emigrated with Lafayette on 18 August and was proscribed on the 20th (Six, ii. 505). Unlike M. d'A, however, he took full advantage of the consular amnesty that followed 18 Brumaire, returned from Holland in the last weeks of 1799, and began in 1800 a distinguished career in the Napoleonic cavalry, voting, however, for Napoleon's abdication in 1814. Named a peer of France by the King on 4 June 1814 and grand cordon of the Legion of Honour on 23 August, he was soon after appointed a member of the commission formed by Monsieur (le comte d'Artois) to reorganize and purge the army. But although he accepted his commission to organize the battalions of royalist volunteers assembling at Vincennes on 12 Mar. 1815, he quickly stood aside and played a waiting game during the rest of the

[*Notes 23 and 24 continued opposite*]

yet seen M. Barbier![25] he has no morning Leisure, & I have not been well enough to receive *du Monde* in an Evening. M. Lajard[26] remembers you with much kindness. Adrienne[27] says 'tis your own fault that she has married another, for she never intended it, if you had come back. She is well & happy. Report is spread here, I know not how! that you are grown very social! Is it true? Write quickly, dearest Alex—& openly & clearly to your faithful Sister—

& most [affec]tionate Mother—FBd'A— |

Write a line, I beg, in MY name, to the dear good kind Archdeacon, with my grateful thanks for his goodness to you. His influence with Mr. Chapman has been of the deepest service, y^r Aunt Broome says.—God bless him for it! Your poor Father still feels the shock of the dreadful blow, though less & less, I bless God! But he will not be quite restored, they say, till Summer!— |

Poor worthy Clem!—I hope he is moderated & recovered? How kind has been Ebdin![28] how amiable, Jones!

Hundred Days. He was not among the peers named by Napoleon (*Moniteur*, 5 June 1815). When the Bourbons returned he was restored to all his honours, and he joined with some zeal in the proscription of Napoleon's supporters, voting for Ney's execution.

His increasingly reactionary devotion renewed his career, and he became in turn ambassador in London from 29 Jan. 1819, Minister of War in succession to Gouvion Saint-Cyr from 19 Nov. 1819, and gouverneur des Invalides from 15 Dec. 1821. He left France with the Bourbons in 1830 returning only in 1848. More accommodating and more successful than M. d'A, he followed the more typical path for a French military careerist.

24 Marie-Alexandre Lenoir (vii, L. 697 n. 5) had been since 1800 an administrator of the Musée des Monuments français and had worked with M. d'A in the Ministry of the Interior. He had called on the d'Arblays on New Year's Day (Diary Entries, p. 547), and it was he whom FBA would ask to oversee the d'Arblay property in Paris when she was forced to flee the capital on 19 March. See further L. 924, pp. 357–8.

25 M. d'A's former colleague, Jean-Pierre Barbier de Neuville (1754–1822), until 1813 chief of the Third Division of the Department of the Interior (vi, L. 595 n. 10 and *passim*).

26 After fleeing to England in 1792 (iv, L. 291 n. 5), Pierre-Auguste Lajard (1757–1837) renewed his acquaintance with the d'Arblays, and it continued after their return to France (v, vi *passim*). With the restoration of Louis XVIII in 1814, he was confirmed, like M. d'A, in the rank of maréchal de camp (roughly equivalent to that of brigadier general).

27 Daughter of the *émigré* Louis-Vigile, comte de Chavagnac (iii, L. 201 n. 5), Adrienne-Adélaïde-Anne (1795–1868) was a childhood friend of AA in England, where she was brought up by the Locke family (iii, L. 215 n. 12). FBA took her to France, together with Alexander, during the entreguerre that followed the Peace of Amiens in 1802. She had married in 1813 Bon-Charles-Henri Euloge de la Couldre (1789–1869), *styled* vicomte de La Bretonnière. For an account of her affectionate visit with FBA on 20 January, see Diary Entries, p. 549.

28 James Collett Ebden (1794–1884) had been admitted pensioner at Caius on

M. d'Arblay
To Madame d'Arblay

A.L. (rejected Diary MSS. 6036–[9], Berg),   11 fev^r
Double sheet 4to   3 pp.   *pmks*   SENLIS   12 Février 1815   wafer
Addressed: A Madame / Madame d'Arblay, / rue de Miromenil N° 8. /
A Paris.
    Edited by FBA, p. 1 (6038), *annotated and dated*: ⊹ (2) (1815.) Re-
ceived at *Paris*, from *Senlis*, where General d'Arblay was then *de* service in
the Artillery, compagnie du duc de Luxembourg—& waiting there my
joining him for a 3 month's residence.
    Edited also by CFBt *and the* Press. *See* Textual Notes.

11. Fev^r

Que tu es aimable et bonne, mon excellente amie! Je ne
puis trop te remercier du joli et charmant billet que tu m'ecris.
Continue à bien soigner ta santé. Tu en auras bon besoin ici.
Surtout fais provision de courage pour supporter le changement
de vie qu'on t'y prepare. Pour toute autre que toi je ne doute
pas que ce ne fut une trés grande jouissance que le tourment
au quel il faut que tu te resignes.[1] Imagine toi, ma bonne amie,
que tu auras à choisir entre une solitude qui pourra paroitre
aux autres trés désobligeante, et une vie dissipée qui certes
sera pourtoi trés fatiguante. Ce dernier parti neanmoins me
semble inevitable; et tout ce que tu pourras faire ce sera d'alleger
le fardeau, en ne recevant que deux jours dans la semaine, et
en annonçant d'avance que ta santé ne te permet pas de
veiller, passé dix heures. Le pis est, qu'il faudra debuter par
faire partout des visites qui te prendront au moins deux jours. |

4 Jan. 1812 and in 1813 and 1814 had won the 1st Classical Prize. He was to
have a long career: B.A. (6th Wrangler, 1816), M.A. (1819), Junior Fellow at
Caius (1816–17), Fellow and Tutor of Trinity Hall (1817–28), Headmaster of
Ipswich Grammar School (1832–43), Vicar of Great Stukeley, Hunts, (1838), and
Rector of King's Ripton (1842). Among his published works are *An English–Latin
Dictionary* (1853) and *Parochial Lectures, on the Church Catechism . . .* (1841).

841.   [1] The burdens of garrison life that FBA feared most were those of receiving
the wives of officers stationed at Senlis and late evenings entertaining them (and
their husbands) with conversation or cards. M. d'A cannot see how she can be spared
the obligation of the wife of a commanding or superior officer, as M. d'A was of the
compagnie de Luxembourg's artillery detachment, to be hostess at mess dinners of
the unit's officers. M. d'A's account in this letter of his own dull and exhausting life
at Senlis seems to warrant all of her misgivings.

Quant au diner, il est bien certain que tu ne pourras pas te dispenser de faire les honneurs de la table des officiers si toute fois elle est montée au premier d'avril, époque la plus eloignée que je puisse t'indiquer pour le commencement de ma residence ici. Refléchis bien à tout cela, ma tendre amie, et commence dès à present à voir un peu plus le monde, afin de t'accoutumer un peu à l'espece d'ennui que traînent à leur suite ses usages et son exigeance

Je te remercie de ce que tu m'as ecrit concernant notre fugitif;[2] et mon opinion est que tu as pris le bon parti, celui d'avoir l'air d'ignorer le contenu de la lettre que tu tiens en reserve pour me la donner à mon retour, c'est à dire aprés demain. Hier j'étais à cheval dès 8^h 1/2 du matin Je n'en suis descendu que pour aller diner, aprés quoi j'ai travaillé. Pour me reposer, j'ai été faire une visite avec ׀ l'etat major dans une maison d'ou je suis sorti à neuf heures precises. J'etais seul, parceque toutes les personnes de ma connaissance etaient engagés au jeu. à près de dix heures j'etais encore à chercher mon chemin dans les rues, et je crois que le jour m'y aurait trouvé, si un particulier à la fenêtre du quel j'ai frappé, parce que j'avais apperçu sa lumiere ne m'eut pas fait reconduire par son fils. Ce matin samedy, j'ai encore été six heures de suite ou à cheval ou pied à terre en plein champ; et je ne fais que [*tear*] rentrer, pour aller vite chez M^r le duc [de Luxembourg] aussitot que j'aurai fait un peu de toilette. Tu vois mon amie que je mene ici une vie très active, qui me fait au surplus le plus grand bien. Aime moi de même et crois à l'eternel sentiment du plus heureux des epoux et des athanases.[3]

Ce samedy à 2^h 1/2.

[2] Probably Edmé-Charles Bazille (L. 839 n. 1).

[3] This name, which the d'Arblays applied repeatedly to one another and to those closest to them, refers to Athanasius (*c.* 298–373), Bishop of Alexandria. Numerous biographical and literary occurrences of this name during the last decades of the eighteenth century and the first decade of the nineteenth show that it had become a fashionable emblem of rural withdrawal and solitude. Charlotte Barrett, in editing FBA's letter of 26 Dec. 1795 to the comte de Narbonne (iii, L. 184), substituted 'two hermits' for FBA's description of herself and M. d'A as 'two *athanases*' who offer to share their 'Hermitage' so that the comte too may 'turn hermit at Bookham till brighter Suns invite you elsewhere'.

The connection with the Bishop of Alexandria may be strengthened by the fact that Alexandre was the Christian name by which M. d'A was known, and it was the name he passed on to his son. A further significance of this name, and one given greater poignancy by the d'Arblays' life together and apart, emerges when we recall what else their contemporaries knew about 'Athanase'. Lemprièrè's *Classical*

Conjointly with M. d'Arblay
To James Burney

A.L.S. & A.L.S. (PML, Autog. Cor. bound), *n.d.*
Double sheet 4to   4 pp.   trimmed   black seal
Addressed: Capt Burney, / James Street, / Westminster.
[*with a direction later in the hand of* JB:] pray direct & send off by post for
Mrs. Broome—

                                                                        Paris—
                                                        Rue de Mirominl—8—
                                                        Fauxbourg St Honore—

'From whence will you write to Me?' said my dear Brother,
when we separated—'From Tours,'[1] I answered—If I wait
till I arrive to give the promised date, when will my Letter
reach you? Melancholy & affrighting accidents have impeded my southern expedition—& have forced & alternately
induced me to silence. I can bear to write ill news, when it is
surmounted by good; but ill by itself ill is so graceless I have
no heart to communicate it when not urged by necessity.
I will not go over the detail of our evils again; I have written
it to Sister Esther & to Alexander;[2] & therefore I am sure you
will not long be ignorant why I have not yet put in my claim
for what I so much desire, intelligence from yourself of your
health & welfare.

For *Our's*, we are in a fair path, I trust, to restoration,
but we travel it slowly, & frequently lose our way, though

Dictionary of 1788, which reflects literary attitudes of the time and which was
known by the Romantic poets of the next generation, speaks not of the Bishop's role
in the growth of monasticism but in terms peculiarly apt to M. d'A. Athanasius,
we are told, was 'Celebrated for his sufferings, and the determined opposition he
maintained against Arius and his doctrines' and he died in A.D. 373 after 'leading
alternately a life of exile and of triumph'. Like Athanasius, the d'Arblays were often
exiled but they were always, like him, firm in their convictions. Both meanings of
the name—hermit and faithful exile—should be understood in these letters; with
the latter becoming more and more what they were, the former more and more
what they wished once more to become.

842.   [1] See L. 838 n. 7.
          [2] The letter to EBB is L. 838; to AA, L. 840.

never our confidence that, at length, it will be attained. Our relapses have been tiresome & painful, but have not robbed us of hope. Darby & Joan,[3] like, therefore, we jog on, & only wish, Darby & Joan like, ultimately together to jog off.

How go on the Bucaneers?[4] I want news of you of all I sorts but chiefly of your health, & of dear Mrs. Burney's, Martin's & Sally's I look upon, as yet, to be superiour to enquiry.[5]

All here is perfectly tranquil; the abolition of the Conscription[6] has gained all Mothers, who have any bowels—though

[3] From their earliest appearance the devotion of Darby and Joan was homely and touching.

> Old DARBY with JOAN by his side,
> You've often regarded with wonder.
> He's dropsical, she is sore-ey'd,
> Yet they're ever uneasy asunder.
> Together they totter about,
> Or sit in the sun at the door;
> And at night when old *Darby's* pot's out,
> His *Joan* will not smoak a whiff more.
>
> No beauty nor wit they possess,
> Their several failings to smother;
> Then what are the charms, can you guess,
> That make them so fond of each other?
> 'Tis the pleasing remembrance of youth,
> The endearments which that did bestow;
> The thoughts of past pleasure and truth,
> The best of our blessings below.
>
> Those traces for ever will last,
> Where sickness and time can't remove,
> For when youth and beauty are past
> And age brings the winter of love,
> A friendship insensibly grows,
> By reviews of such raptures as these;
> The current of fondness still flows,
> Which decrepit old age cannot freeze.

'The Joys of Love never forgot. A Song', in *GM* v (March 1735), 153.

[4] JB's 'History of the Buccaneers of America', comprising the first part of the fourth volume of *A Chronological History of the Voyages and Discoveries in the South Sea or Pacific Ocean* (5 vols., 1803–17), was extensively reviewed in *GM* lxxxvi[2] (1815), 242–6. 'The Buccaneers' was published separately (with a different title-page) by Payne and Foss in 1816, and this edition was reprinted with a new introduction by Malcolm Barnes, *History of the Buccaneers of America. By James Burney, F.R.S.* . . . (1912).

[5] See i, pp. lxix–lxx.

[6] Conscription, which had been instituted in 1799, became a focus of fear and later of opposition to Napoleon's imperial power. The personal and economic losses brought about by it are vividly portrayed in the comments of a disillusioned Napoleonic official: 'Hitherto every call to the conscription has been looked upon as a call to death.... The conscription has been a double calamity to all the productive arts; while it has carried off from them useful hands, it has enhanced the wages of labour.' See G. T. von Faber, *Sketches of the Internal State of France* . . . (trans.,

those who are without complain That they know not, now, *what to do with their Children!* The World at large, however, is so tired of War, that the usual arts of peace will soon resume their reign, & find other employment for Mankind than that of cutting one another to pieces.

I can give You no account of the amusements here, for I have not once been well enough to go out in an evening: &, indeed, were I sufficiently robust to go forth every Night, I much doubt whether I should gain any thing beyond a Yawn for the smartest accounts I could give you of a Ball, an Opera or an assembly, or even the newest flourish of curling the hair, or dizening a Coat. Paris is full of English, I am told; but I have no friends amongst them, & I deny myself the harrass of making new acquaintance. The English in general please here very much. They spend a great ¹ deal of money— which is not apt to breed ill will—& they offer immense food for observation & raillery—which, even with Us, help to keep off ennui & sleep; & which, with my *present* us serve to circulate gaiety, & animate amusement. I intend, when I am a little stouter, to go to a new piece which has a prodigious run here, called *Les Anglaises pour rire.*⁷ The title is so impertinent, that I dare not stay away, lest I should seem sore.

I take the opportunity to send you this hasty *How do* by Mrs. Turner, ci-devant Mad^lle de Boinville⁸—Whose return to [The] *Tight little Island*⁹ I have only known in time to shew

Philadelphia, 1811), p. 252. The danger that AA might be conscripted had led FBA to overcome all obstacles and bring him to England with her in August of 1812. Conscription was abolished by a series of royal decrees in the spring and summer of 1814, though the need had virtually ceased with the abdication of Napoleon and the ensuing peace.

⁷ *Les Anglaises pour rire, ou la table et le logement,* a one-act comedy in couplets by Messrs Sewrin and Dumersan, opened in Paris on 24 Dec. 1814 at the Théâtre des Variétés. It ran in repertory with a number of short plays until the beginning of May 1815 (*Moniteur,* 1 May 1815), but it is unlikely that FBA saw it.

⁸ Daughter of Jean-Baptiste Chastel de Boinville (v, L. 425 n. 8) and his wife Harriet *née* Collins (v, L. 515 n. 21), Cornelia (1795–1874) had married in 1812 Thomas Turner (*fl.* 1803–41, d. *pre* 1856), a lawyer. When she visited FBA on 19 January, they had recalled her youthful frolics with AA to put away the sombre memory of the death of Cornelia's father on 7 Feb. 1813 during the retreat of Napoleon's army from Moscow (Diary Entries, p. 549). In England the Boinvilles lived at Bracknell, where they frequently entertained Shelley, who commemorated his visits there in 'Stanzas, April 1814' and who later praised Cornelia: 'although so young when I saw her, [she] gave indication of her mother's excellencies, & certainly less fascinating, is I doubt not, equally amiable & more sincere' (*Letters,* ed. F. L. Jones, ii. 92).

⁹ See L. 837 n. 11.

you I am somewhat stupified by so much illness & alarm, but
ever & to my last hour, My dear James,

Your really affectionate & unalterably faithful
Sister & Friend
FB d'Arblay.

[*By M. d'Arblay*]

I twoo or too, dear brother, will & must have my share in the
friendly scrawl sent to you. Pray be so kind to remember me
to your better half and to Martyn & his Sister. I hope all are
quite well. Do you danse in London as much as in Paris where
I am said, the English give so many bals. I was to one given
by the princess de Beauveau and hope to be able to see to
morrow another at the same house.[10] | Pray, be so good to
remember me to all friends and relations, and believe for ever &
ever, my dear brother

Your's
A P d'Ay

P.S. Your sister is thank God, pretty well now, and I hope
she will be yet better when the weather shall be quite good— |

10 For M. d'A's account of a former visit to this family, see vi, L. 619. Nathalie-
Henriette-Victurnienne *née* de Rochechouart de Mortemart (1774–1854), who had
enchanted FBA on the first meeting in Paris in 1802 (v, L. 513) and her husband
Marc-Étienne-Gabriel de Beauvau (1773–1849), prince de Beauvau-Craon, had
both become part of the household of Napoleon, she a dame du palais of the
Empress in 1812 (vi, L. 612 n. 2) and he, a chambellan of the Emperor in 1809 and
comte del'Empire in 1810. On 2 June 1815 the prince de Beauvau-Craon was raised
to the even more dangerous eminence of pair des Cent Jours. As the Waterloo
Journal makes clear, the d'Arblays were dismayed by Beauvau's decision to cling
to Napoleon, a decision apparently made in resentment at Louis XVIII's ex-
cluding him from the list of peers at the Restoration in 1814. For FBA's defence of
the Beauvaus, see L. 924, pp. 343-8.

[8, rue de Miroménil, Paris,
pre 22 February 1815]

Conjointly with M. d'Arblay
To Mrs. Broome

A.L.S. & A.L. (Berg), *n.d.*
Double sheet 4to 2 pp. & 1 p. *pmk* 22 FE 1815 black seal
Addressed: Mrs. Broome / Under the Hill / Richmond / Surry.—
Endorsed: Sister d'arblay / March 1815 / & M^r d'arblay

How exquisitely kind was my ever kindest Charlotte in giving us so comforting an account of our Alexander! The history of my silence must now surely be known to you, through my Sister Burney, or Alexander, & therefore I will spare both you & myself the repetition of our *malheurs*. We are both, now, recovering, though by no means yet such as my dearest Charlotte would wish us. We long for better tidings of poor Clement: but the re-establishment of his dearest sister is a true consolation to me.[1] Thank her for her sweet little postscript to your letter, & assure her I would thank her *in kind*, were I less hurried. But this opportunity has been revealed to me only in the middle of the day, & I have so many calls for a few lines, that I have no possible time for one real letter.[2] I am cruelly impatient for another letter from Alex, to hear his X^{mas} history. Your account of him was truly satisfactory, because I saw it was candid & sincere. He speaks with warm gratitude of your kindness to him. Should any opportunity occur, I should be extremely glad to receive the letters, & more still for my near sighted glass. How admirably you have abridged the contents of my Epistles! I am so hurried, I can now only add my thanks, thanks, thanks! with my kind love to Marianne, Clement & Ralph[3]—& when occasion offers to dear Fanny Raper.[4]

843 [1] CBFB's daughter Marianne Francis, now aged 25, was apparently recovering from a series of bilious attacks brought on by emotional crises, her painful decision to reject the addresses of Captain John, *later* Admiral Pakenham (1790–1876) and worries over the health of her brothers. See Gazley, pp. 643–9.

[2] FBA sent this letter and letters 842 and 844 to England with Cornelia Turner (L. 842 n. 8).

[3] The 14-year-old 'Dolph', who had for some time been diagnosed as consumptive (vii, L. 718 n. 16) and was to die at Bath in 1817.

[4] FBA's niece Frances *née* Phillips (L. 838 n. 30), who lived at Cook's Grounds, King's Road, Chelsea.

God bless my most dear Charlotte—I will write longer & better as soon as ¹ possible—but this will assure you we are both preparing to be well, & both full of love & gratitude for your kindness to our Alex & we entreat you to speak for us to the excellent Archdeacon, whose goodness penetrates me with delight as well as thankfulness. Remember me in best manner to his Cornelia⁵—& tell my dear Miss Baker how sincerely I love her, & feel her sweet kindness in giving roof-room to our distressed baggage.⁶ Should our Charlottine⁷ come really to France cannot my dear sister come also? To Ralph it might be essentially beneficial, & he might go to some good Seminary here for his education. I cannot endure your separating from my other Charlotte. Marianne I should think would like to accompany you—& Clement, if he MUST quit his studies, would also be new-manned by such a scheme—Think of it, I beg.

I wrote to sister Esther by post,⁸ unlucckily, a few days ago— Adieu, my dearest Charlotte—pray speak of *your health* very particularly in your next—what is dearest to

your tenderly affecte FBd'A: ¹

[*By M. d'Arblay*]

It is impossible, my dear sister, to be more *reconnaissant* than I am, for your *kind kindness* in giving us so ⟨good⟩ account of all which is to us so much interesting. Would to God that account had been as good in respect of the health of dear Clement to whom I *wish* the fullest accomplishment of all his best *wishes.* a thousand thanks, my dear sister, for all what you do & all what you say concerning our Alex, who cannot fail to feel & enjoy all the good he owes to such a worthy amiable tenderhearted aunt. As to his naughty Cousins whom I have the *mauvais gout d'aimer*, just as much as if the[y] were *aimables*, I heard with rapture they were both single & doubled quite

---

⁵ Cornelia *née* Kuyck Van Mierop (*c.* 1769–1858), who had married the Revd. George Owen Cambridge in 1795, see L. 840 n. 6 and iv, L. 311 n. 5.

⁶ In closing Camilla Cottage and CB's Chelsea apartments in 1814, the d'Arblays stored some of their furniture and effects in White's warehouse, while the rest of their baggage went to relatives such as CBFB and to friends such as Sarah Baker (i, L. 10 n. 6), who lived at Richmond in a house owned by Archdeacon Cambridge.

⁷ Charlotte Barrett (i, pp. lxxii–lxxiii).

⁸ L. 838.

well.[9] So is also I hope Mr Barrett and *his* two frightful little pretty girls and blackpudding milky sons.[10] |

844   [8, rue de Miroménil, Paris,
                                              pre 22 February 1815]

Conjointly with M. d'Arblay
To Charles Burney

A.L.S. & A.L.S. (Osborn), *n.d.*
Double sheet small 4to   4 pp.   *pmk* T.P.P./U.   22 FE 1815   black seal
Addressed: Rev^d Dr. Burney, / Rectory House / Deptford—

[*By M. d'Arblay*]

In the middle of all your fine library,[1] my dear Charles, you cannot have any idea of the many misfortunes I have had to encounter since I left England. In less than ten minutes I was almost drowned, with my backbone broken and knocked down, by the beam of a cart, drawn by a nearly galloping *horsone* (id est) very big & stout horse. After five days of tenderest care from my almost dying Nurse, we left Calais, but we were not able to go beyond Boulogne, in which town we should have been both burn't alive,[2] if we had not been preserved by a kind of miracle, to which you owe the eloquent scribble I send you, in spite of a pretty bad pain pretty lower than my shoulders God knows when we shall meet again, if those bad times don't

---

[9] Charlotte Francis (*supra*) had married Henry Barrett (1756–1843) on 19 June 1807. At the time of this letter the first 'doubled', i.e. paired, children of that marriage, Julia Charlotte (1808–64) and Henrietta Hester (1811–33) had been first 'singled' by Richard Arthur Francis (1812–81) and just recently 'doubled' by the birth of a second son Henry John Richard (1814–29). A third son Arthur Charles (1816–80) was to complete this family in the following year.
[10] A reference to their colouring, in which dark hair contrasted with fair skin. This may have been all the more striking to M. d'A, whose son was 'brown' and 'dark-eyed', as described by CFBt and MF on his arrival in England in 1812 (*HFB*, p. 328).

844.   [1] CB Jr. had one of the finest classical libraries of his age, nearly 14,000 volumes and many manuscripts, including a fine manuscript of Homer. See *The Annual Biography and Obituary for the Year 1819* (1819), p. 222; also Scholes, ii. 237–8.
[2] None of the Boulogne newspapers for this period mentions such a fire and the editors have been unable to find any other explanations for M. d'A's remark.

become milder. We hope however to see again at the end of the summer your little tidy Island. Our intention has been to pay it a new visit sooner, but we must renounce it, because I must, for this year, be *garrisoned* in april May & June; at the end of which I shall be obliged to serve July & August ⏐ at the thuilleries.³ September being the properest time for great manoeuvres, I am afraid I must again spend it at Senlis residence of our Corps. Thus we could not enjoy our liberty before october. But I hope to obtain to see you before that time. Amen, Amen! Till that time be so kind to give us some good account of your health, and of that of Sister Rosette.⁴ How are our Greenwichich friends? pray, be so good to give them my best compliments & whishes, and believe me in Saecula Saeculorum Yours,

Al. d'Ay

[By Madame d'Arblay]

We have heard so late, my dear Carlos, of this opportunity,⁵ that I have but time to greet you with a chaste salutation, & to entreat to receive from you some symptom of remembrance. The cruel accidents, which the chief sufferer has so philosophically rendered ludicrous for your amusement, but which have robbed us both of health & enjoyment, & nearly of existence, since we parted from you at Deptford, will now cease, I hope, to exercise any longer their malignant influence. ⏐ I attempt not any account of them, as I am sure our sister Esther will give you their outline, which your own imagination will easily fill up with probable colouring. But I am quite tired of the subject, though, alas! it is still fresh in its consequences, for we both continue Invalides, though not *BOTH* Hermits; for M. d'A. is obliged to go abroad, & to brave, occasionally, the Elements, & to bustle in the World. But I, who, when at my best, rarely go forth but from some necessity, have kept by our fire side almost entirely from the time of my return to it. I would I could turn aside from our own evils to a gayer prospect of YOUR felicity!⁶ But Alexander gives me the melancholy

³ The artillery company with which M. d'A alternated between garrison life at Senlis, guard duty at the Tuileries (during which time the company lived in the barracks of the Hôtel des Gardes on the Quai d'Orsay), and autumn manœuvres with the other artillery units of the royal army. See also the Waterloo Journal, L. 924 below.

⁴ CB Jr.'s wife, Sarah *née* Rose, called 'Rosette' (L. 838 n. 31).

⁵ See L. 843 n. 2.

⁶ Perhaps the prospect of an additional living (see L. 869 n. 8).

intelligence that poor dear Rosette is—*WAS*, let me hope—
very ill when he saw you at Cambridge. I earnestly wish for
better news. Are you planning any new publication? Alex:
says you were examining Athenaïs,[7] & deep in learned huntings
while at the university. I wish for some account of the colated
Evangelists[8]—& their result. The reverend Dr. *Retardy*[9] is
rather too vellum-like[10] for my taste. Will nobody give him a
hint how he may make himself more agreeable? I am anxious
for information relative to the Museum. I entreat that whatever
you may have for me, either from that learned body, or Mr.
White, or Mr. Leigh, may be paid to | Mess[rs] Hoare, who will
give you a receipt in our names.[11] They have both commission
& directions for placing all that we do not appropriate to
our Alex, through the hands of our sister Broome. We always
build upon returning in the autumn, though we are yet uncertain for what for what time. But I must be much more
established than I feel at present, ere I can brave again the
stormy main—dreadful indeed were the sufferings I owed to it
during my last passage. I hope my dear Charles & his Fanny
are as well as when I left them at Greenwich.[12] I am sorry I
did not see Bright Blossom & my God child elect.[12] I have had

---

[7] This would seem to be Athenaeus, the Greek rhetorician and grammarian
(*fl.* A.D. 200), whose *Deipnosophistae*, a hodgepodge of dinner-table wisdom cast in
the form of a dialogue within a dialogue, may have appealed to the voluptuary in
Charles as it interested the scholar.

[8] In 1812, as FBA mentions in her *Memoirs* (iii. 410) of her father, CB Jr. had
done some work toward 'collating a newly found manuscript Greek Testament';
for this he was given the degree of Doctor of Divinity by the Archbishop of Canterbury, at whose request the work had been undertaken. In conferring this degree the
Archbishop was taking unusual advantage of the ancient and somewhat anomalous
powers vested in his office (Scholes, ii. 236). According to FBA, CB Jr. was to have
undertaken shortly before his death on 28 Dec. 1817 'an examination of a *Fac
Simile* of the Alexandrine MSS of the Greek Scriptures which the Trustees of the
British Museum have been lately engaged in Printing'. See copy of letter (Barrett,
Eg. 3699B, ff. 66–7) to George Cambridge, 12–13 Feb. 1818, and further, x, L.1116
n. 12.

[9] FBA encouraged CB Jr.'s cultivation of 'Dr. Retardy', that is, Charles Manners-
Sutton (1755–1828), Archbishop of Canterbury (1805). Cf. vii, L. 750 n. 3; L. 804
n. 11. This sobriquet she again used in her congratulations when CB Jr. became
Rector of Cliffe at Hoo in Kent (1815): 'the Good Archy is no longer the naughty
Retardy' (L. 922 n. 2).

[10] 'Vellum-like' is an allusion to the tedious and methodical steward in Addison's
The Drummer or the Haunted House (1716). Like 'Dr. Retardy' in this passage, Vellum
was noted for pomp and procrastination. As his impatient master says of him,
'Thou'rt the fittest fellow in the world to be a master of ceremonies to a conjuror'
(III. i).

[11] For business concerning the sale of CB's library and effects, see L. 838 nn. 14,
15, 18.

[12] CB Jr.'s son Charles Parr Burney (1785–1864) had taken over the headmaster-

no news of her Christianism yet. How is Lady Crewe?[13] Pray do not let her quite forget me. Her kindness to me, & her *Friend-ship through life* for my dearest Father will keep her constantly a high place in my Memory. I often think with REAL & great regret of the unfortunate concatenation of events that impeded my availing myself of the goodness of Lady Spencer.[14] The whole time I spent in England was a period of hurry, disturbance, anxiety, or illness: & it has left me nothing but pardons to beg—that I could find no time for enjoyment or comfort.

Adio, my deares[t Carl]ucci—ever & ⟨aye⟩

Yours F B d'A.

PRESENTATION
TO LA DUCHESSE D'ANGOULÊME
24 February 1815

845

A.J., a corrected draft (Diary MSS. vii. 6040–[75], Berg), written *post* 1825 at 11 Bolton Street, London.

Nine double sheets 8vo (7·3 × 4·6″) pinned, making a booklet. The first leaf (6040–1), *recto* and *verso*, is used for titles: Presentation / of F. d'A. / To Son Altesse Royale / Madame / La Duchesse d'Angoulême, / Depuis / Madame la Dauphine /

The text comprises p. 1 (6042)—p. 34 [6075], 34 pp., paged 1–24 and foliated on lower margins.

Edited by CFBt *and the* Press. *See* Textual Notes.

ship of Greenwich School from his father in 1813 (Scholes, ii. 238). His wife was Frances Bentley Young (*c*. 1792–1878), whom he had married in 1810. 'Bright Blossom' was their first child, Frances Anne (1812–60); FBA's 'God child elect' (vii, L. 761), their second, Rosetta d'Arblay (1814–1910). For CB Jr.'s verses to his granddaughter 'Bright Blossom', see vii, L. 724A n. 3.

[13] Frances Anne *née* Greville (i, L. 1 n. 10 and *passim*) was the daughter of CB's early patron Fulke Greville, a woman of great beauty, a brilliant hostess at Crewe Hall to the political and cultural talents of her time, and a lifelong friend of the Burneys. In CB's will she was left 'my Nephew Edward's Copy of Sir Joshua Reynolds's Sleeping Child . . .' (Scholes, ii. 265).

[14] Eldest daughter of Charles Bingham (1730–99), 1st Earl of Lucan, Lavinia (1762–1831) had married in 1781 George John Spencer (1758–1834), 2nd Earl Spencer. For Lady Spencer's invitations to FBA to accompany CB Jr. to Althorp, see vii, L. 730 n. 3 and *passim*.

Having fulfilled,—at length!—my long received injunction[1] of committing to paper my Presentation to His Majesty Louis 18, King of France, I come now to that of my Audience with M^de Duchesse d'Angoulême.—As I had missed, through a vexatious mistake, the Honour she had herself intended me of presentation in England,[2] my own condescending Royal Mistress, Queen Charlotte, recommended my claiming its performance on my return to Paris. This was M. d'Arblay's intention & wish also. But the dreadful accident—

⌈elsewhere narrated⌉

which made him arrive in that Capital only to be placed under the care of the Baron Larrey—my excellent surgeon & Friend—caused nearly 3 months to elapse ere measures could be taken for putting in my solicitation. M. d'Arblay then ⎪ consulted with le Viscomte d'Agoult,[3] his intimate early Friend, how to repair in France my English deprivation. M. d'Agoult was Ecuyer to S.A.R. & high in her confidence & favour: but, not knowing the peculiar circumstances that authorized my application, he confessed that to obtain a private Audience would be very difficult,[4] the Princess having a real dread upon

845.   [1] This request was made by M. d'A in 1818. FBA's account of her presentation to Louis XVIII on 22 Apr. 1814 was composed in Brighton during November and December of 1823 (*HFB*, p. 432). She would seem to have 'come' to the duchesse d'Angoulême only in 1826 or 1827, in any event, *post* 1825 and before her move from Bolton Street in 1828.

It is possible to date the presentation itself quite precisely. The duc and duchesse d'Angoulême left Paris for Bordeaux early on the morning of Monday 27 Feb. 1815. During the preceding week FBA received the following note (Comyn), written by the duchesse de Sérent (n. 7) for the duchesse d'Angoulême, *pmk* 22 Fevrier 1815.

Madame Duchesse d'Angoulême charge la D^esse de Serent de mander à Madame d'Arblay qu'elle la recevera bien du plaisir vendredi prochain entre quatre et six heures, elle regrette que sa santé ne lui ait pas permis de venir plutôt.

la D^esse de Serent partage les regrets de S.A.R. et sera très ais[ée] d'avoir l'honneur de voir Madame d'Arblay

This means that the presentation took place late on the afternoon of Friday 24 Feb. 1815.

[2] See vii, L. 769, for a description of the confused attempt at presentation made by FBA and Lady Crewe in London in April of the previous year.

[3] This discussion with d'Agoult (L. 835 n. 7) took place in the d'Arblay's apartment on Sunday 5 February (Diary Entry, p. 551).

[4] By choosing to be presented to the duchesse d'Angoulême in this private way, FBA sought to avoid the rigid etiquette and expensive dress required of courtiers at the Restoration. The duchesse d'Angoulême, zealously backed by the duc de Duras (n. 8), insisted on a court dress for women that added to the imperial style of Napoleon's court a costly layer of ribbons, laces, and mantillas. In this grotesque dress court ladies who were presented publicly were hurried through a series of rooms and interviews that exhausted them and ruled out any hope of conversation (Boigne, i. 259–63).

her mind of giving an opportunity for any personal requests, as she had been besieged, since her restoration, with petitions impossible to grant, yet, from their Justice as well as urgency, deeply painful to refuse. He advised me, therefore, simply to *faire ma Cour*, as the Wife of a superiour officer in the Garde du Corps du Roi, at a public Drawing Room.

The great exertion & publicity, joined to the expence of such a presentation, made me averse, in all ways, to this proposal: & when M. d'Arblay protested I had not any thing in view but to pay my respectful ˡ devoirs to Her Royal Highness, M. d'Agoult under took to make known my wish. It soon proved that this alone was necessary for its success; for Mme la Duchesse instantly recollected what had passed in England, & said she would name, with pleasure, the first moment in her power, though she was just then preparing to go to Bordeaux,[5] & extremely engaged.—I felt highly obliged, but earnestly begged, through M. d'Agoult, that, such being the case, my presentation might be postponed to Her Royal Highnesses return: to this, however, she would not consent, expressing an impatience on her own part that an interview should not be delayed which had been desired by Her Majesty Queen Charlotte of England.

Of course, this both encouraged & gratified me: but, fearful of commiting any mistake in *Etiquette*, from my utter ignorance of the French Court, ˡ I entreated M. d'Arblay to enquire of M. Mathieu de Montmorency[6] whether there were any peculiarities in such an introduction that I ought to study, or learn.

M. de Montmorency—Now M. Le Duc, with whom we were all much acquainted, & who was then in waiting upon La Duchesse, most kindly promised to be at hand, when the time should be fixed, for obviating all embarrassment by presenting me himself.

This—as he was one of the most amiable & best bred of men, was quite delightful to me.

[5] The duc and duchesse d'Angoulême left for Bordeaux on 27 Feb. 1815 to commemorate the proclamation of the restored reign of Louis XVIII on 12 Mar. 1814 in that city, an event which many saw as the miracle that brought the Bourbons back to the throne of France (see Bertier de Sauvigny, pp. 29–33).

[6] Mathieu-Jean Félicité de Montmorency-Laval (L. 837 n. 16) had been acquainted with FBA since his *émigré* and more liberal days in England in 1792. Previously aide-de-camp to the comte d'Artois, he was now chevalier d'honneur of the duchesse d'Angoulême.

The Viscomte d'Agoult then told M. d'Arblay, that I had best write a billet to Madame la Duchesse de Serent,[7] to solicit an Audience; &, that I should still do well, to quiet all the apprehensions of Madame, if I mentioned the singleness of my intentions, & their freedom from any application.

To this I could certainly have no objection;—yet I thought, with a gratitude | the most fervent how nobly free from all similar precautions was the intercourse with which I was indulged by my own beloved & honoured Princesses in my own '*tight little Island.*'

My best Friend drew up for me this Note—which I retain in His hand.—

À Madame La Duchesse de Serrent.

Madame là Duchesse,
    Penetrée des bontés dont le Roi a daigné m'honorée de lui être presentée en Angleterre par M. le Duc de Duras,[8] Je n'en ai senti que plus douloureusement le regret d'avoir reçu trop tard la Lettre de M. le Cte de La Châtre,[9] me donnant l'avis que j'aurais pû l'être egalement à son Altesse Royale Madame la Duchesse d'Angoulême. Depuis cette epoque ma santé, toujours chancellante, m'obligè au plus grandes precautions contre le Froid, mon mortel Ennemi. Mais, j'ai appris, Madame la Duchesse, qu'à la solicitation de M. le Viscomte d'Agoult | Vous avez eu l'extreme bonté de vous charger de mettre sous les Yeux de S.A.R. mon desir de pouvoir être admise de lui presenter particulierement l'hommage de mon Respect, et d'un devouement aussi sincère qu'il est totalement disinterressé.

    Veuillez, Madame la Duchesse, agréer celui de ma reconnoissance respectueuse.

F. d'Arblay, née Burney.

Ce 20. Fev^er 1815.
Rue de Miromenil, N° 8. |

    [7] Bonne-Marie-Félicité de Montmorency-Luxembourg (1739–1823), duchesse de Sérent (vii, L. 770 n. 6), had been appointed in 1776 dame d'atours to the duchesse d'Angoulême, then princesse Élisabeth, and had been dame d'honneur since the latter's marriage. Her husband, Armand-Louis, duc de Sérent (1736–1822), had been tutor to the duc d'Angoulême and to his brother the duc de Berry since before the Revolution.
    [8] Amédée-Bretagne-Malo de Durfort (v, L. 440 n. 2), duc de Duras, an hereditary officer of the crown as First Gentleman of the King's Chamber, whose part in FBA's presentation is recorded in vii, L. 770.
    [9] For a biography of Claude-Louis, successively comte, marquis, and duc de La Châtre, see ii, p. xvi and L. 836 above.

But I have omitted to mention that on the Sunday preceding these billets, the Duchess d'Angoulême, at Court, had deigned to tell my best Friend that she was reading—& with great pleasure—*Madame d'Arblay's last Work*. He expressed his gratification, & added that he hoped it was in English, as Her *Altesse Royale* so well knew that language. No, she answered, it was the translation she read;[10] the original she had not been able to procure.

On this, M. d'Arblay advised me to send a Copy. I had none bound, but the sett which had come back to me from my dear Father.[11] This, however, M. d'A. carried to the Viscomte d'Agoult, with a Note | from me, in which, through the medium of M. d'Agoult, I supplicated leave from S. A. R. to lay at her feet this only English set I possessed. In the most gracious manner possible, the viscomte told M. d'Arblay, her Royal Highness accepted the Work, & deigned also to keep the Billet. She had already, unfortunately, finished the Translation; but she declared her intention to read, some months hence, the original.

Previously to my presentation, M. d'Arblay took me to the Salon of the Exhibition of Pictures,[12] to view a portrait of Mad^e d'Angoulême, that I might make some acquaintance with her Face before the Audience. It was very deeply interesting, but very deeply melancholy.

All these precautions taken, I went, at the appointed Hour & morning, about the end of February, 1815, to the Palace of the Thuilleries, escorted by the most indulgent of Husbands, in full uniform. |

We repaired instantly to the Apartment of la Duchesse de Serrent.[13] I presume, however, it was merely a temporary room for her, as it was very small, encumbered with common furniture, &, alltogether not merely inelegant, but positively shabby:

She received us with the utmost politeness, She had only with her a young lady, her Daughter, or her Granddaughter;[13]

[10] The French translation of *The Wanderer* (L. 837 n. 15).

[11] This copy of *The Wanderer* would seem to be one of the 'miscellaneous' books that CB left 'for the profit of MY TWO ELDEST DAUGHTERS', EBB and FBA (Scholes, ii. 264). The delivery had taken place, as the Diary Entries show, on 29 January.

[12] In the 1814 Salon, which is where M. d'A took FBA, there were portaits of the duchesse d'Angoulême by no fewer than six painters.

[13] According to the comtesse de Boigne, the duchesse d'Angoulême was

but we all stood while I stayed, as the Duchess said she must not detain me from son Altesse Royale. She made me very civil speeches, & in a tone & manner of extreme courtesie, upon her gratification in this opportunity of becoming acquainted with me; & then spoke more at large with General d'Arblay upon various persons of their mutual acquaintance: After which, she gave us our lesson how to proceed, & delivered us over to some Page of her Royal Highness.

We were shewn into a very ⎪ large apartment. I communicated to the Page a request that he would endeavour to make known to M. de Montmorency that I was arrived, & how much I wished to see him.

In a minute or two, from an inward entrance came forth a tall, sturdy Dame who immediately addressed me by my Name, & spoke with an air that demanded my returning her Compliment. I could not, however, recollect her, till she said she had formerly met me at the Princesse d'Henin's.[14] I then recognized the Dowager Duchess de Duras,[15] whom, in fact, I had seen last at the Princesse de Chimay's,[16] in the year 1812, just before my first return to England; & had received from her a commission to acquaint the Royal Family of France that her son, the Duke, had kept aloof from all service under Bonaparte, though he had been named in the Gazettes as having accepted the place of Chamberlain to the then Emperor. ⎪ Yet such was the subjection, at that time, of all the old nobility, to the

constantly attended by Mme de Sérent and her two daughters, the comtesses de Damas-Crux and de Narbonne-Pelet. The first, Anne-Simonne-Félicité (vii, L. 818 n. 12), the wife of Étienne-Charles, comte *later* duc de Damas-Crux (1751–1846), succeeded her mother as lady of honour; the second Émilie (1770–1856), the wife of Raimond-Jacques-Marie (1771–1855), comte de Narbonne-Pelet, a woman of some intellectual gifts, was a confidante of Louis XVIII (Boigne, i. 429). It is more likely, however, given their ages, that FBA saw one of her granddaughters, one of the many children of Émilie.

14 Adélaïde-Félicité-*Étiennette* de Monconseil (1750–1824), princesse d'Hénin (v, L. 446 n. 23), a constant friend to the d'Arblays (v, vi *passim*), with whom FBA was to flee to Brussels on Napoleon's return to Paris.

15 Louise-Henriette-Charlotte-*Philippine*, *née* de Noailles (1745–1822), the dowager duchesse de Duras, was the widow of Emmanuel-Céleste-Augustin de Durfort (1741–1800), an *émigré* who had died in London (see v, L. 440 n 3). Her son, Amédée-Bretagne-Malo de Durfort, duc de Duras (n. 8 above), held no office under Napoleon.

16 Laure-Auguste *née* Fitz-James (1744–1814), widow of Philippe-Gabriel-Maurice-Joseph d'Alsace-Hénin-Liétard (1736–1804), prince de Chimay (1759), had also given FBA a commission in London (see vi, pp. 711–13 and notes). She had died by the time of FBA's presentation to the duchesse d'Angoulême.

despotic power of that mighty Ruler, that M. de Duras had not dared to contradict the paragraph.

She then said that Her Altesse Royale was impatiently expecting me: And made a motion that I should pursue my way into the next room; M. d'Arblay no longer accompanying me. But before I disappeared, she assured me that I should meet with a most gracious reception, for Her Altesse Royale had declared she would see me with marked favour, if she saw no other English whatsoever; because *Madame d'Arblay* she said, *was the only English person who had been* peculiarly *recommended to her notice by the Queen of England.*

What Graciousness this of my most ׀ revered & beloved Royal Mistress!

In the next, which was another very large apartment, I was received by a lady much younger & more agreeable & more fashionable than Mad⁰ de Duras, gaily & becomingly dressed, & wearing a smiling air with a sensible Face. I afterwards heard it was Madame de Choisy;[17] who, a few years later, married M. le Vᵗᵉ d'Agoult.

Mᵐᵉ de Choisy instantly began some personal Compliments, with which I could well have dispensed, of knowing me *d'avance* by her acquaintance with *mes ouvrages*, &c &c, but finding she only disconcerted me, she soon said she must not keep me back, & courtsied me on to another room, into which she shut me.

I here imagined I was to find M. de Montmorency; but I saw only a lady, who stood at the upper end of the apartment, & slightly courtsied, but without moving, or speaking.[18] ׀

Concluding this to be another *Dame de la Cour*, from my internal persuasion that, ultimately, I was to be presented by M. de Montmorency, I approached her composedly, & with a mere common inclination of the head, & looked wistfully forward to the further door. She enquired politely after my health, expressing good-natured concern to hear it had been deranged, & adding that she was *bien aise de me voir*. I thanked her, with some expression of obligation to her civility, but

---

[17] Anne-Charlotte-Henriette de Choisy (vii, L. 818 n. 11), lady of the bed-chamber of the duchesse d'Angoulême, who was to marry the widower d'Agoult in 1815 (L. 835 n. 7). It was in her rooms in the Tuileries that the most vehement royalists, attached to the duchesse d'Angoulême, met in the evenings after dinner.

[18] It should be remembered throughout this presentation, especially when FBA fails to recognize the courtiers she meets, that she was near-sighted and that she saw them here without the aid of her lorgnette, which she mentioned in vi, L. 603.

almost without looking at her, from perturbation lest some mistake had intervened to prevent my Introduction, as I still saw nothing of M. de Montmorency.

She then asked me if I would not sit down, taking a seat at the same time on a Chair next to the Wall herself. I readily complied; but was too much occupied with the Ceremony I was awaiting to discourse though she immediately began what was meant for a Conversation. I hardly heard, or answered ˡ so exclusively was my attention engaged in watching the door through which I was expecting a summons: till, at length, the following words rather surprised me.—

I must write them in English, for my greater ease, though they were spoken in French. 'I am quite sorry to have read your last charming work in French.'

My Eyes now changed their direction from the door to her Face, to which I hastily turned my head, as she added:

'Puis-je le garder, le livre que vous m'avez envoyé?'

Startled, as if awakened from a dream, I fixed her, & perceived the same Figure that I had seen at the Salon. I now felt sure I was already in the royal presence of the Duchesse d'Angoulême, with whom I had seated myself almost *Cheek by Jowl*, without the smallest suspicion of my situation.

I really seemed thunderstruck. I had approached her with so little formality, I had received all her Graciousness ˡ with so little apparent sense of her condescendsion, I had taken my seat, nearly unasked, so completely at my ease; & I had pronounced so unceremoniously the plain *vous*, without softening it off with one single Altesse Royale that I had given her reason to think me either the most forward person in my nature, or the worst bred in my education, existing.

I was in a consternation unspeakable, & a confusion that robbed me of breath; To have given cause for an opinion so unfavourable hurt me to the quick; & my first impulse was to abruptly arise, confess my errour, & offer every respectful apology I could devize: but as my silence & strangeness produced silence, &, probably, wonder in herself, a complete pause ensued that gave me a moment for reflection; & in that short moment, my ideas, from the accelerated rapidity of conception ˡ caused by the pressure of sudden alarm, instantaneously represented to me that S.A.R. might be seriously hurt, her stately character considered, that nothing in her demeanour had announced her rank; & such a discovery might lead to encreased distance & reserve in her future conduct upon other extra-Audiences, that could not but be prejudicial to her popularity, which already was injured by an opinion extremely unjust, but very generally spread of her haughtiness.[19] It was better, therefore, to be quiet, & to let her suppose that embarrassment, & English awkwardness & *mauvaise honte*, had cast my poor understanding, & yet more my unaccountable manners, into a bewildered obscurity that had produced the effect of complete stupidity.

I kept, therefore, my taciturnity, till, tired of her own, she gently repeated 'Puis-je la gardér—? cette Copie que vous m'avez envoyée?'—civilly adding, that she should I be happy to read it again, when she had a little forgotten it, & had a little more time.

I siezed this fortunate moment to express my grateful acknowledgments for her goodness, with the most unaffected sincerity, yet scrupulously accompanied with all the due forms of profound respect.

What she thought of so sudden a change of dialect I have no means to know;[20] but I could not, for a long time afterwards think of it myself with a grave Countenance. From that time, however, I failed not to address her with appropriate reverence; though, as it was too late, now, to assume the distant hommage pertaining, of course, to her very high rank, I insensibly suffered one irregularity to lead to, nay to excuse another; for I passed over all the *Etiquette d'usage*, of never

[19] The duchesse impressed everyone, including her enemies, with her firmness and courage. But even those who most greatly admired her admitted a severity verging on haughtiness. According to Antoine de Reiset, like M. d'A an officer of the Gardes du Corps, 'Madame la duchesse d'Angoulême n'a aucun goût pour les frivolités; elle ne se plaît qu'aux choses sérieuses. . . . Malheureusement, Madame qui est très bonne est d'abord froid et d'humeur peu liante. . . . Elle se déride rarement, et son entourage est plutôt austère'. See Reiset, iii. 55–6. Her entourage, drab and unyielding, suffered numerous attacks from the opposition. The wittiest and perhaps the most damning of these came from the famous paper the *Nain jaune*, which derided the royalists as the Chevaliers de 'l'ordre de *l'Éteignoir*', literally the Order of Knights of the Candle-Snuffer and figuratively those who snuff out or dampen the gaiety or spirits of others (Pasquier, iii. 59–60).

[20] The duchesse might have attributed FBA's lack of awe to the forthrightness of the English, which was a by-word among the French nobility and royal family. Even before the Revolution Marie-Antoinette was amused to see Mme de La Tour du Pin shaking hands at Versailles with the English ambassador rather than curtseying to him (La Tour du Pin, p. 71).

speaking but *en reponse*; & animated myself to attempt to catch her attention, by conversing with fullness & spirit upon every ⎮ subject she began, or led to; & even by starting subjects myself, when she was silent. This gave me an opportunity of mentioning many things that had happened in Paris during my long ten years uninterrupted residence, which were evidently very interesting to her. Had she become grave, or inattentive, I should have drawn back: but, on the contrary, she grew more & more *eveillée*, & her Countenance was lighted up with the most encouraging approvance.

She was curious, she said, to know how I had gotten over to England in the year 1812, having been told that I had effected my escape by an extraordinary disguise. I assured her that I had not escaped at all; as so to have done must have exposed the generous husband & Father who permitted mine & his son's departure to its dangerous responsibility. I had procured a passport for us both, which was registered in the ordinary manner *chez le Ministre de Police*, for foreign affairs;— *chez* one, I added, whose name I could not pronounce in her Royal Highnesse's hearing;[21] but to whom ⎮ I had not myself applied, & for whom, indeed, I had a repugnance so intense, that I should sooner still have waited the indefinite & heart-sickening progress of events, with all their menaces of being for-ever adverse to my wishes, than have presented myself to him as a petitioner for personal favour. She well knew I meant Savary, Duc de Rovigo, whose history with respect to the murdered Duc d'Enghein has, since that period, been so variously related.

She did not speak, but her look demanded a continuation of my account.

I was then embarrassed; for I had owed my passport to the request of Madame d'Astorge,[22] who was distantly connected

---

[21] Anne-Jean-Marie-René Savary (vi, L. 631 n. 17), duc de Rovigo, minister of police (1810–15). His name was indelibly linked in royalist memories with the plot against the duc d'Enghien and his hurried execution in 1804. The complex and in part factitious plot through which the duc d'Enghien was ensnared remains a source of debate and speculation among historians. There is, however, little doubt that FBA was right in her judgement. During the Hundred Days Savary was created a peer by Napoleon and commandant général de la gendarmerie; he was condemned to death *in absentia* after Louis XVIII's return from Ghent in 1815 but acquitted by a second court martial on his return to France in 1819. An earlier account of FBA's application for this passport appears in vi. 708–10.

[22] Marie-Thérèse-Louise d'Éon de Cély (*fl.* 1783), wife of Jean-Jacques-Marie

with Savary, & who had obtained it to oblige Madame de Tracy,[23] a mutual friend: but to have had any influence with Savary could ill have been a recommendation to Her Royal Highness; & ill, therefore, on my part; could it have been named, since it was for my Advantage that influence had been employed.

I found, however, to my great ⌐ relief, that she possessed the same noble delicacy of forbearance that renders all private intercourse with my own exemplary Princesses as safe for others as it is honorable to myself; for she suffered me to pass by the names of my assistants, when I said they were friends who exerted themselves for me, in consideration of my heavy grief in an absence of Ten years from a Father whom I had left many years at the advanced Age of 75; joined to my quick terrour lest my son should remain till he attained the period of the Conscription, & be necessarily drawn into the military service of Bonaparté. And indeed, these two points could alone, with all my eagerness to re-visit my Native Land, have induced me to make the journey by a separation from my best Friend.

This led me to assume courage to recount some of the prominent parts of the conduct of M. d'Arblay during our Ten Years Confinement, rather than Residence, in France: I thought this necessary, lest our sojourn during the usurpation should be misunderstood. I told her, in particular, of Three high ⌐ military appointments which he had declined; the first was to be head of l'Etat Major of a Regiment under General ⟨Jalizoke⟩[24] whose name I cannot spell—in the Army of Poland;

(1751–1822), comte d'Astorg of Auch, Gers, lieutenant de la compagnie écossaise des gardes du corps (see vi, L. 631 n. 21).

23 Émilie-Pérette-Antonie de Durfort de Civrac (1754–1824), the wife of Antoine-Louis-Claude Destutt (1754–1836), marquis and comte de Tracy. See v, L. 526 n. 21 and vi *passim*.

24 Józef Zajączek (1762–1826), a cavalry officer whose military career spanned Europe, had been recalled to Paris on 17 Mar. 1806 and on 20 September ordered to raise a Polish legion, in which M. d'A was offered 'la proposition de la place de Major general laissée à sa (i.e. Zajączek's) disposition' with pay of 10,000 francs. See A.L.S. Vincennes (France), M. d'A to Louis XVIII, 9 June 1814.

By raising this Polish (or Northern) Legion soon after going to war with Prussia, Napoleon hoped to encourage desertion among Poles in Prussian service and to recruit those who were taken captive. Zajączek, after a number of campaigns with the Grande Armée in Germany and Poland, took command in 1812 of the 1st division of the 5th Corps during the invasion of Russia. He survived this to join the army of the Kingdom of Poland in 1814, becoming a general of infantry in 1815 and a prince of the realm in 1818. See Jan Pachoński, *Legiony Polskie, 1794–1807* . . .

a post of which the offer was procured for him by M. de Narbonne,[25] then aid de Camp to Bonaparte but always to M. d'Arblay the most attached of Friends: the 2[d] was an offer, through General Gassendi,[26] of being Commander of Palma Nuova,[27] whither M. d'A. might carry his Wife & Son, as he was to have the Castle for his residence, & there was no War with Italy at that time. The 3[d] was again a proposal from General Gassendi; & was made the very Day after I left Paris for my visit to my dear Father, in 1812. Gassendi, though he was very partially my Friend, as well as M. d'Arblay's, probably attributed the refusal of Palma Nuova to feelings that had reference to me; & therefore believed the moment of our separation would be more favourable to a military | expedition. The offer was a very high one; it was no less than the command of Cherbourg as successor to M. le C[te] de La Tour Maubourg,[28]

(Warsaw, 3 vols., 1969–71) *passim*; *Cambridge History of Poland*, ii. 226; and Six. His name, which was the despair of the French who tried to spell it, appears as 'Tayouchek' in M. d'A's later account to Louis XVIII of this offered appointment and elsewhere in the papers as an almost illegible scrawl.

[25] Louis-Marie-Jacques-Amalric (1755–1813), comte de Narbonne-Lara (i–vii *passim*). FBA here mistakenly shortens the period of Narbonne's neglect after his return to France in 1800. Although still able to see and seek favours from those who had known him when he was Minister of War (1791–2), his expectations that his talents and experience would gain for him an important post under the Consulate went unfulfilled until 1809. Whatever may have been the reasons for passing over Narbonne (envy and fear of rivalry by Talleyrand and Bonaparte were certainly among them), it was only after the fall of Talleyrand that Narbonne rose again to a position of importance, serving as minister to Munich in 1810, aide-de-camp to the Emperor in 1811–12, and ambassador to Vienna and minister to Prague in 1813, in which year he died at Torgau (Dard, pp. 152–8). For his attempts to secure military employment for d'Arblay, see vi, L. 605 n. 2.

[26] For this offer, see vi. 641–2. Jean-Jacques-Basilien (1748–1828), comte de Gassendi, général d'artillerie (v, L. 468 n. 3), chef de la 6e division du ministère de la Guerre, had confidence in M. d'A not only as an artillery officer but also as a military engineer. This explains why the appointments he proposed to M. d'A in 1812 were those of a fortress commander. They were within the scope of his branch of the War Ministry.

[27] Palma Nuova, or more properly Palmanova, was an important fortress on the eastern frontier of what had been the Venetian Republic. A castle fifteen kilometres from Udine whose fortifications, frequently fought over by the French and Austrians, were in the shape of a nine-pointed star, it was one of the fortresses (along with Legnano, Osoppo, and Venice) surrendered to the Austrian army by Prince Eugène de Beauharnais according to the Convention of Schiarino-Rizzino on 16 Apr. 1814, signed on Napoleon's abdication at Fontainebleau on 11 April. See R. John Rath, *The Provisional Austrian Regime in Lombardy-Venetia, 1814–1815* (Austin and London, 1969), pp. 4–5.

[28] Marie-Charles-*César*-Florimond de Fay (v, p. xlvi), comte de Latour-Maubourg, had been governor of Cherbourg (vi, L. 605 n. 2) and commissaire extraordinaire to the National Guard in the five departments of Brittany since the beginning of 1810. After a year of retirement he was ordered on 21 Mar. 1812 to organize the cohorte du 1er ban dans la 13e division militaire. In 1814 César sup-

who was sent elsewhere, by still higher promotion. Steady, however, invariably steady was M. d'Arblay, never to serve against his liege Sovereign. General Gassendi, one of the most zealous of his personally attached Friends, contrived to cover up this dangerous rejection; & M. d'Arblay continued in his humbler—but far more meritorious office, of *sous chef* to one of the *Bureaux de l'Interieur*.—

I had now the pleasure to hear the Princess say '*Il a agi bien noblement.*' 'For though he would take no part,' I added, '*à la Guerre*, nor yet in the *Diplomatie*, he could have no objection to making plans, arrangements, buildings, & so forth, of Monuments, Hospitals, & palaces:—for, at that period, Palaces, like Princes, were *élevés tous les Jours.*'

She could not forbear smiling; & her smile, which is rare, is so peculiarly ^I becoming, that it brightens her Countenance into a look of youth & beauty.

'But why,' I cried, recollecting myself, 'should I speak French, when your Royal Highness knows English so well?'

'O no!' cried she, shaking her head, 'Very bad!—'

From that time, however, I spoke in my own tongue, & saw myself perfectly understood, though those two little Words were the only English ones she uttered herself, replying always in French.

'Le Roi,' she said, 'se rappelle très bien de vous avoir vu À Londres.'[29]

'O, Je n'en doute nullement!' I replied, rather *naively*,— 'for immediately before I had the honour of being presented to his Majesty, there passed a scene that cannot be forgotten, & that surprised me into courage to come forward, after I had spent the whole morning in endeavouring to shrink backward: the Address of the grateful & warmly attached County of Buckinghamshire, in which ^I his Majesty & your Royal Highnesses so long resided, had just been read, in English, by

ported the abdication of Napoleon and swore allegiance to Louis XVIII, becoming a pair de France on 4 June 1814. Unlike his brother Victor, who stood aside during the Hundred Days, César allowed Napoleon on 2 June 1815 to include him among the pairs des Cent Jours, and he voted on 23 June for the proclamation of Napoleon's son as emperor. Under the Second Restoration he was expelled from the Chambre des Pairs by Louis XVIII and was not restored to his place until 5 Mar. 1819.

[29] FBA's presentation to Louis XVIII had taken place on Friday 22 Apr. 1814 at an open house in Grillion's Hotel that followed the formal receptions of the preceding day. See vii, L. 770.

Colonel Nugent,[30] I think; & with a fervour of congratulation
& Joy that was really affecting: but how much more so, to me,
was the answer of His Majesty, uttered, to my unspeakable
delight, in English, & not read, but spoken, & pronounced in an
accent so elegant, & in words so well chosen, so courteous, so
condescending, so lively, & so completely amiable, that the
moment it was over, & Colonel Nugent & the Addressers had
retired, I involuntarily sprung from behind his Majesty's
Chair, &, to my own eternal surprize at its recollection, I
suffered the ardour of my joy at something that seemed
amalgamating the two Countries to which I almost equally
belonged, to over-power ' all the Rights & Ceremonies of
Etiquette, & I hardly gave time for M. le Duc de Duras to name
me, before I burst forth in expressions of irrepressible admiration & delight. And I could not be sorry—for I felt that his
Majesty could not be offended at a vivacity which his own
courtesie to England excited.'

The Princess smiled, with a graciousness that assured me I
had not mistaken the King's benevolence of which she evidently
partook.

But next—to my no small embarrassment, notwithstanding
my gratitude, she named my son, demanding many particulars
relative to him & his proceedings, that my consciousness of his
earnest, nay, insuperable desire to fix in England, made very
difficult to answer. My responses, therefore, here, were both
brief and unsatisfactory, for ' I did not dare mention that he
had declined, nay, returned the brevet of the Nomination
obtained in his favour by the Duc de Luxembourg, of giving
him a place of *surnumeraire* in the King's body Guard, & in the
Duc's Company, to which M. d'Arblay belonged, lest it should
hurt as well as amaze her, to find him so invincibly attached to
his *mother*-Country.[31]

The conversation then far more pleasantly turned upon the
Royal Family of England; & it was inexpressibly gratifying to
me to hear her just appreciation of the virtues, the good

---

[30] Colonel Edward Nugent (1752–1819) of the Buckinghamshire Local Militia
(see vii, L. 770 n. 31).

[31] Even this supernumerary place in the gardes du corps carried with it the
promise of royal favour and the likelihood of rapid promotion in the army. For
the conflicting wishes of AA's parents concerning his future career, see vii, L. 813
n. 6 and L. 828 n. 1.

qualities, the intellectual endowments, the sweetness of manner, & the striking Grace of every one, according to their different Character, that was mentioned. The Prince Regent, however,— Now George the 4th—was ǀ evidently her favourite. The noble style in which he had treated her & all her family at his Carlton House Fête,[32] in the midst of their misfortunes; & while so much doubt hung against every chance of those misfortunes being ever reversed, did so much honour to his heart & to his Rank, & proved so solacing to their woes & humiliation, that she could never revert to that public testimony of his esteem & good will without the most glowing gratitude. 'O!' she cried, 'il a été parfait!—'

The *Princesse Elise*,[33] with whom she was in correspondence, seemed to stand next. 'C'est Elle,' she said, 'qui fait les honneurs de la famille royale', & with a charm the most enlivening & delightful. She lamented the illness of la Princesse Sophie,[33] who was *très malade*, but *très charmante*. Of the Princesses Augusta & Mary we talked next & she permitted me to make her more familiarly acquainted with their ǀ several excellencies by details that seemed so deeply to interest her, from her knowledge of the opportunities I must have had, during five years residence under the Royal Roof, to discriminate Verity from assumption, that she really appeared as unwilling as myself to break up the conference, which was only done ⟨by⟩ a summons to the King's Dinner. My audience, however, instead of a few minutes, for which the Duchesse de Duras had prepared me, was extended to Three quarters of an hour, by the watch of my kind husband, who waited, with some of his old Friends whom he had joined in the Palace, to take me home.

The Princess, as she left me to go down a long Corridor to the Dining apartment, took leave of me in a manner the most gracious, honouring me with a message to her Majesty the Queen of England, of her ǀ most respectful Hommage, & with her kind & affectionate remembrances to ALL the Princesses

[32] At this fête, held during Louis XVIII's triumphal passage through London in April 1814, the Prince Regent exchanged with Louis the orders of the Garter and Saint Esprit. This exchange provoked the future George IV to the malicious remark that placing it around his knee was like encircling the waist of a young man (Castries, p. 214).

[33] These are FBA's correspondent and friend H.R.H. Princess Elizabeth (see Ll. 835–7) and her sister the 'elfin' Princess Sophia (1777–1848), whose recurrent bad health had confined her to her room for a year and a half in 1813–14.

with warm assurances of her eternal attachment to Both. She then moved on, but again stopt, when going, to utter some sentences most grateful to my Ears, of her high devotion to the Queen, & deep sense of all her virtues.

I listened with profound acknowledgement to so honourable a commission, the result, I imagine, of her knowing that the Princess Elizabeth deigned to correspond with me. I looked respectfully after her while she walked slowly, down the Corridor, of which she shewed a consciousness certainly not displeased, by turning her head before she disappeared, & deigning me a second adieu by its graceful motion.

I little thought that this, my First, would prove, also, my Last meeting with this exemplary Princess, whose ¹ Worth, Courage, Fortitude & Piety are universally acknowledged, but whose powers of pleasing seem little known. I was surprized by them myself at the time, so little had any previous praise prepared me for their exertion; & I still retain a sense of them that makes me grieved not to hear of their popularity. It is true, I saw her under auspices peculiarly favourable; for she was eager herself to do Honour to one whom the Queen of England had recommended to her notice: & the very mistake which drew me, at first, unawares out of the trammels of Etiquette, & beguiled me, next, into an animation that prevented my trying to re-enter them, gave me an opportunity to keep up the discourse with a degree of spirit that, as it seemed to interest & catch her, I only seasoned with due formalities, without changing for the taciturnity of bidden speech. Accustomed so many years to the gaily gracious, & invitingly confidential intercourse with the Princesses—&, indeed, ¹ when Tête à Tête with the Queen of my own Island, I could not be awe-struck into the dull solemnities of Ceremony; & this Princess, who must be too fully conscious of her many ties to my deepest respect to have any apprehension that I could be wanting in it, might be amused, perhaps, as well as surprized, to find herself thus in close conference with a simple & natural converser, instead of—which she might probably expect—an elaborate & pedantic *Blue Monger.*

He, at least, for whose sake I most wished for the Honour of her good opinion, had the infinite happiness to hear, the Day following my Audience, from le Vte D'Agoult that her

Royal Highness had expressed herself in terms the most peculiarly flattering upon the subject of this meeting. And when I
wrote to that faithful Friend of M. d'Arblay, the Viscomte,
my expressions of Gratitude for the kind services, on his part,
which had aided my being presented; & entered with warmth
upon the delight ⏐ which I had experienced from the goodness
with which H.R.H. had deigned to receive Me,—M. d'Agoult
told my dear—happy Husband, that S.A.R. had not only
asked to see the Note herself, but, after carefully perusing it,
desired to keep it in her possession. 'Tis the 2ᵈ she has thus
honoured.

After an Opening such as This—how little could I foresee that
this interview was to be a final one! — — Alas! in a Day or two
after it had taken place, son Altesse Royale set out for Bordeaux
— — and then followed the Return of Bonaparte from Elba—&
then the 100 Days.—& Then the terrible wound in the leg
which hurried us to Bath, to try the Waters — — And then —
— Alas —

Yet Twice *He* visited France afterwards—but I was detained
in England for Alexander, who was preparing for his Cambridge
Examination—& his tender Father would not let him pass that
critical period without his Flapper—to stimulate his exertions,
& watch over his health. ⏐

I ought not to have omitted mentioning that when I came
from the presence of La Duchesse d'Angouleme, I found
M. d'Arblay with M. Mathieu de Montmorency, who was so
ashamed of having arrived too late to fulfil his promise of
Presenting me himself to her Altesse Royale, that he could
hardly look at me. Yet I would not let him know the almost
petrifying blunder into which his failure had led me, lest his
very severe conscience should urge him to make an Apology to
Her R. H. that would betray the whole mystery. Every thing
had ended so well, so greatly to my satisfaction, so happily to my
wishes, that I could not endure to run the risk of sullying the
whole by a confession of my mistake — — and indeed, to have
known my unformal entrance, & my seating myself, almost
uninvited, close to her side, would have put ⏐ him,—& the
whole Court of La Duchesse into Despair. While, being known
only to her R.H. & passing with her merely as *Gaucherie*, or
embarrassment, it would either never occupy her thoughts, or,

if it recurred to them, recur merely with a smile at my English-
ism.

―――――

When—the following Year, & the year after that, i.e. the
Years 1816 and 1817—M. d'Arblay went to Paris, & had the
Honour de lui faire la Cour at the Thuilleries, H.R.H. condescended to enquire for me, with an air—he flattered himself,
—of peculiar interest. ¹

846   [Paris], 17 March [1815]

M. d'Arblay
To Madame d'Arblay

A.N.S. (Berg), 17 mars
Single sheet 8vo   1 p.
Edited by FBA, p. 1, *annotated and dated*: 3.   (1815.) Brought to me by our
Groom, Deprez,¹ from the Thuilleries, where its dear writer had passed the
night *mounting guard*. March ⌜18⌝ 17. / *1815.*

Nous avons de meilleures nouvelles!² je ne puis entrer dan
aucun detail, mais sois tranquille, et aime bien qui t'aime
uniquement.

God bless you!

d'Ay

846.   ¹ Deprez, M. d'A's groom and probably the husband of d'Arblay's house-
keeper (L. 813, p. 435).
   ² The elliptical haste of this note makes it impossible to say with any certainty
what the 'meilleurs nouvelles' heard and reported by M. d'A were. The generals
and courtiers who surrounded Louis XVIII filled the Tuileries with deluded
optimism during these days of Napoleon's approach. But M. d'A may refer here to
the soldierly and confident address to the Gardes du Corps by the Minister of War
at the Tuileries early on the 17th:
   Gentlemen, for the last week you have had no sleep. Now you can take off your
   boots. I shall sleep to-night as peacefully as I did three months ago (Stenger,
   p. 317, n. 1).

M. d'Arblay
To Madame d'Arblay

A.L. (Berg), *n.d.*
Double sheet 8vo   2 pp.
Edited by FBA, p. 1, *annotated and dated*: ⁙ 4 *NB* Brought me by
Deprez, (Groom), from the Barracks. March 18ᵗʰ 1815 (To be kept forever
by my Family. / F. d'Ay)
See further, Textual Notes.

Les nouvelles ne sont pas rassurante. — Mʳ le duc d'orleans a
fait partir sa femme, et ses enfans.¹ Mᵐᵉ de Blacas² est aussi
partie. Rien ne tient³ — ou plutot tout nous trahit. Si mon

847.   ¹ The eldest son of Louis-Philippe-Joseph (1747–93), known as Philippe-
Égalité, Louis-Philippe (1773–1850), duc d'Orléans, duc de Chartres (1785), and
général de division of the French Republic, *later* King of the French (1830–48).
He had married in 1809 Princess Marie-Amélie de Bourbon-Siciles (1782–1866),
daughter of King Ferdinand I of Naples and Sicily (1751–1825). Of their eight
children four were born by 1815: Ferdinand-Philippe-Louis (1810–42), duc
d'Orleans; Louise-Marie-Thérèse (1812–50); Marie-Christine-Caroline (1813–
39); and Louis-Charles-Philippe (1814–96), duc de Nemours.
    He had reconciled himself with Louis XVIII in a tearful audience at Mittau on
27 June 1799. At the urging of Vitrolles, who like the other legitimists distrusted
him as the head of the Orleanist branch of the Bourbons, he had accompanied the
comte d'Artois (Monsieur) and Marshal Macdonald to Lyons to rally opposition
to Napoleon's approach. When Monsieur's appeal to their loyalty failed, he withdrew to Lille, whose garrison remained loyal to Louis XVIII until they heard of
Napoleon's arrival in Paris.
    ² Félicité-Marie (1774–1856), daughter of Yves-Marie du Bouchet de Sourches
de Montsoreau (b. 1749), had been courted at Hartwell by her future husband,
Pierre-Louis-Jean-Casimir (vii, L. 817 n. 7), comte de Blacas d'Aulps. They had
been married late the night before their departure from Dover for France with
Louis XVIII on 25 Apr. 1814 (Stenger, p. 169). Her departure from Paris may
have been prompted by a warning from her brother-in-law the comte de la
Ferronays, aide-de-camp of the duc de Berry, that the duc's army south of Paris,
the only force of any size between Napoleon and the capital, could no longer be
trusted, news which must have been especially disturbing. Her husband, the comte
Blacas d'Aulps, who was in formal terms Grand Master of the Wardrobe, was
unfortunately the King's chief adviser and favourite. Ever since Napoleon's return
from Elba he had deluded the King about an increasingly menacing situation,
stultified the attempts of others to see Louis XVIII, assured the courtiers of the
Tuileries that there was no reason for concern, and mocked Vitrolles's sensible
suggestion that the King should leave Paris for the royalist stronghold of La
Rochelle in the Vendée. This sign of his concern was a drastic change.
    ³ The zealous royalism of the middle and upper classes ebbed away at Napoleon's
approach. In reports written on 18 March two different préfets summed up the
situation in the same words: 'Plus le danger s'accroît, plus le zèle diminue' (Houssaye, *1815*, i. 333). And the defections of the army to Napoleon left Louis XVIII
nothing to lean on but ageing royalists, untrained students, and a courageous but
increasingly ineffectual Chamber of Deputies. Its members shared the unyielding

amie pouvoit partir aussi, je la regarderai plus froidment, car il est presumable que nous ne pouvons faire aucune resistance, ou que nous n'en ferons qu'une bien peu heureuse, et bien courte — si nous partons de Paris! — Vois et Juge de mon embarras — de mon inquiétude! Tout parait perdu — 'hors l'honneur' — [1] qu'il faut *conserver*. — Le mien sera sans tache; et si je meurs victime de mon devoir, je ne perdrai pas pour cela l'espoir de te rejoindre dans un meilleur monde, pusqu'en mourant ce sera là mon dernier veu, ma demande à l'eternel — que je supplie de me rejoindre à mon fils et à sa mere, que j'embrasse de toutes les puissances de mon ame —

Je parais calme — et ne le suis guere — mais je suis et serai ferme.

[xxxxx ½ *line*]

848 [Paris, 19 March 1815]

M. d'Arblay
To Madame d'Arblay

A.L. (Berg), *n.d.*
Single sheet 8vo   greenish   1 p.
Edited by FBA, p. 1, *annotated and dated*: ⊞ (No. 17) Written on Sunday morning March 20—1815 just before going to le champ de mars—de—

Le Moment est venu,[1] mon amie, où d'un instant à l'autre il deviendrait très difficile et peut être impossible de quitter une

opinions expressed here by M. d'A, none more so than those who were, like him, longtime constitutionalists (*constitutionnels*) and liberals. They, who had for so long opposed Bourbon extremists and had gained so little from the King, were his most principled defenders. See also Lafayette, *Mémoires, correspondances et manuscrits . . .* (6 vols., 1837), v. 365.

848.   [1] This was actually written late on Sunday morning 19 March (see Waterloo Journal, L. 924) after M. d'A returned to the Tuileries to rejoin his artillery company, which was reviewed together with the rest of the household troops by Louis XVIII, who galloped past their ranks in an open carriage. M. d'A and the Gardes du Corps were under the impression that they were about to march south to Melun or to the camp at Villejuif to join the army of the duc de Berry for a last-ditch battle against Napoleon, and it was under that impression that this letter was written. In reality the King had decided late on the 18th to leave Paris and escape north to Lille the following day. He had taken this decision, kept a secret until the evening of the 19th, in the light of the disastrous news of the previous two days: Marshal Ney's defection, first known during the night of 17 March (see 'Relation

ville, qui peut être sera bientôt en proie aux plus grands malheurs. Toutes les esperances ont été jusqu'à present si souvent trompées, Tous les bruits un peu rassurans sont si vite dementis que je desire, je l'avoue, une separation qui seule en cas de malheur peut preparer et assurer notre reunion, lorsque cette terrible crise sera tout à fait terminée. J'apprens qu'un des six detachemens d'artillerie, est dejà parti; celui que je commande recevra peut être bientôt le même ordre. La Princesse probablement n'attendra pas longtems. Si elle part, accompagne la et je serai bien plus tranquille.[2]

849   [Paris, 19 March 1815]

M. d'Arblay
To Madame d'Arblay

A.N.S. (Berg), *n.d.*
Single sheet 4to, being a cover addressed: A Monsieur le / Comte de Bethisy[1] / Commandant à Panthe-/-mont rue de Grenelle S. / Germain au coin de la rue / de Bellechasse / *à Paris*   1 p.
Addressed: à Madame / Madame d'Arblay / rue de Miromenil / *N° 8*
Edited by FBA, p. 1, *annotated and dated*: (5)   *Opening Emigration of March 19th 1815.*
   p. 2: II on the Retraite from Paris, March 19th 1815.
   This was written at the Barracks, *près les* Thuilleries—& brought me thence by Cte Chas de Maubourg[2] who found me at his Brother's, the

des événements qui sont passés avant et depuis le 20 mars', *Moniteur de Gand*, no. 2); the disintegration of the duc de Berry's army; and Napoleon's arrival at Auxerre and swift advance on Paris.
   [2] Already on 19 March M. d'A had written a letter entrusting FBA to the princesse d'Hénin in the event that it became necessary to flee from Paris and it was with her party, as we learn in the following letters, that FBA was to leave the following day.

849.   [1] The cover on which this hurried note is written had been addressed to Richard Henri-*Charles* de Béthisy de Mézières (1770–1827), comte de Béthisy. After fighting in the army of Condé and in the Prussian army, he had during the 1790s become lieutenant-colonel 'des hussards de Rohan' in English pay. An *émigré* until his return with the comte d'Artois in 1814, he was named lieutenant in the compagnie de Luxembourg on 1 June 1814 and maréchal de camp on 17 August. He accompanied Louis XVIII to Ghent and became commander of the military district of Dunkirk during the Hundred Days.
   [2] Jules-*Charles*-César de Fay (1775–1846), comte de Latour-Maubourg, was at this time a colonel in the cavalry and a lieutenant in the Compagnie de Luxembourg. He had brought this letter to his brother's house from the barracks of the

Marquis Victor de La Tour Maubourg,[3]—whence I begun my flight from PARIS & BUONAPARTE. It was written[4] while General d'Arblay was preparing to accompany the King, Louis 18. in his flight from Paris & Buonaparte, during the *trop* famous 100 Days: & upon a cover of a letter of the commandant of the Artillery Company to which Genl d'A. belonged.

Ma chère amie, tout est perdu!—je ne puis entrer dans aucun detail. de grace partez — le plutôt sera le mieux
à la vie et à la mort!
Midy! Midy! —[5]
A. d'Ay

850   320, rue de la Montagne,
                       Brussels, 23–26 March 1815

To Alexander d'Arblay

A.L. (Berg), 23–26 Mar. 1815
Single sheet small 4to   greenish   2 pp.   *pmks*   POSTAGE NOT PAID/
TO LONDON   1⟨5⟩ AP .815   AP 27 .815   27 AP .815   CAMBRIDGE
black seal
Addressed: Angleterre. / Alexander d'Arblay Esqr, / ⌈Caius College / Cambridge.⌉
Re-addressed: Redirected from [CAMBRIDGE] ⌈M[rs] Broome, / Richmond. / Surrey⌉
Re-addressed: W[m] Locks Eqr / Norbury Park / Dorking [*on address fold*]:

household troops, which was located on the quai d'Orsay across the Seine from the Tuileries. See L. 924, pp. 360–1.

[3] For Charles's brother Victor, see L. 840 n. 23.
[4] The note was written soon after nine o'clock on the night of Sunday 19 March. M. d'A's declaration that all was lost was his response to the startling news that the King would leave Paris for Lille at midnight.
The plan—such as it was—for the Court, Government, and Army to reassemble at Lille was only promulated when it was too late for anyone to follow the King. Even the loyal troops south of Paris received the order to withdraw to the north by way of Saint-Denis only at 10.30 p.m. on the night of 19 March (Vincennes: Registre de Macdonald). The military household assembled on the Champ de Mars totalled roughly 4,000 men. Their order of march during the small hours of 20 March placed the artillery in the centre, with the grenadiers forming the advance-guard, the black musketeers, the rearguard. They crossed the Pont d'Iéna and then left Paris for Beauvais by the Allée des Veuves and Champs-Elysées, Porte de Saint-Denis (Stenger, p. 321).
[5] Here FBA inserted the superscript (a) and the explanatory note: '(a) Midy! This has reference to a mutual promise of peculiar recollection each day Midy!' This changed later to remembrance each night (L. 873).

Alexander D'Arblay Eqr / Wm Locks Eq⟨r⟩ / Norbury Park / Dorking / Surrey
Not edited, but lines in places, retraced. See Textual Notes.

OH ALEXANDER!—will not even this calamitous moment excite you to write?—Your noble Father—turned of 60—is *at his post* in the Army—with the Maison du Roi — — but *how* employed, or *where*, I am yet ignorant;—& y^r wandering emigrant Mother[1] has been forced to fly even her adopted Country?

We parted last Sunday, March 19th—in the Rue de Miro-minil, without even being able to say to each other where we might mutually write! — — — I am just arrived at Tournay—where I shall wait events—If you will let me see your hand again direct to me—by your beloved Father's honoured name—Mme d'Arblay—

> Chez Thibaut,[2]
> Hotel de l'Imperatrice,
> à Tournay—près Lille—
> dans la Belgique.

Ce Jeudi au soir,
23 Mars—1815,
Tournay.

If a Letter here arrives too late to meet it will certainly follow me. *Ce 26. Mars*—Fresh alarms drove me from Tournay[3] before I |

850. [1] For a map showing the various routes of FBA (with the princesse d'Hénin), M. d'A (with the Maison du Roi) and Louis XVIII (with his entourage and escort), *facing page 2*. Although the route followed by the princesse zigzagged confusingly, as FBA later admitted in her Waterloo Journal (see p. 370), this much is clear: her party reached Tournai and Brussels by travelling north-north-east of Paris to Roye, then west-north-west to Amiens, then to Arras by way of Doullens, thence to Douai, Tournai, and Brussels. M. d'A's company marched north-west through Beauvais and Poix to Abbeville, where the household troops were supposed to join the King who had hurried on ahead, a juncture that never took place. Harried by Napoleon's cavalry and continually threatened by capture at the hands of garrisons who had gone over to Napoleon, all three groups were driven to and then across the Belgian frontier.

[2] In the rue des Meaux off Tournai's Grand' Place.

[3] FBA hoped that at Tournai she could discover the whereabouts of M. d'A and the Gardes du Corps. She was guided by Chateaubriand to the comte de Vioménil (see Waterloo Journal, pp. 387–8), who told her that Louis XVIII was at Ghent but that he knew nothing about the fate of the household troops. The 'fresh alarms' that drove the princesse's party from Tournai would appear to have been caused by the divided loyalties of the Belgian inhabitants of that city, many of whom, as FBA later observed in her Journal, anticipated their return to France as a result of Napoleon's return to power. An ensign in the 5th Line Battalion of the King's German Legion, which had entered Tournai on 20 Oct. 1814, noticed then that 'the

could send off my Letter, which I now finish at Brusselles—It is
a week this Day since I parted from my—mine & your's—
tenderest Friend—Heaven—Heaven preserve him, & grant our
re-union!—

Adieu my poor Alexander! I feel for your penitence & hope
only it will lead you to more consideration for the future!
amen!—the first line I receive shall seal forgiveness for your
cruel negligence, if I may hope that your concern—which I
cannot doubt—will lead not simply to remorse, but amendment. Amen!—Heaven bless my always dear Alex.

Direct à Madame de Burney,
Chez Madame de Maurville,[4]
N° 320, Rue de la Montagne, à Bruxelles.

I would not write to you during this dreadful suspence, but
that I know not how long it may last, & feel sure—with all his
omissions—my Poor Alex will be thankful to Heaven to find
that ONE parent at least is safe. God Almighty spare the OTHER!
—I fled Paris with such disturbance I was forced to aband[on]
every thing! Books—Cloaths Trinkets—Linnen—arg[enterie]
Goods—MSS! ! ! All!—

Last words
Direct to M^e d'Arblay Chez Me de Maurville, Bruxelles. ^I

851   Brussels, 26 March 1815

To M. d'Arblay

A.L. (Berg), 26 mars 1815
Double sheet 8vo   1 p.   *pmk* BRUXELLES   wafer
Addressed: À Monsieur / Monsieur le Chevalier d'Arblay—/ Mareschal
de Camp, / S. Lieutenant du garde du Roi / de France, / de la Compagnie
de Luxembourg, / *À Ypres.* ⟨alon⟩

greatest animosity exists between the Nobility and the tradespeople, and it requires the nicest discrimination of deportment to preserve the good opinion and
acquaintance of the two Classes'. See Edmund Wheatley, *The Wheatley Diary*, ed.
Christopher Hibbert (1964), p. 57.

    ⁴ An *émigrée* to England, where FBA had known her, Mme de Maurville (iii,
L. 237 n. 9), a cousin both of M. de Latour du Pin (vi, L. 575 n. 2) and of the
princess d'Hénin, had come to Brussels in 1814 and taken a house at 320, rue de la
Montagne in the centre of the city near the Grand' Place.

Docketed, p. 4: ⟨F⟩eb.
Edited by FBA, p. 1, *annotated*: ⌐(7/1)⌐ (8)

le Dimanche
Jour de Paque
ce 26. mars, 1815

This Moment I receive the blessed tidings that *la Maison du Roi* est arriveé à Ypres! — —[1]
Blessed & thrice blessed if these lines meet the most cherished des amis!—ONE WORD—one single *BON JOUR* de son écriture me renouvellera l'existence—
Je suis *chez Madᵉ de Maurville*,
Nº 320, Rue de la Montagne,
À Bruxelles.

851.   [1] FBA had undoubtedly received this news in the letter written on or about 26 March (Barrett, Eg. 3698, ff. 137–8b) from the duc de Duras, First Gentleman of the Chamber, whom M. d'A later met in the King's carriage (L. 857):
Chère Madame d'Arblay
Il y a de Bonnes nouvelles de la maison du Roi. Elle est à ypres. M. de Fitz james a recontré ce matin M. de Luxembourg sur la route. il allait d'ypres a Ostende porter au roi cette nouvelle de la part de Monsieur et j'ai vu M. de Lux. tout a l'heure qui m'a dit ce detail. Soyez tranquille il promet ecrire ou envoyer a Ypres pour que M. d'Arblay sache que vous etes ici. Agreez Madame mes tendres sentiments. M. de Duras.
The Maison du Roi had marched from Paris toward Beauvais. The comte d'Artois and the duc de Berry spent the night of 20–1 March at Noailles, but the rearguard, including M. d'A, marched no further than Puisieux, catching up with the Princes in Noailles the following morning. On 21 March the Maison du Roi marched to Poix (where it spent the night); on the 23rd, to Saint-Pol; on the 24th, to Béthune. There it heard that the King, abandoning the plan to concentrate on Lille and make that city the new seat of government, had decided instead to cross the frontier into Belgium. The captains of the companies of the Maison du Roi were told in an order conveyed by Monsieur, the comte d'Artois, that the King could not afford to maintain his household troops, who would in any event not be allowed to enter Belgium under arms. Only those officers who could afford to maintain themselves, as M. d'A thought he should, were invited to follow the King. The remainder were advised to return to their homes. Most did so after the Maison du Roi was disbanded early on the 25th by the comte de Lauriston (*The Times*, 6 Apr. 1815; Romberg and Malet, i. 113–14). The Gardes du Corps who had decided to follow the King slept the night of 25–6 March at Estaire, a village south-west of Ypres on the river Lys, a dismal place 'entourée de marais et de fondrières' (Rochechouart, p. 407). A fever was to keep M. d'A for two days at Ypres (see L. 862 below).

M. d'Arblay
To Madame de Maurville

A.L.S. (Berg), 27 mars
Double sheet 4to 2 pp. *pmk* YPRES wafer
Addressed: à Madame / Madame de Maurville / à Bruxelles
Edited by FBA, *who retraced the text*, p. 1, *annotated and dated*: ✳ 3 ✕
1815 This Letter was brought to me by Madame la Comtesse de Maurville, at Brussels, 29. March, 1815, bearing me the first News of the safety—
nay, existence, of the most beloved of Husbands, after Ten Days utter ignorance of his destiny.[1]
Annotated, p. 4: 2   2

Ypres. ce 27. mars

Madame,
      arrivé ici, et sur le point de partir pour Ostende, je vous
supplie de la faire savoir à Madame d'Arblay, qui est avec
Made la Princesse d'Henin, j'ignore où. Je sais seulement que
cette excellente Princesse devait partir pour Bruxelles ou pour
Bordeaux. J'ai écrit dix lettres, dont peut être aucune ne pourra
leur parvenir: au nom du Ciel tentez l'impossible pour leur
faire connoître qu'ayant perdu mes chevaux, mon domestique,
et tout mon equipage, j'ai obtenu du Mr le Cte d'Artois la
permission d'aller joindre le Roi à Ostende, où je | compte
attendre Made d'Arblay pr nous embarquer et aller en Angleterre, dans sa famille, retablir ma santé, qui a un peu souffert
de la course rapide et très fatiguante que nous venons de faire.
      Soyez Madame, assez bonne pour me repondre à *ostende poste
restante*.

Je suis avec respect
Votre très humble et très
obéissant serviteur,
Le Chevr d'Arblay

852. [1] This hurried note was, as FBA points out, her first word of M. d'A's situation.
Other letters, some of which he probably sent to Bordeaux, have been lost—
except for his letter of 28 March to the duchesse d'Ursel (L. 856 n. 10).

Brussels, 27 March 1815

To James Burney

A.L. (PML, Autog. Cor. bound), 27 Mar. 1815
Single sheet 4to   greenish   2 pp.   *pmks*   T.P.P./U./⟨Duke⟩ St.
11 AP 1815   black seal
Addressed: Angleterre. / Captain Burney, / James Street, / 26 / Westminster, / London.

March 27. 1815—

Give the enclosed—my dear Brother—to Martin—¹ beg him
to receive it the moment it is due, & to pay it, like the former
£500, to Messrs. Hoare, desiring them to give me immediate
notice of its receipt, & the name of the Banker by whom they
can transmit it to me, on my demand, at Brussells¹—I entreat
Martin also to have the kindness to let me know whether a
similar receipt will suffice for the 500 of the 2ᵈ Edition.

Oh James—I know not what is become of my best & dearest
half!—eternally varying accounts kill & revive me in turn—
we parted This Day Week!—how dreadfully!—neither of us
able to devine the destination of the other!—He left me for the
Champ de Mars—a last Review!—& he has followed, or
preceded, the unhappy King.—or—horrible doubt—he is a
prisoner — — In the latter case, I shall re-enter the fatal
Country I have just fled, the instant I receive a power to draw
here for money. I have left & lost every thing I possessed!—
Goods—Cloathes—Trinkets—Books—billets—MSS!. &c but
if He arrive safe in England—I shall be rich with nothing—
for I ¹ shall have a[ga]in the power of happiness—

Adieu dear James—my love to all—

I have not had a line from any one—though I have written
to All—except from my two kind Charlottes—& one Letter
only from my inconceivable Alexander—unless—which I hope,
his other Letters have miscarried. I shall write to him—
I mean I *have* just written—& to Charlotte—speak to my dear

853. ¹ JB's son Martin (L. 838 n. 26), FBA's solicitor, was to arrange payment
through her bankers in London of £500 payable through a banker in Brussels. This
was to be the banking firm of Daniel Danoots & Son (L. 881 n. 13). The earlier
£500 mentioned was the second instalment on the payment of £1,500 allowed
by Longman & Co., for the 1st edition of *The Wanderer*. See vii, L. 761 nn. 5, 6.

sister Esther—Charles & Sarah—I can write now no more—
but

God bless you!

remember me most kindly to Mrs. B. & Sally—& Martin.[2]

All the English have run away from Paris—& such is their
terrour of the conqueror, that they are now flying hence!
Yet I trust & believe that We are safe here. A large body of
English troops passed before my window yesterday, for the
Frontieres commanded by Gen¹ Clinton.[3] They huzza'd the
whole way, & the Inhabitants huzza'd them from ⟨the⟩
windows.

My address is
À Madame Burney—
Chez Madame de Maurville
Nᵒ 320, Rue de la Montagne,
À Brusselles.

The good Madᵉ de Maurville, who has received me in this
distress with the most cordial hospitality, sends her best comptˢ
to Mrs. Burney—
Last notes—Direct to Mᵉ d'Arblay—Chez Mᵉ de Maurville,
Bruxelles.

[2] See i, pp. lxix–lxx.
[3] Lt.-Gen. Sir Henry Clinton (1771–1829), G.C.B., was the younger son of
General Sir Henry Clinton (1738?–95), formerly commander-in-chief the British
forces in America during the American Revolution. After entering the army as an
ensign in 1787, Clinton rose through a series of promotions for distinguished service
in Europe, the West Indies, and India, to become one of Wellington's most trusted
commanders in the Peninsular War and the campaigns of 1814 in southern France.
He had been intended to join Lord Hill* on an expedition to North America
(*Disp.* xii. 6), but its departure from Bordeaux in the spring of 1814 was cancelled.
Clinton therefore was available for immediate service in Belgium when Napoleon's
return to Paris threatened Belgium with invasion. When FBA saw his troops
march past for the frontiers on 26 March, Clinton was moving south to cover
Brussels and strengthen the border fortresses against the French Armée du Nord,
which was by this date in the field under Napoleon's orders. On 27 March the
comte d'Artois wrote to Louis XVIII from Ypres that Clinton had just told
him that the King should go to Brussels and remove any impression that he intended to leave for England—advice given repeatedly by the British commanders
and officials in Belgium during these days of alarm and Bourbon indecision (Romberg and Malet, i. 113–14). Clinton went on to command the 2nd Division of
Wellington's 2nd Corps at Waterloo, for which service he received the thanks of
Parliament.

854   [286, rue de la Montagne],
                       Brussels, 29 March [1815]

To M. d'Arblay

A.L. (Berg), 29 Mar.
Double sheet small 4to   greenish   4 pp.   *pmk*   OSTENDE   wafer
Addressed: À Monsieur / Le Chevalier d'Arblay / Marechal de Camp, /
offi^r de la Garde du Corps / du Roi de France, / Gand / also / à Ostende, /
post Restante / Bruxelles
Edited by FBA, p. 1, *annotated and dated*: 1815   (4/8)
See Textual Notes.

> *chez Me de Maurville, Bruxelles—*
> *ce 29, Mars—*

Oh mon ami! mon ami!—Je viens de lire votre Lettre à
Mme de Maurville[1]—la vue de votre écriture m'a absolument
renouvellé l'existence—J'étois abatue à la mort—Oh comme
je vais me soigner!

Vous joindrai-je tout de suite à Ostende?

Que je vous dise Instamment tout ce qu'il y a de pire—
hèlas—Je n'ai rien avec moi! ⌐excepté ce que je n'ai pas
encore depensé d'argent!¬

All our effects remain—I have even no ⌐cloathes¬, but in a
Napkin!—

All my MSS—my family papers—my dear Father's Memoirs
—all our Argenterie—your billets—my watch, my numerous
little trinkets!—all our linnen—our BOOKS—your various
curiosities—my shawls—all our meubles—all, all left in Paris,
from my hurry of flight. |

⌐My new purchases at so chere an amount of pence! A
Flannel shawl—7^{fr} It amazes—nay awes— But as to money,
I can write James again as is ⟨needed⟩.¬

Je sais, à prèsent, que j'aurais pu avoir apporter mes trinkets—⌐& small affairs,¬ but the suddenness of our departure—
utterly unexpected—with the deeply terrific state of my mind
& Nerves from our awful separation, robbed me of all thought
upon these subjects. I merely locked up every thing I saw,
sealed the keys, ⌐in a bag¬, & told Mme Deprez[2] to carry them

854.   [1] L. 852.   [2] The d'Arblays' housekeeper (L. 846 n. 1).

65

to M. Le Noir[3]—with a note entreating him to keep them in his custody.

I knew not, at that time, but you might yet return at night, & have occasion for them: I can explain all when we meet— I merely state the result & great misfortune at once, ⌐so that if you can ever see any manner ⌐ of reclaiming anything you may know what there is to claim.—⌐ but oh mon ami! mon ami!—I feel too *rich* in being again so blessed as to see your hand—to know you so near me—& *safe*, to be sensible of this evil:—however it has often afflicted me—& the more, as much of it I might have prevented by a happier or abler foresight. Grief-stricken & confounded, *YOUR* departure occupied all my heart—head & faculties—

⌐I paid the Rent to the 1ˢᵗ of April — — all therefore is ours till then. And Mᵉ Deprez to the end of March & gave her 20 francs.⌐

I am truly sorry I did not do better—& I beseech you to spare me all reflections &c—for I have had no practice of this melancholy nature—though *now*—I hope to Heaven I shall never again be tried! but I should certainly emigrate more skilfully!

⌐Sometimes I think of how you could perhaps, even ask for M. de Saulnier[4] should he be in ⟨town⟩?—but every body says we must try at nothing immediately, ⌐ not to excite any notice. Think it all over, & decide whether I shall join you instantly & I shall enquire about conveyances, for I shall come by the Diligence, & you will tell me where to expect you. My Journey hither has cost me 6 pieces of 20 francs & without our expenses at Bruxelles—⌐ I am fixed with Mᵉ D'henin,[5] &c at an equal part—⌐1/3⌐ in all expences of house & house-keeping: but now I know *YOU* safe, & both are poor, I am eager to find a cheaper establishment. I have merely—alas—2 mourning gowns,[6] & a small change of linnen!—but oh mon ami! mon

[3] Marie-Alexandre Lenoir (L. 840 n. 24).

[4] Pierre-Dieudonné-Louis Saulnier (1767–1838), who had been helpful to the d'Arblays earlier in his capacity as sécrétaire-général de la Police (see vi, L. 623 n. 2).

[5] The house of which they rented all but the street level 'was near the Cathedral, & still in a prolongation of Madᵉ de Maurville's street, la Rue de la Montagne'. FBA had the rez-de-chaussée, the princesse d'Hénin, the next level and M de Lally, the third (L. 924, p. 394).

[6] FBA and her sister EBB continued to wear mourning for their father, who had died on 12 Apr. 1814.

plus que jamais Jamais cher ami—what now can affect me? I *supplicate* that our meeting may be without Witnesses!— I *ENTREAT* you to contrive That.—I shall burst if I must constrain my gratitude to Heaven & my joy & tenderness— ⌜Midy—now (think of me)—⌝ I am quite ready to come to you directly—

The Frontiers are all blocked with troops—all communication with France—*legitime* is broken up—but we must endeavour to get a Letter to Mᵉ Deprez—If we set sail without any precaution, all will necessarily be confiscated—at all events, write immediately—mon ami! mon ami!—

Je viens d'écrire à *Gand*—7 |

⌜P.S. Pray in your answer¦ say if you know anything of M. d'Auch,8 or, of Humbert La tour du Pin.9

rien des choses d'Alex.

I have just heard that the soldiers are quartered in the houses at Paris & that all is alarm for the war.

The Guard Nationale waxed at first, but is now disarmed to its great discontent, & the people's disatisfaction.10

My apartment here is unhappily taken for a *month by the Pˢˢ*—it would do perfectly ⟨for both, & at rather less,⟩ if all else were not too dear—

7 Probably because FBA had heard rumours that the King would leave Bruges for Ghent on the following day.

8 Henri-Raymond d'Aux de Lescout (1782–1870), marquis d'Aux-Lally (1815), who had married in 1807 Lally-Tolendal's daughter Elizabeth-Félicité-Claude (1786–1883), an event described by Mme de La Tour du Pin (pp. 350–2, 357–8), to whom M. de Lally had entrusted his daughter's education while the Latour du Pin family was living at Le Bouilh (v, L. 547 n. 4; vi, 756–7 and *passim*).

9 Humbert de Latour du Pin (1790–1816), the eldest of the four surviving children of Fréderic-Séraphin de Latour du Pin (1759–1837), comte de Gouvernet, and his wife Henrietta-Lucy *née* Dillon (1770–1853). See vi, L. 575 n. 2. He had in 1814 entered the Mousquetaires Noirs and he marched north with them when they formed the rearguard of the Maison du Roi (Stenger, p. 321). He returned from Ghent to what promised to be a brilliant military career, but was killed in a duel in 1816 (Boigne, i. 349–51).

10 The Belgians, with the exception of the soldiers who had fought in Napoleon's armies, were happy to see the last of French rule. The 'Garde Nationale' and the people mentioned here by FBA had armed themselves on first hearing of Napoleon's return and his apparently imminent attack on Belgium. They were mobilized on 22 March on the orders of King William of the Netherlands, who also offered the help of the allied army to Louis XVIII when he reached the frontier. The rapid concentration of allied forces made it possible to disarm the Belgian Guard (Romberg and Malet, i, pp. xxi–xxiii).

Is there no nearer embarkation for us than Ostende?

If you can come hither to make our arrangements—representations to Md. Deprez & our goods, &c, come soon. If not let me hasten to you—only name how, when.—

If you think we had best stay on the continent till we can take some measures for our affairs, let it be in some cheap port & oh let us be together!—mon ami! mon ami!

I will write at once to James for word which ⟨bank⟩ is best & to forward or draw our funds.

F. d'A.

I will write à Ostende as to this—consider it further⌐

855   [286, rue de la Montagne],
                                        Brussels, 30 March 1815

To M. d'Arblay

A.L. (Berg), 30 Mar. 1815
Double sheet small 4to   greenish   4 pp.   *pmk*   BRUXELLES   wafer
Addressed: À / Monsieur / le General D'Arblay, / Chev^r de St. Louis, &c—&c / et off^r des Gardes du Corps du Roi de / France. / *à Gand*— / ⟨alodi⟩
Edited by FBA, p. 1, *annotated and dated*: 1815   (8/6)
Edited also by CFBt. *See* Textual Notes.

                                                Bruxelles—
                                                ce 30. Mars—

The happiest—at this moment—in defiance of all worldly evils—the happiest des Athanases[1] vient d'apprendre que le Roi va à *Gand*—J'addresse dont lâ une espece de duplicata d'une longue Lettre que j'ai écris hier *à Ostende post Restante*. — Oh mon ami! hier—le bien heureux 29. de Mars—J'ai reçu votre Lettre à Mme de Maurville — & with it a new lease of life. — — ⌐I wrote at full length, to Ostende—but the post had been long gone ere *the Letter of my Love* had reached me.⌐

855.   [1] See L. 841 n. 3.

If you are at Ostende, you will see at once the state of our affairs—⌐If at *Gand*, I beg you to send to the *post Restante* & desire if a Letter directed to Le Chevalier d'Arblay has come or, if sent back to *Mad^e d'Arblay* (as I instructed) chez Mad^e de Maurville à Bruxelles, or, should you remain at Gand, send it back there to *you* at once. In the Interim, to lose no time,⌐ let me recapitulate the business part of my Letter.

To begin with the worst, & which, at another time, would be *accablant* — — I have saved nothing!—not even my Q[ueen]'s Watch[2]—nor a single of my many trinkets—nor one shawl—nor our billets—though I might have brought them all in my hand basket!

But alas—you left me *La Mort dans le coeur*—yet with a persuasion we had still 3 days before us ere we departed—'Tis, in fact, an irreparable loss—

⌐In short—I have never ceased—since I could think, to regret the *unnecessary* deprivation—but the thing is now irrevocable—

You are safe—& all will be bright to ME comparatively, for the ami of my coeur.

If poor—yet not incomparable loss!

That ⟨unlucky⟩ letter, & with no time on the instant, to endeavour to faire passer une lettre à Mme Deprez,[3] to beg her to convey these ⟨meubles & our plate⟩ unto our chere M^de de G[randmaison][4] & to pack up in the trunk in the little ante-room all my clothes, stores of analeptics, flannel, medicine boxes &c. &c.

I shall write to Anvers, to know whether Me Solvyns is there or her husband.[5] If there I will go to Anvers, when I have your

---

[2] This watch was handed down in the Barrett and Wauchope families until 1960, when it was auctioned by Sotheby's (see item 291 *Catalogue* for sale of 19 Dec. 1960, p. 56): '291 AN ENGLISH GOLD AND ENAMEL VERGE WATCH AND CHATELAINE by Wakelin & Tayler, London, No. 2270, the back enamelled in translucent dark blue with, in the centre, a roundel containing the hair of the Royal Princesses within a split pearl border, the chatelaine with gold links and enamelled gold plaques, at one end a fob seal engraved with a pansy and inscribed A Vous and with two watch keys'.

[3] See L. 846 n. 1.

[4] The widow of Alexandre-Paul Millin de Grandmaison (1739–1811), Marie-Pierre *née* Sonnerat (1759–1848), 'a very favourite friend' of M. d'A (v, L. 514 n. 21). She was later to marry Alexandre-Paul-Augustin-Félix-Élisabeth Barrin (1757–1828), comte de la Gallissoniére.

[5] Mary Ann *née* Greenwood (vi, L. 592 n. 2) and her author husband François-Balthazar Solvyns (1760–1824).

answer, to consult with ⟨him⟩ relative to my Trinkets—papers
—letters—⌐ all the family papers & Memoirs & Letters, & all
of my own inedited mss. !—of my whole life!—

our Goods—Books—Pictures—Curiosities—Meubles——!!!

⌐I paid the Rent till the end of April—all therefore is ours
till then. I paid M^de Deprez to the end of March and left her
20 francs on account. But we must either pay her or dismiss
her.⌐

I left all our keys with M. Le Noir[6]—who was most tenderly
kind.

Fix therefore if we shall depart to England immediately, or
endeavour to find some means to save a part at least of our
property.

And—in the latter case, whether *you* will come to Brussels,
or I shall join you at Ostende—only—let us be together! if
possible—for the remnant of our earthly abode. Amen!
Amen!— come! come! or write, write, incessantly — — ⎫

Lord Wellington is expected here to-morrow.[7] I have only a
small change of Linnen

& 2 Mourning Gowns in the World!—

But I have YOU mon ami! & my affright & despondence have
been such that I have as yet no room—in the relief of my soul,
for a single sigh at any evil — — while so great a BLESSING is the
contrast.—

856   Tournay and Brussels,
                                   23–31 March 1815

To H.R.H. the Princess Elizabeth

A.L. draft (Barrett, Eg. 3695, ff. 86–7b), 23–31 Mar. 1815

One single sheet 4to   greenish paper, paged 1; and one single sheet 4to,
being the 2nd leaf of a letter addressed: À—Madame / Madame la Duchesse
d'Hurst / en son hotel / à Bruxelles. *pmk* MENIN wafer torn

Four pages in all. The draft was begun in Tournay and completed at

⁶ See L. 854 n. 3.

⁷ The comte d'Artois on 1 April had written to his brother Louis XVIII that he
would wait in Brussels for Wellington's arrival, which he hoped for on the 2nd or
3rd. Wellington arrived only on the night of 4 April (Romberg and Malet, i. 122,
125).

Brussels. The first and second sheets are joined by the repetition of M. d'A and the sign ⊙ at lower right *verso* of first sheet and upper left *recto* of second sheet.

A ELIZA. 1

Tournay 23 Mars
1815

Madam—

What dreadful & afflicting scenes & vicissitudes have I witnessed & experienced since my receipt of those valued & condescending lines wh^{ch} gave me the last sensation of pleasure to which my heart was open in Paris!¹ they came to me on the 15th from which period every hour was filled with new disorder, though all was so vague, that till the 19th March I had conceived no idea of the real danger of the state. Even then, nothing was known of the ultimate purposes of Le Roi, nor consequently of the destination *de sa Maison*, to which M. d'A. had the honour to belong. But the histories daily recorded to me of the calm dignity of his Majesty's mind² though exposed to every species of conflict, & of the imperturbable serenity of his manners, while suffering the most excruciating injuries, & most wounding disappointments, reflect equal honour upon his fortitude, his Temper, & his religious principles. No impatience ever escaped him; but a consoling, however modest consciousness of his worth, with a deep though never vindictive sense of his wrongs, kept him firm to his dreadful post. The poor D^{ss} d'Ang[oulême] continued at Bordeaux³—Oh how do I pity that most undeservedly unfortunate of Princesses!

⸺⸺⸺

856.   ¹ H.R.H.'s letter of 13 March (Berg), beginning '*Nobody* has received somebodys letters'. 'The startling event of the Tiny T[iger]'s reappearance . . . makes me dreadfully ⟨want⟩ news.'
   ² The serenity of Louis XVIII could to a less sympathetic eye seem either indifference or incapacity. In some revealing letters written during the King's last days in Paris, the minister of the King of Prussia reported to his superiors that the 'calme du Roi, qui a certainement produit beaucoup de bien, doit à présent aller jusqu'à l'inertie, car on prétend que rien ne l'affecte, qu'il ne donne presque aucun ordre, et que sa bonté l'empêche même de faire exécuter les mesures de rigueur qu'il s'est vu dans la nécessité d'ordonner . . .' (Romberg and Malet, ii. 196).
   ³ On their arrival in Bordeaux on 5 March the duc and duchesse d'Angoulême were greeted with the news of Napoleon's landing and of the duc's appointment to command the right wing of the royal army under his father. The duchesse d'Angoulême remained in Bordeaux while the duc went to Nîmes on 10 March in an

Sunday the 19. M. d'A. left me at Noon, fully equipped for a military expedition, & expecting to march forward to the army opposed to Buonaparte, after a general muster & review of all the troops of *la Maison du Roi* on le *champs de Mars*. Alas—I have never seen nor heard from him since, except on that same Sunday night, about 9 o'clock, when M. Ch[arles] de Maubourg,[4] an officer of la Garde du Corps, delivered me a Note from him, saying

> *Tout est perdu*—*Je ne puis entrer dans aucun detail*—*mais de grace partir! la plutot sera le mieux*—&c.

The P^ss d'Henin had already offered me a place in her Carriage. We set off at 10 o'clock at night.[5] All at Paris then was quiet,— sad, dejected, & astonished. Every body had expected some great blow w^d be struck, though nobody knew by whom, nor when, nor how. Never ¦ but in the Eastern Empires, has a great Revolution been brought to bear with a rapidity so frightful; & never before were Art, Skill & Activity so feebly opposed by disgraceful neglect, & languid, unmeaning mismanagement. The Usurper has only the Army & the Populace;[6]

attempt to raise an army to hold Provence and Languedoc for the King (Houssaye, *1815*, i. 402–15). By 23 March when Vitrolles arrived in the south the royalist defence had begun to collapse. For a time the enthusiasm of the mayor, the citizens, and the National Guard kept the regular troops of the garrison loyal; but a threatened attack on Bordeaux by one of Napoleon's generals and his call for the city's surrender on 31 March persuaded the garrison to capitulate. A last appeal made by the duchesse during a visit to the barracks made no impression, and on 2 April she accepted a safe conduct into exile in England on board H.M.S. *Wanderer* (Hall, p. 76).

The duc d'Angoulême at the head of a dwindling army of regular troops meanwhile carried on a prolonged but unsuccessful campaign directed against the rear of Napoleon's army. Royalist support, which in the south extended downward into the urban and rural lower classes, enabled the duc to continue for over a month until he in his turn was allowed by Napoleon to sail for Spain from Cette on 16 April aboard a Swedish ship (Houssaye, *1815*, i. 416–33). Throughout a multitude of skirmishes, sieges, and changes of side, Napoleon insisted on the least possible bloodshed and the greatest possible clemency for royalist supporters, above all for the King and princes of the blood, who were treated with the greatest respect and concern for their safety.

⁴ Jules-*Charles*-César de Fay (L. 849 and n. 2).

⁵ Mme de Latour du Pin, who did not manage to leave Paris until six o'clock on the morning of 20 March, described the confused departure of her aunt, the princesse d'Hénin and M. de Lally, who lived together in the rue de Miroménil: 'I went to say goodbye to Mme d'Hénin, who had also decided to leave. I found her with M. de Lally, in a state of indescribable confusion, packing, gesticulating, urging on her portly friend' (*Memoirs*, p. 431); and FBA later described at length the confusion of this departure, which threatened to upset her own plans to join their party (L. 924, pp. 362–7).

⁶ Houssaye (*1815*, i. 416–17) summarizes the split within France by saying that

the Army, of which he has corrupted the very essence by permission of pillage, & disdain of all the arts of peace; & the Populace, because, conceiving themselves already the most debased, the[y] believe any change must be to their advantage: but all proprietors, all thinking people, all superiour Officers, all Men of learning, all Gentlemen, & all women whatsoever, gentle or simple, are for the King. When I say ALL, I mean not, of course, to disclaim that there are exceptions; &, alas, many! but I speak of the mass of this classification. 'Tis a Great, firm, high-principled & dauntless *Political chief* that has been wanting, to spurn all jarring interests, be insensible to all personal attacks, & content to leave Posterity for his Judge. SUCH a one here,—as erst in my dear native land, by firmly holding in single view the one great object of ultimate General Good, might have steered the whole to anchor at an equally prosperous port.—but there was no such Pilot, alas, to *Weather the storm!*

Believing, when I quitted my home, that I deserted it only for the neighbourhood of Paris, there to wait news of an impending battle, the affright & distress of my mind allowed me no combinations by which I might have secured some part of my property; I left ALL, save what I could convey in a napkin, ie a small change of linen, & 2 mour[n]ing Gowns! I have learnt—too late—that in emigrating we sh^d carry *with us* whatever we most value. But I have nothing, absolutely NOTHING! Yet my anguish in my uncertainty of the destination & situation of M. d'A.,[7] from the fluctuating accounts that have broken in upon me *just now* relative to *La Maison du Roi*, makes all else immaterial. We arrived without molestation to this place, Tournay. At Amiens & at Arras, the 2 Prefects,[8]

in two-thirds of the country *le peuple* favoured Napoleon, the bourgeoisie, Louis XVIII. Only in the south was there a strong popular movement in favour of the Bourbons. Throughout all France, however, and with very few exceptions, the army defected to Napoleon, and this military support returned Napoleon to power. It also made the return from Elba more of a *coup d'état* than an attempted revolution.

[7] On this date M. d'A was marching toward Saint-Pol (L. 850 n. 1).

[8] The prefect at Amiens was Alexandre-Théodore-Victor (1760–1829), comte de Lameth (for the Lameth brothers, see v, L. 446 n. 20). A general, prefect, and legislator who had fought in the American revolution, Lameth had at first welcomed the French Revolution but was soon driven to flee with Lafayette into Austrian captivity (15–17 Aug. 1792). On regaining his liberty in 1797, he went to England and allied himself with the leading Whigs. Soon expelled by Pitt, he went into business with his brother in Hamburg. He finally returned to France under the

acquaintances of M^e d'Henin, treated us with distinction, renewed our passports & spoke warmly *pour le Roi.* and—
BRUXELLES. I could not finish my Letter at Tournay from excess of disturbance—We were so near Lille, that varying news reached us incessantly. The Prince de Condé⁹ came to the same Inn; fear was excited of pursuit, & we came on hither; & I have been too ill, & too wretched to hold my pen again till to day, March 31ˢᵗ when I have just had a Letter from la D^{ss} d'Hurst,¹⁰ with an account that | M. d'A. nearly demolished

Consulate, rose rapidly through numerous appointments as prefect, becoming a baron of the Empire on 14 Feb. 1810. He renounced this title at the Restoration of Louis XVIII and was appointed in 1814 prefect of the Somme. He soon welcomed Napoleon's return from Elba and on 2 June 1815 was named a pair des Cents Jours.

His fellow prefect at Arras was Jacques-François Lachaise (1743–1823), baron de l'Empire (1809). In his youth Lachaise had a typical career in various cavalry regiments in the royal army. After the Revolution he rose to the rank of général de brigade in the campaigns on the eastern frontiers of France, then retired from the army in 1794 to become active in the municipal government of Beauvais, serving twice as mayor (1795 and 1800–3). He was named prefect of Pas-de-Calais on 11 Apr. 1803 and held that post throughout the Empire and first Restoration until 23 Mar. 1815. The day after FBA breakfasted with him he was removed from his post by Napoleon (*Moniteur*, 24 Mar. 1815).

⁹ Louis-Joseph de Bourbon (vii, L. 770 n. 28), prince de Condé. Of all the Bourbons, Condé was the one who most instinctively readied himself for war against his family's enemies, whether Jacobins or Bonapartists, the Republic or the Empire. As Chateaubriand, who also met him in Tournai on 23 March, observed, 'l'émigration était son dieu Lare. Lui n'avait pas peur de monsieur de Bonaparte: il se battait si l'on voulait, il s'en allait si l'on voulait: les choses étaient un peu brouillées dans sa cervelle; il ne savait pas trop s'il s'arrêterait à Rocroi pour y livrer bataille, ou s'il irait dîner au Grand-Cerf' (Chateaubriand, *Mémoires*, i. 928). Condé followed the King to Ghent and then went to Alost where the Royal army was forming.

¹⁰ Marie-Flore-Françoise-Auguste-Caroline *née* princesse d'Arenberg (1752–1832), the dowager duchesse d'Ursel, who should not be confused with her daughter-in-law, 'the young duchess' (L. 872 n. 9), whom FBA was also to meet in Brussels. On 28 March M. d'A addressed to the dowager duchess the following letter (Berg), later annotated by FBA: 'This Letter, enclosed in an elegant Billet from Madame la Duchesse d'Urse, was my Second welcome news of the Safety of its honoured writer.'

Madame la Duchesse,
Dans l'inquietude la plus vive sur la santé de Madame d'Arblay qui doit avoir accompagne la Princesse d'Henin soit à Bruxelle soit à Bordeaux, j'ose esperer que vous voudrez bien informer cette Princesse du parti que j'ai pris de me rendre près du Roi à Ostende, où j'attendrai des nouvelles de Madame d'Arblay. Si vous en aviez, Madame la Duchesse, daignez m'en donner, et m'adresser un mot *poste restante.* J'ose croire Madame la Duchesse, que dans la nouvelle position où nous sommes tous, vous aurez la bonté d'excuser la liberté que je prends de m'adresser à vous pour obtenir quelqu'information, sur ce qui m'interesse le plus au monde. Les marches forcées que nous venons de faire, et la perte que j'y ai faite de tous mes equipages, et qui pis est de ma santé, qui pourtant est aujourdhui moins mauvais ne me permettent plus d'espérer qu'au repos, et j'attendrai pour m'y livrer que Mad^e d'Arblay m'ait rejoint pour passer en Angleterre, et y

with the harrass of guarding the Artillery, & full of severe rheumatism from constant rains, while on Horse back night & day, in covering the retreat of the Roi, writes from Menan that he is going on to Ostende,[11] to pay his duty to his Majesty, & to endeavour to recover some portion of his lost health—for which purpose he has the permission of Monsg[r] le comte d'Artois.

I shall surely join him there, unless, his duty paid, he thinks it better to come hither. He was already, in fact, made unfit for the campaign by his previous fatigues, for since the disembarkation of the barbarous Destroyer, he has never known rest, & by doing the double service of Garde du corps au chateau,[12] & artillery officer at la Cazerne, l'ecole militaire, he was very hardly employed almost night & day; &, by a zeal beyond his force, but which he could not controll, he was so altered & exhausted before he began his late march, that with a grain less of spirit & of loyalty, he must have declined to undertake it:[13]—& alas his strength had never been restored since his cruel accident at Calais.

passer les restes d'une vie que 61 ans d'agitations continuelles ne peuvent qu'abreger.

Daignez Madame la duchesse m'excuser de vous ecrire sur un pareil chiffon. C'est tout ce que j'ai pu me procurer dans le malheureux village où je suis près d'Ypres. Demain j'espère pouvoir arriver à Ostende.

Je suis avec le plus profond respect
Madame la Duchesse
Votre très humble et
obeissant Serviteur
Le Ch. d'Arblay Off[r] Sup[ieur]
du Gardes du Corps

[11] This letter is missing.

[12] Before Napoleon's appearance the companies of the Gardes du Corps were in turn posted inside the rooms of the Palace of the Tuileries, which during the Restoration was known always to the courtiers by the name FBA uses here, the 'Château'. Other units of the Maison du Roi had special posts to guard: the Cent Suisses at the head of the entrance staircase, the Garde de la Porte at the inner archways, the Garde de la Prévôté in the gardens. The remaining 'compagnies rouges', the Gendarmes, Mousquetaires, and Chevaux-légers, had no fixed posts but took their orders every day at noon from the King himself (Stenger, pp. 237–8). In addition to his guard duties M. d'A was also given command of an artillery detachment in barracks at the École militaire, at the foot of the Champs de Mars near the Pont d'Iéna. The distance and double duty that this involved must indeed have been exhausting. Even worse was the consequence that M. d'A had to keep pace with the slow progress of this foot artillery all the way to Béthune during the flight from Paris.

[13] Many others declined. We know from another participant that very few of the troops in the 'compagnies rouges' assembled as ordered for the march. Even among the Gardes du Corps only a little over half left Paris during the night of 19–20 March (Rochechouart, pp. 405–6).

Le nouveau Roi,[14] in his public entry, passed yesterday before my window. There was no species of enthusiasm, but great respect & decorum, & moderate cries of *Vive le roi*. The unhappy dethroned monarch so near saddened all hearts, & I do not, therefore, augur ill from the want of apparent warmth, which, I hope, was only the effect of a contrast repressing to all demonstration of festivity. He may be better, perhaps, served than the injured King who was received with such triumphant exultation. Worse, he cannot be! I am inexpressibly anxious for M^e la D^{ss} d'Angouleme; of whom ۱ no News is known here. We wait for intelligence through England! An English lady, who found means to leave Paris for this place Sunday the 26. relates, to a lady who has repeated to me, That the 1st 3 days of B[onaparte]'s return were passed in utter consternation, but that the nomination of so Jacobinical an administration—Savary—Real—Dâvoust—carnot—caulaincourt[15]—&c had struck with a panic that renewed all the horrour in the minds of the Inhabitants, of the reign of terrour. The soldiers were quartered in the houses, as if B.

[14] This was William I (1772–1844), King of the Netherlands. Forced to take refuge in England in 1794 (see iv. 20–1), he became Sovereign Prince of the United Provinces in 1813. Crowned King on 18 Mar. 1815, he had first to assure himself of the loyalty of his people, especially the Belgians, who little welcomed the forced unification with Holland. He offered his help and hospitality to Louis XVIII in a letter written from Breda on 28 Mar. 1815 (Romberg and Malet, i. 13–14).

[15] To a royalist the names of Napoleon's new ministers must have seemed a return to the revolutionary days of twenty years before. Anne-Jean-Marie-René Savary (1774–1833), duc de Rovigo and pair des Cent Jours, personally attached to Napoleon since the campaign in Egypt and Ministre de la Police Générale under the Empire, became during the Hundred Days Commandant Général de la Gendarmerie. Guillaume-André Réal (1755–1832), an active but relatively moderate legislator during the Revolution who had welcomed Napoleon's seizure of power of 18 Brumaire, became Prefect of Police. Louis-Nicolas Davout (1770–1823), duc d'Auerstadt and prince d'Eckmühl, pair des Cent Jours and maréchal de France, one of the most famous and loyal of Napoleon's generals, became his Minister of War. Lazare-Nicholas-Marguerite Carnot (1753–1823), comte de l'Empire (1815) and pair des Cent Jours, perhaps the most rigorous and consistent of all the Jacobins who had any influence during the Empire, was named Minister of the Interior. Armand-Augustin-Louis (1773–1827), marquis de Caulaincourt and duc de Vicence, who had risen through his close relations with Napoleon to become the Emperor's personal representative and ambassador to the major courts of Europe, was during these days his Minister for Foreign Affairs. In making such appointments Napoleon sought to retain his popular and military support while keeping it under the control of those who were personally loyal to him. He also needed ministers such as these—experienced in internal control through the police and in external relations with the European rulers he sought at first to placate. The zealous revolutionary Carnot, he took care to tame, by making him a comte de l'Empire on the same day (20 Mar. 1815) that he gave him the necessarily repressive Ministry of the Interior (Houssaye, *1815*, i. 378).

had entered as a foreign Conqueror.[16] He was seldom seen, & working always with his Ministers, & wearing an air the most *sombre*. If the Allies are but quick; if the D. of Wellington heads them,[17] the universal belief here is that he will—*par les siens même*, be culbuté. But that if he gains *time*, his activity & resources are such, that he will again, for a period, reinstate himself upon the Throne.

I shall make this pass, under cover to Mr. Rolleston,[18] by the English minister.[19] *My* Letters—should I be so happy as to receive a line, will be sacred & safe, directed to *me* Chez la comtesse de Maur[ville], a most honourable Friend, at Brussels.

I dare attempt no apology,—no conclusion—but I am ever |

857   Bruges, [31 March 1815]

M. d'Arblay
To Madame d'Arblay

A.L. (Berg), *vendredy* matin
Double sheet 4to   4 pp.   *pmk*   BRUGES   wafer
Addressed: A Madame / Madame d'Arblay chez / Madame la Princesse d'Henin / à Bruxelles

16 After Napoleon's return to the Tuileries the troopers of his cavalry escort were forced by a shortage of barracks to hitch their horses in the Place de Carrousel and sleep there under their cloaks. This gave that part of Paris the look of a bivouac in a city taken by assault (Houssaye, *1815*, i. 368). During the following days many more troops who had marched to the capital and could find no space in barracks were assigned temporary billets in the prosperous neighbourhoods near the Tuileries.

17 Wellington accepted the offered command of the allied army on 25 Mar. 1815 (*Disp.* xii. 277). FBA hoped that he would lead his army immediately into France, thereby provoking Napoleon's overthrow at the hands of his own subjects. Wellington was less sanguine, however, judging it impossible to take the offensive before 10 or 15 May (Romberg and Malet, i. 7).

18 To forestall FBA's uneasiness in writing, the Princess Elizabeth had directed in her letter of 13 March (Berg) that a reply could be sent in the care of Stephen Rolleston (d. 1828), chief clerk, office of the Secretary of State, Foreign Affairs, Downing Street (see *CCR*, 1815).

19 The 'English Minister' was Sir Charles Stuart (1779–1845), G.C.B. (1812), one of the most skilled and experienced of British diplomats, who had served in Spain and Portugal and as an envoy at the Congress of Vienna. British Minister at The Hague (1815–16), he had accompanied William I when on 29 March he went to Brussels to assure himself of the loyalty of his new subjects and prepare to face a possible French invasion. There Stuart learned that Castlereagh had named him ambassador extraordinary to the court of Louis XVIII. He received his letters of credence on 31 March and had his first audience with the King at Ghent on 2 April (Romberg and Malet, ii, pp. xii, 5).

Edited by FBA, p. 1, *annotated and dated*: ✻ (8) 8 (9. lost) March
30.th (1815)   [*with numbers on address fold*]: 5 5
See further, Textual Notes.

Bruges ce *Vendredy* matin

J'ai tant de choses à te dire, ma chere et bien aimée amie
qu'en verité je ne sais pas où commencer; et comme il est
probable que sous trés peu de jours j'irai te voir et me con-
certer avec toi, si effectivement tu es à Bruxelles comme me
l'a dit hier M^r le Duc de L[uxembourg]¹ je crois que je ferai
mieux d'attendre ce moment si desiré. Retenu deux jours à
deux lieues d'Ypres par un debordement de bile qui m'a
affaibli, mais m'a degagé le foie et un peu soulagé la poitrine,
je me sens aujourdhui presqu'aussi bien que lorsque nous nous
sommes quittés. Bref, à un peu de maigreur près, fruit de ma
complication de contrarietés et d'infortunes, non compris
l'excessive fatigue que j'ai essuyée, tu me trouveras beaucoup
mieux ⌐ que je ne pouvais l'esperer après de si rudes epreuves.
N'ayant aucune nouvelle d'Auguste,² et privé absolument de
tout, j'ai été forcé d'acheter à Ypre 6 grosses chemises de
hazard: mais ce que je ne puis remplacer ce sont mes papiers,
mes livres, et surtout mes chevaux. Ne t'afflige pas cependant
mon adorable amie. J'en ai un qui n'est ni beau ni agreable,
et qui est un peu jeune, puisqu'il n'a pas 5 ans; mais il est
neanmoins assez vigoureux. Depuis qu'il a eu un peu de
repos j'en suis assez content. Je voudrais seulement qu'il fut
mieux dressé, et moins ombrageux: mais il n'est point mechant.
Seulement après avoir été l'off^{er} le mieux monté, il est douloureux de me trouver l'un des moins bien, et cela au bout de
8 jours!!! Sans qu'il y ait de ma faute. Je te reverrai, voilà
dans ce moment, tout ce que je veux voir et sentir. Attens moi
donc, et je te le repete ne t'afflige point. Deux minutes de
conversation avec Mr de L. qui est toujours pour moi la
bonté même, et l'assurance qu'il m'a donnée que la Princesse est à Bruxelles où consequement tu dois être aussi, m'ont

857. ¹ Charles-Emmanuel-Sigismond de Montmorency-Luxembourg (1774–1861),
duc de Luxembourg, pair et premier baron de France, emigrated with his father in
1791 with Condé's army (1792), then passed into the service of Portugal (1793–
1802). Appointed captain of the third company of the Gardes du Corps in June
1814, he accompanied Louis XVIII to Ghent, where he became the King's envoy
to William I and commissaire du Roi to the allied army commanded by Wellington.
    ² M. d'A's servant or batman.

rendu la vie. [|] C'est à *Ghistelles* à 2ʰ1/2 *d'Ostende* que j'ai eu ce bonheur inattendu. Je me rendais tristement et au petit pas de mon cheval dans cette derniere Ville, lorsqu'informé que le Roi venait de la quitter, je me suis un peu detourné de mon chemin pour venir l'attendre au relai, où je l'ai effectivement vu arriver. Mʳ de L. qui etait dans la seconde voiture est aussitot descendu pour venir m'embrasser, et me faire toutes les offres de service imaginables. Aujourdhui je pars pour l'aller rejoindre à *Gand,* où je te prie de m'ecrire *poste restante.* J'attendrai ta lettre pour partir pour *Bruxelles* où j'aurais, sans cela, trop de peine à te trouver. Je suis tellement mieux aujourdhui, et mes forces sont deja tellement revenues, que sous trés peu [de] jours il n'y paroitra pas. Deja mon teint de vert et gris qu'il etait me parait presque *couleur de rose!* et comme j'ai pris le parti [de] m'en aller à Gand dans la barque en attachant mon cheval à coté de ceux qui la conduisent, je ne doute pas que ce repos ne me fasse le plus grand bien. Enfin je suis un tout autre homme: car je dois t'avouer que mes pertes si soudaines, si peu prevues, et l'inquietude que tu m'as donnée, jointes à la privation des seules medicamens, dans les quels j'avais une confiance d'autant plus entiere que je les tenais de toi, tout cela m'entrainait [|] assez rapidement vers une dissolution totale, contre la quelle je suis bien resolu de me roidir de toutes mes forces. À revoir, donc ma Fanny, et cela le plutôt possible. J'ai ecrit à Madᵉ de Maurville,[3] même à Madᵉ la Dᵉˢˢᵉ d'Hurst[3] que je n'ai point l'honneur de connoitre, afin de savoir de tes nouvelles et de celles de notre chere Princesse, aux pieds de la quelle je te prie de me mettre. Il est impossible d'exprimer le regret que j'eprouve en pensant que j'ai perdu le precieux petit billet où son ame et son extrême bonté se sont si bien peintes au moment de notre derniere separation!!!

Lally est surement des vôtres. Comment se porte-t'il? Conçoit-on la proclamation du Mᵃˡ Ney[4] qu'on disait un si loyal

3 Ll. 852 and 856 n. 10.
4 Michel Ney (1769–1815), duc d'Elchingen and prince de la Moskawa, the most tragic of Napoleon's marshals, rose from humble origins to early fame in the revolutionary campaigns. He was one of the few generals from the Army of the Rhine whole-heartedly to support Napoleon's imperial ambitions and this, together with his fiery temper, made him both famous and envied. He behaved well in the transition from Empire to Restoration, but his switch of allegiance to Napoleon during the Hundred Days led to his court-martial and execution for

militaire!! Bon dieu quel siecle! Fais agreer mon hommage à Mme la D^esse de Duras⁵ si tu la vois. Son mari qui etait dans la voiture du Roi, a été p^r moi comme à son ordinaire — c-à-d. très gracieux. Ô mon amie — et ta santé? voilà ce dont je n'ai osé te parler; je n'aurois pu m'entretenir d'autre chose!! ǀ

[xxxxx 3 *lines marginal writing*]

858   Ghent, 31 March [1815]

M. d'Arblay
To Madame d'Arblay

A.L. (Berg), 31 mars
Single sheet 4to   2 pp.
Addressed: A Madame / Madame d'Arblay / chez Madame la Princesse / d'Henin / à Bruxelles—
Edited by FBA, p. 1, *annotated and dated*: ⊞   ✕   ⌐6⌐   1815   [*with numbers on address fold*]: 6   6
See further, Textual Notes.

Gand ce Vendredy soir Mars 31.
à l'hotel de Flandre *Drap-Straet*¹

Je suis arrivé ici assez bien, et je suis convaincu que si j'avais de bonnes nouvelles de ta santé, la mienne serait bientôt

treason—a trial and sentence that damaged the Bourbons even more than the defection that prompted them.

On 14 March in the Place d'Armes at Lons-le-Saulnier, Marshal Ney had proclaimed to his troops his change of allegiance from Louis XVIII to Napoleon in an address that began 'Officiers, sous-officiers et soldats, la cause des Bourbons est à jamais perdue' and continued 'Soldats, je vous ai souvent menés à la victoire; maintenant je vais vous mener à la phalange immortelle que l'empereur conduit à Paris', words that may have been written by Napoleon over Ney's signature (Houssaye, *1815*, i. 312–19).

⁵ Claire-Louise-Rose-Bonne de Coëtnempren de Kersaint (1778–1828) had married the duc de Duras during their exile in London in 1797 (vi, L. 631 n. 4), but despite the constant attendance that his post as First Gentleman of the Bedchamber (L. 845 nn. 8 and 15) forced upon her, she dissociated herself during the Hundred Days from the Tuileries clique of ultras, who hated her and declared that she deserved a whipping (Stenger, p. 315). She supported Chateaubriand and Lally-Tolendal during the Hundred Days and became a leading member of the opposition to the extreme royalists (Boigne, i. 348–9).

858. ¹ The Hôtel de Flandre on Drap Straet (or rue aux Draps) was in the centre of Ghent between the river Lys and the canal de Bruges along which M. d'A arrived by barge. The comte d'Artois, the duc de Berry, and the prince de Condé had already reached Ghent and taken up residence in this hotel (Romberg and Malet, i, p. xxiv).

excellente. Donne m'en donc bien vite à l'adresse cy dessus.
Je n'ai encore pu voîr personne, et j'ai dejà eprouvé qu'un
General deguenillé, sans domestique et avec l'air d'un deterré,
jette un pauvre cotton. Don Quichotte avait du moins Sancho
Pança à sa suitte: mais personne! et ce diable de casque[2]
qui me fait suivre constament par une foule de polissons.
Dieu veuille que leur premiere curiosité satisfaite ils ne m'as-
saillent pas avec des pommes cuites et peut être pis. Demain
matin je compte voir M^r le duc de L. — — [xxxxx 1½ *lines*]
Oh la charmante ¹ voiture que la barque de Bruges à Gand. Il y
avait un excellent diner dont j'ai peu profité et fort bonne
compagnie le tout pour 5^f non compris 2^f que j'ai donné p^r
conduire mon cheval et 8 sols p^r sa depense. Lord Fitzeroi
Sommerset[3] ambassadeur d'Angleterre près de Louis XVIII
etait du nombre des passagers avec sa femme et toute sa suitte.
Le Pere Elysée[4] chirurgien et medecin du Roi s'y trouvoit
aussi. Je l'ai vu plusieurs fois chez D'Agoult[5] qui même m'a
presenté particulierement à cet original en lui demandant
ses bons conseils pour moi, en cas de besoin. J'avais quelqu'
envie d'y avoir recoûrs, quoiqu'il ne m'inspire pas grande
confiance. mais comme il n'a pas eu l'air de me reconnoitre.
J'ai été dispensé de cet effort. Ô mon amie quand serons nous
reunis, tout à fait reunis! God bless thee dearest of dears ¹

---

² M. d'A's helmet, which may have evoked his allusion to Cervantes and which
caused urchins to follow him everywhere, was one of grandiose design newly issued
to the officers of the Maison du Roi. It followed a Graeco-Roman pattern and was
topped by crested plumes.
³ Youngest son of the 5th Duke of Beaufort, Lord Fitzroy James Henry Somerset
(1788–1855), 1st Baron Raglan (1852) and field marshal, had risen quickly in the
army to become in 1811 Wellington's military secretary. On 26 March he left
Paris, where he had been ambassador during Wellington's absence at the Congress
of Vienna, and rejoined Wellington's staff in the Netherlands (*Morning Chronicle*,
1 Apr. 1815).
He had married in 1814 Lady Emily Harriet *née* Wellesley-Pole (1792–1881),
the second daughter of the 3rd Earl of Mornington, and Wellington's niece.
⁴ Marie-Vincent Talochon (1753–1817), père Élisée, a Brother of Charity who
became a military surgeon and professor of anatomy. He emigrated in 1791 to take
charge of the hospitals of the Armée des Princes, went to England in 1794, and
became Louis XVIII's physician in 1797. He spent the years of exile and returned
to France with the King. See Jean Pinasseau, *L'Émigration militaire: campagne de 1792*
(1957–64), ii. 41. M. d'A's doubts about père Élisée, who had been doctor to the
chevalier d'Éon, were clearly shared by others, who found him a mysterious, even
sinister member of the royal court (Romberg and Malet, i, p. xxviii).
⁵ The vicomte d'Agoult (L. 835 n. 7).

[320, rue de la Montagne,
Brussels, *post* 31 March 1815]

To M. d'Arblay

A.L. (Berg), *n.d.*
Originally a double sheet 4to, of which FBA later discarded the second leaf
Edited by FBA, p. 1, *annotated and dated*: 1815. (10/8) (9. lost.) Bruxelles, *See* Textual Notes.

Mon ami—mon amico—mon *ALL*! I have just had your delightful Letter[1]—delightful in defiance of all its painful mixture of misery & suffering.—My 1st joy & gratitude at sight of your hand writing to Me de Maurville can NEVER be equalled;[2] but my present less tumultuous happiness fills me with a thankfulness for your preservation that ought to tincture with determined philosophy all the rest of my existence, in opposition to all the evils, of *any other description*, that may assail it. I cannot, however, rejoice, after such fatigues & such illness & such strength-consuming toils, that you have again proferred your services, when I thought you fixed to retire, for the present, to the neighbourhood of our Alex, for repose & recruiting.

But—you have not had any of my Letters?[3] You know not, therefore, either my exquisite felicity at your 1st handwriting, or my cruel difficulties how to give up, or *not* give up, all hopes of recovering any part of our property? ⌐La Morte dans le coeur—a *sort* that I rescued not one of my letters nor a single of my many trinkets—nor our bibelots nor my shawls!— Excess of disorder robbed me of all recollections that we had them, in the hurried moment of unexpected departure—I have written all this AT LENGTH to Ostende post restante directed à M. M. Le. Chev¹ d'Arblay, Marechal de Camp, et Lieutt des Gardes du Corps, du roi de France. If you can send for the Letter, pray do, as it contains many things that were written

859. ¹ M. d'A's letter to the duchesse d'Ursel (L. 856 n. 10).
 ² See L. 852.
 ³ Ll. 851, 854, and 855. FBA's letters through the post and to Lille are missing, as are M. d'A's from Ypres and Menin, which FBA had received by 31 March (see L. 857). Her comments here on the duc de Luxembourg's kindness near Ostend after M. d'A had left Ypres indicate that she had also read M. d'A's letter of 31 March from Bruges (L. 858).

in the belief you only would read them! I sent a rough duplicate also to *Gand.* pray enquire—to M. le General de Lux[em]bourg, & one—I sent thro the post though not *post Restante*! & I wrote also to Ypres, & to Lille, ¹ received 1 only. I bless & save it in requite—If you can come hither, *do now,* I have much I should ask—should I ⟨receive⟩ any dire medical advice back,⁋ I trust you will remember that to demolish yourself is not to serve your King: & the hard service of the present moment, when the War planned & threatened once begins, really demands the endurance & vigour of youth to save its operators from being its victims.

How am I charmed with M. le Duc de L[uxembourg]—³ that much of his quick feeling regard, in jumping from his carriage to embrace you, winds me round him in grateful attachment for-ever.

⌐If you can come hither you have a right to a ROOM—& when once sure here—a BED—for⌐ our house is taken for a month between La Pss M. de Lally & myself. ⌐La Pss has a Man & a Maid, M. de L. his valet—& we have hired a helper in common, our account is to be paid, in partition, de même— I like it not—how at first to do better, I knew not, but at the end of the month [xxxxx 1 *line, in which Mme d'Arblay resolves to*] seek some cheaper way of life. Two—I will not go over *without you,* while I can communicate with & have news & Letters.⁋

My journey, though in the carriage of the Psse cost me 6 nap[oleon]s—in Gold coin for horses, Inns, dinners, &c.

I have no clothes! I only possess a small change of linen, & 2 mourning Gowns! Ceaselessly but too late I regret not having had a better foresight of migratory destiny!⁋

And all my MSS!—My beloved Father's! my family papers!— my Letters of all my life! my Susan's Journals!—!!!—our Argenterie—Linen—BOOKS—prints—*curiosities*

But my consternation in being forced to quit Paris so abruptly, without any means of learning where you were—or acquainting you with my own destination,—& my absence indefinite from our Heart-dear Boy—all this, gave me a sort of stupor— of indifference to every other consideration—O, for what an Animation is it NOW exchanged!

[*the second leaf is missing*]

[320, rue de la Montagne],
Brussels, 27–[31] March 1815

To Alexander d'Arblay

A.L. (Berg) 27–29 Mar. 1815
Double sheet small 4to   greenish   4 pp.   *pmk*   17 [A]⟨P⟩ 18⟨ ⟩   wafer
Addressed: ⌐Angleterre.⌐ / Alexander d'Arblay Esq, / ⌐Caius College, /
Cambridge.⌐
    Re-addressed: at Mʳ Lock's Norbury Park— / near Dorking / Surry
    Docketed: the last folding down of this—to keep—

March 27ᵗʰ
1815.

I know not whether my poor Alex has received my first
Letter[1]—begun at Tournay, & ended at Bruxelles? If not,
This must give him the disastrous tidings of my separation from
the best beloved of BOTH our hearts—who left me on Sunday
the 19ᵗʰ March, to go to a Review of all La Maison du Roi on
Le Champ de Mars. He had not yet received any order for
departing—& I flattered myself to the last moment he would
once again, at least, return!—but he had less hope! he prepared
entirely for a Military expedition, had a noble War Horse, a
servant well mounted on another Horse, splendid new accout-
rements—arms, Baggage, &c—&c—Oh Alex! what a parting
was ours, in defiance of my ignorance of the impending horrours, & delusive belief better days were quick approaching!
Your name was nearly the last he pronounced as we separated
—he forgave you, my poor Alex—& said '*Embrassez le pour moi—
& dites lui que je l'aime—Je crois—plus que jamais*'—but, he then,
in a low voice, added, that he would not write to you, because
he felt too angry at your inconceivable negligence to write
without a reproach which, at such a moment of precarious
existence, he should be sorry to utter. Oh my poor Alex! how
do I pray to Heaven the kindest of parents may be spared to
receive—& you to offer some amends! I feel sure, sure of your
desire. Then, ⎮ after joining our hopes for a speedy—with our
solemn prayers for a Future, an eternal re-union, he quitted

860.   ¹ L. 850, which FBA had finished the day before.

me—yet, at the door, turned back, to cry, with a Face & voice reviving to his duty, '*Vive le Roi!*—' I echoed, with what energy I could assume, the call of Honour—& I have never seen him since!—

He had made me promise to quit Paris in 3 days, if he did not return—he had engaged me a place in the *voiture* of the p^ss d'Henin, who had decided to be gone, if Buonaparte arrived. An officer, sent upon a recognizance by the Minister de la Guerre,[2] had told Mr Victor,[3] before me, that B[uonaparte] could not reach Fontainbleau[4] for 3 days—On this I had relied, for time to arrange my affairs, if forced to depart: but — — I was yet in absorbed grief & horrour at what I had to fear from the impending battle to which your dear Father believed himself hastening, when M^e d'Henin came to inform me B. was already at Fontainbleau—& that we must be off with all speed. She did not determine whether our route should be to Bordeaux, where was La D^ss d'Angouleme, or to Brussels, where she should join her niece, M^e La Tour du Pin—I made ready a small packet of linen, & 2 mourning Gowns—and This is ALL I now hold of my so numerous hoards & possessions in France! unless some happy return to Right & Justice takes place, we shall have the World to begin again—for we have neither cloaths, plate—Goods—Chattels—Linnen—nor any single circumstance necessary for house-keeping & living. But to be joined again to my two dear Alexanders will reconcile me to bearing with every privation.

My poor little packet made, I went to our excellent Genl La Tour Victor de Maubourg, to take leave of Me de Maisoneuve. I found her much disturbed for Maxime,[5]—who always retains his friendship for you—& who was at Metz—under Marechal Oudinot,[5] reported to be faithfully loyal, but ill

[2] Henry-Jacques-Guillaume Clarke (1765–1818), duc de Feltre (1809), had been Minister of War under Napoleon (1807–14), a position he resumed under Louis XVIII on 11 Mar. 1815, succeeding the disgraced Marshal Soult.

[3] General Victor de Latour-Maubourg (see n. 7).

[4] Both reports were false. Napoleon in fact reached the courtyard of the palace at Fontainebleau at 10 o'clock on the morning of 20 March. He had spent the previous night at Pont-sur-Yonne, leaving there for Fontainebleau at dawn accompanied by a small escort from the 13th Regiment of Dragoons (Houssaye, *1815*, i. 360–4).

[5] 'Maxime' (L. 840 n. 21), son of Mme de Maisonneuve (L. 839 n. 4), Victor's nephew and AA's old school friend, was garrisoned at Metz under Marshal Nicolas-Charles Oudinot (1767–1847), duc de Reggio, in the newly styled Grenadiers et Chasseurs de France, formerly Napoleon's Old Guard. Louis XVIII and

surrounded. ꞁ Gen¹ Victor had been so thunderstruck by the reports that had reached him of defection & treachery, that he was quite ill: he was engaged with sundry officers, endeavouring to form some rallying point. While here, came Charles,[6] his Brother, from la Cazerne de la Maison du Roi—whence he brought me this billet from our beloved

'Tout est perdu!—Je ne puis entrer dans aucun detail, mais, de Grace, partez! le plutôt sera le mieux!—'

It was 9 o'clock at night. I had not yet seen Gen¹ Victor[7]—but demanded a moment—he was then equipping himself to wait upon *le Roi*, with an offer of his ultimate services. We shook hands through his door—I could only say 'Je pars!—' & only replied 'Bien des choses de ma part à Alexander!' How kind! but he always honours you with an affection [*tear*]. He concluded I was going to England. But I was on[ly] destined to wander ⟨1st⟩ ANY whither from Paris—[and] next—to seek our dearest Friend. I then went [to] Madᵉ d'Henin. & at 10 at night we set off—with no fixed purpo[se h]ow far to go, or what to do, but to change & settle our projects according to circumstances. The 21ˢᵗ on arriving, at Night, at Amiens, we found that *le Roi* had passed by, in going to Abbeville,[8] but procured no news de *sa maison*. B[uonaparte] had entered Paris the 20ᵗʰ. But no orders had yet arrived at *Amiens*, where the

the duc de Feltre considered the loyalty of these famous regiments at Metz to be key to the loyalty of the rest of the army. Oudinot tried without success to secure their support by offering a commission to every soldier and a title to every officer. On 13 March he expressed his doubts to the duc de Feltre about the attitude of his troops, and on the following day he was forced to telegraph the news that not only had they refused to fight for Louis XVIII but they planned to join the army of Napoleon as soon as they were able. On 18 March Marshal Oudinot made a last attempt to rally the remnants of his command at Chaumont where he had gone after the guard had abandoned him, marching out of Metz to join Napoleon (Houssaye, *1815*, i. 351–3).

[6] See also L. 849.

[7] Marie-*Victor*-Nicolas de Fay Latour-Maubourg (L. 840 n. 23) formed a detachment of mounted volunteers while the octogenarian Marshal Vioménil (see n. 13) raised infantry volunteers in the last days before the King's flight from Paris. Both detachments were meant to hold the Château of Vincennes for the King. The Governor of the Château found Vioménil's two battalions, most of them students, a pathetic force, 'marmots incapable de tenir un fusil'. See letter (Vincennes), the Marquis de Puyvert to General Maison, 17 Mar. 1815.

[8] Louis XVIII left the direct route to Lille by way of Amiens and spent the night of 20–1 March at Abbeville. Napoleon, on hearing around noon of 20 March of the King's flight, left Fontainebleau at two o'clock in the afternoon and travelled slowly through enthusiastic crowds and troops who had come out to meet him from Paris. He entered the Tuileries around nine o'clock that evening (*The Times*, 6 Apr. 1815; Houssaye, *1815*, i. 360).

Prefect[9] came & supped with us.—All here was loyal, but apprehensive & inactive. As every where else! We travelled nearly all night, & stopt to a long Breakfast at the Prefect's at Arras[9]—where all the troops & Inhabitants were for *le Roi*: & the General who commanded them[10] told me he had dined the preceding day at Beauvais with the Princes, the Prince de Poix, the ducs de Luxembourg, *Wagram, Tarente, Raguse*,[11] &c—But the *Maison du Roi* could not travel so fast, & was not arrived!![12] Think of my inquietude!—As yet, however, there

9 The Prefects, *Alexandre*, comte de Lameth, and Jacques-François Lachaise (L. 856 n. 8).

10 François-Antoine Teste (1775–1862), baron de l'Empire (1810). After many campaigns with the Revolutionary and Napoleonic armies, Teste was captured at Kulm on 30 Aug. 1813 and did not return to France until June 1814. He was made a Chevalier de Saint Louis on 8 July 1814 and on 31 August given command of the troops in the department of Pas-de-Calais, but went over to Napoleon on hearing of his arrival in Paris. Recalled to Paris by Napoleon on 15 April, he was given command a week later of the 21st infantry division in the 6th Corps of the Armée du Nord under Lobau. Following Waterloo he distinguished himself in a series of rearguard actions from Belgium to the Loire, after which he was put on the inactive list and not recalled until 30 Dec. 1818.

11 This ill-assorted group made up Louis XVIII's military staff during the flight to the Belgian frontier. The Princes were the comte d'Artois and the duc de Berry; the prince de Poix (v, L. 513 n. 16) was Philippe-Louis-Marc-Antoine de Noailles (1752–1819), lieutenant-général of the King's armies; the duc de Luxembourg (L. 857 n. 1), like the prince de Poix a friend of the d'Arblays, was also M. d'A's commanding officer as captain of a company of the Gardes du Corps.

The next group of three were among Napoleon's most famous marshals. Wagram was Louis-Alexandre Berthier (1753–1815), prince de Neuchâtel and Wagram, formerly the Emperor's chief of staff and now a captain of one of the two new companies of Gardes du Corps. Tarente was Étienne-Jacques-Joseph-Alexandre Macdonald (1765–1840), duc de Tarente, the son of a Scots Jacobite who had entered the French army after the failure of the 1745 rebellion. He was widely admired for his fidelity, which led him to accompany Louis XVIII to the frontier, then to return to France, where he refused all of Napoleon's offers of commands. Raguse was Auguste-Fréderic-Louis Viesse de Marmont (1774–1852), duc de Raguse and captain of the other new company of Gardes du Corps. Many charged him with betraying Napoleon in 1814 (see vii, L. 793 n. 19) by going over to the Austrians, and Louis XVIII as well during the Hundred Days, by persuading the duc de Berry to abandon the Maison du Roi (see n. 18).

In the haste and confusion of their forced march from Paris during the night of 19–20 March, the various companies and units that made up the Maison du Roi (i.e. all of the household troops and royal guards) had become separated and in some cases lost. The best mounted, the Gardes du Corps, Gendarmes, Chevaux-légers, Grey and Black Musketeers, reached Beauvais on the morning of 20 March. The infantry, royal volunteers and d'Arblay's foot artillery, accompanied by a rearguard of La Rochejaquelein's Grenadiers à Cheval, marched on behind, slowed to a marching pace and bogged down in the yellow mud mentioned in numerous accounts of the flight from Paris, reaching Beauvais late in the afternoon of the 20th. There orders were issued to keep to the road to Abbeville (Rochechouart, pp. 406–7; *The Times*, 6 Apr. 1815).

12 Louis XVIII had entered Lille on 22 March at one o'clock in the afternoon. There he conferred with his Marshals Berthier, Macdonald, and Mortier and with M. de Blacas, who concluded that his safety at Lille could not be assured. The King himself was so struck by the hostility of the troops—'Les soldats, mornes et glacés,

was no pursuit. From Arras we proceeded to *Orchies*, the last frontière town of France. Here the wheel of the carriage broke, at 11 at Night. every Inn was full—it could not be mended under 4 or 5 hours—& it rained continually. In this desperate situation, the almost unequalled humanity of a good woman who heard voices in distress, after she was in Bed, led her to arise, & come to our assistance. She made us enter her little parlour, lighted an excellent fire, got each of us a Pillow to rest our heads against a Chair & a Table, & poured us out basons of [1] warm Tea!—With this model of true hospitality, we stayed till 6 in the morning—& at about 9, on the 23d Mars, we left hapless, disordered France, & entered Flanders by *Tournay*—w[h]ere new scares & alarms awaited me—*Le Roi* was at Lille[12]— I saw M. de viomenil[13]—but no news of your Father—The Prince de Conde came to Tournay—in his flight towards Brussels—but no news! I saw an *English* General, whom I addressed—& he assured me *La Maison du* Roi had never reached Lille![14]— & was seeking another direction to the Frontieres!!! We came on the next day to Brussels—& stopt at Made de Maurville's—whence we are now settled in a small house at our united expense, for I brought away all I could of money, though nothing of any other value. I am waiting—with feelings I would not for the world describe, intelligence of our Beloved. *Le Roi* is at *Ostende*[15]—le duc de Berri is here[15]—*la*

gardaient un sombre silence, présage alarmant de leur prochaine défection' declared the official release (in the *Moniteur de Gand*, 14 April)—that his first reaction was to leave that night; but his counsellors advised waiting until morning to avoid appearance of flight. As at the Tuileries, Louis was uncertain. Rumour that orders had arrived from Paris to the prefect of Lille and to Marshal Mortier to arrest the King, finally prompted his departure from Lille at three o'clock, not toward Dunkirk, as his counsellors had advised, but toward Ostend (Romberg and Malet, i, p. xix).

[13] Joseph-Hyacinthe-Charles du Houx (1734–1827), marquis de Vioménil, who had been one of the great nobles and leading generals of the *ancien régime*, was notable even in the Restoration for the rigidity and arrogance of his views. Even though his service after he emigrated in 1791 had been chiefly in the Russian and Portuguese armies and although he had not served at all while in England from 1802 until 1814, he insisted on his return to France in 1814 that he should not only be made a marshal at the age of 80 but also that his promotion should be pre-dated to give him seniority over all of Napoleon's marshals. After following the King to Ghent in 1815, he was given command in turn of the 11th, 12th, and 13th military divisions and made finally a maréchal de France in 1816 (Joseph Valynseele, *Les Maréchaux de la restauration et la monarchie de juillet, c.* 1962). See further, L. 924, pp. 387–8.

[14] For the route of the Maison du Roi, see L. 850 n. 1.

[15] Louis arrived in Ostend from Lille on the evening of 24 March (*Morning Chronicle*, 31 Mar. 1815). The duc de Berry had probably passed through Brussels

Maison du Roi is dispersed![16] *Monsieur* has declared there is no power left for supporting it, & given to each officer his own option to follow, *by his own means*,[16] the Roi—or return to his family, & wait for better days. But some have been lost in a dreadful *marais* where they plunged to rise no more![17]—some have been betrayed by a Traitor[18]—others go to seek their wives & children—& others, *à toute frais & risque*, have pursued the royal tracks. That this last has been the resolution of OUR beloved, if not overpowered with fatigue, we cannot doubt—

March 29ᵗʰ I kept this back—& not in vain, I bless Heaven! to add some tidings—I have had the unspeakable consolation & joy of seeing once more your Father's handwriting, in a Letter to Mᵐᵉ de Maurville[19] dated *March 27.* & enquiring news of your mother. The *Maison du Roi* has been broken up,[20] as a Body, from inability to sustain itself, in the midst of treachery & desertion! Many have returned—licensed by the Princes, to their homes—some have fallen victims to fatigue & direful accidents—others have been betrayed to the Enemy—

on his way from Béthune to Ghent on 24 and 26 March. He then went to Alost, within a short ride from Brussels and Ghent, where on the 29th he had established a headquarters for the royalist troops. The duc de Berry and his father the comte d'Artois are frequently reported in Brussels during these days.

16 These are also the words recalled by Rochechouart, a lieutenant in the Mousquetaires Noires (pp. 407–8).

17 This refers literally to the constant rain that turned the roads to the north into quagmires and figuratively to the swamps of confusion and frustration that trapped so many members of the Maison du Roi. The first issue of the *Moniteur de Gand* gave the state of the roads as the reason for the inability of the Maison du Roi to follow the King (Houssaye, *1815*, i. 391 n. 1).

18 The suspected traitor may have been M. d'A's friend, the comte de Lauriston (see v *passim*), captain of the Mousquetaires Gris, who was ordered by the comte d'Artois to carry out the disbanding of the Maison du Roi. When he began to do so on 25 March he was loudly accused of treason by many of the Gardes du Corps still at Béthune, who were convinced that he was sending them into imprisonment at the hands of the Napoleonic forces. The first number of the *Moniteur de Gand* claimed that Lauriston had disbanded the troops contrary to the wishes of the comte d'Artois (Houssaye, *1815*, i. 391 and n. 1). This was clearly not true, but it increased the feeling referred to by FBA that they had been betrayed. It is, however, possible that FBA refers here to Marmont (vii, L. 793 n. 19). In addition to the charges of disloyalty made against him (n. 11), he was also accused by the Gardes du Corps of hurrying them towards the débâcle at Béthune merely to provide himself with an escort to the frontier (*The Times*, 6 Apr. 1815).

19 L.852.

20 FBA is here translating the French military term for the discharge or disbanding of troops.

others betrayed themselves—your beloved Father—through difficulties that nearly overpowered him—got at last to the King at Ghent²¹—wh[en]ce—finally—I have a Letter from himself.²² Joy for [*wafer*] me, my dear Alex—& write—Write—Tell [me] when you exhibit—&c—yrs ever |

⟨FB ly⟩

direct
à Madame ⟨F⟩ Burney Bruxelles, Madame d'Arblay—chez Madame de Maurville, à Bruxelles.—

861   [320, rue de la Montagne],
                    Brussels, 27–[*post* 31] March [1815]

To Mrs. Broome

A.L.S. (Berg), 27–29 Mar.
Double sheet 4to   4 pp.   *pmks*   FOREIGN/10/AP 181⟨5⟩ AP 1⟨0⟩ /18⟨15⟩   wafer
Addressed: Angleterre—/ À Madame / Madame Broome— / au charge du Captaine Burney, / N° 26 James Street, / Westminster, / London. / to be forwarded / immediately.
Endorsed by CBFB⟨ Sister d'arblay / 1815
Edited by CBFt. *See* Textual Notes.

Brussels—27. March—

Ah my dearest Charlotte—I would not write to you in this moment of anguish & affright if there were any chance you could escape hearing the dreadful blow which again shakes all Europe: but as that is impossible, it is best to tell you that I am

²¹ According to the *Journal de Gand* of 29 Mar. 1815, Louis XVIII had arrived in Bruges from Ostend on that day. From Bruges he went to Ghent, arriving there on 30 March at five o'clock in the afternoon. He was welcomed by the comte d'Artois and the duc de Berry who, travelling from Brussels the night before had settled themselves together with the prince de Condé in the Hôtel de Flandre. The King, dressed in a sky-blue uniform and seated in a state carriage drawn by six horses, was escorted by the mayor, comte Philippe de Lens, and detachments of Belgian and Hanoverian troops to the house of the comte d'Hane de Steenhuyse, who had placed at the King's disposal his handsome townhouse in the rue des Champs in the centre of the town (Romberg and Malet, i, pp. xxii-xxv).
²² M. d'A arrived in Ghent on 31 March, and FBA probably refers here to his first letter from Ghent written that evening (L. 858). The last few lines of this letter were clearly added some time after that date.

safe—even though I am forced, at this melancholy moment, to own to you—that I am alone! that I know not what is become of my far—far dearer part! — — We separated on Sunday the 19th March—he left me to go to a Review at le Champ de Mars. He had had no order for marching at that time, but circumstances led him to believe in it, & he went off prepared, with military equipments,—arms—Horses—baggage—& a domestic—and—though still I had hope he would return from the Review, our leave-taking—Oh my dear Charlotte, was dreadful!—for every thing was black all around, & an engagement with the troops of the usurper appeared to M. d'A[rblay] not only inevitable, but desirable, since not to fight was the same thing as to be conquered. He made me promise, if he returned not, to quit Paris within 3 days,—having engaged by the most solemn request the princess d'Henin to give me a place in her carriage if she took flight—which she was fixed to d[o], should Buonaparte be expected. An officer—I now see a Traitor—had told ¹ Me Victor La Tour Maubourg, in my presence, that B[uonaparte] could not reach Fontainbleau for full 3 days—but alas—my best Friend had not left me half an hour, when M^e d'Henin came to tell me that Destroyer was already at Fontainbleau, & that we must be off with all speed. Still, however, I believed I quitted my home only for a few days, to be in the neighbourhood of Paris, while a Battle with the Rebels should secure their defeat, & bring all loyal subjects back to the Capital. But with my heart full of grief & horrour at the victims which might buy the expected victory, I could make no calculations or combinations upon my interest & my property— &, to my never-ending regret, I brought away with me nothing but a small change of linen, & 2 mourning Gowns! For Cloaths, Goods, Books, MSS—I had no room in the Carriage of a Friend—& of my valuables—watch, Trinkets—&c—I never once thought! At 9 o'clock at night, a fellow officer of the garde du Corps du Roi, M. Chas La Tour Maubourg, delivered me a billet from M d'A. to charge me to depart from Paris with all speed, as *All was over!* At 10 o'clock at night I left that unhappy Capital, in a state of ignorance of its own fate, & of general consternation. We stopt for a few hours at *Bourget*, where we heard that the King had left Paris. But no news of his guard, called *La Maison du Roi*, to which M. d'A belongs. We proceeded to a place called *Roy*, the following night, where we heard that Buonaparte had made his entry into the metropolis. We then changed our course to Amiens, where Mme d'H. had a nephew in high power,[1] & where we decided to remain till we could obtain some certain news. But we found that the King had gone by, to Abbeville, & that there could be no security that orders might not arrive to stop all travellers. We | supped, therefore, & set off in the middle of the night. We had some very bad road to pass, but we arrived the next morning to Breakfast at Arras, without accident. There all still was loyal, & we were perfectly well treated. We proceeded to the frontier of France, meaning to arrive in La Belgique: but the wheel of our carriage gave way, & 4 hours were demanded for mending it, at *Orchies*, where every Inn was full, of fugitives like ourselves —& we were without either house or carriage, in the Rain, in the dead of the night. In this terrible distress, which threatened me, in particular, with the most dangerous consequences, a good Gentlewoman in the neighbourhood heard the *Jeremiades* of the postilions, &, though in Bed, dressed herself to come down into the street, & offer us assistance. I never saw a better creature in my life, more innocently generous & kind. She made us enter her small *Parlour-Kitchen*, lighted a blazing fire to dry & warm us;—made us basons of tea; & got each of us a pillow, for which she aired a clean pillow bear, that we might repose our heads against the back of our Chairs, & try to sleep: while she herself sat up, to nourish the fire, & watch, from time to time, the arrival of our carriage. How I wish we could meet her! or find means to send her some acknowledgement. She disclaimed all recompense, & only sent us off with her hearty good will & wishes. on Thursday, March 23^d we entered La Belgique, at Tournay—quitting the tortured, wretched, revolutionary France, so lately the beautiful scene of restored tranquility & rising prosperity! Here we passed a day spent by me in continual agony, from my uncertainty what was become of M. d'A.—my nearness to the place which I believed him to inhabit, yet impossibility to procure any intelligence The next day we came to Brussels—where we have remained ever since.

861. [1] Alexandre-Théodore-Victor (L. 856 n. 8), comte de Lameth, was prefect at Amiens. FBA probably thought him a nephew of the princesse d'Hénin through confusion with M. de Latour du Pin, who had been prefect there from 1812 to 1814, when he welcomed Louis XVIII on his return from France.

I was quite confined for a time, by colds & feverish fatigue—but the moment I was able I wrote to my Alexander & my Brother James[2]—by an opportunity offered through Mrs. Kirkpatric[3]—who was going over immediately. This Letter was also begun—but I had not been able to finish it—& I have now the blessing to conclude it by telling my dearest Charlottes that on the 29th March I had the exquisite relief of seeing the hand writing of M. d'A. in a Letter to Made de Maurville, to enquire whether she could give him any intelligence relative to myself. He is one of those who have waded through every difficulty to follow the King to the end of his retreat. I have since had a Letter from him, from GHENT,[4] where he was arrived more dead than alive, after an expedition of the greatest harrass & suffering & danger, begun when he was already full of rheumatism, & while yet by no means recovered from his dreadful accident at Calais. Oh that he could go to recruit over the Channel!—write to me, my beloved Charlotte—tell me news of you all—I hear none!—& speak to me of my naughty Alexander from whom we have had but one single Letter![5] God grant he may be well in all ways! my heart aches daily—you, my kindest, & your dear namesake alone have written to me since my departure—

Heaven bless you ever! prays your ever affecte

FB d'A

The poor—excellent—barbarously treated King is now at Ghent—a few faithful adherents & servants—& my best of friends with him—May the united powers of Europe restore him—& may his bitter experience avert the fatal clemency that has been his bane! he spared his Destroyers for his own destruction |

---

[2] The letters to Alexander are 850 and 860, to James, 853.

[3] Possibly Margaret Kirkpatrick, wife of 'William Kirkpatrick, fustian &c. manufacturer, 2 Spring Gardens' (*Pigot's Manchester & Salford Directory*, Manchester, 1813, p. 145). The Kirkpatricks, who do not appear in any of the accounts or lists of English people in Brussels during the Hundred Days, carried letters to England for FBA on what were apparently frequent crossings. Commercial travel could explain their frequency, and this identification gains strength from a contemporary newspaper advertisement: 'Kirkpatrick et comp. de Manchester tiennent cette foire avec un bel assortiment de Manchester unis et rayés, callicos et mouchoirs' (*Journal de Francfort*, 28 Aug. 1815).

[4] L. 858.

[5] Undoubtedly the (now missing) letter of 23 Dec. 1814 that the d'Arblays had received in the New Year (L. 840).

27–post 31 March 1815

Direct Madame de Burney, chez Mad^e de Maurville, à Bruxelles. & write—dearest, write! & give my Kindest Love to all—

862   Ghent, 1 April 1815

M. d'Arblay
To Madame d'Arblay

A.L. (Berg), 1 avril 1815
Double sheet 4to   3 pp.   *pmk*   GAND   wafer
Addressed: A Madame / Madame d'Arblay chez / Madame la Comtesse
de / Maurville   Rue de la Montagne / *N° 320* / A Bruxelles
Edited by FBA, p. 1, *annotated and dated*: ✻· ❖ ❖ × ⌐12⌐ (12.)
(1815)   Narration of the passage from Bethune to Ostend on the dire
Evening of the flight from Paris & Buonaparte with Louis XVIII   [*with
numbers on address fold*]: 7   7

> Gand, 1er avril (Samedy matin), de retour de
> chez M^r de L[uxembourg]¹ que je n'ai point
> trouvé mais qui m'a laissé un petit billet
> refermant le tien — —²

Dieu soit loué, nous ne sommes qu'à 10 lieues l'un de l'autre,
et je te sais près d'une amie; ah que ce mot est doux à pro-
noncer! et que l'idée qu'il presente raffraichit l'ame dans des
momens comme ceux ci! Que de graces je rends au Ciel d'avoir
permis que la princesse³ préferât la Belgique à la Guienne.
Dejà nous pouvons causer par ecrit, et três probablement
avant peu nous pourrons nous entretenir de tout ce qui nous
interesse. J'ai eu sur ma santé les plus vives allarmes, et tu le
concevras quand je t'aurai dit qu'apres avoir debuté par
être 26 heures à cheval, 14 au moins les autres jours et 23 le
dernier, j'ai été à deux fois differentes près de sept heures sur
un pont levis mourant de froid, et sans manteau, à donner au
diable le Commandant d'Ypres qui pour toute reponse à notre

862.   ¹ Here FBA later inserted the superscript + and filled in the name: +
'Luxembourg', M. d'A's commanding officer (L. 857 n. 2).
   ² Probably L. 858.
   ³ The princesse d'Hénin (L. 845 n. 14).

demande d'être admis dans cette ville, nous avait ecrit sans trop de façon

Le Commandant ne veut pas que vous entrez actuellement!!![4]

Le malheur rend moins fier, et il a fallu encore remercier ce personnage quand il lui a plu de laisser enfin *nous entrer.* J'etais alors souffrant, decouragé, denué de tout, n'entrevoyant aucun moyen de reparer la partie que j'ai faite de mes chevaux, et de tout mon equipage, même de mon manteau, que j'avais remis à Bethune à Auguste,[5] dans la ferme persuasion que nous allions nous battre contre un corps de Cavaliers,[6] dont environ 200 lanciers qui venaient de prendre la fuite n'etaient, disait on, que l'avant garde. Depuis j'ai fait dire à Auguste de me rejoindre quand j'ai eu scu que le parti qu'on avait pris de laisser derrierre plus de moitié de l'artillerie et presque tous les domestiques, n'avait d'autre cause que le desir de pouvoir marcher plus vîte, et d'avoir moins de bouches à nourrir dans une traverse où n'etant pas attendu on etait presqu'assuré de ne rien trouver. Nous etions partis le matin[7] de St Pol par une pluie battante, et des chemins du diable; et moi qui voulais faire arriver notre artillerie, j'avais fait beaucoup plus de chemin

---

[4] Entry into Ypres was denied to the Maison du Roi by an officer in Russian service, Bartolomé-Émile de Palavicini (1770–1846), who as commandant of the town claimed to be carrying out the orders of the commander of the Allied troops in that sector. Palavicini, whom Wellington called Paravicini, soon afterward criticized for his conduct as commandant at Ostend (Letter to the Prince of Orange, 27 Apr. 1815, *Disp.* xii. 333), would seem to have been as reactionary as he was obstinate. At Ypres he made an exception of the duc de Richelieu (L. 918 n. 9) because he appeared before the walls still dressed in the uniform of a Russian general, which he had become during his years of service under the Czar. But Palavicini flatly refused to allow the French troops to enter and denounced their commanders to their faces as traitors to Louis XVIII. He finally opened the gates after Richelieu made a direct appeal to the commanding officer, who sought to excuse the obstinacy of his Dutch officer by saying that he had been embittered toward the French by a lifetime of fighting against Napoleon (Rochechouart, pp. 408–10).

[5] Auguste (L. 857 n. 2).

[6] The hostile cavalry mentioned here were in fact the 3rd Lancers, sent to Béthune by General Teste (L. 860 n. 10), the general commanding at Arras. By a double irony Teste, who two days before had been helpful to FBA, now ordered the Lancers to capture the very artillery that M. d'A had brought to Béthune. Although it had lost many stragglers and deserters the Maison du Roi still numbered more than 3,000 men, whom the duc de Berry ordered to follow him to the attack against the 3rd Lancers. Before any clash could take place, however, the duc de Berry himself accosted a squadron commander of the Lancers and ordered him and his men to cry out, 'Vive le roi', but as M. d'A reported, they shouted instead 'Vive l'empereur' but finally withdrew before the assembling horsemen of the Maison du Roi (Houssaye, *1815*, i. 390–1).

[7] 24 March.

que les autres, pour me procurer des chevaux de requisition, qui en effet l'avaient mis dans le cas de suivre à Bethune, où je venais de faire donner l'avoine à mon cheval, et j'allais m'assurer pour manger ma part d'une omelette tandis qu' Auguste qui menait ce pauvre cheval à l'abreuvoir avait l'ordre de revenir sur le champ à 4 pas de là où je l'avais laissé dans la rüe. Tout à coup on crie *'aux armes! aux armes! des lanciers, des Grenadiers à cheval de la Garde'*. Je courus au rendez vous assigné à Auguste. Rien — à l'abreuvoir, pas davantage. Sur la place, tout y etait en confusion Canons, voitures, chevaux, fantassins, pêle mêle et s'empêchant mutuellement d'agir. Monsieur et le Duc de Burry pendant ce tems sortent cependant suivis de quelques personnes et aux cris mille fois repetés de Vive le Roi, vivent les Bourbons — Les lanciers y repondent par celui de Vive l'Empereur et aussitôt ils prennent la fuite — On croit que c'est pour nous attirer dans une embuscade, et l'*on* rentre p^r resortir presqu'aussitôt mais en ordre et n'emmenant que moitié des pieces d'artillerie c. à. d laissant les ǀ Obusiers.[8] C'est cet ordre qui m'a fait croire que nous allions decidement *en decoudre*[9] et comme mon cheval etait fatigué et que la jument etait plus fraiche, je changeai aussitôt avec Auguste que je n'ai plus revu quoique le garde du Corps que je lui ai envoyé p^r lui dire de rejoindre se soit fidelement acquité de sa commission. À la verité ce garde du Corps m'a rendu compte qu'il n'avait pu l'amener avec lui, parcequ'à la poste de Bethune on avait donné l'ordre de ne laisser passer aucun valet. La plus part neanmoins ont trouvé le moyen de rejoindre leurs maitres. Quant à moi pauvre diable, j'ai tout perdu tout absolument, puisqu'arrivé à 4 lieues de Bethune a

[8] *Obusiers* were heavy wheeled mortars, here left behind because they would be useless in any field action against cavalry.

[9] Jacques-Alexandre-Bernard Law (v, L. 425 n. 5) was the general who carried out the order of the Princes for the Maison du Roi to disband (L. 860 n. 18). Descended from a noble Scots family, Lauriston had been like M. d'A an artillery officer. Unlike him he served in the armies of the Revolution and the Empire, distinguishing himself in the ratification of the Peace of Amiens in 1801, at the Battle of Wagram in 1809, and as ambassador to St. Petersburg from 1811 to 1812. Taken prisoner at Leipzig in 1813, he returned from captivity to become in 1814 aide-de-camp of the comte d'Artois, and in 1815 captain of the Mousquetaires Gris. In this capacity he joined the march to Béthune, but after the disbanding of the Maison du Roi he returned to France and retired to his estate of Richecourt. Taking no part in the Hundred Days, he returned to the King's service on 29 June 1815 at Cambrai and became a distinguished commander in the wars against Spain in 1823 when he was made maréchal de France.

travers une boue profonde et tenace où quelques hommes quelques chevaux et beaucoup de bagages sont restés, trouvent
qu'on allait encore plus loin parcequ'on ne pouvait rien s'y
procurer et que les chevaux même ne pouvaient y manger
l'avoine, je me suis vu forcé pour ne pas rester en arrierre de
troquer ma pauvre petite jolie jument que ses molettes fesaient
un peu boîter contre un cheval de la Comp^e assez bon, mais
très jeune et qui une demie heure après avait la plus grande
peine à mettre un pied devant l'autre. Arrivés enfin sur la
grande route de Lille à un demi quart de lieue de la frontiere,
nous y restâmes trois heures au moins, jusqu'à ce qu'on nous
dit de la part des Princes, que S.M. trés reconnoissante de nos
bons services, etait bien fachée de se trouver dans la dure necessité de licentier *momentanement* sa maison,[9] laissant à chacun de
nous de se retirer au sein de sa famille ou d'aller vaquer à ses
affaires où et comme bon lui semblerait. 29 gardes de la Comp^e
seulement ont passé avec les Princes, non compris 3 officiers
savoir MM. de La Roche dragon,[10] de Chabannet[11] et moi,
qui trés malade et prêt à expirer de fatigue demandai le jour
même de mon entrée dans Ypres un passeport à Monsieur
pour Ostende. Mais à deux lieues d'Ypres J'etais si foible et si
mal que sans des volontaires nationaux qui y etaient en can-
tonnement, il m'eut été impossible de descendre de cheval et
probablement d'aller plus loin. Grace à leurs bons soins et à
mon excellent temperament, je m'en suis tiré, et suis tout à fait
quitte de coliques effroyables accompagnées de maux de nerfs
et d'un debordement de bile verte et epaisse puis jaune et puante

[10] Jean-François (1744–1816), marquis de Rochedragon, a cavalry officer under
the *ancien régime* who had become maréchal de camp in 1791 and who, resigning
from the service in the following year, was recalled to the Gardes du Corps and
promoted to lieutenant-général honoraire on 23 Aug. 1814.

[11] Jean-Baptiste-Marie-*Frédéric* de Chabannes (1762–1836), marquis de Curton,
a cavalry officer who had taken part in the siege of Yorktown as aide-de-camp to
Vioménil (1781) and who, renouncing his earlier revolutionary sympathies in 1789,
emigrated in 1790. He was entrusted with several missions as negotiator on behalf of
the Bourbons, was taken prisoner during the expedition to the Island of Yeu (1795)
but escaped to join his family in England where he became an enterprising business-
man. Returning to France in 1802 through the intervention of Talleyrand, he
extended his business interests, building *vélocifères*, light and speedy carriages, which
were used between Paris and Lyons from 1803 to 1806. In 1813 he fled from his
creditors to England, where he became aide-de-camp to the comte de Provence and
succeeded in promoting the surrender of Napoleon's troops at Lille (1814).
Although he accompanied Louis XVIII to Ghent, his impetuous character kept
him from gaining the friendship of the King and earned him the enmity of his
entourage, which he attacked in numerous pamphlets. Put on the retired list as
colonel on 25 Sept. 1816, he moved to London where he founded *L'Argus politique*.

qui a duré deux jours entiers. J'entre dans ce detail parceque Lally[12] que je viens de voir pourra te rassurer pleinement et te dire qu'il m'a même trouvé *assez bon visage.* Ce n'est pas assurement ce que t'avait mandé Mr de L., il y a deux jours, après notre recontre à Ghistelles, relai entre Ostende et Bruges, où sachant que devait passer le Roi que j'allais joindre à Ostende, d'où je n'etais plus qu'à 2 lieues, j'etais venu l'attendre. Ce cher M^r de L[uxembourg] en m'appercevant etait sauté à bas de sa voiture uniquement p^r m'embrasser. Il y etait avec MM les ducs d'Havray[13] et de Grammont.[14] dans celle du Roi etaient S.M. qui avait à sa gauche le p^ce de Poix,[15] et devant lui MM. de Duras et de Blacas,[16] tous avaient les meilleures mines du monde, et S.M. surtout avait l'air aussi | calme que lorsqu'il recevait aux Thuilleries. Depuis ce tems, electrisé par l'espoir fondé que tu etais à Bruxelles avec la bien chere Princesse, j'ai été un nouvel homme. Hier matin j'ai encore vômi un peu de bile verte, mais mon estomach tout à fait retabli a repris ses fonctions dont il s'acquite trés bien à son ordinaire. Tu peus juger si ton petit billet de ce matin et la vue du cher Bon ont arreté cette amelioration dont j'avais tant de besoin. Reste l'embarras de ma situation; et certes il est difficile d'y porter remede. J'en ai fait ce matin dans une lettre le detail ecrit à M^r le duc de L[uxembourg][17] en lui demandant Conseil; et lui fesant entendre qu'à la verité il me parait impossible de demander en ce moment au Roi une indemnité qui me seroit bien due mais que sa position

---

[12] Trophime-Gérard (1751–1830), comte (later marquis) de Lally-Tolendal, a *constitutionnel* and longtime friend of the d'Arblays (see ii-vi *passim*). After accompanying the princesse d'Hénin and FBA to Brussels, Lally, a member of the King's Privy Council since 1814, went to Ghent where in April 1815 he wrote the King's Manifesto to the French People and was named on 2 May 1815 a minister of state in his cabinet.

[13] Joseph-Anne-Auguste-Maximilien de Croy-Havré (1744–1839), duc d'Havré, prince de Saint-Empire, emigrated in 1791 and returned after the Restoration to become pair de France, lieutenant-general and in June 1814 captain of the first company of Gardes du Corps. His accompanying the King prevented him from taking any important part in the Hundred Days (Stenger, pp. 70–1, 338).

[14] Antoine-Louis-Marie de Grammont (vii, L. 770 n. 39), duc de Grammont, pair de France, lieutenant-general (1814), captain of the second company of Gardes du Corps. During the years of emigration he was attached to the household of Louis XVIII as First Gentleman of the Bedchamber. After following the King to Ghent he returned to command the eleventh military division at Bordeaux.

[15] See L. 860 n. 11.

[16] See L. 845 n. 8; and L. 847 n. 2.

[17] This letter to the duc de Luxembourg is missing. In an earlier fragment also intended for him, M. d'A broached the possibility of retiring from the King's service. See A.L. (Berg), [25 Mar. 1815] and L. 852.

ne lui permet guere de m'accorder, mais que d'un autre coté privé de tout, et sans moyens actuels de reparer mes pertes, de maniere à pouvoir faire la campagne d'une maniere utile, je ne voyais guere qu'une place que peut être il pourrait me faire obtenir et dont j'esperais pouvoir me tirer avec honneur, celle d'être comme commissaire de S.M. près du G^al anglaîs[18]— parcequ'alors je ne serais forcé de monter à cheval que les jours d'affaires, et que le traitement de mon grade pourrait me mettre à [même] de remplacer avant peu ce que j'ai perdu. J'attens sa reponse, et la permission d'aller causer de tout [cela] avec toi. Pour le moment je te quitte et t'embrasse comme je t'aime *toto corde meo*. Je ne me crois [plus] malheureux depuis que je puis me rapprocher de toi et de notre cher Alex à qui je te prie d'ecrire. Quel bonheur que tu n'ayes pas été à Bordeaux! Certainement *dans ton etat de santé*, jamais je n'aurais pu supporter l'inquietude qu'il me donnait, et je serais à present un homme mort. Aulieu que à ma respiration près qui n'est pas tout à fait libre, je suis reellement regeneré. Que pourrais-je faire pour cette chere Madame de Maurville à qui je baise bien tendrement les mains et les pieds, en lui recommandant tout ce que j'ai de plus cher au monde l'adorable toi. Adieu chère chère Fanny

Ce 1er avril 1815

P.S. Je suis ici dans le même hotel que le duc de Feltre[19] (Hotel de Flandres rue aux Draps) Ce matin je lui ai rendu visite; il m'a reçu à merveille en me disant qu'il me demandait pardon de ne pas m'avoir reconnu. Jaucourt[20] est venu le voir p^r *parler d'affaires* ce qu'ils ont fait devant moi sans permettre que je les laissasse ensemble. Trois heures après je l'ai encore vu en particulier dans sa chambre où il m'a fait entrer avec

[18] This refers to the mission of the duc de Luxembourg as Louis XVIII's representative with the army commanded by Clinton and later by Wellington.

[19] See L. 860 n. 2.

[20] Arnail-François Jaucourt (ii, pp. xvi–xvii), a soldier and politician whose career during the Revolution and under the Empire was influenced by his relations with moderate circles such as those around Mme de Staël (see vii, L. 736 n. 13), his diplomatic skills, and his fervent Protestantism. He was interim Minister of Foreign Affairs during Talleyrand's absence at the Congress of Vienna and was obliged to make a last-minute escape from Paris early on the morning of 20 March when burning or removing incriminating papers. He was exempted from Napoleon's amnesty and declared an outlaw. From Ghent during the Hundred Days he carried on a correspondence with Talleyrand in Vienna—letters valuable for their records of the period.

Lally, qui te dira que ce Ministre de la Guerre me traite de la
maniere la plus distinguée, et que devant lui il m'a repeté qu'il
me connoissait beaucoup mais beaucoup et de la maniere la
plus avantageuse, par tous les rapports des personnes qu'il
estimait le plus. ¹

863   [286, rue de la Montagne],
                              Brussels, 6 April 1815

To James Burney

A.L.S. (PML, Autog. Cor. bound), 6 Apr. 1815
Single sheet large 4to   2 pp.   *pmks*   T.P.P./U/Duke St   15 AP 1815
wafer
     Addressed: Angleterre / Captain Burney / James Street / Westminster, /
London.

Direct A Made d'Arblay
Chez Made la Comtesse de Maurville
À Brussels

Brussels—April 6th 1815.

Oh my dear Brother I have just seen in an English news
paper a paragraph stating an Epidemical fever at Cambridge¹

863.   ¹ A number of such reports appeared in English newspapers during the last
week of March. One, dated the 23rd and signed 'A.Z.' proposed fumigation since
'the fever, which has for some time past been prevalent in Cambridge, still exists
in an alarming degree' (*Morning Chronicle*, 25 Mar. 1815). The most informative
comments on the nature and extent of the outbreak appear in a letter of the 29th
from a Cambridge surgeon:
> Many cases of remittent and low nervous fevers having occurred in the University
> of Cambridge, more particularly in two Colleges, and four deaths having taken
> place unfortunately in a short interval, much alarm and unfounded rumours have
> been spread. I conceive there can be no doubt of their having arisen from a morbid
> constitution of the atmosphere generally: but aggravated by unfavourable local
> situation, and it will not be found to be peculiarly endemic to Cambridge: that it
> is contagious from one person to the other, I see nothing in the character or
> progress of the disease that can support such opinion. The tutors have very
> properly recommended gentlemen to leave Cambridge for two or three weeks;
> and I am happy to add, the disposition of the disease appears to have nearly
> subsided (*The Times*, 31 Mar. 1815).
A later report, dated 3 April from Cambridge, asserts that fever had broken out at
Trinity and St. John's, that the masters of colleges had sent away their students,
and that there was no real danger, since 'no more than two or three in the University are seriously indisposed' (*Morning Chronicle*, 6 Apr. 1815).

—& that the students are removed elsewhere —— I had written
to my dearest Boy there[2]—whether he has got the Letter Heaven
knows —— Probably. You can tell whether to forward to him
the enclosed[3]—written some days ago, & waiting for this
opportunity—pray inform him one of an earlier date was
sent long since—& charge him to write a line instantly, if—as
God Almighty grant he is well — — — — if otherwise—if
he be ill—oh James, write yourself, & I will quit even his
Father—(though at this moment with agony from suspense of
his destined course, & the sight of his shattered state of health,)
to nurse him myself—

M. d'A. has suffered such unheard of fatigue & privation,
with profound affliction & torturing anxiety, in the course of
the last unhappy month, that he is changed & altered so as to
be forced to demand a *congée* for recruiting his strength. This
has enabled him to come hither—where we are now both
devoured with an inquietude that consumes us for news of our
loved Alexander. I was uneasy before I had this alarm, & I
wrote to my sister Charlotte, through you, not knowing her
direction. Till I hear from or of my Alex, I shall fix no plan
for myself—but the son only can take me from the vicinity of
the Father ¹ while I see him so unwell:—all hope beside of
recovering any part of our property hangs upon watching,
while still on the continent, for someone who can act for us, if
as yet there has been no confiscation.—M. d'A., if (oh what
an If) & when he recovers sufficiently, will re-join the remnant
of *La Maison du Roi* now about the King at Ghent, there to
receive orders. My destination will hang upon circumstance,
unless my Alex is ill — & then all gives way to my solitary &
terrible voyage to nurse him. Pray tell him this—or send this
on to him, & let me have news by return of Post if any way
possible. Every minute languishes in this barbarous uncerti-
tude—Alas, my Heart already seemed bursting from my fears
& distress for my best of all best Friends now nearly a shadow
by my side!—yet evidently, hourly, & rapidly recovering from
what he was at the end of the perilous retreat. He was then so
ill, that he had a *congée*[4] from Mons⟨r⟩ le Comte d'Artois to go &

---

² L. 850 was redirected from Cambridge, first to CBFB's house in Richmond,
then to the Lockes at Norbury Park. ³ Probably L. 860.
⁴ M. d'A's leave, at first granted on 2 April for ten days, actually lasted until the
22nd, when he returned to Ghent.

refit en Angleterre. But—to my infinite regret! on his first amendment, he RESOLVED to wait nearer the scene of action. I wrote to you,[5] or rather Martin, upon business almost as soon as I arrived—& I am in daily hope of an answer. I can now add no more than Love to all from

y[r] ever affect[e]

sister

F Burn[ey]

Particular Love to Mrs. B.—Martin & Sally—

We have not had one word from Mr. W. Lock about our House! nor even heard from Mrs. Lock & Mrs. Angerstein![6]

I have no species of intelligence about my 2[d] Edition.[7] And never did I as now want to regulate my money affairs.

If Martin's answer is not yet sent off, pray, dear Brother, tell him I shall be much obliged for some account of the Irish business.[8]

From the 19. to the 29th I had NO NEWS whatever of M. d'A. I had then a Letter a day till the 2[d] April, when he procured a congée to come & recover his health at Brussels, where he now is—I thank Heaven!—

I have heard from no one but my Alex & my dear Charlottes —yet I would use this opportunity to write again All Round were my mind less disturbed. ¹

[5] L. 853.

[6] M. d'A and FBA built Camilla Cottage on the property of William Locke, Sr. (1732–1810) at his invitation but without any title or deed. When his son and heir William Locke, Jr. (1767–1847) decided in 1814 to sell Norbury Park, Camilla Cottage was lost to the d'Arblays in a forced sale for £620, which Locke offered to pay. This was more than the law required of him, but less (in M. d'A's opinion) than honour demanded; and it was only after a grating correspondence during the spring of 1814, in which Mrs. Locke and Mrs. Angerstein defended Locke, that the house was given up (see vii, Ll. 721–831 *passim*). FBA's postscript here suggests that they had not since heard from, or been paid by, Locke and that FBA suspected continued hurt feelings on the part of Mrs. Locke and Mrs. Angerstein.

[7] For FBA's contract with the publishers of *The Wanderer*, see vii, L. 761 nn. 5, 6.

[8] FBA and EBB had inherited from CB the value and proceeds from the mortgage he held on their former brother-in-law Molesworth Phillip's farm of Belcotton near Termonfeccan, county Louth. When JB refused their offer of a third share (vii, L. 777 n. 1), they gave it to his children, Martin and Sally. Settlement was reached on 25 Mar. 1815 through a foreclosure that yielded £1,754, of which FBA's share was £469 (vii, L. 781 nn. 2, 7).

[286, rue de la Montagne],
Brussels, 7 April 1815

To Charles Burney

A.L. (Berg), 7 Apr. 1815
Single sheet large 4to 2 pp. *pmks* 15 AP 1815 To be De[livered] /
by 10 o'Clo[ck] / on Sund. Morn wafer
Addressed: Angleterre / Rev^d Dr. Burney, / Rectory House, / Deptford /
near / London.

Bruxelles
April 7th 1815

Though not a word has reached me from my dear Carlos
since I left him at his Rectory, I must & will conclude some
Letter has miscarried—& therefore again I write a 3^d time[1]—
since an opportunity offers—for my dolorous ditty would not
be worth postage while I am unable to unfold it with any interesting details. My mind indeed is harrowed with anguish &
apprehension for the future,—& incapable therefore of dwelling
with clearness of recollection upon the past, however recent.
I need not mention many causes for self-terrible occupation &
oppression—when I say that my best Friend leaves me—after
a *congée* of only 10 days to re-join le Roi for service—& when I
add that a cruel News paper from England has just given me
the tidings that an epidemical fever rages in CAMBRIDGE,
whence the students who have escaped it are sent away to their
homes!—

Alas, my dear Charles, what a year has this—beginning from
the 12 of April,[2] & ending *next Tuesday*—when M. d'A.'[s]
congée finishes—been to me!—M. d'A. has never recovered
from the dreadful accident at Calais — & was utterly unfit for
service, when he began his late sad campaign, with the rest of
La Maison du Roi—but his Zeal & force of mind & Character &
loyalty would not listen to any pleas for holding back. The
short, however, but terrible expedition has nearly demolished

864. [1] The second of these is FBA's joint letter with M. d'A dated 22 Feb. 1815
(L. 844); the first is vii, L. 835.
  [2] CB had died at Chelsea College during the night of 11–12 Apr. 1814, while the
sky was illuminated by fireworks set off to celebrate the fall of Napoleon, who had
abdicated on 6 April (*HFB*, pp. 347–8).

him—he is changed! changed! Monsieur, (Comte d'Artois,) gave him permission, at his arrival past the frontiers of France, to retire to [E]ngland—he seemed then so really sinking from fatigue & sufferings. M. d'A accepted it ¹ for the moment, with a real belief he could serve no more—& he was proceeding to Ostende to embark as soon as I could join him. But after 2 days confinement, he grew better, & then went to the *Roi,* at Gand, & only accepted a *congée* for 10 days, from M. le Duc de Luxembourg, who is Capitaine du Gardes du Corps of the company to which he belongs—4 melancholy days only remain for him to pass with me! what his next service may be, or whither, who knows? Lord Wellington is just arrived here — without Him, all public Hope would be lost. — — —

I wish much to know that poor Rosette is recovered—& that your Gout has had fair play,³ & restored your health. I want also extremely to know the fate of the Museum⁴—& what has been paid from the other residuo to Mr. Hoare,⁴ whose Letters we have missed, if he has written any. So have we any, if written, from Messʳ Longman,⁵ & Mr. William Locke.⁶ Unless some speedy happy turn takes place, in public affairs here, we have lost all we possessed in France—Even all my dear Father's MSS. & all my own, & unprinted works, from *my youth upwards,* with all *my* Letters, & my Susan's.⁷—& our Journals! — — Nothing can equal the constant distress of my mind, from subject to subject, when I do not revive to revive my dear excellent Partner — & our Alexander's uncertain situation & health devours us with inquietude. If I hear not of him while I have yet my best support—my now only one—by my side, Heaven knows how I may weather my stormy destiny —for I am happy, perfectly happy *now,* in comparison with what I shall be next Tuesday! Alas, Alas—

³ CB Jr., afflicted with gout, and his wife Sarah ('Rosette') *née* Rose (1759–1821), who 'had been occasionally subject to low spirits'. See vii *passim* and *The Annual Biography and Obituary for the Year 1819,* p. 222.
⁴ The British Museum had agreed to purchase part of Dr. Burney's library (see L. 838 n. 14), and FBA's bankers Messrs Hoare were to receive and pass on payment for her share of Molesworth Phillips's farm (L. 863 n. 8).
⁵ Longman and Rees published *The Wanderer* in March 1814 and sold 3,600 copies in six months, for which their contract with FBA required them to pay her £2,000.
⁶ See L. 863 n. 6.
⁷ SBP had written many vivid and intimate letters to FBA, including a number from Ireland that describe the last stages of her unhappy marriage to Molesworth Phillips. A selection appears in *FB & the Burneys,* pp. 118–305.

Adio—dearest Carlucci!—Love to Charles Parr & his Fanny,[8] not forgetting Mrs. Bick[nel]l[9] & tender love to dear Rosette if well enough— ǀ

We are so uncertain how long we may stay here, that my Letters can only be safe by some private hand; or through some minister. Try to secure such means—as I shall leave some direction if I go, at *Mme. de Maurvilles*, Rue de la Montagne. ǀ

865   [286, rue de la Montagne],
                              Brussels, 8 April 1815

To Esther (Burney) Burney

A.L. (Berg), 8 Apr. 1815
Single sheet large 4to   2 pp.   *pmks*   15 AP 1817   To be Delivered / by 10 o'Clock / on Sund. Morn   wafer
Addressed: Angleterre / Mrs. Burney, / Turnham Green, / Middlesex / near / London.

Brussels—Ap[l] 8th 1815—

Ah, my dearest Esther, when am I to write to you a chearful Letter? A Day longer than I was first offered for writing to England being given me, I cannot refuse myself using it to again address you, though still—alas! alas! only in the sackcloth & ashes of grief—distress & alarm!—a frightful paragraph of a contagious fever at Cambridge has chilled my blood, & added so direful a weight to my already so loaded mind that every minute seems to linger out an hour—though I do all, all I can to smother my apprehensions, not further to oppress my *Partner in All*; himself but just escaped from a malady, the effect of his long fatigues & nearly outrageous exertions, which threatened him with the most serious consequences. I had hardly had time to bless Heaven in grateful fervour for his safety—after our critical & dread separation on the 19th of March, when this so unexpected blow came to quash again all remittance from evil!—for the best is but remittance, since the

8 See i, p. lxxi.
9 Sabrina Bicknell (*c.* 1757–1843), a widow who became supervisor and housekeeper of CB Jr's schools after a bizarre earlier life recounted in i, L. 7 n. 18.

congée of M. d'A. has only been granted, or asked, for the recruit of his shattered health, & that he may procure himself a fresh equipment for his military service! all his original most expensive equipment—his papers, Baggage, military Books & stores—his Horses, & his Domestic—All, in short, but his weapons & uniform, have been left en route, at Bethune, near the frontières, whence the whole *Maison du Roi*, i.e. gardes du Corps, issued with the belief of a Battle—which, however, did not take place. The pursuers, Buonaparte's guards, being but 200, against as many thousand, then making a parade of approach & defiance, suddenly called out *vive l'Empereur* while the Duc de Berri cried *'vive le Roi'*—& precipitately fled. It was concluded, │ however, that this was a feint, & that they had sufficient force near at hand; the Duc, therefore, ordered the *Maison du Roi* to march on, without stopping to retake either Baggage or Domestic. To us this has been peculiarly unfortunate, for *I* had already left Paris, with only a handful of linen, & 2 mourning Gowns—and now M. d'A. also is robbed of every thing! Yet oh—if of Him & my other Alexander I am *not* robbed—if once we have a safe re-union in any peaceful spot, away from Revolutionary events & sufferings & terrours,—methinks I shall be happy under every privation.—

Adieu! my dearest Esther—my best Love to Mr. B[urney] who I hope continues mending, & to Amelia—& when you write, to Maria in particular, & to dear Sophy, Cecilia & Fanny[1]—

How our affairs go on in England I know not—& never yet were money matters so important to me—Not a line has come to me relative to our now unfortunate Cottage—nor to the so long impending 2[d] *Edition* that was sold *before publication*! nor from Charles for our residu at White's, Leigh's, & the Museum! —nor from Mr. White for the goods we left to be sold from West-Humble—nor of the Irish business—nor whether the Mortgage of Mr. Lewes[2] has been deemed worth struggling for.

865. [1] In the polite usage of the age FBA names severally the members of the household likely to read her letter, in this case EBB's four unmarried daughters (i, p. lxix) and her married daughter, the widow Maria Bourdois (L. 838 n. 25; and i, p. lxix).
[2] In his will CB declared that his estate had been lessened by 'the stoppage of the £50 per annum by Mr Lewis' (Scholes, ii. 272), which would seem to be what FBA refers to here—the default on a mortgage by Matthew Gregory Lewis (1775–1818), author of *The Monk* and longstanding debtor of CB (iii, L. 221 n. 9; L. 226 n. 10).

Certainly we are greatly injured, & in a very considerable Sum (I speak of you & me,) if Mr. Lewes keeps a debt so undoubtedly due to our dear Father: Oh, my dear Esther, what a succession of mortal & bodily sufferings have been mine, from the time of his loss, to its anniversary, next Tuesday! I had always kept in mourning, as we had agreed—& 2 mourning Gowns, with a small change of Linnen, is ALL I have saved from All my possessions in Paris! And, since, M. d'A. in his short & *triste* Campaigne, with *La Maison du Roi*, a tout perdu!—military Equipments—Baggage, Books, Maps, papers, Horses & Domestic. &c—all left at Bethune [where] he thought himself preparing for a Combat! ¹

866   [286, rue de la Montagne,
                       Brussels, *pre* 15 April 1815]

To Mrs. Barrett

A.L. (Berg), *n.d.*
Single sheet 4to   2 pp.   *pmks*   15 AP [18]15   To be Delivered / by 10 o'clock / on Sund. Morng / ⟨   ⟩ P.P. ⟨   ⟩ / Duke St. ⟨   ⟩   wafer
Addressed: *Angleterre*. à Madame / Madame Barrett, / under the Hill, / Richmond / near / London.

An opportunity offering for England by which I can send a few hasty lines, I will not lose it without thanking my ever dear Charlotte for her kind conclusion to her dear Mother's Letter.¹ I have no spirits at this moment for meriting postage—but I will not listen to my pen's reluctance when a few words can be franked that will convey a mark of my constant affection to my dear Girl. By the post I wrote last week to my sister Broome²— but directed to your uncle James, as I have not her address. I think she will let you know our sad history, & therefore spare both you and myself its repetition. M. d'A. is at this moment, I thank Heaven, by my side—he has a *Congée* for the recruit of his

866.   ¹ This letter from CBFB with its addition by CFBt has been lost.
   ² L. 861, posted on 10 April. This letter along with Ll. 864 and 865 seems to have been taken to England by Walter Boyd (L. 870 n. 2), the banker, who posted all three in London.

health, which the adventures & exertions & fatigues & mis-fortu[nes] of every sort have nearly demolished. What his stay may be I know not—nor whither his next destination; but as soon as he is refitted, he means to offer again his services to his King. Alas, he will not, this summer, I am sure, be *really* in a condition for the toil of such a War as is preparing! he is thinned & changed inconceivably! & has never recovered from the cruel accident that had so nearly been fatal to him at Calais. *My* sole project has been to watch about the vicinity of his quarters, that—should he be wounded[3]—which Heaven forbid! I may at least be at hand to nurse him—or should he—perhaps worse! be made prisoner, to petition for leave to share his prison.[3] But all this is not mournful enough! a new & greater terrour than all now assails me—an English news paper, of March 28th has just been lent me, that speaks of an Epidemical fever at Cambridge, I and of a transitory removal of the students! imagine what a state my mind will be in till I have news of my beloved Alexander! Should I hear he is ill, I should leave all & hasten to him — — I have written for intel-ligence to your Uncle James[4]—who I am sure will not keep me a post in so dreadful an incertitude. If he *has* been ill, & is recovering, perhaps he had better change the air, & come over to *me*, if well enough for travelling—yet alas—our position here is so little stable, we count but day by day upon a resi-dence! Lord Wellington, nevertheless revives all hopes—& all accounts speak of the *sombre* & consternated state of Paris.[5] Till I had this alarm for my Alex, I had believed it beyond the reach of fortune to present a case that could have drawn me

[3] The first of these feared results of M. d'A's return to service later took FBA to Trèves; the second may have been a reminiscence of Mme de Lafayette's mission to share her husband's prison at Olmütz. This possibility is strengthened by FBA's readiness 'to petition', since she had recently heard that M. d'A was safe in Belgium through a note forwarded by the duchesse d'Ursel (L. 856 n. 10), whom Mme de Lafayette saw in Vienna in 1795 while she waited for her own petition to be ap-proved.

[4] L. 863.

[5] Wellington himself spread such reports about the state of Paris. Thomas Creevey, who was also then in Brussels, noted in his Journal for 22 Apr. 1815 Wellington's opinion that 'a Republick was about to be got up in Paris by Carnot, Lucien Bonaparte &c., &c., &c.,' and that Napoleon was about to be assassinated by his own people (*Creevey Papers*, i. 215). Napoleonic propaganda countered these reports in the official *Moniteur* and the satirical *Nain Jaune*, but contemporary English witnesses in Paris reported that both republicans and royalists there 'were filled with consternation at the evils with which they were menaced'. See Helen Maria Williams, *A Narrative of the Events . . . in France . . . in 1815 . . .* (1815), p. 42.

away from his Father—whom I have but just recovered from
the most eminent danger, & whom I should quit with a heart
rent in twain! God send me quieting tidings! & of dear Clement
—whom my late Letters make me consider at a distance from
Cambridge, & in Kent with his dear Mother, or for him I
should indeed be frightened.[6]

I hope your little nursling[7] is now stouter—& that my dear
Julia & Hetty & Godson are all well, & their fond father
flourishing? I was more sorry than surprised that the patient
sweet Kate[8] is yet uncured. *A year* was the least time, I was told,
for success. My kind love to my dearest Fanny,[8] who had
promised to write to me. But you & your dear *mere* with my
Alex ALONE have shewn me your hand writings! Where is my
dear Marianne?[9] How is Dolph.[9] Present my very best remembrances to my faithful Friend the Archdeacon,[10] who my
Alex has told me has demonstrated a kindness to him that he—
that his Father—& that *I* most of all, can never think of without
grateful delight. To Mrs. Cambridge, his most amiable Partner,
join all you can, & tell my very dear Miss Baker that we never
cease to talk of her so willing, so characteristic aid & friendship.
adieu, my dear [dear] dear Charlotte Heaven bless you!—

I hope Mr. Barret has been so good as to remember my
compts & apologies & regrets the kind Lady Abbess of Ellerker
Abbey.[11]— |

My direction is—chez Mad^e la Comtesse de Maurville—
but our sejour is so uncertain that I hope you will engage

---

[6] FBA's fears for Clement Francis were increased during this outbreak of fever
at Cambridge by past evidence of his poor health. In looking back on the dispersal
of the University during this period, one contemporary witness suggested that both
Oxford and Cambridge were too unhealthy to be the sites of universities. See
Teignmouth, i. 67.

[7] CFBt's nursling was her son Henry John Richard (1814–29). For the other
children mentioned, see i, pp. lxxii–lxxiii.

[8] This may have been Catherine Minette Raper, aged 7, only child of Charles
Chamier Raper and his wife Frances *née* Phillips (L. 843 n. 4), SBP's daughter and
the Fanny mentioned below (see i, pp. lxx- lxxi).

[9] CFBt's sister Marianne Francis (see vi, L. 603 n. 2) and her half-brother
Ralph Broome Jr. (1801–17).

[10] George Owen Cambridge (L. 840 n. 6), Archdeacon of Middlesex, his wife
Cornelia (L. 843 n. 5), and their family friend Sarah Baker (*c.* 1744–1835). See also
L. 843 n. 6.

[11] The Mainwaring-Ellerker sisters, Elizabeth (1751–1831) and Harriet (1759–
1842), residents of Richmond, FBA had known since 1782 (see iii, L. 126 n. 7).
The whimsical title probably referred to Elizabeth, whom in 1799 FBA remembered
as having 'drunk tea with me at Kew Palace, while I had apartments there' (iv.
327).

pre 15 April 1815

Mr. Raper to be so good as to contrive to send to us through the Foreign office—though how *I* know not! but all other ways, our Letters may be left behind & lost—& my restlessness to hear of my Alex will augment daily till I am ⟨relieved⟩. ¹

867   Ghent, 22 April [1815]

M. d'Arblay
To Madame d'Arblay

A.L. (Berg), 22me.
Double sheet 8vo   1 p.   seal
Addressed: À Madame / Madame d'Arblay, / rue de la Montagne n° 286 / à Bruxelles
Edited by FBA, p. 1, *annotated and dated*: ✴ × ⌈8⌉ ⌈13⌉ ⌈16⌉ 13 April 1815 ⌈from Ghent⌉ Written from Gand when summoned thither by the Duc de Feltre for the mission to the frontier.¹ [*with numbers on address fold*]: 8 8

22me

Nous nous sommes trompés, ma chere Fanny, cruellement trompés et la mission dont je suis chargé¹ n'est rien moins qu'agreable dans les circonstances où nous nous trouvons. Ce qu'il y a de plus fâcheux c'est que nous ne serons pas ensemble, car je ne crois ni prudent ni même possible pour toi: de me

867.   ¹ As one of the 'commissaires royaux' with the allied armies, M. d'A was officially instructed to mediate between the Prussian Army of the Lower Rhine (*Niederrheinisch Kriegsheer*), then forming under the command of Marshal Blücher, and the French population on behalf of Louis XVIII's shadow government at Ghent. In the decree that created the commissaires, ordered in council on 25 April but never published in the *Moniteur de Gand*, they were also ordered to supervise requisitions and guarantee payment for purchases made by the allies and to enrol volunteers for the royal army. But the peculiar aspects of this mission arose from the concealed motives of its three chief supporters. The baron d'André, Louis XVIII's former police minister, first broached the subject, in a letter of 31 March to the comte de Blacas, as a way of asserting royal control over both France and the allied armies—'afin que les étrangers ne parussent effectivement que les alliés et les auxiliares du Roi et non des conquérants'; the Duke of Wellington desired the commissaires to forage for the invading allies at French expense; while the duc de Feltre wanted them to entice deserters from Napoleon's army, thereby strengthening the feeble royal army and his own hand as War Minister. See Fleischman, p. 89, and Romberg and Malet, i. 28–34, 127, 139.

suivre sur l'extrême frontiere où l'on m'envoye.[2] Cette mission très delicate[3] et en même tems três difficile, est encore plus embarassante puisqu'il ne s'agit de rien moins que d'agir avec les Prussiens aux quels il ne sera pas aisé de faire entendre raison.[4] Et qui aurai-je à commander des gens qui jusqu'à present sont à trouver des deserteurs dans les quels je n'aurai aucune confiance.[5] C'est bien à présent qu'il faut rassembler tout notre courage —

868   [Ghent, 23 April 1815]

M. d'Arblay
To Madame d'Arblay

A.L. (Berg), *n.d.*
Double sheet 4to   2 pp.   *pmk*   GAND   wafer
Addressed: A Madame / Madame d'Arblay / rue de la Montagne *N*° *286* / à Bruxelles
Edited by FBA, p. 1, *annotated and dated*: ⁂ × ⌐9⌐ (14) April 23. 1815 / *Gand.*
Openings *renseignmens* on the Mission to the Frontiers—on Luxembourg [*with numbers on address fold*]: 9   9
Sketched, p. 4: *a street plan*

[2] M. d'A had first been ordered to Luxemburg, one of the chief Prussian garrisons west of the Rhine since the previous year and a centre of deployment for the movement forward to the Meuse carried out at the urgent request of the King of the Netherlands when Napoleon's return to Paris became known during the last week of March.
[3] The confidential circular addressed to the commissaires by Beugnot (*Mémoires*, p. 576) and other royal advisers begins: 'Il serait difficile de concevoir une mission plus délicate et plus importante' (Romberg and Malet, i. 38).
[4] Unlike the other allies, who were in varying degrees willing to accept the Bourbon distinction between Napoleon (the outlawed enemy of Europe) and France (the victim of his usurping invasion), the Prussians tended, in part because of their experience of defeat and occupation, to detest everything French and consider the last campaigns of the Napoleonic wars to be a War of Liberation (*Befreiungskrieg*). A member of Wellington's staff hinted at this in explaining to him why such commissaires would not be welcomed at Prussian headquarters 'as in the present war much of the national and military spirit is derived from a decided hatred of the French, it is a part of the Prussian system to keep alive this spirit' (*Supp. Desp.* x. 311).
[5] M. d'A's lack of confidence may have been prompted by reflections on the quality of troops likely to desert for the bounty or bribe his orders called upon him to offer—eighty francs for a mounted deserter, twenty francs for one on foot (Fleischman, p. 89).

Hier, ma chere et bien chere Fanny, je serais je crois couché dans la rüe sans Lally[1] qui m'a rendu le três grand service de me donner un lit dans un petit cabinet près du sien. Je me suis couché de fort bonne heure, et j'ai reposé assez bien. J'en avais bien grand besoin n'ayant pas été assis de la journée. Ce matin il est tard et n'ai pas encore eu le tems de déjeuner. Tu me gronderas, mais en auras tu la force quand je t'aurai dit que cela provient du desir que j'ai eu de te rejoindre aujourdhui. Cela est impossible et c'est tout au plus si demain je pourrai jouir de ce bonheur; et pourtant j'ai fait dit on des merveilles Il est certain que je n'ai pas perdu de tems; et que je crois avoir reussi à monter fort bien mon affaire. J'ai pour adjoint M[r] le Cte de Mazancourt[2] Lieut[nt] Colonel fort instruit et connaissant presque tous les G[aux] Prussiens avec les quels il a servi six ans. Quant à mon aide de Camp c'est Mr de Premorel[3] cap[e] et garde de la Comp[e] de Luxembourg. C'est M[r] le duc de L[uxembourg] lui même qui me l'a donnê ainsi que son fils tous deux de la ville même de Luxembourg où consequement je me trouverai tout de suite | en pays de connoissance. Mon traitement est celui de M[al] de Camp employé.[4] Ainsi avec de l'economie je pourrai me tirer d'affaire: mais je serai forcé d'avoir un 3eme cheval et probablement un 2me domestique au quel neanmoins je compte substituer un palfrenier à la journée. Je suis un peu raccomodé avec tout ceci, et nous en causerons plus amplement ce qu'il m'est impossible de faire en ce moment,

868. [1] Lally-Tolendal stayed on at the Hôtel de Flandre in the rue aux Draps, supported and busied there by the editing of the *Moniteur de Gand*, whose first number appeared on 14 April.

  [2] Alexandre de Mazancourt (1776–1842), comte de Mazancourt, emigrated in 1792 with his father, Gabriel-Auguste (1725–1809), comte de Mazancourt, served with him in the Armée de Condé (régiment des Chasseurs nobles) until 1796, then followed the army into East Prussia and Russia and served there until 1801, when he transferred into Prussian service and was promoted major on the Prussian army staff, where he remained until 1808. He returned to France at the Restoration and was named sous-lieutenant in the Gardes du Corps. On his return from Trèves in 1815 he became a major in the dragons de la Sâone, retiring in 1828.

  [3] Pierre-Louis-Raoul-Edmé Durand de Prémorel (1768-*post* 1834) began his military service in 1783 before the Revolution as a sous-lieutenant in the régiment de Bouillon, rose slowly to be promoted lieutenant in the régiment de Poix in 1791, when he emigrated to join the Armée des Princes until 1801. He returned to France in 1802 and, along with his son Alphonse (1798–1857), entered the garde du corps in the compagnie de Luxembourg, holding at the same time the rank of captain in the army. He retired from the army in 1816, a few months after his return from Trèves.

  [4] M. d'A's pay as a maréchal de camp on active service was 1,033 francs, 33 centimes per month (M. d'A to duc de Feltre, 20 Aug. 1815, Vincennes).

où je t'ecris sur mes genoux dans le cabriolet même de Mr Tabarier.[5]

Adieu chère chère amie: j'ai lu avec bonheur la lettre d'Alex.[6] Elle m'a fait un plaisir au quel je m'attendais peu; et je l'ai trouvée beaucoup mieux que tu ne me l'avais annoncé.

à revoir ma bonne amie

869　　　　　　[286, rue de la Montagne],
　　　　　　Brussels, 26 April–6 May 1815

To Alexander d'Arblay

A.L. (Diary MSS. vii. 6606–[9], 26 Apr.–6 May 1815
Double sheet large 4to (10·5 × 8·5″) 4 pp. foliated (208) (209) torn in two 6·9″ from the top, weak in the folds; with outer edges folded and damaged *pmks* P 94 P / BRUXELLES FOREIGN / 12 M⟨Y⟩ 1815 13 MY .815 12 M[Y] 18[15] DARKING green wafer
Addressed: *Angleterre*. / Alexander d'Arblay, Esqr, / at Mrs Broom's, / Richmond, / Surry.
Readdressed: Norbury Park / Dorking Surry.
Again readdressed: 20 Great Cumberland / Place / Oxford Street
And again on fold: 20 G^t Cumberland / Oxford Street / London
Edited by CFBt *and the* Press. *See* Textual Notes.

At length, my long-expecting Eyes meet again your hand writing—after a breach of correspondence that I can never recollect without pain.—Revive it not in my mind by any repetition, & I will dismiss it from all future power of tormenting me, by considering it only as a dream of other times. Cry

[5] Michel-Marie-Étienne-Victor Tabarié (1768–1839), chevalier (1814) and vicomte (1815), began his career in military administration as a commissaire des guerres in the 1790s and became secrétaire général of the War Ministry in 1806 under Clarke (*later* duc de Feltre), whose assistant and ally he remained until Napoleon's abdication. Turning into a zealous royalist at the Restoration, he followed the King to Ghent, where, considered 'le meilleur et le plus utile des hommes qui sont venus nous joindre' (Jaucourt, p. 310), he found the money that enabled the duc de Feltre to finance policies and carriages while the rest of the Ghent shadow cabinet scrimped and schemed. On the return to Paris he was named intendant de la Maison du Roi, but he had resumed his post as secrétaire général by 1816, when M. d'A applied to him for his back pay and pension. See letter (Vincennes), M. d'A to Vicomte [Tabarié], 'Vu le 12 Sept. [1816]'. He later became conseiller and sous-secrétaire d'État, but his influence waned after the duc de Feltre's death in 1818.
[6] The contents of this letter, which is now lost, are given in part in L. 869 below.

'*Done!*' my Alex,—& I will skip over the subject—not, perhaps, as lightly, but as swiftly as you skip over the Hills of Norbury Park. I delight to think of the good & pleasure that sojourn may do you:[1] though easily—too easily! I conceive the melancholy reflections that were awakened by the sight of our dear—dear Cottage![2]—Yet your expressions upon its view[3] lose much of their effect by being over strained, r*echerchée*, & *designing* to be pathetic. We never touch others, my dear Alex, where we *study* to shew we are touched ourselves. I beg you, when you write to me, to let your pen paint your thoughts as they *rise*, not as you seek for, or labour to embellish them. I remember you once wrote me a Letter so very fine from Cambridge, that if it had not made me laugh, it would certainly have made me sick. Be natural, my dear Boy, & you will be sure to please your Mother without wasting your time. How greatly am I obliged to all my dear Family & Friends who so kindly & hospitably have housed you in your houseless state! What anguish have we not suffered from the moment we saw that cruel paragraph upon the contagious fever at Cambridge, till the happy instant that brought fair tidings from your invaluable Aunt Charlotte! Yet, knowing the immense importance to our happiness for the rest of our lives that hung upon its contents, we were almost as fearful of opening it, as you & I were of breaking the Seal of the Letter from Joigny after the long silence of your dear Father.[4] But all our fears were removed, & peace was restored to our minds, nearly by the opening, from the kind consideration which urged that dear Aunt—though still ignorant of our uneasiness, to say 'Your dear Boy is well.—'

To HER it is I trust for keeping you still back from your college till Mr. Chapman[5] himself acquaints her all is entirely safe. What can have been the origin of so dreadful a disorder being spread there?[6] Should there be the least return, or should

869. [1] On leaving Cambridge, AA went first to Mrs. Broome at Richmond, then to the Lockes at Norbury Park, then, to judge from the final address, to the town house of the Angersteins, whose kindness FBA mentions in Ll. 870 and 873.

[2] Camilla Cottage, lost to the d'Arblays in a forced sale (vii *passim* and L. 863 n. 6).

[3] In a letter of 11 April, now missing, which the d'Arblays had received on 19 April (see following L. 870).

[4] This may have been M. d'A's letter of 12 Apr. 1813 (vii, L. 689).

[5] AA's tutor, the Revd. Benedict Chapman (vii, L. 740 n. 1).

[6] One of AA's contemporaries offered the following explanation: 'In the spring of my second year, in 1815, a fever was caused at Cambridge by opening a long-

you feel the least disordered, fly the spot again, & take refuge at Richmond, [where] the air is pure, & where your dear Aunt would secure you a lodging & a Nurse & superintend both. I beg you to send me a compendium, in your next of your money concerns. Your Father desires you will spare [no de]tail to your A[ccount]. |

Let us know what you have *received*, what you have *spent*, what you may have still *unpaid*, & what you yet *want*. But for this last article, we both desire you will not wait our permission to draw upon your Aunt, whom we shall empower to draw upon Mr. Hoare in our names. We know you to have no wanton extravagance, & no idle vanity; we give you, therefore, dear Alex, *carte blanche* to apply to your Aunt, only consulting with her, & begging her kind, maternal advice to help your inexperience in regulating your expences. She knows the difference that must be made between our fortune & that of Clement;[7] but she knows our affection for our Boy, & our confidence in his honour & probity, & will treat him with as much kindness, though not with equal luxury. Your Father charges you never to be without your purse, & never to let it be empty. Your Aunt will counsel you about your *cloathes*. About your necessary *Books*, we trust to yourself. And pray don't forget, when you make *sleeping* visits, to recompence the trouble you must unavoidably give to servants. And if you join any party to any public place, make a point to pay for yourself. It will be far better to go seldom, & with that Gentlemanly spirit, than often, with the air of a hanger on.

How infinitely hospitable has been your Uncle James! But hospitality is his characteristic. You don't mention Deptford? except to speak of the new living,[8] which gives me, indeed, great satisfaction. But I flatter myself you have been at the Rectory? If you were to *finish* your vacation there, it would be the best way, in all probability, to lead you to finish it to the advantage of your re-entry, in putting you upon such thoughts

closed drain in the neighbourhood of Jesus College, which produced mortality among its students' (Teignmouth, i. 67).

7 Clement Robert Francis (i, p. lxxiii) was possessed of a competence at least by the terms of his father's will (P.C.C., Fountain 607), pr. 22 Dec. 1792. Clement Francis Sr. (*c.* 1744–92) of Aylsham, Norfolk, was a surgeon who had served in the years 1778 to 1785 as a medical officer with the East India Company.

8 CB Jr. had earlier in April been preferred to the rectorship of Cliffe in Kent (*GM* lxxxv, i. 369).

115

& such studies as may make the ensuing term ⌐more⌐ prosperous ⌐than the last—for all, Alex⌐, I am unwilling to tell you
my — — surprise at ⌐hearing of⌐ a 2ᵈ place ⌐only⌐ in the
Mathematics.⁹—What is now before you? Is there enough both
of *possibility* to obtain distinction, & of energy & application
to struggle for it? ⌐And is your conscience—or heart at ease,
in your continuing your academical pursuits? deceive neither
us nor yourself, in [this;] for we had better draw you away at
once & put you upon some other way than let another year
be wasted & useless
[*line torn away on lower margin*]

So much, my Alex, from your Mother & your sister respecting Yourself! let me now [share my] own feelings in speaking of
ourselves. My last told you I had had news, at length, of our
best Friend, & my Letter from Ypres was followed by one from
Menin,¹⁰ which told me to join him at Ostende, as he was so ill,
so exhausted by the fatigues of the shortest but most laborious
of Campaigns, that he would take leave there of Le Roi Louis
18. &, by permission of Monsieur, embark to re-establish his
health in England. At that time it was expected that Le Roi
was at Ostende to embark himself. From Bruges, however, I had
another Letter¹¹ — — but ere I come on to the present moment,
I will give you a succinct history of this painful campaign, certain that nothing upon Earth can so greatly interest you.—I
have related already that, at 2 o'clock on the 19ᵗʰ March, we
separated—He then thought he was going forth to *Melun*, with
a party of la Maison du Roi, to join the army collecting to

⁹ In later years as editor FBA was to obliterate such phrases and lines as expressed dissatisfaction at Alex's having taken second as opposed to first place in
mathematics and to supply interlinearly a text denuded of blame:
   But I flatter myself you have been at the Rectory? If you were to *finish* your
   vacation there, it would be the best way, in all probability, to lead you to finish
   it to the advantage of your re-entry, in putting you upon such thoughts & such
   studies as may make the ensuing term prosperous. I am unwilling to tell you my —
   — surprise at your forbearing to write us word of your 2ᵈ place in the Mathematics.—What is now before you? Is there enough both of possibility to obtain
   distinction, & of energy & application to struggle for it? Yet, even if you fail
   entirely—you should not the less write—Can you think our affection hangs upon
   vanity?—We have only insisted upon your regularity at chapel & at Lectures, &
   w[e] fear of your attention to them,—comparatively; & we are fixed to be contented *en attendant*. Don't lose courage dear dear Alex, the second place is the
   nearest to the first. I love you with all my heart!
See further, Textual Notes.
¹⁰ These are missing.
¹¹ L. 857.

oppose the further progress of the invading Enemy. At the *Champ de Mars* there was a general review, at which the King was present: but there, we now know, his Majesty received the fatal news of the desertion of all the troops of the line.[12] Your Father, with the artilery under his command, of the Company of Luxembourg, returned to the Cazerne—& thence wrote me the terrible Note I have copied for you.[13] Cha[s] de Maubourg delivered it to me *Chez son frere* [*tear*] I will beg your Father to write you himself a brief account of the Campaign, for I have [seen] him too little to have learnt it completely.

MAY 2[d] Endless perplexities & difficulties have kept my pen from my hand till now, joined to an expecta[tion] of an answer to my long Letter sent to you through your Uncle James. I will wait, however, now, no longer, to thank you for your 2 most welcome half sheets from Norbury Park & to beg a full reply to the 2 first pages of this Letter. Your dearest Father has not a moment now to comply with my desire of indulging you with the narration I wish to give you; but when he has time he will not—oh no!—want inclination. Meanwhile, I can only tell you he set out, *en retraite*, about midnight, from the Chateau des Thuilleries, with the rest of the company of the Duke of Luxembourg & the other 5 companies, of Grammont, de Poix, d'Avuray,[14] Wagram, & Marmont, with les Cents Suisses, les Gardes de la porte, les Mousquetaires, &c—in short, all *La Maison du Roi*, who went himself in a Carriage with le Prince de Poix, le Duc de Duras, M. de Blacas, & le Mareshal Duc de Wagram, followed by Monsieur, Le Duc de Berry, &c. The King proceeded straight to Lille: which none of la Garde du Corps could reach; for none could change Horses, & many had no Horses to change & the roads were bad, & the rain poured almost continually. Your Father was very unwell, indeed, when he

[12] Louis XVIII had been warned during the night of 18 March that the army at Melun would defect and that the 6th Lancers had already done so. Despite FBA's suggestion of a sudden defection *en masse*, what happened was more drab and piecemeal. 'Désertions successives des troupes' (Villemain, ii. 46) became known in Paris on the 20th as regiments turned away or held back from the march that was meant to take the troops of the line northward to Saint-Denis. Only two Swiss regiments remained loyal, but in the confusion they returned to their Paris barracks in the rue Verte. Of the generals, only Macdonald and Maison went on to Saint-Denis to follow the household troops.

[13] L. 849, copied by FBA in L. 860, p. 86.

[14] Duc de Havré (L. 862 n. 13). For these events and the generals mentioned, see L. 860 and notes.

began the journey, from the havock made on his mind & his health by the suspensive menaces of the fortnight which preceded it: arrived at Bethune, he had just dismounted, sent his Horse to be fed, & ordered an omelette, having tasted nothing but a crust of Bread dipt into brandy all the route, & bivaced[15] only upon straw, in boots & spurs & Casque—but the regale had not reached his lips, when a cry of '*To arms!*' called him away—and he could not even await the return of his fine War Horse, a most beautiful Animal, which he loved *à la folie*; but was obliged to mount a Horse, of the Company, &, casting off his manteau, which he thought might embarrass him in the combat, he was amongst the foremost to answer the call. It proved however, ǀ [nug]atory: a party of the *garde-Imperiale* had insulted les gardes du Corps, by cries of *vive l'Empereur*; but when, by order of le Duc de Berry, the latter would have begun an attack, they turned round, & gallopped off: whether, naturally, from their inferior number, or whether to draw the *gardes du corps* into an ambuscade, is not certain. The risk was too great, at all events, to be run, & the Duc desisted from the attempt. But here, through some errour, or mystery, that has never yet been cleared, there was generally heard & understood a *Licenciement* of La Maison du Roi,[16] given by order of Monsieur & le Duc de Berry, with thanks for their devotion & services, & permission that they might return to their families & Estates, if they pleased, as the King was forced to quit his Kingdom, for the moment, & was unable to maintain any body of troops: those, nevertheless, who were rich enough to provide for themselves, or disposed to run the chances of other provision, his Majesty would see among his followers with great satisfaction. I need not tell you that your Father unhesitatingly left all he was worth in France to pursue the call of Honour, & fly from the irruption of new tyranny & usurpation. But there was no returning to Bethune—&, besides abandon-

---

[15] 'bivouacked'.

[16] After the disbandment at Béthune, fifty volunteers from the École de Droit battalion that had marched all the way from Vincennes rejoined three hundred gardes du corps who had accompanied the comte d'Artois to the gates of Ypres. When finally allowed to enter, Monsieur commissioned them for their loyalty in a moving speech: 'vous arrivez, bien fatigués, pour recevoir vos brevets d'officiers. Nous allons manger un pain de douleur, mais du moins nous le partagerons!' See Alexandre Guillemin, *Le Patriotisme des volontaires royaux de l'École de Droit de Paris* . . . (1822), p. 86. They then halted to care for the sick and disabled, including M.d'A and their own colonel, before marching on to Roeselare.

ning all he possessed in Paris, he now lost his Horses, his war equipage, Baggage, manteau, Domestic, & whatever was not immediately upon his person. And in this starved, spoliated, & sleepless condition, he arrived, with difficulties all but insurmountable, at *Ypres*, where the Commandant kept him *several hours* upon a bridge, in the most pouring rain, & his slight *petit uniform*, before he would resolve upon opening the Gates! He was then hardly alive; & but for a party of *L'Ecole de Droit*, had gallantly followed the *Maison*, on foot, he must have remained, he thinks, to perish upon his Horse! but three youths helped him off, put him to Bed, & waited upon him, during 2 days in which he was in a high fever, unremittingly with the tenderness they would have shewn to a Father. Heaven bless them! with what pleasure you will hear that the whole of this noble little party have been made sous Lieutenants by *le Roi*. Every thing at this moment promises prosperity to the Royal Cause Deserters—or rather Adherents—arrive daily from France. Your Father has just received a new commission, & is pressing to fulfil it. Alas! were his health & [*seal*] like his Zeal & Loyalty! When I know his [direction] I will write again— I am aware how great [is your] impatience. oh—durst I but press you here! but that is [weak]ness—Direct to Mad^e de Burney, *n° 1358 Marché au Bois: Brussells.*[17]

PS. May 6th Alas no, my dearest Alex, I cannot invite you to my side—you are certainly not strong enough to begin so violent a campaign, & if Cambridge is not *QUITE* safe, I beg your kind aunt Charlotte to lodge & board you pick nick, chez Elle, if possible, that you may enjoy country air after thanking most gratefully your Uncle (& Aunt) for his hospitable goodness.—

[*tear*] not, alas, have you here! I know not how long *I* shall be here; but my Letters will follow if I am gone, & be safe.

Every Letter I receive tells me how you are improved in Health, looks, cleanliness, & manners, Thanks dearest Alex! Your Father is transported with pleasure. He sends his kindest Love

---

17 FBA's new address in Brussels, Marché au bois, was near the Grand' Place. It was also close to her first stopping-place with Mme de Maurville (L. 838 n. 30) at 320, rue de la Montagne, in one of the city's network of market streets.

Why not one word to your Sister of Nell?[18] &c—Be amongst the last to go to college—but [*tear*] Keep a *pick nick* account, which I will pay.

Pray don't neglect to pay for your Letters: Your kind Aunt says she expects you at Richmond. Kiss her for me &

We are both delighted to see your hand so improved & legible

Endeavour to visit the excellent Mr. & Mrs. Haggit & Mrs. Yates[19]—Distribute properly & truly my Love to all our Family & Friends.

How fares the Wanderer, in earnest ⟨   ⟩

[*By M. d'Arblay*]

all, all. is improved—thank God! dear dear Alex! Write soon, pray, & don't let pass a week without giving us some news of your health & welfare—

870   [1358, Marché au bois], Brussels, 20 April–16 May 1815

To Mrs. Broome

A.L. (Berg), 20 Apr.–16 May 1815
Two single sheets large 4to   The second sheet has a damaged right margin.   4 pp.   *pmks*   P 94 P / BRUXELLES   Foreign / 22 MA / 1815   22 MY 1815   wafer
Addressed: Angleterre. / À / Madame / Madame Broome, / Richmond, / Surry.
Endorsed by CBFB: [*tear*] d'arblay / 1815
Edited by FBA *and* CFBt. *See* Textual Notes.

Brussels
April 20 1815.

What balm was poured into my aching heart by the Letter of my dearest Charlotte last night![1] it was brought us just as

[18] Unidentified.
[19] Sarah, wife of the Revd. William Haggit (i, L. 22 n. 18), Chaplain at Chelsea Hospital; and Anna *née* Telfer (*c.* 1778–1856), wife of the Revd. Richard Yates (vii, L. 794 n. 2), the Second Chaplain.
870.   [1] CBFB's letter and the other family letters mentioned here are missing.

we had retired from the P^{ss} d'Henin's apartment to our own, at past 11 o'clock. I feared dreadfully, nevertheless, to open it,—& felt a terrour and anguish almost insupportable when I found my direction was known, & that an English Letter arrived, yet saw not the hand of my Alexander —— but the joy with which we came to the phrase 'your dear Boy is well—' paid me—momentarily, at least, for every affliction. And how kind is my other sweet Charlotte's Letter, how truly entering into all that can most interest me, all I can most desire to know. We had had so much of sorrow & misfortune, that we could never have done wishing one another joy— felicitating each the other upon a happiness that put a period to a weight of suffering & suspence that had almost bowed us down each to the earth. A Letter from dear James[1] immediately after confirmed the glad tidings, & we found that the reason of Alex's present silence was his absence from town. And the Letters which I had written to him at Cambridge must, of course, have missed him. One of them, however, which had been written for a private hand, was fortunately still by me, from the traveller's having deferred his voyage, at the terrible time that an accidental news-paper gave me the cruel alarm relative to the contagious fever at Cambridge: & *that* I inserted in a 2^d Letter to James, which I sent off by a Mr. Boyd,[2] & which, I hope, with sundry others sent by the same conveyance, has long since arrived, & will speedily bring me an answer.—

[2] Walter Boyd (*c*. 1754–1837) was a protean financier who rose from obscurity to become joint founder of the Paris banking firm of Boyd, Ker & Cie in 1785 and a conduit for Pitt's money after the French Revolution. Accused in 1792 of financial espionage along with Ker and his younger cousin, partner, and namesake Walter Boyd (1766–1820)—the two were and are often confused—he fled to England (Bouchary, ii. 123–39; iii. 251–2). There he soon founded with the dubious Paul Benfield (*c*. 1740–1810) a new banking firm favoured with the handling of the Imperial loans to Austria. See Karl F. Helleiner, *The Imperial Loans* (Oxford, 1965), pp. 5–12. He was M.P. for Shaftesbury from 1796 until 1802, when he returned to France during the Peace of Amiens to reclaim his confiscated holdings and restore fortunes ruined by the liquidation of Boyd, Benfield & Co. in 1799. He was caught by the renewal of hostilities and interned, first at Verdun and later in Paris (Lewis, p. 297). British attempts to exchange him for a senior French officer failed and he was finally released in 1814 after loss of sight in one eye. See J. G. Alger, *Napoleon's British Visitors and Captives 1801–1815* (1904), p. 265. He had more reason than most to flee Paris at Napoleon's approach and good reason to go to Brussels, where he had longstanding connections with the banking house of Veuve Nettine et Fils. After the Hundred Days he returned to England, seemingly rich again, became M.P. for Lymington (1823–30) and gained in 1828 praises for his serene probity (Lockhart's *Memoirs of the Life of Sir Walter Scott*, 10 vols., Toronto, 1901, ix. 234–5) that may be set against repeated French attacks on him as a reactionary speculator. It was evidently he who carried FBA's Ll. 864–6 to London.

May 16th—This was begun the morning after I received your first Letter, my dearest Charlotte, dated April 11th with my first news that Alex. had escaped the contagious fever at Cambridge. I was indisposed in the midst of my joy while I wrote this page,—& from that time to this I have either been unwell & little capable, or in anguish, & little willing to resume my pen.—This, with regard to my *health,* will require no explanation; & for my *mind,* alas, ⏐ I have but to tell you that during this whole period M. d'A[rblay] has only remained with me while waiting orders—*Daily* expected—to depart.—The uncertainty *whither, when, how,* for what *term,* and on what expedition, would have been full sufficient to keep me in continual agitation: but the view of his still shaken health, diminished strength, & changed appearance — — have added such a weight of sorrow & alarm to suspensive uneasiness that every day, every hour, every instant has been passed simply in preparing for the event which seemed menacing the next! — — The order at length is come—& he is gone!³—Two days I have given to quiet my nerves in meditation—& now I tear myself from that consumption of soul to seek consolation through sympathy & affection. I cannot address myself to one who will more tenderly feel for me than my Charlotte—shall I not say Charlottes? & I would write at the same moment to my dearest Esther, & with the same confidence, but that the situation of my Alex calls for my first attention, & it is to his dear Aunt Broome I must apply to be his present maternal protectress.

I received, at the very instant his dear Father was quitting me, a letter from him¹ informing me he does not return to the university till the last day of October. I am truly glad, in defiance of all loss of time, & intricacy of local arrangement, that he will not risk an air that has been so infectious during the heats of summer. I am sure you will have the same sensation for Clement. I would not, however, for WORLDS, either that he should hang upon his friends, or waste such a period in mere pleasure: & he has written with so due a sense of the impropriety of doing either, that his Letter filled us both, even in that terrible moment, with heartfelt satisfaction, from seeing how usefully, & practically, his understanding is opening to the

---

³ M. d'A had left Brussels on his birthday, 13 May.

Right use of Reasoning, that of directing our conduct in the difficulties of life. I hope he will ere this have received a Letter which will fully put him at his ease, & in the road we wish him to travel: but in case of any accident, I re-write to my ⟨dear⟩ representative our desire on this occasion. Greatly as we are indebted to my kind Brother James, & kind Friend Mrs. Lock, for their most affectionate goodness to our Alexander we should be *grieved*, not *gratified* to have him any longer without a ˡ *home*, a *nest* of his own in which he would make ⌐a point of⌐ studying seriously for a certain number of hours: now from the Morning, now from the Evening, according to circumstances, but *always* from ONE or the other, so as to keep up a regular progress of improvement, & preparation for a satisfactory & creditable re-entrance into College.

If, therefore, my dearest Charlotte can hire him a comfortable room at Richmond, where he may sleep, & have his Books & papers for study—and yet suffer him to *pick nick* with her at meals, she would make ⟨us⟩ truly happy. Certainly not at *less* than a Guinea a week, his appetite & his Beer, which we wish him to quaff, considered: but as much *more* as th[e] encreased price of provisions, &c, may demand. To US, all must be cheap that gives us the peace of mind to know h[im] under so kind a wing. And his chances, then, of often see[ing] his sweet & favourite (I hope!) Cousin Charlotte;—& that meritor[iou]s pattern [of] application & good conduct, Marianne; with now & then the to⟨o⟩ laborious, [but] admirable Clement, & his dear—though I fear *not yet* quite diligent Dolph,—will make such a sojourn as delightful as it will be safe & useful to him. M. d'A: says if *you* travel further, he entreats he may accompany you, & make him keep his own accounts,—& then honour, in our names & with our full confidence, his drafts. He has no extravagence, & if he takes a little to *order*, he may be trusted now as if he were *forty*. We are so pleased with the statement of his situation in his las[t] Letter, that we shall be ready to grant whatever he can desire or want, if he will only counsel with his excellent Aunt, who so well knows how to help his inexperience. Above all, we would not have him remain in London: no, not even if his kind uncle James would take him [u]pon the only t[erms he] can, [&] ought, to suffer him to be taken, *pick nick,*— because we are persuaded the Cou[n]try air will complete the

123

establishment of his health—& Mrs. Loc[k] assures me he is *perfectly well.* Richmond air is always reckoned excel[lent.] If, however, the plans, the situation, or the spirits of my dear Charlott[e] should make this addition to her household oppressive, I entreat her to [make] ¹ some arrangement for his eating where he sleeps. She is sure I shall be sensible how unwillingly she declines my wishes; & I dare not, in that case, propose my other Charlotte, because the higher style of living of Mr. Barret, would make *2* Guineas a week an insufficient pick nickery.

I can never say how much I have been gratified & touched by a Letter from my invaluable Friend the Archdeacon.⁴ Pray give him my most grateful thanks. I shall write to him as soon as I may mention the route that M. d'A: has taken, & as soon as I know myself its intention & ultimate direction. I am sure of his kindest interest in such a communication.—

[If you] have not already placed the May quarter at Hoare's, keep it in hand for this new season of expences: if you have, draw as is necessary, & be sure we desire nothing upon Earth so much as that Alex should be properly provided for & keep a Gentlemanly independence, & be comfortable. My dear sister will understand the *spirit* of this, I am sure; & her *Eleve,* has promised, most affectionately, her aid, [& yo]u will *BOTH* give him such hints as my absence will make truly maternal. Dearly he loves you both, & he will not be ungrateful for your care. Pray urge him to write oftener, & more *openly.* I am now, alas, alone! & his Letters will help to support me. I shall write to him again soon—but hope to hear again first.—How cruel [the] return of your 'propensity' to a cough! Is it conquered, my dearest Charlotte?—[& has] 'Dolph benefitted by the Poney? & Clement by his Jaunts? Pray thank my dear [Marian]ne for her kind intention. I hope sweet little Tooty⁵ is re-establishing? I have been [frighten]ed at the alarming illness of her poor Mamma—Pray tell our Esther I have received her dear Letter, & a very kind one from Maria.⁶ Every body has written now—& I will endeavour to write once in every Week *at least,* during a separation, in the anxiety of which you will

---

⁴ George Owen Cambridge (L. 840 n. 6). His letter is now missing.
⁵ Possibly a child's pronunciation or nickname for CFBt's daughter Julia (L. 843 n. 9), aged 7 years.
⁶ EBB's daughter, Maria Bourdois (L. 838 n. 25).

all bear a part—I am very sure. oh God! what a separation!—
No one knows when hostilities will begin[7]—but the preparations on EACH side are horrific!— —Mrs. Lock & Mrs Angerstein[8] have been quite angelic in their kindness to my Alex—&
their soothing relations. & L^y Keith[9] is a Friend of sterling
faith & firmness. M^rs W[addington] has written—& Chas—&
poor Fanny R[aper]—All but Sarah, who I [believe] at
Che⟨ltenh⟩am.
     Kind love to M^r Ba[rrett] & d^r Miss Ba⟨ker⟩
                         adieu, my kind[est Ch]arlotte
                         —M. d'A [sends] to All his
best Love

N.B. *entre nous*—If Chas should—*cordially*—invite A[lex] for a
part of the vacation, it might be so eminently useful to his
studies, from the order he w^d put in his application under such
a roof, that I beg you to encourage acceptance: but if not
cordial, by no means to ⟨bind⟩ him to go merely for complais-
ance, or œconomy: |

     ps. I have a Letter nearly finished for Alex[10]—but will wait
his answer to my last ere I send it, as I feel you will All rather
hear from time to time than all at once. Tell Alex the return of
post shall bring him an ANSWER TO HIS ANSWER—which I only
hold back that our Letters may not always cross each other.
He never tells me how many of my letters! he ⟨rec^d⟩

For Alexander

     At length, my cher Alex, I have the comfort of seeing your
hand writing [xxxxx 3 *lines, in which Mme d'Arblay complains
of the painful* breach of correspondence, *which, unless* repeated,
she will dismiss from her mind or remember only as a dream of other
times and places.]

---

     [7] Since the preparations of mid May were reversed by the campaigns of mid
June, we should bear in mind that Wellington, Blücher, and the Prince of Orange
still planned, despite constant delays, to invade France from the north, that
Napoleon, still hoping to remain Emperor without a war, had held his armée du
Nord in defensive positions, and that although France was rapidly being encircled
by the allied armies, war had not yet been declared.
     [8] Cf. L. 869 n. 1.
     [9] Hester Maria *née* Thrale (L. 837 n. 3), daughter of FBA's estranged friend
Mrs. Thrale and wife of Admiral the Viscount Keith (see vi, L. 594 n. 8).
     [10] Probably L. 889, begun on 13 May and posted in Brussels on 19 June.

M. d'Arblay
To Madame d'Arblay

A.L.S. (Berg), 16 May
Double sheet 4to   1 p.   *pmk*   LIEGE   seal
Addressed: à Madame / Madame d'Arblay / marché au bois Nº. 1358 / à Bruxelles
Edited by FBA, p. 1, *annotated and dated*: ⌗ ⌐10⌐ (I) (I) New Date 16 Mai—1815 / de Liege— The first Letter received at Brussels / When General d'Arblay left me there, to repair to Luxembourg, by order of the Duc de Feltre to raise volunteers for Louis 18.—But Prince General *Blucher* wrote to desire M d'A would change his destination for Triers or Treves, [*with numbers on address fold*]: *10* I I

Mon amie, ma tendre amie ne peut savoir à quel point cette derniere separation eprouve mon courage. Ce n'est que lorsque je la reverrai que je pourrai entamer le recît de tout ce que j'ai à souffrir. Mais quand serons nous reunis! Je n'ai trouvé ici ni le p^ce Blücher,[1] ni le General chargé du chef de la Police,[2] ni le quartier maître g^a13 et le G^al qui commande en chef[4] dans

871. [1] Gebhard Leberecht Blücher (1742–1819), created Prince (*Fürst*) Blücher von Wahlstadt in 1814, whose long and dogged service as a cavalry officer, general, and field-marshal had made him the most famous, and in England the most popular, of the allied commanders. But, since he 'understood nothing whatever of the conduct of a war' (Müffling, p. 225) he had been appointed Commander-in-Chief (*Oberbefehlshaber*) of the Prussian armies in the field against Napoleon in 1815 on the understanding that Gneisenau as chief of the general staff would organize the army and direct strategy. The latter quickly became supreme commander in all but name, so that letters and orders—such as those directed at M. d'A—though signed by Blücher represented Gneisenau's opinions and wishes.

[2] No such officer or post is listed in the Prussian army's order of battle for May or June of 1815, but it is possible, bearing in mind the title and pecking order used by M. d'A, that he meant Johann August Sack (1764–1831), who as *Général-Gouverneur* of the Lower Rhine had direct control over the police in territory under Prussian administration or control.

[3] Karl Wilhelm Georg von Grolmann (1777–1843), one of the able, ambitious, and nationalistic staff officers who rose through Scharnhorst's reorganized Prussian army and the war of liberation against Napoleon. Grolmann fought in the Spanish army's *Legión extranjera* in 1810–11, was awarded the *Pour le mérite* after the Battle of Leipzig and served as quartermaster under Blücher and Kleist in the 1813 campaign. Promoted general in the following year, he was appointed quartermaster-general in the headquarters of Gneisenau and Blücher in succession to Müffling early in May 1815.

[4] *Gouverneur* to the Prussian royal family in the 1790s, Friedrich Wilhelm von Bülow (1755–1816), created Count (*Graf*) Bülow von Dennewitz in 1814, had commanded East Prussian troops with varying success in 1806–7, rose to the rank of lieutenant-general and distinguished himself in the campaign of 1813, in which he took Halle by storm and defeated Ney at Dennewitz. During 1815 he commanded the 4th Army Corps, at this time quartered in Liège.

cette ville etait d'avis que j'allasse à Namur.[5] Mais après m'être assuré, dans une conference avéc Mr de Mazancourt,[5] que je ne saurais rien de plus du M[al], que je ne ferais qu'importuner, et qu'il etait de plus incertain que je pusse joindre, Je prens le parti d'executer les ordres de ce M[al] en me rendant à Treves[6] ou j'attendrai ceux que je mande au duc de Feltre de vouloir bien m'y adresser.

J'embrasse tendrement mon adorable amie, et la supplie d'ecrire bientôt à Alex, et de faire partir tout de suite sa lettre. Je voudrais ecrire plus longuement et ne le puis. Je pars.

A. d'A.

Ce 16 May.

Nous nous sommes trompés d'un jour et je t'ai quittée le jour même de ma fête. le 13!!!

872   [1358, Marché au bois],
                           Brussels, 13–18 May 1815

To M. d'Arblay

A.L. (Berg), 13–18 May 1815
Double sheet 4to   4 pp.   *pmk* BRUXELLES   wafer
Addressed: À / Monsieur le Chev[r] d'Arblay / Mareshal de Camp, / et Off[r] Superieur / du garde du Corps / de Sa Majesty Louis 18–. / *À Treves*.
Edited by FBA, p. 1, *annotated*: ⊹ (1/2)/2/ Brussels.
See Textual Notes.

[5] Prussian headquarters were now at Namur, but so too were the Saxon troops whose mutiny against Prussia in favour of their own pro-French sovereign had just been quelled. What Mazancourt conveyed to M. d'A as uncertainty about his joining Blücher's headquarters may have been opposition to having such an onlooker at Namur and, in Gneisenau's blunt words, to having any such French envoy at his headquarters, wherever they might be: 'Einen Armeekommissarius der Bourbons in unserm Hauptquartier gedenke ich nicht zu dulden, und er soll wenigstens nichts zu regieren noch zu verproviantieren haben' (Letter of 2 June 1815 to Boyen*, the Prussian War Minister, printed in Pflugk-Harttung, p. 253).
[6] Lt.-Col. Sir Henry Hardinge (1785–1856) reported from Prussian headquarters on 9 May that he had discussed with Gneisenau Wellington's forwarded request from Louis XVIII concerning M. d'A's mission—'The King is very anxious to send the Comte d'Arblay to Luxembourg on this service. The deserters whom he might collect might be sent by tens or twenties from thence to Termonde, and could do no mischief to the Prussian army' (*Disp.* xii. 363)—but according to Hardinge, Gneisenau 'objected to Luxemburg as the place of reception for the French deserters and in lieu proposed Trèves, as answering the same objects, without the inconveniences' (*Supp. Desp.* x. 266).

Read *This* in going to rest but read the *enclosed* immediately—

Saturday Night, May 13!!—1815.
Oh blessed be the *coming* anniversary of This Day! Happier, far happier than This, its precursor! in sweet, soft, faithful re-union may it be blest, after storms & sorrows & sufferings so heart-rending!—Oh how long & how dreadful has been the Tragedy of our separation & my revered Father's Death!— And our new parting has been upon your Birth day!—I knew it only to night—And my fervant prayer That fairer may be its anniversary—in the year to come—I offer up kneeling as I write — — Amen! amen! — — We engaged to interchange a prayer for our re-union—all Three—every night, instead of *midy*,—with what ardour have I here begun mine! amen!
amen!—

Ce Jeudi, *May 18.* How deplorably long, long LONG has weighed upon me every minute from your departure till this day, when you return to me, in fancy, in a few balsamic— however melancholy lines!—
'Tis most fortunate you resolved upon going to Treves, whither I shall direct. A printed summons came to you yesterday, from the Post Master General, to call yourself for A Letter *à votre addresse*, or to send a procuration signed by a notary public—I hesitated what step to take; & then assumed courage to go myself, taking with me the certificate of our residence, to prove who I was. This sufficed, & they gave me the enclosed Letter, which had lain by, for want of a proper direction, for this last fortnight! I was obliged to sign my name for receiving it, in a Book of office, of the date, I think, of the 5th of May!—
I have copied for you some verses which Mme Ch[1] says are *sung at Paris*! I am sorry I cannot get for you the others I have mentioned—*surtout* that with the refrain that though | Buonaparte has taught himself to wear *des mittins*, Paris & France call for their PAIRE / pere / de GANT / Gand / — [2]

872. [1] Possibly the Spanish beauty Jeanne-Marie-Ignace-Thérèse de Riquet de Caraman *née* Cabarrus (1773–1835), princesse de Chimay, whose three husbands were in turn a nobody, a leading revolutionary in the Terror, and a Prince of the Holy Roman Empire. FBA mentions her in the Waterloo Journal (p. 412 below) as an acquaintance during her weeks in Brussels.
[2] Here FBA inserted the superscript +++ with the instructions 'see last page' where she wrote the conclusion of the refrain '. . . GANT / Gand.' This song and

Ah, mon Ami!—est-ce possible que, lorsque nous nous reverrons, vous aurez '*un recit à entamer*' qui ne se pourr⟨oit⟩ être entamer auparavant! '*un recit, dites Vous,*—'*de tout-ce que j'ai a souffrir!*— — ' helas—mon Cher ami! mon cher ami! am I to be put *à une epreuve*—*Can* I be put *à une epreuve* plus fiere—plus tragique que ce que j'ai eprouvè déja?—Cependant, 'tis certain all evils that must be known are shorter & better supported for being known at once. — — Nevertheless, this is no period for details—I will press therefore no explanation now. —I only implore you to study your health, to spare your strength, to persuade yourself to go early to rest, & to watch what *regime* does you good, & fly what is injurious. Leave all else to our re-union—ah, what will not that—our re-union— soften?— —

I have kept my word religiously in forcing myself out every day, & in obliging myself to constant occupation—save in the morning & at night—when rumination siezes me by force!—

Sunday, the 1st lonely day, I spent almost wholly in the Park —so did I Monday—in the retired parts, where children only haunt.—Sunday I received, also, a long & cordial visit from the good Mme de Beaufort,[3] who came to invite me to her daily board! ⌜my tante⌝[4] made me a long & agitated visit in the Evening. Mme La Tour du Pin[5] & Mme de Maurville have been also, but I missed them. M. de Beaufort,[6] too, has made me

refrain appear in the account of a contemporary witness in Paris: 'The ladies of the Halle [les Halles], however, found a means of declaring their sentiments by singing continually a favourite air, in which the burden of the song consisted of a play upon words, and might be read, "Donnez-nous notre *pair* de *gants*" or "Donnez-nous notre *Père* de *Gand*"' (Maria Williams, p. 49).

[3] Sophie-Françoise-Thérèse *née* Helman-Termeeren (1758–1815), wife (since 3 Jan. 1805) of M. d'A's friend Colonel Beaufort (n. 6). She was the daughter of Philippe-Joseph-Hubert Helman (1715–85), seigneur de Termeeren, de Cantecroy, de Mortsel, de Luythagen, who had married in Brussels on 3 Nov. 1748 Marie-Christine van Overstraeten (b. 15 Mar. 1719), dame de Weldene et de Tenberghe. Her father, Nicolas, seigneur de Weldene, entrepréneur général des vivres et fourrages, was created comte (by lettres patentes, 27 mai 1750), and on the death of her husband, Marie-Christine Helman (*supra*) petitioned that the title descend to herself and children. Her eldest son François-Aurèle-Guidon (1749–1816) was granted the title comte Helman de Termeeren. See *Annuaire de la Noblesse* (1887). There would seem to be enough property in the family to support the great wealth that FBA attributes to Mme de Beaufort (L. 919 and *passim*) and M. d'A's interest, presumably for his friend's sake, in her will.

[4] The princesse d'Hénin.

[5] The wife of Frédéric-Séraphim, comte de Latour du Pin, who had taken lodgings in the rue de Namur while she awaited the arrival of her husband (L. 854 n. 9), then one of the four French ambassadors at the Congress of Vienna.

[6] Jean-Baptiste Theuillier de Beaufort (1751–1824), chevalier (1816), M. d'A's

two visits, most friendly; & on Tuesday I dined at his house, tolerably chearfully; but I have declined going again till next week. My own little dinner suits my present state of nerves best. I have written all we settled for our dear Alex—and ᵻ I have written to James—& to Charles—& to Martin—& a very long Letter to Charlotte,⁷ to enforce our scheme of residence for Alex at Richmond—with full powers to make him comfortable & independent.

M. de Lally is charmed you approve the Manifesto,⁸ & says that if you think you can distribute it usefully, he will be answerable for the expence of your printing as many copies as you judge you can disperse with good effect.

Yesterday, Wednesday, I walked in the park in the Evening with Mᵉ d'H[énin]—who joined the young Dˢˢ of Ursel,⁹ & all her pretty Children;⁹ & we were afterwards joined by M. de Liedekirk, pere, & his two ugly daughters.¹⁰ The Pere told me the Russians were arrived in the heart of Germany.¹¹ Lord

friend and fellow officer, who had served in the military engineers and rose from lieutenant in 1774 to chef de brigade in 1800 and colonel directeur des fortifications in 1803. After the death of his wife and Louis XVIII's return to Paris he returned to his birthplace of Pécquigny (Somme), a personal domain of the comte d'Artois (later Charles X), whence in 1816 he wrote to M. d'A (*Catalogue*, p. 233) and where he died eight years later.

⁷ Only L. 870 to CBFB has survived.

⁸ This Manifesto, forcefully summing up the Bourbon interpretation of events, Lally-Tolendal had prepared before 20 April, but the British and Russian ambassadors dissuaded Louis XVIII from publishing it until the end of May, when it appeared under the title *Manifeste délibéré au Conseil du Roi*. M. d'A's approval of the royalist document would not have been lessened by Lally's mention of the commissaires extraordinaires and his promise that deserters who went over to them would receive in a new and loyal army 'un rang qui sera fixé par leurs services' (Romberg and Malet, i. 54).

⁹ Louise-Victoire-Marie-Josèphe-Françoise Ferrero Fieschi (1778–1847), princesse de Masserano, who had married in 1804 Charles-Joseph d'Ursel (1777–1860), duc d'Ursel, former mayor of Brussels and in 1815 Interior Minister for the Southern Netherlands in the new country's royal government. She was the mother at this time of four children, Jean-François-Charles-Marie-Léon, Ludovic-Marie, Marie-Augustine-Caroline, aged 10, 6, 5 years respectively, and of the infant Marie-Auguste.

¹⁰ Marie-Ferdinand-*Hilarion* de Liedekerke Beaufort (1762–1841), comte, married in 1788 Julie-Caroline Desandrouin (1769–1836), by whom he had three children: a son Florent-Charles-*Auguste* (1789–1855), who was to marry in 1815 Marie-Charlotte-Alix (1796–1822), elder surviving daughter of the Mme de Latour du Pin mentioned in n. 5 above; and two daughters, Ermelina (1791–1871), who was to marry in 1821 Alphonse, comte de Cunchy, and Clara (1795–1818), whose father remembered her as 'la plus intéressante personne possible, en même temps qu'elle était jolie' (Liederkerke Beaufort, i. 271).

¹¹ The Russian army, whose total strength was 167,000 men, was advancing through Germany in three columns, which by mid May had reached Fulda on the right, Bayreuth in the centre, and Neckar on the left (Plotho, App., p. vi).

Duke of Wellington gave a dinner to the Prince Hereditaire,[12] & sundry Ambassadors, with music the whole time in the Park—and after the repast, | the Duke & his Company came into the Park, to gratify the awaiting multitude, that were swarming about his door & windows. He walked by the side of the Austrian minister, Vincent;[13] he looked remarkably well. all the mob followed quietly, & well behaved, his every step; all the better sort stood still, when he passed, in a row, as when the King walked on the Windsor Terrace.[14] Quel beau role que le sien! Since his return to military command, he has an Air the most commanding, a high, superiour *port*, & a look of animated spirit. I think he is grown taller!—He has just taken a much larger & nobler House![15] adieu, mon ami!—mon cher —oh *how* cher ami!—

pray preserve p^r Bluchers Letter & signature for Alex— Nothing will so much gratify him. |

Chant Francois du 20 Mars: 1815.[16] Air – du *prem^r pas.*
1 Il est parti
  Ce Roi que l'on révere;
  Il est parti
  Ce souverain cheri.
  Chaque Francais gémit, se désespere,
  Tous orphelins! nous n'aurons plus de Pere!
  Il est parti! — (bis)

[12] William Frederick George Louis (1792–1849), Prince of Orange and later King William II (1843), had been named on 23 Mar. 1815 commander-in-chief of the allied armies in the Netherlands. He had served under Wellington in Spain, but his rash inexperience caused friction with the British and serious losses to the troops under his command at Waterloo.

[13] Karl Freiherr Vincent (1757–1834) entered the Austrian cavalry in 1776, rose to the rank of general in capaigns against the French in Italy and Germany, was appointed in 1814 Austrian envoy to Paris then, after Napoleon's return from Elba, to Ghent and Wellington's headquarters. He arrived in Brussels on 17 May, the day of the dinner mentioned here.

[14] The family procession that followed George III after dinner along Windsor's Castle Terrace was accompanied by tunes played by a band of musicians and watched by spectators who lined the way. An illustration appears in Constance Hill, *Fanny Burney at the Court of Queen Charlotte* (1912), p. 24.

[15] Wellington's new house was on the rue de la Montagne du Parc at the corner of the rue Royale that runs along the north-west side of the Parc de Bruxelles (de Ros, p. 137).

[16] The *Chant François* . . . appears in the anonymous *Chansonnier royal, ou Passetems des bons Français* (2nd ed., 1815), one of several published during and after the Hundred Days. The second song, 'Idolatrer son patrie . . .' does not appear in any of these collections, but the tune was a popular one frequently used for satirical purposes.

2. Il est parti
   Dans cette Nuit d'allarmes,
   Il est parti
   Le fils du bon Henri!
   Son coeur craignait le ravage des Armes,
   Et bénissant ses sujets, tous en larmes,
   Il est parti! — (bis)

3. Ils l'ont trahi
   Ce Prince qu'on adore,
   Ils l'ont trahi!
   Tous ces guerriers flétris
   De le defendre — oh crime que j'abhorre! —
   oui! tout à l'heure ils le juraient encore! —
   Ils l'ont trahi! —

4: Ils l'ont suivi
   ses defenseurs fidèles
   Ils l'ont suivi
   Dêja loin de Paris,
   Pour le sauver des atteintes cruelles,
   Et des fureurs de ses Soldats rebelles
   Ils l'ont suivi. (bis)

5: Fidelite! —
   Que ce mot nous rallie!
   Fidelité
   Au Roi persecuté!
   Nous lui devons nos sermens, notre vie,
   Et de l'Honneur j'entends la voix, qui crie:
   Fidelité!

6: Il reviendra!
   Gardons en l'Esperance,
   Il reviendra
   Le Roi qu'on désira.
   Louis ne peut abandonner la France.
   Et toujôurs bon, toûjours plein d'Esperance
   Il reviendra. (bis) |

Air — *Des portraits à la mode.*[16]

1:

Idolatrer son pa⟨trie⟩ et son Roi;
Du point d'Honneur n'écoûter que la loi;

Etre loyal et fidèle à la fois / C'etoit autre fois La Mode:
Se faire un jeu de faussez son serment,
comme d'habits, changer de sentiment
comme un journal flagorner bassement.
Voilà l'honnette homme à la mode.

2:

Comme un bon Roi aimer tous ses Sujets,
Leur procurer l'abondance et la paix,
Et, quoiqu'ingrats, ne les haïr jamais —
C'était autre fois la méthode:
Mais epuiser d'Hommes son pays,
Au fond du Nord chercher des ennemis,
Et leur livrer et la France et Paris — — !
Voilà le Monarque à la Mode.

873   Brussels, 19–20 May 1815

To Mrs. Locke

L., incomplete copy in the hand of CFBt (Diary MSS. 6610–14, Berg),
19–20 May 1815
Double sheet and single sheet 4to   5 pp.
Docketed, p. 5 (6614), *left margin*: May 20. 1815.
Edited by the Press. *See* Textual Notes.

Marché aux Bois
Brussels
May 19. 1815

To Mrs Locke

Balsamic indeed have been your letters—your accounts—
my ever dear Friend—& how I have needed—how I need
them—my not answering. not writing sooner may speak!
Except from some species of necessity, I have not been able to
hold a pen since my flight from Paris—& while Alex was with
my dearest Friend I knew she would hear of his Parents—&
necessity therefore, directed my hand elsewhere—but now

that he has changed his asylum I feel not alone a necessity to give her some tidings, but—my pen once beginning to run,—an inclination revives to talk to her, & a consolation to do it without restraint.

———

How exquisitely good you have been to my Alex! & how his whole composition seems to have imbibed ¹ pure happiness in your pure air & pure society. His Letters breathe a spirit of gentle content that fills me with as much gratitude in perceiving the *species* of life that suits his taste, as I feel to my indulgent Friend for having given him the opportunity to try it. We wish him, however, now, to have a little nest of his own in which he may seriously & steadily resume his studies with that degree of application & perseverance which alone can conduct him to the happy result of his exertions without which—ultimately all deviations will lead to regret. My dearest Friend will be the first to comprehend how little I mean, by this, to wish him to return to the elaborate course of pursuits that strain the mind & wear the intellects, & throw away the blythe beauty of juvenile happiness.—oh no, I enjoy his delight—I have no joy, indeed, at this moment, like that of reflecting upon its innocence—he has been he says, in Paradise, with no single wish but that his Father & myself were at his side.— ¹ A taste, in such early life, for such virtuous felicity, will lead—I humbly hope—to its permanent attainment.

His freedom from all ambitious views, all tumultuous desires, & the innate charm he finds in the society & the goodness of my beloved Friend & of my Amine, with only his own feelings to stimulate their appreciation, have given both his Father & myself the highest satisfaction. His last letter from Norbury arrived at the very moment of our last separation—it was nearly the only thing upon earth that could have happened to mitigate the bitterness of that instant.

I am here quite alone; in Apartments of my own—*Isolée, isolée!*—The first month of my arrival at Brussels I spent under the same roof with the Princesse d'Henin; we took a house in common with a third part to a third person:—but circumstances have, since, made all three seek separate dwellings. I am unfit, in truth, for any nest but my own! my disturbance, as news circulates & changes of impending events, is too mighty for the burthen additional of constant controul. I am best, when very unhappy, in retiring within myself, [|] not however by running away from social comfort or comforters, but by turning to them at choice, with that wish & aptitude—I had nearly said *resignation* for consolation that will not, in *suspensive* calamity, be always at hand. I can only behave well before witnesses, by indulging—O what a false word!—by suffering a vent to keen emotions in solitude—for then I can mix them with a devotion that alone can overpower—or meet their harrowing effects. I see Mad^e d'Henin almost daily,[1] either here or *chez elle*. She has resided in Brussels formerly some years, when her Nephew, M. La Tour du Pin, was Prefect:[2] She knows, therefore, almost every body—but from her whole set I have only associated myself intimately with one lady, Madame de Beaufort,[3] who has conceived for me so earnest a kindness, that she would never have me out of her house: & who, though neither brilliant nor alluring, is so good, & so sympathizing, that she enters into the whole of my situation in a manner that draws forth my confidence, & makes her society really valuable, & the more as she never takes ill my withdrawing from her, though she is so kind that it makes her look dejected.

It is a week this day, *May* 20th since M: d'A: last left me—I have had one letter[4]—it was dated *Liege*: but he was going farther. He is on a military mission of importance—& alas, of much danger—much, much risk!—redoubted by the shattered state [|] of his nerves & strength, & by a thinness that has utterly changed his appearance. — —

The Duke of Wellington has just taken a larger house which has spread a report of *Peace* throughout Brussels!! Paris is in a deplorable state[5]—& Bonaparte is embarrassed past all

873. ¹ Mrs. Locke had entertained the princesse d'Hénin in the years she was an *émigrée* in England (iii *passim*).
² The comte de Latour du Pin-Gouvernet (L. 854 n. 9), baron de l'Empire (1808) and marquis (1820), who had been prefect at Brussels from 1808 until 1813, was the son of the princesse d'Hénin's elder sister. His childless aunt (iv, L. 575 n. 2) treated him more as a son, helping him to recover his fortune after the Revolution. He had just returned from the Congress of Vienna, where he was one of the four French ambassadors, by a roundabout route through Toulon, Marseilles, Barcelona and Madrid, having delivered at Ghent on 18 May important dispatches from Spain (*Moniteur de Gand*, 19 May).
³ See L. 872 n. 3.
⁴ L. 871.
⁵ Although Paris remained calm during the uprisings and dissensions that

measure. This I have just heard from private & very certain authority in a person newly escaped. — — Adieu my most dear Friends—Your kindest wishes and prayers follow—accompany mine, I am very very sure! |

874   [Trèves], 25 May 1815

M. d'Arblay
To Madame d'Arblay

A.L. (Berg), 25 May 1815
Single sheet 4to   2 pp.   *pmk*   TRIER   seal
Addressed: A Madame / Madame d'Arblay / marché au bois N° *1358* / a *Bruxelles*
    Edited by FBA, p. 1, *annotated*: ⌖ ⌈12⌉ (3/1) Containing the astonishing & magnanimous letter of *Marmont* to *Caulincourt*   [*with numbers on address fold*]: *12   12*   6   3   3
    Edited also by CFBt. *See* Textual Notes.

Ce 25 May 1815.

Ne point recevoir de tes nouvelles quand je pourrais et consequement devrais en avoir, c'est mon amie, ma chere et unique amie, un tourment au quel je n'etais pas preparé et qui me rend tous les autres insuportables. Dejà, je me dis: serait elle tombée malade! Bientôt je me dirai: il faut qu'elle le soit! et Dieu sait, comment je m'en trouverai. Sois bien sûre pourtant ô mon amie! que je ne negligerai rien pour conserver ma santé. [xxxxx 3 *lines*] Du reste je me porte assez bien; mais je [suis tou]jours vexé au delà de toute expression de

marked the west and south, its commercial and cultural life stagnated as the middle classes withdrew their confidence from Napoleon's liberal empire, which seemed increasingly and embarrassingly dependent on lower-class and military support, while the noisy festivities of *faubouriens* and *prétoriens* revived memories and fears of revolution. Napoleon's support among prefects, mayors, and the clergy ebbed away in its turn as it became clear that despite social divisions, forced loans, and disruption of trade, France would soon be overwhelmed by an invasion of the allies, whose declaration from the Congress of Vienna of 13 March had by mid May filtered through most of the country. This united hostility gave the lie to Napoleon's earlier claim that the Emperor of Austria would not declare war on his son-in-law and that peace would continue. The language of revolution was also being used on the royalist side to sum up the state of France during these weeks: 'La lie de la nation est de nouveau soulevée contre le rang, la naissance, la religion, la propriété' (*Moniteur de Gand*, 23 March).

ne recevoir aucune lettre de Gand. Il est presumable qu'à Liege on aura oublié la promesse qu'on m'avait faite de me renvoyer ici toutes celles qui m'y auraient été adressées. Mon premier soin en arrivant ici a été d'ecrire à ce sujet au directeur de la poste et j'attens sa reponse. J'attends aussi et trés impatiement, celle du P^ce Blücher au Gal Kleïst.¹ Il faut en convenir tout cela est bien etrange, et peu agreable. Je ne veus pourtant pas me décourager: mais j'avoue que j'avais besoin du redoublement d'energie que vient de me donner la lecture de la reponse de Marmont à Caulincourt.² Nous avions été três contents de sa justification; et selon moi cette derniere lettre est [bie]n superieure. Elle est inserée (sans date) *dans le N° 136 du Journal de Frankfort.* Il parait que les propositions d'accomodement lui ont été faites au nom de B — Voici comme il les a accueillies.³ Il a commis, dit il, *une faute | immense,*

874. ¹ Friedrich Heinrich Ferdinand Emil Graf Kleist von Nollendorf (1762–1823), from one of the most famous of Prussian military families, entered royal service as a page in 1782 and became a staff officer in 1793. He served as a colonel in the grim campaigns of 1806 and the following year, reaching the rank of major-general by 1813, when he gained a decisive victory at Kulm and the title of count (Graf) from the nearby town of Nollendorf. He led the left wing at Leipzig later that year and distinguished himself in the French campaign of 1814. During the Hundred Days he commanded the 2nd Deutsche Bundescorps and the Prussian Army of the Lower Rhine but was forced by illness to give up his command at the start of the Waterloo campaign. He retired as a field-marshal in 1820. Both M. d'A's comments and the tributes of others make it plain that he was a man of great ability and charm, respected for both his humanity and devotion to duty.

Kleist shared M. d'A's bafflement about his position and on 22 May wrote to Blücher for directions. Gneisenau's reply on the subject ('die Unkunst des französischen General d'Arblay in Trier betreffend') summarized Blücher's objections to having a French officer set up his recruiting 'bureau' inside the fortress at Luxemburg, passes over their joint objection to having M. d'A around their headquarters (Blücher, because he detested the French; Gneisenau, because he had introduced among his staff open discussion of all manœuvres and decisions), and finally leaves it up to Kleist to keep M. d'A under control and out of harm's way (Pflugk-Harttung, p. 252).

² See L. 860 n. 11 and L. 856 n. 15.

³ This curious document, so different in tone and style from Marmont's answer to the accusations made against him in Napoleon's Proclamation of 1 March—an answer printed in the *Moniteur de Gand* of 1 April—is probably a forgery concocted and circulated by the Prussians as propaganda. It first appeared on 5 Apr. 1815 in the *Gazette de Berlin*, together with a letter allegedly written by Marmont to the Austrian Generalissimo Prince Schwarzenberg* (1771–1820), with whom he had negotiated before his notorious defection from Napoleon in 1814. This letter, which accepts with thanks the offer of an Austrian command to fight against his own countrymen, makes sense of the passage, quoted by M. d'A and italicized in the original, in which Marmont supposedly promises to bear the Bourbon standard back to Paris. The Prussians sought to discredit Marmont, the best strategist among Napoleon's marshals, perhaps because they had caught wind of a royalist proposal to give him a new army to be based upon Swiss regiments, including those already in French service (Jaucourt, pp. 278, 283), rather than upon the Maison du Roi. Had this plan worked, Louis XVIII would have had a sizeable force of trained

'J'ai eu la foiblesse d'assurer la conservation des jours de B.; j'en arrachai le serment à ses ennemis et je sacrifiai ainsi l'interest de ma patrie à un sentiment mal eteint d'une ancienne amitié. Voilà le seul tort que ma Conscience me reproche — — —. La conquête donnait aux puissances le droit de partager un pays qui leur arrachait depuis 20 ans toutes leurs richesses, leur opulence. Le nom de Louis les a appaisées. à ce nom sacré, elles ont deposé les armes. Ainsi Louis, sans armes, sans soldats revetu de cette seule force que donne la vertu, et l'ascendant d'un pouvoir legitime, a conquis sur l'Europe en armes, la paix la plus extraordinaire dont jamais l'histoire ait gardé le souvenir. Je me suis voué sans reserve à la defense du veritable souverain, je l'ai honnoré dans la prosperité, je lui serai fidele dans son infortune; et dussent ses revers être aussi durables que je les crois passagers, ma vie s'eteindra à ses côtés heureux de voir couler p^r sa conservation la derniere goutte de mon sang. Voilà M^r mes sentimens, et ma justification. Vous savez si le regne de Louis a pu en affoiblir les ressorts, ce regne si merveilleux dans sa brieveté, ce regne sujet de notré admiration, de notre amour, de nos larmes, ce regne l'eternel objet de la meditation des princes, le desespoir des Tyrans, ira deposer dans la posterité en faveur de ceux qui contribueront au retour des Bourbons, et contre les coupables partisans de l'usurpateur. Je vous le dirai, M^r, avec toute la franchise [de]mon caractère, je n'ai cherché et je n'attens l'approbation, ni de B[uonaparte], ni de vous, ni des hommes qui vous ressemblent, j'ai été etonné, je l'avoue, d'entendre le compagnon d'enfance du malheureux duc d'Enghien me reprocher d'avoir abandonné B — p^r un Bourbon. J'excuse l'erreur de ceux qui ont admiré ce heros sanguinaire jusqu'au regne de Louis XVIII: mais je crois prevenir le jugement de l'histoire, en vouant au mepris et à l'execration qui conque a quitté le Roi p^r s'attacher à B — Je vous declare, M^r, que les lâches ennemis de la Patrie sont à mes yeux indignes de pitié et de pardon; et je pense que la Nation doit, p^r eviter un opprobre eternel, les repousser pour toujours de son sein. Vous voyez Monsieur, par la franche enonciation de mes principes si B — peut encore songer à me seduire. Dites à

soldiers under a capable commander—and the Prussians a much more complicated situation to deal with. Napoleon's supporters exploited the propaganda value of this apparent betrayal by publishing it in the *Journal de l'Empire*. It was, however, denounced as a forgery by a serving French officer in a letter published in the *Journal* on 14 May.

l'assassin du duc d'Enghien et de Pichegru, dites au per-
turbateur de l'Europe entiere, dites à celui qui a plongé la
France dans le sang et les larmes, dites au violateur du
droit des gens et de tous les traités, dites au parjure, au
plus perfide et au plus coupable des hommes, que le serment
que j'ai preté à mon Roi, sera dans peu de jours scellé du
sang des traitres, qu'il n'y a plus rien de commun entre moi
et le persecuteur de ma patrie; *que mon bras va bientot conduire
l'etendard des lys jusque dans la Capitale*; que ma vie est desormais
consacrée à rallier autour du drapeau blanc les sujets fideles
et les sujets egarés; annoncez lui, de ma part, et de celle de
l'Europe entiere, que le sang versé par les assassins va re-
tomber sur leurs têtes, et que le jour de justice est proche.
Signé Marmont.

Je n'ai pu me refu[ser *cut*] au plaisir de te faire [*cut*]ait emu. ǀ

Quel bonheur! On me remet ta lettre[4] au moment où j'allais
fermer celle ci. J'y repondrai dans 3 ou 4 jours. Merci! Merci! ǀ

875   Trèves, 25 May 1815

M. d'Arblay
To Madame d'Arblay

A.L.S. (Berg), 25 mai 1815
Double sheet 4to 3 pp. *pmk* TRIER seal
Addressed: À Madame / Madame d'Arblay / marché au bois Nº *1358* / a
Bruxelles.
Edited by FBA, p. 1, *annotated*: ✳ ⌈13⌉ (4/1) [*with numbers on
address fold*]: *13 13* 4 4   6
See further, Textual Notes.

Jeudi, 25 mai — 1815
Treves —

Pardon, mille et mille fois, ma tendre amie, de l'inquietude
que j'ai eu la sottise de te donner. J'avais effectivement quelque
raison de me plaindre de ce que j'avais à souffrir. J'en avais
beaucoup, et tant que je ne sais plus à present sur quoi portaient

---

4 L. 872.

les plaintes qui t'ont tourmentée. Ma santé, notre bourse, ma position, tout à la fois allait fort mal: mais tout cela va mieux à la bourse près; et bientôt tout ira bien. La lettre que tu m'as envoyée du M^{al}, tes chansons, et plus que tout ton ecriture, ces caracteres que j'ai depuis tant de fois baisés — — tout cela a operé un veritable miracle; et c'est pour t'en remercier que je te griffonne ceci, à la hâte, p^r ne pas manquer le courrier pour le quel je suis à ecrire depuis 4^{h}1/2 du matin. Il en est à present plus de 11. Il faut neanmoins que je te dise encore que les couplets que tu m'as envoyés m'ont été et me seront encore très utiles. Remercie aussi Lally | de la permission qu'il me donne et dont pourtant je crains de ne pas pouvoir faire usage. J'ai fait passer un extrait du manifeste, du rapport de Chateaubriant,[1] et de la reponse de Marmont à Caulaincourt; et j'en attens quelque succès. Amen!

Imagine toi qu'obligé de venir de Liege ici par des chemins diaboliques avec la colique, des menaces de Rhumatisme, et ce qui est bien pire d'assez vives douleurs dans la poitrine, j'ai eu peur de la pluie qu'il m'eut fallu essuyer 7 à 8 heures de suitte. J'ai en consequence été forcé d'acheter à la verité à très base prix une vielle carcasse à 4 roues traînée par un cheval de diligence ou de roulier qui seul vaut ce que j'ai payé.[2] Quant à la voiture qui est fort laide mais sur de bons ressorts, j'ai fait ici reparer les souspentes, et pourrai désormais voyager à couvert, et conserver ma santé qui est à present fort bonne. [xxxxx ½ *line*]

Une autre sujet d'inquietude très vive a été ma jument noire, qui non seulement a été menacée d'être poussive, mais | *morveuse*. [xxxxx 6 *lines* mais] la bête va mieux, mange bien, mais est fort maigrie. [xxxxx 2 *lines*] Malheureusem^t je ne suis pas en etat de lui acheter un autre selle. à cela près me voilà remis, et aussi content que je puis l'être loin de mon unique amie. Adieu, adieu donc. Continue à m'ecrire et envoie moi tout ce que tu pourras trouver dans le genre de tes couplets. car il ne

---

875. [1] Chateaubriand's *Rapport sur l'état de la France au 12 mai 1815 fait au Roi dans son Conseil*, an eloquent defence of Louis XVIII as the guarantor of French liberty and an attack on Napoleon as the renewer of tyranny, appeared in the *Moniteur de Gand* (12 May) and was published separately as propaganda by the 'Imprimerie Royale' set up at Ghent. Royalists soon afterward arranged its clandestine publication in Paris, where it provoked, according to its author, great acclaim and uproar. See Chateaubriand, *Mémoires*, i. 934–6.
[2] M. d'A's horse was suffering from broken wind and glanders.

nous parvient rien ici. J'ai demandé qu'on me fit passer le moniteur universel. Tu devrais appuyer cette demande près de Lally, qu'on ne pourrait refuser. J'en ferai bon usage. Adieu, adieu donc, à notre reunion! —

d'Ay

Treves
Ce 25 May (rue St Simeon n° *1003*.)[3]

876   [1358, Marché au bois],
                          Brussels, 28 May 1815

To M. d'Arblay

A.L. (Berg), 28 May 1815
Double sheet 4to   4 pp.   *pmk*   BRUXE⟨LLES⟩
Addressed: à *Treves* / À / Monsieur le General d'Arblay, / Chev^r de St. Louis, &c &c / & Officier Superiere du garde / du Corps du Roi / de France / à *TREVES*.
Edited by FBA, p. 1, *annotated*: ⁛   (2/2)
See Textual Notes.

Brussels—28 May, 1815

Oh for Wings to answer in person the 2 *side* lines on the first page. '*ÉLOIGNER*' votre tendre—votre fidèle Athanase?—que rien n'a pu éloigner?—nulle epreuve?—& shall she be '*ÉLOIGNÉE*' by *l'idée d'un projet* that fills her sad heart once again with hope of happiness? I read those two precious lines[1] *avec une joie si attendrissante* that it still absorbs my whole being—Oh mon ami! will you indeed, when Honour is satisfied, *planter là* all Ambition, & *planter chez nous vos choux*?[1]—and shall I see you again All yourself?—i e—all, at once, that is RIGHT & that is KIND?—⌐& shall the inimical ⟨duty⟩ that gave you a

---

[3] In the north-central section of Trèves, between the Porta Nigra and the church of Saint Gangolf.

876. [1] These lines, together with several other comments reported or referred to below, come from a letter (now missing) that M. d'A wrote *c.* 22 May after his arrival in Trèves. In this letter he seems to have mentioned Kleist's welcome and his own desire to retire from the army to the private and rustic life that FBA also longed for.

semblance so cold, so hard,[2] so changed be blotted as an ugly dream from my remembrance?⁊ Oh with what tender gratitude shall I owe to you the restoration of my gaiety of spirits, which for so many delicious,—though not wholly unchequered years, I had owed to you before—but which from the time of our eventful, & to me most unhappy long separation, so many nameless—excruciating feelings—fears—& suspences have transformed into almost habitual inquietude nay, suffering?— Those dear *2 lines* which talk with such pointed *desire*, nay *design* of our re-union, melt me with a soft joy balsamic to every past wound—ah mon ami!—if you could see—as I feel my features unbending from long care—sorrow & disturbance, to gentler tranquility, you would bless the pen that wrote those 2 propitious lines!— ꙇ

I am not at all of opinion you would find joining the English army *much* more endurable: the opinion of your Prussian offc^r de Gend'armerie[3] is general through the allied army, though the D[uke] of W[ellington] will repress its consequences as much as is in his power. The French ARMY they go *professedly* to crush; & the French *NATION* they hold to deserve no better for *submitting*, even against their choice, to leave them undisputed Masters of disposing of the sovereignty.

I shall give no hint of this project, not the smallest to any one. It must come first & straight from yourself to the D[uke] of F[eltre][4]—I suppose it must be done from where you are, & that you must await his acceptance, & perhaps nomination of a successor.

I hope you have now received M^l Blucher's Letter,[5] which I enclosed in my own, & sent off to be ready to meet you at *Treves?* — I did not say *poste restante*, as I thought you might probably have your address known,—but if it is not delivered, pray enquire for it.

Two Letters are come from M. de Premorel,[6] but I do not enclose them, as I take it for granted you have sent to him, & that he is with you. His impatience is violent for movement, &

---

[2] This reproach, which had been obliterated, is one repeatedly hinted at in FBA's letters of this period. She thought throughout the Hundred Days that M. d'A showed himself too exclusively concerned with his duty, too little with her fears. The excited emphasis of FBA's opening lines marks her joy at his change of outlook.
[3] The name is lost with M. d'A's letter of *c.* 22 May.
[4] See L. 860 n. 2.   [5] See L. 871 n. 1.
[6] See L. 868 n. 3.

his Letters are full of respect & good intelligence of *les Fidèles*, as I agreed with him to call *les deserteurs*.[7]

I had just written to P^ss Eliz[abeth] of your mission:[8] but whatever you decide to say to the D. of F. will there be fully satisfactory. Your known loyalty & courage will make you judged as you ought to be; & your shattered health & your 61 will speak a language the most impressive. ⎸

M. l'abbé de Montesquiou[9] & Char^s de Noailles[10] are just arrived at Gand: surely Bonaparte must be betrayed par *les siens* or people so marked would not then pass the frontiers.

A decree has just past, signed by Fouché,[11] to call back all Emigrés on pain of confiscation! Whatever we have not had saved will probably now be lost! 'Tis a measure taken to raise ready money. ⌐The horses arrive not! though *ma tante* has received, since, an arm Chair!! & in it was sent some small matter of ours, not worth carriage, but which will make me pay half!! You have 4 *shirts* & 2 *nightcaps*!⌐

M. La Fay[ette] & George are chosen Representatives for La Mayenne & Loire![12]—Mme de G[rand] M[aison][13] says we shall be ruined by useless house rent, & Deprez'[13] wages & nouriture: & offers to let our apertments for us! How good! But there is no possibility now of writing to her. Escapes are all *from* Paris, not *to* it.[14]

---

[7] Deserters from Napoleon's army who came over to Louis XVIII.

[8] L. 877, dated in draft 29 May.

[9] François-Xavier-Marie-Antoine de Montesquiou-Fézenzac (1756–1832), abbé de Montesquiou and duc de Fézenzac (1815), long a political ally of Louis XVIII, became Minister of the Interior in 1814, when he had a hand in drawing up the *Charte* by which the King promised to rule. FBA is mistaken in thinking that he had come to Ghent. Napoleon's return from Elba forced him to flee to England and his portfolio was taken over by Chateaubriand during the Hundred Days.

[10] Charles-Arthur-Tristan-Jean Languedoc de Noailles (v, L. 513 n. 16), *styled* duc de Mouchy, was promoted to the rank of maréchal de camp at Ghent on 31 May and after the second Restoration, to lieutenant-general (17 May 1816).

[11] This decree was Napoleon's, but it was prompted by Fouché's report of 7 May on the activities of royalist dissenters. The texts of both documents were first published on 9 May in the *Moniteur*.

[12] Lafayette was in fact returned for Seine-et-Marne (*Moniteur*, 23 May). His son George Washington de Lafayette (v, L. 517 n. 18), whose distinguished military service had been ignored by Napoleon—who repeatedly denied requests for his promotion—had lived on the family estates at La Grange since 1807. He was elected as one of the deputies for Haute-Loire (*Moniteur*, 25 May).

[13] Mme de Grandmaison (L. 855 n. 4) and Mme Deprez (L. 846 n. 1), 'femme de charge' of d'Arblay's apartments in Paris. See A.L.S. (Berg), Durand de Prémorel to M. d'A, 7 Sept. [1815].

[14] When John Cam Hobhouse (1786–1869), Baron Broughton (1851), set off on what the British in Belgium called his 'forbidden expedition' to Paris he was surprised to find that many others, from disbanded gardes du corps to English tourists,

Poor Mme de Beaufort is very dangerously ill!^15—She has been so kind to me, so cordial, that I am quite afflicted—for I fear there is little hope!! — — ⌐A Letter is come for you from Dufresne,^16 who is with Ma^de de Boinville. He begs your interest to get him employed by the Duke de Feltre in his office—or any thing similar. He wishes to return, but to be employed Royally. There is so much hope of ultimate success in Mr. Boyd,^17 that I fancy he has full expectation of returning to Paris, & of a family re-establishment & of splendour. Yet she evidently, I think, is occupied by the remembrance of Dufresne, who calls himself *de Boinville*—I had a visit from her & her Mother & sister just now.^18 They have brought me, most obligingly, English N[ews] P[apers], which I will run over while I have some paper left to speak of them.⌐ |

Eh bien—je les ai lu jusqu'au 23 du mois! La D^ss d'Ang[oulême] est toujours en Angleterre—Elle a été reçue par la Reine avec toutes les mêmes cérémonies that were accorded

were entering France and travelling freely toward the capital. See Broughton, i. 241–4.

^15 See L. 872 n. 3. The illness, diagnosed as pleurisy, was to prove fatal (L. 924, p. 415).

^16 Alexandre de Boinville de Fresne (1785–*post* 1849), the bastard son of Jean-Baptiste Chastel de Boinville (L. 842 n. 8), was taken by his father to England soon after the Revolution. In 1794 Alexandre's father had married Harriet Collins (v, L. 515 n. 21), of whom the young Boinville was later to write 'Madame de Boinville eut pour moi toute l'affection et la tendresse d'une mère, elle seule reçut de moi ce titre sacré, et je ne connus jamais d'autre'. See A.L.S. (Vincennes) to the duc de Dalmatie, then ministre de la Guerre, 28 Dec. 1840. When the Boinvilles returned to France in 1797, Alexandre went with them, but travelled on to Spain, Italy, and Germany before returning to England. He remained in London with Harriet de Boinville and her other children when his father returned alone to France, and in 1804 entered the British army as an ensign in an infantry regiment. At his father's orders Alexandre left the army and returned to France, entering first the ministère de l'Intérieur (1806–10) and then transferring to the ministère de la Guerre (1811–19, 1820–8), in which he rose to become chef de bureau. Only after his return to France did he learn the truth about his birth—the knowledge of which may explain why FBA obliterated his name in her letters during the very period in which he changed his name. His father then took the step of introducing him to his natural mother, who for the rest of his life hounded him for money, gained a legal judgement that required him to support her, and drove him to write the letter to the Minister of War quoted above, a moving account of a tormented life.

^17 Boyd (L. 870 n. 2) had repeatedly petitioned the French government to restore the personal estates and bank funds seized when he escaped abroad to avoid arrest on charges of espionage. The granting of his petition of 27 July 1814 restored part of his holdings (Archiv. Nat. T 1604) but he went on to demand compensation, which was finally granted by a convention signed on 25 Apr. 1818 (Bouchary, ii. 139). While in Brussels, he appealed (without success) even to Wellington for help in his suit (*Disp.* xii. 429).

^18 For Harriet's sister Cornelia Newton (d. 1816), see v, L. 515 n. 21. Their mother, widow of John Collins (d. *pre* 7 Feb. 1813), is not identified as yet.

to the Emp[eror] of Russia:[19] & she has been visited by P[ss] Charlotte. Le P[rince] Regent voit souvent M. d'O:[20] qui, au reste, disavows his partizans hautement, & thinks himself much injured in honour by the reports. A universal cry is raised ags[t] the Administration of L[ouis] 18.[21] But He will not dismiss one minister. What an unhappy virtue is such individual Generosity when the *world* is at stake! They may be faithful servants, but they have SHEWN themselves incapable Ministers for such a period. All are trembling des suites des suites! C[t] Vincent,[22] the Austrian ambassadour to L. 18 has dined here in great state with the D. of Wellington—p[ses] Eliz & Mary have visited the D[ss] d'Angoulême.

How satisfactory a surprise was so long a Letter![23] How often I shall read it.

I am truly glad you have got a voiture, but I am shocked about y[r] Horses & alarmed for my Protege.[24] I hope *Henry* does not supplant him? Genl Kleist's visit did me good. You will be extremely satisfied with P[r] Blucher's Letter, which counsels you so civilly to resort to Treves. I am quite pleased with your Homerical visit & Book gallantry: but not with your *rhume*—& your *poitrine*! Ah, for Heaven's sake take all possible care! & if ill — — never forget, at least, who is at hand ONLY for You!— How terrible—& how true all that was said to you by the Prussian offi[r] de Gend'armerie!

Certaine *Trames*[25]—de *ma tante*, &c go on, Je crois, & Je

---

[19] These visits and audiences at court took place on 18 and 20 May and were reported in the *Moniteur de Gand* (23 and 26 May).

[20] The Prince's meetings with the duc d'Orléans began on 5 April, when they talked for two hours in the presence of Louis XVIII's special envoy (Romberg and Malet, i. 157–61). The subject of their discussions, and a source of alarm to Louis XVIII and his favourites, was how best to bring about a new restoration in France, where there was widespread support for Louis-Philippe as a moderate solution to the problematic choice between Louis XVIII and Napoleon.

[21] FBA's letters mirror the growing split between the King's reactionary family, ministers, and favourites—chief among them, the hated Blacas—at Ghent and the *constitutionnels* there, in Brussels, Paris, and London (Houssaye, *1815*, i. 477–9).

[22] See L. 872 n. 13.

[23] A further reference to M. d'A's lost letter of *c*. 22 May.

[24] FBA's protégé was M. d'A's valet and interpreter François (see L. 896, p. 232). M. d'A added the groom Henry to his entourage at Trèves.

[25] This plotting (*trames*) involved the liberal and *constitutionnel* faction in Ghent and Brussels, including the princesse d'Hénin (*ma tante*), who was in correspondence with Lafayette. Their muddled conspiracies were provoked by the heedless obstinacy (*entêtement . . . insouciance*) of the Ghent court, which seemed bent on repeating the worst mistakes of the first emigration.

crains that there is an *entêtement* of *insouciance* for public opinion that will be dreadfully hazardous if not conquered in time.

M. de la Tour du Pin is arrived from Spain.[26] M. Mounier is arrived from Germany.[27] Ma tante's friend[28] is here & I believe not in perfect contentment.

Pray—PRAY remember—delighted as I am with a long & confidential *causèrie*—a mere Bonjour, with date of *place*, & [na]me, will always be thankfully received, when you are hurried. Heaven ever bless mon ami!—& re-unite us!—never never more to be parted! |

877   [1358, Marché au bois],
Brussels, 29 May 1815

To H.R.H. Princess Elizabeth

A.L.S. draft (Berg), 29 May 1815
Double sheet 4to   torn away at lower right corner   4 pp. and a single sheet 4to 2 pp. in all 6 pp. showing the obliterations and rephrasings characteristic of a draft. The trial phrasings are omitted in the transcript.

        2 à ELIZA   Brussels, May 29, 1815
                              Brussels

Madam,
Ah, that some good Genius w^d arise—or rather, I ought to say, descend, for *surely Good* Geniuses cannot have subterraneous apartments—to give the counsel, kind, yet true—(qualities rarely united—) whether I had more wisely rest quiet in contented oblivion, with dismal respect, or make an effort to work my way out of it by an humble petition that Yr. R.H. would deign to put aside those waters of Lethe that my 'Mind's Eye' sees even now quaffing to my non-entity, & condescend to

[26] His arrival in Ghent on 18 May was announced in the *Moniteur de Gand* of 19 (mistakenly dated 12) May.
[27] Claude-Philippe-*Édouard* Mounier (v, L. 514 n. 15), who on arriving in Ghent was made deputy to the duc de Richelieu, Louis XVIII's *commissaire* with the army of Czar Alexander.
[28] Lally-Tolendal, who had failed to persuade the duc d'Orléans to allay suspicion by returning from London to Ghent, was one of the leading liberals in the plots mentioned in n. 21 (*supra*).

admit me once more to yr. Royal presence—and afterwards again & again—& again—in This only *questionable shape* in which I have present capacity for aiming at that high Honour.

At all events—there is something so much more agreeable in thinking ones self alive than in being passed by as dead, that I will no longer resist making another essay for peeping out of my solitary corner, with the dear hope that a bright ray of light from 'The Island all Islands excelling,[1] may warm & cheer me at this sad season, & give me some comfort to enable me to return to it with lessened depression.

Almost immediately after my arrival at Brussels, I sent a long ditty, under cover to Mr. Rolleston,[2] with the history of my flight from Paris, & of M. d'Ar's terrible though so short campaign, which, from various peculiar misfortunes, joined to the broken state of ı health in which it was begun, had so exhausted him, that he was incapable of further service, & had obtained, from Monsieur, permission to retire for refitting, but while slowly journeying to Ostend, where his Majesty Louis 18 then was, & whither I was preparing to join him, a few days rest & medicine so wonderfully recovered him, (comparatively) —that he changed his plan, & returned his congé. He then came to Brussels—still so altered as to frighten every body that had known him—but he here received a commission from the Duc de Luxembourg, Cap^n of his company, (relative to Maps & Horses) that detained him more than a month, & gave time for recruiting his strength. He had then a summons to Gand, from the Duc de Feltre, where the King most graciously saw him, & recommended to him the care of his health—& where he received a new & important mission, which has now carried him further afield. It is to precede, where it is possible, the allies, in hanging upon the frontiers of France, for receiving, inspecting, selecting or rejecting Deserters—who now, in This Cause, we have agreed to call Les Fideles. He has had a conference with the Duke of Wellington upon the subject & he is

---

877. ı FBA seems to be quoting freely from the Song of Venus in Act V of Dryden's *King Arthur*:

> Fairest isle, all isles excelling,
> Seat of pleasures and of loves;
> Venus here will choose her dwelling,
> And forsake her Cyprian groves.

² This was L. 856 sent to Stephen Rolleston (n. 18), for over thirty years an employee in the Foreign Office.

in a correspondence with the | good old M¹ pʳ Blücher. Where he is at this moment I know not. He was originally appointed for Luxembourg—but circumstances have made a change not yet decided, in his destination. He has 3 officers[3] of known fidelity under him, besides his aid de camp. 9 other French Generals have at different points upon the frontiers, similar positions. It is a difficult task, & of fearful responsibility—yet it is one that has certainly as many charms as dangers—& he undertakes it with a zeal that *rejeunis* him.

Accounts from Paris of the most encouraging description arrive continually. The shops are said to be without business, the public places without company, & the streets, but for soldiers, appear to be uninhabited. The *'tiny Tiger'*[4] seems to be caught in his own toils, for he is so evidently embarrassed, that though always hunting about for prey, he looks scared, gloomy, amazed—and knows not which way to prowl.

Since the murder of the Duke d'Enghein, nothing, I am assured by a person just escaped from Paris—has so hurt him in men's minds as the account he has printed of Mᵉ la Dˢˢ d'Angoulême, The epithet *furious*[5] given to the heroic exertions of that pious & gentle character, which seems—as my Royal Correspondent so sweetly said, to be 'virtue framed'[6] has shocked all Ears, & excited general indignation, & la Dˢˢ is now signalized, in Paris, by the title of La Femme par Excellence. |

I live now quite alone—in a very good apartment, though amazingly cheap.[7] I have little about me to attract new friends, & I avoid nothing so sedulously as new acquaintance. I have met, however, with far more civilities in this City than I merit, or have been gay enough to return. Yet I often see some parisian

---

[3] Only three were general officers (see list below, L. 897).

[4] A term quoted from the Princess's letter of 13 March (Berg) and often used for Napoleon in contemporary English lampoons and satirical drawings, which repeatedly contrast a pigmy Bonaparte with a robust George III.

[5] It is by no means certain that Napoleon used the term, but it is certain that the insulting phrase 'une femme furieuse' is attributed to Napoleon's supporters in royalist accounts of her spirited defence of Bordeaux (*Moniteur de Gand*, 16 May), which may have been FBA's source.

[6] 'Never were Virtues more thoroughly portrayed than in that person', wrote the Princess Elizabeth in her letter (Berg) of 13 March, when, in speaking of 'the *white Rubband Corp*', she signalized in particular the duchesse d'Angoulême.
In her later editorial years FBA provided the superscript (a) and the recollection: '(a) I could not forbear reciting that proposition to her R.H. [the duchesse] in my conference [see L. 845]—she heard it with a modest blush—but a smile of pleasure.'

[7] The cheapness of everything in Brussels was a wonder to English travellers and French refugees during this period. See, for example, Capel, pp. 45–7.

fugitive friends, & one Belgian Lady[8] has shewn me such excessive kindness—by the most feeling sympathy in all my disasters, & a desire—if I w^d let her—to make her house my own, that she has drawn me from my melancholy *sauvagerie* into a really social intercourse—& not the less readily from her being the wife of a gentleman. M. de Beaufort who was a military Comrade of M. d'A. at Metz or Besançon, when they were both youths, whose Library, as well as his Table (for he is extremely rich) were immediately & warmly at the service of his old Friend, whom he received as a Brother. These are sort of encounters, very sweetning in calamity. Some of our Friends, also, still at Paris, have contrived means to let us know that they will endeavour to save a part, at least, of our property there, should a siezure from M. d'A's belonging to the Maison du Roi, be threatened.

The D. of Wellington lives here in the simplest manner possible for his high Rank—and though, between visiting military posts, conferring with officers of all description, & receiving couriers of all nations, he has not a moment to breath, he yet never looks harried or absent. In defiance of my general seclusion, Music tempted me one night to accompany M. ¦ d'A to hear Catalani sing at the Great Concert Room[9] where were the Reine des pays Bas, & the Hered. prince—the voice of Catalani charmed & astonished me—but well as she is worth looking at besides being heard, my Eyes were rivetted all the night upon The Hopes of World, the D. of W. who was just facing me. I have a faith in him so great that, at his sight, I feel all courage. I was never well enough, unluckily, while he was in Paris to be introduced to his circle, but I once met the Duchess,[10] who was so very good as to immediately recollect having seen me in London at L^y Templetons. Ah! how I sigh to mention it was at an assembly at la p^ss de Beauvaux that I had this meeting!— That poor lady, I am told, is visibly wasting away in consump-

[8] See L. 872 nn. 3, 6.

[9] This was the *Concert Noble* of 27 April (Fleischman, p. 116). Angelica Catalani (1780–1849), the most famous opera singer of the period, was an Italian soprano whose voice was noted for its purity and range. After a false start in a convent at Gubbio, she made her singing debut at Venice in 1796, sang later in Lisbon, Madrid, and Paris, reaching the height of her career in London from 1806 until 1813. She then became manager of the Paris opera, and although this proved a failure she continued to sing with great success until she retired in 1828.

[10] FBA had first met the Duchess of Wellington in July 1813 at the home (65 Portland Place) of Lady Templetown (iii, L. 216 n. 16). See vii, L. 710 nn. 9, 10.

tive grief & shame![11]—I knew HER to be utterly blameless.
M. d'A. has had fresh accounts of her lately from the Duke de
Croix,[12] her Brother in Law. How sorry will L^y Harcourt be![13]—
every body is afflicted for her. She was made dine, lately, at the
'tiny Tiger's' table—& she was so ill during the repast that the
Tiger himself could not help noticing her changed countenance.
She nearly fainted twice!—She is a most sweet & lovely woman,
full of attaching qualities & virtues—& I never think of her
without a pang.

The general opinion here is that hostilities will not begin
till the middle or end of June. How tremendous will be the
opening battle! & how big with consequences! Who can look
forward to it—however sanguine for the ultimate result to the
Just Cause—without awe? |

I have had the infinite satisfaction to hear from L^y Keith
that the benign Magnolia seemed remarkably healthy lately[14]—
& she was allowed, she says, to stand before it, & partake of its
odour, longer than usual—which gave her a gratification of
wh^{ch} she is greatly & duly sensible. She is truly public spirited,
& a high bred *Tory*, she is charmed, she tells me, that her L^d
is brought forward again in this great Cause of Church &
State.[15]

May the perfume of all the charming Flowers—which
entwine the sacred Magnolia be long—long as salubrious as
sweet! & may I ever be admitted to partake of the far-extending
fragrance of the delight giving Honey Suckle!

Permit me, Mad^m with the profoundest respect

& inviolable attachment
to sign myself yr. R.H.:

Sh^d I again be so happy as to be indulged with a cordial—

[11] The princesse de Beauvau-Craon (v, L. 513 n. 2 and L. 842 n. 10), who with
her family had returned to Napoleon's court, was at least able to waste away in
style. By a decree of 7 April she received a gift from Napoleon that included one-
third of the revenues of the estate of Harcourt and the Hôtel d'Harcourt in the rue
de l'Université.

[12] The duc de Croy-Havré (L. 862 n. 13).

[13] The Earl and Countess of Harcourt (v, L. 513 n. 1) bore the English title of
this noble and originally Norman family, and as such they welcomed their kinsmen
when they were *émigrés* in England.

[14] Lady Keith (L. 837 n. 3) and Queen Charlotte. Here FBA reverts to her
botanical code for the English royal family (see v. 361 and L. 837 n. 18).

[15] Lord Keith, though now 69 years of age, was prominent during and after the
Hundred Days both as a naval commander in the Bay of Biscay and as a negotiator
for Napoleon's exile to St. Helena.

which I dare not say how I long for—my name & Brussels are now sufficient direction, for the post man is my only constant visitor. ⎮

878   [1358, Marché au bois], Brussels, 29–30 May 1815

To M. d'Arblay

A.L. (Berg), 29–30 May 1815
Double sheet 4to   4 pp   *pmk*   BRUXELLES   wafer
Addressed: *à Treves.* / À / Monsieur le General *d'Arblay*,— / Officier Superieur du garde / du Corps de sa Majestie / Louis 18.— / Chev^r de St Louis, &c &c / *à TREVES.*
Edited by FBA, p. 1, *annotated*: ✲   (3/2)
See Textual Notes.

ce 29 mai, 1815, Brussells
Lundi matin.

I cannot & will not refuse myself the happiness of telling mon bien bien cher ami, the great delight with which I have just received & read his most unexpected 3^d Letter,[1] dated the 25th—for it has confirmed the work of the 2^d in tranquilizing my so long tortured nerves. ⎡Yet its inquietude would have grieved me, though it was an inquietude hanging only on some inexactitude of the post, had not the dear bit in conclusion, shewn my letter, with Pr Blucher, arrived. I find the post goes to Trèves but 3 times a week. As I wrote but yesterday, I will not send this till the *end* of the week, lest such quick return should frighten you.⎤ Ah ⎡no,⎤ mon ami!—always remember, in defiance of the charm of a long Letter, I shall always—be deeply grateful, while you are thus occupied, for your mere *signature*, with date of *month* & *place*. Let this be *completely* understood; & then, when you can afford me more, my satisfaction will be *complete*.

How I thank you for the D. de Raguse's spirited, admirable,

878.   [1] L. 874.

alive answer to Caulincourt![1] quelle plume de feu! I should like to have it read as the order of the Day upon the entry into France — —

But your health?—ah, how ill I fear it to be fitted for your enterprize! You say not one word upon the subject & hope & project next my heart—but my answer to the opening you have given me to Hope & Happiness was not arrived. I must not say with what excess of impatience I shall wait your reply & resolution. — — I must run away from this subject, or I shall be tempted to enter into plead[ings] that may be *mal à pro pos.*— I must wait silently—not quietly! for that is impossible, your further communications.—Good day, then, good day, till Thursday's post!—

Lundi au soir. The Fates will not spare you from receiving this by the first post, for I have so many things to tell you, that—though no single one of them is *pressée,* the *aggregate,* I think, I ought to send without delay. P^me La D^ss d'Angoulême is just arrived at Gand:[2] & only for a few days!—She returns this very next week to England! Some great & portentous ǀ cause can alone have brought her over for so short a time: it must be to confer upon something not to be committed to paper, not to be entrusted even to the most faithful adherent, & previous to hostilities. To me it appears that it must be relative EITHER to the *ministers* that England wishes to persuade the King to remove & only through this gentle mediatrix can make its wishes known; or some intelligence which that mediatrix, spirited as she is gentle, desires to give herself relative to some project or plot or perspective which she may have learnt in the *Tight,*[3] where she is not surrounded by courtiers. 'Tis certainly some affair of great MOMENT,[4] & great delicacy.

2^d the Duke of Wellington is to have a Review of his principal favourite forces, lately arrived, To-morrow, the 30th May, about 3 lieus off towards Gand.[5] It is imagined the Roi will be there.

---

[2] She arrived on Sunday 28 May (*Moniteur de Gand,* 31 May).
[3] Short for 'Tight little Island' (see above, L. 837 n. 11).
[4] The duchesse d'Angoulême left Ghent on 4 June to return to England, not only to pursue her policy of gaining English support, but also, according to a first-hand source, to dissociate herself from Louis XVIII, who vacillated about everything except court protocol and his own prerogative (Reiset, iii. 195–7).
[5] On this date Wellington reviewed at Grammont the British and King's German Legion cavalry and horse artillery that formed the only resplendent part of his rather dingy army (Fleischman, p. 48).

It is not of more than 15.000 men, but yet, such being the Commander, Expectation is high.

3ly the Duke of Wellington has given another *Ball*.[6] The English ambassadour, on Saturday, gave a sumptuous *dinner*; & last night the Duke gave a superb *supper*. These are looked upon as leave taking civilities!—Ah me!—

Be quick in your resolution!—

4thly I have just had a visit from Mr. Taylor,[7] Inspector general of the Hospital of sick & wounded in the British army — — he has brought me two Letters—& he is of opinion the operations are *very* near, or he should not have been summoned! — ! —

Oh be quick, mon ami!—

Lord Wellington, he told me, will have 150.000 men at his command,[8] but alas, only 40.000 English! This is certain! & much to be lamented.

5thly Ma tante has just told me she hears hostilities will begin in about 8 days! This is the 29th of May!—Ah, see how time presses,—be energetic, & decisive!

6thly The English Ambassadour, Sir Charles Stuart,[9] is gone this morning to Gand, to wait upon La Dss d'Angoulême. His Secretaries are following. I imagine, therefore, he will fix his ministry There during Her stay. |

7thly Le M¹ Blucher came to Brussels yesterday. To confer, sans doute, finally with Lord Wellington. Were you not quite satisfied with his Letter to you? *I* was, completely. But I imagine that neither He nor the D[uke] de F[eltre] will write any more, at this arduous epoch, except to give *fresh* orders. *You*, indeed, cannot want to be *accredité*; who can be so more honourably, than by a Letter from the Duke of Wellington to Marechal Prince Blucher? Nothing, on that score, remains to be wished.

6 FBA and others at first misconstrued the meaning of these affairs. Wellingtons supper on 28 May, as she soon learned and noted below, was given in honour of Blücher, who arrived in Brussels earlier that day.

7 William Taylor (1774–1841), Deputy-Inspector of Hospitals on Wellington's medical staff, had been recalled from half-pay on 25 April (*London Gazette*, 6 May).

8 In the event Wellington had approximately 106,000 troops under his command, but FBA is roughly correct about the small number of British troops—all that could be scraped together from the wreckage of the fine army of 1814, half of which had been disbanded, and many of whose best Peninsular regiments had been sent off on the expedition to America that ended in defeat at the Battle of New Orleans.

9 Stuart (L. 856 n. 19) had in fact established himself at Ghent on 1 April, the day after he received from Castlereagh the letters that accredited him ambassador to the court of Louis XVIII.

153

8^{thly} The neveu of *ma tante* told me, to day, that Vandamme is now *chez Elle*, à Chimay,[10] which is still settled to be in France.— And the neveu told *me*, as well as *her*, that he had reason to believe Buonaparte would endeavour, upon the opening of the War, to make his first attack *here*, as the D. of W. has fewer troops than any of the other powers! & as this is the most open to attack, from the nature & defenceless state of the country.

I tell you this thus openly, to spare your horrour should it happen, & all the sufferings of the exquisite fears & feelings which I know well it would excite, by giving you my solemn word I shall go instantly to make an arrangement with the Boyds, to do whatever They will do: for alas—poor Mme de Beaufort is too ill to afford me the asylum promised!—I could not, at such a time, add any weight to M. de Beaufort—but I will run even now to the Boyds, to prevent leaving you in any suspence, by enquiring into their projects.—

10 at night. Eh bien, I am returned, after a long visit & conference. They were already apprized of the notion that a *coup de main* might bring the Enemy hither — — & in that case, they mean to go to *Anvers*—whither, should I find nothing else more eligible, I shall accompany them. Mr. Boyd is to keep upon the Watch for intelligence,—as I shall, *de mon coté*, through Mme d' H & he will secure Carriages, &c. Therefore be under no uneasiness, for I shall be in good hands, & *Miss Ann*[11] is enchanted at the idea— |

I have made, however, no agreement—I have only made enquiries by which I see this step is in my power, & I have engaged them to immediately acquaint me if they hear tidings that lead to removal. I hope—I MUST HOPE this is a measure that will never be necessary. I am only willing, *en cas* d'*evenement*, to set your mind at ease as to my safety—should we, alas, be still asunder!—But oh — — how anxiously shall I wait your decision! your *final* decision! which, I am well aware, I ought not to influence by my wishes—& therefore I will not dwell upon them. Always write *here* where the people will always

---

[10] The comte de Latour du Pin (L. 873 n. 2), the princesse d'Hénin's nephew, reported that General Vandamme* (1770–1830), one of the most ferocious of Napoleon's generals and commander of the 3rd Corps of the *armée du Nord*, had reached her estate at Chimay, on the French side of the frontier.

[11] Anne Isabelle Boyd (*fl.* 1797–1834), daughter of Walter Boyd (L. 870 n. 2) and his wife Harriet Anne Greene Goddard (*c.* 1762–1833). By 1834 Anne had become the wife of Foster Petrie (*fl.* 1833) and appears to have lived in Paris.

stay, & I shall engage their care of my Letters. Should I be absent. Mme de Maurville is fixed to stay at all events. The streets here are, at this moment, actually covered with English soldiers. The Fête chez Lord Wellington was given, I find, for M^l Blücher. I have no doubt I should personally be safe & unmolested *here*, at a native's house,—but if I could not receive Letters from you I should expire of terrific apprehensions. My 2 Letters from England were entirely on the Irish Business,[12] from Martin & my Sister. Nothing is yet arranged, but Esther is fearfully in haste. Alex was quite well, & in James Street. Why he answers not my first Letter, which begged him to go to Richmond, I know not.[13]—Martin's Letter is dated the 16th May: the day you wrote to me from Liege.

Spain has declared War against Buonaparte[14] & its armies are preparing to pour across the Pyranees.—M. La Tour du Pin is nominated Ambassadour to the King des pays Bas.[15] Lord Wellington's niece, L^y Fitzroy Somerset,[16] has just lain in here: certainly, therefore, he is sure B[uonaparte] cannot come these 3 weeks; he would not else have suffered her to *faire ses couches* where she might be surprised & taken prisoner. M. de Lally is here. I saw him this morning. Some of his Manifestos were sent to Lille,[17] & received with applause:—but the bearer was discovered—& shot!

Mon ami—mon eternellement cher Ami—Listen! I *EARN-ESTLY* entreat you to give up your night studies, to retire early to rest: you will else exhaust your strength—& by trying imprudently to do *All*, be able, from fatigued spirits, & over-strained faculties, to do nothing. Oh Listen while it is yet Time!

[12] Both letters are missing.

[13] L. 869.

[14] The Spanish declaration of war was accompanied by a lengthy diatribe against Napoleon as the overthrower of Louis XVIII, whose propagandists published the declaration in full (*Moniteur de Gand*, 26 May).

[15] Latour du Pin had the year before been accredited to the Dutch court at The Hague and continued to hold that appointment during his absence as one of the French ambassadors at the Congress of Vienna. On his return he resumed his post at what had in the meantime become the court of the King of the Netherlands.

[16] Lady Fitzroy Somerset (L. 858 n. 3), encouraged by Wellington, remained in Brussels for her confinement, and her decision reassured many of the English and French residents (Capel, p. 100). She gave birth to a daughter, Charlotte Elizabeth (1815–*post* 1901).

[17] In a remarkable letter to Wellington (*Supp. Desp.* x. 184–5) Lally advocated the wholesale distribution of this manifesto, by which he hoped to achieve nothing less than the conversion of French opinion into a new and deeper loyalty to Louis XVIII. No one, however, was shot for carrying it to Lille (L. 901, p. 260).

I hope you have sent to M. de Premorel,[18] who is dying to join you. |

Tuesday Mai 30. The solemn Declaration of *Toutes les Puissances à Vienne*,[19] is published. I have just read it. It proclaims War inveterate against Buonaparte & All French men who adhere to him without distinction. Ah God!—*nos choux!*—

⌐P.S. I will not take up your Time, at this busy period, with such long letters except upon PARTICULAR subjects.¬

879   Trèves, 31 May 1815

M. d'Arblay
To Madame d'Arblay

A.L. (Berg), 31 May 1815
Double sheet 4to   4 pp.   *pmk* TRIER   seal
Addressed: À Madame / Madame d'Arblay / marché au bois Nº 1358 / à Bruxelles
Edited by FBA, p. 1, *annotated*: ⌐14¬   (5/1)—   [*with numbers on address fold*]: 14   14   5   5
See further, Textual Notes.

Treves ce 31 May 1815

Je t'ecris ma chere bonne amie de chez le Marechal *ferrand*,[1] tandis qu'on ferre mes chevaux. Tu me demandes pourquoi je choisis ce moment. parceque madᵉ l'Athanase je n'en ai pas d'autre à ma disposition; attendu que n'ayant pas mon aide de camp avec moi je suis obligé de griffonner du matin au soir. J'ai donc pris ⟨ce moment⟩ pour ne pas perdre la poste et te dire que je desire avec la plus vive impatience d'avoir de

---

[18] See L. 868 n. 3.

[19] This document, published in a Supplement to the *Moniteur de Gand* of 26 May, while confirming much of the earlier declaration of 13 March, weakens Louis XVIII's position by separating the war against Napoleon from any attempt to restore him to his throne—a weakness that Talleyrand artfully described as a strength in a letter to the King of 17 May (Talleyrand, p. 425).

879.   [1] Perhaps a word-play on *maréchal-ferrant* (farrier) and *comte de Ferrand* (L. 835 n. 8), Louis XVIII's postmaster-general. M. d'A's emphasis strengthens the possibility.

tes nouvelles. Tu dois aussi savoir que je suis bien plus content de ma santé qui dans ce moment est tout à fait bonne. [xxxxx 2½ *lines*] J'ai pour prendre soin de moi un exemple sous les yeux qui ne me sera pas inutile. Il y a quelques jours que le General Kleith[2] devant faire manoeuvrer une partie des Troupes qu'il commande dans les environs, eut la très grande imprudence de quitter un gilet de flanelle qu'il avait jusqu'alors porté constament. Il fesait ici fort chaud, et rien ne paraissait plus naturel: mais l'endroit où l'on a manoeuvré etant fort chaud, la temperature de l'air s'y est trouvée si differente qu'après ǀ et pendant la manoeuvre, l'air froid qui l'avait saisi lui a occasionné une jaunisse qui depuis 6 jours le retient au lit où il est fort malade quoiqu'un peu mieux. Il aurait été moins aimable pour moi que je lui souhaiterais un prompt retablissement. Juge si je le desire avec impatience. Il est impossible d'etre mîeux pour ton athanase. J'ai aussi beaucoup à me louer du General Müller[3] qui commande les Hessois. Cet officier est le seul qui ait suivi l'Electeur:[4] aussi ce Prince l'a t'il nominé General à son retour quoiqu'il ne fut en quittant la Hesse que Major de Genie. C'est le même qui chargé l'année derniere du siege de Thionville[5] a laissé beaucoup de regrets dans ce pays lorsqu'il l'a quitté, comme vient de me le

[2] Kleist's malady, which was soon to force him to give up his command, was caused by a gall-bladder and liver infection. It overcame him on 25 May during the manœuvres mentioned by M. d'A and forced him to spend two days in a regimental field hospital before he could return to Trèves (Pflugk-Harttung, p. 268).

[3] Moritz von Müller (1780–1837) did indeed play an important rôle in his country's struggle against the French. From *Oberstleutnant* and chief of the Hessian *kurfürstlichen Legion* in 1809 he was promoted to *Oberst* by the Elector, who made him his adjutant at allied headquarters during the 1813 campaign. He rose to *General-major* in 1814 and in 1815, to deputy commander (as M. d'A notes more correctly in L. 880 below) of the Hessian Corps in the *Norddeutschen Bundescorps*.

[4] Formerly Landgrave Wilhelm IX (1785), Wilhelm I of Hesse-Cassel (1743–1821), Elector, had attained his higher title in 1803 when his state was raised to an electorate. He had been forced into exile and fled to Prague in 1808, less than a year after his territories had been swallowed up in the Napoleonic Kingdom of Westphalia. A rising of Hessian patriots in 1809 failed in its immediate goal but created a spirit of national resistance that, with the help of the Prussian army, brought Wilhelm back to his throne in 1813. See Philipp Losch, *Geschichte des Kurfürstentums Hessen, 1803 bis 1866* (Marburg, 1922), pp. 20–94.

[5] Thionville was one of several border fortresses invested during the winter campaign of 1814 by the invading Prussian, Austrian, and Russian armies, whose commanders had, however, learned from Napoleon the futilty of assaulting such strong-points. They therefore generally limited their sieges to encirclement and bombardment—tactics for which Müller's training as a sapper fitted him very well. During both this siege and that of 1815, Thionville was held for Napoleon by Victor Hugo's father, Joseph-Leopold-Sigisbert Hugo (1773–1828).

31 May 1815

dire un Monsieur de Balthazar[6] frere d'un off[er] d'Artillerie de
la plus grande experience guillotiné à Metz il y a 23 ans.[7]
J'etais commandant des Eleves quand ce malheureux jeune
homme a été reçu officier, et Malavillars[8] et moi nous passions
en quelque sorte notre vie chez sa grand-maman Madame
d'Hayange[9] dame du bourg de ce nom près de Metz et pro-
prietaire non seulement des superbes forges qui y sont etablies,
mais encore de presque tous les grands etablissemens de ce
genre. Mon intime liaison avec cette famille venait de ce que
j'avais été attaché environ deux ans | à ces forges avec Gassendy
et plusieurs autres de nos camarades. L'ainé des fils de M[de]
d'Hayange,[10] Mr de Vendel homme du plus grand merite et
au quel j'avais eu le bonheur de rendre un três grand service
sous le Ministère de Mr de Narbonne est mort de chagrin il y a
plus de 20 ans. [xxxxx 14 *lines*]

Je t'ai hier, ma bonne amie, encore plus regretté que de
coutume, si toutefois cela est possible. J'etais à Mr Naile's
Landechen,[11] ce | qui veut dire, le petit pays de Mr Nail

---

6 Georges-Victor-*Alexandre* de Balthazar de Gacheo (1781–1848), baron de
Balthazar, emigrated in 1793 with his family, was raised at the court of Hesse-
Cassel, entered the Swiss régiment de Diesbach (in French service) in 1801 as a
sous-lieutenant, distinguished himself in Italian and German campaigns, and was
promoted lieutenant-colonel. In 1808 he entered the service of Mecklenburg, whose
army he reorganized and trained. He left military life in 1809 and returned to the
Moselle region, where his family, originally of Bohemian origin, had long been
settled, until 1821, when he entered the civil service as a Treasury official, a post
that he held until his death.
7 François-Ignace-Louis de Balthazar de Gacheo (1771–93) had gone on from
his acquaintance with M. d'A as an officer-cadet at artillery school to enter as a
sous-lieutenant the régiment d'Auxonne (artillerie), but with the fall of the monarchy he resigned his commission. Refusing to swear allegiance to the new revolutionary government, he was condemned to death and executed at Metz in the
place de la Comédie in October 1793.
8 Probably Jean-Georges de Hault de Malavillers (1730–*post* 1787), an artillery
officer senior to M. d'A who was promoted colonel in 1767, commanded the
régiment de Toul (which M. d'A had joined as a lieutenant en 2e in 1769) until
1774, when he was posted to the artillery school at Auxonne.
9 Louise de Wendel *née* Le Vayer (1714–1802), the widow of Armand-Louis de
Wendel (*c.* 1705–42) and virtual suzeraine of Hayange, where the Wendel family
established in 1704 the ironworks that created their great fortune, fifteen years
later building the château that M. d'A visited. The ironworks at Hayange were
confiscated when the Wendels, many of whom were army or naval officers, began
to emigrate, but 'Madame d'Hayange' (who was then 80) managed to hold on to
other property whose sale in 1799 provided part of the money with which the
family bought back the ironworks in 1808 for 220,000 francs. See Henry Contamine,
Metz et la Moselle de 1814 à 1870 (Nancy, 2 vols., 1932), i, 200–1.
10 Ignace de Wendel (1741–95), who died an *émigré*. His dealings with Narbonne,
who was War Minister from 7 Dec. 1791 until 9 Mar. 1792, may well have concerned arms manufacture at Hayange or the family's control over the ironworks.
11 Nells Ländchen, a park for which Christophe-Philippe-Bernard-Hugues Nell

chez qui je suis logé. Imagine toi que Monsseaux[12] et même Trianon ne sont rien compares à ce jardin delicieux. C'est reellement le Paradis terrestre. Ecris moi donc, ma bonne amie. J'ai assez bien reussi ici, de toute maniere, et si le Gal Kleïth recouvre la santé, comme je l'espere, je serai fort content de ma position, et je crois pouvoir me flatter d'être ici fort utile. Mais j'en suis encore à recevoir un mot de Gand. Je ne puis concevoir un silence aussi obstiné. Comment se porte Lally? Ne manque pas d'ecrire à la dame Isabeau la belle et bonne.[13] Mille et mille choses à M[r] et M[de] de Beaufort et rappelle moi au souvenir de la Princesse[14] et de Mad[me] de La Tour du Pin et de Maurville & ——.

880   [Trèves], 3–4 June 1815

M. d'Arblay
To Madame d'Arblay

A.L.S. (Berg), 3–4 juin 1815
Double sheet 4to   4 pp.   *pmk*   TRIER   seal
Addressed: À Madame / Madame d'Arblay marché / au bois N° 1358 / À Bruxelles
Edited by FBA, p. 1, *annotated and dated*: (6/I)— 1815   1815 3[d] June 1815   p. 3: × (I) [*with numbers on address fold*]: (15) (15) (6) (6) *See further*, Textual Notes.

Helas! ma bien chere amie! mes desirs ni mes craintes n'ont pu changer: mais tu dois sentir que mes projets ne peuvent plus être les mêmes. Pardonne le moi, et dis toi bien que ma

(1753–*post* 1825), with one of his brothers, purchased land in 1796, consists of parkland around a small lake on which there are five small islands. It rapidly became known as a 'parc d'agrément'. See C. H. Delamorre, *Annuaire topographique et politique du département de la Sarre pour l'an 1810* (Trèves, 1810), p. 162. When Nell, an important figure in the business and social life of the city and a deputy for the Sarre from 1808 till 1814, first visited and improved his park it was over a mile outside and to the north-east of Trèves, near the banks of the Moselle river. It is now one of the city's parks.
12 Monceau, near which park in Paris the d'Arblays had lived during the summer of 1802 (v, L. 517 n. 2).
13 The Princess Elizabeth.
14 The princesse d'Hénin.

seule ambition est de remplir, autant qu'il est en moi, ce que je regarde comme des devoirs sacrés pour tout Français que sa position et ses moyens de quelque genre qu'ils soient, mettent à même d'être de la moindre utilité pour le succès si important d'une cause et si juste et si sainte. Sur cela, je pense, et penserai toujours tout ce que j'ai dit avec tant de vivacité à notre ⟨Tante⟩ quand elle regrettait de voir son ami[1] appellé à Gand pour n'y remplir une place qu'elle ne considera pas comme assez importante pour un homme d'un merite aussi superieur.[1] O mon amie tout ce que tu as trouvé dans les deux lignes que je benis ᴵ puisqu'elles t'ont fait tant de bien, est dans mon coeur; et toujours la même pensée y tiendra la premiere place; mais dans un tems comme celui ci, rester tranquille serait une lacheté dont ma Fanny ne peut desirer que je me rende coupable. Ma santé est excellente en ce moment; et je n'ai qu'à me louer des egards avec les quels je suis traité sans pourtant être très satisfait du reste relativement à ma mission qui porte ombrage et gêne beaucoup. le Gal Kleith a fait mettre une sentinelle à ma porte et le Gal Engelhard[2] comm[dt] du Corps de Troupe Hessois m'a fait l'honneur de m'inviter aujourdhui à une fête qu'il donne à l'occasion du jour de naissance de S.A.R. l'Electeur son Souverain. Je vais je crois faire imprimer aujourdhui un appel aux braves, sur le quel j'aurais bien voulu avoir ton avis: mais le tems qui me presse ne me le permet pas. Il ne me donne pas même ᴵ le loisir de t'en donner copie ici. Je n'ai de possibilité en ce moment que celle de te remercier de tes trois lettres toutes arrivées à bon port.[3] Merci, merci pour toutes trois, mais surtout pour les nouvelles que contient celle du 29 may. Elle est arrivée en même tems que celle du 18 cràrd. il y a au plus 3/4 d'heure Pauvre Pauvre Beaufort! que je le plains! je lui ai ecrit il y a quelques jours ! Continue à me donner de tes nouvel-

---

880.   [1] Lally-Tolendal, as Jaucourt observed in a contemporary letter to Talleyrand, placed a higher value on his propagandist's work than did others at Ghent: 'pour manier la plume, nous avons MM. Lally, Chateaubriand. Celui-là veut que sa première phrase soit payé du titre de ministre du roi' (Jaucourt, p. 261).
   [2] Karl Joachim von Engelhardt (1755–1821) had like Müller been a part of the Elector's staff during his Prague exile and later during the campaigns against Napoleon (Losch, p. 93; Pflugk-Harttung, pp. 121–4), as a result of which he rose to become lieutenant-general in Hessian service. He arrived in Trèves in April and took command of the Kurhessische Corps, within which Müller commanded the 2nd Brigade (Plotho, App., p. 54).
   [3] Ll. 872, 876, 878.

les, et joins toi à moi pour prier le Ciel de nous reunir bientôt
—amen !

A. d'Arblay

Treves ce 3. Juin 1815.

Par le plus grand bonheur, je n'ai point envoyé ma lettre à
la poste, et me voici de retour pour causer avec toi, aussi
longtems [que] cela me sera possible (Ce 4 à 4^h du matin)
que cela ne t'effraye pas. Dès que je ne dors point, je me
leve et me mets à travailler. J'en ai tellement l'habitude actuellement que cela ne me fatigue pas du tout. À aucune epoque de
ma vie même lorsque je retournais au Ministere l'après diner,
je n'ai autant ecrit. Ma santé n'en souffre nullement. Seulement
j'avais hier soir les yeux fatigués mais 4 heures de repos font
que je ne m'en apperçois plus. Cette activité m'est utile,
necessaire et même indispensable: car je puis dire que je suis
seul absolument seul, attendu que Mr de Maz[4] — qui est
fort bon enfant, fort aimable, et assez spirituel, est bien le
plus paresseux de tous les hommes. Hier lorsque je me felicitais
de n'avoir pas fait partir encore ma lettre, parce que nous
pourrions causer quelque tems encore, tout celui dont j'ai
cru pouvoir disposer a été forcement employé à faire subir un
long interrogatoire à un déserteur et à dresser du tout un procès
verbal que je n'ai pu finir qu'à minuit. Le diner s'est passé
à merveille. Le Lieutenant General Engelhard [1] et le Prince
Frederic de Cassel[5] en ont fait les honneurs avec beaucoup de
Grace. J'ai été placé à la droite du Prince et l'off^r General[6]
remplaçant le G^{al} en chef Kleith à la gauche du Lieut^{nt} Gen^{al}
à sa Gauche etait un Prince off^{er} G^{al} dont j'ai oublié le nom,[7]

---

[4] Mazancourt's service dossier which sums him up as 'assez médiocre', supports
M. d'A's opinion.

[5] This was Friedrich Wilhelm (1790–1875), Prinz von Hesse-Cassel, then a colonel
in the service of the King of the Netherlands and commander of the Cavalry
Brigade in the *Deutsche Armee-Corps*, whose over-all commander was General von
Kleist.

[6] George Dubislaw Ludwig von Pirch* (1763–1838), who before Kleist's illness
had commanded the 5th Brigade, was a Prussian *General-major*. M. d'A calls him
by the higher rank to identify him as Kleist's temporary successor. He is usually
called 'Pirch I' or 'Pirch der 1ste' to distinguish him from his younger brother Otto
Karl Lorenz von Pirch* (1765–1824)—'Pirch II'—who was also a Prussian general
serving in Blücher's army.

[7] There were two other generals in the army at Trèves who were also princes:
General-major Wilhelm Heinrich Casimir, Prinz von Solms-Braunfels (1765–1852),

et j'avais à ma droite le General Müller,[8] Commandant en second le Corps Hessois. J'entre dans ce detail pour te montrer les egards qu'on a pour le Souverain que je represente comme etant l'off^{er} present le plus elevé en grade de son armée. Je puis ajouter que personellement, j'ai eu aussi beaucoup à me louer de la manière dont j'ai été traité. Des details à un autre tems. Voici la copie de ce que je veux faire imprimer

> *Appel aux braves* Francais! Sensibles à la voix de l'honneur, quittez l'etendard de la revolte, p^r rejoindre le drapeau sans tache qu'a deployé comme signal de ralliement le monarque le plus digne de rendre heureux un grand peuple. En fuyant ainsi le monstrueux assemblage de l'Anarchie et du Despotisme, pour retrouver, sous le meilleur des Peres, le Gouvernement le plus juste comme le plus doux, vous vous reunirez à des camarades dont le plus grand bonheur sera de vous recevoir comme des freres. — Camarades! c'est p^r remplir l'honnorable mission de ramener des enfans egarés, près d'un Pere, dont ils doivent connoitre l'inepuisable bonté, que je suis venu sur la frontiere ainsi que plusieurs de mes compagnons — Venez nous y joindre. — Vous y trouverez secours pecuniaires, protection, et toute la liberté compatible avec le respect dû aux lois protectrices de l'Ordre social.
>
> Soldats Français, c'est au nom de notre legitime souverain, c'est de par le Roi Louis XVIII, que cet appel vous est fait — surs de jouir, en arrivant, des appointemens affectés à votre Grade, Venez meriter, avec nous, la distinction que son ordonnance du 17 May dernier assure aux braves qui lui seront fideles.
>
> Je joins ici copie de cette ordonnance
>
> Signé. A. P. d'Ay

J'ai voulu dans cet appel bien constater qu'obeissant, comme je le fais aux ordres de mon Souverain legitime par principe d'honneur, je ne puis être confondu avec un vil ambassadeur qui cherche à détourner *de leur devoir* de braves militaires. Mais dusse-je-être fusillé comme l'infortuné colporteur du Manifeste du Roi,[9] je mourrais plus tranquille que ne le sont

who commanded the 1st Brigade of the *Kurhessische Corps*; and *General-lieutenant* Friedrich-Ludwig, Erbprinz (i.e. hereditary prince) von Mecklenburg-Schwerin (1778–1819), who commanded the Mecklenburg contingent in the army.

[8] See L. 879 n. 3.

[9] Kleist's staff officers were clearly suspicious of M. d'A's intentions (Pflugk-Harttung, p. 95)—suspicions which his rousing Proclamation must have increased.

ou que ne doivent l'être les au[tres] [*blot*] dont ils n'ont pas su prévoir et dont ils ne pourront arreter [*blot*].

J'avais l'idée de te prier d'aller à Gand pour y presenter ton hommage à l'heroine du siecle:[10] mais j'y renonce, parce que dans le doute si tu pourrais y trouver un logement, je serais trop tourmenté de te savoir exposée à ne savoir où trouver un azyle — J'ai monté ce matin à cheval et je recois à l'instant une tres aimable lettre du Gal Kleist qui m'invite à partager chez lui aujourdhui un diner de malade avec Mr de Mazancourt.[11]

Au nom de tout ce que tu as de plus cher, ma bonne Fanny, ecris moi autant que possible de bien longues lettres, c'est mon seul bonheur, et j'en serai peut être sitôt privé! —

Tres certainement, ma bonne amie, je n'ai d'autre ambition que celle de planter mes choux que je ne veux point que ma Fanny arrose de pleurs qu'auraient fait couler de justes regrets si elle me voyait tourmenté de la crainte d'avoir encouru quelque reproche. Ah que les intrigans, et les faux amis de l'infortuné Louis XVIII lui ont fait et lui font encore de mal! Ils verront le fruit qu'ils retireront de leur acharnement à propager à inoculer en quelque sorte, partout et jusque chez les alliés le venin de leur medisance. Qu'ils s'appretent à en supporter les effets desastreux. Ils ont sappé dans son fondement la noble confiance qui animait les soutiens d'une cause sainte. Et je ne vois partout à la place de ce moyen puissant de succès, qu'incertitude ouvertement avouée et craintes mal deguisées.

Oh oui, oui et de tout mon coeur, de toute mon ame, je me joins de tout mon être à toi pour adresser au Ciel la priere qui finit ta lettre. *Heaven bless thee—us—all; & re-unite us! id est three. never, never more to be parted!*

Continue, ma chere Fanny à m'ecrire tout ce que tu sauras, et pardonne moi de n'avoir point fait ce que je desire plus que toi!

[xxxxx 14 *lines marginal writing*]

[10] The duchesse d'Angoulême.
[11] See L. 868 n. 2.

[1358, Marché au bois,
                                    Brussels], 29 May–4 June 1815

To M. d'Arblay

A.L. (rejected Diary MSS. 6616–19, Berg), 29 May–4 June 1815
Double sheet 4to   4 pp.   *pmk*   BRUXELLES   wafer
Addressed: *Treves* / À / M. le General d'Arblay, / Offic^r Superieur des
Gardes / du Corps du Roi de France, / Chev^r de St Louis, &c &c / à /
Treves.
Docketed: 9th   0
Edited by FBA, p. 1 (6616), *annotated*: ⸬   (4/2)
Edited also at the Press. *See* Textual Notes.

MONDAY–MAY 29. 1815

I am so much struck with *THE DECLARATION OF LES PUISSANCES*
at Vienna, that, in the fear you have not seen it, I will make
some Extracts.—et quelques abrégés.[1]

⌜*Conference du 12 mai, 1815.*⌝
La commission chargée d'examiner si après les événemens qui
se sont passés dipuis le retour de Napoleon Buonaparte en
France, et ensuite des pieces publieés à Paris sur la Declaration
que les puissances ont fait émaner contre lui le 13 Mars, il
seroit nécéssaire de proceder à une nouvelle Declaration, a
presenté à la Seance de ce jour le rapport qui suit.

*   *   *   *   *[2]

⌜*Pr. Question.*⌝
La position de Buonaparte vis à vis les Puissances de l'Europe
a t-elle changé par les premiers succès de son entreprise, ou
par les événemens qui se sont passés depuis son arrivée à
Paris?
LES PUISSANCES, informées du debarquem^t. de B[uonaparte]
en France, n'ont pu voir en lui qu'un homme qui, en se portant
sur le territoire français à main armée, et avec le projet avoué
de renversé le Gouvernement établi, en usurpant le titre de
l'Empereur des Français (a) avoit encouru les peines que toutes

881.   [1] See above, L. 878 n. 17. The form of FBA's abridged text suggests that
she copied it from the supplement to the *Moniteur de Gand* of 26 May.
   [2] FBA uses these marks throughout her abridgement to show omissions.

les legislations prononcent contre de pareils attentats un homme
* * * ennemi implacable du bien public. Tels fut l'origine
et les motifs de la declaration du 13 Mars Declaration que
l'opinion générale a sanctionée.

Les événemens qui ont conduit B. à Paris, et qui lui ont
rendu, p^r le moment l'exercise du pouvoir supreme, n'ont pu
créer aucun droit, et sont nuls sous le point de vue legal.
* * * Les Puissances connoissent trop bien les principes qui
doivent les guider dans leurs rapports avec un pays indépen-
dent pour entreprendre de s'immiscer dans ses affaires intér-
ieures; * * mais elles savent aussi que la liberté d'une Nation
de changer son systeme de gouvernem^t doit avoir ses justes
limites * * et que les Puissances étrangères ont le droit de
protester contre l'abus qu'elle pourrait en faire à leurs dépens;
et elles ne renonceront jamais au droit d'empêcher que, sous
le titre de gouvernement, il ne s'établisse en France un foyer
de désordres et de bouleversements pour les autres états.
Elles respecteront la liberté de France par tout où elle ne sera
pas incompatible avec la tranquilité générale de l'Europe.
* * * L'abolition du pouvoir que l'on prétend y rétablir
aujourd'hui étoit la condition fondamentale d'un traité de
paix sur lequel reposaient tous les rapports qui, jusqu'au
retour de B. à Paris, ont subsisté entre la France et le reste de
l'Europe. Le Jour de leur entrée à Paris, les souverains dé-
clarèrent qu'il ne traiteraient jamais de la Paix avec B, . * * et
cette Declaration amena l'abdication de Napoleon, et forma
la base de la Negociation. La Nation française ne peut se
soustraire à cette condition fondamentale sans renverser |
le traité de Paris, et tous ses rapports avec le systeme de
l'Europe. La *Volonte*, mème, du peuple français, supposé
qu'elle soit parfaitment libre, ne suffit pas pour rétablir,
dans le sens *legal*, un Gouvernement proscrit par des engage-
mens solennels, que ce même peuple avoit pris avec toutes les
puissances de l'Europe * * * l'Exclusion de B. avoit été
la condition préalable de tout arrangement pacifique avec la
France * * *.

⌐*2de Question.*¬

L'offre de sanctioner le traité de Paris, peut-elle changer
les dispositions des Puissances?

La Traité de Paris a reconcilié la France avec l'Europe. * * *

c'étoit un bienfait immense pour un pays réduit, par le délire de son Chef, à la situation la plus désastreuse. * * * Mais — jamais en traitant avec B. — Elles n'eussent consenti aux conditions qu'Elles accordèrent à un Gouvernement lequel, en offrant à l'Europe un gage de stabilité, les dispensait d'exiger de la France les garanties qu'Elles lui avoient demandées sous son ancien Gouvernem^t (*b*) Cette clause est inseparable du traité de Paris: l'abolir, c'est rompre ce traité. * * * La Question a donc cessé d'être une Question de droit; elle n'est plus qu'une Question de calcul politique, et de prevoyance; dans laquelle les puissances n'ont qu'à consulter que les intérêts réels de leurs peuples, et l'intérêt commun de l'Europe. * * * * L'Homme qui, en offrant aujourd'hui de sanctionner le traité de Paris pretend substituer sa garantie à celle d'un Souverain dont la loyauté étoit sans tâche, et la bienveillance sans mésure, est le même qui, pendant 15 ans, a ravagé et boulversé la terre pour trouver de quoi satisfaire son ambition. * * * * * que la plus grande partie des envahissemens a eu lieu pendant les perfides intervalles de Paix — plus funestes à l'Europe que les Guerres mêmes! C'est ainsi qu'il s'empara du Piemont, de Parme, de Genes, de Lucques, des états de Rome, de la Hollande * * * &c même du Portugal et de l'Espagne.[3] * * * La Paix avec un Gouvernement placé entre de telles mains, et composé de tels élémens, ne seroit qu'un état perpetuel d'incertitude, d'anxiété et de danger. Aucune Puissance ne pouvant effectivem^t désarmer, * * le peuple seroient écrasés de charges de toutes espèces; l'industrie et la commerce languiraient par-tout; rien ne serait stable dans les relations politiques * * * et l'Europe en alarmes s'attendrait à une nouvelle explosion. * * une Guerre ouverte est préférable à un pareil état de choses.

⌐*3me* QUESTION.¬

Est il nécéssaire de publier une Nouvelle Declaration

La Declaration du 13 Mars a été dictée aux Puissances par des motifs d'une justice decisive: ces motifs subsistent encore dans toute leur force, — * * En consequence, la commission est d'avis qu'il serait inutile d'émettre une Nouvelle Declaration.

---

[3] This list appeared as note 7 in the *Moniteur de Gand* for 26 May.

Suivent les signatures dans l'ordre alphabetique des Cours.[4]

l'Empereur, convaincu de la position critique où il a placé la France, et de l'impossibilité où il se trouve de la sauver lui-même, a paru se resigner et consentir à l'abdication entière, et sans aucune restriction.

Lettre du Mar^chal Ney au Prince de Benevent, Fontaine-bleau, 5 avril, 1814. voy. Moniteur du 7. avril 1814.[5]

(a) l'article prem^r du 11 Avril 1814, est conçu en ces termes: L'Emp. Nap: renonce pour lui et ses successeurs à tout droit de Souveraineté et de pouvoir, non seulem^t sur l'Empire fr: et sur le royaume d'Italie mais sur tout autre pays. —[6]

Thursday
Bruxelles, ce 1^r Juin
1815

Mon Ami! mon si cher Ami! Vous voulez donc absolument me re-animer? Encore une Lettre!— ⌐Ah — — shall I go back to those times so dear to me! When to write to your Athanase seemed as essential to *your* happiness as to receive your Letters was to her!! — — but youth done—⟨hélas⟩ how smooth, how even *chearfully* comparatively!—will my hours flow to-day, with such a thought! — — but let me haste to speak of M. de Pre-morel[7] — — is it possible he is not yet with you? He has sent 5 Letters—but concluding you had written, as you intended, from Liege to beg he would join you, I thought it needless to send by post intelligence that he would give you himself. Yesterday, however, I was really concerned to find by a Gentleman he sent hither, Le Chev^e Louis d'Argy,[8] de Sedan, that he was still waiting your summons.

Is it [a del]ay? I don't suppose that your decision for yourself

---

[4] In their original order the signatories were Austria, Spain, France, Great Britain, Portugal, Prussia, Russia, and Sweden.
[5] Note 4 (in its entirety) in the *Moniteur de Gand* (*supra*).
[6] Originally note 1.
[7] See L. 868 n. 3.
[8] 'Louis' may be a mistake or a nickname for Charles-Augustin d'Argy (1795–*post* 1846), chevalier and later (1818) comte d'Argy, who had been born in South-ampton while his parents were *émigrés* in England. He had just excaped from Sedan where since 10 Oct. 1814 he had been a capitaine-commandant in the 1er régiment des cuirassiers de la garde du roi. When that regiment, formerly part of the Imperial Guard, went over to Napoleon in March, Argy remained loyal to Louis XVIII, whom he then followed to Ghent.

is for a moment to preclude your requesting him? NOT a word upon the subject most interesting to me of all others is there in this last Letter—I looked for it with an eager anxiety quite indescribable—but you had not yet received my answer — — the Letters are cruelly long on the road. Your Jeudi le 25 May arrived NOW to-day Jeudi le 1ʳ Juin. It is only 3 times a week they set out hence, or arrive.

M. de Lally as I have mentioned in my last is gone to Gand, to pay his devoirs to La dˢˢ d'Angoulême; so is Mᵐᵉ d'H[énin], but I will urge whoever is first to return ici about des Moniteurs. (I answer today to a Letter en route—one since parting! I [have] yet to write for the 2 of Friday.)⁷¹

How you comfort me by your assurances of renewed health — — Pray guard it beyond all things. Without it, what is life but toil, lamentation, & uselessness? I know how sorry you will be that I can still give you no better account of poor Mᵐᵉ de Beaufort![9]—I must keep back for leaving paper to add the latest news—but it is *bien doux* to me to write at different periods, so as to seem in converse with you the more frequently.

Saturday, June 3ᵈ:—M. de Beaufort has just sent me your Letter to him[10]—How I feel its tender solicitude! alas, it compels me, nevertheless, to own the melancholy tale, now good Mᵐᵉ de Beaufort is no more! I know so well how you built upon her kindness, that I could not bear to tell you This my so new & unexpected disappointment. I went twice a day during her short illness but she was confined, by medical order, to see only her Relations. Even Mᵐᵉ de Maurville was not admitted. Her illness was a pleurisie. What a loss! Let me hasten, however, to tell you that the idea of B.—'s coming hither loses ground every moment. I believe it was a false alarm. M. d'Argy, who ¹ came so lately from Sedan does not believe it at all probable. He would not dare, he says, quit France by this Quarter, when he knows so many troops, of all NATIONS, ready to enter it by every other. The encreasing quantity of British troops in this Town just now is amazing. The Natives have hardly room to walk in their own streets.

---

⁹ Mme de Beaufort (L. 872 n. 3) had died on 26 May.

¹⁰ M. d'A's letter 'en route' is that written from Liège 16 May (L. 872) The '2 of Friday' are Ll. 875 and 876. The postal service that carried his letters to FBA left Trèves for Brussels via Luxembourg every Monday, Thursday, and Saturday at 5 a.m. (Delamorre, p. 432).

The brave scotch Highlanders are proudly amongst the fore-most.[11] They all conduct themselves here in a manner the most exemplary. How awful is this pause! How, & in what manner will it terminate? I shudder—but try vainly to run from the subject. I will call *you* from it, however, for a moment, by telling you how I have been entertained by a recital of a Gentleman just come from Paris that has reached me. B. had again given out his expectations of the arrival of his Empress & Son:[12] a mob gathered round the Thuilleries, shouting '*Vive l'Imperatrice! Vive Marie Louise!*' till he appeared at the Window, to thank them, saying she was not yet arrived, but he doubted not would soon come. A wag among the crowd suddenly sung to his next neighbour '*Va-t-en voir s'elle vient, Jean!—*' the neighbour repeated the verse—it was caught by a third—& presently became a chorus—which B—could not help hearing, as, looking furious with indignation, he shut his window. But the chorus was too general to be dangerous; there was no ONE, two, ten, twenty or fifty to be marked & arrested,—& therefore all laughed, but all sung on, & all escaped with impunity. If you read This, as I always wish you to do my Letters, when you are going to Bed, may the *refrain* sing you gaily to sleep. Amen—

The Banker's direction is Daniel Danoutts, & Co, Brussels.[13]

Bankers: — —

Is it possible the D[uke] of F[eltre][14] has not yet listened to your so just representation?[14] I am the more sorry as it is

[11] Three Highland regiments—the 42nd or Royal Highland Regiment of Foot (Black Watch), the 79th or Cameron Highlanders, and the 92nd or Gordon Highlanders—were then garrisoned in Brussels. Their popularity may have been increased by their picturesque uniforms, but it was also based on their courteous and helpful attitude toward the citizens who were obliged to offer them billets (Fleischman, p. 48).

[12] As early as 21 April Napoleon had tried to counter the embarrassment caused by Marie-Louise's continued absence by distributing posters that falsely announced her return to Paris by way of Rambouillet, but the announcement backfired and increased public mockery when some of these posters were mistakenly put up in Rambouillet itself (Reiset, iii. 160). Royalists sang songs about the absence of the Empress, including one that ran 'Ah! dis donc Napoléon, / A! n'vient pas ta Marie-Louise!' (Thiry, p. 140).

[13] The firm, more commonly known as 'Danoot et fils', had important connections in London and Paris (Bouchary, ii. 108). Their Brussels office was in the rue d'Aremberg. See also above, L. 853 n. 1.

[14] The duc de Feltre (L. 860 n. 2) advanced 5,000 francs to M. d'A to cover the costs of his mission (see Feltre's letter of 17 April in Rochechouart, pp. 418–19), a sum soon spent. M. d'A's official correspondence for 1815 and 1816 was to be filled with appeals for the repayment of his expenses.

ALWAYS still more difficult to get expences REFUNDED than
anticipated. If any one would [in]vest for you, is it not your so
constantly ami [Le] D[uc] of Lux[embourg]?[15]—How cruel
that 6 Days is the [qui]ckest a Letter can arrive from one to the
oth[er,] consequently for an answer we must wait 12 Send me
your decision—y[r] *choux planter*
read the P.S. at top. [1]

P.S. *Bonjour*, This *4th June*[16]—Birth Day of my ever loved &
honoured King! Must there not be a HEAVEN if only for HIM?
Ah, mon ami—*There* may we, too, meet!

882   [1358, Marché au bois],
                              Brussels, 5–6 June 1815

To M. d'Arblay

A.L. (rejected Diary MSS. 6620–[3], Berg), 5–6 June 1815
Double sheet large 4to   4 pp.   pasted in pages 140–1 of the Scrapbook
Fanny d'Arblay and Friends. France. 1679–1820   wafer
Addressed: À / Monsieur le General d'Arblay / off[r] Superieur des gardes
du Corps / de Sa Majesty le Roi de France, / Chev[r] de St. Louis, &c &c— /
à Treves.
Edited by FBA p. 1 (6620), *annotated*: 5/2   Visit of the Duke de Luxem-
bourg—
See further, Textual Notes.

Monday, June 5th 1815.
Brussells—

I have so *much* to say, I must take my largest paper, to begin
with the really important. The Duke de Luxembourg[1] this
moment quits me. He entered without being announced,
no one being at hand, & I did not recollect him. He named

[15] See L. 857 n.1.
[16] In remembering George III's birthday FBA may have had in mind the
notice he took of her on 4 June 1796 (i. 188), for instance, and of the sadder
ceremonial days of his final illness described by the Princess Elizabeth (see L. 888
n. 11).

882. [1] The duc de Luxembourg (L. 857 n. 1) had in fact been made a 'com-
missaire royal' at Wellington's headquarters over a month previously, as Sir
Charles Stuart pointed out in a letter to Castlereagh dated 27 April (Romberg and
Malet, ii. 78–9).

himself, in the most flattering sentence, & made me a visit truly agreeable. We talked over all the most interesting topics with great openness. He considered me evidently as *YOU*, & He considers *YOU* as every thing a woman can wish for in her husband—ie—as the faithful deposit of his confidence & sympathy. —— To see that, to gather it from all that dropt from him, & to observe his *approvance* of his opinion of *our liaison*, did not a little contribute to render his conversation interesting, and his visit delightful to me. But to business. *Le Roi* is upon the point of naming him Commissaire Extraordinaire, with high titles & powers, | belonging to the Army of the Duke of Wellington:

(I had already had this intimated to me by accident) but at his acknowledging it —— your wish to belong to the same [Army; and] *MINE, NEXT* to planting les Choux!!!—made me instantly express a regret that you should be attached to the *Prussian* Army. He then asked me several questions—more than I could answer—of your success.[2] I could only assure him of your indefatigable efforts, of mind & body, to fulfil all you could undertake in a cause in which dwelt your whole heart. He hoped you were pleased with M. de Premorel, & with Alphonse,[3] speaking very highly himself of BOTH: M. de Premorel, he said, was a man of the most perfect honour & principle: & his son peculiarly interesting. I praised both very sincerely, & avoided to name the long separation, which I hope to Heaven is now ended. Then he enquired about your Horses: he takes an *affectionate* interest in All that belongs to you; *affectionate* is so truly the ⟨ex⟩pression of his air & voice in naming you, that it gave me | courage to dilate upon your warm attachment to him, & respectful devotion & unlimitted confidence—& how much it would solace *ME*, in knowing its solace to *YOU*:—in a War so terrible at best!—if it could be possible your services could be at his side, & under his auspices.

He listened with the most flattering look of pleasure. I am sure he sincerely loves you.—After a little pause, he asked your direction—but presently added that he doubted not *I* wrote

---

[2] Here FBA inserted the superscript (2) and the explanation (p. 1): '(2) Unluckily I had not then received your Letter of May 31—so satisfactory on that subject.'

[3] See L. 868 n. 3.

every day. O no! M. le duc! I cried, smiling however, pas tout à fait! car — — les Lettres ne passent à Treves que 3 fois par semaine!—ainsi je ne puis pas être plus indiscrète que cela!' 'O,—il vous le paye bien!' he answered—(Flatterer!) Je ne doute nullement qu'il vous écrive tous les Jours de poste. — —' He then told me that, IF you did not continue your present mission — —

What he meant I know not;—have you revealed to him the *choux planter* project?—Oh mon ami! could That be realised!— IF—&c—and IF his own took place,—he should be most happy to have you always near him.

He did not expound the *IF* with regard to you, & I did not press him: I felt, & feel, if the dear *Choux planter* may finish our toils, *I* must have no share in its regulation. I am all, all attention to that.

But the *IF* with regard to himself, he let me [know], with a proper, though a very modest dignity: namely, that unless the English Commander would engage to render his place, in point of power, distinction, & independance, suitable to his rank, & to his holding it immediately under the controll of his own Sovereign,—he should beg leave to be recalled to the side of His Majesty, which his post as Capitaine des Gardes, made incumbent he never should quit, but for some great & appropriate service. |

In the mean while, This situation of his *own* being yet uncertain, he would not have you, on HIS account, think of leaving your present mission till you hear from him. Should his OWN appointment be fixed in a manner *convenable*—(I was obliged to help him, he so modestly hesitated to that word)—he should be most ready & willing & pleased to make use of his own influence for personally arranging your junction with him.

Finally, however, he said he would endeavour, *after* tomorrow, to write to you himself. I earnestly pressed that he would, knowing how far more comfortable, in matters of moment is a *direct* communication than *any* other. Nevertheless, —though I fear no post goes till Wednesday, I write all this at ONCE, in case of any chance Courrier for Treves on Tuesday. Oh why have I not the reply to the Choux plan? I did not dare hint at it! But I talked of your health, & your breast, and your rheumatic tendencies: & he looked much concerned.

He is now here, apparently, to conclude some plan with the D. of Wellington. Perhaps by *Wednesday*, when he means, if possible, to write to you, he may know more of his own situation,[4] & speak more positively of yours. At all events, it will not be *de trop* to hear of his amiable visit to me, which was peculiarly welcome & soothing to me, in many ways.

How I regret, for the sake of some deserving woman, he should not be married! with ideas such as his—so rare!— think of the conjugal indulgence, how happy might he make a virtuous & tender Partner! He looks very ill, & much altered. One of his Eyes was so red that it quite disfigured him.

Though nothing was said on the subject of hostilities, it was clear by his manner that he does not expect they will begin *de sitôt. Why* opinion has changed I know not, but I am told they are not expected, *NOW*, to commence before the end of this month. What a reprieve to me is the delay! ⌐Ah Heaven bless him for his ⟨true⟩ answers to me.⌐ The Duke had enquired my direction, at our old lodging.

———

⌐And now let me record a little adventure that will amuse you. I carried my yesterday's Letter to the Post, myself, to make excuse to ask after the Treves' Letter day. in returning, a Gentleman, who was just over looking me, said, Permettez-⟨moi⟩ Madame, de vous demander où est la Rue d'Assaut. I told him I knew not the way to it—but when I turned to answer, he exclaimed, Mon Dieu! Mad^m d'Arblay! ⎹ I then recognized Dufresne[5]—Was not the rencontre & the Question ingenious & diverting? He felt it strongly, for after the 1st *How do,* said he was enquiring his way to Mr. Boyd,[6] in order

---

[4] Luxembourg's position was even more delicate than M. d'A's, for the duke, as a 'commissaire royal', was ordered to insist that Wellington hand over to him the 'civil government of all the departments occupied by the army'—a bold claim that would in effect restore Louis XVIII and extend his rule with the march of the allied armies. M. d'A, on the other hand, was a 'commissaire ordonnateur' whose chief duty was 'to give receipts payable by the government' for provisions and supplies needed by the allied armies in their advance into France—an appointment that did not carry with it the claims to sovereignty made by the 'commissaires royaux'. Both appointments are discussed by Stuart in a letter to Castlereagh, from which the above phrases have been quoted, dated 21 April from Ghent (Romberg and Malet, ii. 57–8).

[5] Alexandre de Fresne (L. 876 n. 16).

[6] Walter Boyd (L. 870 n. 2) and possibly his granddaughter Anne (L. 878 n. 11).

to ask Your direction. I appeared to think this very plausible. but it told me much more than if he had said nothing, & proved his confusion at having so unexpectedly accosted me by such a speech. He accompanied me home, & I invited him into my *sallon*, & had a very long conversation with him. Imagine how glad I was to hear that he was just come across from England, but from Ghand. He had written to the Duke de Feltre, who accepted his services, & directed him to come hence, & has instantly employed him. He had procured leave of 3 days absence, to *visit Bruxelles*. I am really & truly rejoiced for this worthy young man, & so, I am sure You will be to hear, also that the Duke has promised him, when they arrive at Paris—double pay and double rank. I hope this will accelerate what I am internally persuaded the fair Anne⁶ desires as much as himself, of that, however, I shall not positively judge ⟨until⟩ I see her next. I told him—did I right? Your embarrassment? & he promised most heartily, to try to be of some service. I thought it an opportunity not to lose, as his is the ⟨ideal⟩ department. I let him know your disasters in money matters, & that without some attention was paid to them, you would be seriously distressed, or forced to take up from our pittance in England. "Oh that, cried he, will be ⟨disastrous⟩ at present! he must not think of it!—I will speak to ⟨Blacas⟩ of M. de Beurnonville being head of your Mission, & the appointment of the D. [of Luxembourg] with Lord Wellington. But he knew not of difficulties which kept it suspended. I [hear] La Duˢˢ d'Angoulème returned to England yesterday! but—not there to abide! She is to be cond[ucted] on the opening of Hostilities, either to the Vendée, or again to Bordeaux! What a noble Creature!

Tuesday, June 6—and just this corner to thank you for your Letter de *chez le Marechal*, ⟨   ⟩ the last is to me the most welcome date. But why still no news de Premorel? You will break his heart. Is it right to nigle him thus? I hope Genˡ Kleist is quite recovered. I am charmed at the villa which you have visited with your Hôtes, & still more with your ⟨carriage⟩, your interior & with the family of Mᵉ d'Hayange. How I ⟨long⟩ that you are in good health. I write in better spirits. But [xxxxx 5 *quarter lines*] stillᴫ

Ma ⟨ta⟩nte, &c ne sont pas revenus—

[M. de la Roche Jaquelin[7] heads a royal party in the West, that have taken Bressuires, & attack *Parthenay*: say the English News-papers

The fear of B[uonaparte]'s coming hither is wearing away— The D[uke] of W[ellington] has so stored the Frontiers, & put every fortress into such excellent order & strength. I shall record you in my next an interesting discourse I have had with one of the Highlanders upon Poor Th⟨—⟩![8]

883   Trèves, 5 June 1815

M. d'Arblay
To Madame d'Arblay

A.L. (Berg), 5 juin 1815, including M. d'A's translation of a letter to him from General Kleist de Hollendorf, 4 June 1815.
    Double sheet 4to 4 pp. *pmks* TRIER seal
    Addressed: A Madame / Madame d'Arblay / marché au bois N° 1358 / À Bruxelles
    Edited by FBA, p. 1, *annotated*: 16— (7/I) German Dinner chez le Gen¹ Kleist—avec le prince Fred de Hesse [*with numbers on address fold*]:
7 7 16 16
    See further, Textual Notes.

Treves le 5 Juin 1815

[xxxxx 7½ *lines*] plus j'y reflechis, plus je me persuade que si les circonstances du moment mettaient Bonaparte, ou quelqu'un de ses adherents à mème de faire une pointe au Brabant,[1]

---

[7] This attack was part of the insurrection in the Vendée led by Louis du Vergier, marquis de La Rochejaquelein (1777–1815), who had been rewarded in 1814 for his own and his family's loyalty to the royal cause with the rank of maréchal de camp and command of the mounted grenadiers of the king's bodyguard, which he accompanied during Louis XVIII's flight from Paris (see L. 860 n. 11). He had in fact been killed in the Vendée on 4 June at Pont-des-Mathis, the day before FBA made this comment.
    [8] Unidentified.

883. [1] During the early days of June the allies, lulled both by reports of Napoleon's apparent inaction and by their own growing strength, lost their fear that the French could and would soon strike north into Belgium. They began rather complacently to plan instead a concerted invasion of France, led by Wellington and Blücher, that was to cross the frontier on 12 July near Maubeuge (Müffling, *History*, pp. xi–xii).

il leur serait impossible de s'y maintenir. Tu sais sans doute qu'au moment où je t'ecris 80,000 Russes doivent être arrivés sur le Rhin.[2] Mais ce que tu ignores sans doute aussi et que tu ne pourras probablement connoitre par toi même, c'est un diner militaire Prussien. Eh bien, je vais te le dire *par le menu* quoique j'aye dejà beaucoup ecrit ce matîn. Mais causer avec toi n'est jamais que plaisir et délassement. Il n'y a que le tems qui n'est guere à ma disposition. Heureusement ce n'est pas le cas en ce moment. Il faut que je commence par te donner copie de l'invitation fort aimable dont je t'ai dejà parlé; et je le dois d'autant plus que les nouvelles dont on me remercie sont celles que je tenais de toi et que je n'ai fait que traduire.

'Recevez mes remerciemens, Monsieur le General, pour les nouvelles que vous m'avez fait tenir. je ne manquerai pas de vous informer de même de tout ce qui pourrait vous interesser.

J'ose vous prier, Monsieur le General, de me faire l'honneur de diner chez moi aujourdhui en societé de Mr de Mazancourt, auquel je vous prie de présenter mes civilités. Mais je vous prie de ne vouloir compter que sur la fortune du pot. Ce n'est absolument qu'*un diner militaire.*

Comptant sur l'honneur de vous voir, je finis cette lettre avec l'assurance de ma haute consideration.

Signé Kleist de Hollendorf
Treves
le 2 juin
1815.

C'est à 3^h que je dine ordinairement; si cette heure vous est seant, Je vous prie M. le Géneral de vouloir l'accepter.' |

Cette lettre ne me fut remise qu' à mon retour d'une promenade à cheval. J'acceptai, et presqu'aussitôt je partis pour me rendre à l'Evèché où loge le general Kleist.[3] Presque tout le monde etait dejà rassemblé, et il eut la bonté de me presenter à deux ou trois personnes avec qui je causai, mais je ne te

---

[2] The long-awaited Russians had not yet reached the Rhine in such strength, but by 5 June the vanguard of their left wing had reached Mannheim and the Czar himself had joined its main body at Heidelberg (*Supp. Desp.* x. 369, 498).

[3] Kleist had taken over as his residence and headquarters the palace of the former Prince-Bishops and Electors, whose classical mansion makes up the south range of the quadrangle that surrounds the Trèves Basilica and whose grounds form the park known today as the *Palastgarten.*

puis dire leurs noms que je ne me rappelle pas. Je sais seulement
que l'un d'eux est un Prince Prussien general commandant
d'un des Corps cantonnés dans les environs.[4] On annonça
que le General etait servi et sur le champ il vint à moi en me
disant mon General quand il vous plaira, me priant de l'oeil
et de la main *to lead the way*, ce que je fis quoique malgré
moi et un peu honteux, mais dans la persuasion qu'il devait
savoir ce qu'il avait à faire. Nous etions 21 assis à une table
longue et etroite puisque les bouts dont le G^{al}[1]. Kleist occupions
le plus haut ne fournissaient de place qu'à deux personnes.
Cette table etait couverte de 10 à 12 plats tous de petite patis-
serie qu'on sert ordinairement au dessert, deux seulement
contenaient des cerises. J'en fus enchanté, parceque je jugeai
que le repas ne serait pas si long que celui de la veille puisqu'on
servait en ambigu,[5] car j'etais persuadé qu'on allait achever
de couvrir la table du reste du diner. J'etais seulement surpris
qu'on ne l'eut pas encore fait. Cependant rien ne paraissait.
Enfin une porte de coté s'ouvre et un domestique decoré
parait avec une assiette de soupe excellente qu'il deposa devant
moi où je la laisse attendant un instant que le General le
Prince et quelques autres eussent les leurs. Quatre domestiques
decorés comme le premier etant les seuls parceque ceux des
personnes invitées n'ont pas été admis, ce service n'a pas laissé
que d'être long. Ce qui l'a eté davantage c'est le tems qui
s'est ecoulé ensuite jusqu'au moment où deux plats de petits
patés delicieux mais gros comme des maisons ont paru. Le
premier m'a été offert et je l'ai pris; puis le Prince en a fait
autant et le General alors s'est servi, et les deux plats ont fait
à droite et à gauche chacun leur demi tour de la table, la
même ceremonie a eu lieu pour chaque mets qui a paru
ensuite tout coupé sur deux plats, le premier etait composé
d'excellentes tranches de boeuf bien minces, aux quelles ont
succedé I des cotelettes et de petites carottes bien fines sur un
plat separé, de sorte que pour cette fois, chaque domestique
avait deux plats au lieu d'un. Je ne dois pas oublier ici de te
dire que par une sorte d'analogie je me suis servi double
proportion de carottes car j'en ai pris deux cuillerées, ce qui a

---

[4] Friedrich-Ludwig, Erbprinz von Mecklenburg-Schwerin, mentioned in L. 880
n. 7. He and his principality were neighbours and close allies of Prussia, though he
was not strictly speaking either Prussian or in Prussian service.
[5] A dinner at which the various courses are served together.

été apperçu et reparé, graces au soin delicat d'un aide de camp qui a refusé d'en prendre.

À la suite de ces cotelettes sont arrivés deux puddings qu'on a dit excellens et qui en avaient bien la mine; mais je n'en ai pas gouté. Puis ont paru deux plats de rôt egalement coupés et suivis d'une salade dans deux saladiers, le tout couronné par de jolis petits pots de crème qui n'etait pas prise, mais qui pourtant etait agreable au gout.

Tout cela n'est qu'inusité pour des français, mais voici ce qui m'a paru vraiment original. Après avoir attendu au moins 20 minutes, j'ai vu de nouveau ouvrir la porte de coté, et deux domestiques portant chacun une assiete sur la quelle etaient de jolis petits couteaux de dessert artistement arrangés et presentant la forme d'un soleil, sont avancés d'un air grave et les ont distribués comme le reste avec un serieux qui m'a presque fait perdre le mien. Heureusement je me suis contenu et j'ai le premier derangé cette simetrie en me saisissant du premier couteau et me disant nous allons surement voir paroitre quelques fruits precoces, ou pour le moins un morceau de fromage: autrement à quoi peuvent servir ces couteaux completement inutiles pour manger des cerises des macarons et des dragées. Point du tout rien n'est venu, et les deux domestiques commençant par les cerises qu'ils ont egalement et dans le même ordre presenté à droite et à gauche, ont exactement fait de même pour tous les autres plats de dessert qui n'ont pas été augmentés. Je remarquerai seulement qu'un des convives ayant pris environ 8 cerises son voisin s'est condamné à n'en prendre qu'une son voisin 2 le 3eme egalement deux, de maniere qu'il n'y a plus paru.[6]

Quant au vin il a été servi avec profusion et etait excellent, mais dans le commencement tout le monde autour du General attendait que lui même lui en servit; j'ai été le seul qui ne connoissant pas cette etiquette ait negligé de m'y soumettre. Le Caffé ne m'a rien offert de particulier nous l'avons pris dans le sallon où nous sommes retournés avec les mêmes ceremonies. Ecris moi souvent et longuement, et donne moi

---

[6] Throughout M. d'A's amused account there is an implied comparison with the French order of courses, which had been codified recently enough that the old disorder might still be *inusité*, yet firmly enough that the bill of fare, it was said, need no longer be listed. See, for example, John Scott, *A Visit to Paris in 1814* (Philadelphia, 1815), p. 135.

exactement des nouvelles de ǀ ta santé dont tu ne me parle pas. Il ne me reste que le tems de te dire que la mienne est excellente. Adieu. adieu chere et toujours plus chere amie — Ne m'oublie pas près de Beaufort et donne moi de ses nouvelles. Adresse toujours ici tes lettres qui me suivront —

884   Trèves, 9–10 June 1815

M. d'Arblay
To Madame d'Arblay

A.L.S. (Berg), 9–10 juin 1815
Double sheet 4to   2 pp.   seal
Addressed: À Madame / Madame d'Arblay / marché au bois Nº 1358 / à Bruxelles
Edited by FBA, p. 1, *annotated and dated*: ⸬ ⌜17⌝ (8/I)   9 juin   1815.
(1815) [*with numbers on address fold*]: 8   8   17   17
See further, Textual Notes.

Point de lettre de toi ma chere, chere, et toujours plus chere amie. ce que renfermaient tes deux dernière,[1] ton attente, ton désapointement que ta raison ne peut condamner, mais que ton coeur ainsi que le mien ne peut que trouver bien douloureux, tout cela me fait desirer encore plus de tes nouvelles. J'ai besoin de savoir que tu soignes ta santé par dessus tout pour rendre possible notre reunion, pour la quelle je fais bien exactement et avec toute la ferveur possible la priere convenue. God, God bless thee and I and *him*. dear Alex! must I not hear from him!
Treves ce 9. Juin 1815

                                                        A d'Ay

P.S. Ecris moi toujours ici et donne moi promptement de tes nouvelles. Nous attendons à chaque minute l'ordre de partir,[2] mais rien ne vient excepté Mr de Premorel et son fils

884.   [1] Letters 876 and 878.
   [2] Kleist, embarrassed by M. d'A's determination to accompany the Prussian army, stated in a letter of 16 June to Blücher, 'Ich wünsche diese Zugabe eben nicht; dies kann ich Ew. Durchlaucht versichern' ('I don't want this addition; I can assure your Serene Highness of this'). See Pfugk-Harttung, p. 254.

qui sont arrivés hier soir et que je n'ai pu encore faire loger, parceque tout est plein — |

Ma lettre n'ayant pu partir hier parce qu'il n'y a pas de poste le Vendredy, je la r'ouvre ce matin 10 pour te dire que je reçois en ce moment même la tienne du 29³ renfermant l'extrait de la conference de Vienne en date du 12 May dernier. Je la connoissais, mais je te remercie beaucoup de la peine que tu as prise car j'ai eu et j'aurai souvent encore le plus grand plaisir à la relire. Helas je n'en dirai pas autant de l'ignorance où tu es encore sur le parti definitif que j'ai du prendre, car ma bonne amie il est impossible en y reflechissant que tu puisses penser que ce tems-cy soit celui où l'on peut et doit planter des choux quelques raisons qu'on ait d'ailleurs pour le desirer. ô mon amie personne ne peut le desirer autant que moi mais personne aussi n'est plus eloigné de faire ce qu'il croit peu en mesure avec ce qu'il se doit à lui même et plus encore peut être c'est-à dire au moins egalement à son souverain malheureux et qui a daigné non seulement l'honneur d'un regard de bienveillance, mais encore lui a donné une preuve de distinction particuliere. Deux choses seules ont pu un moment me faire hesiter, la 1ᵉʳᵉ la crainte de n'être d'aucune utilité malgré mes efforts pour meriter et gagner en quelque sorte le traitement dont je jouis; la seconde le mauvais etat de ma santé. Depuis ce tems je suis parfaitement retabli, et ma santé qui se fortifie chaque jour ne me laisse aucune crainte pour l'avenir depuis que j'ai pris sur moi d'acheter une voiture qui me mettra à l'abri du danger certain que je courreois si je baignais et couchais sur la dure avec mes maudits rhumatismes. En second lieu, je suis tellement bien et sur un ton si amical avec les généraux de diffᵗᵉˢ nations qui se trouvent ici, que je suis bien persuadé que personne ne pourrait tirer un meilleur parti que moi de ma situation. Comment avec tout cela pouvoir planter des choux pour son propre compte! Cela ma chere Fanny, est de toute impossibilité, et toi, la plus vertueuse, la plus noble, la plus courageuse des femmes, la plus attachée surtout à ma reputation, la plus devouée pr la cause si juste des Bourbons, à la personne sacrée du Roi, à cette heroine de ton sexe l'inimitable Duchesse d'Angoulême, tu seras la premiere à te repentir d'une demarche que le desir

³ L. 881.

de me raprocher de toi pour ne plus m'en separer m'aurait
seul fait faire. On disait de la femme de Cesar qu'elle ne devait
pas même être soupçonnée; Ne doit on pas dire au moins de
ton mari, qu'il cesserait d'être digne de t'avoir donné son nom,
si ce nom n'etait pas honoré par ceux qui auront été à portée
de le connoitre. ô mon amie, mon amie! adoucissons le plus
possible l'absence en nous ecrivant aussi souvent que poss[ible]
Amen! ⎮

Le 76ᵐᵉ d'infanterie de ligne de l'armée de B[uonaparte]
envoyé dans la Vendée y a été ecrasé.⁴ Que tarde t'on à
marcher au secours de ces braves Vendeens! les laissera t'on
devenir les victimes de leur zele, tomber sous le grand nombre
de Bonapartistes qu'on ne manquera pas d'envoyer contr'eux.
La nouvelle de la déconfiture du 76ᵐᵉ Regᵗ me parait certaine.
Elle m'a été donnée par le chef d'état major⁵ du Gᵃˡ Kleist.

885   [1358, Marché au bois,
                    Brussels], –9–11 June [1815]

To M. d'Arblay

A.J.L. (rejected Diary MSS. 6624–[27], Berg), –9, 10, 11 June [1815]
Double sheet large 4to   4 pp.   pasted in pp. 140–1 of the Scrapbook:
Fanny d'Arblay and Friends. France. 1679–1820.   wafer
Addressed: À / Monʳ le General d'Arblay, / Officier Superieur des armées /
de sa Majestie Le Roi de France, / Chevʳ de Sᵗ Louis, &c / Treves.
Edited by FBA, p. 1, annotated and dated: ✠ Brussels, June 8ᵗʰ   (2)
Edited also by CFBt and the ?Press. See Textual Notes.

N.B. read at your leisure.
rien de pressé—c'est pour
vous endormir la nuit—

I will prepare a Letter against my next invitation for sending

⁴ Actually the 26th regiment, and it could hardly be said to have been 'ecrasé',
though the 2,000 peasants under La Rochejaquelein who on 17 May attacked the
26th inflicted serious losses, forcing it to flee from Saint-Pierre-des-Echaubrognes,
where the clash took place, as far as Châtillon-sur-Seine (Thiry, p. 303).
⁵ Karl Ernst Job von Witzleben*, distinguished Prussian officer, was recalled in
1815 to become Kleist's chief of staff. Kleist clearly had a talented staff—one of
Witzleben's colleagues for a time was Clausewitz.

one by giving you the sum total of Lord Castlereagh's final speech upon the Question of Peace or War—which has carried the Cause of War by a great majority.[1]

AUSTRIA engages for 150.000 men in *Italy*: & an army of equal extent, (150.000.) towards, or upon, or crossing the *Rhine*. In all 300.000.

RUSSIA, under General *Barclay de Tolly*,[2] is at the head (Lord C[astlereagh] says) of as fine an Army as has ever been called out in ANY Country. The Force, quick advancing to the *Rhine*, is of 225.000 *effective* men, the great mass of volunteers following it, & not counted, fully sufficing to supply all accidents.— Another Russian Army was assembled on the frontiers, of 150.000, under General *Wittgenstein*, which should be put in motion to join the other, should circumstances require its aid. All in the most perfect condition.

PRUSSIA has 6 corps, making 236.000 men in an effective state.

Wirtemberg, *Baden*, *Hesse*, *Saxony*, the *Hanse towns*, & *small states on the Rhine*, would, united, bring into the Field 150.000. *Bavaria* alone had 60.000 of the very best description.

The *British* force would be 50.000. The *Netherlands* also 50.000.

EXCLUSIVE, therefore, of the Russian additional 150.000— in case of need. The collective ACTUAL force, for immediate service, amounts to one million Eleven thousand effective men!!!

England, though she gave but 50.000 effective men, was to

---

885.   [1] Robert Stewart (vii, L. 741 n. 28), Viscount Castlereagh and 2nd Marquess of Londonderry (1821), Foreign Secretary from 1812 until 1822 and senior British plenipotentiary at the Congress of Vienna, delivered his final and decisive speech in support of the alliance against Napoleon in the House of Commons on Thursday 23 May, and both the speech and the debate it provoked were reported widely (see, for example, *The Times*, 26 May). The treaties and letters that confirmed his promises of concerted armed action were presented to the House on 22 May (*Journal of the House of Commons*, lxx. 313, col. 1).

   [2] Mikhail Bogdanovich Barclay de Tolly (1761–1818), Prince (1815) and Marshal (1814), of Scottish descent, was born in Livonia, entered the Russian army in 1786, served against Turkey, Sweden, and Poland in wars that filled the years from 1788 until 1794, distinguished himself in the 1806 campaign against Napoleon at Pultusk and Eylau, for which he was promoted lieutenant-general. He was minister of war from 1810 until 1812, devised the Fabian tactics that finally defeated Napoleon's invasion. Replaced after Smolensk by Kutusov*, he was recalled in 1813 to become commander-in-chief of the Russian forces, an appointment he held through the battles of Dresden, Kulm, and Leipzig and the campaigns of 1814 and 1815. He returned to Russia with his many honours and died in East Prussia at Insterburg.

provide, by subsidy, for 100.000 more, in order to meet the number of her great allies. This lord Castlereagh calculates at 2.500.000 livres sterling from the British Parliament.

Every English soldier, he added, cost his country between 60. & 70. livres sterling for his equipment.

Called upon by the opposition to speak of *SPAIN*,[3] she had agreed, he answered, to the Treaty of Vienna, but nothing was yet decided as to what degree of exertion she would actively make in the Cause.

The same enquiry being made as to *Danemark*; she, also, he said, had aceded to the treaty, but had entered, as yet, into no positive stipulations.

PORTUGAL was also quite uncertain as to its operations, though sure for its good Will.

SWEDEN could not yet settle its *quota*, but Lord Castlereagh professed himself as ˥ certain of its cordiality as of that of Austria—of which he had that morning received the Definitive signature in all its Diplomatic forms.

This statement struck even Mr. Whitbread dumb.[4] Lord Wellington is now at full liberty to act by his own entire judgment. — — Heaven guide it! Amen!

June 9ᵗʰ I have just had a conversation the most terrific with a British under-officer, by an accident; an intelligent, well behaved & well educated man—I ought to write you what he says, though it has made me shake all over with horrour. He seems in all the vigour of youth, yet has been in the service 23 years! He has been in 17 Battles, & severely wounded; but always soon his own man again. He has served through-out Spain with Lord Wellington, &, even in *cold blood*, would now, cut off his right hand to save that of his noble commander. But — — oh *But!* The *surrender*, by the Inhabitants, *of Buona-*

[3] Louis-Antoine de Bourbon (1775–1844), duc d'Angoulême and son of the comte d'Artois, was eager to lead a Spanish army over the Pyrenees, but the British were alarmed at the prospect of the unruly conduct of any such army that was not paid and controlled from London (see letter from Sir Charles Stuart to Castlereagh, 9 June, Romberg and Malet, ii. 167–9).

[4] Samuel Whitbread (1758–1815), the leading Whig politician and opposition spokesman of the period, whose pointed questions of 22 May about the aims and costs of the alliance (see *The Times*, 23 May) had forced Castlereagh to give his later detailed exposition, was only briefly silenced by the news that Austria had ratified the treaty of 25 March. The following day (26 May) he delivered a sweeping but unsuccessful attack on the treaties, the alliance, and the war itself (*The Times*, 27 May).

parte, or the *Destruction of all France* was the word of command &
the decision of the Invasion!—For this effect, Lord Wellington
carried with him 16. million of Congreve's Rockets![5]—& 16
million of Carcases with hooks![6] —! — The Country, he said, if
the French resisted & persisted, must be a burning heap of
ashes! How sick I turned! O God!—Yet Lord Wellington,
he said, *wished* to spare the nation: & had prepared proclamations to send in, just at his Entry into France, to tell his determination, & give the people a choice.

100.000 pieces of Cannon, he said, were arrived,[7] 50.000 of
which were stupendous. The other 50.000 lighter & more
portable.

The *Carcases*, he said, were of a fire of so noxious a nature,
that no man could breathe within 20 yards of the spot on
which they burst!

All these combustibles are already on the frontiers. Chiefly
at Mons. But OSTEND,[8] he says, whence he is just come, has
such a collection of fire arms, warlike stores, & Instruments of
destruction, as no place in the known world ever collected
before. It is surrounded with canon, & immense inundations
are also prepared every where.

Every thing now, he added, is ready! The Duke of Wellington
is completely prepared. All his cavalry is come. He has every
Horse that England could spare! The last of his Reserve
arrived at Brussels from ostend yesterday!— |

I ventured to ask if hostilities were soon to begin—my
voice hardly audible with the terrour he had given me. *No!*
he answered; the Duke chose to be entirely prepared for events,
& for any attempt of Buonaparte's; but, if not urged from his

---

[5] William Congreve (1772–1828), 2nd baronet (1814), inventor, M.P. (1812–16,
1818–28), and artillery officer, first produced his spectacular but unreliable rockets in
1805. Employed in battle at Leipzig in 1813, under Congreve's own command, and
in the south of France in 1814, they were never much used or liked by Wellington,
who approved them only for setting towns on fire, though he did have one rocket
troop under his command at that time armed at most with a few thousand pro-
jectiles (*Supp. Desp.* x. 23). FBA's figures in this passage are wildly overstated.

[6] Spherical shells filled with inflammable material that spurted out through
three holes as it spun in flight. Wellington used them chiefly in bombarding towns
and fortresses (*Disp.* vi. 577).

[7] On 8 June Wellington had only 204 artillery pieces in the whole of his allied
command, and of those roughly 100 were manned by British or K.G.L. gunners. He
had 174 cannon at Waterloo, most of them 9-pounders with only a few 18-pounders
and heavy 5½-inch howitzers.

[8] Mons was one of the chief allied bases during the Hundred Days. Ostend was
the chief port for supplies and reinforcements coming from England.

own purpose, he wished & meant to defer the conflict till the Harvest should have secured food for the survivors.[9]—Oh Heaven! how dreadful yet how humane!—I must leave some paper to answer—when it arrives!—your next Letter—ah— I dare not—must not tell you how disappointed I have been at not receiving one to day! nor how ill I have borne my disappointment—mais pensez ce que c'est pour moi que votre decision sur notre *plantation de choux!*—

June 10th La reponse est arrivee[10]—& it was the fault of the Post that I had it not yesterday—not that of my dear—dearest Ami!—for it is kind, kind!—full of little animating *morceaux* that from every corner seem to shew a reluctance to quit the *causerie* that is destined to console your poor Athanase—ah! how does she want consolation! this last raised hope thus cut off!—Certainly I attempt no demur—It was You gave the hope—not *I* who pleaded for it. I have always felt that, upon the subject of Honour, tenderness, even virtuous, conjugal tenderness, ought to be mute. You know it well! but I had flattered myself some circumstances had arisen that had reconciled duty with peace—without a murmur, I assure you, solemnly, I yield to what you have last represented—for I cannot but approve your reasoning—yet you will not believe— cannot expect I yield without deep, deep regret.—But This— as a Theme over, I must now touch upon no more. Let me go back to what is more consolatory—your bettered situation, your most just appreciation by others, & — — the kindness of those dear morceaux, like so many re-iterated Adieux— that meet & soothe my best affections.—And how very comforting to me are your assurances of recruited health! Be circumspect & watchful, nevertheless, of your *regime*. Never lose the remembrance of the dangerous mistake you made in Paris, after my departure at our unhappy separation;[11]— you changed your diet, took wine, coffee, un peu de liqueurs tous les jours—& wrote me word you found yourself *à merveille*—

9 Lady Caroline Capel *née* Paget (1773–1847), a knowing observer during these weeks in Brussels, hints at another reason for Wellington's wait for the harvest by noting Belgian complaints about the strain and expense of feeding and housing so many foreign troops (Capel, p. 107). Wellington decided early in this campaign to continue Peninsular practice of buying all needed provisions. Without the spring grain harvest there would have been no grain to buy and no way to feed his army.
10 L. 880.
11 After FBA left for England in 1812.

but all that gave you a false fire—sensations of spirits & exaltation beyond nature,—& certainly *contributed* to, though it sufficed not to *cause* your terrible illness—for you wrote me word, afterwards, that M. d'Esparron put you entirely upon a milk regimen.[12] Be careful, therefore, I pray, & watch yourself as I would watch you—if possible. | But never persuade yourself you can really live upon 4 or even 5 Hours sleep. If you take no more in Bed, be sure you take more when up, whether you are conscious of it or not. You are else in some unnatural state, & will be surprised by some new evil; for *6 Hours* rest, Buchan, Tissot,[13] & all the best authors who study health & longevity, affirm, from long experience & investigation, to be the recruit which the MIND & *spirits*, as much as *health* & the BODY, *require for conservation*. What goes beyond nature, *wastes* the vital powers, by making them *live too quick*.

I plead, however, only for your going earlier to *rest*—the *rising* early I think excellent.—The fear of B[uonaparte]'s arrival is quite over now—or rather it is changed into contempt! We have 15.000 English troops now in Brussells! Every house is stored—but the Inhabitants do not murmur as they attach to them an idea of safety.

June 11ᵗʰ Your 7ᵗʰ Letter is just arrived[14]—my beloved friend —& I shall pass a day of genial revival. Their effect upon me in every sort of way is nearly wonderful to myself! Oh remember a single *Bonjour, dated*, when you are pressed for time, will at least keep me from such fits of *morne melancolie* as undermine, secretly & slowly, but surely, the poor harrassed machine, of which the inside outworks the outside. Such a mere word will not, indeed, solace *mes ennuies* like these two dear precious last Letters, of June 4ᵗʰ & 5ᵗʰ—but it will keep off killing suspense, which harrows the soul more intolerably, if possible, than positive evil. Since so kindly you desire your athanase's Letters, also, another shall be begun directly, for I expect tomorrow some English news papers. And to write to you, when I

---

[12] M. d'A's physician, Pierre-Jean-Baptiste Esparron (vi, L. 617 n. 5).

[13] William Buchan (1729–1805) was the author of *Domestic Medicine; or the Family Physician* (1769), a widely used guide to self-diagnosis and treatment. The equivalent work in French was *Avis au peuple sur sa santé . . .* (1761) by the famous Swiss physician Samuel-André Tissot (1728–97).

[14] L. 883.

think you have time to read me, excites my *second* best sensations. The *First* best—need I name?

Poor M. de Premorel has certainly missed your Letters, for he is in despair at not joining you. He has visited the Directeur. du cercle de Neufchateau,[15] & engaged his interest for your mission. And he has been else where, & as ACTIVE as has been in his Power. *Beatrix*,[16] near Neufchateau, I think is his address. I am quite grieved about him. He seems cruelly hurt, yet writes with unabating respect. I have begged the Chev^r d'Argy[17] to tell him I was sure some Letter must have miscarried & that you were at Treves. Yet you talk of quitting it? Ah—for where? I will observe the address of Alex. I divine why I am very tolerably well. |

Let us N° our Letters[18] This is my 6th I have received (5).[19]

The Champ de Mai[20] took place the 1st of June!—A month alas to Day—*June 10th*—is passed since you have left me!— Oh how heavily!—How I languish to know whether le D. de Lux[embourg] has written: Ah! mon ami!! Why *sign* the Proclamation?[21] 'Tis surely a chevalresque extravagance!

[15] In the administrative language of the German and Austrian territories, to which Neufchâteau belonged, 'Kreis' or 'circle' continued to be used after the district passed under French control early in the Revolutionary wars. The 'directeur' under the old system was governor of the region and president of its local assembly, which had its seat at Neufchâteau (sixty-one kilometers north-west of Luxemburg).

[16] Bertrix—a village roughly seventeen kilometers west of Neufchâteau.

[17] See L. 881 n. 8.

[18] FBA's six letters since M. d'A's departure were 872, 876, 878, 881, 882, 885.

[19] FBA had had in fact received six of M. d'A's letters—871, 874, 875, 879, 880, 883.

[20] This postponed military and civil assembly, which was named after those held in March and May (hence the names *champs de mars* and *champs de mai*) by the Frankish kings, was staged by Napoleon as a collective pledge of loyalty to his imperial rule and as a celebration of its military power. For an excellent eye-witness, see John Cam Hobhouse (1786–1869), Baron Broughton, *The Substance of some Letters written from Paris during the Last Reign of the Emperor Napoleon . . .* (2 vols., 1817), i. 408–23.

[21] By signing the proclamation issued from Trèves (L. 880), M. d'A revealed himself publicly as a supporter of Louis XVIII, and under the edicts passed on Napoleon's return that had become a capital offence.

M. d'Arblay
and Madame d'Arblay
To Alexander d'Arblay

A.L. & A.L. (Berg), [13 mai], 11–12 June 1815
Double sheet large 4to   4pp.   *pmks*   P   94   P   BRUXELLE
FOREIGN / 19 JU 1815
Addressed: Angleterre / to the care of / Mrs. Broome, / For her Nephew
AD / Richmond, / Surry / near London.
Docketed, p. 1 : *c.* 32
Edited by CFBt. *See* Textual Notes.

'le 13. de mai, 1815
— at Brussells.'

La campagne va bientôt s'ouvrir, mon cher Alex; et dans
trois heures j'aurai quitté ta mere pour me rendre où l'honneur
et mon devoir m'apellent.¹ Honnoré d'une mission particu-
lière et que peut être de la plus grande utilité pour la noble
cause que j'ai embrassée, je fais à cet espoir le sacrifice de ma
tranquillité, de mes gouts et peut être de ma vie; car, à mon
âge, et accoutumé depuis trop longtems à une vie paisible je
ne me dissimule pas que je suis peu preparé aux fatigues que
peut être je suis appellé à souffrir. Je dis peut être puisque dans
le fait, il est presumable que je ne suis pas destiné à une bien
grande activité, et que le rôle que j'aurai à jouer dans le drame
nouveau qui se prepa[re] ne sera pas aussi brillant que j'aurais
pu l'esperer il y a vingt ans. Quoiqu'il en soit, mon ami, et
quelques soient les chances que j'aye à courrir, ce dont je suis
sûr, c'est que je ne te laisserai point pour heritage une reputation dont tu ayes à rougir. C'est avec douleur que je me separe
de la compagne la plus adorable: mais [ce]tte dôuleur est bien
adoucie par l'idée que tu n'as point tromp[é] mes esperances,
et j'en suis sûr tu rempliras toutes celles que me fait naitre ce
bon commencement—Adieu mon ami, je t'embrasse comme je
t'aime; je ne sais rien de plus fort, comme de plus v⟨rai⟩
à te dire. Je te donne ma benediction, et te recommande la

886.   ¹ L. 869, finished on 6 May but started on 26 April.

meilleure ⟨connaissance⟩ la plus tendre et la plus chere de ⟨mes⟩ amies, en même tems que je te recommande à elle. Puisses tu à la fin de tes exercices academiques, et sans perdre de vue le but principal de tes etudes et l'objet presqu'unique de tes gouts, te livrer a quelqu' occupation utile qui, en augmentant ton aisance, ajoute egalement à celle que ta mere ne devra qu'à son seul genie, parce que les circonstances imperieuses dans lesquelles je me suis trouvé ont rendu presque sans but et sans resultat la vie laborieuse que j'ai menée. God bless you Both!

à 8ʰ, moins quelques minutes au moment de monter en voiture, je veux te dire que j'ai baisé deux fois ta lettre en même tems que celle à qui je dois un tel fils

[*Madame d'Arblay beginning on page 3 of the letter (overleaf) eventually became aware that d'Arblay had written a letter on page 1, which letter she dated (bottom of page 1)* 'le 13. de mai, 1815.— at Brussells. '] *with the comment*: His Birth Day!—O may many— & happier be its anniversaries—'

June 11ᵗʰ 1815.—

MADAME d'ARBLAY—A BRUXELLES—is all the direction necessary for me now. The Postman is always best acquainted with my abode.

WHY I have no answer to the Letter I sent the beginning of the second Week in May[1]—& just a few days before I lost sight of our mutual best & dearest Friend, I can form no idea! In it HE wrote two or three lines that alone should have secured a reply. I am quite, quite in the dark how to comprehend such silence. Indifference I cannot believe it. Insensibility is impossible — — Inattention?—Forgetfulness? — — Negligence? — — procrastination—paresse?—Oh Alexander! can they be pushed so far?

I had much, much to tell you of your dearest Father—but this mystery must be cleared away, or This fault cancelled by an ingenuous acknowledgement, ere I write again. It would be an utterly false indulgence to give you information which you do not even seek. If you persevere in this conduct, you must *learn* from others all those interesting particulars which, if you would earn them by enquiry, you would have yourself to *communicate*.

With what pleasure, Oh Alexander, should I detail to you the minutest circumstance belonging to him whose Name we have the honour to bear, if your Letters, by their frequency and affection, shewed you would merit & appreciate the accounts! — — It is still time for the future! I am never—you have long long known, inexorable.

My *1ˢᵗ Letter* after my flight from Paris was to *you*.² I Directed it to Cambridge, as I knew not of the fever. This was March 26ᵗʰ, I think.

I wrote to you, *early in April*, a whole history of all I then knew of your Father's campaign—it was before our re-union, but I knew he was *safe*, & I had had Letters from him.

A *3ᵈ Letter* I sent you from Brussells the beginning of the 2ᵈ week in May.³ This is my *4ᵗʰ*. Had I received Answers, it might have been my 14ᵗʰ! And my correspondance with YOU, as with your Father, I should have considered, with the utmost satisfaction, as a sort of pension to be paid from our Income, to the Post office rather than to the Apothecary.⁴ |

I copied This for your Father, without seeing, unluckily, that I took his own precious Letter.⁵ I have now to copy it over again, to send to him.

AUSTRIA engages for 150.000 men in Italy: & an army of equal extent, 150.000, in another quarter towards the *Rhine*; making in all 300.000 Men.

RUSSIA, under General *Barclay de Tolly*, was at the head of as fine an army as ever had been called out in ANY country; the force which would arrive at the *Rhine* would a[mou]nt to 225.000 *effective* men, the great mass of Volunteers following it, & not counted, fully sufficing to supply all accidents. Another Russian army was assembled on the *frontiers*, of 150.000, under General *Witgenstein*: & This also should be put in motion to join the other, if circumstances should

² L. 850.
³ L. 860.
⁴ Before FBA completed this letter, one from AA had arrived as she indicates here by the superscript (2) and the note '(2) I have received from you—1ˢᵗ Letter, April 13. from Norbury Park. 2ᵈ The conclusion of a Letter of my dear Mrs. Lock's, April 16. 3ᵈ & Last, also Norbury Park, May 8. & finished by Mrs. Lock. That Letter so pleased me, that I should have instantly written again, but that I had anticipated my answer by my previous Letter, just gone, & that I wrote upon its subject to your Aunt Broome [L. 870].'
⁵ By accident or design FBA has begun her letter on paper M. d'A had used on 13 May to start a letter to AA, then used again to copy out Castlereagh's speech.

require its aid.!! The 225.000 was near the *Rhine* already, in the most perfect condition.

PRUSSIA has 6 Corps, making 236.000 Men in the whole, in an effective state.

Wirtimberg, Baden, Hesse, Saxony, the *Hanse Towns,* & small *states on the Rhine,* would, united, bring into the field a force of 150.000. *Bavaria* had an army of 60.000 Men of the very best description.

The *BRITISH* force would be 50.000. The NETHERLAND force the same.

There were actually 30.000 of them in service, in the field. The remainder was in a state of preparation, & expected to be soon ready. Exclusive, therefore, of the Russian addition, if wanted

The Collective actual Force for immediate service would amount to *ONE MILLION* Eleven thousand men!!!!

England, in giving only 50.000 effective men—was *by subsidy* to provide, in all ways, 100.000 more—which Lord Castlereagh calculates at 2,500.000. livres sterling, from the British Parliament—!

The English army, he added, though undoubtedly amongst the most gallant & the bravest, was by no means amongst the cheapest that could be brought to the field; EVERY MAN cost to Government between 60 & 70 livres sterling, for his equipment!

called upon by the opposition to speak of *Spain*—she had acquiesced, he answered, to the treaty of Vienna, but nothing was yet decided of the degree in which she would act.

The same question put for *Danemark,* she had aceded, he replied, to the spirit of the treaty, but nothing more.

Portugal was yet uncertain, as to its operations, though not as to its good will. *Sweden* could not at present fix its *quota,* but Lord Castlereagh was as sure of its cordiality as of that of Austria.[1]

Your Letter of May the 7th was all we could wish[6]—it arrived the instant your Father was departing to join the army —We were both so pleased with it, that it lightened to *me* the misery—to *him* the deep pain of the separation. He had

---

[6] The letter from Norbury Park (n. 4), now missing.

written what begins with '*La Campagne va bientot s'ouvrir*—'[7] to leave with me, for being sent to you as soon as your answer arrived to the Letter we had sent a few days before: but he added the 2 lines beginning '*a 8 heures et demi*' when he had girt on his sword, & pronounced his sad adieu—

He conceives not that you have not written—I hope I shall never let him know it—He went off persuaded I should divide my correspondance between the Father & the Son,—& reap consolation in my deplorable solitude & apprehensions from Both!—!!—Oh! if you considered how unhappy is my present Life! — — ǀ

I know not even where you are—nor what you do—nor how you live! I *hope* you are with your Uncle Charles—& preparing for confirmation: but I shall direct to your dear Aunt Broome, *chez qui* I would have you arrange a *nest* for yourself & a *pick nick* if possible; but at all events an independence from *hanging on* upon any body.

All this, at length, I have written to *you* the beginning of May —& to that dear Aunt as soon as I had read your Letter[8] of May 7th—An *incidental* information reached me of *May 16.* that told me you were neither at Richmond nor Deptford?— Is your silence, at last, the effect of conscious shame in disregarding the injunctions parental I have written?—Could you write so VERY proper & respectable a Letter as that which has won you such bless[ed] words from the kindest of Fathers, yet not have character enough to act up to it?—Alas—

Attend to This INSTANTLY. For God's sake don't neglect!—

June 12th I have this moment received a Letter, with a power of attorney, from Martin.[9] Pray *IMMEDIATELY* write him word *The proposition must come from Mr. W. Lock, through Mr. Murray.*[10] Having never had any answer, on account of Mr. William's absence, we are impatiently *waiting* for one. I

---

[7] M. d'A's wistful comment may help to explain his determination here and later at Trèves to stay at his post long after it had become pointless for him to do so. He felt himself to be grasping, perhaps, for the last time at the military and personal glory gained by so many of his contemporaries but denied to him by his exile and marriage.

[8] In one of the family letters mentioned by FBA in L. 870, none of which have survived.

[9] Martin Burney (L. 838 n. 26) was acting as the d'Arblays' solicitor in their dealings over Camilla Cottage (L. 863 n. 6).

[10] Alexander Murray (vii, L. 728 n. 6) was William Locke's solicitor.

beg Martin to see Mr. Murray, & THEN write explicitly & definitively. I can send no *pros.* & *cons* to The Army!—
M. d'A. did not see Mr. William in Paris, nor has ever heard from him on this subject. Mrs. Lock says the neglect is all Martin's.
pray do not neglect to pay the postage of your Letters. Every body has written to me the most flattering accounts of your progress in *l'usage du monde* & of your greatly encreased attention to the proprieties of dress, hours, conversation, &c —
— Mrs. Lock—Amine—Charlotte Barret—Mrs. Raper—Fanny Burney—EVEN your Uncle James![11]— — Ah when may I see the progress I so sigh to behold!—
I had closed my Letter—but I have not the heart to let it go without even telling you where your best Friend now is[12]—*Treves* was his last date. But he expected soon to change his quarters—Will you know whither? The means are still in your power. O Alex!
The only reparation you can make that I can cordially accept, will be your taking a *large* sheet of Thin paper, & filling it with a full answer to all my several Letters treat upon—adding frankly yʳ own plans & feelings, & affairs—& writing *all* yʳself to be *wholly* unreserved on all subjects.

887   [Trèves], 12 [June 1815]

M. d'Arblay
To Madame d'Arblay

A.L. (Berg), 12
Double sheet 4to 4 pp. *pmk* TRIER seal
Addressed: A Madame / Madame d'Arblay place / du marché au bois Nᵒ 1358 / A Bruxelles
Edited by FBA, p. 1, annotated and dated: ⌐19¬ (10) Juin / (1815) [*with numbers on address fold*]: 6 10 10 19 19
See further, Textual Notes.

Ce 12 à 10ʰ du soir
Je ne sais, ma bonne amie ce que je t'ai ecrit aujourdhui.

¹¹ These letters are missing.   ¹² M. d'A.

J'etais si pressé Je n'ai pu relire ni cette lettre ni celle que j'ai ecrite presqu'en même tems à M^r de L[uxembourg]¹ qui t'a fait une si aimable visite. J'en viens de recevoir une à l'instant même bien extraordinaire. Je sortais de table, car il faut que tu saches que dinant de très bonne heure et ne pouvant prendre du thé avec mon amie, je suis obligé de faire un repas à la verité très leger et composé p^r l'ordinaire d'un bon bouillon et de legumes. Ce second repas fini, j'etais rentré dans ma chambre p^r faire tirer mes bottes, et je venais d'envoyer François² faire une commission. Quand à Henry, il coucha près de mes chevaux. Tout à coup ma porte s'ouvre, et je vois entrer un homme superbe, de la figure la plus interessante vetu d'un uniforme allemand très propre, et portant sur son bras un sac de toile³ à peu près comme les chanoines portent l⟨ivres⟩ au messe. Je ne doute point qu'il ne soit venu m'apporter quelque grande nouvelle, et peut être l'ordre de partir; d'autant que ce matin même le Gen^al Kleist que j'imaginais me l'avoir envoyé, m'a repeté que s'il a quelques nouvelles concernant l'ouverture de la Campagne, j'en serai instruit aussitot. Ce militaire m'adresse la parole d'un air tout à fait noble quoique suppliant. Je lui repons en français que je ne parle pas allemand: mais que s'il ne peut s'expliquer dans ma langue, je vais appeller quelqu'un pour me servir d'interprete. Il me salue respectueusement, ne veut pas s'asseoir, mais attend sur le pas de la porte dans l'attitude d'un homme qui aurait entendu ce que je lui ai dit. Une demoiselle de la maison arrive; et veut bien prendre la peine de lui demander de ma part ce dont il a été chargé pour moi. Grace à l'obligeance de cet interprete, j'apprens que ce militaire n'est point une ⌐ ordonnance;⁴ qu'il est né bavarois, et qu'il fait partie d'un escadron de cette nation en garnison à Treves;⁵ que plus de cinq ans il a eu l'honneur de faire la guerre avec les français, qu'il a eu le

---

887.   ¹ See L. 857 n. 1.
   ² M. d'A's interpreter, earlier employed and recommended by Henry Grattan Jr. (1789–1859). See further, L. 896, p. 232.
   ³ Canons carried bags that held their missals—and sometimes hot bricks to keep them warm during the singing of the office.
   ⁴ An orderly or dispatch-rider from Kleist's headquarters.
   ⁵ To screen the gaps between the allied armies on the Rhine and Moselle, the Bavarian Marshal de Wrede* had earlier stationed 48 squadrons of cavalry between Germersheim and Trèves (see his letter to Wellington of 20 April in *Supp. Desp.* x. 108–9). M. d'A's would-be recruit was a trooper or non-commissioned officer in one of these units.

bonheur de se conduire toujours comme un brave homme, et qu'ayant eu cinq blessures, qu'il ne s'est jamais mis dans le cas, pendant tout ce tems de recevoir aucune punition, ni même aucune reprimande, mais que malheureusement il s'est oublié avant hier soir et n'est rentré que ¾ d'heure après la retraite;[6] ce qui a été cause qu'on l'a maltraité si indignement qu'il vient me trouver pour me supplier de le faire partir sur le champ pour rejoindre l'armée Royale de braves français qui ne donnent pas de coups de bâton aux gens d'honneur qui ne demandent pas mieux que de se bien battre mais ne veulent pas être battus; qu'en un mot il veut quitter le service bavarois parceque ⟨qu'il⟩ a reçu pour une faute involontaire et bien legere, 50 coups de bâton,[6] qu'il ne peut digerer; et qu'il ne lui est pas plus possible de pardonner que d'oublier. &c. &c. J'ai eu toutes les peines du monde à faire entendre à ce brave homme que je prenais toute la part possible à sa situation, mais qu'il m'etait absolument impossible de faire ce qu'il desirait. à mesure qu'on me traduisait, sa figure, d'une mobilité extrême, exprimait avec une rapidité inconcevable, jusqu'aux moindres nuances de diverses sensations en apparence peu faites pour aller ensemble; on y voyait de la reconnoissance pour l'interêst qu'il m'inspirait, et une sorte d'angoisse de ne pouvoir obtenir ce qu'il etait venu demander; tout cela, sans gestes trop marqués, et d'un air aussi noble que touchant. Je ne crois pas avoir vu de ma vie de plus beaux yeux levés au Ciel l'implorer et l'accuser en même tems. J'etais reellement penetré de cette situation tout à fait nouvelle; et je crois en verité ǀ que cela me donnait une onction en parlant qui donnait ou plutot pretait à ce que je disais une partie de ce charme qu'on admire dans la veritable eloquence. Ce qui me le fait croire c'est que cet infortuné qui n'entendait pas un mot de ce que je disais me comprenait si bien au bout de quelques instans ecoulés rapidement et tout à fait remplis, qu'a mesure que je parlais, tous ses traits me faisaient vite reponse; de sorte que celle que me faisait ensuite de sa part notre interprete ne m'apprenait rien de nouveau. Aprés avoir epuisé tous les lieux

---

[6] At the sounding or beating of retreat, here in the sense of curfew, all troops were expected to return to barracks. The Bavarian's punishment does seem excessively severe and may have been inflicted by the brutal *Feldgendarmerie* of the Prussian army—a further reason for his attempt to switch into the French *armée royale*.

communs pour convaincre de ce dont j'etais bien effectivement persuadé, (que sa punition n'etait que suite d'une discipline malheureusement necessaire pour pouvoir conduire ceux qui pensaient moins delicatement que lui) j'ai ajouté en lui prenant la main, que loin de le degrader comme il le pensait, elle l'avait mis à même de se faire connoitre et de deployer des sentimens qui me donnoient pour lui beaucoup de consideration; et qu'enfin j'etais si eloigné de le regarder comme un homme deshonnoré; qu'au contraire je me sentais tout à fait porte à l'estimer; et qu'enfin ne pouvant pas l'engager dans l'armée royale, parce que ce serait manquer à ce que nous devons aux Alliés, je serais au moins charmé de trouver l'occasion de lui être utile. Promettez moi lui ai-je dit encore, de ne pas faire de coup de tête, de retourner vers vos camarades qui ne peuvent pas vous voir d'un autre oeil que moi. *Alors posant* son sac par terre, Non Monsieur s'est il ecrié, je ne puis vous promettre cela; je suis un homme perdu, puisque vous ne pouvez pas me prendre avec vous; Jamais je ne pourrai Je n'avais pas besoin qu'on m'expliquât rien de tout cela; je lui ai pris la main qui etait brulante comme un vrai charbon; Je le veux lui ai-je dit; et je vous promets de mon coté de parler à vos chefs. Il ne vous sera rien fait. Au contraire, ils auront appris de moi à vous connoitre et à vous distinguer, si comme je n'en doute point vous vous conduisez de maniere à ne plus vous attirer une pareille punition, qui n'a ⎸ rien de deshonnorant par elle même toute penible et humiliante qu'elle vous paraisse — En attendant faites moi le plaisir — j'ai alors tiré ma bourse, et lui sa main d'un air qu'il me serait impossible de definir et que j'appellerais noble si cette epithete n'etait bien plus justement applicable à l'air avec le quel il accepte la très petite piece d'argent que je lui offris en le priant de ne pas me donner la mortification de croire que j'avais pu le désobliger, en voulant le prier de boire un coup à ma santé. En mème tems ses larmes qui coulaient abondament a travers ses mains qu'il avait portées sur ses yeux quand il avait retiré d'entre les miennes celle que je tenais, s'etaient taries. Cependant il ne m'a rien promis, je n'ai point de mon coté pensé à insister et nous nous sommes quittés, moi en le priant de venir quelque fois me voir, lui en [me] baisant à diverses reprises ma main que je ne pouvais retirer, tant il la serrait.

(Mardy soir) J'arrive avec Mr de Mazancourt des forges[7] de — où j'avais promis à Melle Balthasar[8] dans ma premiere visite d'aller demander à diner à son frere[9] qui nous a reçus de la meilleure grande manière Toute cette famille d'Hayange est en verité aussi aimable que respectable. Je t'ai parlé de la capacité bien rare de Mr de Vendel[10] qui sans un sol et avec la seule reparation de son pere a racheté les biens ou du moins la principale partie des biens de M[de] d'Hayange sa grand mere.[11] Ne bien non seulement il a tout payé; mais il jouit en ce moment de pres de 8,000£ ce qui fait environ 200,000[frs]de rente, et il a fait en outre la fortune de tous ses parens à qui il a cedés quelques uns de ses etablissemens de forges, où qu'il emploie d'une manière aussi lucrative qu'agreable. Par exemple c'est lui qui a cedé à son cousin germain M[r] de Balthazar les forges que j'ai vues; et qui dans l'arrangement qu'il fait avec lui ne tient aucun compte, ni d'un chateau superbe que 3,000[f] de reparations rendront tres habitable[12] [xxxxx 4 *lines on right fold*].

[p. 3, xxxxx 24 *interlinear lines*]

[p. 1, xxxxx 9 *interlinear lines*] monde entier pour longtems la proie du plus infame comme du plus honteux despotisme, celui qu'exerce une armée qu'aucun frein ne retiendrait plus!

Ah Fanny Nos choux si nous existons alors!! Que ne m'est il permis d'aller les manger dès à present; En attendant, nous pouvons toujours les planter Et c'est Alex qui doit etre chargé de ce soin.

[xxxxx 29 *lines in margins*]

[7] The ironworks at La Quint, down stream from Trèves near Ehrang, bought by the Wendel family in 1810 (Contamine, i. 201).

[8] Sister of François-Ignace-Louis de Balthazar de Gacheo (L. 879 n. 7), Anne-Louise (*c*. 1780–1853), whom M. d'A met on his first visit to Hayange.

[9] Alexandre de Balthazar (L. 879 n. 6), who spent the summer of 1815 working with his kinsmen the Wendels at La Quint and Hayange (Serre, ii. 39).

[10] François (1778–1825) had been a naval cadet before the Revolution, after which he emigrated and fought in the campaigns of the 1790s. He returned to France in 1803 and became almost at once the organizing genius of the family's recovery of power and wealth. In this he was aided not only by his talents as an iron-master, but also by the political and financial abilities of Alexandre de Balthazar and Hercule de Serre (Trèves Journal, L. 932 n. 66), both of whom were his first cousins and close friends.

[11] See L. 879 n. 9.

[12] A wild overvaluing of the franc. If the sterling figure is correct, its equivalent would be roughly 200,000 francs. But there can be no denying Wendel's shrewdness —the sum he paid to buy back the Hayange iron-works in 1808 (220,000 francs) was little more than his annual revenue in 1815.

To M. d'Arblay

A.L.S. (rejected Diary MSS. 6628–[31], Berg), 11–13 June 1815
Double sheet 4to   4 pp.
Addressed: *Treves.* / À Monsieur le General d'Arblay, / Offic^r Superieur
de la Maison de sa: Maj: / le Roi de France, / Ch^{ev} de St. Louis, &c, / à
Treves.
Edited by FBA, p. 1 (6628), *annotated*: (7/2)
Edited also by CFBt. *See* Textual Notes.

Pray Read the First half page *immediately*. The rest
pour vous endormir at night.

Dimanche, June 11th 1815.

The softly soothing idea which these 2 last Letters[1] inculcate
of reciprocity in the feeling that makes *your* Letters *mon* seul
bonheur — — encourages me to begin immediately writing,
though I shall not be so indiscreet as to send off the sheet till
I hear again, unless some news or intelligence ought to hurry
my Letter. I will keep a sheet always open, & write—if only a
line—EVERY day: for that, to every day will give one moment of
sweet intercourse to soften off the black shades of every other.
It will remind me of Bookham—of West hamble—of Dunkirk[2]
—where I *never* spent one day absent from my meilleur ami
without Writing—& *scarcely* one without hearing from him.
The life I now lead of lonely rumination upon every period of
my past existence, will make this plan renovating to some of
my best & happiest feelings. Will you not, then, kindly encourage it? Oh yes! I am sure you will.

M. de Beaufort has been to see me. He behaves very un-
affectedly, & seems truly sensible of his loss in so worthy
a friend.[3] He made a warm offer of his services, should I

888.   [1] Letters 880 and 883.
    [2] Great Bookham and West Humble were residences of the d'Arblays in the
years 1793–1802 (*HFB*, pp. 241–2, 271–2); FBA and AA were delayed at Dunkirk
on their way to England in 1812 (vi. 627 ff.).
    [3] For the death of Mme de Beaufort, see L. 894, p. 222.

find any way to make him useful. But all fear of a visit here from France is over, & I doubt not but I may rest tranquil— (personally!) during the dread contest — — O mon ami! why that *signature* to your Proclamation?[4] I regret it with affright & dismay. Besides, is it not inviting immediate confiscation of all our poor possessions & property? Your Fame & Name, at all events, are out of danger; they will not be judged by any decision, or catastrophe inflicted by your *Enemies!* be very sure of that. & if the thing is not done, forbear the signature!—Give only an address to *the commanding officer of the King's party* at Treves—or elsewhere. That will answer all the purpose. Ah, why run any unnecessary risk from Imaginary punctilio? By your Enemies you will be equally traduced, take what precautions you may—& by your Friends vindicated, without taking any. I MUST send this off next post, in a small tiny hope something may have deferred the impression. *Au reste*, I think it admirable, save not BRIEF enough. Every thing has been said so often & so well that a short *concentration* of pithy matter has the best chance of striking forcibly. No post, alas, goes hence till Wednesday the 14th—yet what *remains* of the Impression may you not curtail of the signature? Oh listen! listen!—

I have been disappointed of my News-papers which hitherto I have had regularly twice a week. I fear Mr. Kirkpatrick must be gone.[5]

Lundi, June 12th I begin to strongly apprehend something is deeply forming for new measures. Our Louis is *safe* every way, I see—but plots & plans are sewing with fresh seeds for *les suites,*[6] and oh I fear, I fear, the contagion has been innoculated where it will be most dangerous! 'Tis a dreadful *siecle!* how happy is our philosophic, nearly apathetic Alex! ǀ

I have seen my—erst—so partially fond friend only once for a fortnight![7] I have reason to think your last *vivacité* has made a sore impression. *I* have been worked at since, with great energy; but I was as undisguised, though not as alarming as yourself—& I fancy we should both be *d'une aimable absence*! But what is

---

4 See L. 880, pp. 162–3, and 885 n. 21.
5 William Kirkpatrick (L. 861 n. 3).
6 FBA suggests that the Orléanist intrigues she is about to describe in such oracular terms will have serious consequences ('*les suites*').
7 The princesse d'Hénin (ii, L. 68 n. 17).

MOST surprising, *Fanny Raper's* Friend[8] has but ONCE been to see me since your departure!—She, now, is unboundedly of the same side we deem so evil of the present question. The tide can no longer, I fear, be stopt! the round Letter makes way perceptibly![9] The CHIEF,[10] however, no one dares attempt annoying.

My dear dear Friend with what pleasure do I resume my pen, to tell you what will give YOU the same pleasure it has given me!—I have so little to do at this period with giving or receiving pleasure, that I feel an inexpressible thankfulness that I now experience & can bestow it — — I have just got *two* Letters from Isabelle la belle et bonne,[11] They have come to me from Sir Chas Stewart's office,[11] with no other direction than our name & Bruxelles.

I am quite, quite enchanted! they are sweeter than ever! more open, flowing, & confidential. One was written June 2^d from the great Chateau, the very day of receiving that which I last wrote—the other June 4th from her own new little Cottage in the Forest,[12] of which she gives me a full & most delight-

[8] Mme de Maurville (iii, L. 237 n. 9).

[9] The letter O—the duc d'Orléans, whom even the sympathetic Wellington urged to return and to accord public support to Louis XVIII (Letter dated 6 June 1815, *Disp.* xii. 447–9).

[10] Louis XVIII.

[11] These were the letters (Berg) of 2–3 June and [5–6] June sent by the Princess Elizabeth through the Foreign Office (see L. 856 n. 18). Sir Charles Stuart (L. 856 n. 19) was the Ambassador at The Hague (1815–16).
In the first, written at Windsor Castle, the Princess mentioned plans for the King's birthday (4 June): 'To morrow is our most valued day in the Year it will be spent quietly & solemnly being Sunday all the plants [the Princesses] will surround the Parent Tree at their own home—'

[12] The second letter (a continuation of the first) was written at the cottage near the river in Old Windsor, which the Princess had rented on long lease from a local grocer (see Olwen Hedley, p. 289). Miss Hedley says further (in a kind letter of 7 June 1978 to the editors) that the Princess enlarged the room on the garden side and formed 'rustic arcades' before both fronts. According to T. E. Harward, *Windsor Old and New* (privately printed, 1929), p. 254, the cottage was demolished in 1873. An aquatint of it, made in 1812 by J. Clark after David Cox, may be seen in the British Library.
It gave the Princess 'no small pleasure to have retired into the midst of Green fields & all the beauties of nature'. On the verandah was 'placed a seat from whence You can see the country around' and, true daughter of 'Farmer George', the Princess appraised 'the Hay field close by', hoping to 'have a good Year for the benefit of my animals. I am rich in calves having already had three born upon my own ground, & a fourth coming'. She revelled in 'the simple state that every thing is here', describing also for FBA the interior of the cottage, which included two small rooms 'north and south' with 'a large double door between them which when opened makes one good Room—the paper Green, the whole painted light Oak,

ful description. But the charm of charms is her manner of naming Him who is the Essence of my Existence—or—alas! NON-existence!—She highly approves your appointment, & is so sanguine, she can see no sort of doubt of the most perfect success: but what most touches me, is that while my other friends try to tempt me over to them, during this terrific suspension of all living comfort, SHE, while saying 'you have no idea how you are thought of here, & valued, & pitied, & longed for—'¹³ yet afterwards adds 'your caro sposo's Conduct, however, makes one not wonder at your affection for him, & your devotion to him. — —' & therefore *she* says not a word to me of going over. — —

What a relief to many fears—what a brightening to many glooms is this! She says she did not write sooner, because uncertain of my direction, my last having talked of my going to join you at Ostend. |

How pleased I am you are thus amicably connected with the brave Prussian officers. The Sentinel at your door is a compliment to your King of which I am most happy you should be the exciter. But you talk of going further? Whither? Whither? —Oh that you may join the Duc de Luxembourg!

I have just had a visit from M. de Lally—amical & obliging. He has promised me to interfere immediately for procuring you the Moniteur. He is going to Gand again to-morrow. With regard to the Duke de F[eltre] he could promise nothing; but he listened to me, & if opportunity offers, I am sure he will not neglect using it. He, alas, does not believe the D[uke] of W[ellington] will wait *La Moisson*!¹⁴ he does not think it possible to keep so many thousand men unemployed & fed, after all is

---

which must ever give You & me a feeling of *Exaltation* for tis to that Tree we owe our fame, The curtains a pretty linnen . . .'.
For the visit of the Queen and the Princesses on 5 June, see L. 893 n. 5.

¹³ 'You have been thought of, pitied & longed for more than words can tell', wrote the Princess in her letter of 2–3 June (*supra*), '& happy will it make all here to know that you are safe, tho great anxiety will be felt for Your natural affection & devotion to your better half—who deserves every thing that is good from his firm attachment to his Head, who is ever Benevolent & good.'
By [5–6] June the Princess was acknowledging FBA's account of M. d'A (L. 877): 'It gives me great pleasure to hear You say that Your Caro sposo is recovered & most anxiously do I pray that so good a cause as ours may triumph. . . . I hope . . . Your mind is by this time at ease about Him You love best—'
¹⁴ The harvest, the importance of which is mentioned in L. 885 n. 9.

ready for action. Oh mon Ami!—*What* a fearful day will be that of the opening campaign! My soul sinks with horrour when I think of it! — — But I had great satisfaction in hearing M. de L[ally] say that every where M. le duc de Angoulême was risen in public opinion by the unaffected bravery Personal he had shewn in the most trying circumstances & danger.

M. de Talleyrand is expected here every day, in his way to Gand.[15]

Je pense que 'certaines personnes' ont trop *d'espoir*, encore, pour avoir du remords! remorse comes rarely but with *failure*.— Helas, comme je vois, aussi par tout, what you so justly express 'incertitude ouvertement avouée, et craintes mal deguisées!'— I am now told That Notre Heroine ne veut pas entrer avec les Etrangers[16]—& that that is the reason she has again disappeared: also, that she waits an appel to enter either at Bordeaux or La Vendée, when the Allies make their opening on the other Frontiers. The Duke d'Ang[oulême] continues in Spain, to animate an attack par les pyranees. Oh France! why sleepest thou thus profoundly! or dost thou expect a levy *en masse*? or build upon thy strong places?

M. de Lally told me they have printed his Manifesto in a Paris paper, with *alterations & omissions*.[17] He is—you will believe, quite *non-compos*. *He*, also, sees much more danger than use in your printing your name! *His*, who is far from the scene of seizure, enforces his doctrine, without augmenting his risk.

The Emperor Alexander has proclaimed himself King of Poland.[18]

The Duke of W[ellington] is declared Commander in chief of the Forces of the Netherlands[19]

[15] A reference to Talleyrand's success in shifting masters while staying in office himself.

[16] The duchesse d'Angoulême, who, as FBA notes, throughout the Hundred Days favoured more independent and warlike policies. Her pet scheme, described in a letter of 13 June from Sir Charles Stuart (Romberg and Malet, ii. 172), involved landings along the coast of both the Vendée and Normandy.

[17] Lally's Manifesto (L. 872 n. 8) was taken up and reprinted by several journals and papers after its first clandestine appearance in Paris in mid May.

[18] The proclamation, made in Vienna on 25 May and printed in the *Moniteur*, 16 July 1815, was a blow to both Napoleonic and Polish hopes, for by an agreement announced on 9 June, also at Vienna, Posen (Poznan) was to go to Prussia, West Galicia to Austria.

[19] This declaration was made by King William of the Netherlands, whom

⌐I have a new Letter from Martin about the Irish business.[20] James himself says the offer is accepted by us, & does not think our worthless *debitors* will pay it or probably any thing. I am glad, however, we have sent our signature, for poor Esther & Mr. Burney would else think the loss was all our fault.⌐[21]

The British minor officer I mentioned in my last,[22] told me that signal posts & Barrels were to be placed along the whole of the lines of the Allies, for quick communication of the moment of general attack. Some English officer has told Mr. Boyd that the plan is for All the Allies to arrive—through Fire & Sword! on the same day upon the suburbs of Paris! for which purpose the Austrians, Russians, & Prussians will enter France first, though progressively, according to the distance of their several frontier of entrance from the capital: but as La Belgique is *la plus près*, Lord Wellington & his Men will enter last!!! O if at that period the post should fail me!—But Mr. Boyd—whom I have seen to day, assures me it is the unanimous opinion of All the military he sees, whether French or English, That the Allies will hold themselves bound in honour & humanity, as well as in politics, not to let the small French parties enter either before, or with them, on the commencement, as *Their* danger is so incalculably the greatest from the Enemy's assumption of treating them as REBELS. Oh! God!—let no rashness— no false notions precipitate *you* to mischief! To all that is *essential* to The Cause, & to Your Honour, I submit:—but Oh! go no further!

I finish this long Letter This Day, June 13th—the melancholy Birth Day of your poor melancholy Athanase:[23]—yet, melancholy—lonely—trembling as it is—it is almost *happy* compared with its *last* anniversary, spent in the long Anguish of hearing NO NEWS, NONE! of all she held most dear upon Earth! — — I am going to make myself a Bouquet of your

Wellington considered the most difficult person to deal with he had ever met (*Supp. Desp.* x. 168). Under pressure from the British government and from Wellington it was drafted at Brussels on 15 May, but not made public at The Hague until 2 June (see the *Moniteur de Gand*, 10 June 1815).

[20] See vii, L. 781 n. 1; and above, L. 863, p. 102.
[21] EBB and FBA were CB's residuary legatees. For EBB's husband, see i, p. lxix.
[22] L. 885, pp. 183–4.
[23] FBA turned 63 on this birthday. For the applicability of the name Athanase, see L. 841 n. 3.

Letters since this last parting. The finest perfumes of Arabia will not smell so sweet as every kind passage I shall collect in them will read to your own

F B d'A.—

Adieu, mon cher—CHER ami—I am better, & struggle hard for serenity, & to get a more lively colour than they have worn of late to *mes pensees*. I am going now to my Bouquet. The passages that speak of your ameliorated health are those that will have the odour the most salubrious. Adieu! Adieu! à notre re-union! à notre re-un[ion!] Here and Hereafter!—Is that *Hereafter* de trop?—

The formalities & etiquettes of your Dinner militaire amused me much.

ᵀHow earnestly I long to hear the de Premorels are with you. Me de ⟨P.⟩ speaks of proclamations spread from Namur, about M. de Castries[24] but not in his name.ᵀᴵ

---

889   [Trèves], 13 June [1815]

M. d'Arblay
To Madame d'Arblay

A.L. (Berg), 13 juin
Double sheet 4to   1 p.   *pmk*   TRIER   seal
Addressed: À Madame / Madame d'Arblay / place du marché au bois / Nº 1358 / à Bruxelles
Edited by FBA, p. 1, *annotated and dated*: ⁑ ⌐20⌐ 11 de Treves. Ce ⌐14⌐. / 13./ Juin. 1815 [*with numbers on address fold*]: 11   20

Mille et mille paisibles jours de bonheur à ma fanni, — à qui j'écris pour lui apprendre qu'on vient de préparer pour Sa M. Louis XVIII le chateau de Banrath[1] à deux Lieues de

---

[24] Edmond-Eugène-Philippe-Hercule de la Croix (1787–1866), marquis de Castries, had returned from captivity in Russia in 1814 to become sous-lieutenant in the gendarmes de la garde du roi and, during the Hundred Days, Louis XVIII's commissaire at Namur. After the Second Restoration he resumed his career as a cavalry officer, commanding a regiment in Spain in 1823, reaching the rank of maréchal de camp in 1828, and retiring in 1830.

889. [1] Benrath, a Hohenzollern château built 1756–60, may have been prepared

Dusseldorf de l'autre côte du Rhin. S. M y est attendue incessament, et je desirerais que mon amie prit cette direction; parce que là je serais sans inquietude pour son existence, et que j'aurais la certitude d'avoir de ses nouvelles et de pouvoir constament lui donner des miennes.

Ce 13. juin[2]

Ceci ne veut il pas dire que nous allons commencer? — 98,000 russes viennent de passer le Rhin[3]—j'apprens tout cela à l'instant même.

890   [1358, Marché au bois], Brussels, 14–16 June [1815]

To M. d'Arblay

A.L.S. (Berg), 14–16 June
Double sheet 4to   4 pp   *pmk*   BRUXELLES   wafer
Addressed: *Treves.* / À / M^r le General d'Arblay / Off^r superieur du Gardes du Corps / de sa Majesty le Roi de France, / Che^r de St. Louis, &c &c / Treves.
Edited by FBA, p. 1, *annotated*: (8 / 2) 8th Letter.
See also Textual Notes.

Messrs Daniel Danoots & Son, & Co,
Bankers, Bruxelles.
At your leisure. Il n'y est rien qui presse—Hors la reponse!—

Wednesday, June 14th Every day I will keep to my purpose of saying *Bonjour* to mon ami, since his own kind request keeps pace with the tender thoughts that prompt such constant circulation of intercourse. Yesterday—the poor 13 ^th I was so fraught with dejection, that but for the *Bouquet* I gathered for myself from your Letters, I should have been quite ill. To-morrow I hope for a new plant to my *physic Garden*—

for the arrival of one of the German princes on the Rhine. No account of Louis XVIII's plans during the Hundred Days suggests that Benrath was intended for him.

  2 The date, like M. d'A's opening wishes, marks FBA's birthday.

  3 There were numerous reports during these days of June concerning the arrival of this Russian army (see, for example, *Supp. Desp.* x. 369), but by the date of Waterloo only one exhausted corps of 14,000 had caught up with the Czar at Heidelberg. See Alan Palmer, *Alexander I, Tsar of War and Peace* (1974), p. 327.

Thursday, June 15ᵗʰ The plant is come—& a very sweet one, indeed! of the most reviving nature. I had already given the direction to the Bankers, but I will write it at top. *Bruxelles* is enough even for ME, now! the post man is so frequently my visitor, that all else is superfluous. You will find I had already yielded with respect to *nos Choux*—but you certainly forget, my dearest Ami, *I* never began that plan! I only answered— with alacrity, it is true, a proposition you made *yourself*. Ah no! delighted as I should be, I have always been sensible *I* ought never to take the lead in a proposal of that nature, when once you are engaged. And here, I must do myself the justice to remind you, I have never once pleaded with you to retreat—however eagerly I have hung upon every minute of delay. Yes, I am indeed *'attachée à votre reputation—'*[1] & feel the truth of what you say, that, without it, I should only water *nos choux* with my tears. Never, never have I had an idea of the possibility of happiness under any sort of disgrace, even though but a fanciful one. Here, however, Fancy is out of the Question; I feel & acknowledge every true French man should come forth, according to his powers, to aid his injured King.

According to his powers,—but ah—go not beyond them!

The openning is expected to be inexpressibly dreadful— but, by many, to be decisive! Oh how to be pitied will be the victims of that openning, who never will reap its fruits!—

I *will soigner my santé,* my kind Ami!—to day's Letter is *Bark* to me:[2]—it braces my poor nerves—which *yesterday* & its *reflections,* had anew unstrung. What you tell me of YOUR health has given me a glow of satisfaction unspeakably strengthening to me.

———

I am extremely glad indeed Messʳˢ de Premorel are with you. I beg my best compᵗˢ to them *both.*

I have had no English newspapers this fortnight. Nor have the Boyds, who think Mr. Kirkpatrick is gone on,[3] & suddenly.

---

890. [1] L. 884, in which M. d'A gave up in the name of duty his own earlier hopes that they could soon retire ('planter nos choux').

[2] Peruvian or Jesuits' bark, the source of quinine, which was used in a powdered form to reduce fever. The word was also used in the figurative sense given it here by FBA (*OED*).

[3] See L. 861 n. 3.

Mme de Maurville has not seen him either. This is a terrible loss to me. I live more & more retired. *Ma tante* ne me cherche presque pas; & there is constantly so much desire of whispering when I am there, that I do not purpose to go any more unless by invitation. I had rather be d'une *aimable absence*, than of an obtrusive presence. Mme de Maurville has called only twice since your departure—ⁱʳ& both times for short & ordinary visits, since that discussion of l'*echange* pour faire passer de l'argent,⁴ she has seemed obviously alienated from us! How strange a World! And how very cruel!ⁱⁱ M. de Beaufort is engaged, I *believe*, in solemn rites, & with his wife's relations wholly. The Les Tour du Pins I *believe* are gone to la Haye. I did not know the intention till too late to return Madame's last visit, & therefore have not seen her. M. de la T[our] du P[in] is nominated Minister to Les pays bas for Louis 18.⁵

I have subscribed to the Library you chose for me, & I am reading Dewez. Hist. de La Belgique,⁶ to seek some account of *Treves*. I find it was the seat of many of the latter Roman Emperors, & you ought to see there antiquities such as are at Rome, since the Emperors had their Triumphs often there. Triumphal arches, Baths, Temples, Termes, roman ways, obelisks, sculpture, are said to abound there. It was for many years the Capital of La Belgique.

—————

I have just been told, by a British officer, that the D[uke] of Wellington has ordered that 4 days provisions for the whole army round should accompany its entrance into France.⁷ After that, it is to find quarters & provisions as it can. But he will not run the risk of feeding upon, or pillaging the loyal from immediate want. He will give time to select their unhappy prey, & favour the right side.—Murat, you must

⁴ Mme de Maurville (L. 838 n. 30), who was always hard pressed for money, may have proposed some scheme based on foreign exchange or letters of credit that was refused or criticized by the d'Arblays. The French phrase used by FBA suggests that there may have been something odd or shady about the proposal. See further, L. 902 n. 1. ⁵ See L. 873 n. 2.

⁶ A prolific historian and man of letters, Louis-Dieudonné-Joseph Dewez (1760–1834), author of *Histoire générale de la Belgique, depuis la conquête de César* (Brussels, 7 vols., 1805–7). 'The Library' was probably the 'Cabinet Littéraire' nearby in the Marché au bois. See Romberg, pp. 176–7.

⁷ And yet Wellington and his staff were so surprised by Napoleon's advance into Belgium that the allied army fought the Waterloo campaign on empty stomachs. See Christian von Ompteda, *In the King's German Legion* . . . (1894), p. 305.

know, is taken into Austria.[8] ⌐Oh that they may *livrer* that wretched man who causes such devastations universal!⌐[9]

I have written a long Letter, at last, to my valuable Friend, Archdeacon Cambridge.[10] |

M. Mounier,[11] so long desired, is arrived, & now at Gand, & of the K[ing]'s Council.

The other day, at the Library, a young lady, who had just changed some Books, said to me 'Pardon, Madame—mais— ne parlez vous pas anglais?' 'Mais oui,—et vous, Mad^elle?—' she answered in English, & told her her mama was an English lady. 'And you, I said, look English too?' 'O yes! cried she, with great vivacity; 'I had an English Father; & I have an English Mother; but I was born in the East Indies myself: though I am a very good English! for if I could catch Buonaparte I would hang him directly!' This made me laugh heartily, for she is not taller than the youngest Boyd. But she is spirited & clever. She then entered into conversation, very animatedly, & when I was coming away, took my hand & pressed it several times, & entreated to introduce her Mama to me. I told her I was a recluse, & made no acquaintance. 'O! she cried, but my Mama will be so fond to know you!—I'll tell you her name, if you please?' "Certainly." "Rhamus.[12] Do you know that

---

[8] Joachim Murat* (1767–1815), King of Naples and Napoleon's greatest cavalry commander, had been defeated by the Austrians at Tolentino in the Marches of central Italy on 2 May, after which he fled to France. He was not captured until 8 October, when he landed with a handful of men at Pizzo in Calabria in a last attempt to regain his throne. He was court-martialled by his Bourbon captors and shot on 13 Oct. 1815.

[9] Napoleon.   [10] This letter is missing.   [11] See L. 876 n. 27.

[12] The Ramus family, which seems to have come over to England with Queen Charlotte, filled many posts in the Royal Household ('clerk of the spicery', 'clerk of his majesty's kitchen', 'Gentleman of the Ewry'). Nicholas Ramus (d. 8 Feb. 1779) and his son William (d. 22 Sept. 1792) were pages of the backstairs to King George III and a son of the latter, William, junior, was Page of the Bedchamber to the King from 1772 until 1789, the year of the King's illness, when he was dismissed for offensive curiosity with respect 'His Majesty's looks and gestures' (R.H.I., Windsor). This was the Ramus FBA would have remembered from her years (1786–91) at court and he may have been 'the very one' in the mind of her young interlocutor, who was born, she said, in the East Indies, where by 1789 several members of the Ramus family were firmly established. The dismissed page, if he went to Bengal, could have been aided by his uncle Henry Charles Ramus (d. 1822), whose career (writer, factor, merchant, and commissary) is recorded in a 'List of the Honourable Company's Covenanted Servants in the Bengal Establishment'. Henry's sister Benedicta (d. 1811) had married 15 Feb. 1777 John Day (d. 1808), advocate, who through Ramus or Court influence was knighted (1777) and appointed in the years 1779–85 Governor General of Bengal. See *Memoirs of William Hickey* [1749–1809], ed. Alfred Spencer (4 vols., 1919–25), i. 283; ii. 151; iii. 299–306.

name?" "There was one of the K[ing] of England's pages bore it—but—" "O! that's the thing!" she cried—but he's been dead a long number of years! I can't remember him!' she then renewed her suit: but though I liked her, & her sprightliness, & warmth, very much I would not risk a new acquaintance that I may not like at all, & of whose character & conduct I am wholly ignorant. She came back to me at least 10 times to repeat her request, always taking my hand, & profoundly courtysing. I suppose she had some how or other gathered my name. It is not else likely so young a person would now have taken such a fancy to me. But my melancholy garb makes me now conspicuous. I am known by it, I have been told. ⌈If mes Malles do not arrive, I must go into half Mourning i.e. black & Coloured ribbons, &c I am terribly shabby, en attendant but I see nobody.⌉

⌒

I have now to tell my dearest Ami that I have had a *confabulation* with Mr. Kirkpatrick. He has been *up the country*, upon business for about a fortnight. He has promised me the News papers again soon. I begged him to give me some intelligence. Lord Wellington, he answered, told his times & projects to no one: but the reason of delay now, he added, was the non-arrival of the Russian army, which, however, was *expected* by the *21st* June—& — — it was *believed* the first movement hence would be on the *25th*—but *certainly* before the end of the month. He confirmed the assertion That France will be a pile of ruins if B[uonaparte] is not given up! |

⌈But the best of the business is, this good man has got over for you the analeptics, andersons, & James's powders.[13] I have just paid him 18 shillings for the packet. How can I direct to be sure you may not miss them? At least, as you KNOW they are within call, do not spare for what you possess, if you feel occasion—which Heaven, however, forbid.—Your last Bulletin has really revivified me.

How sorry I am to tell you that in the list of B[uonaparte's]

---

[13] Of the analeptics, strengthening or restorative medicines in general, Anderson's Scots Pills (vi, L. 620 n. 2) and James's Powders (i, L. 7 n. 2), named after their concocters, were favoured patent medicines.

new peers,[14] not only M. de Beauvau is named,[15] but M. de La Tour Maubourg![16] Not OUR OWN La Tour Maubourg.[17]— Gassendi,[18]—also F[lahaut][19] but no one else that I care about, I believe, though I have not read the list myself.

—————

Report, here, says, Carnot[20] & Fouché are ready enough to stop the War by giving up B[uonaparte] but, the allies won't negotiate with the Jacobins. Poor Mr. Lajard,[21] young Boin[ville][22] told me, began to look *rather blue*—i.e. effrayé et epeuré, before he—Boin[ville]—left Paris. How I hope the *Vendeens*[23] will be sucoured in time! Mr. Kirk[patrick] gave me the infinite relief of assurance the allies meant not to be preceded or, even accompanied, by *any* French! When they have cleared the way, *All* the French are to form around the King & M. d'Orleans, then, will come over, to take the command, if Louis 18 will accept his services. Il tient ceci de bon part.

Friday—June 16ᵗʰ—I have retained this bit to bid you Bon Jour before the whole goes to the post.⁊ To-morrow I shall begin a new sheet. Your re-iterated request takes from me the fear I had of overwhelming you. Read my Letters *pour vous delasser*, when tired of writing & working & business.

[14] This list first appeared in the Paris *Moniteur* on 6 June. Those named came to be called *pairs des Cent-Jours*, and when the Hundred Days ended most of them came to be called to account for their approval of Napoleon's return to power.

[15] The prince de Beauvau (L. 842 n. 10 and v, L. 513 n. 2) was named in the list (*supra*) according to his Napoleonic title as 'Le comte Beauvau'.

[16] Marie-Charles-*César* de Fay, marquis and comte de Latour-Maubourg (L. 845 n. 28).

[17] Marie-*Victor*-Nicolas de Fay, marquis and comte de Latour-Maubourg (L. 840 n. 23).

[18] For Gassendi's earlier career and friendship with M. d'A, see v, L. 486 n. 3 and above L. 845 n. 26. It should also be remembered that his friendship with Napoleon stretched back into their days when as young artillery officers they served together before the Revolution and after it at the siege of Toulon. See Joseph du Teil, *Une Famille militaire au XVIIIᵉ siècle* (1896), pp. 388–9, 415.

[19] Possibly August-*Charles*-Joseph de Flahaut de la Billarderie (1785–1870), comte de Flahaut, whom the d'Arblays had met at Joigny in 1802 (vi. L. 630 n. 2 and ix *passim*).

[20] Although Carnot (L. 856 n. 15) remained firmly attached to Napoleon, Fouché was negotiating during this period with both Louis XVIII, whose loyal subject he affected to be, and Wellington, whom he began to interest in an Orléanist succession (Romberg and Malet, ii. 162, and *Supp. Desp.* x. 60–2).

[21] After a long career (L. 840 n. 26) as a defender of moderate and constitutional policies, Lajard seems to have been dismayed by this return to despotic rule. See L. Gallois, *Biographie des ministres français depuis juillet 1789 jusqu'à ce jour* (Brussels, 1826), pp. 176–7.

[22] See L. 876 n. 16.

[23] Vendéens.

—And take—my dear dearest Ami! the recompense for your own in the knowledge how they soothe the sad *ennuies*, & even re-waken to *Life* & *HOPE* the most faithful & devoted Wife & amie that ever man possessed—

FB d'A—

⌐We have scarcely a Day here withou train.²⁴—How do I long to know if some of these ⟨arrive⟩. It is 12 days even in presuming return of Post, ere we can reply to each other.⌐²⁵

All idea of B[uonaparte]'s coming hither is now scouted. 'Tis laughed at, ⟨nor⟩ are D[uke] W[ellington]'s forces here at present. The brave Highlanders are going forward²⁶—& others are to succeed them & be quartered on Brussells.

891   [1358, Marché au bois,
                           Brussels], 15–19 June 1815

To M. d'Arblay

A.L. (Berg), 15–19 June 1815
Double sheet 4to   4 pp.   *pmk*   BRUXELLES   wafer
Addressed: *Treves.* / À / Monsieur le Général d'Arblay, / officier Superieur du Garde du Corps / de sa Majesty Le Roi de France, / Chevʳ de Sᵗ Louis, &c &c / À Treves.
Edited by FBA, p. 1, *annotated*: (14 / 2)
Just Before Waterloo.
Rough & confused & inaccurate sketch of the opening of the Campaign between Buonaparte & Wellington & Blucher.
Annotated by M.d'A, p. 4: (19 et non pas 20) Cette erreur m'a causé une inquietude terrible qui a été heureusement dissipée par l'almanach.
Edited also by CFBt? See Textual Notes.

²⁴ The prolonged rain before Waterloo, which virtually all contemporary accounts comment on, had the important result that Napoleon's great strength in cavalry and artillery had no decisive effect (the horsemen were impeded and the shells often buried themselves in the soft ground). He waited long before opening the battle, chiefly to let the sun dry out the field.
²⁵ This was too pessimistic, for as FBA's opening remark in L. 891 makes clear, she could receive a letter from Trèves in three days and could therefore hope to send a reply by return of post that would reach her in seven or eight days.
²⁶ As FBA wrote this on the morning of 16 June, the battle of Quatre Bras was about to begin. The Highlanders (especially the 42nd, 79th, and 92nd Regiments) distinguished themselves in this delaying battle that gave Wellington time to concentrate his forces for the main battle at Waterloo.

June 17th 1815.

Oh my beloved Ami—what dreadful times are these! May you but still be at Treves!—& quickly, quickly be able to let me see that date which is now my fondest desire—for I have just received your Letter of the 12th where you answer to M. le D[uke] de L[uxembourg][1]—& I entirely enter into your reasonings & feelings,—they are now, indeed, *my own*, so completely they have operated upon my mind: & others, which I cannot now write, that the change of affairs has given rise to, combine to make me earnestly desire your continuance with Genl Kleist at Treves. So be it! Amen! — —

To the present state of Brussells.

Thursday, the 15th—early in the night, a Bugle Horn called me to the window:[2] I saw a few soldiers,[3] & thought them collecting for some change of sentinels: but about 3 in the morning I was awakened by a *Hub bub* in the street, that made me rise, & run hastily again to the window: it was not light, & a sound of a few voices, in passing stragglers, made me once more conclude there was nothing material, & go quietly to Bed again. But at six o'clock *Friday the 16th* the same sounds called me forth to examine the neighbourhood, & enquire of the maid, who was arranging the sallon, what was the matter? Can you conceive this flemish phlegm? From *FLEMISH, PHLEGM* must certainly be derived! She answered that she knew of nothing; & the Masters of the house gave me no species of intelligence though well aware of my deep private interest in public matters! —& I forwarded to you my Letter without any communication upon a subject which was then known all over Bruxelles, except to my lonely self!—

You will certainly have learnt, long ere this can reach you, that the Enemy has broken into La Belgique.[4] No clear account of the particulars has yet been published. M. de Beaufort came to me immediately with an offer of services; Mme d'Henin came, also, to say she would remove herself to Malines, or anvers,[5]

891. [1] L. 887.

[2] This was the first sounding of the alarm at Brussels (Galesloot, ii. 113).

[3] Probably the Brunswickers, who at that hour were passing through Brussels from their encampment at Laeken north of the city (Capel, p. 112).

[4] FBA is quite right about this—the news that the French were already at Charleroi had spread throughout Brussels that morning and was published in *L'Oracle* for 16 June.

[5] Departure to Antwerp was also the safest course in Wellington's eyes, and he

& lend me Therese[6] to attend me, if I wished it: & Mme de Maurville offered me a Bed in her house, if I preferred staying, yet not resting alone. Every body revived into friendly attention. To the Boyds I went myself. |

What a day of confusion & alarm did we all spend! In *my* heart the whole time was Treves! Treves! Treves! That day, & *This*, which is now finishing, June 17th I passed in hearing the cannon—!—seeing the wounded & disabled return, & the ready-armed & vigourous victims march forth to the same destruction!—I was with the p^ss at least 10 times—spent 2 Hours chez M^e La Tour du Pin,—who was returned to Brussells,—calling upon & receiving the Boyds & Me de Maurville —as well as M. de Beaufort—joining in & changing plans 20 times in an Hour—&, while occupied thus variously in words & actions, filled, entirely filled within with one sole only all concentrating thought—of Treves! Treves! Treves!—

Finally, it is arranged This Day

Sunday,[7] June 19th—Exactly 3 months since I flew from Paris.

That I shall set out to-morrow morning, at 5 o'clock,

If Danger here approaches

with the family of the Boyds, for Antwerp. (Anvers.)[5]

If better prospects arise, I remain at Brussells.

As also if—unhappily, our conveyance fails us!

Direct always in future à Mad^e *de* Burney,[8] Bruxelles— *No street, Nothing else.*—[9]

I will make the post man send it on if I am gone—by directions left:

and a line à Mad^e *de* Burney, post Restante, Anvers.—[9]

For Heaven's sake, one line each way! *no* signature!

I have just—at last—had a Letter, delicious for us both— from our Alexander.[10]—still, alas at James's—[11]

At Anvers, Mr. Boyd says I can draw upon the Danoots, here, or from Hoare's in England, without difficulty. How soon I

proposed it to an English lady in a note written just before Waterloo (*Supp. Desp.* x. 501).

  6 The princesse d'Hénin's maid.
  7 Actually Sunday 18 June, the day of Waterloo.
  8 FBA's change of name and omission of her address were intended to conceal her identity as the wife of an active royalist.
  9 A further step to avoid detection in the event of a French victory.
  10 AA's letter has not survived, but FBA's answer appears below in L. 896.

must do it, ¹ if we do not meet!——for I have now only 10 napoleans left in all.¹¹ And travelling—& incidental expences in removals will soon swallow them up.

You, also, Mon Ami! mon cher ami! will always be able to draw upon the *tight*,¹² *wihout* me, if M. de Feltre fails you—& if this place should be taken. Since I have *heard*—since I *HEAR* the canon!¹³—Oh mon ami!—one line! *one word!*—

Daily!

Daily!—

For the present awful moment!—

all the people at Brussels LIVE in the streets or at the windows —the whole population is in constant view.

They assure us the Chiefs on each side are in constant view, too, of one another!

The poor Duke de Brunswic¹⁴ was killed close to the side of the D. of Wellington.—& le Comte de Vincent,¹⁵ the austrian minister extraordinary, has been wounded to day in the same position.

Sunday Night.

The various News of this horrible day has altered my projects every hour. All, at first, was ill—& I accompanied the Boyds to the water side, to embark in a Barge for Anvers: but our vessel was siezed for some wounded officers, & we could get no other.¹⁶ The news then changed, &, in the Evening, I was assured Lord Wellington & M¹ Blücher united had gained a complete victory. 800 prisoners were brought in¹⁷—made by

¹¹ The napoleon was a gold coin worth 20 francs, which at the exchange rates of the time equalled 16 shillings. FBA had therefore only £8 with which to make her escape from Brussels, where all the banks had closed and where widespread panic and requisitioning had made horses, carriages, and boats both scarce and expensive.

¹² FBA means that M. d'A will be able to get money by drawing on their bankers in England if Brussels falls and Louis XVIII's court leaves Ghent.

¹³ Apart from the noise, shock waves from the Waterloo cannonade were strong enough to break window-panes in some Brussels houses. See Henri-Marie Ghislain, comte de Mérode-Westerloo, *Souvenirs* . . . (Brussels 2 vols., 1840), i. 350.

¹⁴ Frederick William (1771–1815), Duke of Brunswick and kinsman of the British royal family, had been shot in the chest and killed at the Battle of Quatre Bras on 16 June.

¹⁵ Vincent (L. 872 n. 13) was slightly wounded at Waterloo on 18 June.

¹⁶ Wellington's medical officers were forced by the heavy casualties at Quatre Bras and Waterloo to start at once to evacuate wounded by barge to Antwerp. The Brussels hospitals were inadequate and the roads were clogged by refugees, deserters, and advancing troops (*Supp. Desp.* x. 598).

¹⁷ There were in fact roughly 8,000 French prisoners captured at Waterloo, but

report as many thousands—But now, the last news of all, tells us the Enemy is working at turning the right wing of Lord Wellington,[18] who is in great danger, & that Brussels is threatened with being taken to-morrow morning! |

I am come therefore, to the Boyds, to be in readiness for departing for Anvers to-morrow—or rather This morning at 4 O'clock. We none of us go to Bed, but they are all gone to lie down, in their cloaths; & I have tried to do the same, but excessive inquietude prevents my sleeping. I must now make up this confused scrawl, with repeated petition for a Line to Mad^e *de Burney, poste restante,* Anvers. Heaven bless & preserve you, O mon ami!—and grant that, This frightful storm weathered, we may be re-united in dear, soft, gentle & confiding peace for the rest of our mutual days! Amen. Finished *Three o'clock* on *Monday Morning, June 19th*

We have all been employed in making Charpie![19]—Ah, ma chère Mad^e de Tessé!—!—[19]

Mr. Boyd & his family have been upon La place Royale to see the prisoners who were almost all severely wounded, & were in immense numbers. & to see 2 tri-coloured Drapeaux, & two large & beautiful Eagles.[20] The English have continued arriving, on foot, in carts, & on Horse back, grievously wounded also. NEVER yet, all agree, has there been so bloody a battle fought! We have had as yet no consistent details—but the continued sight of the maimed, wounded, mutilated & tortured victims to this exterminating warfare is shocking & afflicting beyond description.

P.S. I open my Letter to say, that, just as we were setting

FBA is probably right about the number who reached Brussels on the night of the battle.

[18] This was a false report, though it was, according to Wellington's later comments on Waterloo, the manœuvre that Napoleon should have attempted (*Supp. Desp.* (x. 530–1).

[19] 'Unravelled linen' or lint used in making bandages, a task that many ladies in Brussels took on themselves. 'During the 16th, 17th, and for many succeeding days, we were all employed in scraping lint, and preparing cherry water for the wounded' (de Ros, p. 136). M. d'A's old friend Mme de Tessé (v, L. 510 n. 11) had prepared charpie for use in FBA's operation (her mastectomy) of 1811 (see vi. 605).

[20] These trophies, which on 19 June Wellington promised to send to the Prince Regent (*AR* lvii. 178) were among the first to be displayed after Waterloo. They were probably the eagles of the 45th and 105th Regiments, both of which were captured by British dragoons in an early charge, together with the colours of the 105th and 25th Regiments, the last of which was taken by the 28th Foot (Dalton, pp. 257–63).

off for Anvers, an English officer brought us word the Enemy had so been pushed & routed at *Wavre* that he had fought his way en retraite back to Genappe[21]—and that Brussells is saved!—though the *War* is only beginning. I must run to Copy you a bulletin that I am told is just published. I have this moment read it. Added to what I have told you of the *position*, is 100 pieces de cannons *present* from the Enemy![22]—I stay here, therefore, decidedly—so direct as usual, only *Bruxelles, sans rue.*

P.S. 2ᵈ No official news is given since 3 in the mornᵍ of the 19ᵗʰ—! Lord Wellington & Mˡ Blücher were then both following the Enemy.[23] We are terrified lest they have gone too far! I will write again to-morrow if I can learn any tidings. We think Bruxelles as safe now as before the War. Oh for equal satisfaction from Treves! Treves!—Treves!—

892   Trèves, 19 June 1815

M. d'Arblay
To Madame d'Arblay

A.L. (Berg), 19 juin 1815
Double sheet 4to   greenish   4 pp.   *pmk*   TRIER   seal
Addressed: A Madame / Madame d'Arblay Place / du Marche au Bois Nº 1358 / à Bruxelles.
Edited by FBA, p. 1, *annotated*: ⌜22⌝ (13) [*with numbers on address fold*]: 6   13   13   22   22
See further, Textual Notes.

Du Cabaret ce 19 Juin 1815

Pardon ma bonne amie, mais je ne veux pas dans un moment comme celuici perdre un jour de poste sans te donner de mes nouvelles. Ma santé est excellente mais, my spirits are not so.

---

[21] This was a seesaw battle between the French and Prussians that lasted throughout 18 and 19 June, when the news of disaster at Waterloo forced Grouchy* to retreat through Gembloux to Namur while the remnants of Napoleon's main force retreated through Genappe to Charleroi (Houssaye, *1815*, ii. 455–78).

[22] A return of ordnance for 20 June lists 122 cannon captured at Waterloo (*Supp. Desp.* x. 547).

[23] Only Blücher and the Prussians continued the pursuit during the night of 18–19 June. Wellington's army was exhausted and his cavalry had been virtually destroyed by repeated charges.

Toute ma pauvre (*machine—morale!*)¹ est bouleversée depuis ce que tu m'as mandé. Quelle terrible catastrophe se prepare! Veuille le Ciel que mes présentimens me trompent mais je ne puis voir comme ceux qui pensent que des moyens extrêmes de cette violence puissent jamais avoir le resultat qu'ils en attendent. Qu'ils reflechissent à tout ce qu'ils peuvent leur preparer non seulement de regrets mais de dangers! Quels moyens ne seront pas justifiés par de ⎸ telles menaces surtout lorsqu'effectivement on aura commencé à les mettre à execution. De quel droit d'ailleurs confondre ainsi l'assassinat d'une innocent et la juste punition du coupable? qui doute ou peut douter que les deux tiers de la France voulaient et veulent encore le Roi et la paix; et qui osera dire qu'il est possible aux gens desarmés et sous le glaive d'une infâme soldatesque, de faire autrement qu'ils ne font. Sont ils les maitres de remettre sur le Thrône celui que la Trahison en a fait descendre? Non sans doute pourquoi donc abuser de la force et la deployer d'une maniere à la rendre impuissante pour le bien? Si son action n'etait dirigée que contre l'armée ⎸ revoltée, peut etre pourrait on s'etourdir sur les suittes, mais —— je ne veux pas pousser plus loin ces reflexions. O mon amie que je voudrais te savoir en Angleterre! du moins les plus chers objets de mes affections, —il y a deux jours j'aurais dit *les seuls*—mais ce que tu m'as ecrit me fait sentir que j'ai laissé derriere moi des personnes qui me sont encore bien cheres! Au nom du Ciel menage toi les moyens de t'eloigner au premier signal, à la premiere crainte. Pauvre France! et pauvre Louis XVIII! [xxxxx 1½ *lines*]

Dis à Alex mille et mille choses pour moi, et dis lui aussi pourquoi je ne lui ecris point. Je donnerais tout au monde pour avoir un mot de lui. Dechire un petit morceau d'une de ses letters et envoie le moi. ⎸

J'ai demandé la medaille de la Fidelité² pour mes com-

---

892.   ¹ That man is a machine had become an eighteenth-century commonplace through the influence of La Mettrie's *L'Homme machine* (1747). What so upset M. d'A was FBA's account in L. 888 of the allied plan to drive 'through Fire and Sword' toward Paris.
    ² Created by a royal decree (printed in Guillemin, p. 219 n. 1), dated 17 May at Ghent, and intended for those who had rallied around Louis XVIII during the Hundred Days, this was a silver medal attached to a blue and white ribbon. It was to be worn on the left side by those whose fidelity had been demonstrated to the satisfaction of a court council presided over by the comte d'Artois. M. d'A was later able to add this token of loyalty to his Ordre du Lys, which he had received during the spring of 1814 but which had been cheapened by wholesale distribution;

pagnons et pour moi. Je crois certes la meriter car personne n'a jamais fait un plus grand sacrifice. La date de ma lettre t'etonnera mais je n'ai pu me refuser aux instances de Mr de Mazancourt, et le dejeuner se prolongeant plus que je n'avais pensé je t'ai griffonné ceci.³ Adieu adieu ma chere amie— Ecris moi Toujours ici. ¹

893   [1358, Marché au bois,
                                       Brussels, 10]–20 June, 1815.

To H.R.H. Princess Elizabeth

A.L. draft (Berg), –20 June 1815
Double sheet 4to 4 pp. showing the false starts and overwriting characteristic of a draft.

The waters of Lethe?¹ No, no, no! thank Heaven, no!— ungenial beverage! I am all revived in finding how far it has been from those lips which I had feared, with so much sorrow, had been sucking in its oblivious juice. With what real & grateful happiness do I receive this fresh mark¹—more flowing, more peaceful, more engaging, I think, than ever—of a remembrance which so condescendingly honours me, & which, at this awful moment of mingled menace & hope, has a power unspeakably precious of giving la couleur de rose to *des pensées*, which continual, & almost always lonely rumination, was cruelly at work to tinge with hues *les plus noirs*. (And yet,—who should I have believed only 6 months ago, that should have predicted that I was destined to love, honour & delight in Nobody?)² I had not, I own, the smallest idea I had such a

only, however, after he applied once again to the duc de Feltre on or about 1 July. See A.L.S. (Vincennes).

³ M. d'A here excused the lapse of six days between this letter and his last (L. 889).

893. ¹ FBA's fear (expressed in L. 877, 29 May) that with respect to her the Princess had quaffed the 'waters of Lethe' must be dispelled, the Princess said, by her 'long Epistle' of 2–3, [5–6] June (8 full 4to pages): 'This . . . will prove that somebody has not swallowed the waters of Lethe in 〈regard〉 to her friend, though in many cases what a delightful draught that would be.'

² It was in a letter (Berg) of 28 Dec. 1814 (see L. 837 n. 1) that the Princess had initiated the correspondence between Nobody (herself) and somebody (FBA) though throughout the war the letters were sent without signatures.

misanthropical tendency—But we never know ourselves till the day of trial; for most certainly, now, Nobody has a place in my mind, my estimation, & my gratitude, that Nobody—I am sure, can imagine!

I am charmed at the good opinion retained of the engrafted tribe:[3] I have myself seen, by a singular chance, mingled with a very peculiar confidence, some productions of the principal plant that were perfectly deserving the fair mede of praise with which I see them honoured. For the *weak* & the *little* Branches, however I deplore their ⎮ decay, I cannot disguise from my view of the scenery around, that no vegetation thrives, in this season, that is not naturally vigorous, & fitted to bear the inclemencies & to resist the shocks of the Elements. For the root, however, white & hoary, & the sprig, tried in storms yet sustaining every blast, the sprig par excellence, we—I speak for two halves that unite in one unbroken whole—are interested with a zeal & fervour that have no bounds. O certainly yes! those waters of Lethe, that to me would have been so noxious, if made use of to wash away the speeches lodged in the old breach, would be most salubriously employed, & purify the whole ambient atmosphere, till it became 'Lilly bright & shiny.'

But the interest excited by all these engraftings, though warm & sincere, must always, with me, be short of what will ever superiorly remain for my own original parent plants & precious shoots. How beautiful, how refreshing the account of the cheering union around the sacred Magnolia at that lovely cottage,[4] of which the views, grounds, & even the decorations, are now, with all their agricultural emblems,[4] before my Eyes! elegant in simplicity, ⎮ gay in the purity of innocent enjoyment, springing from the general harmony of cherishing Nature's first, best, & dearest ties! I was kept, as I read, in as much in a fever about

[3] Perhaps the Maison de Bourbon. To the Princess with her life-long interest in gardening, landscaping, and farming, a botanical idiom came naturally, and her comments on personages in the guise of engraftings, branches, buds, and shoots, though evidently intelligible to FBA, are lost on the editors. FBA, however, in her reply, seems to be referring to Louis XVIII, his Manifesto, the duchesse d'Angoulême, whom both she and M. d'A revere, the political climate of Brussels, if not of France, and the backstairs intrigues of the second Restoration. She echoes the Princess's hope that 'an old breach' may be washed out by the 'waters of Lethe'.
[4] 'The Princess's Cottage at Old Windsor.' See L. 888 n. 12 and the Princess's letter (Berg) of [5–6] June. With authentic features, at least, hay crops and cattle, the mock cottage sported 'agricultural emblems' as well, for the Princess, out of 'a whim' of her own, kept nearby 'a common Country basket filled with instruments of Husbandry' including 'a Rake & a Hoe to support the violence of the virtuous'.

the weather, and whether or not the Rain would be so good as to go to Spain,[5] as if I had been present & watching the varying Clouds. The peculiar pleasure which the dignified Magnolia must reap from seeing the state of perfection to which the *full blown fruit* has attained[6]—appears to me a providential consolation to many a blight—

June 20 1815

Oh Madam, what a victory!—how glorious, how stupendous! beyond—except perhaps the Battle of Trafalgar ANY of ANY sort recorded in our Annals! not from its actual greatness alone, but from the undoubted & superb & organizing effect it must essentially have upon all the Nations of the World!—

I had lain down my pen, from hearing that Sr C. Stuart was gone to G and,[7] &, almost immediately afterwards the commencin^g of hostilities made me defer writing till I could obtain some news—not to send to the Hill![8] I know well I should there always be anticipated, but to recover enough of calm to write yet now, I am as far from calm by Joy as I was removed | from it then by terrour. But I am sure I shall be pardonned, for EVERY sweet plant now will be sensitive as well as that tender one[9] to which this delicious event if gently told, will be strengthening as well as reviving.

How great, how noble, how miraculously happy are events!

[5] The Princess had evoked 'the old adage, 'Rain rain—go to Spain' as sitting at the open window of the cottage she scanned the sky in fears for her plans for the day. 'This day [5 June] will bring the Magnolia & the other plants [the Queen and the Princesses]. 'Where there is heart room one is sure to find house Room, & most likely at Dinner will be sixteen at supper above twenty.' Here is none of 'the shew of magnificent places', no 'rich Plate', but only 'flowers in Chrystal vases', 'comfort—neatness, & chearfulness, & every thing that suits a farmers wife'. 'Good humour & Amnity will naturally preside at the Board, Good will certainly & I doubt not that The Will will be taken for ye deed.'
On [6] June the Princess could report that 'the party yesterday went off to perfection'. Twenty sat down to table. 'The Magnolia bore it with its usual strength & was surrounded by all the plants.'
[6] In the botanical assembly surrounding the magnolia on all occasions of state, celebration, or crisis, the Princess depicts her own ample presence as the '*Full blown Fruit*', the humour of which appellation may be appreciated in a glance at her portraits, of which one is shown by Dorothy Margaret Stuart, *The Daughters of George III* (1939), *facing* p. 186.
[7] The sequence of his letters suggests that Sir Charles Stuart (L. 856 n. 19) returned to Ghent on Monday 12 June (Romberg and Malet, ii. 170).
[8] The term used by the Princess for Windsor Castle.
[9] 'That tender one' or 'the Sensitive Plant' is the Princess Sophia (L. 845 n. 33 , who 'tho better still requires all the care of the Hot House', can admit her sisters for only a short time, and, able to go out of her own door only once or twice a week, seldom makes an appearance (Princess Elizabeth's letter, op. cit.).

Dear incomparable old England—as it stopt the torrent of revolutionary rage among the people, will stop it now, I trust, amongst the Dynasties!

Poor little Jerry they say is dead.[10] I could never have believed the death of honour reserved for him—indeed I dare say he had no ambition of that end even for himself. *Murat* always brave, deserved *that* distinction, & has obtained it.[11] Vandamme c^d not too soon be cut off from the Centre which he disgraced,[12] & I only wish his rival in ferocious cruelty d'avoust,[12] as quick an exit. And I wish a round robin of ditto to many a Brother foul-fiend at Paris. Reports of Bertrand vary.[13]

2 eagles & 2 Drapeaux Tricolore arrived at the Place Royale on Sunday. *5 more* I am assured are on the road. The canon taken are UPWARD of 200! The Prisoners cannot yet be counted. A miserable ill dressed set passed my window just now; I imagine they were in the rear for la garde imperiale was always equipped with the utmost eclat. A general Mouten[14] also passed yesterday, followed by an insulting crowd, calling out 'Tuez le moi, qu'il soit tué—!' but they were quieted when they found their mistake, they had thought him Buonaparte—

All Saturday & Sunday the English were running hence to Antwerp.

The fright, the horrour here cannot be depicted—& I, Heaven knows, had my share! ONCE, on the Sunday, they

---

[10] Ruler of the Napoleonic Kingdom of Westphalia from 1807 to 1813, Jérôme Bonaparte (1784–1860) had returned to France after his brother's escape from Elba to command a division of the army that invaded Belgium. He was lightly wounded in the left side at Quatre Bras and in the head at Waterloo but rallied a few troops whom he led back to Laon, then went on to Paris. An exile in Germany, Italy, and Switzerland until 1848, he was made in 1850 a maréchal de France and in 1852 président du Sénat.

[11] Not of course true. See L. 890 n. 7 (*supra*).

[12] Vandamme (L. 878 n. 10) lived on until 1830; his fellow Bonapartist Davout (L. 856 n. 15), until 1823.

[13] Henri-Gratien Bertrand (1773–1844), comte de l'Empire (1808), who early in his distinguished military career became Napoleon's favourite aide-de-camp and in 1813 his grand maréchal du palais, was perhaps the most loyal of the Emperor's followers, later accompanying him to Elba and St. Helena. FBA's interest in him may have been increased by his marriage in 1808 to Fanny Elizabeth Dillon (1777–1862). For talks with Bertrand reported to Wellington on 15 June see *Supp. Desp.* x. 479–80.

[14] Apparently Georges Mouton (1770–1838), comte de Lobau (1809), commander of the 6th corps d'armée at Waterloo, was captured and brought to Brussels. Facing proscription at the hands of Louis XVIII and deportation by the King of the Netherlands, he was allowed to remain and live in Brussels through the intercession of Wellington (*Supp. Desp.* x. 596 and xi. 273).

shouted aloud with piercing outcries 'Les Français arrivent ils sont à nos portes!

894   [1358, Marché au bois, Brussels], 20 June 1815

To H.R.H. Princess Elizabeth

A.L. incomplete draft (Berg), 20 June 1815
Double sheet 4to   3 pp.   The beginning is missing.

I had already sent my small baggage to a family with which I had engaged to depart for Antwerp the next morning—but supposing all departure now too late, & terrified at the idea of being alone in a lodging, where I was only known as wife of a General in ACTIVITY of service ags^t Buonaparte—& *also* of La Maison du Roi—I determined to fly to the house of a lady, M^e la Comtesse de Maurville,[1] who had promised, *en cas d'evenement* to receive me as a part of her own house, by the name of Mad^e de Burney—for alas—my so partial & excellent new friend, Mme de Beaufort, seized with a pleuretic fever, was suddenly dead!—!

In traversing the streets, the disorder & despair I witnessed strongly affected me *THEN* with concern, but now, on reflexion, with pleasure; for there could be no greater proof of the real horrour in which B[uonaparte] was seen. The shops (*open* here ordinarily on Sundays!) were suddenly shut up—the goods hidden—the common people in groups, always curious, however trembling, in the middle of the streets, the others at the windows, & running away from them, alternately every other minute—& poor women with Babes at their breasts screaming aloud their apprehensions that their Infants would be all victims!

With M^e de M[aurville][1] as safe, at least, as a Native, I remained shut up till about 10 o'clock at night—witnessing from the window—continual, incessant arrivals of wounded, maimed, ill, or dying! on foot, on Horse, on Brancards; on carts,

894.   [1] See L. 838 n. 30.

& in waggons!—a sight to break one's heart!—yet upon which the Eye, forever seeking some information, or hoping for some change, while filled with commiseration, was fixed as by Magic! —— at last, ¹ an English gentleman, belonging to some army office, came in to tell us he was just returned from the Field of Battle! & he *thought* all was going on well—& that the report that had so dreadfully alarmed the Town of the arrival of Les Français was *TRUE*, though *without* alarm, for Les Français Were indeed, & by hundreds arrived—as Prisoners!

I then went—seeing O what sights in my way! to la rue de l'assaut²—& found my friends there still decided to go, but powerless to find any Horses, or means. None of us—Fathers, Mothers, nor 5 young ladies, went to Bed all night—in the Morning, at 7, we were promised a Barge—for Antwerp; but an English gentleman, who called in, Capt. Marshall,³ tho' he advised us all to go, & had sent off his own wife, told me he did not think there was any danger for Brussels for *that* Day, (Monday)—

Then, quoth I, there can be none at all! for if B. does not obtain Brussels by a Coup de Main, he can only obtain it by the loss of Paris—since, if he stays longer away, the allies will enter in his absence,—& the Victory of a Town will cost him a Kingdom.⁴ I therefore returned quietly to my apartment. Mr Mrs & Miss Boyds went on for Antwerp.

Most happy, indeed, was I not to encrease my distance from the Person for whose sake I am distant from all others.

Where He now is I know not—his Last Letter is dated—Treves, Juin 14.⁵ but he was at that moment going forth—though whither, nor even how, he does not tell me. He only bids me always direct to Treves, whence his Letters will follow,

² The house of Walter Boyd (L. 870 n. 2) in the rue d'Assaut was only a five-minute walk from FBA's new refuge with Mme de Maurville in the rue de la Montagne. Both streets are in central Brussels between the Grand' Place and the Place Sainte-Gudule.
³ Possibly Captain William Marshall (1775–*post* 1839) of the 79th Regiment of Foot or Cameron Highlanders, who had been severely wounded at Quatre Bras on 16 June (*Bell's Weekly Messenger*, 9 July, p. 218) and may therefore have been allowed to return to Brussels (Dalton, pp. 190–1).
⁴ FBA's summing up of the choices open to Napoleon and his army after Waterloo—and of the lessening threat to Brussels—was even more accurate than it seems, for Vandamme, at the risk of being cut off from France, urged Grouchy* on 19 June to lead his army behind the advancing allies and attack Brussels (Houssaye, *1815*, ii. 475).
⁵ Actually 13 June (L. 889).

& he writes in good spirits, & declares himself in quite recovered health — — which softens to me the last word!—
Nous allons commencer — — He knew nothing of what has passed
this way—Nothing, indeed, ' at that time had passed. Every
Letter is 6 days en route—though he tells me, should I find it
prudent to remove, to let it be to Dusseldorf,[6] Germany being
much safer, *en cas de revers* than les pays bas. He has been
extremely well treated at Treves, by Gen¹ Kleist, &c as the
officier superieur there in the service of the French King: he is
invited to all the festivals, a sentinel is placed at his door, &c &c
And he has had, he assures me, far more success in his mission
than he had dared hope.

The D. of Wellington is just gone back to the army. He came
hither, yesterday, whⁿ the Battle was over, and a long pursuit of
B—who has, however, escaped once more: but so beaten, that
how he will be recᵈ in France, or whether received at all, is
doubtful. *MYSELF*, I suspect he will sneak off in some disguises
on board some shabby brig, & sail away for America.[7]— —What
effusion of blood will be saved shᵈ he be so very good as to do
that mean thing!

Mean while, the D. de Fitz James is commissioned to go from
the D[uke] to Louis 18. to advise his Maj. de se rendre à
Tournai[8]—& thence to go at once into France, as soon as the D.
of W. &c shall have prepared him a proper opening. This, to
yr. R.H. I may tell—my authority for. M. de la T[our] du
P[in] who was present himself, & shared the mission—& who
told it me.

How astonishing! the D. then thinks this great Battle already
decisive!

Almost all the Maison du Roi, not employed in separate
missions, came from Alost hither yesterday morning. Probably

⁶ To be near the château of Benrath (L. 889 n. 1).
⁷ A report made by Colonel Henry Dillon to Wellington (*Supp. Desp.* x. 479–80)
supported FBA's suspicion as to Napoleon's actual plan in the event of defeat or
deposition.
⁸ Édouard de Fitz-James (1776–1833), duc de Fitz-James (1805) on the death of
his father (vi, L. 631 n. 28), was an ardent royalist with strong English connections.
His mission from Wellington to Louis XVIII was chiefly one of protocol, since the
duc de Feltre had already received and accepted Wellington's proposal of 19 June
that the King advance into France at once, not by Tournai as FBA suggests but by
Grammont, Ath, and Mons (*Disp.* xii. 492 and *Supp. Desp.* x. 553).

to consult with the D. of W. upon accompanying the R[oi] to Tournai!

June 20. 1815 ¹

895   [1358, Marché au bois,
                       Brussels], 19–21 June [1815]

To M. d'Arblay

A.J.L. (Diary MSS. vii. 6636–[9], Berg), 19–21 June
Double sheet large 4to (10·1 × 8·2″)   4 pp.   foliated in ink   212   213
pmk BRUXELLES   wafer
Addressed. Treves. / À / Monsieur le General d'Arblay, / off͏ʳ Superieur des gardes du Corps / de sa Majesty Louis 18— / Chev͏ʳ de S͏ᵗ Louis, &c &c, / *à Treves*
Edited by FBA, p. 1 (6636), *annotated*: ⁜ ⌜9ᵗʰ⌝ 15 / 1   Battle of Waterloo
Edited also at the Press. *See* Textual Notes.

Monday, June *19ᵗʰ*

The sitting up all Night, however little merrily, made me, I know not how, seem to have lived a day longer than real time, for I thought to-Day the 20ᵗʰ when I finished my Letter of this morning.¹ I have now, therefore, to rectify that mistake, & tell you that there is, therefore, no chasm in the known history of the D[uke] of Wellington. But, to my infinite regret, with all the great, nay marvellous feats he has performed, he is less, not more, in public favour, from not being approved, or rather, I think, *comprehended*, in the openning of this tremendous business. As I am sure the subject must be of deeper interest to you than any other, at such an instant, I will tell you all I know, i.e. all I have heard & gathered, for I *know* nothing, & add my own consequent conjectures, as soon as I have first acquainted you that I separated from the Boyds at about half past 7 in the morning, too much satisfied with the news of Lord Wellington's victory to endure to distance myself still further from ALL I

895.   ¹ L. 891

love MOST upon Earth. They, therefore, still alarmed, went to Anvers—& I am again at the little Bureau upon which my dearest Ami has sometimes written in la Marchée aux Bois.

The first news the D. of Wellington was known to receive of the invasion of les *pays bas* was at a Ball at the Duchess of Richmond's.[2] He would not break up the party, more than half of which was formed of his officers,[3] nor suffer any interruption. Some time after, however, he went out, & when he returned distributed cards of orders to the several commanding officers. But he stayed to Supper—after which 50 red Coats retired abruptly. Not so the Duke—and he is now much — — —

Ah mon Ami—two Letters arrive[4]—at the same instant—that curtail all subjects but what belong to themselves — — *Nous allons commencer!*—Great God of Heaven preserve & prosper the beloved Partner of my soul — — — I dare enter upon nothing I can only say the first of the two Letters—written before the order of *commencer* was issued, is one of the fullest, & sweetest, dearest & most salubrious I have in my possession—& I shall read & re-read its ⏐ interesting contents with heart-felt pleasure

Tell, tell me, my beloved Ami, *where when* you would have ME remove? I will not ask *how*, I will find that out. To be NEARER to you—to hear more frequently—oh what a solace!—

But I fear making some mistake without a direction more positive. If the Roi fixes in Germany, there is no doubt we shall

---

[2] Lady Charlotte Gordon (1768–1842), the eldest daughter of the 4th Duke of Gordon (1743–1827), had married in 1789 Charles Lennox (1764–1819), later (1806) 4th Duke of Richmond and Lennox, who brought his entire family to Brussels in 1814 to live 'on an Economical Plan' (Capel, p. 57). Their famous ball before Waterloo was held in what had been the showroom of the coach-builder from whom they leased the house in the rue de la Blanchisserie. Wellington, who said even on his arrival late on the evening of 15 June 'we are off tomorrow' (de Ros, p. 123) stayed for the ball-supper and dispatched his many officers (see the complete invitation-list in de Ros, pp. 124–32) in the way described by FBA. The ball ended around 2 a.m. on 16 June with the farewells of the daughters of the Duchess of Richmond to the Duke of Brunswick and to the young James, Lord Hay (1797–1815), both of whom were killed later that day at Quatre Bras.

[3] Cf. the explanation offered by Lord Fitzroy Somerset: 'As it [the ball] was the place where every British officer of rank was likely to be found, perhaps for that reason the Duke dressed & went there.' Cited by Lady Longford, *Wellington, the Years of the Sword* (1969), p. 417, who adds: 'Morale-building, duty, convenience—they all played their part in getting Wellington to the ball. Why not admit also that the Irish devil in him wanted to go? He would go; and see "those fellows" damned.' The event, as everyone knows, supplied Byron with some of his most famous lines, *Childe Harold's Pilgrimage*, canto iii, stanzas 20–8.

[4] Letters 887 and 889.

have our mutual communications far more readily & safely than by my remaining in any other place:

The Prince Hereditary of Orange has been wounded[5]—& the D[uke] of W[ellington] has gallopped hither to see him. Nap^n in complete *deroute* is returning to Paris! AND—he has lost all his baggage!— Almost all la maison du Roi is now come hither from Alost. It is supposed to be embodied for La Vendee! — —[6] Oh what times! I dare not write upon them! I dare but hope—& pray—and — — Love!—Oh Heaven! how tenderly! — adio—adio! — —

Alex's Letter is quite interesting & amiable—for us *both*— though it is to me.

The maimed—wounded—bleeding—fainting arrive still EVERY MINUTE! there seems a whole—& a large ARMY of mutilated soldiers! Jerome is said to be killed,[7] & Vandamme to have lost both legs.[8] Our loss is yet incalculable!

Oh my beloved Friend! our re-union! our re-union! — —

Every Creature that was moveable is gone to Anvers, or England, but myself—but my intense desire not to lose ground or time in my Letters, made me linger to the last—and NOW, thank Heaven! all danger here is at an end, & All fugitives are returning. |

I have left this for a word at the last minute This is *Wednesday, June 21st* I shall hold myself in readiness to follow your instructions, but not move without them, as this great immortal victory may change them. Every body is expected back again here, to await the issue of the entrance into France   But I have now positive NEWS to give you of the *Roi*—who is not to go to Barenth[9]—but to Tournai—& thence, as fast as an openning can be made for him, into France itself. I have This immediately from a person to whom the commission was *half* given: *half*, I say, for the D. of W. spoke it to *two*: but the one who is to carry it to Gand is M. le D. de FitzJames. It is M. de la T[our] du P[in] who himself told it me yesterday at Mme de Maurville's.

---

[5] The Prince (L. 872 n. 12) was wounded at Waterloo by a musket-ball that struck his left arm near the shoulder. See F. de Bas and T'Serclaes de Wommersom, *La Campagne de 1815 aux Pays-Bas . . .* (Brussels, 3 vols., 1908), iii. 6.

[6] See L. 888 n. 16.   [7] Not true. See L. 893 n. 10.

[8] Vandamme (L. 878 n. 10) was wounded, but not seriously, on 20 June near Namur.

[9] Benrath (see L. 889, p. 204).

It is now thought the *Maison du Roi* will accompany his M[ajesty].

quel interressant homme que Votre Bavarois![10] — — et que CELUI qui l'a console!—O quel abus abominable de *forces militaires!*—

Mr. Kirkpatrick tells me Murat is dead of his wounds— Vandamme lost his two thighs, & is dead also; Jerome died of a Cannon Ball at once. Poor M. de Vincent, austrian, has a Ball still in his arm, which they cannot extract.[11] Lord Fitzroy Sommerset has an arm shot off;[12] Lord Uxbridge a leg—![13]— Col. Hamilton [i]s killed.[14] Lobau is here, prisoner. I shall continue to write all the particulars I can gather. It has been the most bloody Battle, that ever was fought, & the victory the most entire. |

The Imperial Guard is almost annihilated! They fought like Demons. Napoleon cried out continually to them, the prisoners say, à Bruxelles! mes Enfans! à Bruxelles! a Bruxelles!'[15]

[10] The Bavarian cavalryman whose grievances M. d'A heard at Trèves and reported in L. 887.

[11] See L. 891 n. 15.

[12] Somerset (L. 858 n. 3) had his right arm amputated after it was shattered by a shot fired from the top of La Haye Sainte farmhouse (see M. d'A's sketch of the Waterloo battlefield, *facing* p. 224.

[13] Henry William Paget (1768–1854), 10th Baron Paget of Beaudesert, 2nd Earl of Uxbridge (1812), and for his services at Waterloo, 1st Marquess of Anglesey (1815), commanded Wellington's cavalry, which he led with the brilliant but reckless style he had shown earlier in Portugal and Spain. Paget's military career began in 1793, when he raised an infantry regiment (later the 80th foot) on his father's Staffordshire estates, and continued in Flanders (1794), Holland (1799), and the Peninsula (1808–9). He had risen to the rank of lieutenant-general before Waterloo, where his right knee was shattered in one of the last cavalry charges. His sister, Lady Caroline Capel (1773–1847), was not long afterward shown by the owners of the house in which his leg was amputated and in whose garden it was buried, the following inscription: 'Ci est enterrée la Jambe de L'illustre, brave et Vaillant Comte Uxbridge . . . Qui par Son Héroisme a concourié au triomphe de la Cause du Genre humain, Glorieusement décidée par L'Eclatante Victoire de cet Jour' (Capel, p. 148 n. 1). Among his many other distinctions and honours, he later became Lord-lieutenant of Ireland (1828–9, 1830–3) and field-marshal (1846).

[14] James Inglis Hamilton (1777–1815), who commanded the 2nd (or Royal North British) Regiment of Dragoons (Royal Scots Greys) at Waterloo, was born the son of a soldier in America and baptized James Anderson. On his father's return to Scotland the boy was educated by his former commanding officer, and on entry into the Scots Greys as a Cornet took his name and kept it thereafter. He rose through service with his famous regiment to become its lieutenant-colonel in 1807 and brevet-colonel just before Waterloo in 1815. After several charges against French infantry, cavalry, and artillery, during which both of his arms had been cut off, Hamilton seized the reins in his teeth and charged again, this time to his death. When his body was finally found it showed several more wounds, including a musket shot through the heart (Dalton, pp. 58–9).

[15] In the French Archives Nationales there is a poignant letter written by an unknown officer of *chasseurs* just before Waterloo which closes 'Demain nous serons à

They were reported one day to be arrived here—I never saw—never, indeed, FELT such consternation! Not only Money, Jewels, & valuables of pecuniary sorts were shut up—but *Babies* from the arms of their terrified mothers & nurses!— I flew out myself, to take refuge, unmarked, unnamed, unknown, in the apartments of Mme de Maurville—& I never witnessed such horrour & desolation.

O how I rejoice my tender ami knew not of all this terrour till it was over! what solicitude for your poor Athanase has not that spared you!

896   [1358, Marchè au bois],
             Brussels, 12–23 June 1815

To Alexander d'Arblay

A.L. (rejected Diary MSS. 6632–[5], Berg), 12–23 June 1815
Double sheet 4to   4 pp.   p. 1 (6632) and p. 3 (6634), paged (?), 210, 211 *pmks* BRUXELLES   FOREIGN / 29 JU 1815   29 JU ⟨18⟩15
Addressed: Angleterre / à Madame / To the care of / Madame Broome, for her Nephew AD. / Richmond, / Surry—
Docketed, p. 4 (6635): 193 vol. VII
Edited by CFBt, *the* Press, *and* ?FBA. *See* Textual Notes.

Bruxelles, June 12^⟨th⟩,

Your full, satisfactory, & interesting Letter,[1] or, rather, your 5 Letters in one my dearest Alex, is just arrived, & has given me the more pleasure that it arrives before my last, filled with uneasy remonstrances at your silence, had reached you—or even, perhaps, left *les pays bas.* I will now instantly let you see the value of your '*scrawl, such as it is,*' by narrating all you must most want to know, & putting you, by a brief retrospection, in clear possession of your dear Father's situation. You know the whole history of his accompanying *Le Roi* with *sa maison*

Bruxelles' (AB xix 3375, i), an indication that Napoleon's over-confidence had spread throughout the army (Houssaye, *1815*, ii. 320–1). When the Emperor's baggage was captured after Waterloo the Prussians found proclamations announcing victory that were dated from 'Brussels, at the Imperial Palace of Laeken' (Henry Lachouque, *The Last Days of Napoleon's Empire*, 1966, p. 24).

896.   1 The letter is missing.

in the Retreat from Paris begun March 19th at midnight, or there abouts; for to disguise the intention, the different companies of *la maison* were ordered off at different Hours, though all embodying the King. You know, too, that a particular commission from the Capitaine of his Compagnie, Mon^r le Duc de Luxembourg, kept him at Brussels afterwards for some weeks, seeking Horses, Maps, &c. He was then summoned by the Minister de la Guerre, le Duc de Feltre, to Gand, to receive a new & important mission, by order of the King. He there found that his Majesty had appointed 10 officers of known fidelity to be fixed on 10 frontier places,[2] in order to receive, select, or [det]ect, Deserters from Buonaparte, & form them into Batalions, & give an account of them to the Duc de Feltre. A post of extreme difficulty & delicacy. This is the List.

[2] The ten *commissaires* were scattered along the frontier from the Channel (Furnes, near Dunkirk) to Switzerland (Basel) and their views of their missions were as far apart as their postings. Furnes, for example, became the base for a scheme to retake Dunkirk and Calais (Romberg and Malet, i. 68–9), while Basel became a little Alost or Coblenz with its *garde royale de l'Est* (*Moniteur*, 7 September) composed of *émigré* and local nobles.

FBA's list corresponds roughly with other available lists and information, but gaps and uncertainties remain. Rochechouart, as chief of staff of the armée royale at Ghent and Alost, is perhaps the best source, but the list that appears in his *Souvenirs . . .* (p. 419) does not give postings and alters some of the names. Of those mentioned by FBA, the editors have been unable to identify 'Vassemont'; while Stenger (p. 342) makes no mention of Boissach and says instead that the commissaire at Kehl was one 'M. Roesch'. But the others can be identified through military and political records as follows: 'Marq^s de Castries' (L. 888 n. 24); 'C^t de la Poterie', Louis Leroy de la Poterie (1762–1847), comte and *émigré*, who apparently went from Mons to the Vendée, then returned with Louis XVIII to command the 4th regiment in the garde royale and sit as an extreme right-wing deputy, retiring in 1832 as a maréchal de camp; Jean-Charles-Annet-*Victorin* de Lasteyrie (1768–1833), marquis de Saillant, an *émigré* who returned to become one of Napoleon's chamberlains (1809) and a prefect (1811); 'Count de la Rochefaucault', Frédéric-*Gaetan* de La Rochefoucauld (1779–1863), marquis de Liancourt, a sous-préfet under the Empire who returned from his exploits on the Swiss frontier (*Moniteur*, 17 August) to become a moderate deputy and opponent of Polignac's reactionary ministry; 'C^t de Quinsonas', Emmanuel-Victor Pourroy de l'Auberivière (1775–1852), marquis de Quinsonas, a Knight of Malta who emigrated and on his return to France soon after the Revolution entered the Russian service, in which he became maréchal de camp, returning after the Second Restoration to sit as a reactionary deputy and command the 1st brigade of the garde royale; 'Chev^r Berthier', Anne-Ferdinand-Louis de Bertier de Sauvigny (1782–1864), *émigré* and comte, an active royalist under the Empire, colonel of the chevaux-légers of the garde royale and an extreme right-wing deputy after the Second Restoration; 'C^t de Gouvello', Louis-Paul de Gouvello (1754–1830), vicomte de Gouvello (vii, L. 770 n. 12) had lived in England from 1795 until the First Restoration (apart from military service with the English in Santo Domingo in 1797–8), and was in 1814 appointed sous-lieutenant in the bodyguard of the comte d'Artois. He was promoted to the army rank of maréchal de camp and decorated in the following year for his services during the Hundred Days and retired to his estate in the Nivernais in 1816.

Tournay, C^t de Gouvello	*Luxembourg*, Chev^r d'Arblay
Furnes, Visc^t de Saillant	*Mons*—C^t de la Poterie
Deux ponts, Baron de Vassemont	*Courtray*, Chev^r Berthier
Namur Marq^s de Castries	*Spire* C^t de Quinsonas
Kell le Cap^n Boissack	*Bale*, le Count de la Rochefaucault.

The Minister then named M. le Count de Mazancourt *adjoint* to your Father, & M. de Premorel, his aid de Camp. Alphonse de Premorel, son of the latter, was joined as a volunteer to the little group of which your Father is Chief.

Notre ami then, upon his return to Brussels, by order of the Duc de Feltre, demanded an Audience of the Duke de Wellington, to concert upon measures, &c—The Duke said he would himself write upon the subject to Prince Mar^l Blücher, & desired notre ami to remain here till the answer arrived. Notre ami wrote to the Mar^l also himself. Nevertheless, no answer came, & he spent 10 days here vainly awaiting it. In this time, the 2 Messrs de Premorel dined with us daily, & M. le C^t de Mazancourt occasionally. Your Father, you may believe, was put immediately upon full pay,—for else the whole party, ourselves included, must have made interest to dine with Duke Humphry.[3] A Duke of whose convivial entertainments you have perhaps never heard—but your Uncle James will give you the explanation, when you see him; no one, of our's, or of any other family, keeps a table of more hospitable contrast to that of his starving Grace. ǀ

This delay, though to me, you will believe, a secret reprieve & benediction, inquieted notre ami, & made his party impatient. He therefore sent his aid de camp to Gand, to confer with the D. de Feltre, & the D. de Luxembourg. The answer however was that Mar^l Blücher's reply must be awaited, as Luxembourg was entirely under Prussian orders. At the end of a few days more, notre ami, more & more disturbed, sent off M. de Mazancourt to Liege, to endeavour to see the Mareshal: & dispatched les Messrs de Premorel *chez eux*, which is in the

---

[3] A proverbial phrase, meaning 'to go dinnerless', which is said to have originated soon after the hospitable Humphrey Plantagenet, Duke of Gloucester, was killed in 1446. Although he was buried at St. Albans, the notion spread that his tomb was in St. Paul's, where loiterers with no prospect of a dinner explained that they were dining with Duke Humphrey (*Oxford Dictionary of English Proverbs*, s.v. 'dine').

neighbourhood of Neu-Chateau, ⟨Bertiz⟩ & paliseul[4] in the Duchy of Luxembourg, to pick up deserters *en attendant*. But Mar[1] Blücher was gone to Namur, & M. de Mazancourt wrote word that the superiour Officer remaining at Liege assured him the Mar[1] had answered the Letter of notre ami! M. de Mazancourt then followed, & got a conference with Prince Blücher himself; who repeated that he had answered *M. le Marechal de Camp d'Arblay's* Letter; & when M. de M. told him not a line had arrived, he gave a tremendous stamp with his foot, & uttered a little gentle volley of soft words that I leave you to conjecture. Upon this intelligence, Notre ami set off at once for Liege. He sent his 3 Horses, loaded with Baggage of military equipment, with his servant,[5] to go gently, & travelled himself, to save time & arrive more quickly, in the Night Diligence. His servant, Fran[çois] is a German, of Cologne,[5] whom he takes as Interpreter; for he has another Hen[ry] for his Horses. François had travelled with *Mr. Grattan,*[6] *Jun*[r] & he seems to me an excellent creature. We had him here about 3 weeks before the departure. I have met Mr. Grattan at Lady Crewe's, & his written *eloge*, which François showed me, that he [François] had behaved *parfaitment bien* is very comforting to me: for I liked extremely all the Grattans on the Day I met them *Chez le Roi Louis 18. when I was introduced to them by kind Lady Crewe*—who I am charmed to hear has been so good as to remember you. Lady Keith, too!—My dearest Mrs. Lock & sweetest Amine! what do I not owe to their friendship, & to the affection of all my family, shewn lately through my Alex's agency!

Notre ami had not left his forlorn & sorrowing Partner 2 days, when an order came from the post office that he would go thither, or send a public Notary, to receive an official Letter. I took courage to go myself, declaring who I was, & his departure. They then delivered me the so long awaited Letter of Pr. Mar[1] Blücher, which had remained 3 weeks at the post office, from a wrong direction! The mistake was discovered by accident. Your dear Father writes me word that the Letter is *perfect*; polite, gentleman-like, & military, yet humanely

---

[4] The names of these towns are Neufchâteau, Bertrix, and Palizeul.

[5] For M. d'A's servants, a valet *cum* interpreter and a groom, see L. 876 n. 24.

[6] Henry Grattan Jr. (L. 887 n. 2), whom, with Mrs. Crewe, FBA had met at Grillion's Hotel in April 1814 at a reception given by Louis XVIII (vii. 300–6).

entering into your Father's conciliatory Mission, & promising to abet it, but declining to let him enter Luxembourg, & desiring he would go to *Treves*. Thither he went, & there he has been ever since, with his party. And I have the pleasure to inform you, that he has had, upon the whole, far better success in his mission than he had expected. ¹

Brussells, June 14ᵗʰ
1815.

How truly provoking that a Letter so long expected should be so long upon the road! only now is come the so impatiently awaited answer: yet it is dated May 24ᵗʰ However, it is a dear Letter, my Alex, & pleases me completely—unless I except that touch of l'*amour propre* that makes you so sensitive to my attack upon a few laboured flowers of rhetoric,⁷ that you will laugh at yourself, when I shew you them hereafter. For it is only in the immediate moment of composition that we are so tenacious of applause. But write me all your Letter, I beg, by *yourself*, I perceive then I have a *Brother* & a son too; when you share your paper, I hardly find either one or the other. And your Letters are too necessary to my repose to ever be costly.—

Your Secret has deeply interested me;⁸ & I will speak of that before I enter upon the account which shall then absorb the rest of my paper, of your dearest Father. And you, my own Alex, will be as happy as I am that you have earned the relation without having received my exhortation. O let not[hin]g *ever more* [oc]casion a silence on your part to draw forth another.— To be satisfied with *you* is the Second greatest delight I have in the World.

Upon further thoughts, I will turn my paper, & There write of your Padre—& keep this snug for a sister's confidential *moitié*,—for all our dear Family & Friends will be so anxious to share your news, that I will not embarrass you by any mixture of subjects.

⁷ FBA objects here to AA's habit of making up his letters by stringing together quotations and allusions. For a sample of this, see L. 927 below.

⁸ AA's secret was his attraction to his lively cousin Sarah or 'Sally', now 18 years of age, the daughter of FBA's brother James and his wife Sarah *née* Payne (i, p. lxix). With this development, along with time lost in chess, the dangers in 26 James Street were compounded, and FBA was anxious that Alex remove to Norbury Park or to Mrs. Broome in Richmond.

Sure as you have so often asserted yourself that you[r] heart was adamant, your Sister has read your confession without much surprise, though she takes you to her heart, & would, were you here, to her arms, with pleasure for your confidence. Not, however, from the thing, but from the feeling that prompts you to reveal it. I cannot doubt the object, though you forbear naming her till your next: nor can you, I am sure, doubt the satisfaction I should in many points have in your success: my inalterable love of her Father,[8] who I think has, *au fond*, one of the best of human hearts; & my long & faithful esteem & friendship for her Mother,[8] are circumstances of deep importance. Herself, too, I took early into my affection, & I think her clever, amusing, full of talents, & glowing with good humour & gaiety of happy spirits:—but alas! a steadier character is what *both* want. *She* requires some one to help her through the thorny paths of life as a Guide; *you*, some one to attract you to the domestic virtues as a Model. You candidly *own*, that though she is much improved, there is still great room for improvement; yet, in another corner, you say she is already an angel upon Earth! This inconsistency is always allowed ˈ to be pardonable where *la belle passion* predominates; & yours, I hope, is not *incurable*, since you avow that your next Letter may reveal a *past* instead of a *present* flame. I make therefore the less simple to put you on your guard, & to urge you, if not already at Richmond, to hasten thither. Your lingering so long in a visit may betray what ought to be held sacred till you have, as you will say, a *name* & a *fame*, which will lead to competence & independence. And then—I own, I would wish you to be wholly free & disengaged, to look around you with more experienced Eyes for judging what may make you permanently happy. I cannot write on this delicate matter to notre ami at this eventful moment, & we meet now no longer, but I know he has other views—views to which he thinks the *name, fame*, &c when arrived, with his own distinction, & the partial manner in which your madre is seen, might draw you imperceptibly, but surely. Now too, especially, when you are so partially & kindly estimated yourself, that they talk of you as one of themselves: & love you with a kindness that warms me with glowing gratitude. Keep up, at all events, their predilection, which is truly gratifying to me. I shall write immediately to my kind

Mrs. Lock, who *mothers* you, my Amine[9] says, in her bosom! You have not answered one word of all I have said of your studies, residence, &c. You will be more respected by every body for taking a little more of Clement in your application & diligence![10] The *name* & *fame*, my Boy, are still in your reach—but I fear you will let them pass by, & only live to regret always looking at your watch in time to see that you are too late! Your fond Father, however, will not have you constrained: he thinks you required some dissipation, & is glad to have you gain l'*usage du monde*, & make yourself friends, & enjoy, for an interval, your happy existence. From that relaxation, *he* says, you will spring into assiduity, & return to College to make a brilliant *entrée*, even after the necessary mode & fashion of the Dons themselves, since no other will lead you to independence, & a power of CHOICE for your way of life, & for your life's partner. When young himself, he always, he says, worked harder & more profoundly after any dissipation, in order to obtain his own forgiveness & good opinion. I shall see, he pretends, that you will do the same.

P.S. *June 23*d Ah my dear Alex—what trouble[d] times! This Letter, begun the moment I had yours, has been packed up, & almost to Anvers in our last affright—But all is safe *here*, now, I trust! though I have passed a fearful week, & am in the most suspensive pain for our dearest & best of Friends. I had a Letter yesterday—still from *Treves*, but he was prepared to depart—he says not whither—He knew nothing then of the eruption of the *Fleau* into these parts[11]—within 9 miles of Brussells!—We are now—*I am* now—for I am nearly left alone—in all the *horrour* & *hope* of perpetual expectation of news —all my friends went off—

Give Thanks to your dear Aunt Broome—aunt Sarah—& cousins Charlotte & Fanny & Love to All—my next Family Letter must be to [dear Au]nt Hetty.[12] You, my Alex, know how & when to get another [at you]r own pleasure. adieu, my Love.

You don't say a word of your own plan that we had so much

---

[9] Mrs. Locke's daughter Amelia Angerstein (L. 838 n. 27).
[10] Clement Francis (L. 838 n. 12).
[11] The furthest advance made by Napoleon, the 'Fléau' or 'Scourge' of Europe.
[12] These aunts and cousins are, in the order FBA names them, CBFB, SHB, CFBt, Fanny Raper, and EBB (i, pp. lxix–lxxv).

812507   I   235

approved of going to Uncle Chas if INVITED to stay¹³ nor why you forget y^r own objections to hanging on poor Uncle James¹⁴ nor one syllable of money matters.

P.S. send me as quick as possible a few lines so written that I may cut them off from my Letter, & insert them to the kindest of Fathers—who demands the sight of your hand impatiently. I won't send your Letter itself, for I must have an entire *Sister's* Letter.

I hope you did not really send that Letter to Mrs. Waddington?¹⁵ as a Badinage c'est bien, & it made me laugh heartily.

I hope you gave my message to Martin, or wrote it?¹⁶ He must be so good as to send me the specific *proposal of Mr. Murray:*¹⁶ Mrs. Lock says Mr. Murray has the commission from Mr. William. I am very glad you had that meeting at the Panorama.¹⁷ The Reviews I never see, & my mind is so occupied, I never think of: but what Heart-affection does not my dear James shew by thus feeling them! My Heart thanks him so will my M.d'A when he knows it but now ⟨We⟩ have no intercourse except ⟨for the business [*tear*]⟩

Pray remember me to every body. My next Letter shall be to Mrs. Lock; has she not received one dated May 22!?

¹³ AA was meant to go, if invited, to CB Jr. to study and prepare for confirmation during the extended Cambridge vacation (L. 870, p. 125).

¹⁴ A few days before FBA had written to M. d'A that AA was 'still, alas, at James's' (L. 891 p. 213), at her brother's house in 26 James Street (Buckingham Gate).

¹⁵ See i, L. 5 n. 10 and vii *passim*.

¹⁶ JB's son Martin Charles (L. 886 n. 9), attorney, who was acting for the d'Arblays with respect to the sale of Camilla Cottage (L. 863 n. 6), and Alexander Murray (L. 886 n. 10), acting for William Locke, Jr.

¹⁷ 'A picture or a landscape or scene, arranged on the inside of a cylindrical surface around the spectator as a centre (a *cyclorama*), or unrolled or unfolded and made to pass before him so as to show the various parts in succession' (*OED*). Both the name and object were invented by Robert Barker (1739–1806) of Edinburgh, where the first panorama was exhibited in 1788. It soon became popular in England, especially for pictures of battles, landscapes, and views of cities. During the spring of 1815 the panorama most in the public eye was the work of Barker's son, Henry Aston Barker (1774–1856), which was exhibited at the Panorama in Leicester Square. The first of its two parts was 'The Battle of Paris', the second a 'Panorama of Elba' (*The Times*, 3 April, 5 and 15 May). The name used by FBA and the date of AA's letter strongly suggest that this is the panorama visited.

[1358, Marché au bois,
                              Brussels], 22–23 June 1815

To M. d'Arblay

A.L. (rejected Diary MSS. 6640–[3], Berg), 22–23 June 1815
Double sheet 4to   4 pp.   *pmk*   BRUXELLES   wafer
Addressed: *Treves.* / À / Monsieur le Genéral d'Arblay, / Offi^r superieur
des gardes / de sa Majestie le Roi de France, / Chev^r de St Louis, &c &c /
&c / à Treves.
Edited by FBA, p. 1 (6640), *annotated*: ⋇ ⋇ (15/2) Battle of Waterloo —
Rejected at the Press. *See* Textual Notes.

Jeudi, Juin 22^d 1815.
How more than ever precious is now the sight of your hand!
—I received it to day with a joy inexpressible.

Can I grieve you have not accompanied your favourite
General?[1] No, alas, no—for good as *HE* is, his party, I am told, is
all inflamed against ALL France so as to be bent upon granting
no quarter! We have had scenes even here, with stragglers,
that frightfully avow their schemes of exterminating vengeance!

I will write directly, according to your desire, to Gand;
& to our friend; for I am ignorant whether M. le Duc[2] is
there. He was here lately; but nobody now can be found.

The Duke of Wellington is gone entirely from Brussells. He
merely arranged for the Hospitals, & ordered off all that could
bear, & find, arms, belonging to him.[3] His Quartier général,
when I heard last was at Wavre, or Waterloo: but I have been
able to get no news of it to-day with certainty.

897.   [1] Kleist von Nollendorf (L. 874 n. 1), whose civilized views were as FBA suggests a contrast to the vengeful threats of such Prussians as Karl Justus von Gruner
(1777–1820), governor-general of the Prussian Rhine. In a proclamation that deeply
shocked both royalist and Bonapartist opinion when republished in Paris, Gruner
gave official support to the Prussian view that their war was against France itself
and that their aim was not to restore Louis XVIII and depose Napoleon but rather
to destroy the French as a people, divide their country into the regional kingdoms
that resulted from the collapse of the Carolingian empire, and repeat (as Gruner
concludes) earlier Germanic victories over imperial Rome (*Gazette de France*, 4 May).
[2] The duc de Feltre (L. 860 n. 2).
[3] In a General Order of 20 June, issued from his headquarters at Nivelles,
Wellington, after briefly thanking his troops for their service at Waterloo, reverted
to his more usual stern tones to provide for the wounded, order the return of all
absentees and deserters, reminding his soldiers that 'their Sovereigns are in alliance
with the King of France, and that France therefore must be considered as a
friendly country' (*Supp. Desp.* x. 538–40). By the 22nd Wellington's headquarters
were at Le Cateau.

The dreadfulness of the late Battle exceeds all precedent![4] *Piles* of Dead—heaps, Masses, *hills* of Dead! French, English, Belge & Prussian, are horrible. The wounded still are coming in—& the *Charettes* are now sent back for the sick & maimed Prisoners. The English who *began*, passed 2 days & a Night without food! There was no cessation of slaughter!

The accounts of individuals vary so, that all I have told you is contradicted, & new tales are current. But there are no leading persons here who affirm or make positively known anything.

Sir Charles Stuart also is gone to Gand. There is no longer any English ¦ Ambassadour here. But I had the great satisfaction, by the most happy chance, to send a packet to the tight by the last Courrier who went hence.[5] I called myself, with a long Letter for the Bonne et Belle, at Sir Charles's, to make enquiry how I might act—& heard he was gone entirely from Brussells, as were all the Secretaries, & even domestics. Much disappointed, I was coming away, when they mentioned a courrier going for London—I begged to see him—Times of disturbance give me courage. He was getting his Horse, & had not a moment. I followed to the stable yard. He came to me, & proved to be a most Gentleman-like man, who had served, under Lord Burghersh,[6] all the last campaign. I had a long discourse with him, & he took my packet, & promised it should be delivered by himself immediately on his arrival. How fortunate! for I may now have no other opportunity.

---

[4] Supplying first-hand observations also on the aftermath of Waterloo was Charles John Shore (1796–1885), 2nd Baron Teignmouth, who rode over the battlefield on that same day. 'I saw several hundreds naked, and in a putrid state; some heaps of them are collected, and will be burnt. . . . The bodies both of men and horses were much swollen; those of the horses had, without exception, burst. Some of the men, as they were all swollen, seemed gigantic . . . the stench was great. . . .' (i. 80–4).

[5] FBA means that she has managed to send a letter to Princess Elizabeth ('the Bonne et Belle') at Frogmore, despite the departure of Sir Charles Stuart (L. 856 n. 19).

[6] John Fane (1784–1859), *styled* Lord Burghersh, 11th Earl of Westmorland (1841), was commissioned in 1804 as a lieutenant in the 7th Foot and began at once a rapid series of promotions that attracted, even in those days of purchase and patronage, hostile comment and criticism: captain (1805), major (1810), lieutenant-colonel (1811), colonel (1814). An uproar in Parliament forced George III to rescind his first promotion to major in 1809 (*Later Corr. Geo. III*, v. 290–1). Burgersh was, however, an able officer and served in the Peninsula, southern France, and Italy as an aide-de-camp and military diplomat (during the Hundred Days with the Austrian army campaigning against Murat). He sat as M.P. for Lyme Regis (1806–16), founded the Royal Academy of Music in 1823, served as resident minister in Berlin (1841–51), and reached the rank of general in 1854.

'Tis to Gand Sir Charles is gone. I suppose he will accompany le Roi to the Frontiers. It is supposed He will make his entry by Lille,[7] as that is thought the place that will first declare for him.

I see no more of the Gardes du Corps here now. They are gone to their destination.

Oh how are you to appear in safety in a French Uniform!— pray, for Heaven's sake, consider to what dreadful mistakes it may make you liable!

In the last Battle, near Night, the Belgians, from the likeness of their uniforms,[8] were taken for French by the English, & fired ᴵ upon! A wounded soldier here told me the English were quite in despair when they found their mistake.

All the Prisoners I have seen here look a complete set of dirty, ragged, coarse Jacobins! in soiled old carter's Frocks.

I am since told that these Frocks were cast over them after they were taken, & had been despoiled of their uniforms by their captors!—

The garde imperiale were all cut up & killed,[9] that did not escape by B[uonaparte]'s side! One whole regiment went, every man!

The poor brave Highlanders have fared little better!

Yet B. has got back to Paris—& has published a bulletin that he has conquered Lord Wellington!—!!![10]

He mentions, you will believe, only the surprise upon Charleroy, where he took 1500 men & 6 pieces of cannon: but not a word of LOSING every one of them, with ALL the material of his army! Baggage, &c &c.

⌐⁀⌐

[7] Lille was famous during this period for its strong royalist leanings, which were thought to affect even the regular garrison (*Supp. Desp.* x. 732), but in the event Louis XVIII, with an escort of gardes du corps, by-passed Lille and entered France by way of Bavay and Cambrai (Reiset, iii. 218–23).

[8] Until lately the Belgian regiments were in fact part of the French army, and the change of government had not yet been followed by a change of uniform.

[9] This is only a slight overstatement. At least one battalion of the Young Guard was wiped out in the last stages of the battle (Houssaye, *1815*, ii. 422) and the Imperial Guard suffered heavy casualties by forming squares against the British and Prussian cavalry. This exposed them to infantry and artillery fire that first reduced their squares to triangles and then to small pockets of resistance against the general allied advance.

[10] This bulletin, dated 15 June from Charleroi and published in the *Moniteur* on the 18th, was, given its date and place, a fairly accurate statement of Napoleon's position and opening success.

I have just seen an English wounded soldier who had been made Prisoner on the 18th Sunday; I asked how he became free? he answered he had been carried into a Wood, with many others, where he was very ill & roughly used, stript of all his baggage, & of his shoes, & whatever did not leave him naked; but that in the Night, they were in too much trouble to watch, & he crawled upon all fours out of the wood, & crept on till he joined a party of his comrades.

⌐I have written to de Boinville to plead that I be taken to you with M. Durand now in defiance of all ambition even though at first I joined in your objections;¹¹ but since I have had each fresh proof of the almost universal deviation from right in All quarters, thus I shall be comforted. For all things else if I know you by the name of one who truly feels his real duty, to whom each will find no hesitation, prepare your utmost firmness of purpose—for that which sickens us must unavoidably be re-solved ┃ as what to any and each *French* man would at this moment be deemed a disgrace, a *personal* quarrel! You must act & think for yourself, mon ami, in this uncertain time, & rather shew by your example than by your precepts what ought to be done.⌐

M. & Mme de la T[our] du P[in] returned yesterday, I have heard, from Anvers; & Mme d H[énin] comes back to night. The Boyds have not yet re-appeared. I can give you no account of Mme de Beaufort's Will:¹² Public affairs are so absorbing, I have had no opportunity to enquire. M. de Beaufort I hardly ever see; but he is always polite & obliging, & interested for you: but instead of less, he grows *MORE triste,—much* more.— Mr. Kirkpatrick¹³ is too busy & troubled now to think of sending me the N[ews] papers, which I miss cruelly. At this moment I am going to subscribe for *reading quick*, if possible, to the Oracle¹⁴—for I cannot live without any intelligence.

¹¹ M. d'A's earlier and ambitious notion was that FBA would maintain contact with the courtiers in Brussels and Ghent, thereby encouraging his advancement. FBA's exposure to the malicious intrigues around Louis XVIII—the 'personal quarrel' would seem to refer to the hatreds that divided Blacas and Monsieur on one side from Talleyrand and the duc d'Orléans on another—has convinced her that she would be better off at Trèves, where she hopes to go with de Fresne [de Boin-ville's] authorization from Ghent and in Durand de Prémorel's company.

¹² The will has not been located but for family wealth and property, see L. 872 n. 3.

¹³ See L. 861 n. 3.   ¹⁴ *L'Oracle*, the Brussels daily newspaper.

How kind, how very kind (and reviving) is your attention in writing! I should certainly *succomber* without it! I shall write myself by every post, i.e. 3 times a week, during this critical situation—for I well know—& have *always* & at ALL times known that my dearest ami can never suppose me in any great distress or embarrassment & not be wretched if without intelligence.

⟵⟶

A new Regiment, the 43ᵈ of English, has just passed before my Eyes![15] *pour remplacer* their poor slaughtered Countrymen!—*Every* major was killed! 2 colonels, one after the other! the brave Genˡ Picton, who was in all the victories in Spain![16]

Heaven bless you, mon ami!—Heaven preserve & bless you!—not once a day, once an hour, once a minute such is my prayer—but *all* day long—but *every* moment!—

Finished Friday morning 23ᵈ June—all here quiet. scarcely a military unmaimed to be seen!—except the just arrived from England, or elsewhere, to march on!—

Your collegue de Namur, *M. de Castries*, was at Brussels a few days ago:[17] & perhaps may be here now.

[15] The 1st battalion of the 43rd Foot, which had just returned from America, where it fought at the Battle of New Orleans. Listed as 'under orders' for the Netherlands on 17 June (*Supp. Desp.* x. 500), it apparently reached Ostend only on 20 June.

[16] Sir Thomas Picton (1758–1815), G.C.B. (1815), one of the best British field commanders of the period, entered the army in 1771 and served at length in the West Indies and Netherlands. He is, however, most famous for his command of the 3rd division in Wellington's Peninsular army and his part in the victories at Fuentes d'Onoro and Vittoria and in the siege of Badajoz. He was promoted lieutenant-general in 1813 but excluded by the ministry from the list of those honoured for Peninsular service. He commanded the 5th division at Quatre Bras and despite a serious wound received there he went on to Waterloo, where he was killed while leading his 2nd brigade to the attack.

[17] See L. 888 n. 24.

M. d'Arblay
To Madame d'Arblay

A.L. (Berg), 23–24 juin 1815
Double sheet folio   4 pp.   *pmk*   TRIER   seal
Addressed: A Madame / Madame de Burney / poste restante / à Bruxelles
Readdressed: Marché au Bois / 1358
Edited by FBA, p. 1, *annotated*: ⊞ ⌈24⌉ (15 / 3) (15 / 3) Sur le General
Kleist—le Gen¹ Kamenski et les Jours précedent la Battaillé de Waterloo.
dated, p. 4: 1815 [*with numbers on address fold*]: 15   15   15   24   24   24
See further, Textual Notes.

Treves le 23 Juin 1815
  Ou es tu à present, ma bonne amie? Quels jours que celui que
j'ai passé hier et celui qui l'a precedé! mais par quelle heureuse
nouvelle nous avons été dedomagés avec quel enthousiasme
nous avons fini la journée en criant Vive Vive notre bon Roi.
Comme il doit etre heureux! [xxxxx 3 *lines*] Mon coeur nage
dans la joie quand je pense aux immenses resultats d'un tel
evenement. [xxxxx 3 *lines*] Bientôt notre bon Roi, sans autres
armes que ses vertus, exercera sur le noble coeur de ses appuis
heroiquement puissans, toute l'influence que doit lui accorder
non seulement leur generosité mais leur interêst bien entendu:
En effet cet interest n'est pas simplement de le faire remonter
sur le Thrône, mais d'y maintenir lui et sa dynastie. [xxxxx
3 *lines*] Quelle douceur pour moi de pouvoir ainsi m'ouvrir
librement avec toi et de me dire, non seulement j'ai pour
compagne l'amie la plus chere la plus noble la plus genereuse,
la plus aimante, mais la plus *congeniale* la plus parfaitement
d'accord avec moi sur tous les points de ma croyance politique.
Vive le Roi vive Monsieur Vive le couple heroiquement
français, Mʳ et Mᵈᵉ la Dᵉˢˢᵉ d'Angouleme, Vive le duc de Berry
que je crois brave et loyal, et dont la fougueuse jeunesse ne peut
manquer de recevoir du tems et de l'experience une leçon que
la calomnie même ne rendra que plus profitable¹ Vive aussi ce
duc d'orleans, qui désavoua les coupables mêmes de ses parti-

898.   ¹ Unlike the other Bourbons, who were courteous and refined, the duc de
Berry was notorious for his coarse and bullying manner (Stenger, pp. 49–50).

sans interessés Vive cet infortuné duc de Bourbon,[2] qui cherche
la mort au champ d'honneur et n'est sorti de la solitude à la
quelle sa juste sensibilité pour la plus grande de toutes les pertes
l'a condamné que pour rendre encore utile à son pays le reste
d'une vie passée dans le desespoir. Puisse t'il au lieu de cette
mort déplorable qu'il recherche rencontrer une compagne digne
de lui, et prevenir ainsi l'extinction de son illustre race Amen!
Amen! encore encore et encore. Ces braves Vendeens! recevront
donc le prix de leur noble et genereux effort. Notre bon Roi
aura bien quelques Marechaux à creer sans doute! Quel plus
digne compagnon peut il donner à Macdonald, et quel plus
digne successeur à Berthier que la Roche Jacquelin,[3] à qui je
donne ma voix; et à qui je crois, aprés y avoir bien reflechi
personne de santé ne pourra la refuser.[4] Celui là au moins peut
recevoir sans aucun scrupule et les graces et l'argent de notre
bon Roi. Mais moi qui malgre tous mes efforts ne peus rien
faire j'en suis en verité honteux, et dieu sait pourtant si j'en
profite, et si je ne serais pas au contraire tout à fait ruiné tout
à fait sans ressource si je n'en trouvais pas une inepuisable dans
l'incroyable et plus que genereuse conduite de mon incomparable Fanny. God bless her & my dearest Alex! Je passe au
recit de toutes les agitations que nous avons eprouvées ces deux
derniers jours. Avant hier le Gal Kleith repassant ici pour aller
aux eaux d'Aix la Chapelle[5] etait si malade que ce ne fut qu'avec
la plus grande peine que je pus arriver jusqu'à lui et le voir en
presence de son medecin, qui ma prie en grace de le faire parler
le moins possible. L'attachement sincere que je lui ai voué plus
puissant encore que cette recommandation me permit tout au
plus, sur sa santé quelques questions auxquelles un signe de
tête peut repondre; et quand il voulait parler je prenais le plus
grand soin de l'en empècher. Cependant les bruits les plus

---

[2] The only son of the old prince de Condé (L. 856 n. 9), Louis-Henri-Joseph de
Bourbon (1756–1830), duc de Bourbon, was 'infortuné' as the father of the murdered
duc d'Enghien (L. 845 n. 21). M. d'A praises him here for going to the Vendée on
Napoleon's return from Elba to rally support for Louis XVIII and act as his
governor-general for the Eastern regions of France. The failure of his plans forced
him to take refuge in Spain at the end of March (Romberg and Malet, i. 72–6,
130–3).   [3] For these Generals, see L. 860 n. 11 and L. 882 n. 7.
[4] One who belongs to the sound part (*sana pars*) of the body politic—a notion
that the widespread defections of the Hundred Days helped to revive in reactionary
political rhetoric.
[5] Early on 17 June Kleist had marched westward from Trèves to join the allied
concentration against Napoleon, but on the 18th he was forced by a crisis in his
illness to leave the army near Luxemburg (Pflugk-Harttung, pp. 270–1).

alarmans se repandaient de tous cotés; et les nouvelles desas-
treuses qui d'abord n'avaient aucune consistance ne parurent
tout à coup que trop fondées, quand on sut qu'il n'etait arrivé
aucune lettre du Brabant[6] et surtout quand on vit evacuer avec
precipitation les magasins de l'armée pour les transporter par
terre et par eau à Coblentz. Dès qu'on m'en eut rendu compte
j'envoyai Mr de Premorel chez le Commandant.[7] Un peu moins
rassuré au retour de cet emissaire, je fus moi même chez ce
Commandant qui ma dit qu'il n'etait guere mieux instruit que
nous et qu'il se croyait en conscience obligé de me repeter ce
qu'il avait dit à mon aide de Camp. c. à. d. qu'il ne pouvait
ajouter foi au bruit qu'on faisait courrir de la deffaite des
Prussiens; qu'il pensait que leur retraite devant les Troupes de
B. ne pouvait provenir que de quelque manoeuvre pour les
attirer et les combattre avec plus d'avantage, qu'en même
tems il ne pouvait me dissimuler l'incertitude de sa position
devenue telle qu'un parti de 20 hussards pouvait dans la nuit
s'emparer facilement et de lui et de la Ville de Treves, où
son devoir etait de rester. Quant à vous, mon general, Votre
position et le risque que le decret de B. vous fait courrir exigent
une conduite toute differente et si j'etais à votre place je ne
perdrais pas un moment pour m'eloigner, et j'irais d'abord à
Creuzenach[8] et de là à Mayence L'avis de Mr de Mazancourt
etait de nous retirer au contraire sur Coblentz.[9] Après avoir
murement pesé le pour et le contre je me decidai pour cette
derniere place comme plus rapprochée de la ligne d'operation
et des corps d'armée aux quels mes instructions m'attachent
plus particulierement, bien decidé en outre à saisir la premiere
occasion de rejoindre les corps agissans, et qu'on disait en pleine
retraite. J'etais vraîment desolè de ne pouvoir compter sur la

---

[6] The region that includes Brussels, Ghent, and Namur (where the Prussians had
their headquarters).

[7] Surviving Prussian records fail to identify this apparently junior officer, left
behind in Trèves with a corporal's guard when the various German army corps left
on 17 June. M. d'A wrote to him on 20 August but the letter (Berg) bears no name
or address ('On me flatte, mon cher commandant').

[8] Or Kreuznach, south-west of Mayence (Mainz) on the Nahe river.

[9] Although the Prussians sent back stores and equipment to their base at Coblenz, their army marched westward to Arlon and then into France. M. d'A was
kept utterly in the dark about Prussian plans and movements. In his zeal to catch up
with their army, however, he was following his orders from Ghent, which included
the dangerous suggestion that he should accompany the Prussians 'même en
avant s'il est possible'. See A.L.S. (Vincennes) from M. d'A to the duc de Feltre,
1 July 1815.

cooperation de quelques hommes, n'eut ce été qu'une cinquan-
taine cela me paraissait suffisant | vu la nature du pays et les
risques que courrerait necessairement un parti considerable s'il
se hasardait à y penetrer. Une fois decidé à partir, et occupé des
preparatifs indispensables pour quitter Treves à peu près en
même tems que l'immense quantité de voitures chargées des
effets contenus dans les magasins qu'on evacuait, je crus
m'appercevoir que ceux qui le moment d'auparavant avaient
l'air tout effrayés de me voir deliberer etaient devenus presqu'-
indifferens sur le resultat de notre conference ou du moins
paroissaient être entierement rassurés. J'en fis hautement la
remarque et decidai que je resterais. Sur le champ on changea
de langage; mais je persistai en prenant neanmoins les precautions convenables pour n'être pas tout à fait pris au de-
pourvu, par precautions convenables j'entens celles qu'on
peut prendre quand on n'a aucun ordre à donner et qu'il n'y
a d'ailleurs personne qui put en recevoir, attendu que notre
garnison reduite à quelques gendarmes est toute sur les chemins
pour donner connoissance de l'Ennemi en cas qu'il veuille
pousser une pointe jusqu'ici. Après avoir passé la nuit à peu près
sur pied je faisais brider pour partir, lorsque M^r de M — me dit
qu'il croyait que nous ne courrions plus aucun risque parceque nous avions devant nous des bavarois qui avaient remplacé
les prussiens. On venait de me dire le contraire chez le Com^dt
de la place qui etait même passé chez moi pour me donner
l'avis que nous n'avions absolument personne des notres devant
nous, depuis Luxembourg jusqu'à Sarguemines.[10] Si ce que vous
venez d'avancer est exact dis-je à Mr de Mazancourt est exact,
nous n'aurions pas besoin de partir, mais il faut absolument
savoir sur cela à quoi s'en tenir. Je lui proposai alors de monter
mon petit cosaque;[11] ce qu'il fit et 3 heures et demie après il
revint, et me rendit compte qu'il n'avait absolument rien vu
quoiqu'il eut fait au moins 7 lieues. En consequence notre depart
fut resolu; et bientot tous nos chevaux au nombre de 8 arrive-
rent et je n'avais plus qu'à monter en voiture. Lorsque mon
hote[12] vint me dire que toute la ville avait les yeux sur nous et

[10] Or Saargemünd, as the crow flies roughly seventy kilometres south-east
of Trèves.
[11] A small horse, perhaps one of the Cossack ponies that entered France and the
Rhineland in great numbers during the campaign of 1814.
[12] M. Nell (L. 879 n. 11).

que si je partais elle serait dans la plus affreuse consternation; qu'elle croirait tout perdu du moment où l'on dirait M^r le Gen^al est parti. Ma reponse etait toute simple. Je lui dis que si les inquietudes que donnerait mon depart se trouvaient sans fondement ou plutot si les craintes [qu'il ferait] naitre se trouvaient sans resultat fâcheux, la ville serait bientot rassurée tandis qu'au contraire [si les] craintes etoient fondées et si les ennemis par exemple arrivaient, la ville que je ne pouvais en ⟨aucune⟩ maniere ni mettre à l'abri de leur incursion, ni defendre contre leurs violences se reprocherait sans doute du sort qu'en ce cas ils ne manqueraient pas de me faire subir. Sans aucun doute s'ecriait il: mais il n'y a aucun risque. Sur cela Mr de M. a fait l'offre de rester et de venir ensuite me rejoindre. Pendant toute cette discussion la nuit qui s'approchait à grands pas me fit remettre mon depart a la pointe du jour mais une demie heure au plus aprés cette determination arriva la nouvelle de la victoire du 18 et je me felicitai d'être resté. (le 24 Juin). Hier Je fus interrompu par un message du Com^dt qui me fesait dire que retenu chez lui pour affaires indispensables, il me priait d'aller chez lui où je me rendis aussitot, pour y apprendre que le P^ce de Wreda Gal Bavarois avait reçu l'ordre d'attaquer à Midy 1/2 et d'emporter la position de Sarrebruck.[13] Le Com^dt ajoute qu'il avait depèché tout ce qu'il avait de gens à cheval disponibles, et que n'ayant plus personne il me serait obligé si j'envoyais quelqu'un afin que nous pussions être avertis à tems, dans le cas où quelques ⟨fuyards⟩ ennemis un peu avantureux et au fait de notre *defenceless* position, n'entreprit de faire un peu parler de lui en venant nous surprendre. Je fis encore le sacrifice de mon petit cosaque qui sous Mr de Premorel est allé sur la montagne la plus elevée a 3 ou 4 lieues puis est revenu le soir rendre compte qu'il n'avait rien vu rien rencontré rien entendu. | Nous qui n'avons pas été si loin que lui, nous croyons bien avoir entendu le canon, mais je n'en jurerais pas.

(à 9^h du matin.) la poste devrait être arrivée. Tu puis juger avec quelle impatience nous l'attendons. Ô mon amie quand je songe à ta position durant cette terrible affaire! Il y a je crois

---

[13] Writing to Wellington on 20 June, Wrede* confirmed this plan to force a crossing of the Saar either late on 23 June or the following morning, then advance in concert with Kleist (*Supp. Desp.* x. 548).

tout au plus 6 lieues de Bruxelles à Jemappes![14] Dieu veuille que
tu ayes su à tems les bonnes nouvelles qu'on nous a envoyées.
Sans cela tu es surement à Anvers où je compte t'ecrire si par
malheur je n'ai pas de lettres de toi. Quant à nous il est presumable que nous ne couchions pas ici, ou reellement nous
sejournons dans une position par trop desagreable, puisque
nous courons à chaque instant le risque d'etre pris et fusillés
sans gloire quelconque à acquerir pour nous dedomager de ce
que cette aimable perspective a de trop attrayant. Je compte
après l'arriveè du Courrier me diriger sur Namur pour attendre
de nouveaux orders en mème tems que je m'approcherai
davantage du Theâtre de la Guerre conformement à mes
instructions. J'aurai soin seulement de laisser à chaque station
mon adresse pour la suivante.

(à 10^h 1/2) Je reste ici, ma chere Fanny, du moins pour quelques jours encore. Ouvre bien les yeux et lis: La poste n'est pas
encore arrivée, mais je sors de chez le Com^{dt} où j'ai causé assez
longtems avec le Lieut^{nt} Colonel Kamenski[15] premier aide de
camp du Cte Barclay de Tolly qui demain arrivera avec son
quartier general à *Kaisers Lautern*.[16] J'ai sur le champ ecrit à
ce General pour lui demander la permission de me reunir
à lui jusqu'à ce que j'aye reçu de nouveaux ordres de mon
Gouvernement. J'attendrai en consequence sa reponse à moins
que le Courrier ne m'indique une autre destination. Je viens
moi mème encore à la poste.

(à une heure) God be praised! voilà ta letter[17]—ô ma chere
chere amie, dans quelle crise tu t'es trouvée! J'en causerai une
autre fois avec toi. je ne puis en ce moment que remerciant le
ciel de ce qu'il a permis que tu sois encore à Bruxelles. Rien de

[14] The distance was more than double that suggested by M. d'A—60 kilometres
rather than 24 (1 French league equalled roughly 4 kilometres)—but the historical
significance of Jemappes may have been uppermost in his mind and fears. It was
the site in 1792 of a French victory by which the Revolutionary armies were able
to overrun the Austrian Netherlands.
[15] Sergei Mikhailovich Kamensky (1771/2–1835) was the son of Marshal Mikhail
Fedorovich Kamensky (1738–1809) and the brother of another Russian general.
He had distinguished himself in the campaign of 1812 and commanded the Narva
Infantry Regiment (Plotho, App. 12) during the invasion of 1815, when he also
held the post of chief adjutant to the Russian commander. He appears to have
retired from the army soon after his return from France in 1816. See *Biografichiski
Slovar'* (St. Petersburg, 1897), viii.
[16] Barclay de Tolly (L. 885 n. 2) notified Wellington of his arrival at Kaiserslautern and congratulated him on his victory at Waterloo in a letter dated 25 June
(*Supp. Desp.* x. 585). [17] L. 891.

nouveau pour moi qu'une lettre de M^r le Cte de Leautaud,[18] notre aide major, qui se trouve à Gand comme par Miracle et me recommande son beau frere à son passage ici, si sa bonne fortune l'y conduit. Quel bonheur que ce debut mais quel malheur que B. ne soit pas au nombre des morts! Je te quitte mon amie car j'ai à ecrire à Gand, ou ma lettre sera surement lue avec interêt.

899   [1358, Marché au bois],
                        Brussels, 24 June 1815

To M. d'Arblay

A.L. (rejected Diary MSS. 6644–7, Berg), 24 June 1815
Double sheet 4to   4 pp.   *pmk* BRUXELLES *foliated* 214, 215
Addressed: *Treves* / A Monsieur / Monsieur le General d'Arblay, / offi^r superieur des Gardes du Corps / de sa Majesty le Roi de France, / Chev^r de St Louis, &c &c / à Treves.
  Edited by FBA, p. 1 (6644), *annotated*: ⁂ ⁂ 16/1 Battle of Waterloo.
Rejected by the Press. *See* Textual Notes.

Brussells,
Saturday, June 24 1815

With what inexpressible joy have I just received your Letter dated the 19th *du Cabaret!*[1] to know you at Treves during these scenes of desolation & slaughter, not merely for your so loved existence—though surely for me that were enough!—but to know you have not been killed *mentally* with witnessing—or aiding!—the dreadful carnage of the 15th 16th 17th 18th & 19th in the early Morning, is Heaven to my soul! Oh how I bless General Kleist![2] The soldiers here themselves say It was murder rather than fighting, on both sides!

The wretched prisoners are now brought in every hour, in a condition so horrible, the streets seem pestilential as the Car-

---

[18] Auguste de Léautaud-Donnine (1771–*post* 1827), comte de Léautaud, a senior officer in the Compagnie de Luxembourg who became a maréchal de camp in 1820.

899. [1] L. 892.
  [2] For refusing to allow M. d'A to march with his army.

riages pass with them.³ Even all the shopkeepers bathe their faces with Eau de Cologne to support the effluvia! There were so many English & Belgians wounded & maimed to remove, that the carriages for the prisoners were not at liberty—though ALWAYS in motion, till the blood, *drying* upon them, & their garments, caused, I imagine, this nearly putrid effect. The Dead!—the Piles of dead, are now burying, by 3000 peasants!— to prevent a pestilence so many are employed at a time!— ǀ

Are not your scruples about your pay a little far-fetched? You are in a post that has been given you, & you fulfil all the duties that it affords you opportunity to fulfil. While you continue to send your regular accounts to the D[uke] de F[eltre] of your operations, 'tis for *him* to judge whether it be worth while to hold you to the post. To give your dismission, instead of being seen as extra-scrupulous in generosity, might be construed into contempt of your *besogne*. It seems to me that just now *exactitude* in service, & *strictness* in observing the minutest directions, is incumbent upon every one under the Royal Banners. The D. de F. will not keep you there when *HE* thinks you unnecessary. And that must be left to his own judgment. Mr de Castries,⁴ from Namur, was here at all the late Battling there. You are sure he was *ordered* away. M. de la Poterie,⁴ also, is *remplacé*,—therefore your line of action is not *forgotten*. But this is no period to embarrass the Minister with minor representations. I shall soon have an answer, I doubt not, from de Boinville.⁵ We may gather some thing from that.

I am far far from surprised my account of the plan should thus have shocked you; I hope, however, it has been exaggerated.⁶ In the first place, as many prisoners are made as possible; no cruel enmity leading to extirpation is shewn, & they are brought in, now, with the same care as our own troops or the Belges. The *first* were grossly insulted—*surtout* some General⁷— ǀ but at present, that the victory is decidedly ours, the poor wretches are pitied, & humanely used, & many french here send offerings to them. We are all at work more or less in

³ The 'fear of pestilence' was so great that many of the English thought once again of fleeing Brussels (Capel, p. 119).
⁴ For these *commissaires*, see L. 896 n. 2
⁵ See L. 876 n. 16.
⁶ The allies' sweeping plan to invade France and converge on Paris (mentioned by FBA in L. 888 and viewed with alarm by M. d'A in L. 892).
⁷ Mouton, comte de Lobau (L. 893 n. 14).

making Charpie. For me, I am about amongst the wounded half the day—the *British, s'entend!* The rising in France,[8] for the Honour of the nation now, & for its safety & independence hereafter, is brilliant & delightful, spreading, in some directions, from La Manche to La Mediterrannée:—the *focus* of loyalty is Bordeaux. *Monsieur* is gone to Mons already, with a part of the Maison du Roi.[9] Le Roi left Gand the 22ᵈ All alost, &c surround, follow, or precede him. The noble Blücher has entered France at ⟨Mortes⟩ le Chateau.[10] '*Suivez-les vite!*' he cried, '*Mes Enfans! ou demain nous les aurons encore sur les bras!*' The D[uke] of W[ellington] has avowed he more than once thought the Battle lost! The efforts made by B[uonaparte] were stupendous, & his Imperial Guards fought with a *devoument,* an enthusiasm, that shewed they thought victory & their leader MUST be ONE. It was not till 6 o'clock that the D[uke] felt his real advantage. He was every where in the field, & ran the most terrible risks; for which he is equally blamed & admired: but the stake was so prodigious! the victory or defeat so big with enormous consequences!—Oh mon amico! Can you wish me NOW in England—NOW, when the very moment is arrived which would have brought me hither, had I quitted you? recollect my dreadful, convulsive, almost dying sufferings at Sea—& think of me not only *going*—but *RETURNING* alone—! at *all risks,*—as undoubtedly if you should either be wounded, or a Prisoner I should do—& then compare the present inconveniencies & *désagrémens* & distastes—nay, even *dangers,* in *staying* here, with what I escape, in such a case, by *returning?*—

Besides—believe me!—the kind kind attention of every post, at this critical terrible period, repays all the evils of the intervals. —Heaven Heaven protect & bless you! I finish *Dimanche*— *June* 25ᵗʰ ⏐

The Boyds are come back—Mr. Boyd has called upon me— All agree the armies are now all on the frontieres of France,

---

[8] What FBA refers to here was a wave of royalist-inspired unrest and insurrection that continued during Napoleon's invasion of Belgium (Houssaye, *1815,* iii. 2–3). As the news of his defeat spread southward the violence increased, especially in the Vendée around Bordeaux, and in Marseilles (ibid. 148–67).

[9] This was actually the duc de Berry, who took with him a squadron of gardes de corps as an escort for Louis XVIII. Even in this emergency his choice was loudly criticized by the captain of one of the excluded companies as a breach of military etiquette (Romberg and Malet, i. 146–7).

[10] Solre-le-Château (Plotho, pp. 84, 90).

some at Maubeuge—others at Valenciennes but no public bulletin was given either Friday or Saturday here!—

The business, with respect to B[uonaparte]—must now, I think, be short — — Oh be it happy!—& safely to his fondest, truest—only permanent amie restore faithfully her beloved Protector & Support! — —

I cannot send you our Alex's last Letter, for I am answering it & it is long & embarrassed & we ought to make it out *together*. Ah when? But there is a very dear bit in this I trust to the post.

How am I charmed—yet how astonished—you knew nothing of the invasion of B. on the *14*. At Treves on the *19ᵗʰ*! │

Your last Letter, dated *June 19.*¹¹ Monday, is the 13ᵗʰ arrival. —This is *my* — — 12ᵗʰ

900   [1358, Marché au bois],
Brussels, 25–26 June 1815

To Mrs. Locke

L., excerpts in the hand of CFBt (Diary MSS. 6648–52, Berg), dated 15 June, 25–26 June 1815

Double sheet and a single sheet 4to 5 pp. pp. 1, 3, 5 foliated 216, 217, 220.

Docketed p. 5 (6652), *left margin*: 15 June 1815 The dating and docketing suggest that the excerpts may have been taken from two or three letters, or possibly from an A.J.L.

Edited by CFBt *and the* Press. *See* Textual Notes.

Brussels.
June 25. 1815

To Mʳˢ Locke

Tis a solace indeed,—at a period of unintermitting dismay, alarm, incertitude, for what is most dear to me upon Earth— tis indeed a solace to hear the voice of Happiness, & to hear it from a source that makes it vibrate through every terror to my

---

¹¹ The first of these dates is not astonishing, since Napoleon did not cross into Belgium until 15 June.

Heart!—. My beloved Friends letter of the 26ᵗʰ May[1] reached me only a week ago—just, just before this last affrighting, afflicting, murderous invasion—I began a letter immediately of warmest congratulations to my dear Augusta,[2] but ere I had sent it, these new horrors arrived—& it was packed up with my luggage for Antwerp—

But ere I go on with myself, or even with my dear *nouvelle mariée*, let me first do that which both you & she will first desire, speak of my other *Moitié*. I told you our history to our last separation which took him to *Liege*—Thence he proceeded to *Treves*, where he has been stationed ever since. His mission is to receive & examine, &c, Deserters from Bonaparte: Les Fidèles, plutôt, au Roi. A business of infinite delicacy, so many are the Spies & Emissaries that ǀ are ready to insinuate themselves on this side,[3] to gather information under every possible form and pretence. However, to *serve* the cause & the King in whatever manner it may be prescribed, is the fullest desire of M: d'Arblay. Nine other officers have the same commission, all upon Frontier Towns.[4] This station he has never quitted, though he has made various efforts to place himself more actively. But his mission has been successful, & I — — — you will easily believe!—am well contented it has not been changed. Le Comte de Gouvello,[5] husband to Lady Crewe's friend, has the same mission at Tournay. At *Mons*—whither now all the Royal Family are going, M: d'Auvergne has just been sent on the same errand,[6] to replace M: le Comte de la Poterie.[4] M. d'Arblay has an Aide de Camp, an Adjoint, & a volunteer

---

900. [1] This letter is missing.

[2] Mary Augusta Locke (1775–1842), Mrs. Locke's elder daughter, who by her marriage on 29 May to Rear-Admiral Sir George Martin (1764–1847) became Lady Martin. FBA's later references to 'my dear *nouvelle mariée*' and 'the dear Bride' refer to her.

[3] Spying assumed great importance during the Hundred Days, not only because of the divisions within France, but also because of the state of peace that forced all sides to substitute spies for usual military methods of reconnoitre and observation.

[4] See L. 896 n. 2.

[5] Louis-Paul, vicomte de Gouvello (L. 896 n. 2), and his wife Gasparde-Louise-Julie de Bourbon de Busset (1779–1853).

[6] Probably Joseph-Denis-Édouard-Bernard de la Tour d'Auvergne (1766–1841), comte de Lauragais de Saint-Paulet and baron de l'Empire (1814), a descendant of Turenne who rose quickly in the army to become a maréchal de camp in 1788. Although he added a Napoleonic title to his own, Auvergne remained strongly royalist and voted with the right as a deputy in the Chamber of 1815–16. He was given Turenne's heart by Louis XVIII as a family relic and retired in 1835, still with the rank of maréchal de camp.

officer of the Maison du Roi, Compagnie de Luxembourg, always with him; & others occasionally. This small party, of which he is Chief, follow his suggestions & directions in aiding his purpose. His Table is theirs—& he is therefore, you will justly conclude, upon full pay: otherwise!—! with 2 domestics, 4 Horses, a *Voiture de Campagne*, (i.e. a *half Cart*)[7] and, as the Superior ⎸ officer at Treves in active service for Louis XVIII, forced to innumerable *convenable* expences—*otherwise*, he must *try* to make debts for which, there, he could make no credit. And indeed the expences of such situations are so great, that unless some happy *suite* takes place, he will be apt, in the end, to say to those who have thus distinguished him like Swift to Harley and Bolingbroke,

> Well—Friends—since you have done your worst
> Pray leave me—where you found me first! ———[8]

He, however, while able to go on at all, thinks not, at this awful period, either of Gain or Loss. The *Cause*—so good! his *Country*, so culpable and unhappy—Those alone are the subjects that occupy his mind. And his Letters upon the latter, on the devastation he sees preparing all around him, are as melancholy as mine are from my perpetual apprehensions for his personal safety. He has written & printed a Proclamation, inviting his Countrymen to join him, which is to be thrown by every means into France, & which he has signed with his name.[9] This I think much too rash! so does Mons[r] de Lally, who has signed *his own*,[10] but who is away ⎸ from the Frontiers, & not military, nor

---

[7] A light two-wheeled vehicle drawn by a single horse.

[8] FBA here quotes the closing lines of *Part of the seventh Epistle of the First Book of Horace Imitated*, in which Swift answers Harley's mocking question 'What makes your Worship look so lean?' by reminding him of his own penniless condition and its cause:

> The Doctor in a Passion cry'd;
> Your Raillery is misapply'd:
> Experience I have dearly bought,
> You know I am not worth a Groat:
> But it's a folly to contest,
> When you resolve to have your Jest;
> And since you now have done your worst,
> Pray leave me where you found me first.

Poetical Works, ed. Norman Davis (Oxford, 1967), p. 111.

[9] M. d'A's proclamation is missing: it was not published in any of the surviving Trèves newspapers. A similar proclamation by his colleague La Rochefoucauld (L. 896 n. 2), urging soldiers to desert and officials to give up their posts, was reprinted in *Bell's Weekly Messenger* for 9 July.

[10] See L. 872 n. 8.

engaged in the scene of hostilities. You must have been pleased, I am sure, with the manifests of M: de Lally, from whom I had a visit but lately: He resides at Ghent, near the King, but comes occasionally to Brussels. Everybody ran away at the late Invasion—Madame d'Henin,—Mad^e La Tour du Pin & her daughter, Mad^{lle}, & her married daughter Mad^e de Liedekerke[11]—the Boyd Family—& in short every person I knew except Mad^e de Maurville, who determined to wait the event. For myself, I began the flight—but after sitting up all Sunday night in a house from whence I was to depart at 4 in the morning, surrounded by my little packets—for Baggage here have I none!—The Carriage failed the party with which I was to travel—& at seven o'clock, an English Officer who came to conduct us to a Barge that was to glide us to Antwerp, told me Bonaparte would have too much to do to be at Brussells that day, (Monday the 19th) 'Then he will not come at all!', I cried, 'for if he cannot take Brussells by a *Coup de main*, at once, to stay another Day will be to risk Paris! for the Allies will enter France in his absence.' On this presumption I ventured to return, packets & all, to my apartments, though my friends went on. And here I am! though in a most unpleasant, unsettled state.

I must wait for brighter days which all say are fast approaching, to write to the dear Bride,[2] but she will accept & feel my warmest wishes & hopes for her happiness.

June 26—I have now just had a letter from M: d'A. dated June 19th in which he expects orders to move every minute, but when he had not heard of the Invasion of *Les Pays Bas*![12] The odd slowness & apathy, or philosophy, of these perfectly good & worthy sleepy souls, is really astonishing.

P.S. We know the victory of D.W. *quite complete*—and Bonaparte hopeless—But what else is to ensue—whether Civil War, alas! or *what*, all here are ignorant.

[11] Cécile de Latour du Pin (1800–17) and her elder surviving sister Marie-Alix-*Charlotte* (1796–1822), comtesse (1813) de Liedekerke-Beaufort (L. 872 n. 10).
[12] The letter is missing.

901   [1358, Marché au bois],
                          Brussels, 26–28 June 1815

To M. d'Arblay

A.L.S. (Diary MSS. vii. 6654–[7], Berg), 26–28 June 1815
Double sheet large 4to (10 × 8·3″) 4 pp. *pmk* BRUXELLES wafer
Addressed: *TREVES.* À Monsieur / Monsieur le Général d'Arblay, /
Off^r Superieur des Gardes du Corps / de Sa Majesty le Roi de France, /
Chev^r de St. Louis, &c—&c / à TREVES.
Edited by FBA, p. 1 (6654), *annotated*: 16 / 2 Waterloo
Edited also at the Press. *See* Textual Notes.

BRUXELLES.
Ce Lundi,
ce Blessed Lundi, June 26. 1815

Why have I not a Balloon to be the first to tell you this
enchanting news!¹—or, rather, Wings to fly to you with it
myself! Buonaparte has yielded to Lord Wellington! — — —²

The particulars—how, which way, &c, are told too variously
for building upon their correctness—but the Fact SEEMS undoubted—SEEMS, I am compelled to say, for nothing official has
been here printed. The sleepiness of this quiet & good, but most
drowsy & hum drum people exceeds belief: Especially when I
consider que les Francs et les Belges came from one parent
stock, i.e., the *Germains.*

O Mon Ami! will not PEACE now re-visit us! — — My hand
shakes—& my spirits are agitated past all description, with an
inward fear that all this will not be confirmed. O for an English
Gazette!—

The whole City, in spite of its apathy, looked smiling, & even,
some few, grinning with contented joy, as I walked out early.
I except some others, evidently & gloomily overset. But these

901. ¹ Balloons were first used for manned flights and military observation soon
after the first experimental flights in 1783. The English Channel was crossed in 1784
and 1785, for example, and captive balloons were first used in war in 1794. See
'Aeronautics', *Enc. Brit.*
   ² Although Napoleon had abdicated in favour of his son on 22 June and the
French provisional government wrote to Wellington three days later to ask that
he be allowed to go into exile in the United States (*Supp. Desp.* x. 583–4), there
had been no surrender and no direct communication between Napoleon and
Wellington.

last are few. The people of this house, & every shop-keeper had heard the news, though without any positive authority.

But, about noon, I had a visit from M. de Beaufort—who came, kindly smiling himself, to bring me the first of the news. He had *JUST* learnt it, at the Commandants'—M. le Colonel Jones.[3] His account was That Buonaparte had sent to the Duke propositions, by an officer General. *1st* To Abdicate, in favour of his Son & a Regency:[2] *or 2dly*, in favour of Prince Eugene,[4] the great favourite of the Emp^r of Russia; *3dly*, In favour of the Duke of Orleans! |

The Duke sent him word he must yield at Discretion, or Fight. He had nothing to do with *Abdicating*, for he was NOTHING! He *had* already Abdicated, when he was Emperor.

The Army then sent a deputation, demanding a TRUCE to prepare a Peace, for sparing the further effusion of human blood.

The Duke answered, Their King might spare it, when re-seated on his Throne; but that *FOR THEM*, & *FROM* Them, the application was now too late.[5]

---

[3] Leslie Grove Jones (1779–1839), British commandant at Brussels during the Hundred Days, served first in the navy, which he left in protest over the unjust flogging of a cook aboard H.M.S. *Revolutionnaire*, entered the 1st Foot Guards as an ensign in 1796, served with this regiment at home and abroad (chiefly in the Peninsular campaigns), rising by 1813 to the rank of captain in the regiment and lieutenant-colonel in the army. His control over visas and residence permits made him important to the English in, or travelling through, Brussels during this period (see Broughton, i. 240) and his blunt friendliness endeared him to at least some of them: 'He is very intimate with us, he comes in and out of the House at all Hours like a tame Cat' (Capel, p. 63). While with the army of occupation at Cambrai in 1817, Jones wrote a radical pamphlet *Principles of Legitimacy*, published in 1827 after he retired from the army to enter politics. He wrote abrasive letters to *The Times* in favour of reform, signing himself 'Radical', but was forced by lack of money to give up his hopes for a new career in Parliament.

[4] Eugène-Rose de Beauharnais (1781–1824), son of the Empress Josephine, stepson of Napoleon, viceroy of Italy (1805), and Prince of Venice (1807),—both Napoleonic titles—and, later, Prince of Eichstaedt and Duke of Leuchtenberg (1817)—Bavarian titles conferred by his father-in-law King Maximilian Joseph (1756–1825)—rose rapidly in the armies of the Consulate and Empire, distinguished himself at Marengo and went on to become the most popular and perhaps the most able ruler of the Napoleonic dynasty, into which he was adopted as a son and heir in 1806. He commanded the 4th (Italian) Corps in Russia in 1812 and the wreckage of the Grande Armée in the last stages of the retreat, commanded in Germany in 1813 and Italy in 1814, when he defeated the Austrians on the Mincio. Napoleon's fall forced him to retire to Bavaria in June 1814, and although named a pair des Cent-Jours, he gave his word not to serve for or against Napoleon. Although less often mentioned as a candidate for the French throne than the duc d'Orléans, he was known to be favoured by the Czar (Palmer, p. 288) and by some liberal Bonapartists. For his early career see v, L. 529 n. 11.

[5] Unconditionally. Wellington refused even to discuss terms of a separate truce or peace.

After this, I spoke all the kind things you have written of M. de Beaufort, who heard them with tears in his Eyes, & who is still & evidently more melancholy. Does he feel her loss more than he felt her presence? I have heard no relation of the Will;[6] but it is impossible for me to doubt that so very attached a wife should have failed in the tender duty of shewing a regard beyond the Grave.

In the course of the Morning, came the P^ss escorted by M. de Lally. They gave me, & kindly came on purpose to give me, the same particulars: with many added, of deep interest—but of a sort I shall not write till I am sure my Letters come straight into your own hands: & you talk so often of their *following* you, that I durst run no rash risks at such a moment.

After all this, in the Park, whither I went to breathe an instant, at it's epoch of real emptiness, 5 o'clock—I met a Gentleman whose face I thought I knew. He looked a reciprocal look of a similar idea, but walked on. Presently, however, we both looked back, & caught each other making the same second investigation—He then returned, & ¹ seizing my hand, with an air of cordial affection, exclaimed 'Mon Dieu! Mad^e d'A:!—' & I then recalled our old friend le voisin [*M. de Boursac*].[7]

He was extremely affectionate & kind^B He had escaped the same day that we did: but *ses dames sont toujours à Paris*. I believe he is with M. le P[rince] de Condé. He has promised to come & see me speedily; he enquired most heartily after you & said he had done so already, & had learnt you were at Treves. He told me further news — —[8]

That in *Les Chambres*, various voices had demanded army intelligence, & where was the Emperor. At first, the Ministers present said les Nouvelles were not mauvaises; & the *Emperour* was with his army; but being hard & hardily pressed, Carnet acknowledged *all to be bad*, & the Emperor in Paris!—After much dissention, & contention, & [violence,] a Majority took imperious lead, & declared Buonaparte *déchu*.

---

⁶ See L. 897 n. 12.

⁷ For Louis-François-Joseph de La Cropte (1753–*post* 1819), vicomte de Bourzac, his wife and daughter, see vi, L. 585 n. 2, L. 607 n. 2. Before the Revolution he was aide-de-camp to the prince de Condé. For the explanation of 'le voisin', see J. 924, p. 413.

⁸ FBA here compresses Bourzac's report, itself pieced together from the *Moniteur* and the *Journal de l'Empire*, on the stormy sessions in both Chambers (of deputies and peers) of 21–4 June.

A Committee was then formed to make a proposal to the Allies—THREE took the lead[9]—And said They would make any sacrifice to recover peace—resign the Emperor;—become a republic; take another & new form of Government—or revert to a free Monarchy—*ANY THING*, for Peace—except—re-instating the late Power! — — — oh mon ami—I hope this is exaggerated—& surtout that it is FALSE, entirely false that one of these Three is one of our most valued friends! — — Not Victor, you are very sure—nor yet his Brother[10] — — but — — M. de La Fayette!

Difficulties—contrarieties—Factions—Mischiefs we must expect—& meet with fortitude—but ONE voice, clear & UNIVERSAL, in a chorus angelical, cries, affirms, & confirms, That the Armies fight no more!—

If you were to see me in this happy, happy Moment—you would not know me—I have not felt so blyth since — — — since when?—Since the Evening you came home from the first short & frightful Campaign—when happiness—after long—long Journeying elsewhere, suddenly & sweetly made me a visit—

Tuesday, June 27ᵗʰ I have again seen M. de Boursac, & I have been to the Boyds, once but no *new* News is afloat to day. The King is at Cateau Cambresis, under ˡ the immediate protection of Lord Wellington.—whose proclamation[11] if I can possibly procure I will copy for you to-morrow early. How amazing that on the *21ˢᵗ* you should not have heard, at Treves, of the Invasion of les pays bas!—I am truly sorry for Gen: Kleist: but oh how happy to think & hope *you* still at Treves!—I am happy, also, I decided against going to Anvers: already, I am forced to

---

[9] After the battle of Waterloo and the obvious collapse of Napoleon's regime, the provisional government formed in Paris tried to negotiate a separate peace (one bought at the cost of Napoleon's abdication) by appointing three emissaries who were instructed to cross the Rhine to Haguenau and open negotiations with the allied sovereigns—especially with the Czar.

The three were Lafayette, who swayed the deputies away from Napoleon and over to himself in the opening speech of the session on 21 June; Horace-François-Bastien Sébastiani de la Porta (1772–1851), a general and comte de l'Empire; and Marc-René Le Voyer d'Argenson (1771–1842), a prefect and comte from a great family of the noblesse de robe. All three liberals, cool to both Bonapartist and Bourbon schemes, Fouché sent off on a hopeless mission (see L. 903 n. 8) to clear the way for his own negotiations with Wellington and Louis XVIII.

[10] Victor de Latour-Maubourg (L. 840 n. 23) and César (L. 845 n. 28).

[11] Louis XVIII's proclamation of 25 June, a paternal announcement of his return that included promises of rewards for the good and punishments for the guilty (*Supp. Desp.* x. 580-1).

tell you I must have recourse myself to Messrs Danoots in a short time. With my most scrupulous œconomy, I can only hope to wait till I hear from you next, as an answer is always 12 days in arriving. I have been compelled to purchase some few matters of wearing apparel,—nothing coming from Paris— though merely matters of necessity, for I live more retired than ever, & have NO pleasure in ANY expence of which neither you nor Alex partake. The Aegide,[12] ou plutôt, *les siens*, would much have disappointed you; had you seen them *de plus prés*. When you come to *close quarters*, they are ordinary & uninteresting; I mean in *discourse*. I except, however, the Eldest, who is far the best fashioned of the tribe. But I am truly glad not to have been forced upon beginning an intimacy it would have been a burthen to me to sustain.

Wednesday, June 28!—O how *il me tarde* d'avoir de vos nouvelles! & to know your destination! I shall love Treves all my life! To-morrow is post day, Dieu merci! — — & my kind Ami has not once failed his impatient suffering athanase since this alarming period, that would make failure almost mortal. I cannot get the Proclamation[11] till next post! I hope it will reach you otherwise. I have no room to relate the pourquois; for I have another thing to tell you. I enquired of our voisin how it happened that *you* had received no order to move, when one of your Collegues, M. de Castres,[13] certainly had, since he had been at Bruxelles. He answered me—That M. de C. had received no order, for he had seen him, & believed he was even

---

[12] Aegidé, which is the French form of Aegida—the chief town of the Adriatic district of Capo d'Istria—may be a coded reference to the family ('les siens') of Giovanni Antonio Capo d'Istria (1776–1831), count of Capo d'Istria, the Russian diplomat who had been born on Corfu and was hence originally of Venetian citizenship. But Capo d'Istria, whose life and career make him a paradigm of the change in Europe from dynastic to nationalist politics, was also and throughout a Greek patriot who in 1827 became President of the newly independent Greek republic, after which he signed himself as Joannes Capodistrias. He entered the diplomatic service of the Czar in 1809 and had a great influence, usually of a liberal and conciliatory kind, on Russian foreign policy during the last stages of the Napoleonic period. He had by then become joint minister of Foreign Affairs, but increasing disagreements and the opposition of Metternich led him to resign, leave Russia, and settle into private life at Geneva in 1822. His return to public life as the Greek President soon involved him in the bitter conflicts of the young republic, conflicts that led to his assassination in 1831. Although he never married, Capo d'Istria had a large number of brothers and sisters who often visited or accompanied him during his postings in Russia and Western Europe. It is therefore possible that FBA means by 'the Eldest' Viaro Capo d'Istria (1774–1842), a lawyer and political figure who shared many of his younger brother's ideals and opinions.

[13] See L. 888 n. 24.

here still: but when the Fr[ench] arrived, or were undoubtedly arriving before Namur, he came away of his own accord, AS A THING OF COURSE, & of *common sense*, since, had he been taken, he must instantly have been shot by the Buonapartists, on account of his mission: & that without serving any purpose, as he had no troops, & no command.

The Maison du Roi IS, or is to be, *dissoute*:[14] I asked what was become of its members? He replied Those who had *leave*, or *orders*, accompanied the King: the others addressed M. de Feltre, & waited where was most *convenable* for directions. But ALL, of ALL descriptions, have left Gand. At Alost there is still a Depôt.

with respect to the person *fusilé* for M. de L[ally]'s *Manifest*,[15] it was M. de L. HIMSELF who told me. But happily, it has proved a misinformation. NOTHING, at this moment, must be QUITE CREDITED, but upon *proof*:—is it not THEREFORE that you QUITE credit the tender faith of your inalterable

F B d'A.—y ?—

⌐De Boinville is with the D[uke] of Feltre in France—by mistake, he missed my letter, for he must else have answered it. I have much uneasiness at the moment relative to the *parties divers*—!¹⁶

Le Voisin tells me le Duc de Bourbon has been all this time in Spain—but is now certainly in La Vendee. M. d'Angouleme still in Spain at the last News.

902   [Trèves], 28 June 1815

M. d'Arblay
To Madame d'Arblay

A.L. (Berg), 28 juin 1815
Single sheet 4to   2 pp.   [*cover missing*]
Edited by FBA, p. 1, *annotated*: ⌐25⌐   (16/3)

¹⁴ The household troops, together with the units of royal volunteers, had in fact followed the King.
¹⁵ Cf. L. 878, p. 155.
¹⁶ The conflicting factions within France and around Louis XVIII.

Ce 28 Juin 1815

J'ai eu et j'ai encore en ce moment un mal de dents qui me fait beaucoup souffrir; du reste je me porte à merveille, et souhaitte fort pouvoir apprendre de ta santé dont tu ne me dis rien qu'elle est aussi bonne que la mienne. Ô ma chere et toujours plus chere amie! quel baume pour moi que tes lettres; et combien je te sais gré de les faire si longues dans un moment où tu dois avoir si peu de momens à ta disposition. Pour moi mon tems est tellement pris depuis cinq à six jours par de fastidieux details, et par d'eternelles ecritures qu'a peine ai-je eu le tems de te donner signe de vie, et qu'il m'est absolument impossible de causer avec toi. En ce moment mème je t'ecris ceci en presence de 4 personnes, ce que comme tu penses nuit *un peu* à toute effusion de coeur. Remercie, je t'en supplie Made la Cesse Maureville pour moi, et toi qui sais si bien à quel point je suis eloigné de vouloir nuire à qui que ce soit, Explique lui bien qu'elle m'a peu rendu justice en prenant en mauvaise part ce que j'ai dit trés inocement des Schalls[1] qu'elle avait fait venir de Londres.[1] Tes deux dernieres lettres m'ont fait eprouver deux sensations bien opposées, un plaisir inexprimable, et une peine si vive que c'est seulement ce matin que j'ai pu jouir de quelques instans de sommeil. L'idée des dangers que tu as courus me l'avait fait perdre. O ma chere Fanny je ne puis en verité prendre sur moi de te remercier d'une marque de tendresse qui nous a exposé à une si terrible separation! Que serais-je devenu, si tu etais tombée entre les mains de B. Ce que tu me dis de ces montagnes de morts, parmi les quels se sont trouvé confondus, sans doute, une foule de malheureux extenués par la faim fait horreurs.

Au milieu, cependant, de tant de choses tristes et même accablantes quel bonheur que celui d'avoir pu donner à tems tes lettres au Courrier partant pour cette little tidy happy Island! Celle d'Alex que tu as reçue n'est pas pour toi seule — hein? Donne m'en au moins quelques petits extraits. Après les

902. [1] Mrs. Barbauld is a witness against her sex in the smuggling in these years of 'lace and silk shawls' to England. This enterprise interested lady travellers more than did 'museums of art or new scenes of nature'. They 'think of nothing but running in silks and satins'. See *A Memoir of Mrs. Anna Lætitia Barbauld . . .*, ed. Grace A. Ellis (Boston, 1974), pp. 295–8 *passim*. The pseudonym 'shawls' and 'chaâle', the more usual spelling of the anglicanism, point to some shady traffic both in exchange (L. 980 n. 4) and lucrative contraband, such as the coveted Mechlin or Brussels lace.

tiennes que rien ne peut remplacer, j'aime autant les siennes qu'un brevet de M[al] de France que j'aurais merité. Une chose dont je ne me serais jamais douté c'est que ce Pays n'a aucune relation directe avec Bruxelles de sorte que c'est trés inutilement que j'ai fait chercher ce matin un moyen de te faire passer 200 ou 300[f]. Il devient donc indispensable que tu prennes chez le Banquier cet argent et je te supplie de le faire. adieu chere bien chere et toujours plus chere amie! Mille choses à Beaufort!

903 — [1358, Marché au bois], Brussels, 29–30 June 1815

To M. d'Arblay

A.L. (rejected Diary MSS. 6658–61, Berg), 29–30 June 1815
Double sheet 4to 4 pp. *pmk* BRUXELLES wafer
Addressed: *Treves*. / À Monsieur / Monsieur le General d'Arblay, / off[r] superieur des gardes du Corps / de sa Majestie le Roi de France, / Chv[r] de St. Louis, &c &c &c / à Treves. / Trier
Edited by FBA, p. 1 (6658), 1815 *boxed and annotated*: ⁜ N° ⌜16⌝ (16/4) Brussels after Waterloo—
Edited also by the Press. *See* Textual Notes.

Bruxelles,
Thursday 29th 1815. June

O Cette chère Treves!—Treves encore June 24th! Comme Je l'aimerai toute ma vie! What an interesting Letter! but how cruelly pale the Ink! It must be upon trust, I think, that your own Eye can follow your writing. The indecision, & want of character you have been plagued with I know well how to feel for! But I hope you will now have fresh orders,—& punctually *await* them, all being changed by this immense immortal incalculably Grand victory.—Wellington is indeed at the Head of this nether World!

Oui, mon bien cher ami, oui! in the great—just now great*est* point, that of political opinion, there is not a *nuance* in our thoughts & feelings.—Indeed, I always flatter myself that in ALL which is *innate* we have sympathy; where sympathy drops, or fails, I always soothe myself with believing it is from difference of education—& habits, &, indeed, of *sex*, & *country*— for how often do we catch ourselves, in what we utter spontaneously, *thinking & feeling*, and *saying* the same thing!

Brussells now is beginning fast to recover its usual air. All the English wounded who were able to bear the Voyage & Journey, are sent home, to make way here for les Belges; & all the Prisoners not too dreadfully mangled are sent also away. There was really an apprehension of a pestilence, so shocking were the wounds, & so numerous the poor sufferers, both conquerors & conquered. The noble D. of Wellington came himself to see about the Hospitals As soon as the Battle, & immediate pursuit of Buonaparte, were over.

What a stupendous victory! France seems to have nothing more but *ses places fortes* to oppose to the conquerors,—for now all the allies are entered.

You write, you say, to Gand; no doubt orders are left there to forward Letters to the Minister;[1] but neither minister nor secretary nor clerk remain.

10 at night.—I must now give you all I have amassed of intelligence: For though it may be anticipated, there is a *chance* it may be new.

I have a certain account that the King was yesterday morning, June 29th at Peronne.[2] Cambray has been taken almost without even the pretence of resistance.[3] Maubeuge holds out. So does Valenciennes. (Remember, I speak of the 29th) There have been great difficulties & dissentions & party cabals, &c. &c—&c!!! that I cannot enter into—I give but results.

M. de Blacas is set off for Naples, on a *plenipo* mission;[4] but

903. [1] The staff of the Minister of War (Feltre) accompanied the King as his personal escort (Rochechouart, p. 428).

[2] On 29 June the royal party was still at Cambrai, which it left for Péronne on the morning of the 30th (Reiset, iii. 227).

[3] The town fell quickly to a British assault on 24 June, but the governor of the citadel, in a gesture of great value to the Bourbons, surrendered to Louis XVIII on the following day (*Supp. Desp.* x. 582).

[4] Attacks on Blacas (L. 847 n. 2) had become so widespread that the King was finally persuaded to dismiss him before re-entering France. On 23 June the minister set off from Mons for England to collect his family—and seven million francs deposited there as a parting gift from Louis XVIII (Houssaye, *1815*, iii. 135–6). He presented his credentials in Naples in mid October (*Moniteur*, 17 November) and soon after was appointed ambassador to Rome (there is no evidence that he was meant to go on to Vienna).

he is to be ambassadour at vienna as soon as all is fixed in France.

M. de Tallyrand is just gone to join his Majesty, & become prime Minister.[5]

The Proclamations of the several Chiefs I should fain send you; but they are too long to Copy, & I see them but for a moment: take however their essence. They are infinitely important, & curious beyond measure.

Lord Wellington—Lord of ALL in This grand Coalition by this superb & so hardly won triumph—Lord Wellington says to this effect—[6]

France must know I enter its territories at the head of an army already victorious: but not an Enemy!—I come an enemy only to The Usurper, & his adherents: the Usurper, denounced by all nations, & with whom NONE will make PEACE or even a TRUCE. But let France know, & believe, the troops of the various Nations under my command belong to Sovereigns who are FRIENDS and ALLIES to Their lawful King, Louis 18. They come, therefore, not to conquer, or oppress, but to aid both the Monarch & the people to conquer their usurping oppressor. Should any of them forget or neglect this amity, upon the smallest misdemeanour, let it be to ME that the French address themselves! They shall be righted. The French, however, must so behave as to merit the protection I assure them of. They must remain quietly in their houses, & deliver to the commissaries appointed what is claimed by a written order, with a receipt: they shall then endure no contributions. Contribution & confiscation shall be reserved for those only who adhere to the usurper, or who communicate with him, or his adherents, or who absent themselves from their houses after my arrival. Such, without any compensation, shall provide for the necessities of the army.[1]

This I have written only by Memory, & from a translation. ⌐Is it not all you can wish? Not so the Austrian proclamation.¬[7]

[5] Talleyrand condescended to Louis XVIII at Mons, but the King rejected his advice and accepted his resignation. Wellington, alarmed at the consequences of this, persuaded both to compromise and brought about a reunion at Cambrai that made Talleyrand Foreign Minister once again.

[6] What follows is an accurate paraphrase of Wellington's Proclamation from Malplaquet on 22 June (*Disp.* xii. 494–5).

[7] FBA's sketch of Schwarzenberg's* Proclamation from Heidelberg on 24 June softens its tone and adds to it the final clause about French freedom of choice. The full text (see *Moniteur*, 10 July) stresses the rights of Europe rather than the rights of France.

Prince Scwertzenberg says he comes not to direct a great Nation in its choice of Government or Governors: he comes with peace & Laurel branches, so the abdicated Napoleon be but renounced. With him all must be finally & utterly & eternally finished: for all else, he leaves the French freely to make their own decision & choice.

⌐So here the King is left to take care of himself.¬

The Chamber of pairs & deputies, in a committee, have addressed the Duke, beseeching to end the War, & promising to form any Government whatsoever, so the Bourbons are but excluded![8]

My last particular information, & from good source, is That the Prus[ns] are so very vindictive & cruel & rapacious, that their own officers cannot undertake to keep them within *des bornes!*— they have already begun upon some frontier town, most savagely!—Therefore, Lord Wellington & the *good* as *brave*, the noble Blücher have agreed to let the King go *FIRST* to Paris, *without them*; though they will be near enough to ensure his safety. They, then, will arrive as *VISITORS*, which will take from the wild soldiers the idea & hope of entering as Conquerors & plunderers! & save Paris & the Parisiens. What a heavenly plan! I have heard it with rapture.

I hope to Heaven you will not move from Treves till you hear from the D[uke] de Feltre. The *maison*, I understand, is to be *dissoute*. The whole of those, military & civil, who were at Gand & Alost, are said to be at *Mons: With* the King, are but few: immediate Ministers, & les Capitaines de sa garde. M. Mounier is at Mons.[9] M. de Lally went thither this morning.

The D. of W. was every where in person in the Battle— Never have so many English fallen! never was fighting so hard! It was B[uonaparte]'s last resource & last effort, & his Imperial Guards were Lions all, & rushed on with an ¹ enthusiasm & fire worthy a better Chief & better Cause. Lord W. does all possible honour to B. for his Military abilities, & to his Elect for their

[8] FBA here seems to combine and garble the unsuccessful approaches made to Wellington by Lafayette's commission (*Supp. Desp.* x. 597) on 26 June and the letter written to the Duke by Fouché, acting as 'Le président du Government' late on the 27th.
[9] See L. 876 n. 27.

bravery, & says he never fought so hard & sanguinary a Battle, & never was so near being beaten. He highly praises Mar¹ Blücher, Gen¹ Bulow, & the poor D[uke] of Brunswick:[10] yet, with all their timely aid, but for that great stroke of GENIUS, which will immortalize his name as the Centrical division has done that of Nelson;[11]—but for that stroke, which so well timed the moment in which, (after so many received, yet repulsed, attacks, from 10 in the morn. till 7 at night,) he then gave that tremendous charge; ordering, all at once, Infantry, Cavalry, & Artillery to dash, in one great blow,[12] from his whole line, upon the heights & the plain;—but for that stroke, it would at last have been a drawn battle:—but that unexpected & abrupt, confounded, appalled, Conquered!—it was irrecoverable: & without another effort, all *flew* or *fell*! Buonaparte amongst the rest! the yet remaining Imperial Guards like the youngest Conscripts!—In the account given by themselves, this is acknowledged!!! Immortal Wellington! Vive! Vive! Vive!

Yet how narrowly has he escaped! Two of his aid de Camps have been killed by his side—& three of the confederate Generals, who attended to give an account to Russia & Austria of the Battle, M. Pozzo de Borgo,[13] & M. de Vincent (doyen de diplomatie)[14] both were wounded. Poor M. de Vincent's Ball

[10] See L. 871 nn. 1, 4 and L. 891 n. 14.

[11] The splitting in two of the Allied (French and Spanish) fleet at Trafalgar, by which Nelson was able to destroy or capture (most) of Villeneuve's ships.

[12] Wellington ordered this general advance after the collapse of the attack by Napoleon's Guard. It took place as night fell and was supported by the Prussian vanguard, attacking on his left.

[13] A Corsican nobleman who later became a Russian general and diplomat and in 1825 a French comte, Carlo Andrea Pozzo di Borgo (1764–1842) turned early against the Bonapartes (who backed the Jacobins during the Revolution) and brought Corsica under an English protectorate (1794–6). A French invasion drove him into a life of wandering opposition to the Revolution and later to Napoleon, first to Italy and England, then to Austria (1798–1804) and to Russia (with interruptions from 1804 until 1814). At Napoleon's first abdication in 1814 he was the Russian high commissioner to the French provisional government, took part in the Congress of Vienna, and followed Louis XVIII to Ghent as the Czar's ambassador. He was grazed by a bullet at Waterloo but returned at once to negotiating with Talleyrand and Wellington to bring about the return of the Bourbons and the protection of French interests. He remained in Paris, mitigating the reactionary policies of Charles X (the former comte d'Artois) and reconciling the Czar to Louis-Philippe, until 1835. His francophilia then finally became too much for his Russian master, who transferred him to London, though he returned to Paris in 1839.

[14] Vincent (L. 872 n. 13) was the senior ambassador with Louis XVIII at Ghent and hence 'doyen' of its little diplomatic corps. In a letter to Wellington of 22 June he declared that he hoped soon to be rid of this bullet, which he describes as the only enemy force still left in Belgium (*Supp. Desp.* x. 559).

cannot be extracted from his wrist, & he suffers torture! though at first the wound was thought nothing. Nor is the Prince of orange nearly recovered. Murat, at last was not there:[15] & Jerome is got back to Paris.[16] We know not at this moment exactly where B. is—*I* think escaped on board a ship & off for America!—The Jacobins are at the head of Paris. But they cannot resist an army. Alas—what dissentions will not outlive this terrible calamity!—How will you grieve about M. de la F[ayette]!—Mar[1] Marmont is *here*.[17] I saw him just now, *a*scending the steps I was *de*scending, at Mᵉ d'H[énin]'s.—! I shall continue to write every post at this critical time. How very, very kind is your regularity! what should I do if in ignorance of your situation & proceedings! Your Letters are my existence— adio—El mio caro!—adio ‖

P.S. June 30ᵗʰ a *Bonjour* ere this goes to the post to my dearest Ami. B[uonaparte] is at Paris, struggling to have a Regency for his son! To be sure that would be an abdication! La Bedoyere has declaimed against perjured oaths![18] Massena[19] said, in the

[15] See L. 890 n. 8.

[16] See L. 893 n. 10.

[17] Marmont, the duc de Raguse (L. 860 n. 11) returned from Aix-la-Chapelle, where, with the permission of the King of the Netherlands (*Supp. Desp.* x. 455), he had spent two months recovering his health and waiting upon events. He arrived in Brussels on or about 25 June, but joined the King only several days later at Roye on the road to Paris. See *Mémoires du duc de Raguse de 1792 à 1841* . . . (9 vols., 1857), vii. 128.

[18] Charles-Angélique-François Hutchet de La Bédoyère (1786–1815), chevalier de l'Empire (1809) and comte (1815) as a pair des Cent-Jours, entered the army in 1806 and immediately distinguished himself in Spain, then at Essling and the siege of Ratisbon, as a brave officer and fiery character. Prince Eugène (L. 901 n. 4) promoted him to chef de bataillon in 1811, and Napoleon made him a colonel after the battle of Lutzen in 1812. Although of an old and noble Breton family he became a die-hard Bonapartist after the first Restoration and even while commanding the 7ᵉ régiment de ligne at Grenoble he was noticed in secret police reports as a loud supporter of Napoleon (Letter to Beugnot of 10 Aug. 1814 in Eugène Welvert, *Napoléon et la police*, 1943, p. 122). On the Emperor's return from Elba, La Bédoyère marched his regiment south and defected with it at Vizille. His was the first large unit to go over to Napoleon, and he was as a result marked out for revenge by the royalists. He was promoted to général de brigade and made a peer, fought to the end at Waterloo, and returned to Paris to defend Napoleon and his dynasty in the Chambre des pairs. The bitter attack FBA refers to here was made late in the session of 22 June and brought the rebuke from Masséna (1758–1817), prince d'Essling, quoted here (*Moniteur*, 23 June). La Bédoyère fell into the hands of the restored royalists and, despite many attempts to save him, was court-martialled and shot on 19 August.

[19] André Masséna (1756–1817), duc de Rivoli and prince d'Essling, perhaps the greatest of Napoleon's marshals, was born in Nice and entered the Royal-Italien regiment in 1775. He left the army and went to live in Italy but returned and became an officer at the Revolution, rising to the rank of général de division in

Chambre—Jeune homme—vous vous oubliez:—' How I blush for some of our own Friends'[20] alas—

904   Trèves,
                                                   30 June–[1 July 1815]

M. d'Arblay
To Madame d'Arblay

A.L. (Berg), 30 juin—samedy matin
Double sheet 4to   4 pp.   *pmk* TRIER   seal
Addressed: A Madame / Madame de Burney / poste restante / à Bruxelles
Readdressed: Marché au Bois
Edited by FBA, p. 1, *annotated and dated*: ⌐26⌐ (17/I) (1815) of General Kamenski.; Barclay de Tolly; &c [*with numbers on address fold*]: 17   26
See further, Textual Notes.

Treves ce 30. Juin

Nous avons ici tant d'alertes, les unes sur les autres que je ne sais, ma bonne amie, si je t'ai dit que Mr de Rochechouart,[1] chef d'Etat Major du Ministre de la Guerre, en me prevenant du depart du Roi pour Mons, m'a ecrit que je recevrai *sans delai*

1793. His early campaigns in Italy and Switzerland and his brilliant victory over the Russians at Zurich (1799) made him a marshal in 1804. He further distinguished himself at Aspern-Essling and Wagram, but his reverses began in the Peninsular war after 1810. After his return to France Napoleon shunted him aside and into disaffected negotiations with Fouché and the royalists. He held Marseilles for Louis XVIII during the Hundred Days but later became one of Napoleon's peers and refused to sit on Ney's court-martial.

[20] The loyalty of Napoleon's 'greatest marshal' (*supra*) to the Bourbons contrasts sadly in FBA's mind with the disloyalty of the Beauvaus (L. 877 n. 11) and the tortuous attempts of Lafayette (see L. 901 n. 9).

904   [1] Louis-Victor-Léon de Rochechouart (1788–1858), comte de Rochechouart, was a child *émigré* who entered military service with the régiment de Mortemart in Portugal in 1801, then passed by way of Paris into Russian service. He soon became an aide-de-camp of the Czar, a protégé of the duc de Richelieu, and, after several campaigns, a colonel (1814). He then entered the French army as a maréchal de camp, and the Maison du Roi as a lieutenant in the mousquetaires noires and, accompanying the King to Ghent, became chief of staff to Clarke, the duc de Feltre. On the Second Restoration he was appointed commandant of Paris. He was to be forcibly retired in 1831 and for over two years travelled throughout Europe at the service of the deposed Charles X, returning to France and the writing of his memoirs in 1834.

une nouvelle destination. Depuis ce tems rien n'est arrivé; mais c'est demain jour du courrier; peut être serons nous assez heureux pour recevoir l'ordre de partir d'ici. Amen! amen — (Samedy matin) Je viens de passer une nuit des plus fatiguantes, tout habillé, et sur le qui vive, par ce qu'on avait fait courir le bruit que Vandamme, poursuivi mais echappé, à travers les bois, etait depuis deux jours à Prüm,[2] et n'avait de retraite que sur Thionville, qu'il devait gagner en passant par Treves. Il etait bien naturel en ce cas qu'il en fit la tentative; et certes elle etait sans danger puisque nous n'avons ici personne à lui opposer, et que rien ne lui aurait été plus facile que de lever une assez forte contribution, que les circonstances actuelles l'auraient probablement mis dans le cas de faire tourner à son profit. Heureusement rien de tout cela n'est arrivé; et j'en ai été quitte pour faire tenir nos chevaux sellés toute la nuit: mais cela est vraiment ennuyeux, et devient insuportable. J'esperais que nous aurions aujourd'hui l'ordre de partir: mais non. Rien; absolument rien. Excepté pourtant ta lettre, qui est bien quelque chose! Ah combien j'aurais été malheureux de ne point en avoir de toi! avec quel ravissement j'y ai trouvé l'assurance toujours plus chere de ta tendresse! oserai-je te dire que j'en suis bien bien digne? Cela est pourtant vrai. Mais tu ne m'en diras pas moins que je suis un fat! Ô mon amie tes lettres sont ma vie! Tout ce que tu me dis sur ma position ici est parfaitement raisonné, et pourtant est tout à fait hors de mesure. c.à.d. ¹ que ta maniere de raisonner est très exacte, et tout à fait juste, en partant de la supposition que j'ai des instructions aux quelles sans aucun doute je devrais me conformer, sans ennuyer les ministres du Roi des petits details de conduite que je voudrais leur soumettre. Mais si je n'ai point d'instruction; ou si mes instructions sont devenues sans objet; que diras tu? Eh bien Ecoute.

Mes instructions portent: que je dois favoriser la desertion des partisans de Bonnaparte, et suivre les mouvemens des armées des alliés, agir de concert avec eux, et même par moi même si je le trouve convenable; mais en me rapprochant le plus possible de la ligne d'operations.

---

² Or Pruym, a town in the Rhine province of Prussia forty-five kilometres north-west of Trèves. The report that Vandamme (L. 878 n. 10), wounded at Namur on 20 June, still commanded Grouchy's* rearguard, was false.

Les Troupes alliées à qui j'ai offert mes services, m'ont toutes refusé poliment par l'Organe de leurs Generaux les plus fameux. Voici à ce sujet la derniere lettre que m'a fait ecrire le Marechal Comte Barclay de Tollé Generalissime des armées Russes.[3]

Pardon. Je ne la trouve pas sous la main, et serais desolé de l'avoir egarée: c.à.d. très faché de ne pas l'avoir pour Alex, à qui surement elle ferait plaisir. Le Chef[4] d'Etat major gen^{al} me mande de la part du Marechal, que ce serait avec un très grand plaisir qu'il me Verrait avec lui à son Etat major general, mais que dans les armées Russes aucun off^{er} allié ne peut être admis dans cet Etat Major sans un ordre exprès de Sa Majesté l'Empereur et Roi.

A propos d'Empereur, n'est il pas singulier que nous sachions depuis 3 jours que Napoleon a été deposé à Paris par le Senat, et que tu ne m'en disas pas un mot? Les Gazettes de ce jour confirment cette grande nouvelle.

Elles disent aussi que le Senat a envoyé une deputation à Wellington pour lui demander de faire connoitre le Gouvernement qu'il croit propre à sauver la France, et qu'il sera accepté pourvu toute fois que ce gouvernement n'ait pas à sa tête un Bourbon!!! Conçoit on une pareille demence, plus frappante encore quand on voit à la tête du Gouvernement provisoire d'où part cette absurde proposition. Foucher, Carnot, Caulaincourt Trio bien fait pour se faire respecter! — Trio qu'il faut bien se garder de séparer, et qu'en consequence il faut envoyer à Botany bay, ou à Katshamka —[5] Le Bonaparte de son coté a abdiqué, mais en faveur de son fils. Les Chambres neanmoins ont approuvé cette abdication, mais p[ure] et simple, et le dit B. a été deposé. Ce ne sera une belle histoire que celle de cette pauvre France durant la periode actuelle! Eh bien quelque chose de plus absurde et de plus ridicule encore se prepare, si les intrigans ne renoncent à leurs projets. Ils ont dejà fait, et ils ne cessent de faire beaucoup de mal; Neanmoins ils ne reussiront pas, j'espere, à supplanter notre bon Roi. Tu apprendras,

---

[3] See L. 885 n. 2.

[4] Ivan Ivanovich Dibich-Zabalkansky (1785–1831), also known by his German name, Johannes Karl Friedrich Anton Diebitsch (Plotho, App., p. 56), then a lieutenant-general and baron, later a field-marshal and count in Russian service (*Biografichiski Slovar'*).

[5] Kamchatka, the large peninsula on the east coast of Siberia that was, like the penal colony at Botany Bay, a byword for distant isolation.

Ma bonne amie avec plaisir que Mr de Kamenski,[6] l'aide de camp du M^{al} Barclay de Tolly, m'a fait dire, au moment de quitter Treves avec ses Cosaques,

'que S.M. l'Emp^r de Russie avait fait dire au M^{al} que son intention etait que ses armées ne jouassent pas d'autre marche en France que celle de

"Vive henry quatre!" &c—7 |

Je voudrais mon adorable amie, pouvoir t'aider dans les soins que tu rens aux pauvres blessés que je plains de toute mon ame, et j'approuve ce noble emploi de la plus belle vie que je connoisse: mais ma chere Fanny, je ne puis m'empêcher d'être effrayé par le recit que tu me fais des horribles blessures des malheureuses victimes de nos dissensions. Rien de plus dangereux surtout dans la saison actuelle. Je te supplie, et si cela est necessaire, je t'enjoins de prendre du Vinaigre des 4 valeurs[8] et de t'en laver le visage le sein et les mains avant d'aller vaquer à cette pieuse *business*. — [xxxxx 3 *lines*]

Fais moi tout de suite reponse à *Namur poste restante*. Je compte y être du 7 au 10 de ce mois. Les Bavarois ont passé *Nancy*, les Prussiens et les Anglais etaient il y a 2 ou 3 jours à Compiegne. Ils doivent être à present devant Paris! et Nous resterions à *TREVES*, où nous n'avons été joints que par quelques fuyards de l'armée de B. Pas un seul homme de l'interieur ne s'est presente![9] Je ne connais pas en verité de position plus delicate, plus difficile, et plus ridicule, quoi qu'assurement elle ne soit pas sans dangers. On a grand soin sur cela de me mettre à l'aise, car à peine nous est il arrivé un detachmt — qu'on nous l'enleve. |

6 See L. 898 n. 15.

7 M. d'A's delight at the Czar's order that his army play this Bourbon tune might have faded had he recalled that in 1814, after the fall of Paris and Alexander's triumphal entry, it was repeatedly played and sung in his honour with a different refrain: 'Vive Alexandre! / Vive ce roi des rois!' See Boigne, i. 230 (n. 1, p. 513).

8 'Thieves' Vinegar' or *Acetum Aromaticum* (see v, L. 463 n. 2).

9 M. d'A reported his meagre success in a letter (Vincennes) of 1 July addressed to the duc de Feltre at Ghent. 'La Gendarmerie m'a encore amené deux fuyards de l'armée de Buonaparte; mais il n'ont pas voulu absolument s'engager pour faire partie de l'armée Royale, et le Commandant de la place, sur leur refus formal, les a fait mettre en prisons.'

[1358, Marché au bois],
Brussels, 1 July [1815]

To M. d'Arblay

A.L. (rejected Diary MSS. 6662–[3], Berg), 1 July
Originally a double sheet 4to, of which the second leaf is missing 2 pp.
Edited by FBA, p. 1 (6662), *annotated and dated*: 1815 (17/2) Brussels
Rejected at the Press. *See* Textual Notes.

Saturday, Ce 1ʳ Juillet—

Ah mon ami — qu'êtes vous donc devenu et que n'ai-je de vos
nouvelles? Have you quitted Treves?—could not François — if
you were too hurried, write one line? — I am a prey to the most
terrible uneasiness & so must remain till Monday! for to-
morrow there is no Post. I will send this—since you bid me
continue writing to Treves—but know not how to add any
thing more—

Yet—should you be there, & have no quicker intelligence I
ought to tell you That I read last night the King's Proclamation,[1] drawn up by M. Talyrand, which is perfect!

He will pardon *ALL* but Individuals peculiarly culpable—
of those he will select very *few*, & only the *worst*, to banish or
bring to Justice.

He declares he has *himself* forbidden *All the Princes of his
house* to accompany the Allies into France

And has himself restrained the ardour of all his faithful
adherents, who would have fought for him *avec l'Etranger.*

B[uonaparte]—is said to be trying to escape to Havre, or
some sea port,[2] with all his surviving officers.

If ⌐he be suffered¬,—in 2 years he will again lead us the same
dance of death he has so frightfully taught us at this moment.
The numbers of dead, whether of Conquerors or Conquered,
have not yet been counted!—nor even all the wounded—many

905. [1] Louis XVIII's Proclamtion from Cambrai of 28 June, drafted and counter-
signed by Talleyrand, repudiated his earlier unforgiving manifesto (L. 901 n. 11)
and outraged the *ultras* led by the comte d'Artois in admitting past mistakes. many
of which are obliquely attributed to the 'intentions les plus pures' of Monsieur
(*Supp. Desp.* x. 615–16).
  [2] Accompanied by a small staff, Napoleon left Malmaison for Rochefort at nine
o'clock on the morning of 29 June.

are still on the field of Battle, where they are dressed,—their wounds, I mean!—while waiting for carriages, which are constantly on the road!! ¹

Brussels is a Walking Hospital!³ Maimed & Wounded unhappy men of War are met at every step, either entering, carried in Carts, from the Fields of Battle, or the adjoining Villages, to be placed in Infirmaries, Work houses, Churches, & also at private houses. Every body is ordered to receive all their Dwelling can hold. It is even written on the doors of most houses how many are already refuged in them. The Belgians behave with the utmost humanity to the miserable objects of fallen Ambition,—or contentious strugglers on either side. Almost all the Natives prepare to run from the City, in apprehension of some Contagious fever, from the multitude of Sick!—

O Write! My best beloved! my noble husband! Write—or make Francois write—

At so fearful a time not to have certainty of your health & your position is Agony! nothing less,—mon trop cher ami!

906   Trèves, 2 July 1815

M. d'Arblay
To Madame d'Arblay

A.L. (Berg), 2 juillet 1815
Double sheet 4to   4 pp.   *pmk* NAMUR seal
Addressed: A Madame / Madame de Burney / poste restante / à Bruxelles.
Readdressed: Marche au Bois / *N 1358*
Edited by FBA, p. 1, *annotated*: ⁑ ⌜27⌝ (18/1) [*with numbers on address fold*]: 18   27

Treves
ce 2. Juillet 1815.

Je recois ma bonne amie ta seconde lettre c.a.d. la 13ᵐᵉ le même jour que la 12ᵉᵐᵉ et je m'empresse de te repondre par une

---

³ The extraordinary measures taken by the mayor and citizens of Brussels to care impartially for all the wounded are outlined in the official *Gazette générale des Pays-Bas* for 27 June and in Galesloot, ii. 119–23.

occasion qui se presente.[1] J'espere que cette lettre te parviendra assez à tems pour t'empêcher de m'ecrire à Namur comme je te l'ai ecrit, comptant être dans cette Ville sous 8 à 10 jours. J'avais effectivement l'intention de quitter Treves demain 2 Juillet que j'eusse ou non l'autorisation du Ministre, que j'en ai prevenu en lui mandant que je me conformais en cela à l'article de mes instructions ainsi conçu.

'Vous suivrez les mouvemens des Troupes alliées, observant d'être aussi près que possible de la ligne d'operation, et meme en avant s'il est possible.'

Les nouvelles que j'ai reçues depuis et par les quelles je vois que le Roi est actuellement en France et probablement même près de Paris changent absolument cette determination; et me voilà de nouveau et bien malgré moi confiné ici jusqu'à ce qu'il plaise au Ministre de m'en tirer. En effet —— — On est venu m'interrompre et je ne sais à present ce que je voulais dire. mais voici ce que je dis.

J'ai tenté vainement de marcher à la suite de l'armée anglaise de l'armée Prussienne et de l'armée Russe. J'ai même eu un moment ¦ de reussir près des Russes que je croyais dans l'ignorance de l'espece de convention d'après la quelle les Alliés n'ont pas permis que nous courussions le moindre risque. Après avoir ainsi employé inutilement le verd et le sec,[2] ainsi que j'en ai la preuve par-devers moi, puisque j'ai des lettres des G^aux Blücher Kleist et Barclay de Tolly,[3] il ne me restait plus que de rejoindre la petite armée de Louis XVIII. Point du tout, j'apprens par les journaux qu'au moment où j'ecris ce Monarque doit être aux portes de Sa Capitale, dans la quelle il aura surement fait son entrée, longtems avant que je pusse le rejoindre et le suivre pour être le plus près de la ligne d'operation deviendrait des lors une chose tout à fait ridicule. Il ne l'est guere moins de rester ici pour y voir arriver deux ou trois personnes.

Aujourdhui neanmoins j'ai eté de quelqu'utilité, en empechant de pauvres diables de fuyards de l'armée de Bonnaparte d'être envoyés au delà du Rhin.[4] Je les ai reclamés après avoir

906.   [1] L. 899 was the 12th letter written by FBA to M. d'A since his departure from Brussels, and L. 901, the 13th.
   [2] 'Employer le vert et le sec'—a proverbial phrase meaning 'to use all one's resources'.   [3] See L. 885 n. 2.
   [4] As deserters from Napoleon's army they would be sent off to prison fortresses

274

grondé le Commandant à qui j'ai fait lire l'article de la lettre du
General Kleith portant: qu'il a eu les ordres les plus stricts de
se conformer à ma volonté pour tout ce qui concerne ma
mission. J'ai donc eu gain de cause; et les hommes m'ont été
rendus: mais deux ou trois soldats par ci par là qui ne font
pas une bien bonne acquisition pour l'armée royale peuvent
ils motiver mon sejour [|] prolongé en ce pays. Me voilà
pourtant condamné à y rester jusqu'à ce que je recoive des
ordres ou du moins jusqu'à ce que je sache si les off^{ers} qui ont eu
la même mission que moi, ont changé de destination. Si tu en
sais quelque chose ne manque pas de me le mander. M^r de
Castries[5] par exemple est il retourné à Namur, ou a t'il suivi
le Roi. Mr de la Poiterie[6] a bien été rappellé mais a t'il été
remplacé? — Cela est bien ennuyeux. Je charge le garde du
Corps qui mettra cette lettre à la poste de Namur[7] de m'ecrire ce
qu'il aura appris dans cette ville sur ce sujet. Je me reglerai sur
ce qu'il me dira, si toute fois je ne recois pas quelqu'ordre
d'ici là.

Sans doute il faut bien que nous ayons recours à l'argent qui
est chez le Banquier. moi mëme je serai forcé d'y prendre
environ 400^f si je ne suis pas payé de ce mois cy. au demeurant
nous pouvons le faire [sans] scrupule, la perte que nous eprou-
vons et que j'aurais voulu prevenir en etant plus que compensée
par ce que j'ai eu le bonheur de recevoir. Au total, nous
sommes de toute l'emigration le couple qui aura le moins
souffert. N'achete point de malle. Tu n'en auras pas besoin,
car j'espere bien que nous retournerons ensemble à Paris. Quelle
inconcevable versatilité que celle des Français: j'en suis en
verité honteux. Dieu et toi vous savez si j'ai desiré le renverse-
ment de l'usurpateur. Neanmoins la maniere dont la chute est
arrivée fait trembler pour l'avenir. Je benis [|] à present le Ciel
et la Goutte qu'il a envoyée à notre Bon Roi que je plaignais de
ne pouvoir monter à cheval pour se mettre à la tête de ses
troupes. Jamais je crois B. ne s'est montré plus General que

in Germany, but as 'fidèles' they could remain at Trèves under M. d'A's protection.
⁵ See L. 888 n. 24.
⁶ The comte de la Potherie (L. 896 n. 2), recently replaced at Mons.
⁷ M. d'A apparently gave this letter to one of three gardes du corps who passed
through Trèves together and left on 3 July (A.L.S., Vincennes, M. d'A to duc de
Feltre, 1–3 July).

dans cette courte campagne. Sa manoeuvre audacieuse etait excellente. Elle a été bien combinée et parfaitement executée.⁸ Et parcequ'il perd une bataille dont le gain a tenu a bien peu de chose, il est renversé de son thrône par ceux mêmes qui l'y avaient placé en triomphe 8 jours auparavant!!!

Ecris moi toujours ici; je t'embrasse comme je t'aime ainsi qu'Alex, à qui je te prie de l'ecrire. Dis moi donc quelquechose de sa lettre.

Il n'est que trop vrai qu'un de nos amis est actuellement compromis d'une maniere bien fâcheuse et bien penible pour ceux qui lui sont attachés.⁹ Cela au reste ne peut influer sur mes actions, pas plus que sur mon opinion, qui a toujours été et sera toujours qu'il n'y a de salut pour la France que dans la fidelité au Roi que le Ciel semble avoir conservé tout exprès pour les circonstances actuelles. Il est facheux pʳ Mʳ le Duc d'orleans d'avoir été nommé d'une maniere si etrange par B. et son parti, qui lui attache les crimes de son Pere. Sois tranquille, ma bonne amie, le Roi triomphera. Tu dois, dans de pareilles circonstances avoir été enchantée de ce que je t'ai mandé à ce sujet de l'Empʳ Alexandre *près* du quel la deputation Carnot est allée.⁹ Je ne ⟨conçois⟩ pas qu'on l'ait laissé passer — — des passeports à [*blot*]; c'est en quelque sorte les reconnoitre.

907   [1358, Marché au bois],
                       Brussels, 1–3 July 1815

To Esther (Burney) Burney

A.L. (rejected Diary MSS. 6664–7, Berg), 1–3 July 1815
Double sheet large 4to   4 pp.   *pmks* BRUXELLES   13 JY 1815
Addressed: *Angleterre* / à Madame / Madame Burney, / Turnham Green, / near / London.

⁸ Napoleon's concentration of five army corps on the Belgian frontier, followed by his rapid advance of 15 June, which divided the allied from the Prussian forces and forced both to retreat.

⁹ Although Carnot (L. 856 n. 15) had been named to the 'commission exécutive' of France's provisional government, the deputation to the allied sovereigns, chief of whom was the Czar, was led by Lafayette (L. 901 n. 9). M. d'A in his incomplete last sentence doubts that the deputation, which he describes as a scouting expedition, should even be given the passports needed to get to Haguenau, where negotiations had in fact begun on 1 July.

Endorsed by EBB: July 13. 1815
Edited by FBA, ?CFBt *and the* Press. *See* Textual Notes.

Brussels, 1ˢᵗ July, 1815

I have long meant to write to my ever dear Esther,—& destined hers to be my next Letter—but continual vicissitudes, changes of prospects, of expectations,—of health & of spirits, have kept my pen off till this moment. All now SEEMS fair—& promises fairer—& *voilà* the instant to seize for writing to so dear a sister, who has had from me for so long a time Letters so sad or so alarming that they must have made her heart ache even more than silence. I have just been assured That the King of France will enter Paris this day, or to-morrow.[1]

This joyful news, by which alone the Peace of the World, & tranquility to mankind can again be sealed, revives me into new existence. The Duke of Wellington, who, of course, precedes & guides him;[2]—The Duke of Wellington who, in fact, is at this moment King of France!—For in His hands is all military power—& what other power has wretched France long known?—Buonaparte is said to have again run away—to which I should have no objection if sure he would never run back again. But I fear he has a vehement disposition to shewing himself a living illustration of the famous 4 lines of Butler

> He that is in Battle slain
> Can never rise to fight again;
> But——He who fights—& runs away
> May live to fight another day!— —[3]

His family also,—i.e. his favourite officers, for what other family does he cherish?—report has sent off with him. If this be so, those who ought to have watched his motions saw less well into his character than a certain small fugitive *Emigrée* in

---

907. [1] Louis XVIII did not enter Paris until the following Saturday, 8 July. On the 1st the King was at Roye, where he heard of the capitulation of Paris (Reiset, iii. 227, 236).

[2] A contemporary and hostile witness describes Louis XVIII as 'waddling down into France' by the route to Paris taken by Wellington and his army (Teignmouth, i. 83–7).

[3] Apparently FBA's garbled recollection of two lines from *Hudibras*:
> For those that fly, may fight again,
> Which he can never do that's slain
> (Part iii, canto 3, 243–4).

Brabant;[4] who no sooner heard that he had lost the Battle, than she cried 'If so, be sure he'll disguise himself, get aboard the first skiff he can find, at the first Port he can reach, & bribe himself off to America.'[1]

Nevertheless, I need not tell you that the best of news gives Hope, only, & Joy, not peace, not happiness, while M. d'A. is absent upon military service, & while I know not whether the allies with whom he resides, i.e. the Prussians, will accede to the noble plan of Lord Wellington, & of the Emperor of Russia, to re-place Louis 18, as before, without vengeance or pillage.[5] He is still at *Treves*, where Alexander will have told you he has been established upon the honourable, though difficult & dangerous Mission, of examining Deserters from Buonaparte. He is sometimes, he says, engaged till midnight in making interrogatories, with suspicious personages, assisted by 3 officers, an adjoint, an aid de Camp. & a volunteer of the Maison du Roi, who are constantly with him, & under his orders. The horrour he would have to suffer a *mauvais sujet* to *glisser* through his hands, you can easily conceive. But the quantity that contrive, under various disguises, to elude the vigilance of B's custom-house officers, & Gens d'armes, & Barriers, is truly wonderful. There is, unfortunately, no direct communication with Treves from Brussels, so that I can never have an answer to any thing I write in less than a fortnight. He assures me his health is at present good, except when any change of weather makes him feel that cruel blow upon his chest. I need not, certainly, mention that he is upon full pay,—nevertheless, with the Horses, domestics, Table, & military equipment requisite for a General in activity of service, the pay is always, in France, inadequate to the expences.[6] For the ci *devant Officiers superieurs* were commonly chosen from among those rich enough to dedicate their private fortune to the service, not, as CHEZ NOUS, to *make* a fortune for private uses & enjoyment. At this moment, also, he has been obliged to advance for his Companions, who,

---

[4] FBA herself, who made this shrewd prediction soon after Waterloo (L. 894, p. 223).

[5] Although less permissive about looting and revenge than Blücher, the Czar was by no means so lenient toward the French as Wellington (*Supp. Desp.* x. 592).

[6] From the sum of 5,000 francs received by M. d'A for his mission to Trèves (Rochechouart, p. 419), he was obliged to advance 741 francs to Mazancourt and 559 to Prémorel (A.L.S., Vincennes, M. d'A to the duc de Feltre, 20 August).

all ruined Gentlemen, had not means to purchase Horses for beginning the Campaign. It is to be hoped all this will now be handsomely settled.

Had not all accounts from England, & your own *surtout*, assured me of the re-establishment of the health of dear good Mr. Burney,[7] I should have opened ¹ my Letter with enquiries upon which I am so truly interested. But to hear that he is able even to resume business is a satisfaction I own I never expected, & I felicitate *you*, his constant & most affectionate Nurse, upon the success of your tender cares, *almost* as heartily as the excellent Patient—Patient in every sense of the word, himself upon his recovery.

Pray when you write to dear Maria,[8] beg her to accept through you my thanks for her very kind Letter, till I can write myself. I have written my congratulations to my dear Mrs. Lock,[9] who tells me she has passed a most comfortable & even delightful hour or two with you *one* Wednesday, & hoped to repeat the same pleasure on *another*.

You may imagine how disturbed I have been about *my* & *our*, Manuscripts![10]—I have no news of them, yet; but several of our friends have given me [to] understand, by various adroit methods, that care has been taken of *all* that is most essential that we left behind. All the Mss I possess—all the works, begun, *middled*, or done, large or small, that my pen ever scribbled, since the grand Firework of destruction on my 15ᵗʰ Birthday,[11] are now There!—unless seized by the Police. And with them all our joint Mss of my dearest Father—his Letters—his Memoirs—his memorandums!—And all my beloved Susan's Journals, & my own that she returned me, with every Letter I have thought worth keeping, or not had leisure for burning, from my very infancy to the day of my flight! The variety of uneasy sensations this causes you can readily picture to yourself; though the most serious is involving in my loss my dearest Esther's share of the

---

⁷ Charles Rousseau Burney (i, p. lxix) had become ill in 1814 (vii *passim*). The recovery welcomed here was brief and his sufferings continued until his death in 1819.

⁸ EBB's daughter Maria Bourdois (L. 838 n. 25).

⁹ On the marriage of her daughter Augusta (L. 900 p. 252).

¹⁰ CB's correspondence, which at this time FBA meant to publish (see xii *passim*). The proceeds would accrue to FBA and EBB, shared equally as residuary legatees of CB's estate.

¹¹ The fire in which FB burned all her juvenile writings (see *HFB*, p. 1 and *DL*, i. 128).

result of the meditated publication relative to our revered Father. Here, at Bruxelles, in the solitude in which I generally pass my time—without my family—my *maternal* occupations, or my *conjugal*.—& without my house-keeping, my work, or a single Book—how usefully & desirably I might have dedicated my time to the examination & arrangement of those papers! But when I left Paris, in the carriage of a Friend, & only upon a few hours warning, I could merely bring a change of linnen, in a napkin, to be packed up by her maid in her own *vache*. There was not even a Trunk, nor even a Band Box of mine. We set out at ⌐ 10 o'clock at night, Sunday the 19ᵗʰ of March, & my mind was in the unhappy state of believing M. d'A[rblay] had left me, that very day at 2 o'clock, to go forward with his Company to combat the approaching usurper. *He* thought it, too; — — but the troops of the line were traitors, & the King only used his own household troops to cover his own retreat. I shall soon, however, now, *probably*, know the real situation of my affairs, & whether my *good & chattels* have escaped the police, or been sacrificed.

July 3ᵈ I had hoped to finish this Letter with *positive* good news: but alas to day the accounts that have reached me, & from some English officers whom I have met at a Belgic Lady's house, are truly uncomfortable. They say there must still be another Battle, & upon Montmarte, close upon Paris![12]—The King of les pays bas being now established at La Haye, & the British ambassadour having also quitted Bruxelles, no official accounts come hither first; so that, except for private intelligence, we receive real news *later*, perhaps, than *you* do!—while the D. of Wellington—England's deserved Pride & Honour!—was here, all news visited *us* first. I have just had a Letter from M. d'A.[13] who, the 27ᵗʰ June was still at *Treves*. Pray let Alex know this— or, rather, tell him to *write & ask*: for alas—I cannot wonder at his inaccuracy with *others*! He is really terrible de ce côté là. How grieved I am at your intimation of 'The *rich* person of the Family!'[14] And how is it *POSSIBLE* Mr. White can thus delay our

---

[12] Although the political climate within Paris was increasingly defeatist, the city was still defended by an army of 117,000 men, 600 cannon, and a thick belt of trenches and redoubts, one strong point of which was the heights of Montmartre (Houssaye, *1815*, iii. 280–1 and *Supp. Desp.* x. 650–1).

[13] L. 902.

[14] CB Jr., who, as his sisters thought, delayed in settling CB's estate. For the sale of books by the auctioneer John White of 3 Prince's Gate, see L. 838 n. 13.

accounts?[14] I hope the Irish business is finished;[15] but I have no news; ⌐& Martin will not see Mr. Murray[16] for us.¬ God grant us to come over, & settle our own affairs, without agents or Lawyers! I earnestly hope Alex is at Richmond, in a little nest of his own, as I have desired. He can never prepare for a bright return to Cambridge but from a place where he can pursue his studies *uninterupted*. I would by no means have him resist *society* or *pleasure* occasionally: but his career in life will by no means be what it ought, if his studies take not the principal portion of his time. I have said this to our Brother James, whose kind hospitality, though I am truly obliged for it, is, I fear, too alluring. *Inexpressible*—but not *unimaginable* to my ever dearest Esther is my solicitude about that dear excentric youth—whenever *his Father* gives me any rest — — *He* starts uppermost to rob me of it.

adieu—& God bless you. Loves around— |

How is it possible you have not your precious posthumous Letter?[17]—Was it not in the parcel I brought you myself? I certainly *think* it was—& *most* undoubtedly *meant* it should be. No, dear Etty, no! I never took you for a stock or a stone! I would not lose you that Letter for worlds! |

I had already answered y[r] Letter by Mr. Tailor[18] before it arrived—What think you of Mr. Lewes's business?[19] |

I am extremely glad for Richard,[20] pray tell him so. And my

[15] The foreclosure of the mortgage held by CB on the property of his son-in-law Molesworth Phillips (i, p. lxx) in county Louth. See L. 683 n. 8.

[16] The solicitor (L. 886 n. 10) in charge of the forced sale of Camilla Cottage.

[17] A letter to EBB, presumably found in CB's papers.

[18] William Taylor (L. 878 n. 7) of Wellington's medical staff, who was apparently returning to England with the wounded.

[19] The frequently mentioned default on a mortgage held by CB, on the part of 'Monk' Lewis (L. 865 n. 2).

[20] In this year EBB's son, the Revd. Richard Allen Burney (1773–1836), who in 1802 had been presented to the living at Rimpton, Somersetshire, by the Rt. Revd. Brownlow North (1741–1820), Bishop of Winchester (see v, L. 462 n. 8), had been favoured once again by the North family. The Bishop's son-in-law, the Revd. William Garnier (*c.* 1772–1835), prebendary at Winchester (1800) and somewhat of a pluralist, having come into the living at Brightwell, Berks., in 1815, gave over the duties to Richard as 'stipendiary curate', along with the use of the commodious rectory, at least temporarily.

Richard, whose emolument as Rector of Rimpton was £350, then procured a curate for the duties there and moved to the Rectory at Brightwell, a beneficial arrangement that was to last for sixteen years. The story emerges in 'The Worcester Journal' for the years 1815, 1831, and is confirmed in the Diocesan Records (14 Apr. 1815) and the Parish Records (1815–31).

peculiar Love to my God Child, Cecilia.²¹ I have given my kind Charlotte commission to draw for the money, when due, for good Letty²²—to whom pray remember me— ǀ

908   [1358, Marché au bois],
                                    Brussels, 3–[10] July [1815]

To Mrs. Waddington

A.L.S. (Diary MSS. vii. 6668–[71], Berg), 3 July
Double sheet large 4to (9·2 × 7·9″) 4 pp. foliated 223   224 *pmks*
[GOSP]ORT/24 JY   25 JY 181[5]   25 JY 1815   wafer
Addressed: ANGLETERRE, / À Madame / at Madame Waddingtons, / Lanover, / Near Abergavenny, / Monmouthshire
Edited by FBA, CFBt *and the* Press. *See* Textual Notes.

July 3ᵈ
Bruxelles.—

How is it that my ever dear Mary can thus on one side be fascinated by the very thing that, on the other, revolts her? how be a professed & ardent detester of Tyranny; yet an open & intrepid admirer of a Tyrant?¹ O had you spent, like me, 10 years within the control of his unlimited power, & under the iron rod of its dread, how would you change your language! by a total reverse of sentiment! yet was I, because always inn-offensive, never molested: as safe There, *another* would say, as in London; but *you* will not say so; the safety of deliberate prudence, or of retiring timidity, is not such as would satisfy a mind glowing for freedom like your's: it satisfies, indeed, NO *mind*, it merely suffices for *bodily* security. It was the choice of

²¹ EBB's daughter Cecilia Charlotte Esther (i, p. lxix), now aged 27.
²² CB's niece Letitia Brookes (iii, L. 150 n. 6), who had nursed his aged sisters and to whom he bequeathed in his will (see Scholes, ii. 263) the rent of his house in York Street. See also vi, L. 594 n. 3.

908. ¹ Questions apparently provoked by GMAPW's admiration of Napoleon, as expressed presumably in a letter now lost, to which this is the reply. Free now to speak, FBA tells what it had meant to live under a military dictatorship. Cf. her public statements made in wartime, e.g. in the Preface or Dedication of *The Wanderer* (i, pp. xiv–xv).

my Companion, not of my Taste that drew ME to such a residence. PERSONALLY, for the reason I have assigned, I was always well treated, & personally I was happy: but you know me, I am sure, better than to suppose me such an Egotist as to be really happy, or contented, where Corporal Liberty could only be preserved by Mental forbearance — — i.e. subjection.

The panic impressed upon all the Inhabitants, whether natives or visitors, by the late Invasion, & its consequences, would have cured any one not absolutely incurable of a revolutionary taste; & my dear Mary has too fair & too liberal propensities ever wilfully to blind herself against visible facts, or to deafen herself against powerful, yet candid conviction. The Belgians have for so many Centuries been accustomed to sanguinary conflicts, & violent, or mercenary, change of masters, that I really thought, from the placid state in which, when seeking here an asylum, I found them, that they were utterly indifferent to the result of the neighbouring struggle, & would just as willingly have fallen again into the hands of Buonaparte as not. They never, of their own accord, opened upon the ¹ subject, nor considered nor treated us poor fugitives but as common Visitors. I imagined they had gone through too many political changes, to deem one, or two, more or less, an addition worth ruffling their serenity. And Buonaparte, whether from hearing of this passive philosophy, or whether from motives yet unknown, certainly expected not alone that they would not oppose, but that, on the contrary, they would join him. This idea, with respect to the Belgian troops, was, indeed, spread, & most alarmingly, here. The Duke of Wellington was warned by several persons not to trust them: & it is generally understood That he determined They should neither be trusted in front, lest they should join the Enemy, nor in the Rear, lest they should run away from their friends. Nevertheless, when the day of the most bloody battle that ever Rival Warriors fought, arrived, I found I had taken the calm of their Natures for mere indifference to their fate; [for when] a cry was shouted through the streets That The French were come! That *Buonaparte et les Français étoient à la porte de la Ville!*—the consternation that ensued, the horrour that was depicted on every Countenance, shewed they were alive at least to the evils that menaced themselves—and how few, how very few are really awake to any other!² We do not appear to be asleep, because our Eyes are wide open; but dormant lies every feeling that belongs to whatever is not animated, in some or other shape, by SELF, except in the very, VERY few whom Nature has gifted—or condemned—'to feel for OTHER's woes'.³ —— ——

[10 July 1815] It is now within 3 days of 2 months since I last saw M.d'A: he has been sent upon a mission, of the King's, first to Liege, next to Luxembourg, & then to Treves, where he has passed 6 weeks: he has now left it, but ¹ I know not, yet, for what other destination. You will not believe me very tranquil in the ignorance; but I am tranquil in nothing during this wandering, houseless, homeless, Emigrant life. This is no siecle for those who love their home, or who have a home to love. 'Tis a siecle for the Adventurous, to whom Ambition always opens resources; or for the New, who guess not at the Catastrophes that hang on the rear, while the phantom Expectation allures them to the front.—

The 2ᵈ restoration seems now fast advancing. I have just had a Letter from the quarter General of the King from *Roye*, written by a friend in the King's *suite*,⁴ who says His M[ajesty] has been received there with enthusiasm.—I, you well know, must hear that with pleasure, for my only consolation during the[se] tremendous conflicts, & prospects eternally va[ryin]g, in which of late I have lived, has been that the principles & feelings of M. d'A: have coincided with his duty. You were quite right not to have had a doubt as to the line he would pursue; belonging to the *Maison du Roi*, & having ALWAYS refused to serve Buonaparte, he must not only have been perfidious,⁵ but indefinable to have hesitated. I am extremely glad, therefore, you would take no measure for MY affairs

---

² Most of the Belgian and Dutch troops fought bravely at both Quatre Bras and Waterloo, and those regiments that collapsed were more victims of the Prince of Orange's tactical stupidity than cowards or traitors. For a somewhat overstated defence of their role, see F. de Bas and T'Serclaes de Wommersom, especially i, pp. vii–x.

³ FBA here adapts the line 'Teach me to feel another's Woe' from Pope's 'Universal Prayer'.

⁴ De Fresne (alias de Boinville, L. 876 n. 16), who had set off for Paris with his patron Tabarié (L. 868 n. 5) and the rest of the duc de Feltre's staff.

⁵ This pejorative use with reference to a person—meaning 'shifty' or 'unprincipled'—is rare, but the one example given in *OED* is from a contemporary translation of a French text.

but with My concurrence, for whoever, at that period, remained in Paris, & in power, must both think & act so very differently from M. d'A: that he would have been offended to have owed to them even a solid benefit. He is *très* what those on the other side the question call *exalté*[6]—& oh what painful scenes must we go through if we get back to our deserted home! You will wonder to hear me say *IF*; prosperous as all now seems; but the changes which this Country has now for so long a time gone through, have been so astonishing, ǀ so sudden, so unexpected, That they take at least away all presumption, if not all confidence in public transactions. The various parts, from various circumstances as well as propensities, taken upon the late Eruption of Mount Corsica,[7] will have severed asunder half the families amongst my best friends! In particular she who is most dear to me[8]—a very sister in tender affection, useful friendship, & endearing sympathy, will stand between two Brothers,[8] each equally loved by her, who have decidedly & actively taken two opposite sides!⸺⌐With regard to a very very delicate subject, my dearest Mary, upon it now I have nothing to fear of rashness: I flatter myself, therefore, she will well weigh—& then, I am persuaded, make a decision which seems circumspect—all with her fond devotion to those who so entirely love you.⌐ You make me much wish to see Waverley[9]—Alex, also, writes to me of it with rapture. Sismondi's 'Literature' also I should like to see.[10] But I am out of the way of Books & Book people. I subscribe, nevertheless, to a Library,[11] but it has almost no foreign works. How vexing that Alexander should have so endless a vacation just when he cannot pass it with us. Your angelic Emily I still must hope

[6] Fervently royalist, but with overtones of delirium: 'Celui . . . qui est dans une sorte de transport' (*Littré*).

[7] Napoleon's usurpation.

[8] Mme de Maisonneuve (L. 839 n. 4 and vi *passim*), sister of César de Latour-Maubourg (L. 845 n. 28), who had been named as one of Napoleon's pairs des Cent-Jours (L. 890 n. 16), and Victor, who remained staunchly royalist (L. 860 n. 6).

[9] Scott's successful first novel was published anonymously in 1814. FBA was later to read most of Scott's novels (xi, xii *passim*).

[10] Jean-Charles-Léonard Simonde de Sismondi (1773–1842), Swiss economist and cultural historian, published his *De La Littérature du midi* in 1813. Although Sismondi earlier advanced the claims of Mediterranean culture, just as his friend Mme de Staël advanced those of Germany, as a model and reproach to an age sunk in Napoleonic militarism, he took the Emperor's side during the Hundred Days, of which he left an excellent record in his *Lettres inédites . . . écrites pendant les Cent-Jours*, ed. P. Villari and G. Monod (1877).

[11] The 'Cabinet Littéraire' in the Marché au bois (L. 890 n. 6).

will *weather the storm.*[12] Embrace her for me with tenderness; but
I am alarmed for my bright Augusta! What has she to do with
headaches? does she apply too much? My wise, prudent, yet so
kind hearted & feeling Name sake alone seems fashioned to
sustain the siege of application in her elaborate studies. M. d'A
is quite chagrined to miss the Drawing & Letter so obligingly
designed for him.[12] You may imagine how impatiently I
desire—yet tremble to know the actual state of my affairs in
Paris, & the state of my MSS. I have had no sort of information. Whenever the King gets to Paris, the post will, of course,
be again open. Should you go to town, you will see, I hope,
my excellent sister Broome, & my very dear Fanny Raper,
and, probably, my excentric Alex, for he goes not to Cambridge
till the end of October. I dare not ask if you have had any more
recent account of him—Yet nothing would more usefully serve
& oblige me than to know.

Adieu, dearest Mary—for
Life yours truly,
FB d'A.

909   [1358, Marché au bois],
Brussels, 3 July 1815

To Mrs. Broome

A.L. (Berg), 3 July 1815
Double sheet 4to 4 pp. *pmks* 25 JY 1815 25 JY 1815 wafer
Addressed: *Angleterre* / Mrs. Broome, / Richmond, / Surry. / If absent, to
be / opened by Mrs. Barret.
Endorsed by CBFB: Sister d'arblay / July. 1815

Brussells, July 3ᵈ
1815

For the Universe would I not add to the harrass of my dear
& ever kindest Charlotte,[1] who shews her true affection to me

[12] For Mrs. Waddington's three surviving daughters, see vii, L. 636 n. 1. The
ailing Emelie was now 21 years of age, Augusta, the youngest, only 13. The eldest,
Frances (1791–1876), later Baroness Bunsen, was the designer of the 'Drawing &
Letter' mentioned here.
909. [1] Apologetic and roundabout allusions to the requests (ventured by FBA in

286

full as much in what she declines as in what she fulfils of my desires or commissions; for if any false & mis-understood scruples should make her undertake, for MY sake any business that would perplex or fatigue her gentle spirits, or shake her shattered nerves, I should no sooner hear or discover it than I should be quite unhappy, & NEVER AFTER could venture to make her even the smallest request, lest it should lead to some mischief,—which her more TRULY kind frankness will always, I trust, avoid.[1]

Report at this moment assures me that Louis 18 is proceeding to Paris, amidst the acclamations of the people of every town through which he passes. It must be owned those acclamations are so changeable there is no honouring them with any full or firm confidence: nevertheless, they *may* be sincere; & I have had so much of alarm & discomfort, that I am as eager to quit 'the despair party' as poor Merlin could be,[2] & to hope we may once again taste a little repose.

I quite approve your idea that my Alex should board where he sleeps—& am most uneasily impatient to hear the plan is executed. I was quite *consternated* to receive another Letter from him dated James Street![3] And what you now say—& my Brother himself sees & says, torments me inexpressibly. I will certainly mention it only to Charlottina[4] & you—& least of all to dear James, unless he hinted at the matter. Alex for YEARS will neither in experience nor fortune be in a situation to become a *Family Man*: & engagements incautiously contracted when they *cannot* be fulfilled, or *ought not*, commonly make both parties, & all that belong to them, unhappy. Pray write to me— or beg my second Charlotte to write, all that you BOTH think upon this subject.[3] If *I* thought any serious mischief menacing, I would arrange instantly some new plan, to remove him to a distance. And without hinting *why* but to your two selves. I have been thinking of *Bath*: Maria and Sophy would be most

L. 870, for instance) that CBFB attempt to aid and guide AA in his parents' absence.

[2] An early acquaintance of the Burneys, Joseph Merlin (i, L. 3 n. 117; *DL*, i. 504–5), some of whose colourful phrases seemed to make part of the Burney vocabulary. For 'a curious Merlin Table' and other inventions once in the possession of Dr. Burney, see the will of the latter (Scholes, ii. 268, 271).

[3] From JB's house in Buckingham Gate. FBA is here worrying over AA's admiration of his cousin 'Sally' (L. 896 n. 8).

[4] AA's cousin Charlotte Barrett (i, p. lxxii), later distinguished from her mother Charlotte Broome as FBA's 'second Charlotte'.

kind companions,[5] for his leisure, & social enjoyment, & yet comply with my desires of contributing to *flap* him upon his studies, hours, health, dress, &c—How I wish I had time to write to my second Charlotte by this oppor[tu]nity, that I might with a better grace beg a full & true account of all she can glean of *danger*, or *idea*, or *fact*, upon this too, too interesting topic; for I have much reluctance to drawing in my *first* dear Charlotte to so troublesome a commission. But I have so many Letters *DUE*, & when I have not yet written even once,— that I have no chance upon *this* occasion to write two to Richmond.

To save yourself unnecessary trouble, my kind Love, pray put 5 G[s] at a time into a Box, or purse, from *Mathias*,[6] apart for Alex—for his Letters, pocket money, or washing, or any expenses whatever; & never mind writing them. It will be a fatigue the less to *you*—& to me equal satisfaction.

I supplicate you to remind him of his little debts—of gifts to servants,—&c. My other Charlotte has promised to keep me in intelligence as to his *health*, & his *diligence*.

How infinitely kind is the Congress for my Boy at Richmond & Twickenham! The Archdeacon's goodness is amongst my first comforts. Mrs. Cambridge's & Mrs. Baker's I am thankful for truly.[7] |

I need not tell *YOU* how little we can bear *extravagance*, but I beg again & again you will let Alex want nothing that can make him comfortable, & keep his attire in good repair. Remember—though only *entre-nous, you* can draw for him at any time. I fear his being negligent as well as inexperienced in money matters. A Letter has just reached me of *June 1⟨5⟩[th]* from my dear Fanny Raper,[8] which tells me Alex is at length at Richmond. What a relief!—He has 2 long Letters of mine

---

[5] AA's cousins Maria Bourdois (L. 838 n. 25) and her sister Sophia Elizabeth Burney (i, p. lxix).

[6] CBFB's old friend Thomas James Mathias (iii, L. 157 n. 6), the Queen's Treasurer, who issued FBA's pension, quarterly instalments of which CBFB at this time collected. The Mathias family lived in Scotland Yard.

[7] Archdeacon George Owen Cambridge (L. 840 n. 6), who was acting in place of CB Jr. at this time as AA's guardian. His wife Cornelia and a mutual friend Sarah Baker (L. 843 nn. 5, 6) FBA would have had in mind from her last months in England when she stayed with CBFB at Hill Street, Richmond, within a short walking distance across Richmond Bridge to Twickenham Meadows, the home of the Cambridges (vii, L. 805 n. 8).

[8] FBA's niece Fanny Raper (i, p. lxxi). Her letter has not survived, nor has AA's letter that arrived with it.

unanswered, though there is one of *June 2^d* in the packet with Fanny's. Beseech him to write a long letter quickly. *Not* together, my dearest Charlotte, for *your* Letter will not be what I require if it comes not from yourself alone: or rather—my other Charlotte—for I have a secret hope she will generously answer this, & trust to my gratitude when I am less encumbered with claimants. — —

M. d'A. is still at Treves:—& not any reply can I ever, on any occasion, obtain in less than a fortnight from him, as there is no direct communication from Brussels thither. This fatigues us both. I am in hopes we now shall soon, however, meet, as the King, Louis 18—can certainly no longer require any officer to be placed on the Frontiers to receive Deserters. I do not enter into public news, because, since Lord Wellington is in Paris, I doubt not but you have information sooner in London than we have at Brussels, where we are served, *officially*, only after the Hague, all the D[uke] of W[ellington]'s dispatches going, of course, to the King des pays bas first. The Hereditary Prince is still here, because too weak to join the army.[9] His wound has injured his appearance very much, for he has bled & suffered till he is so thin he can hardly walk. Oh what an execrable scourge to mankind is War!—Yet if Buonaparte escapes—we may expect it again in a very few years. ⸗

Whither I shall move—or *when*, I know not. No Letters yet come from Paris—& I have not any intelligence of the state of my affairs in our Apartments. A decree was passed by B[uonaparte] to confiscate all the property of every officer of la Maison du Roi who did not enter into B.'s service—Judge if I am not impatient to hear whether any of his Brigands visited our small habitation! I have sent this very day, by a private hand, a Letter of quiet enquiry. A lady amongst our friends, who had emigrated here, & even to England, has the courage to go straight to Paris immediately. But she is with a suite of friends, who have 3 carriages, & out-riders.[10] The roads are said to be dreadfully infested with robbers & pillagers of all sorts.

There must be a *new* £22:10. due at Mr Mathias'[6] this month.

[9] The Prince failed to recover fully, as he reported to Wellington (*Supp. Desp.* xi. 306), until December of 1815.
[10] Probably Mme de Jaucourt (L. 910 n. 11), formerly Mme de la Châtre (ii, pp. xv–xvi).

I think he promised to pay to your signature? if not, he must
be so good as to give you the receipt to forward to me. It may
come, anyway, while unsigned. I can only *return* it by some friend,
or opportunity. But I hope, & think, he will take *your* signature,
when you go to town, & can call in Scotland Yard.

Fanny R[aper] tells me Mrs. Waddington is in town—I
wrote to her[11]—a long letter—at Lanover a week ago—or
less; just before Fanny's Letter arrived. I have written also to
Esther—to whom—& to James—Charles—Sarah—& all the
nieces & nephews. My kind love as you see them—& surtout
to my excellent cousin Edward.[12] And pray thank cordially
dear Marianne[13] for her Letter.

Adieu my ever dearest Charlotte God bless you ever! — —
My very kind remembrance to mon cher ami M^r A[rthur]
Young.[14] And to Mr. Barret.

Pray kiss about my Babes.

When our sister tells *you* good Letty's money is due,[15] I
have told *her* I have given—& *HERE I GIVE*—you the power
to draw for it on M. Hoare: or to pay from Mr. Mathias,
according as the finances hold.— |

910   [1358, Marché au bois],
                              Brussels, 3–4 July 1815

To M. d'Arblay

A.L. (Berg), 3–4 July 1815
Double sheet 4to   4 pp.   wafer
Addressed: Treves. / à M. / M. le General *d'Arblay* / offc^r Superieur des
Gardes du Corps / du Roi de France / Che^r de St Louis, &c / Treves.
Edited by FBA, p. 1, *annotated*: ⁙ (18/2)
Edited also, possibly, by CFBt. *See* Textual Notes.

11 L. 908.
12 Edward Francesco Burney (i, p. lxxv), the artist.
13 CBFB's daughter Marianne Francis (i, p. lxxiii).
14 As FBA at this time seemed to know, Mrs. Broome was at this time visiting the
famous agriculturist, a long-time friend and a connection of the family, at Bradfield. See CBFB's letter to him (BM, Add. MSS. 35133), *pmks* JY 1815 and 9 Sept.
1815.
15 See L. 907 n. 22.

Read at once. pray omit *poste restante*, which delays my Letters.

Brussels—
Monday, July 3ᵈ 1815.

How truly am I thankful—though not to YOU, M. l'athanase!
—to find my alarm groundless, & that I had ONLY three days of
affright & shaking uneasiness to spend from some omission of
the post day between the 24ᵗʰ & the 28ᵗʰ which you do not
motivé.[1] Want of *TIME* I can never allow, to *me*, to whom the
mere date of *place* & *month* would be always a *Letter*, & a
welcome Letter, in informing me *WHERE* you were, & *when*
at the latest period of writing. Alas! how can I have peace in
ignorance of those points, at a moment when the happiest
accounts of one day, are followed by the most contradictory &
fearful of another? You encourage me also to write always on—
by words to me resistless—yet what is *your* desire to hear—
compared with *mine*, at present? All *here* is undoubtedly safe:
but all near *you* seems in flames. Saarbrouck! Saarlouis! that
unhappy Roden ⟨marker⟩![2] How can you expect me to breath
but by all the reiterations of your safety the scanty post will
give?—For your most kind regularity till then, take, however,
my most grateful acknowledgments And spare yourself that,
in any particular emergency, I will accept a line from
François, ordered by you, not only without a murmur, but with
contentment.

The date of *Treves* is always a Joy to me—yet I dare so
little expect it, that I always believe every time I see it will
be the last. Your call upon M. de F[eltre] for all your appointments, in the Copy you have sent me, is Now so serious, that I
trust it neither will nor can remain any longer unanswered.

How sorry I am, mon cher ami, how sorry for your mal au
dents!—

I can say nothing explanatory about the schawls, as I did
not understand the affair, & fear only to make *bad worse*; en

---

910.   [1] The Prussian advance seems to have disrupted the Luxemburg and
Cologne mails, by which M. d'A's letters were delivered to Brussels.
   [2] Saarbrücken and Saarlouis, both border fortresses south of Trèves, were
attacked by the advancing allies. Rodemak, a walled town and castle ten miles
north-east of Thionville, had been fortified and garrisoned by 350 gardes nationaux.
On 25 June they beat back an assault by 3,000 allied troops, who lost 300 men
and abandoned the siege. See *Dictionnaire du département de la Moselle* (Metz, 1817),
pp. 347–8.

outre: our *gratitude* need not be very uneasy, for the first *offer* I have mentioned, which was friendly & kind, was by no means followed up with *cordial*, or even *any* but indispensable *suites*. All is just as before you went; the late terrour brought back a fairer view—but it was no sooner over, than the same conduct & Converse we have so grieved at, has been renewed with asperity & *chicanerie*. Indeed, ⌐ opinions such as I think highly dangerous to propagate, & such as I should hold myself culpable to permit any doubt of my disapproving, have lately been uttered so liberally, with assertions That ALL of the Tight were of the same way of thinking,[3] that, yesterday, I thought it quite incumbent upon me to risk all personal displeasure, & even less of good will, rather than not make one attempt, with all the force in my power, to represent the evil to *themselves*, their Country, & All the World, of thus disheartening all our rising hopes, & blighting all our fairer prospects, by perpetually placing in the darkest light all that breathe ⌐Hope &⌐ Success, after so much sorrow past, & such desolation escaped. I had infinite difficulty to procure any hearing: surprise, agitation, anger, & alarm were all awaked with inconceivable activity; every word was stopt, to bring forth a Justification of things *not attacked*; but every meaning of what *was* attacked, was left in the lurch, as if not comprehended. I begged them only to consider what could be the effect of inspiring universal disgust & dissaffection: the *fact* was denied—but in two minutes *proved!* by repetitions of the same tales & predictions to which I alluded. If the *Tight*, I said, thought so, it was from *themselves*, from their own depreciating & dispiriting discourses. Flames now glowed;—but my zeal & true affection, mingled with my accusation, softened them down; a *half* charge, however, was pronounced, that her confidence had been abused—her confidence in her bosom friends had been betrayed! *I* now fired,—& firmly, & indignantly, because most truly, protested, I have *never* named her; & *never* had, nor would, nor should but in a manner to correspond with the Friendship

---

[3] This murky passage, which FBA kept obscure through fear of interception, recounts a painful argument with the princesse d'Hénin and Mme de Maurville, both of whom were beginning to abandon hope in a Bourbon restoration and to suspect that England preferred the duc d'Orléans. FBA had little success in winning over this 'despair party', but her response was quite correct. England's policy was not to dicker with the French, as Wellington was plainly told, but rather to insist upon 'the restoration of the King' (*Disp.* xii. 534).

with which she had so long honoured me. She looked perplexed; yet *pleased*, though not *satisfied*; but she fired again presently, though full as much with shame as with *anger*, when I said I would apply, to strengthen & ⌐succour myself, & my own way of feeling & of wishing, to the *Writings* from THIS ROOF, not the speeches![4] She made 100 apologies for the *Pen*,[5] not one of which was worth even confuting! Ah mon ami! how true is it there is one path only that causes no embarrassment in discussion! the *straight-forward*! all other, however dexterously trodden, lead to so many briars, thorns, pits, & depths unexpected, that confusion is always at hand to overset every defence.

In parting, I was approaching to embrace—but the averted look determined me not to risk a rejection, & I came away without the final, but very kind & soothing harangue I wished & meant to make. We were not alone—*schawl*[6] was by, & always of Her side, of course: but she hinted she would discuss the point another time, more *convenably*. I know not what she meant.[3]

I am very sorry for her displeasure—but much relieved to have spoken *positively*. I have *often* gone half way; but it is so difficult to be heard, by one who will talk all the talk, & fly all the reply, that I could never do it effectually till yesterday. And even then, I said not by any means all I could have urged, for she interrupted at every other word, even when I *demanded* & *required* an audience.

To shew my desire to avoid all offence—for what I said *ought* to prove my sincere regard—as I told her,—I called again to-day: but she was out. She is better; & I am glad to find, however I have astonished & displeased her by my plainness, it has not renewed her palpitations.

Tuesday, July 4th Yes, my dearest ami, our Alex.'s Letter is to *me*; and ⌐a *sister* Letter, he says, as it conveys a secret;[7] but by the *end*, he gives me leave to read it *with you*; therefore I shall write *bit by bit*, its contents, as room & time admit.

---

[4] The resounding Bourbon manifestos Lally-Tolendal had written at the princesse d'Hénin's (L. 872 n. 8).

[5] Lally-Tolendal. The apologies concerned his political fits of pique (see, for example, L. 876 and L. 878).

[6] Mme de Maurville (L. 838 n. 30).

[7] AA's lost letter of 2 June, in which he told FBA of his admiration for his cousin Sarah Burney. See L. 896 n. 8; L. 909 n. 3.

The *secret*, however, I must wait revealing till I am more sure my Letter will arrive to you at once for you always seem expecting removal. But this very pleasant ending let me mention: my dear⁋ faithful Lady Keith not only wrote to him twice while he was in the Country, but immediately invited him to Dinner upon hearing he was in Town.—And after that, she lent him her Opera Ticket. And Alex went & flourished in the Pit, which seems much to have delighted him. Nor is this all; she ˡ gave him a Ticket for a particular place in which to see the key stone of a new Bridge,[8] over the Thames, placed by Lord Keith: & another for a friend to accompany him. ⌐He took Martin with himself.⌐9 At the place, Lʸ Keith saw him, & immediately spoke to him—There was a great repast given by her Lord in a new built room: eh bien—she invited him in, & the Friend who was with him. And he says it was superb:— & a very select & high company. How very good she is! How kindly, nay indulgently faithful to her early friendship!—

At Madᵉ d'H[énin]'s I heard that Mᵐᵉ de Laval is at Brussels —with Mᵉ de Tizkywitz,[10] & Mᵉ de Jaucourt.[11] They have been here above a week; but I have not known it. our news, which has been all that is prosperous, is to day most alarming: B[uonaparte] is said to prepare a stand at Mont Martre! Is it possible the parisiens will suffer such a demolition—such an assault, & such pillage as must ensue? And for a *hopeless* Cause! An English officer told me, yesterday, he was SURE Lord Wellington would save Paris if it were *any way* possible; & from being *consumed*, he thought his efforts would succeed; but if there was a *siege*, no one believed it *possible* to save it

[8] Southwark Bridge. The ceremony took place on 23 May at noon and 'the company afterwards repaired to the temporary bridge erected on the works, where there was a cold collation' (*AR* lvii, 'Chronicle', p. 35).

[9] AA's cousin Martin, JB's son (i, p. lxx).

[10] The sister of Prince Poniatowski (1763–1813), one of Napoleon's maréchaux d'empire, Maria Theresa (1765–1834) lived apart from her husband Count Vincent Tyszkiewicz (1757–1816). A friend of both Mme de Laval and Mme de Jaucourt, she had accompanied them to England in 1793 after their flight from Paris.

[11] Formerly the wife of the duc de la Châtre (ii, pp. xv–xvi), Marie-Charlotte-Louise-Aglaé-Perrette *née* Bontemps (1762–1848), was, in 1793, like her present husband, the comte de Jaucourt (L. 862 n. 20), a member of the *émigré* colony at Juniper Hall. On her second flight to England early in the Hundred Days, her husband advised her to take a three-month lease (Jaucourt, p. 286). At the end of this perfectly timed arrangement she returned to Brussels and prepared to follow her husband to Paris.

from pillage by the *Prussians*. The English Governm[t.] has already, MOST NOBLY, decreed recompences to All the army,[12] *au lieu* of pillages.

Tuesday 10 at night. I have just conversed with 3 English officers, separately, (all wounded) who have All 3 given me different news of the present position of the Armies, according to what had separately reached each. The 1st had been told that the Prussians under Blücher were *en pleine retraite*,[13] after having been worsted by Buonaparte, who was in Paris, preparing for his defence; that L[d] Wellington had halted for the Prussians, unable to do more than keep his ground: & that an immense dyke had been cut around Paris, to let in the waters of the Seine & *arreter* the advance of the allies. The 2[d] officer had been assured That L[d] W[ellington] was at St. Denis,[14] stopping for re-inforcements, as B[uonaparte] was upon Montmartre, with the most formidable artillery, & works, that ever have been employed.

The 3[d] told me he had just been informed that B. had disappeared—that the Jacobins had possession of all power, & that Lord W. was at St. G[erm]ains, in treaty, to save Paris, if those wretches will not delay too long—for the Prussians are now at Versailles, pillaging the Palace & the Ville!— Nothing of all this is sure—but some mischief, I much fear, has happened; & that L[d] W. has advanced too forward—for no troops have yet been able to join him. The Bavarois, under Wrede* are the nearest.[15] How much I fear mon ami's being put into some crippled Fortress, where he may be kept for months—perhaps years! as Governor—and *nos choux*? Without the spur of *AMBITION*, how *triste* are the honours that keep us, in our latter days, from our own fire sides! And oh what a separation from our Alex!—How magnificent is the Parliament of England! it has voted 1 million livres sterl[g] To the Army!

[12] For the details of this prize-money, which ranged from £1,274. 10s. 10d. for each general officer to £2. 11s. 4d. for the rank and file, see *Supp. Desp.* x. 750.

[13] Although Napoleon had left for Rochefort, Blücher had indeed suffered a serious defeat at Versailles, where the French were victorious in a cavalry battle on 1 July (Lachouque, pp. 161–2).

[14] On 1 July Wellington moved his headquarters from Louvres to Gonesse. Prussian headquarters were at Versailles, and although the situation remained confused, the two armies began to move in concert around Paris (*Supp. Desp.* x. 637–8).

[15] They were in fact much further off. On 1 July Wrede* was marching westward from Nancy.

200.000£ of which is for the Duke.[16] The rest in due proportions amongst Generals, colonels, captains, Lieut[ts] Ensigns, & Soldiers. I am delighted that my Letters procure you some relaxation—[17]

[xxxxx 1 *line of marginal writing*]

911   [1358, Marché au bois],
                          Brussels, 4–5 July [1815]

To M. d'Arblay

A.L. (Berg), 4–5 July
Single sheet 4to   2 pp.   wafer
Addressed: N⁰ 2. / Au / Chevalier d'Arblay, / &c– / N⁰ 2.
Edited by FBA, p. 1, *annotated and dated*: ⌗   1815   (3/18)   4 Letters Lost.
See Textual Notes.

                       Tuesday, *July 4*[th]
                              Midnight—

Mon ami! mon cher Cher ami! what joy! what extacy!— Just as my Letter was filled, & folded—& our house all retiring to rest—a ring at the door gave an alarm—& in rushed— into my room, & my arms—the princess d'Henin to tell me all was arranged, by That Angel Lord Wellington!—that the King should enter Paris next Thursday, July 6th without ANY of the allies—without even HIMSELF! (Lord W.)

M. de Lally, who has followed the King, & been admitted to an Audience, & to all the Counsels, has stolen from them to write this—& 3 pages of detail—with ink flowing through tears of Joy! — —

M. Mounier,[1] he says is crying like a Child—M. de Jaucourt *subdued* with excess of happiness—All round do nothing but embrace—& laugh—& weep!—The Letter is the most affect-

---

[16] Wellington's share of the million pounds in prize-money (n. 12 above) was £61,178. 3s. 5d., but on 22 June Parliament voted him an additional sum of £200,000 (*AR* lvii, 'General History', p. 50).

[17] L. 904.

911.   [1] See L. 876 n. 27.

ingly delightful I ever read. But, what astonishment!—B[uona-parte] is NOT ONCE mentioned in the Letter!—

Neither is he in one M. de Jaucourt, with the same exquisite News, has written here to his wife!

Nor yet in one received from the King's party by the D^ss d'ursel.—²

It is supposed he is with the *debris* of his army, behind La Loire.³ The King is now proclaiming That Army *dissoute*. Valenciennes still holds out⁴—so do various places—because not knowing, or not believing this divine event.

Lord Wellington has done the Whole! as Masterly in the Cabinet as in the Field! And he has done it, by going on at all risks foremost,—for had the Prussians, &c arrived, it is probable his negociations would have been overpowered by the earnest desire of plunder.—

The Messenger sent by the Governor of Paris⁵—that horrible d'avoust,⁶ with acceptance of the terms of Lord Wellington, his Grace desired might be well treated; that no *acharnement* of l'*amour propre* might mar the treaty. He dined, therefore, with some of the King's Gentlemen.

I shall gather all possible particulars for the next part,—pray give very attentive orders about the safety of your Letters, should you leave Treves while any are on the road: for I shall

---

² The dowager duchesse d'Ursel (L. 856 n. 10) rather than her daughter-in-law (L. 872 n. 9), whom FBA calls the 'young duchess'.

³ Napoleon reached Rochefort on 3 July, but took no part in the retreat of his former troops, who were regrouped as the Army of the Loire by 10 July and ordered by the terms of the military armistice of 3 July to remain south of the river. Louis XVIII had already dismissed from his service 'tous officiers et soldats passés sous le commandement de Napoléon Bonaparte et de ses adhérents' (*Moniteur de Gand*, 14 April) in a document backdated to 23 March. The decree disbanding the old army (and creating a new one loyal to the Bourbons) was not signed until 16 July and not made public until 12 August.

⁴ The allies had invested Valenciennes by 21 June, but like many other French fortresses it held out through the summer. The provisional government in Paris warned the governors of all such fortified places that any surrender before either an assault or a breaching of their walls had taken place would cause them to be court-martialled for treason (*Supp. Desp.* xi. 84).

⁵ Probably Francis Macirone (1780–*post* 1823), an officer of Italian and English parentage and former aide-de-camp of Murat. Fouché and Davout sent him both to deliver their proposals and to sound out Wellington's attitude toward a Bourbon restoration brought about through their machinations. This aspect of his mission may have accounted for his welcome from Louis XVIII's entourage, but Macirone, who came recommended by people known to Wellington in Paris, had already dined with the allied commander on Wednesday, 28 June (*Supp. Desp.* x. 653). He later continued his career as a soldier of fortune in South America and Spain.

⁶ Louis-Nicolas Davout (L. 856 n. 15).

continue writing till you tell me not:—It is such a consolation
to *me* to hear you say my Letters procure any to you! my
dearest dearest amico! what a blessed termination at length
of so much misery!—⌐Pray write for I can only wait for the
next post, before I take up money, as I have at this moment but
30 Nap[oleons] left in the world. I cannot take up less than
20—for many reasons—unless your next letter gives me some
direction how to do otherwise—Heaven bless you,⌐ caro mio
ben!—caro carissimo!—

⌐*Wednesday* July 5ᵗʰ

I kept this for a Bon Jour—⟨and⟩—viz. demain—Thurˢ
our Bon Roi ᴇɴᴛʀᴇʀᴀ—every body now will say, notre bon
Roi!—⟨am I last to hear I wonder?⟩ I want to share in your
pleasure! My enjoyment is only half till I know yours—⌐

912   Trèves, 4–6 July 1815

M. d'Arblay
To Madame d'Arblay

A.L. (Berg), 4, 6 juillet, 1815
Double sheet 4to   3 pp.   *pmks*   TRIER   TRIER   seal
Addressed: A Madame / Madame de Burney / Poste restante / à Bruxelles
Readdressed: Marché au Bois / N. 1358
Edited by FBA, p. 1, *annotated and dated*: ⸬   ⸬   ⌐29⌐   20   (1815)   4.
July   ⌐July 6ᵗʰ⌐   [*with numbers on address fold*]: 16   29
See further, Textual Notes.

Treves ce 4 au soir

Mon dieu, ma chere chere amie, que je serai malheureux
si demain je ne suis pas plus heureux qu'hier c. a. d. si la
poste ne m'apporte pas de tes nouvelles. Ne me suis-je pas
mis dans la tête que tu es malade parceque j'ai été un seul
jour de poste sans avoir une lettre de toi? J'ai beau me dire à
chaque instant que cela n'a pas le sens commun, d'autant que
la veille c.à.d. avant hier j'avais eu deux lettres de toi,[1] une
par Luxembourg et l'autre, le soir, par Cologne. Tout cela

912.   [1] Ll. 903 and 905, respectively.

n'empeche pas que je ne sois d'une inquietude mortelle, et que j'ai l'imagination frappée au point de ne pouvoir me distraire un moment de l'idee que ta santé, dejà si delicate, n'aura pu soutenir le danger de soigner dans cette saison des blessés du genre de ceux dont tu parles. Je suis dans une ville ou pour cette seule raison, et dans une saison bien moins dangereuse puisque c'etait au mois de Septembre, plus de 1300 personnes sont mortes.[2] Des familles entieres ont peri, et plusieurs maisons sont restées defaites. Et encore ces personnes ne faisaient pas comme toi, que je suis pourtant loin de désaprouver, car c'est precisement ce que je voudrais faire moi même si j'etais à Bruxelles au lieu d'etre à Treves. Ce que j'en conclus c'est qu'il faut que tu quittes cette ville, et que tu ailles dans quelque campagne attendre l'instant de notre reunion, qui ne peut etre eloigné. [xxxxx 2 *lines*] avec quelle impatience j'attendrai demain l'arrivée du Courrier. S'il ne m'apporte rien, je ne sais en verité ce que je deviendrai. Je n'avais pas besoin de ce nouveau tourment! Quest-ce que c'est que ce maudit et absurde Senat qui après avoir entendu la lecture de la lettre d'abdication de Bonaparte,[3] proclame Empereur Napoleon II, et pretend que tout le monde actuellement reuni sous un bambin va sauver la Patrie,[4] que Napoleon 1er avec tous ses talens, n'a pu garantir de sa chute. Il parait certain au surplus que les souverains ont refusé de voir les Ambassadeurs de ce repaire.[5] En effet comment ayant refusé de reconnoitre Napoleon, auraient ils pu reconnoitre les agens de l'homme qu'ils ont proscrit.[6] Au surplus l'invraisemblable dans tout ceci se trouvant assez souvent vrai, il ne faut

[2] During the autumn of 1813 several towns along the Rhine and Moselle took in sick and wounded soldiers from Napoleon's retreating armies. Thousands died from the plague they spread, and local accounts suggest that M. d'A is not exaggerating the number who died in Trèves. See Gottfried Kenterich, *Geschichte der Stadt Trier* (Trier, 1915), pp. 682–3.

[3] Napoleon abdicated on 22 June. Since both chambers also decreed the creation of their own 'Commission de gouvernement' (Houssaye, *1815*, iii. 93–4), which was to hold actual power, the proclamation on the following day of the King of Rome as Napoleon II was equivocal.

[4] A condescending term that called attention, as the royalists repeatedly did, to both Napoleon's Corsican origins and the helpless infancy of his heir.

[5] The deputation to Haguenau led by Lafayette (L. 901 n. 9).

[6] This was Karl Justus (later von) Gruner (L. 897 n. 1), who went on to become chief of the allies' political police in France. On the day M. d'A finished this letter to FBA, he wrote to warn the duc de Feltre of the appointment of 'un Mr Justus Gruner qui ne jouit pas en ce pays d'une excellente reputation' (A.L.S., Vincennes, 6 July).

plus s'etonner de rien; et douter de tout Ce qui neanmoins est de la plus grande verité c'est la nomination d'un Gouverneur general des provinces françaises conquises par les armées alliées. [xxxxx 6 *lines*] Pauvre Pauvre France! Vas tu être assez humiliée? [xxxxx 1 *line*] Puisse au moins les Alliés n'user momentanement du pouvoir terrible qu'ils doivent à la victoire que pour infliger aux brigands la punition qu'ils se sont attirés; et puisse l'excellent ׀ Louis XVIII n'avoir ensuite à s'occuper que du bonheur des sujets fideles dont il sera constament entouré. Amen. [xxxxx ½ *line*].

(Mercredy matin) Dieu veuille que j'aye une lettre de mon amie Amen. Dieu soit loué en voici une, bien interessante comme toutes celles qu'elle ecrit mais combien elle me donne à penser. Tranquille sur le premier objet de mes pensées, me voici de nouveau tout à la politique, et ma foi mes idées sur cette importante matiere ne sont pas toutes couleur de rose. Il parait que ton *heavenly project*[7] convenu entre Lord Wellington et Blücher n'a pu avoir lieu puisque ce dernier est actuellement devant St Denis,[8] d'où il a depêché un courrier au Roi de Prusse, en annonçant que Paris fesait des preparatifs pour sa defense; lui de son côté se propose à bombar[der] cette ville. Pauvre Pauvre France! [xxxxx 1 *line*] Nous sommes ici bien tristes, et je soupire bien après l'instant où je pourrai quitter Treves.

Je t'embrasse adieu

Treves ce 6. Juillet. 1815 —

[7] FBA's phrase in L. 903 was 'heavenly plan'.
[8] Like the rest of the capital's northern periphery, Saint-Denis had been heavily fortified, and early on the morning of 30 June its garrison of two battalions beat back a Prussian assault. This setback decided Blücher to shift his advance to the south, bypassing Paris and leaving the northern approach to Wellington and Louis XVIII.

[1358, Marché au bois],
Brussels, 6 July [1815]

To M. d'Arblay

A.L. (Berg), 6 July
Double sheet 4to   4 pp.   wafer
Addressed: à ⌜*Namur*.⌝ / À M. / M. le Général d'Arblay, / Off^{cr} superieur
des gardes du / Corps de sa Majesty / Le Roi de France, / Che^r de St Louis,
&c / Trèves / à ⌜*Namur*⌝ / ⌜Post Restante.⌝
Docketed p. 4: Juillet
Edited by FBA, p. 1, *annotated and dated*: ⅏ ⅏ + 1815 ⌜N° 16/1⌝
⌜18⌝ (19)
See Textual Notes.

Pray, pray Always Date *Time* & *Place*.

Bruxelles,
July 6. Thursday

Que de bonheur, mon bien aimé ami, que de bonheur, que
d'espoir de vous addresser à Namur![1] C'est si près, il me semble
that I could almost go thither to drink Tea with you! ⌜Yet
the *two* Letters of this morning perplex & make me very
anxious for a *third* as you have given *no date* OR *The time* to the
short one, & I cannot make out when it was written. The
long & very dear one of June 30 & July 1st tells me to direct to
Namur. The last one, with only *Trèves* etc —— says a Letter
for me was to have been put into the post at Namur by a
Garde du Corps,[2] & laments that no Letter was received *from*
me! I vow I⌝ have never missed one single post since the
Invasion of Buonaparte, well aware what would be your
solicitude, your kind solicitude in any suspense as to my position.
⌜Sur la longue Lettre la post mark without is *Trèves*—*sur la
courte*, it is *Namur*. Je n'entends rien; ⟨as told⟩ the duke of Orléans
to *le comte*.[3] I cannot conceive you to be *already* at Namur when
you write, for you say your Letters arrive the 7th to the 10th

———

913.   [1] In L. 904, which FBA refers to below, M. d'A said he hoped to reach
Namur between 7 and 10 July.
   [2] 'Garde du Corps', according to M. d'A's explanation in L. 906 n. 5.
   [3] Perhaps '[write of] the Duke of Orléans to le comte [Lally-Tolendal]'. The
passage is obscure.

I direct thither, however, & you will let me know your arrival & the destination. I shall only write as you give me direction.⌐

I wrote you *La décheance* the moment I heard it:[4] but my Letters to Treves, like your replies, are 6 days on the road: besides that they depart hence only 3^{ce} a week, & never the same day they arrive.

⌐I shall now defer till next week taking up money, by buying nothing but *immediate food*, that I may know more clearly what to do. The exchange, they say, moves rapidly. I hope now I shall recover my ⎸ wardrobe. Nevertheless, unless it arrives hither soon, I MUST buy some wearing apparel in another week —— or keep my bed!⌐

Evening.

I have just been dining at M. de Beaufort's. He came last night to beg me to meet Me de Maurville, & I would not refuse. I felt very melancholy, in thinking of the worthy & friendly Hostess I missed.—

O my dear Ami!—what will you do here? you are fit in no way for any present society! the injustice, ingratitude, & calumny that attack all *we* honour & love, by every means that positive decency does not keep off, would make you wild with pain, or indignation!

Nevertheless—I am so flustered with Joy at the thought of your approaching so much nearer, that I can hardly hold my Pen.—Ingrat! cependant!—*Ingrat as well as 'fat'!* you will not thank me for staying within call, BECAUSE I ran some little risk?—

Yet—*Without* a risk, how should I deserve your thanks?—

However, I will *earn* them now, after your own Fashion of liking,—for I have done what I am SURE you will be pleased with your Athanase for doing;—I have been waiting upon Me de Laval![5]—& my *sauvagerie* & *all that*, being conquered thus voluntarily, will gain me, I expect, one of your very best smiles. I had the good Fortune to find her alone, though she is here with two ladies. She received me with her wonted air of par-

---

[4] Napoleon's abdication.
[5] See ii, p. xv and v, L. 469 n. 6. M. d'A had shared the grief of Mme de Laval at the death in 1813 of comte de Narbonne (vii, pp. 211–15) and sympathy seemed to have softened the adamant stand FBA had taken with respect to the ménage in the rue Roquépine (v, vi *passim*).

tiality, & a cordiality almost touching. She talked of you most affectionately, & gave me abundance of news, & all after our united wishes & opinions. Yesterday she returned my Visit, & I found her, as I always do, one of the most agreeable conversers, for sense, observation, candour, & unaffected *Esprit* que Je *connoisse*. Her son[6] is with Monsieur, to whom he is aid de Camp. M^e la D^ss d'Ang[oulême] sent him over to that end. The Vs^t D'agoust[7] remains with her A[ltesse] R[oyale].

11 at night.

There is no fresh news arrived today. I have seen M^e d'Henin, & heard from Me de Laval & Me de la Tour du pin. The account of today's Great Entry cannot arrive before Sunday,[8] 9th I shall entreat Me de Laval to take a line for me to Me Depres[9] —And also to poor Me de Maisonneuve! It is said *ALL* the new made Peers are to be disgraced. Our dear Genl Victor is not amongst them. Nor any body, I believe, for whom we are much interested, except M. de Maub. & M. de Beauvau And for them—& theirs—O how am I grieved![10] — — And O—for M. de La F[ayette]—Ah! how melancholy a mixture of shame, repentence, mortification,—OR secret vengeance & despair, must sadden the gaiety of the Restoration! France can only be a *happy* sejour for those YET to be born!—I shall enquire if I may send a Letter *by post* through Me de Laval, & if yes, write to our dear Uncle.[11] ⌐Though perhaps he even yet has the Despot's troops & partisans around him—so then a few days later may be safer & wiser. We have no accounts as yet, here, of that part of France.— ¹

And I am concerned you have then been fatigued! Yet not that the *alerte* was a false one! The very name of that Vandamme[12] fills me with horrour. But how truly gallant, chevalresque, & noble is the order of the Emp[eror] Alexander

⁶ Mathieu-Jean-Félécité de Montmorency-Laval (ii, p. xv; v, L. 446 n. 21; vii *passim*).
⁷ Vicomte d'Agoult (L. 835 n. 7).
⁸ Louis XVIII actually entered Paris at three o'clock on the afternoon of 8 July (Reiset, iii. 236).
⁹ See L. 846 n. 1.
¹⁰ The comte César de Latour-Maubourg and the comte de Beauvau, both of whom appeared on this lists of Napoleon's new peers (*Moniteur*, 6 June).
¹¹ Jean-Baptiste-Gabriel Bazille, M. d'A's maternal uncle (see genealogical table in iii, *facing* p. 1; or vi, *facing* p. 476).
¹² See L. 878 n. 10

relative to the verses of vive Henri Quatre.[13] The Waterloo proclamation, also is perfect, in the same sense as that of the D[uke] of Wellington. A great mystery hangs over the present state of B[onaparte]—no one has any but contradictory accounts. De Boinville writes me word he has written to you, that your appointment can be paid only by your sending your *brevet* signed to the *Inspecteur aux Revenus* S. parseval,[14]—but he adds, if your mission is not at an end, he could almost advise you to join the King's A. de C. However, as he has no authority, since M. de Rocheouart has written that you are to have orders,[15] it seems, more proper & en regle, to stay for them. Added to which, you would necessarily be too late to enter Paris —& it may be the D[uke] of F[eltre] has some other plans for you. *THE* Duke's head-quarters were then, July 1st beyond Senlis, where an engagement had taken place a day or two before. D'Avout is said to have an army outside Paris. The R[oi] was received with enthusiasm. de Boinville's Letter[16] is dated Roye, July, 4th

I hope my Letters at *Trèves* will be safe, as they are written without reserve. I know you have seen Alex's Letter, but I re⟨mem⟩bered you only asked for possession of his handwriting. I have a new Letter now here to-day—Yet—dated June 2nd! still from James St![17]

adio, il mio amable!—Tell me if you are recovered the Vandam^me alert & the⁊ Toothache.

⌐There are no mortal *vapours* within my reach. I have always been liberal of Eau de Cologne, & very careful.⌐ 10,000 prisoners all sent to England!—⌐Beurnonville[18] is now marching⌐ fast—

13 Perhaps a garbled reference to the Czar's order concerning the playing of 'Vive Henri Quatre' (L. 904 n. 7).
14 François-Marie de Parseval (1771–1840), a military bureaucrat who entered the Maison du Roi at the Restoration as the sous-inspecteur aux revues of the Compagnie Écossaise. See *Emplacement des Troupes du Royaume de France à l'Époque du 1er Janvier 1815* (1815), p. 5. During the Hundred Days he followed the royal household to Ghent, where he authorized payments made to M. d'A and the other royal *commissaires* (Vincennes C^14 60). 15 See L. 904 n. 1.
16 Louis XVIII and his entourage arrived in Roye on 1 July and remained there until the 5th (Reiset, iii. 227–8).
17 This letter is missing.
18 Pierre Riel (1752–1821), later comte Riel de Beurnonville (1808) and marquis de Beurnonville (1817), rose above his humble origins by enrolling as a volunteer in 1774 with the régiment de l'Île-de-France (now Mauritius) and gaining a commission during twelve years' service in the Indian Ocean. He returned to

(*a word! I can be ready*) [xxxxx 2 *lines marginal writing*]
Here is news relative to the Beau Cheval.
[xxxxx 18 *half-lines*]¹⁹

914   Trèves, [6–8 July 1815]

M. d'Arblay
To Madame d'Arblay

A.L. (Berg), vendredy–samedy
Originally a ?double sheet 4to, of which FBA later discarded the second
leaf   2 pp.
Edited by FBA, p. 1, *annotated and dated*: ⌗   ⌜30⌝   (21/I)   Treves
July 6ᵗʰ   7. & 8ᵗʰ   (1815)
p. 2: Treves le 8. Juillet 1815
See further, Textual Notes.

Que j'aime la phrase suivante, ma chere amie, et comme je
suis fiere de la trouver ecrite de ta main et adressée à moi,
pauvre athanase! *How often do we catch ourselves in what, we utter
spontaneously, thinking & feeling and saying the same thing.*¹—C'est
là le charme et la gloire de mon existence; et je te devrai, ma
bonne Fanny, de la trouver encore agreable, malgré tout ce qui

France in 1788, when he entered the garde ordinaire of the comte d'Artois with the
rank of lieutenant-colonel in the army. He was promoted to lieutenant-general
during his service with the army of the Rhine in the campaigns of 1792, when he
fought at both Valmy and Jemappes, but in the following year he became involved
in the military reaction against the revolutionary Convention. Dumouriez handed
him over to the Austrians in 1793, when he was imprisoned (like Lafayette) at
Olmütz. In 1795 an exchange returned him to France, where he resumed both his
military career and his dabbling in royalist politics. After switching his support to
Bonaparte he became ambassador to Prussia and Spain under the Consulate and
senator of the Empire in 1805. He returned from retirement in 1812, but in 1814
turned his military and political influence against Napoleon and in favour of the
Bourbons. Louis XVIII conferred many honours on him and during the Hundred
Days made him his envoy to the army of Blücher, whose rapid advance Beurnonville accompanied to Paris. Later in 1815 he was named head of the commission
that dealt with the politically explosive claims to rank and pay made by former
officers and leaders of royalist insurgents: he was made a Marshal of France in
1816. See Joseph Valynseele, pp. 51–2.
    ¹⁹ The information given here about an ailing horse is repeated in 33 obliterated
half-lines in L. 919, pp. 325–6, where an attempt is made to read the passage.

914.   ¹ M. d'A is here quoting from L. 903, p. 263, above.

semble se reunir en ce moment pour la rendre insuportable. Juge de ce que j'ai du eprouver depuis trente six heures que ton silence d'un seul jour m'avait donné les plus vives inquietudes, sur ta santé; O mon amie! conservons nous l'un pour l'autre, lorsque [ce digne Monarque] dont les bienfaits n'ont trouvé que des ingrats, n'aura plus besoin de mes services. Un bruit sourd se repand ici que les prussiens sont entrés à Paris après un combat trés sanglant,[2] dernier effort d'un parti aux abois. [xxxxx 4 *lines*] Au demeurant ce malheur tout grand qu'il est n'est pas encore le plus à redouter. Ce qui me parait le plus affligeant c'est ce que tu me dis de la proclamation du prince de Schwarzemberg[3] si differente de celle des Anglais, si pure, si juste, si noble. Bon dieu qu'est-ce que c'est donc que l'esprit de parti! Rien de tout cela [ne m']est applicable, et je ne puis plus voir qu'egoisme et calculs purement personnels dans ce que j'avais pris pour du patriotisme et de l'elevation dans les sentimens. Je t'avoue je rougis de mon erreur et suis effrayé et presqu'honteux et humilié de la foule de dangers qu'elle m'a fait courrir; ne fut-ce que celui de me faire soupçonner d'approuver, et peut être de regretter de ne point partager une conduite que non seulement je trouve inexcusable, mais que j'abhore, et qui même, soit dit entre nous, ne m'inspire qu'horreur, eloignement, degout et mépris. En même tems je deplore la perte irreparable d'amis de trente ans, à qui j'etais devoué,[4] et qui m'ont rendu service toutes les fois ¹ que cela a été en leur pouvoir. Reconoitre les obligations de ce genre,[5] et surtout les soins qu'ils ont pris de toî dans ta maladie serait pour moi la plus grande de toutes les jouissances: mais quant aux sentimens que je leur avais voués, et dont je fesais gloire avant tout ceci, ils sont detruits à jamais.

Vendredy matin Trois courriers arrivés ou dans la nuit ou ce matin nous ont apporté les nouvelles les meilleures possible.

² The Prussians did not enter Paris until 7 July, and the last battle outside Paris took place at Issy on 3 July. M. d'A may have heard of the fighting that broke out in Paris on 4 July between the National Guard and mutinous troops who refused to accept either Napoleon's abdication or the capitulation of Paris (Houssaye, *1815*, iii. 308–9).

³ See L. 874 n. 3.

⁴ Lafayette, whose conduct M. d'A inveighs against in the passage that follows this obliterated identification.

⁵ The Noailles family. Mme de Tessé (v, p. xliv and L. 510 n. 11), the most generously helpful of friends to the d'Arblays (see v, vi, vii *passim*), was an aunt to Mme de Lafayette. The prince de Poix (L. 860 n. 11) also had for many years proved a helpful friend to M. d'A (see ii, L. 112 n. 1).

1er Vandame et Grouchy ont été battus.[6] 2° aprés plusieurs autres combats près de Paris, Les Alliés doivent être entrés hier 6 à Paris, par capitulation ce qui heureusement sauve cette Capitale, qui ne sera ni brulée ni pillée. 3° le Roi était le 4 à Senlis! Les troupes de ligne doivent se retirer derriere la Loire.

Samedy [8 juillet] Je viens de lire la proclamation du Roi. Je pense comme toi qu'elle est parfaite, et pourtant à la seconde lecture on se demande si elle produira l'effet qu'on en attend. J'en doute. J'ai lu aussi ta lettre,[7] et ne puis comprendre que tu ayes été un seul jour sans en recevoir de moi qui n'ai pas manqué d'ecrire tous les courriers. J'oserai ajouter qu'il me semble qu'on aurait du en retrancher ce qui est relatif à l'inactivité dans la quelle on a laissé les officiers qui sont passés avec le Roi, et n'ont en rien contribué à le faire remonter sur son thrône. Pour ma part j'en suis honteux quoiqu'assurément je n'aye rien à me reprocher, puisque j'ai tout mis en usage pour jouer un rôle un peu moins ridicule. [xxxxx 2 *lines*] l'abandon dans le quel on me laisse Je crois qu'on m'a tout à fait oublié; Tout cela n'est pas gai: mais ce qui m'a tout à fait attristé c'est ta lettre, et le tableau de Bruxelle, et des dangers qu'on y court. Souviens toi ma bonne amie, que tu m'as promis de faire ce que je te dirais. C'est ma vie que la tienne.

En consequence j'exige absolument qu'au reçu de la presente lettre 1er tu ailles chez notre banquier prendre l'argent que nous y avons et au quel je n'ai pas touché. 2° que tu passes de la chez mon ami Beaufort, et que tu le pries en mon nom et au tien de te trouver dans un bourg ou village à quelques lieues de Bruxelles un azile[8] ou tu puisses être convenablement toî et Marie.[9]

[the second leaf is missing]

[6] Neither was in fact involved in any decisive defeat. Vandamme commanded the rearguard of the retreating armée du Nord, which Grouchy* handed over to Davout on 28 June.

[7] L. 905.

[8] In the end FBA may have agreed with M. d'A's opinion that this part of L. 905 should have been deleted. Its second leaf is missing. M. d'A was understandably afraid that their letters might be intercepted, and L. 905 may have continued the indiscreet political revelations and criticism of L. 903.

[9] FBA's maid.

M. d'Arblay
To Madame d'Arblay

A.L. (Berg), 10 juillet 1815
Double sheet 4to   4 pp.   *pmk*   TRIER   seal
Addressed: A Madame / Madame de Burney / poste restante / à Bruxelles
Edited by FBA p, 1, *annotated*: ⋇ ⌜31⌝   (22)   [*with numbers on address fold*]: ⌜3e⌝ ⌜26⌝ ⌜31⌝   22
See further, Textual Notes.

Treves ce 10 Juillet 1815.

Si j'avais été prés de toi, ma bonne amie, je t'aurais facilement tranquillisée, en te demontrant l'absurdité des nouvelles de tes trois prisonniers.[1] Je voudrais bien que tu pusses me rendre, en ce moment, le même service, en me rassurant sur les suites de la noble demarche du Roi, entrant seul à Paris, exposé et à la merci du premier federé[2] qu'aura armé contre lui le desespoir de tant de brigands restés encore dans cette immense cité. Le plan du Duc de Wellington est digne de ce grand homme c'est tout dire Et neanmoins il est absolument impossible de n'en pas être trés allarmé, pour peu qu'on reflechisse à l'immense interêst attaché à la personne Sacrée de Louis XVIII. C'est bien dans la sincerité de mon ame que je regrette et que je regretterai toujours de ne pas être près de lui dans ce moment où sa sureté est menacée. God save him! Amen [Amen.]

[xxxxx 18 *lines*] ¹

Je suis reconnoissant de ce que Lady Keith a fait pour Alex que je ne puis desaprouver d'avoir fait ce qu'il a fait. et pourtant j'en suis trés trés faché. Rien de plus important dans le monde que les premiers pas qu'on y fait, et les premieres personnes avec les quelles on s'y montre influent beaucoup sur l'opinion que l'on y donne de soi pour le reste de la vie, et de cette opinion depend le plus souvent par la suite la conduite

915.   ¹ FBA had in fact heard the alarming news reported in L. 910 from three wounded English officers (p. 295, above).
  ² Civilians who volunteered to fight for Napoleon during the Hundred Days were given the same name as those who enrolled in the revolutionary *Fédérations* of 1789–90.

qu'on s'impose, et la ligne sur laquelle on marche. Ceci n'a pas besoin je crois de commentaire. J'ajouterai cependant encore que ce n'est pas avec les Bronghton qu'il faut paroitre en public, quand on veut être de la societé de M^{de} Delville,³ je dis *être de la societé* de, et non pas être *protegé par*. Un brave Cap^{ne} de Vaisseau ou Amiral, peu importe, peut être singulier, même affecter une sorte de mepris des bienseances, sans faire rougir de sa compagnie, mais une femme vulgaire, fut elle Duchesse, et eut elle d'ailleurs les qualités les plus opposées à ses manieres trop communes donne toujours mauvaise opinion du jeune homme, assez malheureux pour lui servir de chevalier. [xxxxx 6 *lines*]

Ma lettre au duc de Feltre est achevée⁴ — on la copie, et je saisis ce moment pour revenir causer avec toi. Ce que j'ai à te dire est fort important et tu ne dois le regarder que comme un texte dont les commentaires sont à faire. C'est à toi de t'en charger. Au fait.

Je suis desormais inutile ici, completement inutile. Je l'ai été jusqu'à present le moins qu'il m'a été possible mais reellement j'y suis actuellement sans esperance de rendre aucun service equivalent à l'argent que je coute; et pourtant je n'ose partir, attendu que dernierement encore il est arrivé un enorme paquet de journaux trop ¹ anciens pour faire aucun bien. Je n'ai point sollicité ma mission, j'ai fait au contraire l'impossible pour faire tomber sur d'autres le choix du Ministre: mais une fois que j'en ai été chargé definitivement, j'ai tout mis en usage pour m'en acquiter le moins mal possible. Les lettres des Generaux en chef des armées alliées prouvent que ce n'est pas ma faute si je n'ai pas suivi de prés leurs mouvemens et partagé leurs dangers malgré l'extréme repugnance que j'eprouvais d'attacher mon nom aux mesures que je prevoyais qu'ils seraient obligés de prendre &c. &c &c J'ai d'ailleurs eprouvé, que ma bonne volonté et tout le zele dont je suis capable n'etaient pas suffisans pour remplir dans une saison

---

³ The double allusion is to characters in FB's novels. The Brangtons are the vulgar cits in *Evelina*. Mme Delville of *Cecilia* epitomizes pride in rank or family. M. d'A seems to think that the invitation in question would have been more creditable to Alex if it had come from Lord Keith himself rather than his lady, an early friend of AA's mother.

⁴ In that letter (Vincennes) to the duc de Feltre, Minister of War, M. d'A had asked for his recall from Trèves: 'De grace, Monseigneur, veuillez me tirer bientôt d'ici et me rapprocher de vous . . .'.

rigoureuse les devoirs d'un general de mon grade. C'est
une verité que je n'ai pas non plus cachée au duc de Feltre
en le prevenant que si la lutte dans la quelle nous etions engagé
venait à se prolonger, je serais obligé de quitter avant l'hiver,
c'est à dire en Novembre. Actuellement si la Maison du Roi,
trop couteuse est reformée et dissoute comme tu l'as ecrit dans
ta derniere lettre, et si je ne [suis] pas placé pour quelque tems
encore près de Sa Majesté, ou du moîns à Paris, pour être à
portée de lui rendre encore le peu de services dont je suis
capable, dans mon grade de M^{al} de Camp, je demande decidement ma retraite qu'on me payera comme et quand on le
pourra. Depuis l'âge de 13 ans 1/2 j'ai servi avec zele, et n'ai
eu d'interruption actuellement que j'en ai 61, que le tems
que j'ai passé en Angleterre à la verité je compte dans mes
cinquante et quelques années de service près de 10 ans passé
dans le bureau des batimens civils. Tu sais de quelle maniere.
C'est à toi de faire valoir tout cela près du Duc de Luxembourg,
et du duc de Feltre, qu'il faut absolument que tu voyes, et de
qui tu seras bien reçue. Je te donne sur cela carte blanche,
puisque je suis bien sure que tu ne feras dans tout ce que tu
entreprendras rien que de convenable, et de parfaitement en
mesure avec l'honneur que j'ai d'être le compagnon de ton
honnorable vie. Le Roi j'espere ne me traitera pas plus mal que
les off^{ers} de la Ligne qui l'ont payé de tant d'ingratitude.[5]
Si j'obtenais ma *demi paye* et une lettre de satisfaction, je me
croirais trop riche. Je serai content à moins, et serai très
satisfait si l'on m'accorde 4000 et le brevet de Lieut^{nt} General
pour retraite. Autrement je n'en voudrais pas, quoique
presque tous mes cadets, entr'autres le frère de Dumas[6] l'ayant
eu sans difficulté. — Arrange tout cela dans ta bonne tête,
et pars tout de suite pour Paris, c'est à dire aussitòt que les

[5] Early in the Hundred Days, with very few exceptions, the officers of the regiments of the line went over to Napoleon, taking their troops with them. The
officers of the household troops and Swiss regiments remained loyal to Louis XVIII.
[6] Guillaume-Mathieu Dumas, *dit* de Saint-Marcel (1755–1826), royalist
brother of the more famous general and comte de l'Empire, Mathieu Dumas
(1753–1837). Guillaume, who was like M. d'A a supporter of Lafayette and an
émigré, went over to the Austrians with Dumouriez in 1793. By some oversight he
was promoted a month later to the rank of général de brigade, which made him
junior to M. d'A, whose own irregular promotion to the equivalent general rank of
maréchal de camp dated from 1792. After several years of active service with the
frontier guards of Napoleon's customs service, Dumas was pensioned off on 1 Oct.
1814 and, on 23 January of the following year, given the honorary rank of
lieutenant-general.

communications seront rouvertes et sures. Je te supplie de n'y pas manquer, et de ┃ me donner bien exactement de tes nouvelles tous les courriers. Celui qui va partir me presse adieu. Reponse tout de suite, et que ce soit pour m'annoncer ton depart. [xxxxx ½ *line*]

916   [Trèves], 11 July [1815]

M. d'Arblay
To Madame d'Arblay

A.L.S. (Berg), 11 juillet
Single sheet 4to   1 p.   *pmk*   TRIER   seal
Addressed: A Madame / Madame de Burney   poste restante / A Bruxelle
Readdressed: Marché au Bois / A / *Bruxelle*
Edited by FBA, p. 1, *annotated and dated*: ⌜32⌝ (23/2) 1815

Ce 11 Juillet à 8ʰ1/2

Mr de Premorel[1] vient, ma chere Fanny, de me mettre la mort dans l'ame en me disant que le bruit courait que le Roi n'etait pas entré dans Paris;[2] qu'il y avait beaucoup de troubles dans cette ville, et qu'en consequence les Generaux Blucher et Wellington lui avaient conseillé d'attendre que tous les alliés fussent reunis pour se rendre dans cette Capitale. J'ai voulu remonter à la source de ce bruit, et cela m'a été impossible. J'ai fait venir un journal allemand où il pretendait qu'il etait question de cette nouvelle. Je me le suis fait lire, et n'y ai rien trouvé de semblable ni même d'approchant. Malgré cela me voilà aux champs,[3] et je suis au desespoir de t'avoir ecrit de partir pour ce repaire de tous les crimes et de toutes les trahisons. Pour Dieu, ma chere chere amie s'il en est encore tems, regarde ma derniere lettre comme non avenue et ne va pas t'exposer sans moi dans cette Ville epouvantable. Point de lettre de toi je n'ai que le tems de dire pr Athanase!

d'A—

916.   ┃ This was the father, Pierre-Louis-Raoul-Edmé Durand de Prémorel (L. 868 n. 3).
    ² Although untrue, this rumour of upheavals in Paris that prevented the King's return was widespread during these days. See, for example, the anonymous report in *Supp. Desp.* x. 672–5.
    ³ A figurative expression meaning 'greatly perplexed'.

917 [1358, Marché au bois],
Brussels, 3–12 July [1815]

To Alexander d'Arblay

A.L. (Berg), 3–12 July
Double sheet large 4to   4 pp.   From the 2nd leaf a segment (*c.* 2 × 0·8″)
has been torn away with the wafer   *pmks*   [G]OSPORT / JY 2⟨4⟩ 1815
25 JY 1815   25 JY 1815   wafer
Addressed: Alexander d'Arblay Junr Esqr, / At Mrs. Broome's / Rich-
mond. / Surry, / or at Henry Barret's Esqr /
Scribbling, p. 4, arithmetical numbers.
Edited by unknown editor. *See* Textual Notes.

Bruxelles July 3^d—

Another Letter from my dear Alex,[1] though written before
he could have received either of my two last, shall make me
again write, as an opportunity—which is very rare, from my
retired way of life — — offers for sending to England. I had
else meant to wait for an *answer* to my two last, both of which
must now have reached you, as their dates were [11–12 and
12–23 June].[2] But, my dear *étourdi*, you have a terrible knack
of never *answering*, even when you do write. I earnestly charge
you to read over the same two I allude to at the instant your
pen is in your hand, that I may not always have to repeat the
same directions, or counsels, or enquiries, or *what not*? from
never knowing whether you have even read them. Your
quotations are very amusing—only not very apropos; if you
gave them AFTER you have answered my subjects of solicitude,
they would charm me: but before those matters in which my
heart, my cares, & my BUSINESS are engaged are settled, they
rather torment than delight. *Why* do you not tell me for what
reason you were still, when you wrote on *June the 6th* in Town,[3]
after our desire you would breathe the purer air of Richmond?
And *why* have you forgotten your own so good reasoning upon
the subject, & your sense of the impropriety, & encroachment,
of remaining with your generous Uncle any longer? *He* cannot
tell you to go! He would sooner share with you his last Crust.

917.   [1] AA's letter is missing, as is the earlier one of 2 June (see L. 909 n. 8).
[2] L. 886 and L. 896.
[3] This letter is also missing.

But your own Letter, & way of thinking upon this visit was so just, & gave both your Father & myself so much satisfaction, that I really want & require a candid explanation *why* you could reason so well, have your reasoning approved, yet act as if you never reasoned at all?—Ah Alex!—give me again a sister's Letter[4]—& and tell me honestly—was it the little blind boy that made you forget yourself? that told you by staying in town you might catch glimpses of which there were no peeps in Richmond? Or was it the dangerous, time-wasting fascination of Chess?—or a general desire of a longer fit of dissipation? or simply a sort of non-challence, that urged you to stay where you were, for no other reason but because where you were, you were?—*OR* — — ¹ have you again the manie to cast upon the last 8 weeks the studies that are expected to produce fruits from 8 months? c.à.d.—not to begin seriously preparing for your *rentreè* in Cambridge till September instead of sharing the preparation with *occasional* pleasures & interruptions from March?

My poor dear Alex!—are you never aware how Time flies—& how it carries Youth upon its Wings?—

Answer all this, I beg! you are now your own Master, from our unavoidable absence: do not make the misfortunes which separate us disgrace as well as sorrow!

Remember, too, what you have told me a name & a fame might do for you!

Let me now resume my account of your dearest Father.

July 12ᵗʰ I was interrupted,—& now am told now of an opportunity of sending to England that requires my Letter in half an hour au plus tard. I will not let want of diligence lose it: Imitate my alacrity, & write immediately; but READ my late Letters, & ANSWER them, before a single Verse runs away with you.

I am charmed to hear from Fanny Raper's kind intelligence you are at length at Richmond.[5]

All hope is again alive for universal peace! yet all depends upon the fate of Buonaparte; therefore I uneasily await what that may be. Your dear Father has all this time been kept at

---

⁴ Like that of 24 May (mentioned by FBA in L. 896, pp. 233–4), in which Alex had told of his attraction to his cousin 'Sally', JB's daughter (i, p. lxx), 'an angel upon Earth'.
⁵ In a letter dated 15 June (L. 909 n. 8).

Treves: which I deem a real hardship, at a moment when, one of the most faithful subjects of La Maison du Roi, he ought to have been summoned to escort the King, in common with his comrades, into the capital. I think there must have been some cruel neglect, or mistake in this business yet he has written repeatedly for permission to join the King! some say the Minister at War, M. le Duc de Feltre, though an excellent & really worthy man, has been too much disturbed to have the composure necessary for such abundant avocation. It is possible he has omitted some order that ought to have been given. Your dear Father writes me word his patience is exhausted, & ¹ his Companions, M. le Comte de Mazancourt,⁶ his adjoint, & his aid de Camp, M. de Premorel, & the other volunteer officer, are all so *triste* at their situation, that nothing less than their born & bred severity of military discipline & order could keep them from gallopping off to join their Corps.

I have no news yet of our affairs at Paris, you may suppose: but as the King is there, & the post is to open in a day or two, I hope soon to know the fate of All—*CHIEFLY* of the Mss. I hope our dwelling was so private, & our way of life so tranquil, that we shall not have been marked: But B[uonaparte] passed a decree, about a month ago, of confiscation to every officer [de] la Maison du Roi who did not re-enter France; & even of military trial—& punishment!—

Imagine how I was struck, when, at the time of the late most alarming Invasion of the Pays bas, & during the horrible Battle which for 4 complete days were fighting within Canon shot of us—imagine, I say, how I was struck, while waiting at the English commandant's, Colonel Jones's, for a signature to my passport, for running away to Antwerp, I saw a young man enter, who addressed the secretary for 'a *billet of residence for Captain Burney!*'—⁷

I started, & immediately made enquiry who he meant. He answered 'Captain Burney, m'aam,' in English; still more astonished, & almost thunderstruck, I made so many questions,

---

⁶ See L. 868 n. 2.

⁷ William Burney (1793–1879) was then a captain in the 44th (or East Essex) Regiment of Foot, whose 2nd Battalion fought at Waterloo. Burney, a youthful veteran of Italian and Peninsular campaigns, who had already been wounded twice at Quatre Bras, later served in the Burmese War, transferred as a major to the Cape Mounted Rifles from 1834 to 1844, when he retired on full pay, and was finally promoted colonel in 1854.

& so rapidly, & with so much uneasiness, that the Person, surprised also, left the secretary to come & give me a minute account: & I then learnt Captain Burney was a land officer, of the 44th Regiment, whose Friends lived at Portsmouth. He had a billet sent him for one of the first houses in Bruxelles. He had been wounded in the head.

A few days after, a Lady—Made de Maurville, came to me *de la part* de Made la Baronne de Spagen,[8] to say how happy she should be to receive me at her house, if I would visit my Relation, just fixed with her, & wounded in the victory of the Duke of Wellington. I answered that I could not but be happy to know such a Relation, if such a one I had; but that I had been told by my Brother, Dr Charles, there was no affinity between us: *OUR* family [1] coming from *Ireland,* where we were among the *MACS:*[9] & *his* being English. He did not care, however, to give the point up, &, after various manoeuvres, I accompanied Me de Maurville to the Baronne's. I found him a very pleasing young man, sensible, conversible, manly, yet modest. He is but 22. A bullet has been cut of his head, which has been *flattened,* in one part, by his skull! such was the force with which it had entered. His escape has been narrow indeed. He came to see me, with Made la Baronne, immediately after & I have again returned the visit, & again received them. And I shall now this night—this moment, indeed, post to La place Royale[10] with this sheet for my Alex. The young man is so amiable, I could wish you to know him. The good Baronne is so pleased with him, she carries him about with her every where, as if he were her son. She has 2 other young wounded English officers with her, the Messrs *Shenley,* Brothers,[11] & Both under Twenty! One will, I fear, be a Cripple for life: he has no patience, & hops about upon his Crutches as if he were dancing to make sport. He is not yet 17! — — the other, who is 19, is a pattern of prudence in *comparison!* My young Captain will return in

---

[8] Joséphine-Hortense de Spangen *née* de la Fons de la Plesnoye (*c.* 1775–1835) was the second wife—her own sister had been the first—of Charles-Joseph de Spangen (1763–1824), whom she had married in 1807. See also L. 924 n. 208.

[9] See Scholes, 'Antecedents', i. 1–3.

[10] Site of Brussels' main post office.

[11] William Shenley (1799–1853), then a second lieutenant in the 1st Battalion of the 95th Regiment of Foot, remained on army service despite his crippling injury until he retired on half-pay in 1828.

Godfrey Shenley (1796–*c.* 1860), a first lieutenant in the 95th's 3rd Battalion, was to retire on half-pay at the end of 1818.

2 months if quite restored. He is *apparently* quite recovered now, but he has des etourdiss⟨ements⟩ very alarming. Oh what a dreadful business has this monster of ambition made for thousands! The wounded are *still arriving*!—many were—& *are* too badly mangled for removal sooner, & m[a]ny still remain, in all the farms & cottages ⟨&⟩ villages. Adieu, my ever dear Alex—write *quite* by yourself, that *your sister* may see your [*tear*] heart—& may *answer* as well as write! Adieu—adieu— always [direc]t *Bruxelles*—My Letters [wi]ll be safe at the post office if I remove, [as I] send for them—

918   [1358, Marché au bois],
                                 Brussels, 10–12 July 1815

To James Burney

A.L.S. (PML, Autog. Cor. bound), 10–12 July 1815
Double sheet 4to   4 pp.   *pmks* GOSPORT/⟨ ⟩ JY ⟨1815⟩   25 JY 1815   wafer
Addressed: Captain Burney, R.N. / James Street, / Westminster. / 26

Bruxelles, July 10ᵗʰ 1815.

Little as I am habituated to the liberality of giving two Letters—(or even, I am afraid! One Letter)—for one, I am indebted to my dear Brother for so much more solid kindness than Epistolary punctuality, that I will not let an opportunity of again thanking him pass gracelessly by. Besides, if Letters are to be considered in their best light, i.e. as marks of Friendship,—how many have you not written me—of late—without holding a Pen? I would not exchange, for Value, your hospitality & kindness to my Alexander, for the best collection of Epistles left by Cicero, Pliny, or even Madame de Sevigné. Nor is even this the only way in which my heart has received, & welcomed, the *Billet doux* which my Eyes have never read: that same Alex has given me a *trait* of your truly brotherly feelings upon the harsh treatment given to my poor Wanderer,[1] in nearly the only DIFFICULTY in which I had not myself involved her, that came home to my bosom, which silently, but warmly, even from this distance, embraced you, my dear James. Nevertheless, sincerely as I am sensible to your animation in favour of this my youngest Child, I am myself gifted, happily, with a most impenetrable apathy upon the subject of its criticisers. I have never read, nor chanced to meet with one word upon the subject. I never expected it would have any immediate favour in the World; & I have not yet shut out from my spying Glass a distant prospect that it may share, in a few years, the partiality shewn to its Elder sisters. Much was against its chances upon its first coming out. There is no such Foe to public success at high Expectation, though there is no such Friend to personal emolument. And Here, [1] Expectation was founded upon Impossibilities, or Improprieties: half the Public expected, from my long residence in France, Political anecdotes, or opinions, & the other half expected, from the title of the Work & my own unsettled life, The History of the Author. The first Volume, nevertheless, was received by the reigning Critical Judges, with almost unbounded applause;— Sir James Macintosh;[2] Lord Holland; Mᵉ de Stael; Sir S. Romilly, Lord Byron, Mr. Godwin,[2]—& others whose names I do not recollect, sung its panegyric: but THEN, the illusion of their own fancies was not over; one party was not yet quite sure That the Wanderer might not still appear in the Writer: or, rather, the Writer in the Wanderer; & the other, had not yet lost all hope that the scene would change to The Continent,[3]

918. [1] After reading Hazlitt's review of *The Wanderer* in the *Edinburgh Review* (February 1815), James Burney cut short his friendship with Hazlitt in a letter (printed in Manwaring, p. 250):

May 17th, 1815.

Sir,

It would be strange, if not wrong, after years of intimate acquaintance, that cause of offence should happen between us, and be so taken, and be passed over in silence, and that acquaintance still continue. Your attack on my Sister's early publications disatisfied me, and the more in coming from a quarter I had been in the habit of believing friendly. If I had seen it before publication, I should have remonstrated against some of your remarks, because I think them unjust. Your publication of such a paper showed a total absence of regard towards me, and I must consider it as the termination of our acquaintance.

[2] Those who in 1814 saw advance copies of *The Wanderer* include Lord Byron, Sir James Mackintosh, Lord Holland, Sir Samuel Romilly, and Mme de Staël. See vii, L. 706 n. 2; L. 718 n. 14; L. 744 n. 3; and L. 754 n. 7. Here added to the list so favoured is William Godwin (1756–1836), author of *Political Justice* (1793).

[3] In writing *The Wanderer* in London in 1813–14 when England and France

& bring the Reader into the midst of the political bustle. The second volume undeceived both parties: & THENCE began a Disappointment which,—*I HOPE*, carried with it a propensity to be displeased through the rest of the Work. Time only can shew the Flattery, or the reality of this idea. If it be true, some future eminent Reader, who, some years hence, shall take it in hand, without any reference, or even knowledge of the circumstances attending its first publication, & who will read, therefore, without prepared prejudice, or partiality, will pronounce '*This is the Genuine*—' Or—'*This is a Spurious* sister of the Young Damsels who were previously honoured with public approbation.'⁴

I ought not, also, to omit another point that has made against any immediate success in Fame—& that is, its immediate success in profit. There can be no doubt that the Bookseller's price did not more widely raise Expectation & Curiosity, than Enmity & Jealousy.

All these concomitant matters, however, will die—& the Book will either Revive, or Expire from the cool & unbiassed judgement of those who may read it, without thinking of its Critics; or even of its Author, hereafter.

If, at the same time, the First vol. had not met with such favour, when seen by *Stealth*, & ere the Plan of the Work, or the Premium of the publishers ¹ were known, I should not encourage this notion. But I think nobody, impartially, will pronounce The First Volume to be the Best — — Ergo — —

But enough; I should not have entered thus largely upon this egoistic subject had not the interest taken in it by my dear James repeatedly reached me. And, I have been writing so long, & so many Letters upon the state of affairs here, that I am not sorry to be called to some other topic; & the less, as a laconic statement up to the moment will save you from reading, or hearing a repetition of all my other Letters.

A Lady—the princess d'Henin,—has this instant—*July 12ᵗʰ* —called to tell me that an 'Express arrived here last Night from

were still at war and d'Arblay still employed in Paris, the author could risk no statements dangerous to him or to herself as a future resident there. Far from a critique of France, the novel is an attack on the illiberalism of the British towards foreigners, one cause for the disappointment in it. Some of the experiences of the French heroine Juliet in England, FBA must have seen her husband suffer in the years 1793–1801. ⁴ FBA's earlier novels *Evelina, Cecilia,* and *Camilla.*

Paris, with an account that all was well & quiet in that extraordinary Capital; that Buonaparte was gone off, nobody could, or *would*, say certainly whither; that he had *himself* desired an application might be made to Lord Wellington for his *passport*, & *sauvegarde*, but that Lord Wellington answered "That to The Man against whom he came to make War, he would certainly grant neither; too many brave men having already been sacrificed in his Defeat, to suffer an English Soldier to risk the loss of even ONE more of his Brave comrades by a future contest." The King, Louis 18. has new modelled the ministry,[5] by a sort of *amalgamation* absolutely indispensable for entering the Metropolis without Blood shed. Mar¹ Gauvion de Sᵗ Cyr[6] is made minister of War, in the place of the Duke de Feltre,—a worthy man, of Irish descent, but who is not thought equal to the dangers & difficulties of such a moment as the present. The rest you will have in the News papers; or perhaps have already; for I am told courriers are sent across the dear protecting *Ditch* daily. *Fouché* has been obliged to be guarded, for it is thought there could be no security against the rest of the Jacobin administration, without one of the Band, who could avert, by knowing their wiles & their snares. Talyrand, who is accounted the strongest Headed man in France, is prime minister. M. de Jaucourt,[7] who was also ¹ at Juniper, is at the head of the Marine. M. Louis continues with the Finance.[8]

---

[5] The new ministry created on 8 July removed most of the extreme royalists from the cabinet and excluded the princes from its deliberations. They were replaced by moderates, many of whom had been born into the senatorial class and advanced under revolutionary and imperial administrations (Bertier de Sauvigny, pp. 116–17).

[6] Laurent Gouvion-Saint-Cyr (1764–1830), comte (1808) and then marquis de (1817), left his early life as a painter in Paris to enlist in 1792, after which he rose from the ranks to hold numerous commands in the Armies of the Rhine and Italy. He served as both ambassador and general in Spain and became a marshal early in the Russian campaign of 1812. During the campaign of 1813 he was captured at Dresden and returned to France in 1814 after the First Restoration of Louis XVIII, who made him a peer and gave him command of an army that was meant to campaign against Napoleon from its base at Orléans. But his troops refused to follow his orders and Saint-Cyr waited on events until after Waterloo. Louis XVIII made him minister of war in succession to the duc de Feltre: he held this post from 8 July until 25 Sept. 1815, and then again from 1817 until 1819.

[7] See L. 862 n. 20.

[8] Joseph-Dominique Louis (1755–1837) was a laicized abbé who became French minister to Denmark in the early days of the Revolution. Forced to flee to England in 1791, he returned to France in 1800. Created baron de l'Empire in 1809 and in 1811, a conseiller d'État, he became Louis XVIII's finance minister in 1814, when his stringent economic policies did much to restore French credit. But the reductions in the army and bureaucracy brought about by these policies created a large and

Le Duc de Richelieu is minister of the Interior.[9] We make YOU a present of M. de Blacas![10] And beg you to be in no hurry to send him back.

My better half—for I subscribe willingly to your so naming him—is still at Treves—or *was*, when he wrote last, July 5ᵗʰ There is no direct communication thence with Brussels, which cruelly separates us from news of each other. What will be his next destination—or whether any—I know not.

This will be carried over to England by a namesake of ours, though not of our family.[11] But he is amiable as well as brave, & has so much desire to belong to us, that I hardly know how not to think myself his Relation when I hear him called by my *ci-devant* name. He was wounded in the 2ᵈ Day's action, the 16ᵗʰ, & carries over the Bullet that was cut out of his head, as a present to his Father—to whom, *so* brought, it will surely be a most welcome one. He is but 22, yet a Captain, in the 44ᵗʰ Regiment. If you happen to see, I am *sure* you will be pleased with him. His family is settled at Portsmouth, & he has 2 months congé, from the giddiness left in his head since the Wound. He is modest, sensible, & unaffected.

I hope, my dear Brother, you have urged your tardy, too reluctant Guest, to Richmond & his Studies? I am a little uneasy lest he adopts a life of mere pleasure & amusement, though without such an intention. My family & friends are almost *too* kind to him! though he, like his favourite Uncle, will perhaps cry 'Hush, Mammy, hush! They SHOULD be too kind!—'

dangerous group who welcomed Napoleon's return from Elba. Louis, who struck his contemporaries as able, brutal, and utterly absorbed in matters of finance, was restored to this portfolio after the Hundred Days and finally held it once again under Louis-Philippe.

⁹ Armand-Emmanuel du Plessis (1767–1822), duc de Richelieu, was born into the high aristocracy and had barely begun a military career when the Revolution broke out. He emigrated to join Condé's army in October of 1789, but in the following year entered Russian service and rose to become Governor of the Crimea. He returned to France only in 1814, when Louis XVIII made him First Gentleman of the Bedchamber. During the Hundred Days he followed the King to Lille, whence he was sent to Vienna as commissaire du Roi with the Czar and his army. He refused to replace Blacas, not wanting to be associated with Fouché, but he later replaced Talleyrand in September and became head of the ministry that brought France into the Holy Alliance and condoned the White Terror. Although a rigid man, Richelieu's sense of honour and probity attracted trust from others, especially from the foreign leaders that France then so depended upon, and he played an important role in freeing his country from the disastrous consequences of defeat and foreign occupation.　　　　　　　　　　¹⁰ See L. 847 n. 2 and L. 903 n. 4.

¹¹ Captain William Burney (L. 917 n. 7).

My best love to dear Mrs. Burney, & to Sally: & to *Martin*, when he has executed my commission!

Adieu, my dear Brother—ever & aye in all truth & affection
Yours FB d'A.

Oh,—how do I long to have again a home!—This Revolutionary manner of existence is fatiguing, affrighting, & consuming. ¹

P.S. You will believe how I long for news from my Paris home! of our Goods & Chattels in general — — & my various MSS. in particular. No letters yet pass. ¹

919   [1358, Marché au bois],
                       Brussels, 10–13 July 1815

To M. d'Arblay

A.L. (rejected Diary MSS. 6672–5, Berg), 10–13 July 1815
Double sheet 4to   4 pp.   *pmk* BRUXELLES   wafer
Addressed: à *Treves*. / M. le Général d'Arblay, / officier superieur des gardes / du Corps de sa M. Le / Roi de France, / Chev^r de St. Louis, &c &c &c / à Treves
Edited by FBA, p. 1 (6672), *annotated*: ⊞   (21/2)
Edited at the Press. *See* Textual Notes.

⌐N.B. REMEMBER not *Poste Restante*
⟨& please!⟩ *Remember* ⟨day OR⟩ *date* on Letters!⌐¹

Ce Lundi, 10. de Juillet
Bruxelles, 1815.

Croyez vous, donc, mon bien aimé ami! croyez vous qu'une Lettre comme celle que je viens de reçevoir² aujourdhui is calculated to make me repent that I have been willing to run some little risk—nay, ANY, the greatest, to be near you in case of accident or distress? To see a solicitude for your poor Athanase so similar to her own for you—ah, my dearest ami—that

919.   ¹ The mails arrived in Brussels in the early morning, and letters directed to local addresses were delivered at once. Those directed to *poste restante* were kept back for sorting, thereby causing a delay that FBA is here trying to avoid (see Romberg, pp. 107–8).
        ² L. 906.

is not the way you must take to lead her to seek eleswhere than in You, in You alone, for happiness—!—But how I grieve, GRIEVE to look forward to the chasm you will find in my Letters through the unfortunate mis-direction of Namur! ⌐Two posts past but can the Letter of 2 ⟨Sun⟩ be lost—& now there is a post again to Trèves to-morrow on the 13th—That post goes but 3 times a week so that there are *3 days* between its passing once, & 2 Days the other times. I foresee how you will again be disappointed with much pain.⌐

I have been enquiring about your Collegues, & have just learnt That M. de Castris[3] did *not* return to Namur: he accompanied the King into France. M. d'Auvergne,[4] also, attended him from Mons. But I have been able to pick up no other intelligence.

⌐I have written to you at full length to Namur all I can cull from our Letters relative to your Beau Cheval. I will soon copy the same paragon Horse here & on t'other side.

I give you some portion also of Alex's Letter⌐

Hélas,—my too partial ami! how have you conceived me to be so piously employed as to run a danger of infection from les *pauvres blessés?*—the little I have been able to do was without risk—it was only for those who were *maimed*, & without fever. None came hither, which I much regret, as then, I should certainly better have merited your kind idea. All I have met with, or tried to serve, have ǀ been in other houses. How they have had exemption here, I know not. With regard to the dreadful Battle, Lord Wellington has been asked, whether he really found Buonaparte so superior to other Generals as to merit his reputation? *COMPLETELY!* he answered, he had never, he said, met with such an opponent, nor with any one that resembled him. It was far the hardest victory he had ever won—though, as yet, he has never lost a Battle. But here, he found so much to do, & was frequently in such great danger of being worsted, that he lost all sort of caution for himself, in the fervour of his zeal, gallopping up & down in the heat of the action, from Regiment to Regiment, Cannon Balls flying round his head, & envellopped by the smoak. Yet never a moment losing his *sang-froid*, which is said—at such junctions, & joined to such energies, to be almost supernatural. He most

[3] See L. 888 n. 24.   [4] See L. 900 n. 6.

handsomely says, in his own account of the Battle sent to London, that the timely arrival of Bulow[5] would have prevented Buona[parte] from reaping any advantage in *advancing,* even had he been *vainqueur*: & it was to that arrival that Lord W[ellington] owed the mighty courage that gave the mighty effort by which the Battle was so stupendously, so completely, so brightly won! for when Lord W. saw that a reinforcement was at hand, which, in case of failure—i.e. of a retort in kind,— would cover his retreat—it was then, & instantly, That, after seeming the whole time upon the defensive, though never giving ground, he ordered that unheard of UNIVERSAL attack, from all points at once, That ǀ utterly confounded the Enemy, astonished him off his guard, frightened away all presence of mind for rallying, & caused an instantaneous, tumultuous, & most disorderly flight—which not a man resisted!—not an officer attempted to controll—B—himself was drawn away with the tide, &, leaving behind all his Baggage, Equîpage, War materials, & even his personals, he re-crossed, no one knows how, or under what disguise, the Barriers, & then ran off to Paris. Voilà a 2ᵈ time he illustrates Hudibras's notion of Combatting![6] He who fights & runs away—&c

Tuesday, July 11ᵗʰ

How cruelly this *Namur* direction will thwart our correspondance. I wrote Thither all about the *Beau Cheval,*[7] which here I copy again—and I called for your PERFECT *approbation* of a measure I took to please you; since my staying here, watching & waiting, Hoping & Fearing, & ALL absorbed in my dear perverse Better half—(who would have me AWAY at the very moment, that, if absent, would have brought me back!—) But since that, you say, you cannot thank me for— Thank me at least, as my Namur Letter will ⟨convey⟩ That I conquered my *sauvagerie,* &c- &c. &c. & waited upon Me de Laval[8]—& spent 2 or 3 Hours with her very satisfactorily & agreeably. She returned my visit immediately. I did ditto. She ditto again—& again I, ditto, this Morning. Her conver-

---

⁵ Bülow's Fourth Corps was the first Prussian force to intervene at Waterloo. They were first sighted at one o'clock as they advanced toward the battlefield from Chapelle-Saint-Lambert to the north-east.
⁶ Cf. L. 907, p. 277.
⁷ See L. 913, p. 305.
⁸ See also L. 913, p. 302.

sation is really charming. | I consulted with her upon your position. She saw its delicacy, & could not pronounce. Without that Letter of M. de Rochechouart, to tell you *you should receive directions*, there can be no doubt you might come away, & join the King. M. de Castre⁹ did not return to Namur; even the Garrison, there, they tell me, is breaking up, as useless. M. de Castre went with the King—so did M. d'Auvergne, from Mons.⁹ But of all the others I can gain no tydings. Nor yet that Lille is *our's*.¹⁰ ⌐I do not write about B[eau] Cheval *en attendant*. But if I hear any contrary I will write totally.⌐ Helas, this last *alertie* has occasioned more *weening* of cordiality, all around, than ever!—¹¹ How unhappy must be the state of social intercourse in Paris! All agree that it will be the most fearful place of residence, from different sides taken by Friends, & in Families, for many years in the whole Universe. No news from Paris is arrived since that of the King's *entrée*! which was only on Saturday—& Alas! *with* the Allies! There was no other security. I have another Letter from Alex, dated *June 2ᵈ*!! ⌐The naughty Boy after all my exhortations was still in James Street!!! But I have since, in a Letter from Fanny Raper, dated June 28ᵗʰ, heard he was gone *on a visit* to Mʳˢ Broome!!

Tuesday 10 at night. July 11ᵗʰ I am Just told Lord Wellington has written to invite the Dˢˢᵉ of Richmond¹² to Paris, to be present at the ⟨*Court*⟩ *du Roi*, which is to take place while all the sovereigns are there. You are right to be attached to M. de B[eaufort]¹³ for he is very much attached to you. But you often surprise me by lamenting his loss as if it was that of a real bosom partner. Was there any appearance, during Life, of such an affection? on *her* part, she had certainly proved there *had* been that warm preference, but even on hers, *I* fancied it was worn out. Probably by disappointment from some⌐ fond dream. It was called here an exceeding good *menage*, because he was always polite ⌐& sometimes affectionate—*I* miss her extremely.

---

⁹ The commissaires Castries and La Tour d'Auvergne (nn. 3, 4 *supra*).

¹⁰ Lille held out through the summer, though unlike most of the other French fortresses it was being held for the King and neither besieged nor assaulted (Houssaye, *1815*, iii. 500 n. 3).

¹¹ Napoleon's threatening advance on Brussels caused the different factions among the French to keep on ostensibly good terms until the issue was decided.

¹² See L. 895 n. 2.

¹³ See L. 872 nn. 3, 6.

To me she was regularly good & partial. He was very *un-affectedly* concerned at her death! & therefore respectably. He has certainly lost a Friend never to be replaced; but if he has appeared to have lost a Friend of his Heart, his grief w^d have appeared hypocritical. & yet—he grows MORE—not less sad—from what feeling, or what cause, I know not. Nobody mentions her will.⌐¹³

⌐It appears to me that you have always written my most kind Ami—& that the Post alone has been in fault on either side. How I thank you! oh—how has it now disappointed me! I thought you once more restored ⟨to me⟩ when comes⟨ ⟩⌐

⌐July 13 Bon Jour!—a bien Bon jour!—⌐

[xxxxx 1 *line*]

[*At the bottom of page 3 of the above letter Madame d'Arblay relayed reports she had received on one of d'Arblay's horses*]

LE BEAU CHEVAL

avril 8

⌐Mr. de G. M.¹⁴

Auguste¹⁵ est revenu sans votre cheval. Il l'a laissé à Lille, chez l'artiste veterinaire le Sr Pommeret,¹⁶ rue St Caterine, N⁰ 96, p^r le guérir du vertige dont il a été atteint.¹⁷ Il m'a montré un certificat tout en regle, de l'artiste, visé pour la légalisation de la signature par le maire, et pour la ⟨verité du⟩ fait par le Gen¹ Dijon.¹⁸ Vous de ⟨ ⟩ de ⟨ ⟩ à Lille p^r le reclamer. Il a été deposé sous votre nom, comme

---

¹⁴ Unidentified.

¹⁵ See L. 857 n. 2.

¹⁶ Unidentified.

¹⁷ M. d'A's 'Beau Cheval' would seem to be one left behind at Lille during the forced marches of the household troops. Later in the summer of 1815, in a letter addressed to the minister of War, he justified his claims for arrears in pay and allowances by explaining, 'Malgré la perte que j'avais faite à Bethune de tout mon equipage, J'ai eu constamment à Treves deux Domestiques, une voiture et 5 chevaux qui avec celui retiens à Lille d'où je n'avais point faire venir composaient les 6 accordés à mon grade.' (M. d'A to [the comte Gouvion-Saint-Cyr], Vincennes, 11 Sept. 1815.)

¹⁸ Armand-Joseph-Henri Digeon (1778–1836), baron (1817), an artillery general who distinguished himself during Napoleon's campaigns in Germany, Italy, and Spain. During the First Restoration he was appointed lieutenant in the Gardes du Corps (on 24 June 1814). After the King's flight from Paris, during which he commanded part of the artillery, Digeon returned to France from the Belgian border and did not resume his post with the household troops until 1 July 1815. It is a curious, but in the light of this passage possibly a significant feature of his military career that in 1808 he was involved in irregularities concerning the purchase of horses (Six, i. 358 col. 1).

⟨vous   ⟩. Pour peu que vous le caissier, le traitm^t et la nourriture absorberont sa valeur.

Après, Avril 26.

Mr de G. M. dit 'votre cheval est Guéri. Sr Pommeret vient d'écrire qu'il allait le renvoyer ⟨   ⟩ p^r l'occasion je vous prévient que ⟨   ⟩ je le fait vendre de suite, attendu que les frais qu'il occasion croit absorber sa valeur.' [xxxxx ½ *line*]

Auguste, à un passage à Lille, laisse dans cette ville le beau cheval malade. Il fut confié a un Sr Pommeret, lequel en est ⟨   ⟩ de Bruxelles ⟨   ⟩ demander c'est un M^r ⟨Legendre Officier⟩ qui l'a remis entre les mains de l'artiste Pommeret.⊓

920   [1358, Marché au bois],
                    Brussels, 13–14 July [1815]

To M. d'Arblay

A.L. (Berg), 13 July
Double sheet 4to   4 pp.   *pmk*   BRUXELLES   wafer
Addressed: *Treves*. / à Monsieur / Monsieur le General d'Arblay, / Officier Superieur des Gardes du Corps / de Sa Majesty le Roi de France, / Chev^r de St Louis, &c &c &c / à Treves.
Edited by FBA, p. 1, *annotated and dated*: 1815   (23/1)
See Textual Notes.

ce Jeudi
Bruxelles July 13th

Instantly, & without one moment of hesitation, would I comply with your kind desire, & plant myself in some neighbouring village, but that all here, since I wrote the Letter which has given you the idea, is altered. The *Roi des pays bas* addressed a request to Lord Wellington relative to the sick, whether English or Enemy; & now, both one & the other are moved to England as speedily as it is possible. ⌐I think, & hope, I have written you this in Letters you must ere now have received.⊓

Indeed mon Ami,—your having no Letter of recall, or of

direction, I think, now, inexcusable, where ever the blame may lie.[1] Who more merited a summons to attend the King upon his *entrée*? ⌐My account of de Boinville's Letter is, I suppose, at Namur!—but *he* now gives no *positive* advice, & contradicts his own opinion in his second note. Now, however, his doubt is at an end.¬ M. le D. de Feltre is no longer *Ministre de la Guerre* & all of the few people I see & speak to here, think you may come away immediately;—only first writing, with all the forms, to the New Minister,[2] to acquaint him with the uselessness of your position, with your vain efforts to be heard by his predecessor, & of your claims of payment.

⌐Perhaps, also, it might be more EXACT to wait one post for his advice —— yet to what purpose? He may be told as well to direct it hither, I should suppose.¬

Gouvion de St. Cyr is the New Minister.[2]

M. de Feltre is not disgraced: he has some other post.[3]

M. de Jaucourt has the Marine: M. Louis[4] still the Finance; [Fouché] to the Police (remember your divination!)[5] *Molé*[6] & *Pasquier*[7] are ˥ [Ministers, though] I forget how:—but what

920.   [1] The Vincennes archives include a list of *commissaires* (C[14] 60) drawn up at Ghent in May, that may help to explain why M. d'A was so often ignored during this period. Both his name and the number corresponding to his name on the list are omitted. Since this list was used by Rochechouart and his staff to send out circulars and general instructions, M .d'A received only letters sent to him personally, such as the one from Rochechouart (mentioned in L. 904) that promised him a new posting and new orders after the Battle of Waterloo.

   [2] Minister of War (see L. 918 n. 6).

   [3] See L. 860 n. 2.

   [4] See L. 918 nn. 7, 8.

   [5] The missing name is Fouché. M. d'A was gloomily impressed by his powers of survival and success, and this new appointment seemed to confirm the fears expressed in L. 904.

   [6] Mathieu-Louis Molé (1781–1855), comte de l'Empire (1809), a politician, administrator, and writer who was first brought to public notice through his *Essai de morale et de politique* (1806). He was presented to Napoleon, who in that year (1806) appointed him to the Conseil d'État in the advisory roles of 'auditeur' and 'maître des requêtes'. A devoted supporter of Napoleon and his dynasty, he accepted appointments as conseiller d'État (1809) and minister of Justice (1813). Though created a peer during the Hundred Days, he refused to sign a declaration against the Bourbons and withdrew to take the waters at Plombières. He was made a cabinet minister (ponts et chaussées) in the announced appointments FBA refers to here and was made navy minister in 1817. Throughout his long career Molé wrote with shrewd partiality about both men and policies and his memoirs—*Le Comte Molé . . ., sa vie, ses mémoires* (6 vols., 1922–30)—give a vivid picture of both his personality and his prejudices.

   [7] Étienne-Denis Pasquier (1767–1862), baron (1821) and duc (1844), was a conseiller au parlement in 1787, a prisoner under the Terror, conseiller d'État under Napoleon, and prefect of police (1810–14). During the first Restoration he held the portfolio of ponts et chaussées and after the return from Ghent that of garde des sceaux. He became président of the Chamber of Deputies in 1816 and

ALL parties must decide to be right, that wish not for new troubles, Le Duc de Richlieu[8] is placed in the palace in the place of M. de Blacas.

But oh—dissentions already are brewing! Heaven send the fermentation to be stopt in its first rise! The prussians are said to demand the demolition of Le pont de Yena![9]—of its *NAME* they have reason to complain, & it ought to be changed—but of the Bridge!—

And Lord Wellington, in the Capitulation, articled the preservation of all monuments of art. They say he opposes the demand.

If it be granted, the Austrians may demolish *Austrelitz*[10]— And where may demolition end?

⌐Nobody can tell me anything of your Colleagues: but why should you not write to them? *Deux Ponts* is so near![11] That might be your best direction.

I have not yet heard of anyone who has received Letters by post from France—when I do, I will write to our dear Uncle.[12]

I have *nam'ed* him in a letter to Me Deprez,[13] that I entrusted to Me de Laval, who will send it by her own man. And I have charged her (Me Deprez) to give me news immediately of all lost. And to go in our joint names with thanks to M^e de G[rand] M[aison][14] & M. Le N[oir][15] & to give me the address of Me de Mais[onneuve]—for malheureusement I know not how to write to her without such intelligence.⌐

Ah—how diminished ENCORE is our already so straightened

---

remained thereafter one of the leaders (Molé was another) of the opposition to royalist extremism.

⁸ See L. 918 n. 9.
⁹ Prussian threats to destroy the Pont d'Iéna, named after Napoleon's crushing victory over them in 1806, became a great scandal of Paris in the early days of foreign occupation. According to one first-hand witness, Louis XVIII at first offered to rename the bridge 'Pont de l'École militaire', but when Blücher refused this solution, the King gave up attempts at compromise and said that he would if necessary be blown up with the offending bridge (Reiset, iii. 245–6).
¹⁰ The Austrians and Russians did not seem to have such destructive plans for the Pont d'Austerlitz, which commemorated their defeat in 1805. The Czar summed up their attitude by saying it was enough for him to have passed over it with his troops (Reiset, iii. 247).
¹¹ Otherwise Zweibrücken, south-west of Kaiserslautern. A commissaire had also been posted there (L. 896 n. 2).
¹² Gabriel Bazille (cf. L. 913 n. 11). For the Russian invasion of Yonne and 'The Occupation of Joigny', see vii, Appendix III.
¹³ See L. 846 n. 1.
¹⁴ See L. 855 n. 4.
¹⁵ See L. 840 n. 24.

328

set of friends!—⌐M. de la F[ayette]—M. de Beau[vau] and family! M. de Maub[ourg]—*à hélas!*¬ And what contestations, what querelous doubts & want of confidence far wider will spread!

HERE it is difficult to speak! and more than you can conceive! —ah mon ami! how good always, but how VERY apropos is the great kindness of your Letter of this morning,¹⁶ for I am sick with *disgust* & *affright* at some conversation ¹ which preceded its arrival. Clouds—clouds—if not of danger, at least of ill-will, are hovering still in the air—& Egotism still swallows every grain of public spirit. Yet always with false constructions & raisonnemens, that paint the most pernicious selfishness in the light of virtue & liberality!

How I sigh to join you once more, my dearest ami! Two whole months have finished this Day since you left me!

Our Alex is inconceivably tormenting. His last letter but one pleased me infinitely; his last of all ⌐contains nothing worth inspecting. It¬ is almost wholly a string of quotations from different poets!—⌐not opened or introduced with any reference to what he means to say, or to imply, & apropos to nothing, copied from printed Books! He was still at James Street, which greatly vexes me; though one Letter, of the 6ᵗʰ of June, from Fanny Raper, says he was *then* at Richmond: on a *visit* to Mrs. Broome. I had begged he might have a nest of his own! a visit of such a length, & when he ought to be master of his time, that he may resume his studies, is quite out of the question. I have just written to him again & warmly represented the impropriety of such a way of *hanging* upon his relatives & Friends, especially as he had so well seen that it would be wrong, & in searching himself, in the Letter we received, the unhappy, but dear forever dear 9ᵗʰ of May, just before our departure! for certain is he a child!—I told you that would happen—¬

They say Mᵐᵉ La Dˢˢ d'Angoulême has printed, en angle-terre, the most superb proclamation upon the Entrée de Roi, that has yet appeared.¹⁷

¹⁶ Probably the touching L. 914, which included M. d'A's reproaches against those whose conduct was prompted by 'egoisme et calculs purement personnels'.
¹⁷ The editors have not been able to find any such proclamation by the duchesse d'Angoulême. It does not appear among the lengthy reports of speeches and de-clarations concerning the King's entry into Paris carried by the English news-papers (viz. *The Times* of 13 July).

Why is my dear Ami thus dispirited by the [*tear*] negligence of others? Is it HE is to blame that he stays ⌐ for orders which he is told will be sent him without delay? You made me smile from Ear to Ear when, after that *élan* which says how well you *merit my tenderness*, you add that, *nevertheless*, I shall call you *un fat* for saying so!—If I *doubted* it, (your *merit*,) you could not possess it! *cependant*—I am horribly anxious to know whether this *élan* is the bursting forth of self applause upon any near, or particular occasion that deserves my greatest joy[18]—or whether it is only the bursting forth of general self applause—that is of All & every part of your late procedure?

Will you tell me *which*? *I* pray! when you have time, & *bonnement*. Meanwhile, be it which it may, *ma tendresse*, mon cher Ami⌐ is YOURS with the whole of my heart, and the whole of my Existence so help me God!—

I have an account to give you of a new acquaintance, a Belgian lady, whom I like very much. Mad^e de Spagen.

I heard yesterday our good M. Larrey was taken prisoner by the Prussians & is now at *Louvain*,[19] attending the wounded who are there! Poor M. Larrey! He has been, for some consultation, The p^ss told me, at Bruxelles! I would I had seen [him.] I am at least truly glad his valuable life is safe. He was in this last bloody conflict!

oui! mon beloved ami, oui! *conservons nous l'un pour l'autre!*— amen! amen![20]

⌐I do write *bits* every day, but the post goes only 3ce a week. Pray leave precise orders that y^r letters may be safe that come, ⟨held⟩ onto for you.⌐ I have very singularly made a new male friend, as well as the Female I have mentioned—a very pleasing young English officer,[21] I am sure you would like him. ⌐

⌐By the greatest good luck I have required no money—I

---

[18] FBA is guardedly asking if M. d'A's 'self-applause' arises from a decision to give up his appointment and retire with her to England—a decision that would give her great joy.

[19] After being wounded by the Prussians and rescued through Blücher's intervention, Larrey was sent with one of the Marshal's aides-de-camp to Louvain, where he was well cared for in the house of a local lawyer. He recovered quickly and visited nearby military hospitals that housed French soldiers wounded in the Waterloo campaign. He reached Brussels on or about 24 June, when he wrote to Feltre and offered his services. His offer was refused with Feltre's annotation, 'Reply that as M. Larrey is a prisoner-of-war of the allies, the Minister has no orders to give him'. See Robert G. Richardson, *Larrey: Surgeon to Napoleon's Imperial Guard* (1974), pp. 222-3.

[20] Quoting from L. 914.   [21] Captain William Burney (L. 917 n. 7).

had just come to my 2 last Napoleons, in waiting your answer, & had fixed my next order to the Banker when Mme de Laval pays the 140 fr. you had laid out for the [xxxxx 4 *or* 5 *words*]. I hope this will do till we meet—⟨How do I long for⟩ word soon about the fate of my mss. [xxxxx 10 *or* 11 *words*].

July 14. Friday. Bon Jour!—bien bon jour!—⊓

921   [Trèves], 15 July [1815]

M. d'Arblay
To Madame d'Arblay

A.L. (Berg), 15 juillet
Single sheet 4to   1 p.   *pmk*   TRIER   seal
Addressed: A Madame / Madame de Burney / poste restante / A Bruxelles
Readdressed: Marché au Bois / N. 1358
Edited by FBA, p. 1, *annotated and dated*: ✲· ⌈33⌉/I   (24)   (1815.)
This cruelly agitated & nearly illegible Letter, arrived after I had quitted Brussels, and followed me to Treves—where I had joined its invaluable— inappreciable Writer, in consequence of the Letter to colonel de Beaufort. (NB. M. d'A. wrote constantly—But the letters arrived—alas! irregularly—)

Chere et adorable Fanny! Si je ne dois pas renoncer pour toujours à notre reunion hâte toi de m'ecrire, — je suis mourant d'inquietude. 5 jours sans m'ecrire dans des circonstances pareilles quand tu sais que j'etais dejà si peu rassuré sur ton imprudence et quand je faisais tout pour te faire quitter Bruxelles — point de lettre de toi aujourdhui apres n'en avoir pas eu mercredy m'a mis dans un etat indicible. J'ai cru en consequence devoir employer à remplir mes devoirs cinq heures qui m'ont epuisé et cependant je n'ai fait que dicter et cependant ⟨   ⟩ parole d'honneur de recevoir touts mes freres et de rassembler tout mon courage pour les rassurer et leur ⟨aider.⟩[1]

Treves
Samedy 15 Juillet

921.   [1] These closing remarks are a garbled reference to M. d'A's undertaking to rally French deserters and assist officers from the Maison du Roi who were passing through Trèves. Both groups appear in the list that M. d'A forwarded earlier to the duc de Feltre (A.L.S. Vincennes, 1 July).

To Charles Burney

A.L. (McGill), 10 July 1815   with 3 lines (p. 3) by CPB
Double sheet 4to   4 pp.   *pmks* TREVES¹   19 AU 1815   19 AU
1815   *franked by* ⟨*Arnheim*⟩   red seal
Addressed: Angleterre, / À Monsieur / Monsieur le Docteur Rev^end /
Charles Burney, / Rectory House, / Deptford. / near *Londres*.

Brussells, July 10.
1815.

Congratulations can never, I ween, be out of season, even
though they may seem out of Time—again, therefore, let me
repeat mine, the most sincere, the most rejoicing, that the Good
Archy is no longer the naughty Retardy. What a desireable
variety, also, for ME to talk of congratulations,² who, for so long
a time past, have had no trafic but with condoleances!

It seems a preferment made for you on purpose, since it
leaves unbroken the complete possession of your noble Library.
The short distance, too, from Town is so conducive to the
enjoyment of society, the exertions of literature, the love of the
arts, & the endless pursuit of that endless object, knowledge,
that I would not barter it for a Bishopric further a field. And
dear, generous Rosette, in thinking over the Fame, Name, &
celebrity, as well as the pride, pleasure, & use of your Book
Room, will chearfully resign herself to the smallness of her
Drawing Room, which will always be sufficient for select
society, if,—as the Learned (*you* know, PERHAPS! —) have said,
the Interlocuters should never be more in number than the
Graces, nor fewer than the Muses.

But what is this I mean—Can you tell?—If you can, pray
do!—by talking of MY congratulations, when I have those to
recite that should make them 'hide their diminished heads'³
in blushing bashfulness? Know then, Dear Doctor, a friend,

922.   ¹ The postmark suggests that this letter was not sent until FBA had got
M. d'A's signature in Trèves (see n. 17 *below*).
   ² CB Jr. had in April been preferred to the rectorship of Cliffe-at-Hoo in Kent
(L. 869 n. 8).
   ³ *Paradise Lost*, iv. 23.

who, while we are thus Ditch-Distanced, must be nameless, has informed me That my gracious Royal Mistress has Herself desired I may be told of *the part she takes,* & *the joy she wishes me,* in the preferment *so well bestowed* by his Grace the Archbishop upon my Brother Dr. Charles.[4]—And to This, the same person was ordered to add the condescending felicitations to me of Their Royal Highnesses the Princesses. |

I hope my fellow Gossip will have the goodness to *settle the balance,* as poor Mr. Sleepe used to say,[5] for me with my fair representative:[6] for which purpose our Sister Charlotte will produce the Rhino:[7] for as she is so kind as to act for me with regard to the expences of Alexander, she has always some cash of mine in hand. Pray join my benediction to your own for the little one.

Upon the subject of sponsors,—again I must ask my dear *Godpapa* if he will not take some measure for the confirmation of his Godson?[8] I assure you it has been remarked, to his disadvantage, at Cambridge, that he never takes the communion, except by those to whom he has told the reason. He can do nothing in this affair himself; & were I in England—I could do nothing so well as what I do now—nothing *better,* I mean—i.e. applying to the Commander in Chief of Holy Rites in the Family, to counsel the preparations, & direct the results.

I remember well that, when I was preparing for confirmation myself, I had such an idea I should undergo an examination, & I was so fearful of some *wry* question that might discountenance me, That I learnt nearly the whole common prayer Book by heart!—Besides reading the Bible *quite through* 3 times! I was so indefatigable, I rose to nothing else; & never went to rest while I could procure light for my labours. Alex would not be much led to imitate me, if he knew that, after all

---

⁴ It gives the Magnolia (the Queen) great satisfaction as well as the 'poor Nobody', wrote the Princess Elizabeth on [5–6] June, op. cit., 'to Hear that the excellent & worthy Brother of dear Mad. d A: had been promoted to a good living by the *principle.*'

⁵ The indigent relative of the Burneys, James Sleepe (i, L. 7 n. 7), beloved for his malapropisms and sweet nature, whose kindness to CB Jr. in his youthful scrapes the latter never forgot, repaying him in the end with care and shelter.

⁶ FBA was 'godmother elect' to CPB's second daughter Rosetta d'Arblay Burney (see vii, L. 761 n. 2). Born on 12 Mar. 1814, the child had been baptized on 4 Mar. 1815 at St. Alfege's, Greenwich, her grandfather CB Jr. officiating.

⁷ A cant term for money (*Dictionary of the Vulgar Tongue*, 1811). Mrs. Broome had in hand the quarterly payments of FBA's pension (see L. 909 n. 6).

⁸ CB Jr. was AA's godfather (iii, L. 179 n. 2).

this hard work—the fat clumsy stumpy worthy Bishop of Norwich[9] clapt his hand upon my head, & off it, as fast as he possibly | could, & never made a single interrogatory, nor uttered a single doubt or demur upon my fitness or unfitness for his blessing.

At this moment,—as the style of my Letter will have led you to conjecture, all my hopes Here of Restoration & of Peace are in excellent good train.

You tell me Martin will write to me about Longman? When? He answered my Letter about the £500 *undoubted*[ly], & which could only require my receipt, & placed it for me at Hoare's: but not a word has he given me upon my Enquiries as to the *2ᵈ Edition*, & its sale; though, as you well know, for you had it from Mr. Straghan himself,[10] not only the 2ᵈ & the 3ᵈ Edition, with my consent demanded & accorded, were printed, but the *4ᵗʰ*, without even my knowledge.[11] Even my poor excentric Alex himself is not more impracticable to act upon relative to *penmanshipness*, than our good & worthy Nephew,[12] who neither upon that business nor my Cottage forwards me any intelligence.

[Here Charles Parr Burney inserts three lines]

⟨Sims⟩[13] & I are calling & chatting with your good dear Sister & are off immediately for the 'Battle-field.'—We sleep at Brussels to-night again, & to-morrow proceed to Cologne on our Road to Basle.

[Madame d'Arblay resumes]

Have I not surprised you now, my Carlos? & most agreeably? with a sight so unexpected at that of your Charles's hand in the midst of my Letter? Having lost an opportunity by which I meant it to pass to the dear Tight little Island, it was on my Bureau when your dear son astonished & extremely pleased me by entering into my *sallon*, on *Sunday, July 16ᵗʰ*, in the very

9 The Right Revd. Philip Yonge (*c.* 1720–83) was Bishop of Norwich at the time of FB's confirmation.

10 Andrew Strahan (iv, L. 292 n. 37), who would seem to have printed *The Wanderer* as well as *Camilla*.

11 Sales of *The Wanderer* came to a standstill with the end of the second edition. Even though Longman and Rees had sold 3,600 copies by then, they were left the third and fourth edition on their hands.

12 Martin Burney (i, p. lxx), FBA's solicitor.

13 CPB (i, p. lxxii) and an unidentified travelling companion had appeared in Brussels on 15 June. See further, J. 924, p. 456.

moment of his arrival at Brussels: & the next morning, *July 17th*, upon his calling again, I presented him this *feuille*—which I have only kept back since from the post to give you the last tidings of one so dear to you. He had a stomach complaint which detained him the 18th, joined to a desire his comrades entertained of going to visit Laeken,[14] the palace now of the Roy du Pays bas, but erst of the Empess Josephine: & which Nap[oleon] had destined for his reception, after beating Lord Wellington; for he had already printed his ⎮ proclamations to La Belgique, with that date: but as it happened that Lord Wellington thought proper to inflict the chastisement which Nap. intended his Grace should receive, the Palais remains a Monument, neither won nor lost, for the curious to visit. Charles came to see me again on Tuesday evening, free from pain, & ready to depart the next morning. I was truly glad of his visit, &, at first thought him remarkably well looking. though [a] '*littel complaint*' changed, momentarily, his bright hue of health to one savouring rather of languour. The change of air will soon restore the vivid tint, I have no doubt. I enquired after him at the Hotel de Flandre ere I would send this to the post, & heard he was quite recovered, & set off for Louvain with his party.—But how is it, my dear Carlos, you forbore sending me an Express, *expressly*, of the Birth of another Charles Burney?[15] *Charles by himself Charles*, as your very affectionate & loyal son calls him. He is prouder to transmit him so to posterity, than even as Charles Parr. Pray felicitate the happy & most pleasing mother for me, as well as — — when that may be!—my dear Rosette! ah, my dear Carlos—I enter not upon that affliction[16]—I hope, indeed, it is *annulling* every day!—you shall have the signature,[17] when I have the opportunity to get it signed by M. d'A., always at Treves: but you do not say whether this 45 includes the 36. still in hand when you wrote last, [ab]out the Ch[elsea] instruments, the Prints: & all? How happy I am for good Mr. Burney's recovery.[18] Don't let my

[14] For the château of Laeken or Laaken, see J. 924, pp. 409–10.

[15] CPB's son Charles Edward Burney (1815–1907), born 'at Croom's Hill, Greenwich' on 9 June (*GM* lxxxv[1]. 562).

[16] A reference to Rosette's states of depression (L. 864 n. 3).

[17] M. d'A's signature was needed to signify his and FBA's acceptance of the payment of £45, made to them by CB Jr. as an executor of CB's will, for the items mentioned here. See also vii, L. 769 nn. 2–5 for details of these provisions.

[18] Charles Rousseau Burney (L. 907 n. 7).

dearest Father's *'honoured & dear Friend through life,'* Lady Crewe, forget me. I have something to say to her L^p about the restored Letters; when I am able to know whether I shall recover my MSS.[19] I entreat, therefore, that she will not destroy them:— or, only *partially.* I have no intercourse as yet with Paris. I have *written,* but received no answers.

I have just read your Letter by dear Charles & return 'von chast embrass' with all my whole Heart, my ever & inalienably dear Carlucci— I

923   [1358, Marché au bois],
            Brussels, 17–19 July 1815

To M. d'Arblay

A.L. (Berg), 17–19 July 1815
Double sheet 4to 4 pp. *pmk* BRUXELLES wafer
Addressed: *Treves* / À Monsieur / le General d'Arblay, / Officier Superieur des Gardes du Corps / de sa Majesty Le Roi de France, / Chev^r de St Louis, &c &c &c / à Treves.
Edited by FBA, p. 1, *annotated*: (23/3)
See Textual Notes.

            ce Lundi Matin
           17. Juillet 1815

An Opportunity offering to send my beloved ami a few lines through *Cologne,* ⌐which may perhaps reach him & sooner than by my usual post day, *Mercredi,*⌐—I seize it, to tell him I have just received his short & melancholy bit written the 11th, when he had heard such evil tidings respecting Paris.[1] The King, however, did enter his Capital on Saturday, July 8th— and was received with clamorous & general Joy. Two Letters

---

[19] On CB's death (1814) Lady Crewe would in all probability have requested the return of the confidential letters that throughout her life she had sent to him. The 'restored Letters' may refer therefore to a Packet returned to her by CB Jr. (his father's executor). 'All of Lady Crewe' FBA was later to locate and return in 1816. See her report (Comyn) of 7–14 May 1816 to CB Jr. (ix, L. 990). Of these letters to CB, only eleven are known to survive (see *Catalogue*).

The passage is ambiguous, however, and the letters referred to may be those written by CB to Lady Crewe, letters whose return FBA had already requested (vii, L. 832 n. 2).

923. [1] This letter is missing.

written the following Monday, July 10ᵗʰ I have heard, & they testify the truth of his really loyal & felicitous *entrée*. ⌐I have mentioned them to you in my Letter of yesterday, the 16ᵗʰ July.⌐ But—the same alarming reports are now spreading also here—on what founded, I have not yet learned. I am uneasy— & I am perplexed—but every thing concurs to forbid my setting off in the present state of things. ⌐I write this, therefore, chiefly to set your mind at ease by an assurance I shall take no measures till I know your opinion of my *commentaire* upon your *sante*.⌐

I will endeavour to gather some intelligence before I finish my Letter.

Lundi au soir. I have met with no satisfaction! no Diligence has yet arrived from Paris, nor gone thither! ⌐I had the enquiry made at La Messagerie des Diligences.[2] The Letters, nevertheless, came on Saturday, for the first time. But I have seen no one who has been able to give me *positive* assurance that they ¹ have received one. At present, therefore, I could not get to Paris, even if all our *accounts* &c. were arranged. Nor shall I think it safe, or right, to go in the First chaise whenever it sets off! pˢˢᵉ Henin dares not yet depart.⌐

I grieve to see, by to Day's Letter,[3] that you have not calculated the *impossibility* there was you should receive Letters from me during the last week, as I had directed to Namur! — I am so, so sorry! I know so well the *blank* of the disappointment, when nothing prepares for or explains it. Who do you think carries this, & will put it into the present post to Treves? *Cologne*, I think?—our Nephew, Charles [Parr] Burney of Greenwich! He is going to visit Switzerland. He brings me a Letter from Alexander—our poor Alexander! who begins now to sigh for our reunion, *en trio*, as *necessary*, he says, for his health, spirits, & happiness! — — dear—dear Alex!—

I am very sorry you cannot see again Charles, who most affectionately wanted to go to Treves, *chemin faisant*, but he has been told, by his Banker, that all the routes about Luxembourg are dangerous,[4] from the quantities of worthless & desperate

---

² In the Place Royale. ³ This letter is missing.
⁴ During July there were repeated attacks on allied troops and royalist officials throughout the eastern districts of France. That they were taken very seriously can be seen from edicts against them by the Russian governor-general in the *Journal de Francfort* of 16 and 18 July.

fugitives who were in the rear of the army of Buonaparte & from les *traineurs de toutes les Nations*! For Heaven's sake do not enter France—should that be your destination, by those parts! *Alsace* is in complete insurrection, it is said! — —ǀ

Oh that we were with our *Choux* & our Boy! — Do not answer this as a *proposal*! it is only a *wish*! — I know well your impediments, & difficulties & am most unresistingly ready to await their removal.

But Oh how I weary of this lengthened absence.

⌐I shall write again by Wednesday the 19th post, lest this, which is to go I know not how, should miss you.

I now recall the D. de Lux[embour]g is at Louvaine through which Charles, & his party, will pass, I shall write to him, for Charles was here saturday to see him.⌐

Every body is *preparing* to go to Paris; but nobody has yet the courage to set out—except the 3 ladies I have mentioned, Mesdames de Jaucourt & de Laval, & pss Twckebywitz5 And they have [direc]tions, if not an escort, from the ministers: besides 3 Carriages, & out-riders.

Some say the army on the Loire amounts to 50.000. Another dreadful Battle is expected.

⌐I have not written to your Uncle, till I know whether foreign letters go further than Paris, or something of the state of Joigny. But I have given a commission to Me Desprez, that I at once undertake, after Her report.⌐ Adio, mio ben!—When—when shall we meet! When profit from the awaked feelings of our dearest Boy!—Lille was said yesterday to have capitulated,—⌐& the Dilligence was expected to-day here. I have particularly copied an account ǀ of le Beau Cheval, & I find the Dilligence is now arrived & the Governor at Lille awaits a French Officer sent by Louis 18, in order to yield.

Every one of your letters are **6 days** upon the road! Therefore, as they never go hence the same day the post arrives, 2 weeks delay to *questions*! answers for them received must be in 13 days!—How I wait!⌐

Bon Jour to my own ami! This is mardi, 18. Juillet, 8 o'clock in the morng. I expect Carolus every moment.

⌐An excellent young man here, the nephew of le Hôte, who has been early trained to the use of Horses, but is now a coiffeur,

---

5 Marie Theresa Tyszkiewicz (L. 910 n. 10).

begs if you come hither without *des Gens* to keep, you will let *him* be employed. He has a Mother in Paris whom he longs to see & he will work his way thither by such exchange.¶

Charles ne part pas, et ceci va par la poste— Bonjour ce 19.— no stage yet arrived.

THE WATERLOO JOURNAL

924   [11 February–July 1815]

A.J. (Diary MSS. 6076–[6421], Berg), FBA, a Journal narrating events from 11 February to July 1815, but written, at least in part (and probably in its entirety) in 1823, as Madame d'Arblay inadvertently indicates by her comments p. 248 [6325], where she gives the date of writing as Thursday 15ᵗʰ June, 1823. She was then living at 11 Bolton Street, London.

The Journal comprises 138 single sheets 8vo (*c.* 7·1 × 4·3"). Some of the leaves cut from a cahier still retain the stitching; others lack the conjugate leaves. Interleaved at irregular intervals are 19 double sheets (*c.* 7·1 × 4·45"). In all, 342 pages of text. For a detailed description of the physical make-up, see the Textual Notes.

The manuscript has the appearance of a draft subsequently revised by the writer. The Journal was revised further and much abridged by editors, presumably at the Press, who, working successively in pencil, red ink, and black ink, changed and suppressed a good part of the text. This editorial work is described in the Textual Notes.

I have no remembrance how, where, whence, nor from whom I first heard of the return of Buonaparte from Elba. Wonder at his temerity was the impression made by the news, but wonder unmixt with apprehension. This inactivity of foresight—has been ever since, my own unappeasable astonishment. But it was universal. A torpor indiscribable, a species of stupor utterly indefinable seemed to have enveloped the Capital with a mental mist that was impervious.¹ Every body went about their affairs, made or received Visits, met & parted, without speaking, or, I suppose, thinking ¹ of this event as of a matter of any importance. My own participation in this improvident blindness is to myself incomprehensible. Ten years I had lived under the

924.   ¹ This curious inertia in Paris is also reported by Benjamin Constant in his *Journaux intimes* for the period. See *Œuvres* (Pléiade ed., 1957), pp. 775–7.

dominion of Buonaparte; I had been in habits of intimacy with many of the peculiar friends of those who most closely surrounded him; I was generously trusted, as one with whom information while interesting & precious, would be inviolably safe—as one, in fact, whose Honour was the Honour of her spotless Husband, & therefore invulnerable: well, therefore, by Narrations the most authentic, & by documents the most indisputable, I knew the Character of Buonaparte ¦ & marvellous beyond the reach of my comprehension is my participation in this inertia. Yet it was less, perhaps, owing to a supine confidence in the so recently established Government, or even to the potent prevalence of my wishes for its permanence, than to the state of exhaustion into which all my political faculties had fallen, in consequence of the too intense, the boiling, the raging effervescence in which during the Ten years I have mentioned in Paris, & the two that followed in England, they had relentlessly been kept. Every forced stretch of Intellect, whatever be its ¦ direction, must have the same termination; either that of suddenly snapping short the over-pressed powers of Thought, or of causing to them that non-elastic relaxation that totally defeats all their super-vehement exertions. In the Ten Years I have mentioned, my mind was a stranger to rest; though the rare domestic Felicity which had fallen to my lot held a certain counter-balance against my Anxieties that saved me from being overwhelmed by their weight. I can by no means ¦ therefore, look back to them as to a period of unhappiness, though no recollection of them remains that is unsullied with disturbance. In those ten years, so full, so eventful, so fearful, so astonishing, the idea of Buonaparte was blended with all our Thoughts, our projects, our Actions. The greatness of his Power, the intrepidity of his Ambition, the vastness of his conceptions, & the restlessness of his spirit, kept suspense always breathless, & Conjecture always at work. Thus familiar therefore to his practices, thus initiated in his resources, thus aware of his own Gigantic ideas of his Destiny, ¦ how could I for a moment suppose he would re-visit France without a consciousness of success, founded upon some secret conviction that it was infallible, through measures previously arranged, & assistance indubitably anticipated? I can only, I repeat, conclude, that my Understanding—such as it is—was utterly tired out by a long harrass of perpetual alarm & sleepless apprehension. Unmoved, therefore, I reposed in the general apparent repose, which, if it were as real in those with whom I mixt as in myself, I now deem for All a species of Infatuation.

I mean not, however, to assert that such was, internally, the case with all others; I assert only that ⎮ such, with others, was its semblance, & with me, unequivocally, its reality.

I ought, however, to mention that we lived but little at that period in the World, & even rarely with our own chosen set: I was lately recovered from a dangerous Fever; & General d'Arblay was not yet — — alas, he was *never* recovered from a dreadful accident, that had happenned to him while too kindly— & too closely he was guarding ME from alarm or hurry upon our landing at Calais in November, 1814. He now, was indispensably, & almost exclusively engaged in preparations for a 4 months Professional residence at Senlis,[2] in the Artillery Compagnie of the Duc de Luxembourg. I, too was busied in making arrangements to follow him, thither: ⎮ my Apartments had already been settled, & even my society selected, by his assiduous care. A Letter to reconcile me to relinquishing my darling love of retirement, which he wrote to me from Senlis, Fevʳ 11. 1815—I have preserved:[3]—My dear Alexander will see by it the gentle persuasion with which he reasoned where he might have commanded! — — such was his ever kind practice with his happy Wife! Whether or not M. d'Arblay himself was involved in this obscure failure of foresight I have mentioned, I never now can ascertain:[4] To spare me any evil tidings, & save me from even the shadow of any unnecessary alarm, was the first & constant solicitude of his indulgent goodness. ⎮ But such great positive events, or the big suspence of their expectation, or all-absorbing anxiety at the view of failing health, occupied from this time—or rather, from this time to the very end of our Earthly Union, oppressed all my faculties, [that] I never thenceforward was sufficiently mistress of the PRESENT

[2] Of the five companies scattered in a circle around Paris at Versailles, Saint-Germain, Beauvais, Meaux, and Melun and rotated in and out of the capital for guard duty at the Tuileries, M. d'A's was the only company stationed at Senlis. The postings and organization of the Maison militaire du Roi appear in *Emplacement des Troupes du Royaume de France à l'Epoque du 1ᵉʳ Janvier 1815*, pp. 5–7.

[3] L. 841.

[4] M. d'A's shock at the desertion of the army suggests that otherwise he would have expected them to withstand Napoleon.

MOMENT to possess leisure, or even interest, for discussing the Past. The coming Day had my heart in its hands! the coming Day, on which so fearfully hung the re-establishment of strength, spirits, & happiness in Him upon whom hung mine! I cannot therefore be sure whether our apathy upon this point were mutual—though certainly there is no other point, from the ∣ beginning to the end of our connexion, to which the word Apathy could to either of us be applied.

At this period he returned to Paris, to settle various matters for our Senlis residence. We both, now, knew the event that so soon was to monopolize all thought & all interest throughout Europe; but we knew it without any change in our way of life; on the contrary, we even resumed our delightful airings in the Bois de Boulogne, whither the General drove me every morning in a light elegant Caleche[5] of which he had possessed himself upon his entrance into the King's body Guard the preceding year; & I have no retrospection that causes me such amazement as the unapprehensive state of mind that could urge either of us to the enjoyment of those drives when aware that Bonaparté had effected an invasion into France. ∣

Brief, however, was this illusion, & fearful was the light by which its darkness was dispersed. In a few days we heard that Buonaparte, whom we concluded would be stopt at his landing, & taken Prisoner, or forced to save himself by flight, was, on the contrary, pursuing, unimpeded, his route to Lyons.[6]

From this moment, Disguise, if any there had been, was over with the most open & frank of human beings, who never even transitorily practiced it but to keep off evil, or its apprehension, from others. He communicated to me NOW his strong view of danger; not alone that measures might be taken to ∣ secure my safety, but to spare me any sudden agitation. Alas! none was spared to himself! more clearly than any one he anticipated the impending tempest, & foreboded its devasting effects. He spoke aloud, & strenuously, with prophetic energy, to all the military with whom he was then officially associated; but the greater part either despaired of resisting the torrent, or disbelieved its approach. What deeply interesting scenes crowd upon my

---

[5] A well-sprung four-wheeled carriage suitable for such 'airings' because it was open in front.

[6] For Napoleon's route see Map *facing* p. 224.

remembrance of his noble, his daring, but successless exertions! The King's body Guard immediately *de service*, at that time, was the *Compagnie* of the Prince de Poix:⁷ a man | of the most heart-felt loyalty, but who had never served, & who was not more incapable of so great a command at so critical a juncture from utter inexperience, than from an entire absence of all military talent. In the same measure as the evil grew more prominent, more prominent appeared his incapacity. Nevertheless his real affection for the King, Louis 18. & his still greater ardour for the Royal Cause, would have indued him with personal courage to have sacrificed his Life to the service of the Crown, if his life could have sufficed without military skill, or intellectual resource, for it's preservation. |

I will not here pass by the family of de Beauvau,⁸ so prized by us all, & to us all so kind & amiable. My dear Alexander will take peculiar interest even in their Name.

M. le Prince, & Madame la Princesse de Beauvau had sustained their loyalty with unshaken fortitude, through all the vicissitudes & temptations of Buonaparté's power, till a message was sent to M. de Beauvau, from the Emperor, demanding that the Prince's two sons, Charles & Edmund, should be educated at St. Cyr. To avoid this cruel separation, & rescue his sons from the mixt & inferiour classes of youth then brought up at that seminary, M. de Beauvau consented that they should both | enter the Army of the Emperor, & be prepared for military service, if he, M. de Beauvau, might be permitted to follow up the preparation in person. This was granted: & I have met repeatedly the anxious Father accompanying them to the Riding School, & attending to their lessons of Fencing, Marching, & the use of Arms. Soon after, but I do not [rec]ollect by what process, M. de Beauvau became *Chambellan* to the Emperor.⁹

As such, upon the marriage of Buonaparte with Marie

⁷ See L. 860 n. 11.
⁸ With the establishment of his dynasty and Empire, Napoleon sought out and attracted to his court and army the great aristocratic families that had either remained in France or returned after emigration. For the biographical details of the Beauvau family, see v, L. 513 n. 2; for its complicated relations with Napoleon, see L. 842 n. 10 (*supra*).
⁹ Beauvau, appointed chambellan in 1809, had been sent to meet the new Empress at Stuttgart (20 Mar. 1810). For the dispatch of other chamberlains on similar errands, see Frédéric Masson, *Napoléon et l'amour* (Lagny, 1933), pp. 94–5.

Louise, M. de Beauvau was sent to Stutgard, with a Letter to the Bride elect from her destined spouse. M. de B[eauvau] was so kind as to call upon me immediately after his ˡ return to Paris, to narrate, in full detail, his Embassy to Wurtemberg. The Queen—ci-devant Princess Royal of England, had received him even joyfully, for she remembered him & his lovely Wife in England. The sister of Buonaparte, Madame Murat, then Queen of Naples, had also been sent to Stutgard to salute the Bridal Empress: & strange was the sight to M. de Beauvau to see that lady not only quite at her ease with the British Princess, but familiarly take her by the arm to saunter from one room to another. The young Empress Elect received the Letter in silence, & with perfect calm & composure; & M. de B. then hastened back to make his report to the Emperour.¹⁰

During the absence of M. de B. upon this mission, I frequently saw ˡ Madame de Beauvau, & heard from her the full detail of an audience she had herself had with the Emperor. The occasion was to plead for relief to her Grandmother, the Duchess Dowʳ of Harcourt,¹¹ who had been Gouvernante to the last Dauphin, & who was now in a state of almost distress,— her lost Woods, & last hopes of recovering any revenu, having been illegally claimed by false pretences, though by a man of high birth. To represent the rights of the ancient Duchess this interview was solicited. Buonaparté granted it with glee. The lineage, character, & beauty of Madᵉ de Beauvau had, no doubt, often reached his Ears. The consequence of the meeting was an immediate nomination of Madᵉ de B. as one of the ladies of Marie Louise.¹¹

Buonaparte thenceforward took every opportunity of shewing

---

¹⁰ Napoleon and Marie-Louise had been married by proxy in Vienna on 11 March and on the 13th Marie-Louise left for Paris. As 'surintendante de la Maison' Queen Caroline of Naples supervised the move to France. See Frédéric Masson, *L'Impératrice Marie-Louise, 1809–1815* (1902), pp. 50–9.
¹¹ Françoise-Catherine-Scholastique d'Aubussen (b. 1733), who had married in 1752 Henri-François (1726–1804), comte de Lillebonne, 4th duc d'Harcourt. For their granddaughter Mme de Beauvau, see v, L. 513 n. 2, and for her appointment as dame du palais de l'impératrice, vi, pp. L. 612 n. 2; L. 619 n. 5; and viii, L. 842 n. 10. Early in the Hundred Days Napoleon once again restored the confiscated property in question to Mme de Beauvau, who was quick to resume her imperial appointment as 'dame du Palais'. Article II of a decree signed by Napoleon and dated 7 April from the Tuileries states in part, 'Un tiers des biens provenant de Madame d'Harcourt, consistant dans les bois de Cervières . . . appartiendra pareillement et au même titre à Madame de Beauvau' (see the anonymous *Échos des salons de Paris . . . 1815*, p. 74).

to the new & high born Attendant ⏐ his appreciation of her merit. Her softness, good sense, pleasing conversation, high manners, & dignified, though unassuming deportment, joined to her very uncommon personal attractions, soon, to his penetrating notice, marked her as the most distinguished Female of his Court; & he once, with an elegance of thought as well as expression, that occasionally, though rarely, burst from him, said: 'When I placed Madame de Beauvau about the Empress, I meant to place a model.' Alas for the poor de Beauvaus! the courtesies, of every description, that were thence showered upon them, so melted the hardness of their original feelings against Buonaparté, that, on the restoration of the Bourbons, they were amongst the last to join the royal standard:—or rather, from their belief that Bonaparté was Unconquerable, they did not join it at all; ⏐ for Louis 18. informed of their backwardness, resentfully, & without enquiring into their position, upon coming to his Throne, left out the name of M. le Prince de Beauvau in his new Register of Peers. This gave a wound incurable to the Family: and M. de B. & his two sons, & his eldest Daughter, were irritated past all bounds of discretion or of patience, & everywhere uttered their political animosity with the most dauntless defiance of consequences. This of course was known at Court, & of course, widened the breach most dangerously. General d'Arblay ⏐ exerted all the influence with which their attachment to him, & his noble character & engaging deportment endowed him, to prevail with them to pay their immediate hommage to the restored Monarch. But all was vain. Nevertheless, M. d'A[rblay] stood so high in their estimation, that, upon the return of Napoleon from Elba, he scrupled not to renew his attempt. Still it was fruitless. Madame la Princesse d'Henin made similar efforts, with similar ill success. So, I believe, did M. de Lally. We were all deeply concerned at the obduracy of M. de Beauvau, fearing that ruin & disgrace must be its consequence. ⏐ My personal anxiety for this really charming family urged me now to propose to General d'Arblay that I, also, should make an essay to open the Eyes of M. de Beauvau to the right path which this critical moment presented for his conduct. With his ever partial view of my intentions, Your Father, my Alex, eagerly cried 'Ce sera bien digne de toi—' Accordingly, we went together, on the ensuing evening, as if purporting simply a social visit. We were received with their usual cordiality, & the two young ladies, the lovely Natalie, & the beautiful Gabrielle,[12] | each gave M. d'Arblay their hands, while holding & hanging upon his own for many minutes, with a pleasure amounting to fondness; while Charles & Edmund, equal sharers in the almost enthusiasm of regard which the General had excited in this delightful Race, eagerly watched the moment when they could catch his attention from their sisters.

They soon fell into a gay, general conversation — — for still there was no alarm, for no one believed that Buonaparte had dared form even | the project of approaching Paris in Person. Privately, then, I opened upon my purpose to Madame de Beauvau, who had placed me next to her upon a small sofa. She listened to me with a flattering willingness that invited | my openness & courage. I ventured therefore to represent in strong Colours the striking effect that might be produced to his own & his Family's honour, if M. de Beauvau could bury in patriotic loyalty his resentment, & generously, at so critical a moment, present himself to the King. The secret wishes of Madame de Beauvau evidently accompanied mine; but an undeviating acquiescence in the will of M. de Beauvau was the inalterable rule of her conduct. She told me, nevertheless, that she had already been to Court herself, without opposition from her husband, & that she meant to go thither again. She then gently urged me to | address M. de Beauvau in person, assuring me he would undoubtedly take my counsel in good part, whether he followed it or not. I declined, however, using a freedom with him that Ten years of open, & often affectionate & confidential intercourse seemed to authorize with herself: but I was not sorry to see that he was struck with our mutual air of earnest discourse, & that, though he stood aloof, he incessantly turned towards us with anxious curiosity, & remained utterly inattentive to the social pleasantry carried on with M. d'Arblay by his Children.

[12] By July 1823 when the Beauvau family visited London the second daughter Nathalie-Irène-Marie-Victurnienne (1798–1852) had become the wife of Auguste-François-Joseph Le Lièvre (1780–1826), chevalier de Lagrange et de l'Empire and colonel of the first regiment of chasseurs à cheval; and the eldest son Charles (L. 840 n. 19) had married in 1815 Lucie-Virginie (1795–1834), daughter of Antoine-César de Choiseul (1756–1808), 3rd duc de Praslin (1791). For the remainder of the family, see v, L. 513 n. 2.

As soon as I perceived Madame de Beauvau deeply impressed, & full ⏐ of meditative reflexion, I held my Peace. At this pause, M. de Beauvau approached, & planted himself behind the sofa. His sweet Wife tried to excite him to demand the subject of our long conference. She easily succeeded, & when he begged to be satisfied, referred him to me. I shook my head, & protested I could by no means intrude upon him my opinions. 'And why not?' he cried, and became eager in solicitation. 'I have no right,' I cried, 'to your attention; yet I earnestly wish to offer some thoughts to your consideration; & therefore, to give my ⏐ cause some little chance of success, I will not utter a word of it! but leave it in far better hands.—'

I then abruptly arose, & M. d'Arblay, who had engaged the young ladies that he might facilitate my enterprize, gave me *le bras*, & we departed.

I was in full hope of success, at that moment, from the influence of Madame de Beauvau, who seemed content to bring forward in my Name sentiments that she would not hazard in her own. But I could not follow up my advantage— This was my last visiting day in Paris before my Flight to the Low Countries. And, ⏐ in the great dispersion from varying events that ensued, I did not—that I can recollect—see any of this amiable Family again,—till — — about 8 Years afterwards — —[12] when they all visited me in my sad widowed Home, in Bolton Street!—the Prince & Princess,—the lovely Natalie— la belle Gabrielle—the noble Prince Charles—the *spirituel* & engaging Prince Edmond,—& the worthy Son in Law, le Marquis de la Grange, & Daughter in Law, La Princesse Charles, ci-devant fille du duc de Praslin.[12] They honoured & cheered me with their charming society, repeatedly taking tea with me *à l'anglaise*, & shewing a sympathizing feeling for my unhappiness that few were better qualified to comprehend, from similar affections—& from perfect knowledge of its source! ⏐

This species of Episode in the opening of the famous Hundred Days, is a standing and striking proof of the deadness I have already remarked of Paris to its impending dangers. Had I not myself entered upon the subject, from the warm desire I felt to see M. de Beauvau restored to royal favour, the Evening would have passed ⏐ away, without even an allusion to the Landing of

Buonaparté, & have passed away in pleasantry, gaiety, & social amusement. That he would make any attempt upon Paris, or plan, or even suggest approaching it, seemed to occur to no one. It was calmly taken for granted he would speedily escape back to Elba, or remain in the South a Prisoner. And it was only amongst deep or restless Politicians that any inquietude was manifested with respect to either of these results.

I frequently saw my dear & valuable Friend Madame de Maisonneuve, but I have no recollection of her marking any species of apprehension. Madame la Princesse d'Henin, indeed, whom, also, [|] I was in the happy habit of frequently meeting, had an air & manner that announced perturbation; but her impetuous spirit in politics kept her mind always in a state of energy upon public affairs. M. le Comte de Lally Tolendahl I do not remember seeing at this period, but I conclude, from his deep intellect & warm loyalty, he must have been amongst the earliest to open his Eyes to the coming mischief.

I often reflected upon the difference that would have appeared in the two Nations of France & England under similar circumstances: had an Invader of any Name or Renown, effected a footing on any part [|] of our Coast, what a ferment would instantly have been excited in our metropolis! Not a street but would have rung with cries of News, true or false; not a Mail Coach would have appeared, but the populace would have stopt it for information; & not an hour would have passed without some real, or pretended Courier, let loose upon the multitude, to convey or to invent intelligence; for few, at such momentous periods, are fastidious with respect to Truth; something fresh to feed conjecture suffices to appease the famine of Ignorance for, on such occasions, we loath taciturnity far more than falsehood.

But when Buonaparté actually arrived at Lyons,[13] the face of affairs changed. Expectation was then awakened, consternation began to spread; & Report [|] went rapidly to her usual work of Now exciting nameless terrour, & Now allaying even reasonable apprehension.

To me, tremendous grew now every moment. I saw General d'Arblay imposing upon himself a severity of service for which he had no longer health or strength; & imposing it only the

[13] Napoleon left Lyons on 13 March (Houssaye, *1815*, i. 302–3).

more rigidly from the fear that his then beginning weakness & infirmities should seem to plead for indulgence. It was thus that he insisted upon going through the double duty of Artillery officer at the Barracks, & of *Officier Superieur* in the King's Body Guards at the Thuilleries. The smallest | representation to M. Le Duc de Luxembourg, who had a true value for him, would have procured him a substitute; but he would not hear me upon such a proposition; he would sooner, far, have died at his post.

He now almost lived either at the Thuilleries or at the Barracks. I only saw him when business, or military arrangements, brought him home. But he kindly sent me billets by his Groom, to appease my dread suspence, every two or three hours.

Le Marquis General Victor de La Tour Maubourg was now appointed by the King, Louis 18, to raise a troop of Volunteers for the Cavalry; while the same commission was | entrusted to M. le Comte de Vioménil for the Infantry.[14]

The project upon Paris became at length obvious: yet its success was little feared, though the horrours of a Civil War seemed inevitable. M. d'Arblay began to wish me away; he made various propositions for ensuring my safety; he even pressed me to depart for England, to rejoin our Alexander & my family. But I knew Them to be in security,—while my first Earthly tie was exposed to every species of danger; & I besought him not to force me away. He was greatly distressed, but could not oppose my urgency. He procured me, however, a Passport from M. le Comte de | Jaucourt,[15] his long attached friend, who was Minister *aux Affaires Etrangères ad interim*, while Taleyrand Perigord was with the Congress at Vienna. M. de Jaucourt gave this Passport *Pour Madame d'Arblay, née Burney*; avoiding to speak of me as the Wife of a General Officer in the Body Guard of the King, lest that might, eventually, impede my progress, should I be reduced to Escape from Paris: while, on the other hand, to facilitate my travelling with any friends, or Companions, he inserted *Et les personnes de sa suite*. This is dated 15 Mars, 1815.

It is now before me.

---

[14] See L. 860 n. 13.
[15] See L. 862 n. 20; L. 918 n. 7. Jaucourt's wife left Paris on or about 15 March (Reiset, iii. 111).

I received it most unwillingly; I could not endure to absent myself from the seat of Government—for I | little devined how soon that Government was to change its Master.

Nevertheless, the wisdom of this preparatory measure soon became conspicuous, for the very following day I heard of Nothing but purposed emigrations from Paris; Retirement; Concealment; embarrassments, & difficulties. My sole personal joy was that my Younger Alexander, was far away, & safely lodged in the only Country of safety.

But on the 17ᵗʰ Hope again revived. I received these words from my best Friend,[16] written on a scrap of Paper torn from a parcel, & brought to me by his Groom, Depres, from the Palace of the Thuilleries, where their | tender Writer had passed the Night mounting Guard.

Nous avons de meilleures nouvelles. Je ne puis entrer dans aucun detail, mais sois tranquille—et aime bien qui t'aime uniquement—
God bless you—

This News hung upon the departure of Marshall Ney, Duc de [d'Elghingen,] to meet Buonaparté, & stop his progress, with the memorable words uttered publicly to the King, That he would bring him to Paris in an Iron Cage.

The King, at this time, positively announced & protested That he would never abandon his Throne, nor quit his Capital, Paris. |

Various of my friends called upon me this day, all believing the storm was blowing over. Madame Chastel & her two Daughters were calm,[17] But, nevertheless, resolved to visit a small *terre* which they possessed, till the Metropolis was free from all contradictory rumours. Madame de Cadignan[18] preserved her imperturbable gaiety & carelessness, & said she should stay, happen what might, for what mischief could befall a poor widow? her sportive smiles & laughing Eyes displayed

---

[16] L. 846.

[17] Anne-Félicité *née* Canot (b. *c.* 1770), the wife of Antoine-Louis-Benjamin Chastel d'Oriocourt (1761–*post* 1831), an employee in the ministère de la Guerre from 1803 until his retirement in 1817. Their elder daughter Nicole-Augustine-Angélique was born on 4 Nov. 1796; the younger, Catherine-Louise-Félicité, in 1802.

[18] The American-born Catherine Hunter (v, L. 513 n. 6), widow of the *émigré* comte de Cadignan (1767–1804), known to the d'Arblays in the 1790s.

her security in the power of her charms. Madame de Maisonneuve was filled with apprehensions for all her Brothers,[19] who were all in highly responsible situations, & determined ¹ to remain in Paris, to be in the midst of them. The Princess d'Henin with unbounded generosity, came to me daily, to communicate all the intelligence she gathered from the numerous Friends & connexions through whom she was furnished with supplies. Her own plans were incessantly changing; but her friendship knew no alteration; & in every various modification of her intentions, she always offered to include me in their execution, should my affairs reduce me, finally, to flight.

Flight, however, was intolerable to my thoughts—I weighed it not as saving me from Buonaparté; I could consider it only as separating me from ¹ all to which my soul most dearly clung. Madame d'Henin was undecided whether to go to the North or to the South; to Bordeaux, or to Brussels: I could not, therefore, even give a direction to M. d'Arblay where I could receive any intelligence:—& the Body Guard of the King was held in utter suspence as to its destination. This, also, was unavoidable, since the King himself could only be guided by events.

The next Day—the 18th of March—all Hope disappeared!— From North, from South, from East, from West alarm took the field, Danger flashed its lightnings, & ¹ contention growled its thunders. Yet in Paris there was no rising, no disturbance, no confusion—All was taciturn suspense, dark dismay, or sullen passiveness. The dread necessity which had reduced the King, Louis 18, to be placed on his Throne by Foreigners, would have annihilated all enthusiasm of Loyalty, if any had been left, by the long underminings of revolutionary principles to be destroyed.

What a Day was this of gloomy solitude! not a soul approached me, save, for a few moments, my active Madame d'Henin; who came to tell me she was preparing to depart, ¹ though as unfixed as ever to what spot, unless a successful Battle should secure the Capital from the Conqueror. I now promised that, if I should, ultimately, be compelled to fly my home, I would thankfully be of her party, & she grasped at this engagement

[19] The Latour-Maubourgs (v, vi *passim*).

with an eagerness of pleasure that gave me an indelible proof of her sincere & animated friendship. This intimation was balm to the tortured heart of my dearest Partner,—& he wished the measure to be executed, & expedited: but I besought him as he valued my existence not to force me away till ǀ every other resource was hopeless.

He passed the day almost wholly at the Barracks. When he entered his Dwelling, in La Rue de Miromenil, it was only upon military business; & from that he could spare me scarcely a Second. He was shut up in his Library with continual Comers & Goers—& though I durst not follow him, I could not avoid gathering, from various circumstances, that he was now preparing to take the field, in full expectation of being sent out with his Comrades of the Guard, to check the rapid progress of the Invader. I knew this to be his earnest wish, as the only chance of saving the King & the Throne—but he ǀ well knew it was my greatest dread; though I was always silent upon this subject, well aware that while his Honour was dearer to him than his life, my own sense of Duty was dearer to me also than mine. While he sought therefore, to spare me the view of his arms, & warlike Equipage & habiliment, I felt his wisdom as well as his kindness, & tried to appear as if I had no suspicion of his preceedings; & remained in acquiescent stillness, almost wholly in my own room, to avoid any accidental surprize;—& to avoid paining him with the sight of my anguish. I masked it as well as I could for the little Instant he had ǀ from time to time to spare me—but before dinner he left me entirely; having to pass the night *à Cheval* at the Barracks, as he had done the preceding night at the Thuilleries.

The length of this afternoon, Evening & night was scarcely supportable:—his broken health—his altered looks—his frequent sufferings, & diminished strength, all haunted me with terrour, in the now advancing prospect of his taking the field— And where?—And How?—No one knew!—yet he was uncertain whether he could even see me once more the next day!— — These lines[20]—these valued— ǀ these invaluable lines—were the only break into my utter solitude, & the wretchedness of my ignorance of what was going forward. They were brought me by Deprez, the General's Groom.

[20] L. 847.

A Mad^e Mad^e d'Arblay

Les Nouvelles ne sont pas rassurantes — M. le Duc d' Orleans a fait partir sa femme et ses Enfans — Madame de Blacas est aussi partie. Rien ne tient — ou, plutôt, tout nous trahit — — Si mon amie pouvoit partir aussi, Je le regarderai plus froidement — car il est presumable que nous ne pourrons faire aucune résistance! ou que nous n'en ferons qu'une ¹ bien peu heureuse, et bien courte — si nous partons de Paris! — Vois — et juge de mon embarras, de mon inquietude! — Tout parait perdu — 'hors l'honneur —' qu'il faut conserver. — Le mien sera sans tâche — et si Je meurs victime de mon devoir, Je ne perdrai pas pour cela l'Espoir de te rejoindre dans un meilleur monde — puisqu'en mourant ce sera là mon dernier vœu, ma demande à l'Eternel — que je supplie de me rejoindre à mon fils et à sa mere — que j'embrasse de toutes les puissances de mon Ame —¹

Je parais calme — et ne le suis guere — Mais Je suis — et serai ferme.¹

I come, now, to the detail of one of the most dreadful days of my existence; The 19th of March, 1815—the last which preceded the triumphant Return of Buonaparté to the Capital of France.

Little, in its opening, did I imagine that Return so near, or believe it would be brought about without even any attempted resistance. General d'Arblay, more in the way of immediate intelligence, & more able to judge of its result, was deeply affected by the most gloomy prognostics. He came home at about six in the morning, harrassed, worn, almost wasted with fatigue & illness, & yet more with a baleful view of all around him, & with a ¹ wounded sense of military honour in the *inertia* which seemed to paralyse all effort to save the King & his cause. He had spent two Nights following armed—on Guard; one at the Thuilleries, in his duty of Garde du Corps to the King, the other on duty as Artillery Captain at the Barracks. He went to Bed for a few hours, & then, after a wretched Breakfast, in which he briefly narrated the state of things he had witnessed, & his black apprehensions of their desperation, he conjured me, in the most solemn & earnest manner, to yield to the necessity of the times, & consent to quit Paris with Mad^e d'Henin, should she ultimately decide to depart. I could not, when I saw ¹ his sufferings, endure to augment them by any further opposition— but never was acquiescence so painful! to lose even the knowledge whither he went, or the means of acquainting him whither I might go myself—to be deprived of the power to join him, should he be made Prisoner, or to attend him, should he be wounded — — I could not pronounce my consent—but he accepted it so decidedly in my silence, that he treated it as arranged, & hastened its confirmation, by assuring me I had relieved his mind from a weight of care & distress nearly intolerable. As the Wife of an Officer in the King's body Guard, in actual service, I might be seized, he thought, as a kind of Hostage, & might probably ᴵ fare all the worse for being, also, an Englishwoman.

He then wrote a most touching Note to the Princesse d'Henin, supplicating her generous friendship to take the task not only of my safety, but of supporting & consoling me.

After this, he hurried back to the Thuilleries, for orders,— apparently more composed,—& that alone enabled me to sustain my so nearly compulsatory & so direfully repugnant agreement.

Grief & Terrour now seemed to struggle within me for pre-eminence; the first for myself, the second for one so much dearer to me,—Oh what torture was my portion in the dread interval of this absence & His next return!

It was speedy—he came, as he had departed, tolerably ᴵ composed, for he had secured me a refuge—& he had received orders to prepare to march.

To Melun,[21] he concluded, to encounter Buonaparté, & to Battle. For certain News now had arrived of the Invader's rapid approach—All attempt to conceal this from me must now be vain:—he acted more nobly by himself, & by his Wife, for in openly, & chearfully, & with rising hope, acknowledging it was for the Field that he now left me, he called upon me to exert my utmost courage, lest I should enervate his own.—

To such a plea had I been deaf I had indeed been unworthy his honoured Choice—& I should have forfeited for-ever the high opinion it was my first pride to see him fondly ᴵ cherish for his grateful Partner — — The event, therefore, seeming inevitable, I suddenly called myself to order, & curbing, crushing

---

[21] The duc de Berry had fortified his army camp at Melun, where the household troops were meant to join him for a decisive battle against Napoleon (Houssaye, *1815*, i. 332–3 and L. 869 n. 12 *supra*).

every feeling that sought vent in tenderness or in Sorrow, I imperiously resolved that, since I must no longer hang upon him for protection, or for happiness, I would, at least, take care not to injure him in his Honour or his Spirits. Still, therefore, I kept in my room, without intervention or enquiry, while he made his final preparations for departure. At half past two, at noon, it was expected that the body Guard would be put in motion. Having told me his history, he could not spare me another moment till that which preceded his leaving his home to join the Duc de Luxembourg's Company.—He then came ¹ to me, with an air of assumed serenity, & again, in the most kindly, soothing terms, called upon to *give him an example of Courage.* I obeyed his injunction with my best ability—yet how dreadful was our parting!—We knelt together—in short but fervent prayer to Heaven for each other's preservation—& then separated—At the door he turned back, & with a smile, which, though forced, had the inexpressible sweetness of approvance, he half gaily exclaimed: 'Vive le Roi!' I instantly caught his wise wish that we should part with apparent chearfulness, & impressively re-ecchoed his words—and then he darted from my sight.—

This had passed in an anteroom; but I then retired to my Bed-Chamber, where, all effort over, I remained ¹ for some minutes abandonned to an affliction nearly allied to despair, though rescued from a positive junction with it by fervent devotion.

But an idea then started into my mind that yet again I might behold him. I ran to the Window of a small anteroom, which looked upon the inward court yard. There, indeed, behold him I did—but Oh with what anguish! just mounting his War Horse—a noble Animal, of which he was singularly fond, but which at this moment I viewed with acutest terrour, for it seemed loaded with pistols, & equip'd completely for immediate service on the field of Battle—while Deprez, the Groom, pre- pared to mount another, & our cabriolet was filled with Baggage, & implements of War—²² ¹

I sunk overpowered—I could not be surprised, since I knew the destination of the General; but so carefully had he spared

²² A light two-wheeled vehicle drawn by a single horse. The cabriolet was often used by senior officers to carry their kits during campaigns.

me the progress of his preparations, which he thought would be killing me by inches, that I had not the most distant idea he was thus armed & encircled with Instruments of Death—Bayonets—Lances—Pistols—Guns—Sabres—Daggers—oh! gracious God! what horrour assailed me at the sight! I had only so much sense & self-controul left as to crawl softly & silently away, that I might not inflict upon him the suffering of beholding my distress—I returned to my Chamber—yet again, at the sound of the Horses' Hoofs, I could not refrain from hastening to have yet another glance, from the Drawing room window, as, followed by his Groom & his cabriolet, he came ⎪ from under the *port Cochere* into la Rue de Miromenil. What an impression did that last glance leave upon my spirits! In his Helmet,[23] for which his military Cap had lately been altered, by a recent order of the Duc de Berry for all the Body Guard, I had not before seen him. It gave an added length to his face & figure that made them seem yet more wan & meagre than when he quitted me. Furrowed looked the former, with care, watchfulness, & previous illness; & thin & infirm the latter from suffering & fatigue. Yet the expression of his face was fixedly calm; & his air announced a firm resolution to die at his post, if at his post he could not live with ⎪ Honour & Loyalty.

Again, after a single glimpse, I shrunk back,—but when [he] had passed the Windows, I opened them [to] look after him.—The street was empty. The gay constant Gala of a Parisian Sunday was changed into fearful solitude.[24] No sound was heard, but that of here & there some hurried footstep, on one hand hastening for a passport, to secure safety by flight; on the other rushing abruptly from, or to some concealment, to devize means of accelerating & hailing the entrance of the Conqueror. Well in tune with this air of impending crisis was my miserable mind, which from Grief little short of torture sunk, at its view, into a state of ⎪ morbid quiet, that seemed the produce of feelings totally exhausted.

Thus I continued, inert, helpless, motionless, till the Princesse d'Henin came into my apartment. She knew from whom I had just parted, and How, and Why!—& her generous spirit was highly capable to judge, to pity, & to sympathise in my

[23] This was a grandiose brass helmet of Graeco-Roman design, topped by a large plume.   [24] This was Palm Sunday, 19 March.

sufferings. But her first news was that Buonaparte had already reached Compiegne,[25] & that to-morrow, the 20th of March, he might arrive in Paris, if the army of the King stopt not his progress.

It was now necessary to make a prompt decision—my word was given—& I agreed to accompany *her* whithersoever she fixed to go. | She was still suspended, but it was settled I should join her in the Evening, Bag & Baggage, & partake of her destination.

Every thing now pressed for Action & exertion: but the pressure was vain; neither of them were in my power. I could execute nothing corporeally, for I could arrange nothing intellectually. My ideas were bewildered; my senses seemed benumbed; my Mind was a Chaos. My husband & Protector was gone to Battle—& its fatal consequences; I could neither follow, nor await him; I must abruptly depart, without letting him know whither;—without knowing it myself — —

How long I wandered about my Apartments under the influence of this species of vague incapacity I | cannot tell. I can only remember it was broken in upon by the entrance of M. Le Noir[26]—& that the sight of an almost bosom favourite of M. d'Arblay, with whom he was in constant intercourse at the Ministère de l'Interieure, awakened me to some consciousness of my situation.

That gentle, ingenuous, meritorious young man, whose mind is the seat of virtue, & whose head is fraught with knowledge & understanding, was so sensibly struck, so grieved, so alarmed, by the sudden departure of M. d'Arblay, that the sympathy I saw excited soon melted the almost frozen faculties of my soul, & dispelled the vague horrour that obscured my mental view, & gave up my whole unhappy being to a nameless, and | most useless consternation. In recounting to him what had passed, I drew my wandering thoughts to a point, & in satisfying his friendly solicitude, I recovered my scared senses. I then determined to take with me whatever Madame d'Henin could admit into her carriage that was valuable & portable, & to lock up what remained, & entrust to M. Le Noir my keys. He consented

[25] Site of a royal château north of Paris. Either the princesse d'Hénin or FBA here confuses it with the palace at Fontainebleau, where Napoleon made his last stop on his advance toward Paris from the south.
[26] L. 840 n. 24.

to take them in charge, & promised to come from time to time to the House, & to give such directions as might be called for by events. I gave to him full power of acting, in presence of Deprez, our *femme de charge*, who was to carry to him my keys when I had made my arrangements; & I besought him—should he see no more either of the General or of myself, never to part with his trust but to our Son. ¹

He solemnly ratified the engagement with his word of Honour, & with feelings for us All nearly as deep as my own, he took leave.

I was now sufficiently roused for action, & my first return to conscious understanding was a desire to call in & pay every bill that might be owing, as well as the Rent of our Apartments up to the present moment, that no pretence might be assumed from our absence for disposing of our goods—Books—or property of any description. As we never had any avoidable debts, this was soon settled but the proprietor of the House was thunderstruck by the measure, saying the King had reiterated his proclamation that he would not desert his Capital. I could only reply that ¹ the General was at his Majesty's orders, & that my absence would be short. I then began collecting our small portion of plate, Jewels, & Trinkets, &c, but while thus occupied, I received a message from Madame d'Henin, to tell me I must bring nothing but a small change of linen, & one Band Box, as by the News she had just heard, she was convinced we should be back again in two or three days. And she charged me to be with her in an hour from that time.

Perplexity upon perplexity now arose what to take—& a general confusion made my choice very inadequate to my after demands. I did, however, what she directed, & put what I most valued, that was not too large, into a Hand basket, made by some French Prisoners in England, that had been given ¹ me by my beloved Friend, Mrs. Lock. I then swallowed, standing, my neglected dinner, &, with Madame Deprez, & my small allowance of baggage, I got into a Fiacre, & drove to General Victor de La Tour Maubourg, to bid adieu to my dearest Madame de Maisonneuve, & her family.

It was about 9 o'clock at Night, & very dark. I sent on Madame Deprez to the Princesse, & charged her not to return to summon me till the last moment. The distance was small.

I found the house of the Marquis Victor de La Tour Maubourg[27] in a state of the most gloomy dismay. No *Portier* was in the way, but the foot door of the *Port Cochere* was ajar, & I entered on foot, no Fiacre being ever admitted ⏀ into *les Cours des Hôtels*. Officers & strangers were passing to & fro', some to receive, others to resign commissions, but All with quick steps, though in dead silence. Not a servant was in the way, & hardly any light. All seemed in disorder. I groped along till I came to the Drawing Room, in which were several people, waiting, as I believe, for orders; or for an Audience, but in no communication with each other, for here, also, a dismal taciturnity prevailed. From my own disturbance, joined to my shortsightedness, I was some time ere I distinguished Madame Victor de La Tour Maubourg,[28] & when, at last, I saw her, I ventured not to address—to approach her. She was at a Table, endeavouring to make some arrangement, or package, or examination, with papers & Boxes, *I think*, before ⏀ her, but deluged in Tears, which flowed so fast, she appeared to have relinquished all effort to restrain them: And this was the more affecting to witness, as she is eminently equal & chearful in her disposition. I kept aloof, & am not certain that she even perceived me. The General was in his own Apartment, transacting military business of moment. But no sooner was I espied by my dearest Madame de Maisonneuve, than I was in her kind arms;—& her soothing affection, her tender sympathy, were so glowing in participation with my sorrows & alarms, that any one who had known her less perfectly than I did, might have imagined she had no Son, no Brothers, no ties ⏀ under Heaven but those which bound her to me. Far, far otherwise; she was a doating Mother, & an adoring Sister; but she had long since taken me to her heart with the most generous friendship; & in that enlarged Heart I stood, & I stand next, immediately next to the native ties of blood. And all her noble family are content to see me in that place.

She took me apart to reveal to me that the velocity of the

[27] The comte Victor's house was at 9, rue d'Aguesseau (*Almanach royal, 1814–15*, p. 69), a nearby street that ran between the rue de Surène and the rue du Faubourg Saint-Honoré. The courtyards of such houses could be entered by private coaches, but not by public cabs or *fiacres*.

[28] Petronella-Jocoba *née* van Rijssel (1772–1844), who had married the comte Victor at Utrecht in 1804 (vi, L. 557 n. 7).

advance of the late Emperor was still more rapid than its report. All were quitting Paris, or resigning themselves to passive submission. For herself, she meant to abide by whatever should be the destination of her darling Brother, Victor: who was now finishing a ¹ commission that no longer could be continued, of raising volunteers—for there was no longer any Royal Army for them to join!—Whether the King would make a stand at the Thuilleries,²⁹ as he had unhappily promised; or whether he would fly, was yet unknown; but General Victor de Maubourg was now going to equip himself in full Uniform, that he might wait upon his Majesty in person, decidedly fixed to take his orders, be they what they might,³⁰

With daring danger thus before him, in his mutilated state, having undergone an amputation of the leg & thigh on the field of Battle at Leipsic,—who can wonder at the desolation of Madame Victor when he resolved to sustain the risk of such an offer!—My own friendship ¹ for him, nearly akin with that I nourished for his all but Twin sister,³¹ & by him returned with feelings almost similar to her own, made me earnestly desire to bid him adieu before my meditated & uncertain flight. Madame de Maisonneuve wished me this indulgence—wished, also, for its momentary break into the arduous toil of her Brother: but Madame Victor was incapable to interfere; & no one could be found to carry to him my request.

During this painful difficulty, what was my emotion at the sudden & most abrupt entrance into the Room of an officer of the King's Garde du Corps! in the self-same Uniform as that from which I had parted with such anguish in the morning! A transitory Hope glanced like Lightening upon ¹ my Brain with an idea that the Body Guard was all at hand—but as evanescent as bright was the flash! the concentrated & mournful look & air of the officer assured me nothing genial was awaiting me; & when, the next minute, we recognized each other, I saw it was

---

²⁹ This bold scheme was proposed by Marmont, who offered to hold the Tuileries for the King by turning it into a fortress garrisoned by the Maison du Roi (see his *Mémoires*, vii. 86–90, and Houssaye, *1815*, i. 345–6). Although this proposal was discussed up to the moment of the King's flight from Paris, it is hard to believe that he could ever have approved, let alone participated in, anything so heroic. Chateaubriand, who supported this plan along with Lafayette, later presented himself as its author (Chateaubriand, *Mémoires*, i. 921–3).

³⁰ See L. 840 n. 23.

³¹ Victor had been born in 1768; Marie in 1770.

the Count Charles de La Tour Maubourg,[32] the youngest Brother of Madᵉ de Maisonneuve; & he then told me he had a Note for me from M. d'Arblay.—
Did I breathe then? I think not! I grasped the paper in my hand, but a mist was before my Eyes, & I could not read a word. Madame de Maisonneuve held a hurried conference with her Brother—and then came to me, & informed me that the Body Guard was all called out, the whole 4 ¹ Companies, with their Grooms, Servants, Equipage, Arms & Horses, to accompany & protect the King in his flight from Paris! But whither he would go,—or with what intent,—whether of Battle or of Escape, had not been announced. The Count Charles had obtained leave of absence for one Hour, to see his Wife (Madˡˡᵉ de La Fayette) & his Children;[32] but M. d'Arblay, who belonged to the Artillery company, could not be spared even a moment. He had therefore seized a cover of a Letter of M. de Bethizy,[33] the Commandant, to write me a few words.
I now read them—& found—

Ma chere Amie — tout est perdu! — Je ne puis entrer dans aucun detail — de Grace, Partez! — le plutôt sera le mieux.
à la vie et à la mort — midy — midy —
A. d'A[34] ¹

Scarcely had I read these few dear, but terrible lines, when I was told that Madame d'Henin had sent me a summons.
I now so earnestly demanded to see General Victor for a moment, that some one, I know not who, had the complaisance to carry him my request: but soon returned, saying it was impossible for the General to quit the officers with whom he was making military arrangements. I then begged his Brother, the Count Charles, to tell him I would come to the ante room, merely to say at the door adieu,—*God bless you!* he knew & loved that English phrase. This was accorded me with vivacity. I went.—he came out, a smile of extreme kindness softening off the disturbance it could not, nevertheless, conceal, & his every feature ¹ as expressive of his animated Friendship as of his pro-

---

[32] Jules-*Charles*-César de Fay (L. 849 n. 2), comte de Latour-Maubourg. He had married in 1798 Lafayette's daughter Anastasie-Louise-Pauline (1777–1863) and had at this time two daughters, Célestine-Louise-Henriette and Louise, 16 and 10 years of age, respectively.   [33] See L. 849 n. 1.   [34] L. 849.

found distress. We shook hands, also *à l'anglais,* 'Mille tendres amitiés,' he cried, à Alexandre!—' He concluded I was flying to England—& he would not venture to name my *other* Alexandre!—nor could he say a word more; while 'Adieu! au revoir!'—and *'God bless you!'* was all I attempted, to utter: and I shut him again up with his officers.

I now could but embrace my Madame de Maisonneuve in silence—& depart. I ventured not to speak to poor Madame Victor. Madame de Maisonneuve accompanied—or rather led me downstairs,—with a disinterestedness of regard the most rare; she seemed to forget herself wholly in her tender anxiety for her parting Friend. We could say nothing of ¹ writing, neither of us knowing where a Letter might be addressed, nor under what Government received. Not a syllable was spoken by either of us as we descended,—She passed the *cour* with me,— empty as before, & the foot door ajar, still, but just as I was preparing to cross the threshold, an immensely tall man, muffled in a folding great coat, & with a Hat flapped low over his face, met me—I stopt—he was passing with disordered steps on,—when Madame de Maisonneuve said 'Mon Frere!—'³⁵ It was the elder M. de Maubourg—who then touched his Hat to me, with a look & manner wholly *disorganized,* & passed rapidly forwards. Madame de Maisonneuve sighed deeply, but still went on with me to the Fiacre—tender then was her silent pressure—& my return to it: & I drove off.—I got into the Coach, ¹ in which was Madame Deprez, who gave the man his direction—& we drove off—my true, affectionate, grieving Friend standing motionless without the Port Cochère to look after me so long as the Vehicle was in sight.

Arrived at Madame la Princesse d'Henins, all was in a perturbation yet greater than what I had left, though not equally afflicting. Madame d'Henin was so little herself that all her fine qualities, her generous zeal for others, her refined good breeding, her fascinating manners, & most winning charm of converse, seemed clouded, if not lost in the conflicting opinions that every moment presented a new view of things, & urged her impatiently, nay imperiously to differ from whatever by any other was offered. ¹

Now she saw instantly impending danger, & was precipitately

³⁵ César, for whose military and political career see L. 845 n. 28.

for flight, now she saw fearless security, & determined not to move a step: the next moment, all was alarm again, & she wanted Wings for speed; & the next, the smallest apprehension awakened derision & contempt.[36]

I, who had never yet seen her but all that was elegant, rational, & kind, was thunderstruck by this effect of threatening evil upon her high & susceptible spirit. From manners of dignified serenity, she so lost all self possession as to answer nearly with fury whatever was not acquiescent concurrence in her opinion: from sentiments of the most elevated nobleness, she was urged by ¹ every report that opposed her expectations, to the utterance of wishes & of assertions that owed their impulse to passion, & their foundation to prejudice; & from having sought, with the most flattering partiality, to attract me to be of her party, she gave me the severe shock of intimating that my joining her confused all her measures.

To change my plan now was impossible: my Husband & my best Friends knew me to be with her, & could seek me, or bestow information upon me in no other direction; & I had given up my home, to which to return, or any where in Paris to stay, was to constitute myself a Prisoner: nevertheless, it was equally a sorrow & a violence to my ¹ feelings to remain with her another moment after so astonishing a reproach.

Displeasure at it, however, subsided, when I found that it proceeded neither from weakened regard, nor a wanton abuse of power, but from a mind absolutely disorganized. The State was not more completely dislocated by this new Revolution, than the whole Composition, mental & intellectual, of this poor Madame d'Henin. It is not that she was insane; far otherwise; her fine understanding had all its force where her feelings & her humour met with no contradiction: but, like Swift's Stella, 'her spirits mounted to a flame'[37] that threatened to fire all around her, at the smallest attempt; ¹ by Argument, by Persuasion, or even by an hint, to point out any mode of proceeding, or of judging, that differed from her own perceptions.

These, indeed, differed from themselves every moment. Her

³⁶ Mme de Latour du Pin described this scene in her *Memoirs*, p. 43.

³⁷ A reference, and one that stresses Stella's obstinacy, to Swift's lines 'Your Spirits kindle to a Flame, ¹ Mov'd with the lightest Touch of Blame, . . .'. See 'To Stella, Who Collected and Transcribed his Poems', *The Poems of Jonathan Swift*, ed. Harold Williams (Oxford, 3 vols., 1958), ii. 727–32.

expectations could not rule events, & consequently laid her continually open to disappointment; though even without that force of necessity, the vehemence of her agitation urged her incessantly to some change.

M. le Comte de Lally Tolendahl, the Cicero of France, & most eloquent man of his day, & one of the most honourable, as well as most highly gifted, was, I now found, to be of our fugitive party. He was her admiring & truly devoted Friend, ǀ & by many believed to be privately married to her. I am myself of that opinion,[38] & that the union, on account of prior & unhappy circumstances, was forborne to be avowed. Certainly their mutual conduct warranted this conclusion. Nevertheless, his whole demeanour towards her announced the most profound respect as well as attachment; & her's to him the deepest consideration, with a delight in his talents amounting [to] an adoration that met his for her noble mind & winning qualities. She wanted, however, despotically to sway him, & little as he might like the submission she required, he commonly yielded with the highest veneration to her will, to avoid, ǀ as I conceive, the dangerous conjectures to which dissention might make them liable.

But at this moment, Revolutionary terrours, & conflicting sensations, robbed each of them of that self-Command which till now had regulated their public intercourse. Etiquette, which had scrupulously encircled them with its distancing minutenesses; & Delicacy which had guided their reciprocal sentiments as rigourously within, as Etiquette their Conduct without, were both not merely powerless, they were annihilated; & while she, off all guard, let loose alike the anxious sensibility & the arbitrary impetuousity of her Nature, He, occupied with too mighty a trouble to ǀ have time, or care for his wonted watchful attentions, heard alike her admonitions or lamentations with an air of angry, but silent displeasure; or, when urged too pointedly for maintaining his taciturnity, retorted her reproaches, or remarks with a vehemence that seemed the Echo of her own—yet in the midst of this unguarded contention, which had its secret incitement, I doubt not, from some

---

[38] FBA seemed not to know that Lally-Tolendal's wife was still living. In 1785 he had married Elizabeth Charlotte (1758–1850), eldest daughter of Sir John Wedderburn Halkett (1720–93), 4th Baronet of Petfirrane. She was to die in Paris on 6 Feb. 1850 (*AR* xc. 208).

cruelly opposing difference of feelings or of ideas upon the present momentous crisis, nothing could be more clear than that their attachment to each other, though it could not gentleize their violent tempers, ¹ was, nevertheless, the predominant passion of their souls.

The turbulence of these two animated characters upon this trying occasion, was strongly contrasted by the placid suffering, & feminine endurance of Madame la comtesse d'Auch,³⁹ the Daughter & sole Heiress & Descendant of M. de Lally. Her Husband, like mine! was in the body Guard of Louis 18, & going, or gone, no one knew whither, nor with what intent; her Estate & property were all near Bordeaux; & her little Children were with her at Paris. The difficult task, in the great uncertainty of events, was now [he]r's to decide, whether to seek the same refuge that her Father & Madame d'Henin should resolve upon seeking, or whether to ¹ run every personal risk in trying to save her lands & fortune from confiscation, by traversing, with only her Babies & servants, 2 or 300 miles, to reach her Chateau at d'Auch³⁹ ere it might be siezed by the conquering party. Quietly, & in total silence, she communed with herself, not mixing in the discourse, nor seeming to heed the disturbance around her: but, when at length applied to, her resolution, from her own concentrated meditations, was fixedly taken, to preserve, if possible, by her exertions & courage, the property of her absent & beloved Husband, for his hoped return, & for her Children.

This steadiness & composure ¹ called not forth any imitation; M. de Lally breathed hard with absolute agony of internal struggles of secret debate; & Madame d'Henin now declared she was sure all would blow over in a false alarm, & that she would not hesitate any longer between Brussels & Bordeaux, but remain quietly in Paris, & merely sit up all Night, to be on the watch: adding, in the fever of her disturbance, that if Madame d'Arblay had not joined them, she should merely have gone *au Val*, to the Country seat of Madame la Princess de Poix,⁴⁰ & there have awaited events.

³⁹ Lally's eldest daughter Élisabeth-Félicité-Claude (1786–1883), the wife since 1807 of the marquis d'Aux-Lally (L. 854 n. 8) and the mother of Arnaud-Jacques-Henri-Félix-Gérard (1808–84) and Léontine-Géraldine-Henriette (1810–77). Auch is in the Armagnac region west of Toulouse.
⁴⁰ The château de Mouchy (see map, p. 2). This mention of the earlier plan

How grieved, with a mind filled, like her's, with generous feelings, & ˡ every power of delicate combination, must she have been at this tardy representation, if it ever occured afterwards to her memory! but such was her disorder, that I believe, far from reflecting upon it in her cooler judgment, she scarcely knew she uttered such a speech then. She seemed to be talking her passing & confused thoughts aloud, merely to unburthen herself from them as they arose, almost without consciousness, & completely without attention or reference to their effect.

M. de Lally determined to go now in person to the Thuilleries, ˡ to procure such information as might decide his shattered & irresolute Friend.

When he was gone, a total silence ensued. Madame d'Auch was absorbed in her fearful enterprise & Madame d'Henin, finding no one opposed her, for *my* thoughts were with no one PRESENT, walked up & down the room, with hasty motion, as if performing some task. Various persons came & went, Messengers, Friends, or people upon business: she siezed upon them all, impatiently demanding their news, & their opinions; but so volubly, at the same time, uttering her own, as to give them no time to reply, though as they left her, too ˡ much hurried themselves to wait her leisure for listening, she indignantly exclaimed against their stupidity & insensibility.

But what a new & terrible commotion was raised in her mind, in that of Madame d'Auch, & in mine, upon receiving a pencil-billet from M. de Lally, brought by a confidential servant, to announce that Buonaparte was within a few hours' march of Paris! He begged her to hasten off, & said he would follow in his Cabriolet when he had made certain arrangements, & could gain some information as to the motions of the King.

She now instantly ordered Horses to her Berlin,⁴¹ which had long been ˡ loaded, &, calling up all her people, & dependants, was giving her orders with the utmost vivacity, when intelligence was brought her that no Horses could now be had, the Government having put them all in requisition.

I was struck with horrour. To be detained in Paris, the seat

to go only this far explains why FBA's letters describing the flight from Paris mistakenly supply the names of places on the estates of the Noailles family northwest of Paris.

⁴¹ Or berline, 'an old-fashioned four-wheeled covered carriage, with a seat behind covered with a hood' (*OED*).

of impending Conquest, & the destined Capital of the Conqueror; detained an helpless Prisoner, where all would be darkly unknown to me, where Truth could find no entrance, Falsehood, no detection—where no news could reach me—except news that was fatal— ' Oh good God! what dire feelings were mine at this period!

Madame d'Auch, who had taken her precautions, instantly, though sadly, went away, to secure her own Carriage, & preserve her little Babies.

Madame d'Henin was now almost distracted—but this dreadful prospect of indefinite detention, with all the horrours of captivity, last[ed] not long; Le Roy, her faithful Domestic from his Childhood, prevailed upon some stable Friend to grant the use of his Horses for one stage from Paris,—& the Berline & 4 was at the Port Cochère in another moment. The servants & Dependants of Madame d'Henin accompanied ' Her to the Carriage in tears & all her fine qualities were now unmixt, as she took an affectionate leave of them, with a sweetness the most engaging, suffering the females to kiss her Cheek, & smiling kindly on the males who kissed her Robe. Vivacity like hers creates alarm, but, in France, breeds no resentment; & where, like her's, the character is eminently noble & generous, it is but considered as a mark of conscious rank, & augments rather than diminishes personal devotion.

We now rushed into the Carriage, averse—yet eager!—between 10 and 11 o'clock at Night, 19ᵗʰ March, 1815. '

⌐──────⌐

As Madame d'Henin had a Passport for herself *et sa famille*, and M. de Jaucourt had given one for me to M. d'Arblay For Madame d'Arblay *et sa suite*, we resolved to keep mine in reserve, in case of accidents, or separation, & only to produce her's, while I should pass to be included in it's privileges.

The decision for our route was for Brussels. The Femme de Chambre of Madame d'Henin within, & the Valet, Le Roy, without the Carriage, alone accompanied us, with the two Postilions for the 4 Horses. '

Madame d'Henin, greatly agitated, spoke from time to time, though rather in ejaculations upon our flight, & its uncertainties, & alarms, than with any view to conversation; but if she had any answer, it was of simple acquiescence from her good & gentle Femme de Chambre; as to me — — I could not utter a word—My Husband on his War Horse—his shattered state of health—his long disuse to military service—yet high wrought sense of military honour, which would seek no refuge from danger through infirmities, or age, or sickness — — all these were before me—I saw, ¹ heard, & was conscious of nothing else—till we arrived at Bourget,⁴² a long, straggling small Town. And here Madame d'Henin meant to stop, or at least change Horses.

But all was still, & dark, & shut up. It was the dead of the Night, & no sort of appearance or effect of alarm seemed to disturb the inhabitants of the place. We knocked at the first Inn: but vainly: after waiting a quarter of an Hour, some stable man came out, to say there was not a room vacant. The same reply was with the same delay given us at two other Inns: but, finally, ¹ were more successful, though even then we could obtain only a single apartment, with 3 Beds. These we appropriated for Madᵉ d'H. myself, & her Maid; & the male servants were obliged to content themselves with mattrasses in the Kitchen.

The Town, probably, was filled with fellow flyers from Paris.

A supper was directly provided, but Madame d'Henin, who now again repented having hurried off, resolved upon sending her faithful Le Roy back to the Metropolis, to discover whether it were positively true that the King had quitted it.

He hired a Horse, & we then endeavoured to repose — — but Oh how far from ¹ ME was all possibility of obtaining it!

About 3 in the morning, M. de Lally over took us. His information was immediately conveyed to the Princesse d'Henin. It was gloomily affrighting. The approach of Buonaparté was wholly unresisted; All bowed before that did not spring forward to meet him.

Le Roy returned about 6 in the morning. The King, & his Guards, & his family, had All suddenly left Paris, but whither had not transpired. He was preceded, encircled, & followed by his 4 Companies of Body Guards; i.e. those of The Prince de Poix, the Duke de Grammont,⁴³ The Duc de Luxembourg,⁴⁴ &

---

⁴² Le Bourget, site of the present-day airport.
⁴³ See L. 862 n. 14.   ⁴⁴ L. 857 n. 1.

the Duc d'Aumale:[45] The 5th or New ¹ Compagnie, under the Duc de Reggio, Marshall Oudinot,[46] was also, I believe, of the Procession.

Horrour & distress, at such a flight, & such uncertainty, were not mine only, however greatly there were circumstances that rendered mine the most poignant; but M. de Lally had a thousand fears for the excellent & loved husband of his Daughter, M. le Comte d'Auch; & Madame d'Henin trembled, for herself & all her family, at the danger of the young Hombert La Tour du Pin.[47]

No longer easy to be so near Paris, we hastily prepared to get on for Brussels, our destined harbour: M. de Lally—now accompanied us, followed by his Valet in a Cabriolet.

Our journey commenced in almost total silence on all parts; the greatness of the change of Government thus ¹ marvellously effecting; the impenetrable uncertainty of coming events, & our dreadful ignorance of the fact of those most precious to us, who were involved in the deeds & the consequences of immediate action, filled every mind too awfully for speech: & our sole apparent attention was to the passengers we overtook, or by whom we were overtaken.

These were so few, that I think we could not count half a dozen on our way to Senlis. And those seemed absorbed in deadly thought & silence, neither looking at us, nor caring to encounter our looks. The road, the Fields, the Hamlets, all appeared deserted. Desolate & lone was the universal air. ¹

I have since concluded that the people of these parts had separated into two divisions; one of which had hastily escaped, to save their lives & loyalty; while the other had hurried to the Capital, to greet the Conqueror: for this was Sunday,[48] the 20th of March.

Oh what were my sensations in passing through SENLIS! Senlis, so lately fixed for my 3 months abode with my General, during his being *de service*, & where already he had secured me not only a dwelling, but admission, with flattering distinction,

[45] This was in fact the duc d'Havré et de Croy (L. 862 n. 13), who commanded the compagnie Écossaise of the King's bodyguard.
[46] The 5th company was actually commanded by the prince de Wagram. Oudinot (L. 860 n. 5), the duc de Reggio, was at that time at Metz.
[47] See L. 854 n. 9.
[48] A mistake for Monday.

to a society the most amiable!—When we stopt at a nearly empty Inn, during the change of Horses, I enquired after Madame ˡ Le Quint,⁴⁹ & some other ladies who had been prepared to kindly receive me—but they were all gone! hastily they had quitted the town, which, like its environs, had an air of being generally abandoned.

The desire of obtaining intelligence made Madame d'Henin most unwilling to continue a straight forward journey, that must separate her more & more from the scene of action. M. de Lally wished to see his friend the young Duc d'Orleans,⁵⁰ who was at Peronne, with his sister & part of his family; & he was preparing to gratify this desire, when a discussion relative to the danger of some political misconstruction ˡ the Duke being at that time upon ill terms with Monsieur, comte d'Artois,⁵¹ made him relinquish his purpose. We wandered about, however, I hardly knew where, save that we stopt from time to time at small hovels in which resided tenants of the Prince or of the Princess de Poix, who received Madame d'Henin with as much devotion of attachment as they could have done in the fullest splendour of her power to reward their kindness; though with an entire familiarity of discourse that, had I been new to French customs, would have passed to me marks of total loss of respect. But after a ten Years unbroken residence in France, previous to this added period, I was too well initiated in the ways of the ˡ dependants upon the Great belonging to their own tenantry, to make a mistake so grossly unjust to their characters. We touched, as *I think*, at Noailles, at Sᵗ Just, at Mouchy, & at Poix—but I am only *sure* we finished the day by arriving at Roy,⁵² where still the news of that Day was unknown. What made it travel so slowly I cannot tell; but from utter dearth of all the intelligence by which we meant to be guided, we remained, languidly, & helplessly, at Roy till the middle of the following Monday,⁵³ the 21ˢᵗ March.

⁴⁹ Unidentified.

⁵⁰ The duc d'Orléans, appointed on 16 March commander-in-chief of the troops in the département du Nord, had been at Lille since the 19th. The sister mentioned here was Adélaïde (1777–1847), and for his wife and children, see L. 847 n. 1. FBA, who wrote this in her old age, calls him 'the young Duc' to distinguish him from his father, Philippe Égalité (1747–93).

⁵¹ This continued to be true throughout the Hundred Days, when the comte d'Artois considered the duc d'Orléans to be a more dangerous enemy than Napoleon.

⁵² See map, p. 2.   ⁵³ Actually Tuesday, 21 March.

About that time, some military entered the town, & our Inn. We durst not ask a single question, in our uncertainty to which side they belonged, ⎮ but the 4 Horses were hastily ordered, since to decamp seemed what was most necessary: but Brussels was no longer the indisputable spot, as the servants overheard some words that implied a belief that Louis 18. was quitting France to return to his old asylum, England.⁵⁴ It was determined, therefore,—though not till after a tumultuous debate between la Princesse & M. de Lally, to go straight to Amiens, where the Prefect was a former Friend, if not connexion by alliance of the Princess; M. Lameth.

We had now to travel by a cross road, & a very bad one, & it was not till night we arrived at the suburbs.

It was here first we met with those difficulties that announced, by ⎮ vigilance, with disturbance, a kind of suspended Government, for the officers of the Police who demanded our passports, were evidently at a loss whether to regard them as valid or not. Their interrogatories, mean while, were endless, &, finally, they desired us, as it was so late & dark, to find ourselves a lodging in the suburbs, & not enter the City of Amiens till the next morning.

Clouded as were alike our perceptions & our information, we could not but be aware of the danger of *to-morrow*, when our entrance might be of a sort to make our exit prohibited. Again followed a tumultuous debate, which ended in the hazardous resolve of appealing to the Prefect, & casting ourselves upon his ⎮ protection.

There were 3 Messʳˢ La Meth,⁵⁵ who had all acted prominent parts in the Revolution,& not such as had seemed chastly spotless with regard either to political principles or moral severity. But the gradations of praise or censure with which they were severally viewed I cannot assign, for I know not which of the Three was the present Prefect; though, having been placed by Louis 18 at Amiens, he was probably the one most esteemed.

⁵⁴ A reasonable belief, since throughout this week the proposal continued to be made. In his flight to Belgium the King stayed close to the Channel ports in case a crossing to England became necessary.

⁵⁵ For the Lameth brothers, see v, L. 446 n. 20. The prefect Alexandre, comte de Lameth (L. 856 n. 8 *supra*), observed a discreet silence during the change of regime and purge of prefects that followed it. When it became clear that he was to be kept in his post, however, he published a proclamation welcoming Napoleon's decrees (*Journal du département de la Somme*, 10 May).

This appeal ended all Inquisition. We were treated with deference, & accommodated in a decent room, while the passports of Madame d'Henin & of M. de Lally were forwarded to the Prefecture.

We remained here some time, in ⎸ the utmost stillness, no one pronouncing a word. We knew not who might listen, nor with what Ears! But far from still was all within, because far from confident how the Prefect might judge necessary to arrest; or to suffer our proceeding further.

The answer was, at length, an order to the police officers to let us enter the City, & be conducted to an Hotel named by M. Lameth.

My Passport being held back, I only made one of *la famille* of la Princesse.

We had an immensely long drive through the City of Amiens ere we came to the indicated Hôtel. But here, Made d'Henin found a note, that was delivered to her by the Secretary of the Prefecture, ⎸ announcing the intention of the Prefect to have the honour of waiting upon her.

She was flattered, but fluttered,—We had been shewn to a large & handsome apartment: & when M. Lameth was named, M. de Lally & I retired to our several Chambers.

Her tête à tête with him was very long; & ended in a summons to M. de Lally to make it a trio.

This interview was longer still—& my anxiety for the news with which it might terminate, relative to the King, the Body Guard, & our detention or progression, was acute.

At length, I, also, was summoned: Madame d'Henin came out to tell me upon the landing place, hastily & confusedly to say ⎸ that the Prefect did not judge proper to receive her at the Prefecture, but that he would stay & sup with her: & that I was to pass for her *premiere femme de Chambre*, as it would not be prudent to give in my Name, though it had been made known to M. Lameth.

I easily conceived that the Wife of an officer so immediately in the service of the King, must not be specified as a Host of a Prefect, if that Prefect meant to yield to the tide of a new Government. Tide?—nay, torrent it was, at this moment, & any resistance that had not been previously organized, & with military force, must have been vain. I made, however, no enquiry; I was ¹ simply acquiescent, &, distantly following Madame d' Henin, remained at the end of the room, while the Servants & the Waiters adjusted matters for supper.

In a situation of such embarrassment I never before was placed. I knew not which way to look, nor what to do—Any presentation to the Prefect was out of the question, & to make one at a Table where he presided unasked & unnoticed, was impracticable. No name having been assigned me, they knew not how to address me, & the awkwardness went all round. Discovery, at such a crisis, might have been fatal, as far as might hang upon detention; & detention, which would rob me of all ¹ means of hearing of M. d'Arblay, should I gather what was his route, & be able to write to him, was death to my peace. I regretted I had not demanded to stay in another room; but, in such heart-piercing moments, to be in the way of intelligence & of motion is the involuntary first movement.

When all was arranged, & Madame d'Henin was seated, M. de Lally set a Chair for me, slightly bowing to me to take it. I complied, & Supper began. I was helped, of course, the last; & not once spoken to by any body.

The repast was not very gay, yet by no means dejected. The conversation was upon general topics, & M. de Lameth was entirely master of himself, seeming wholly without emotion. ¹

I was afterwards informed that News had just reached him that Buonaparté had returned to Paris, but not officially. Having heard, therefore, nothing from the new Government, he was able to act as if there were none such; & he kindly obliged Madame d' Henin by giving her New passports, which, should the conquest be confirmed, would be safer than Passports from the Ministers of Louis 18 at Paris. I was here merely included in her family, & he advised that my Name should be concealed. There was peculiarly less danger for Madame d'Henin, to whom M. Taleyrand, while he held the Seals of Buonaparté, had accorded the preservation of her title, as being her's from a Prince of the Low Countries, or La Belgique, ¹ & therefore not necessarily included in the Revolutionary sacrifice of rank.⁵⁶ Her claim, therefore, to the honours of her Name having, of course, never been disputed on the King's side, &

---

⁵⁶ The principality of Hénin-Liétard, near Lens in the Pas-de-Calais, dating from 1579, had never been a French title.

having been ratified on that of Buonaparté, while in power, made her now one of the persons the least liable to involve any Magistrate in difficulty for being allowed to pass through his domain, whatever might be the issue of the present public conflict.

M. Lameth could not, however, answer for retaining his powers; nor for what might be their modification even from hour to hour: he advised us, therefore, by no means to risk ¹ his being either re-placed or restrained, but to get on as fast as possible with his passports, while certain they were efficient. He thought it safer, also, to make a circuit, than to go back again to the high road we had quitted. Our design of following the King, whom we imagined gaining the Sea Coast, to embark for England, was rendered abortive from the number of contradictory accounts which had reached M. Lameth as to the route he had taken. Brussels, therefore, became again our point of desire: but M. Lameth counselled us to proceed, for the moment, to Arras, where ¹ M. —— —— I lament I forget his name⁵⁷—would aid us either to proceed, or to change, according to circumstances, our destination. Not an instant, however, was to be lost, lest M. Lameth should be forced, himself, to detain us.

Horses, therefore, he ordered for us, & a Guide across the Country, for Arras.

I learnt nothing of this till we re-entered our Carriage. The Servants & Waiters never quitted the room, & the Prefect had as much his own safety to guard from ill construction or ill report as ours. Madame d'Henin, though rouged the whole time with confusion, never ventured to address a word to me. It was, indeed, more easy to be ¹ silent, than to speak to me either with a tone of condescendsion or of command; & any other must have been suspicious. M. de Lally was equally dumb, but active in holding out every *plat* to me, though always looking another way. M. Lameth eyed me with the extremest curiosity, but had no resource against some surmize save that adopted by Madame d'Henin. However, he had the skill, & the politeness, to name, in the course of the repast, M. d'Arblay, as if accidentally, yet with an expression of respect & distinction, carefully, as he spoke, turning his Eyes from mine, though it was the only time that, voluntarily, he would have met them.

---

⁵⁷ Jacques-François Lachaise (L. 856 n. 8).

The Horses being ready, M. Lameth took leave very respectfully of Madame [|] d'Henin, & with marked distinction of M. de Lally, while, in striding across the apartment, he contrived to make me a bow not inexpressive of courtesie.

It was now about 11 at Night! The road was of the roughest sort, & we were jerked up & down the ruts so as with difficulty to keep our seats. It was also very dark, & the drivers could not help frequently going out of their way, though the Guide, groping on, upon such occasions, on foot, soon set them right. It was every way a frightful night. Misery both public & private oppressed us all, & the fear of pursuit & captivity had the gloomy effect of causing general taciturnity, so that no kind voice, nor social suggestion [|] diverted the sense of danger, or excited one of Hope.

At what hour we arrived at Arras, on Wednesday the 22^d March, I cannot tell. But we drove straight to the Prefecture, a very considerable Mansion,[58] surrounded with spacious Grounds & Gardens, which to me, nevertheless, had a bleak, flat, & desolate air, though the sun was brightly shining. We stopt at the furthest of many Gates, on the high road, while Madame sent in to M. (I forget his name)[57] the Note with which we had been favoured by M. Lameth.

The answer was a most courteous invitation of entrance, & the moment the Carriage stopt at the great door of the Portico, the Prefect, M. [Lachaise,] [|] hastened out to give Madame d'Henin *le bras*. He was an old Soldier, & in full Uniform, & he came to us from a Battalion drawn out in array on one side the Park. Tall, & with still a goodly port, though with a face that shewed him worn & weather-beaten, he had the air of a Gentleman as well as of a General officer; & the open & hospitable smile with which he received the Princesse, while, bareheaded & bald-headed, he led her into his palace, diffused a welcome around, that gave an involuntary cheeriness even to poor dejected me. How indescribably gifted is 'the human face divine',[59] where strongly marked with Character, in those who

---

[58] Formerly the episcopal palace, this mansion had been rebuilt in 1780 in sumptuous neo-classical style. Although pillaged and sold off during the Revolution, it was restored and turned into the hôtel de la Préfecture under the consulate. See Achmet d'Héricourt and Alexandre Godin, *Les Rues d'Arras* (Arras, 2 vols., 1856), ii. 311.

[59] *Paradise Lost*, ii. 45.

are invested with power, [|] to transmit, or to blight comfort to those who fall into their dependence, even by a glance.

As Madame d'Henin demanded a private audience, I know not what passed; but I have reason to believe we were the first who brought news to Arras that approached to the truth of the then actual position of Paris. M. Lameth, for political reasons, had as studiously avoided naming M. de Lally as myself, in his Note: but M. de Lally was treated by the mistress of the house with the distinction due to a Gentleman travelling with la princesse: & as to me, some of the younger branches of the family took me under their protection, concluding me to be an humble Companion: & very kind [|] they were, shewing me the Garden, Library, & views of the surrounding country.

Meanwhile, an elegant Breakfast was prepared for a large company, a Review having been ordered for that morning, & several General Officers being invited by the Prefect.

This repast had a chearfulness that, to me, an English woman, was unaccountable, & is undefinable. The King had been compelled to fly his Capital; no one knew whither he was seeking shelter; no one knew whether he meant to resign his Crown in hopeless inaction, or whether to contest it in sanguine civil War. Every family, therefore, with its every connexion, in the whole Empire of the French was actually involved, or indispensably involving, [|] in scenes upon which hung Prosperity or Adversity, Reputation or Disgrace, Honour or Captivity, Existence or its extinction; yet at such a crisis the large assembled family met with chearfulness, the many Guests were attended to with politeness, & the goodly fare of that medley of refreshments called a *Dejeuner* in France, was met with appetites as goodly as its incitements.

This could not be from insensibility; the French are any thing less than insensible; it could not be from attachment to Buonaparté, the Prefect loudly declaring his devotion to Louis 18; I can only, therefore, attribute it to the [|] long Revolutionary state of the French Mind, as well as Nation, which had made it so familiar to Insurrection, Change, & Incertitude, that they met it as a man meets some unpleasant business which he must unavoidably transact, & which, since he has no choice to get rid of, he resolves to get through to the best of his ability.

We were still, however, smelling sweet Flowers & regaled

with fine fruits, when this serenity was somewhat ruffled by the arrival of the Commander of the forces[60] which had been reviewed, or destined for review, I know not which. He took the Prefect aside, & they were some time together. He then, only bowing to the ladies | of the house, hastened off. The Prefect told us the news that imperfectly arrived was very bad, but he hoped a stand would be made against any obstinate revolt; & he resolved to assemble every officer & soldier belonging to his Government, & to call upon each separately to take again, & solemnly, his Oath of allegiance.

While preparing for this ceremony, the Commander again returned, & told him he had positive information that the defection was spreading, & that whole troops & Companies were either sturdily waiting in inaction, or boldly marching on to meet the Conqueror.[61]

Our table was now broken up, & we were wishing to depart, ere | official intimation from the Capital might arrest our further progress. But our Horses were still too tired, & no other were to be procured. We became again very uneasy, & uneasiness began to steal upon all around us. The Prefect was engaged in perpetual little groups of consultation, in the very large apartment of our repast, chiefly with general officers, who came & went with incessant bustle, & occasionally & anxiously were joined by persons of consequence of the vicinity. The greater the danger appeared, the more intrepidly the brave old Prefect declared his loyalty; yet he was advised by all parties to give up his scheme till he knew whether the King himself made a stand in his own Cause. |

He yielded reluctantly; & when Madame d'Henin found his steady adhesion to his King, she came up to him, while I, as usual, was holding back, from all but my new young friends, who never forsook me, & said to him that, finding the firmness of his devotion to Louis 18, she was sure she should give him pleasure to know he had at that Moment under his roof the Wife of a General officer in the actual escort of his Majesty. He instantly came up to me, with a benevolent smile, & we had a conversation of deep interest, upon the present state of things.

<hr/>

[60] The general commanding at Arras was baron Teste (L. 860 n. 10).

[61] Since Teste went over to Napoleon on the following day and ordered the attack on the Maison du Roi at Béthune (L. 862 n. 6), he was both bringing bad news and justifying his imminent change of allegiance.

I had the heart felt satisfaction to find that my honoured Husband was known to him, not alone by his reputation, but personally, & to find that, & to ǀ hear his praise has always been one & the same thing!—alas!—those sounds on these sad Ears vibrate no more!—[62]

During this discourse, thus rendered enlivening to me, I discovered that my worthy Host had not an idea of possessing M. de Lally under his roof; & I had the very great pleasure of procuring to that valued & honourable Friend a welcome such as he merited; for no sooner had I mentioned him, than the Prefect became almost young again from the extacy of his joy. What! he cried, de Lally? de Lally Tolendahl! that excellent citizen, that exalted character, that first rate Man of Parts & Virtues united! is he here? is he my Guest!— ǀ

M. de Lally, who was taking a ruminating stroll, was no sooner thus apostrophized, than the hearing, which is never obtuse where our own names are mentioned, became sufficiently acute to bring him to our side; though not a Word, save that which, identified with ourselves, is caught even from a whisper, where the loudest call might pass unheeded, reached his Ear. And pleasant it was to contemplate the honest expansion of sudden delight in his open face, when he saw himself suddenly drawn from a depressing & subaltern place, to be elevated to that distinction which was so justly his due, & which ǀ he enjoyed as highly as he deserved. Ten years, at least, seemed snatched from his Complexion, & twenty from the weight upon his spirits. The Prefect, repeatedly embracing him, protested that his house had, that day, received its greatest honour.

Our impatience to be gone now lost its eagerness, though nothing had intervened to take away its prudence: but we keep small account of time where we are pleased—ah, why does that oblivious neglect of its calculation occur so seldom!—

At length, however, about noon, we set off, accompanied by the Prefect & all his family, to our Carriage.

I have forgotten to mention that, from the commencement of our flight ǀ We made a common travelling Purse, each entering into it 6 Napoleons,[63] to be replenished as they were extin-

---

[62] General d'Arblay had died on 3 May 1818 and few persons in London in 1823 had ever known him.   [63] Roughly three pounds.

guished, of which Madame d'Henin was Treasury. The servants, as I had none with me, were kept by a separate account.

We were All somewhat roused from our deep dejection, by observing the general tendency to loyalty at the Prefecture of Arras, & by the personal kindness as well as allegience of the brave Prefect: though we grieved to have returned his hospitality by leaving him so much less happy than we had found him.

At Douy we had the satisfaction to see still stronger outward marks of attachment to the King & his Cause, for from far the greater ꞁ number of Windows, in every street through which we passed, the Windows were decked with emblems of faithfulness to the Bourbon dynasty,—white Flags, or Ribbands, or pocket Handkerchiefs. All, however, without commotion, all was a simple manifestation of respect. No Insurrection was checked, for none had been excited; no Mob was dispersed, for scarcely a Soul seemed to venture from their House.

Our wish, & our intention was to quit the French territory that Night, & sleep in more security at Tournay; but the roads became so bad, & our Horses grew so tired, that it was already dark before we reached Orchies.

M. de Lally, from Douy, went on in his Cabriolet, to lighten our weight,[64] as Madame d'Henin had a good deal of Baggage. ꞁ We were less at our ease in thus perforce travelling slower, to find the roads, as we preceded from Douy, become more peopled. Hitherto they had seemed nearly a blank. We now began, also, to be met, or to be overtaken, by small parties of troops. We naturally looked out with earnestness on each side, to discover to whom or to what they belonged; but the compliment of a similar curiosity on their part was all we gained. Some times they called out a 'Vive!—' but without finishing their wish; & we repeated—that is we bowed to the same hailing exclamation, without knowing, or daring to enquire its purport.

At Orchies, where we arrived rather late in the evening, we first found ꞁ decided marks of a Revolutionary state of things. We stopt a considerable time at an Inn, before we could obtain any attention, or even discover by whom we were neglected: all

[64] Since Lally was enormously fat, the relief in weight must have been considerable.

seemed in disorder; but merely the disorder of ignorance what path to take; not of any predominant feeling, or of any plan either to promote or impede the hovering change of dynasty. The constituted authorities appeared to be left to themselves. No orders were sent by either party. The King & his Government were too eminently in personal danger to assert their rights, or retain their authority for directing the Provinces; & Buonaparte, & his followers & supporters were too much engrossed by taking possession of the Capital, & too uncertain either of the extent or the durability of their success ׀ to try a power which had as yet no basis, or risk a disobedience which they had no means to resent. The people, as far as we could see, or learn, seemed passively waiting the event; & the constituted authorities appeared to be self-suspended from their functions till the *droit du plus fort* should ascertain who were their masters.

I confine these observations, however, only to our own particular route. Loyalty to the Bourbons, or enthusiasm for Buonaparte, might, perhaps, be buoyant else where: but from Paris to Tournay I saw nothing that resembled vigour even of wishes for either side.

Nevertheless, while we waited at Orchies for Horses, something like the menace of disorder began to menace this apparent apathy. News arrived by straggling parties which, though only whispered, created evidently some disturbance, ׀ & a sort of wondering expectation soon stared, from face to face, asking by the Eye what no one durst pronounce by the Voice; what does all this portend? and for what ought we to prepare?

It was past Eleven o'clock, & the Night was dark & damp, ere we could get again into our Carriages; but the encreasing bustle warned us off, and a nocturnal journey had nothing to appal us equally with the danger of remaining where we might be overtaken in the conscious act of escaping. We eagerly, therefore, set off; but we were still in the suburbs of Orchies, when a call for help struck our ears, & the Berlin stopt. It was so dark, we could not at first discover what was the matter; but we soon found that the carriage of M. de Lally was broken down.

Madame d'Henin darted out of the Berlin with the activity of 15. Her Maid accompanied her, & I eagerly followed. ׀

Neither M. de Lally nor his man had received any injury;

but the Cabriolet could no longer proceed without being repaired. The Groom was sent to discover the nearest Black-smith, & M. de Lally was obliged to remain close to his Carriage, to guard his Effects. Madame d'Henin would not leave him in this miserable state; nor would I leave Mad^e d'Henin. We grouped, therefore, together, full of uneasiness, lest our journey should be retarded. A man came soon to examine the mischief, & declared that it could not be remedied before day light. We were forced to submit the vehicle to his decree; but our distress what to do with ourselves was now very serious. We knew there was no accommodation for us at the Inn we had just quitted, but that of passing ı the night by the Kitchen fire, exposed to all the hazards of suspicious observations upon our evident flight. To remain upon the high road stationary in our Berline might, at such a momentous period encompass us with dangers yet more serious. A mizzling Rain which dropt continually, made it necessary we should come to some determination, for, as it was too dark to discern any path, we could neither move nor stand still but in mud. We were yet ruminating, & unresolved, when a light from the Windows of a small house attracted our attention. We had not looked at it above a minute, when a door was opened, at which a sort of Gentlewoman somewhat more than elderly stood, with a Candle in her hand, that lighted up a face full of benevolence, in which was painted strong compassion on the view of our palpable ı distress. She was herself obviously but just risen from her Bed, & hastily equipped with decent covering. She fixed us, with an expression that shewed her much less inquisitive who or what we were, than earnest to devize some means to do us service. Her countenance encouraged us gently to approach her, & the smile with which she saw us come forward soon accellerated our advance; & when we reached her threshold, she waited neither for solicitation nor representation, but let us into her small dwelling without a single question, silently, as if fearful herself we might be observed, shutting the street door before she spoke. She then lamented, as we must needs, she said, be cold & comfortless, that she had no fire, but ı added that she & her little Maid were abed & asleep, when the disturbance on the road had awakened her, & made her hasten up, to enquire if any one were hurt. We told as much of our story as belonged to our immediate situation, & she then instantly assured us we should be welcome to stay in her house till the Cabriolet was repaired.

Without waiting for our thanks, she then gave to each a Chair, & went herself into a small out house, whence she fetched great plenty of fuel, with which she made an ample & most revivying fire, in a large stove that was placed in the middle of the room. She had Bedding, she said, for two, & begged that, when we were warmed ⏐ & comforted, we would decide which of us most wanted rest. We durst not, however, risk, at such a moment, either being out of the way, or separated, or surprized: we entreated her, therefore to let us remain together, & to retire herself to the repose her humanity had thus broken. But she would not leave us. She brought forth Bread, Butter, & Cheese, with Wine, & some other beverage, & then made us each a large bowl of Tea. And when we could no longer partake of her hospitable fare, she fetched us each a Pillow, & a double Chair, to rest our heads & our feet, & planted each of us next to some Table, or Dresser, on which we could somewhat lounge our weary arms.

Thus cheered, quieted, & refreshed, we blessed our kind Hostess, & fell ⏐ into something like a gentle slumber, when we were suddenly roused by the sound of Trumpets, & warlike Instruments, & the trampling of many Horses, coming from afar, but approaching with rapidity. We all started up, greatly alarmed. We listened in total silence, & only by our looks made known our reciprocated apprehensions. Presently, the group, perceiving, I imagine, through the ill-closed shutters, some light, stopt before the house, & battered the door & the Window with sundry weapons, demanding admission. We hesitated whether to remain where we were, or to endeavour to conceal ourselves; but ⏐ our admirable Hostess, bid us be still, while, calm herself, she went out, & opened the street Door, where she parleyed with the party, chearfully & without any appearance of fear, & telling them she had no room for their accommodation, because she had given up even her own Bed to some Relations who were travelling, she gained from them an applauding *houra*,[65] & their departure.

---

[65] FBA was mistaken in thinking that this was applause. 'Hourra!' was the battle-cry of Polish and Russian light cavalry and here probably meant 'Forward!'

She then informed us they were Polish Lancers,[66] & that she believed they were advancing to scour the Country in favour of Buonaparté. She expressed herself an open & ardent loyalist for the Bourbons, but said she had no safety except in submitting, like all around her, to ⌐ the stronger powers.

Again, by her encouraging persuasion, we sought to compose ourselves; but a second party soon startled us from our purpose, & from that time we made no similar attempt. Horrified I felt at every blow of the trumpet, & the fear of being made Prisoner, or pillaged, assailed me unremittingly.

At about five o'clock in the morning our Carriages were at the door. We blessed our benevolent Hostess, took her name & address, that we might seek some other means of manifesting our gratitude, & then quitted Orchies.

For the rest of our journey till we reached the frontiers, we were annoyed with incessant small military groups ⌐ or Horsemen; but though they surveyed, or encircled us curiously, they did not yet seem authorised with powers for stopping passengers, & therefore, though suspiciously regarded, we were not stopt. The fact is, the new Government was not yet, in these parts, sufficiently organized to have been able to keep if they had been strong enough to detain us. But we had much difficulty to have our passports honoured for passing the frontiers; & if they had not been so recently renewed at Amiens, I think it most probable our progress would have been impeded till new orders & officers were entitled to make us halt.[67]

Great, therefore, was our satisfaction when, through all these difficulties, we entered Tournay—where, being no ⌐ longer in the late restored Kingdom of France, we considered ourselves to be escaped from the dominion of Buonaparte, & where we determined, therefore, to remain till we could guide our further proceedings by tidings of the plan & the position of Louis 18.

We went to the most considerable Inn,[68] & had each our separate Apartment without interrogatory or dilemma. It was

[66] Of the six regiments of lancers in the French army at that time, three were for the most part Polish. They were famous for their courage and for their loyalty to Napoleon, who had an escort of Polish lancers from Elba to Paris. Within a year they were all to be disbanded (*Almanach royal, 1816*, pp. 570–1).

[67] Napoleon's advancing cavalry had in fact been given orders to allow the King's household and royalist supporters to leave France, even where necessary to hurry them over the border into Belgium.

[68] Probably the Hôtel de l'Impératrice.

late in the morning; but we all retired to rest, which, after so much fatigue, mental & bodily, we required, &, happily, obtained.

The next day, we had the melancholy satisfaction of hearing that Louis 18, also, had safely passed the Frontiers of his lost Kingdom.

As we were less fearful, now, of making enquiries, M. de Lally soon learnt ׀ that His Majesty had halted at Lille,[69] where he was then waiting permission & directions for a place of retreat, from the King of Holland, or the Netherlands. But no intelligence whatever could we gain relative to the Body Guards, & my disturbance encreased every moment.

There was far more commotion at Tournay than at any other town through which we passed, for as the people here were not under the French Government, either old or New, they belong in fearful passiveness: yet they had all the perplexity upon their minds of disquieting ignorance whether they ׀ were to be treated as Friend or Foe, since, if Buonaparte prevailed, they could not but expect to be joined again to his dominions. All the commotion, therefore, of divided interests & jarring opinions, were awake, & in full operation upon the faculties & feelings of every Belgian at this critical & decisive moment. ׀

———

The horrour of my suspence, at this tremendous period, relative to the safety & the fate of Monsieur d'Arblay, reduced my mind to a sort of chaos that makes it impossible to me to recollect what was our abode at Tournay. I can but relate my distress & my researches.

My first thought was to send a Letter to my General at Lille, which, if he was There would inform him of my vicinity, & if not, might, perhaps, find its way to his destination. At all events, I resolved only to write what would be harmless should it fall even into the hands of the Enemy. I directed these few lines to M. le Chevalier d'Arblay, *officier superieur, du Corps de* Garde de Sa Majesté Louis 18.

But when I would have sent them to the post, I was informed there was no post open to Lille. I then sought for a Messenger;

[69] The King left Lille on 23 March.

but was told that Lille was inaccessible.[70] The few Letters that were permitted to enter it, were placed in a Basket, the handle of which was tied to a long cord, that was hooked up to the top of the Walls, & thence descended to appointed Magistrates.

Vainly I made every effort to my power to avail myself of this method; no one of my party, nor at the Inn, knew, or could indicate any means that promised success, or even a trial.

Worn, at length, by an anxiety I found insupportable, I took a decided resolution to go forth myself, stranger I as I was to the place, to its language, & it's customs, & try to get my Letter conveyed to the Basket; however difficult, or costly, might be its carriage.

I mentioned not my intentions to Madame d'Henin, who would warmly have opposed them, lest I should fall into any danger; I felt none so severe as that to my peace of mind in remaining inactive. I knew, also, that she, & M. de Lally, were both so much engrossed by their own affairs, as well as by their uneasiness for their Son in Law & Nephew,[71] that, till dinner time, there was much probability I should not even be missed.

Quite alone, therefore, I sallied forth, purposing to find, if possible, some sturdy Boy, who I would be glad of such remuneration as I could offer to pass over to Lille.

Again, however vain was every attempt. I entered all decent poor houses; I sauntered to the suburbs, & entered sundry cottages; but no enquiry could procure me either a Man or a Boy that would execute my commission. French was so generally known, that I commonly made myself understood, though I only received a shake of the head, or a silent walking off, in return to my propositions. But, in the end, a Lad told me he thought he had heard that Madame La Duchesse de St. Agnes[72] had had some intercourse with Lille. Delighted, I desired him I to shew me the house she inhabited, We walked to it together, & I then said I would saunter near the spot, while he entered, with my earnest petition to know whether Madame could give me any tidings of the King's Body Guard. He returned, with an answer, that Madame would reply to a written Note, but to

[70] The gates of Lille were closed after the King's arrival, but they were reopened to travellers and mail by 26 March (*Moniteur*, 30 March).

[71] See n. 32 *supra* and L. 854 nn. 8, 9.

[72] Emma-Victurnienne-Nathalie de Beauvillier *née* de Rochechouart (1790–1824), duchesse de Saint-Aignan, a younger half-sister of the princesse de Beauvau.

nothing verbal. I bid the Boy hie with me to the Inn; but, as I had no writing tackle of the billet sort, I sent him forward to procure me proper implements at the best stationers. How it happened I know not, but I missed the Boy, whom I could never regain; & I soon after lost my Way myself. In much perplexity, I was seeking ׀ information which way to steer, when a distant sound of a party of Horse caught my attention. I stopt. The sound approached nearer; the Boys, & idle people in the street, ran forward to meet it; & presently were joined, or followed, by the more decent inhabitants. I had not the temerity to make one among them, yet my anxiety for news of any sort was too acute to permit me to retire. I stood, therefore, still, waiting what might arrive, till I perceived some out-riders gallopping forward in the Royal Livery of France. Immediately after, a Chariot of Four, with the arms of France, followed, encircled with Horsemen, & nearly envellopped by a continually encreasing crowd, whence, from time to time, issued a feeble cry of Vive le Roi!—while two or three ׀ other Carriages brought up the rear. With difficulty, now, could I forbear plunging into the midst of them, for my big expectations painted to me Louis 18 arrived at Tournay, & my bigger hopes pictured with Him his loyal Body Guard. They were soon, however, passed by, but their straggling followers shewed me their route, which I pursued till I lost both sight & sound belonging to them. I then loitered for my errand Boy, till I found myself, by some indications that helped my remembrance, near the spot whence I had started. Glad, for safety's sake, to be so near my then Home, though mourning my fruitless wandering, I hastened my footsteps: but what was my emotion on arriving within a few yards of the Inn, to observe the Royal Carriage which ׀ had gallopped past me, the Horse Men, the royal Livery, & all the appearance that had awakened my dearest Hopes! The Crowd was dispersed, but the quantity of Servants, & Waiters, & Soldiers, & people all together, made it difficult to me to enter; I was too urgent, however, for repulse, & my eagerness had, probably, an air of conscious Right, for neither my name nor my business were demanded, & though I was looked at with surprize, I was offered no offence nor impediment. on passing the Gate way, I saw that the Porter's Lodge, or perhaps Book Keeper's, was filled with Gentlemen, or officers in full uniform. I hurried on,—

& meeting with some attendant to whom I was known, personally, belonging to the Inn, I hastily enquired Who it was that had just arrived—My answer was Le Prince de Condé.[73]

A thousand projects now occurred to me ׀ for gaining intelligence from such high authority, & I would have hastened to my chamber to consider which of them to execute: but in the large Court yard I espied Madame d'Henin, sauntering up & down, while holding by the arm of a gentleman I had never before seen. Anxious to avoid delay, & almost equally desirous to escape remonstrances on my enterprize, since I could listen only to my restless anxiety, I would have glided by unnoticed: but she called after me aloud, & I was compelled to approach her. She was all astonishment at my courage, in thus issuing forth alone, I knew not where, nor whither, & declared that I was *méconnoissable*; but I only answered by entreating her to enquire the names ׀ of some of the Gentlemen just arrived, that I might judge whether any among them could give me the information for which I sighed.

No sooner did I hear that M. le comte de Viomenil was of the Number,[74] than, recollecting his recent appointment at Paris, in conjunction with Victor de Maubourg, to raise Volunteers for the King, than I decided upon seeking him. Mad^e d'Henin would have given me some counsel, but I was in an agony of intractable misery, & could not hear her;—as I hurried off, however, the Gentleman whose arm she held, offered me his assistance in a tone & with a look of so much benevolence, that I frankly accepted it, & leaving Mad^e d'Henin all astonished, I took his proffered ׀ arm, & we sallied in search of a Person known to me only by Name. My stranger Friend was now of singular service to me. He saved me every exertion, by making every enquiry, & led me from Corridore to Corridore, from Waiter to Waiter, from Porter to Porter, above, below, & through every avenue to almost every apartment, asking incessantly if M. le Comte de Viomenil was not in the Inn.

At length we came to a man who was loaded with a Tray of viandes, & from him we learned that M. de Viominil was dining, quite alone, in an upper Chamber.

My kind-hearted conductor led me to the door of the room

[73] L. 856 n. 9 and L. 860 n. 21.
[74] L. 860 n. 13.

asigned, & then tapped at it; & on an answer of 'Entrez!—' he let go my arm, & with a bow & look of uncommon ǀ sensibility, that shewed him penetrated by my too palpable distress, he silently left me.

I found M. de Viominil at table, & by no means wearing an aspect of a Kindred sort with that I quitted. He heard my enquiries so unmoved, that I had twice or thrice to repeat them ere I was sure he heard them at all. He then, without raising his Eyes from his plate, said he could give me no possible account of His Majesty, save that he was at Gand, but that of the Body Guard he knew positively nothing.

It may be that he was too deeply wrapt up in his own misfortunes to spare any attention to those of another; or that he deemed it ǀ an impropriety to divulge any circumstance relating to the flight from Paris & Buonaparte: this last idea occurs only as I am now writing; & apologises for his forbidding taciturnity. I left him most reluctantly; & he saw me depart without uttering a word, or deigning me a look.

I afterwards [learnt] that my benevolent strange Chevalier was no other than the celebrated M. de Chateaubriant.[75]

I saw nothing more of him, save for a moment, when, in passing by a small stair-case that led to my chamber, a door was suddenly opened, whence Madame d'Henin put out her head, to invite me to enter, when she presented me to Madame de Chateaubriant,[76] a very elegant woman, but of a cold, reserved, ǀ nearly haughty demeanour.

[75] François-René de Chateaubriand (1768–1848), chevalier and later vicomte de Chateaubriand, writer and political figure, entered the literary and social life of Paris in 1787 but left it after the Revolution to travel in America and live the life of an *émigré* in England until his return to France in 1800. In 1801 he published *Atala*, which not only made his literary reputation but also coincided with and supported Napoleon's re-establishment of the Catholic Church. Seeing himself as the Emperor's equal and rival, he considered his works and opinions to be important historical events. This conceit was in part justified by the immense influence of his writings and by his defence of legitimacy, which he coupled with increasing hostility to Napoleon. He welcomed and paved the way for the return of the Bourbons, with whom his later relations became nearly as vexed as his earlier dealings with the Emperor. He followed Louis XVIII to Ghent, where he became the interior minister of the exiled government—an irony he relished. After the Second Restoration he reverted to the crabwise and brilliant political career that gained and lost him offices and allies. The last part of his life, after the coming of Louis-Philippe, was chiefly occupied by the writing of his great *Mémoires d'Outre-Tombe* (1849–50).
[76] Céleste Buisson de La Vigne (1774–1847) was married to Chateaubriand in 1792 while still a minor. Soon afterward her husband left to join the Armée des Princes, later emigrating to England, and she was forced to spend the grim revo-

I expressed eagerly, but I have since thought injudiciously, the pleasure I had experienced in seeing the author of The Itinerary to Jerusalem,[77]—a work I had read in Paris with extraordinary interest & satisfaction: but I believe the [*Génie du christianisme*] & perhaps the Atala,[78] were works so much dearer & more prized by that Author, as to make my compliment misplaced. However, I so much more approve, & enjoy the natural, pleasing, attractive, instructive, & simple though ingenious style & matter of the Itinerary, than, I do the inflated & overpowering sort of heroic I eloquence of those more popular performances, that the zest of dear hallowed Truth would have been wanting had I not expressed my Choice. The Itinerary is, indeed, one of the most agreeable Books I know.

M. de Chateaubriant hung back, whether pleased or not, with an air of Gentlemanly serenity.

I had opportunity for no further effort; we left Tournay, to proceed to Brussels, & heavy was my Heart & my Will to quit, thus in ignorance, the vicinity of Lille.

I have very little remembrance of my journey, save of the general cleanliness of the Inns & the people on our way, & of the extraordinary excellence, sweetness, lightness, & flavour of the Bread, in all its forms of Loaves, Rusks, cakes, rolls, tops, & bottoms.[79] I have never tasted such else where. /

At the town at which we stopt to dine, which *I think* was Atot,[80] we rencontred M. et Madame de Chateaubriant. This was a mutual satisfaction, & we agreed to have our meal in common. I now had more leisure, not of time alone, but of faculty, for doing justice to M. de Chateaubriant, whom I found extremely amiable, utterly unassuming, &, though somewhat spoilt by the egregious flattery to which he had been accustommed, wholly free from airs or impertinent self-conceit. Exces-

lutionary period with his mother and sisters. Although he often lived apart from her and had many great passions for other women, she remained loyal to him. made friends in his circle, and stood by him in his decline.

[77] *Itinéraire de Paris à Jérusalem et de Jérusalem à Paris* . . ., first published in 1811.

[78] *Génie du christianisme, ou beautés de la religion chrétienne* appeared in 1802. FBA left three lines blank, but this title supplied by a later editor is probably correct. Originally written as an episode in the *Génie du christianisme, Atala*—a romantic tale set in the wilds of America—made Chateaubriand famous when he published it separately in 1801.

[79] 'The flattish halves of small rolls sliced lengthways, and browned in the oven' (*OED*).

[80] Ath, roughly thirty kilometres north-east of Tournay on the road to Brussels.

sive praise seemed only to cause him excessive pleasure in himself, without leading to contempt or scorn of others. He is by no means tall, & is rather thick-set; but his features are good, his countenance is very fine, & his Eyes are beautiful, alike from colour, shape, & expression, while there is a ꟾ striking benevolence in his look, tone of voice, & manner.

Madame de Chateaubriant, also, gained by further acquaintance. She was faded, but not *passée*, & was still handsome, as well as highly mannered; & of a most graceful carriage, though distant & uninviting. Yet her loftiness had in it something so pensive, mixt with it's haughtiness, that though it could not inspire confidence, it did not create displeasure. She carried about her, also, a constant call for simpathy as well as respect, in being the Niece of M. de Malsherbes, that wise tender, generous, noble defender of Louis 16.[81]

The conversation during, & after dinner was highly interesting. M. de Chateaubriant opened upon his situation with a trusting unreserve that impressed me with an opinion of the nobleness of his mind. Buonaparte had conceived against him, he said, a peculiar antipathy, for which various motives ꟾ might be assigned: he enumerated them not, however; probably from the presence of his Wife, as his marriage with a Niece of that Martyr to the service of the murdered King, Louis 16, I conclude to be at their head. The astonishing & almost boundless success of his Works, since he was dissatisfied with his principles, & more than suspicious of his dissaffection to the Emperor's Government, must have augmented aversion, by mixing with it some species of apprehension. I know not what were the first publications of M. de Chateaubriant;[82] but [his *Christianisme*] was in such high estimation when first I heard him mentioned, that no authour was more celebrated in France;

[81] Malesherbes (ii, L. 49 n. 10; L. 68 n. 9), his defence of Louis XVI, and his own execution on 22 Apr. 1794, together with d'Arblay's concern and that of the comte de Narbonne, FBA would have had in memory since the days of the *émigré* (or Juniper Hall) colony at Mickleham (ii *passim*). Executed on the same day were Malesherbes's granddaughter Aline-Thérèse Le Peltier de Rosambo (b. 1761) together with her husband, Chateaubriand's eldest brother, Jean-Baptiste-Auguste de Chateaubriand (b. 1759), comte de Combourg. This seems to be the connection between the two families, notwithstanding FBA's notion about the relationships of the author's wife.

[82] Apart from some early poetry, Chateaubriand's first publication was the *Essai historique, politique et moral sur les révolutions* ... (London, 1797), a liberal, even free-thinking, work he later disowned.

& when his *Martyrs*[83] came out, no other Book was mentioned, & the famous critic, ¹ Geoffroy,[83] who guided the taste of Paris, kept it alive, by criticisms of alternate praise & censure without end. Atala,[84] the pastoral heroic Romance, bewitched all the reading females into a sort of idolatry of its writer; & scarcely a page of it remained unadorned by some representation in painting. The enthusiasm, indeed, of the Draughtsmen & of the Fair Sex seemed equally emulous to place the Authour & the Work at the head of Celebrity & the Fashion.

Of all this, of course, he spoke not; but he related the story of his persecution by Napoleon concerning his being elected a member of the French Institute. I was in too much disturbance to be able to clearly listen to the narrative; but I perfectly recollect that the Censor, to soften Napoleon, had sent back the ¹ Manuscript to M. de Chateaubriant, with an intimation that no public Discourse could be delivered that did not contain an *eloge* of the Emperor. M. de Chateaubriant complied with the ordinance; but whether the forced praise was too feeble, or whether the aversion was too insuperable, I know not; all that is certain is that Napoleon, after repeated efforts from the Institute of re-election, positively refused to ratify that of M. de Chateaubriant.[85]

Another time, a cousin of this Gentleman was reported to be engaged in a conspiracy against the Emperor.[86] M. de Chateaubriant solemnly declared he disbelieved the charge; &, as his

---

[83] *Les Martyrs, ou le triomphe de la religion chrétienne* (1809). Louis Geoffroy (1743–1814), the literary critic of the *Journal des Débats* from 1800 till 1814, and contributor to the *Année littéraire*, was noted for his polemical bent and distaste for eighteenth-century styles and cultural values.

[84] *Atala, ou les amours des deux sauvages dans le désert*, which led to a critical debate soon after its publication in 1801, had as FBA observes a fatal charm for women and illustrators. See further the notes to the Pléiade edition (1957) of the *Mémoires*, ii. 1149–50.

[85] Although elected to the Académie française in 1811, Chateaubriand was not allowed to deliver his inaugural address, which the academicians found unacceptable and which Napoleon thought subversive. FBA's recollection, and perhaps Chateaubriand's account, were less accurate than she claims. Napoleon had in fact pushed Chateaubriand's candidacy before an Academy hostile to his Christian and romantic enthusiasms, and the offending discourse was actually full of praise for the Emperor.

[86] Chateaubriand's cousin, Armand-Louis-Marie de Chateaubriand du Plessis (1768–1809), who since 1794 had been a Bourbon courier between England and France, was driven by a storm on the coast of Normandy on 9 Jan. 1809. He was imprisoned in Paris and, despite Chateaubriand's appeal to Napoleon, executed on 31 March of that same year. The writer, by his own grisly account, took away the body for burial (*Mémoires*, i. 638–42).

weight in Public Opinion was so great, he ventured to address a ı *supplique* to Napoleon in favour of his kinsman —— —— but the answer which reached him the following day, was an account of his Execution![86]

Madame de Chateaubriant spoke very little, & rarely said even a word save to her husband, for whom her Eyes spoke an attachment the most tender, yet unquiet. He, in return, treated her with deference & softness; but I afterwards learned that the idolatry at which I have hinted caused her the most acute disturbance,[87] & gave to him a pleasure so animating as dangerously to break into the domestic tranquility of his fireside.

We separated from this highly interesting pair with regret; & the rest of our Journey to Brussels was without event—for to passport difficulties ı we became accustomed, & grew both adroit & courageous in surmounting them. ı

[BRUSSELS]

And Now, my dear Alexander will be glad, I should think, of a narrative of my residence at Brussels—a residence in which the most acute pain was contrasted by the most exquisite Felicity—while both were terminated by Terrour the most tremendous.

We drove immediately to the house in which dwelt Madame la Comtesse de Maurville.[88] You must remember that excellent person, she had many years lived in England, an Emigrant, & there earned a scanty maintenance by keeping a French school. She had now retired upon a very moderate pension, but was surrounded by intimate Friends, ı who only suffered her to lodge at her own home. She received us in great dismay, fearing to lose her little ALL by these changes of Government. I was quite ill on my arrival; excessive fatigue, affright, watchfulness, & misery, overwhelmed me. I kept my bed a day or two; but with the aid of Dr. James's medicines,[89] & my own earnest efforts to employ every faculty as well as every moment in researches after the King's Body Guard, I then recovered, & again went to work.

[87] A genteel glance at Chateaubriand's numerous liaisons.
[88] Mme de Maurville (iii, L. 237 n. 9 and L. 838 n. 30 *supra*).
[89] See i, L. 7 n. 2.

At Brussels all was quiet & tame. The Belgians had lost their original antipathy to Buonaparte, without having yet had time to acquire any warmth of interest for the Bourbons. Natively phlegmatic, ⏐ they demand great causes, or strong incitement to rouse them from that sort of passiveness that is the offspring of Philosophy & Timidity,—Philosophy, that teaches them to prize the blessings of safety, & Timidity that points out the trembling dangers of Enterprize. In all I had to do with them, I found them universally wort y, rational & good hearted; but slow, sleepy, & uninteresting.

Exceptions, however, to this general observation I had the happiness to meet with—& perhaps they may be numerous. My sojourn was too short, & my life was too obscure to authorize any positive opinion.

In the sick room to which I was immediately consigned, I met with every ⏐ sort of Kindness from Madame de Maurville, whom I had known intimately at Paris, & who had known—& appreciated my beloved—exemplary Sister Phillips in London.[90] Madame de Maurville was a woman that the Scotch would call long-headed; she was sagacious, penetrating, & gifted with strong humour. She saw readily the vices & follies of mankind, & laughed at them heartily, without troubling herself to grieve at them— She was good herself, alike in heart & in conduct, & zealous to serve & oblige, but with a turn to satire that made the defects of her neighbours rather afford her amusement than concern.

I was visited here by the highly accomplished Madame de la Tour du Pin,[91] Wife to the favourite nephew of Madᵉ d'Henin;[91] a woman of as much courage ⏐ as elegance, & who had met danger, toil & difficulty in the Revolution with as much spirit, & nearly with as much grace, as she had displayed in meeting universal admiration & hommage at the Court of Marie Antoinette, of which she was one of the most brilliant latter ornaments. Her husband was at this time one of the French Ministers at the Congress at Vienna;[92] whence, as she learned a few days after my arrival at Brussels, he had been sent on an embassy of the deepest importance & risk to La Vendee, or

90 SBP (i, p. lxx).
91 See vi, L. 575 n. 2 and L. 854 n. 9 *supra*.
92 See L. 873 n. 2.

Bordeaux. She bore the term of that suspence with an heroism of fortitude that I greatly admired, as I well knew she adored her husband. M. La Tour du Pin had been a Prefect of Brussels under Buonaparte, though never in favour, as his internal loyalty to the Bourbons was well known. But Buonaparte loved to attach great ǀ Names & great Characters to his Government, conscious of their weight both at home & abroad, & trusted in the address of that mental diving machine,[93] his secret police, for warding off any hazard he might run through latent ill-will, from employing the adherents of his Enemies. His greatly capacious, yet only half-formed mind, could have parried, as well as have braved, every danger, all opposition, had not his inordinate ambition held him as arbitrarily under controul as he himself held under his own controul every other passion.

Madame de Maurville soon found us a House of which we took all but the Ground floor: the rez de chaussée was mine, the first floor was Madame d'Henin's, & that above it was for M. de Lally. It was near the Cathedral, & still in a prolongation of Made de Maurville's street, ǀ la Rue de la Montagne.

Nothing was known at Brussels, nothing at all, of the fate of the Body Guard, or of the final destination of Louis 18. How circumstances of such infinite moment, nay, notoriety, could be kept from public knowledge, I can form no idea; but neither in the private houses of persons of the first rank, in which, through Mme d'Henin, I visited, nor in any of the shops, nor by any other sort of intercourse, either usual or accidental, could I gather any intelligence.

Madame la Duchesse de Duras, *ci-devant* Madlle Kersaint,[94] who had visited me in Paris, & who was now in hasty emigration at Brussels, with her youngest Daughter, Madlle Clara de Duras,[95] seemed sincerely moved by my distress, & wrote to various of her friends, who were ǀ emigrating within her reach, & who had recently been in highly powerful situations, to make enquiry for me. I visited her in a shabby Hotel, as I think de la Flandre, where I found her without *suite* or equipage, but in

---

[93] A striking comparison derived from the diving bells and similar devices in use since the late seventeenth century.

[94] L. 857 n. 5.

[95] Claire-Henriette-Philippine-Benjamine de Durfort de Duras (1799–1863), 'la charmante Clara' of Chateaubriand's *Mémoires* (i. 904, 931), later by marriage marquise de Duras-Chastellux and duchesse de Rauzan.

perfect tranquility at their loss, & not alone without murmuring, but nearly indifferent to her privations; while Mad¹¹ᵉ Clara ran up & down stairs on her mother's messages, & even brought in Wood for the stove, with an alacrity & chearfulness that seemed almost to enjoy the change of hardships from Grandeur. Indeed, to very young people, such reverses, for a certain time, appear as a frolic. Novelty, mere novelty, during the first Youth, can scarcely be bought too dear. ¹

From M. de la Ferronaye⁹⁶ Madame de Duras procured me intelligence that the Body Guard had been dispersed & disbanded, by the Duke de Berry, on the frontiers of La Belgique; they were left at liberty to remain in France, or seek other asylum, as His Majesty Louis 18, could not enter the Kingdom of Holland with a military Guard of his own.

This News left me utterly in the dark which way to look for hope or information. Madame de Duras, however, said she expected soon to see the Duc de Richelieu,⁹⁷ whose tidings might be more precise.

In one of my visits to this lady I again met M. and Madame de Chateaubriant; but my mind was too troublously pre-occupied to take the pleasure I might otherwise have felt from their acquaintance. Madame de ׀ Duras really entered into the subject of my misery, & seemed capable to fully comprehend it. She once told me, also, gaily, that she owed her mariage to me, as she had resolved when very young, never to marry till she met with a Delville:⁹⁸ such to her had appeared at that time the Duke de Duras—*d'un tout aussi noble caractère*—she said:—but I fear that at this present period, more than 10 years later, her ideas, & her comparisons, had no longer the same Object. She was *romanesque*, however, & professedly apat[het]ic to the

⁹⁶ Pierre-Louis-Auguste Ferron (1777–1842), comte de la Ferronays, a fervent royalist and aide-de-camp to the duc de Berry, was one of the most trusted diplomats under the Restoration and later in 1828 became French foreign minister. See also above, L. 847 n. 2.
⁹⁷ Armand-Emmanuel du Plessis (L. 918 n. 9), comte de Chinon, duc de Fronsac, and after 1791 duc de Richelieu, emigrated to Russia where he became a protégé of the Czar and, by 1803, governor of Odessa. Returning to France at the Restoration, he replaced Talleyrand as Prime Minister in September of 1815. His first ministry lasted until 1818 and was characterized by his increasingly moderate conservatism and his skilful handling of foreign affairs. He negotiated the withdrawal of allied troops and the entry of France into the Quintuple Alliance. Richelieu returned to office in 1820 after the assassination of the duc de Berry, resigning at the end of 1821.
⁹⁸ Mortimer Delville, the hero of FBA's novel *Cecilia*.

reverses of Fortune. She showed to me a Drawing of a small hut on the summit of a high, isolated Mountain, & protested she looked at it, with the view of one Day realizing her wishes of making it the model for her final habitation. Whether in solitude, or with a Partner, I did not enquire. |

Ten wretched days passed on in this torturing ignorance— from the 19th to the 29th of March, 1815 — — when Madame de Maurville flew into my apartment, with all the celerity of fifteen, & all the ardour of twenty years of Age, to put into my hands a Letter from General d'Arblay,[99] addressed to herself, to enquire whether she had any tidings to give him of my existence, & whether I had been heard of at Brussels, or was known to have travelled to Bordeaux, as Made d'Henin, Cousin to Made de Maurville, had been uncertain, when M. d'Arblay left me in Paris, to which of those Cities she should go.

The joy of that Moment—O the Joy of that Moment that shewed me again the hand writing that demonstrated | Life & Safety to all to which my Earthly Happiness clung, can never be expressed, & only on & by our meeting, when at last it took place, could be equalled. It was dated *Ypres, 27. Mars.* I wrote directly thither, proposing to join him, if there were any impediment to his coming on to Brussels. I had already written, at a hazard, to almost every town in the Netherlands. The very next day, another Letter from the same kind incomparable hand, arrived to Madame la Duchesse d'Hurste—[100] who enclosed it to me in a billet of great politeness & good will. She was a person of very good parts, & of great dignity. I had met her sometimes at the Princess d'Henin's, &, formerly, at Madame de Tessé's.[101] This was succeeded by news that the King, Louis 18, had been followed to Gand by his Body Guard. Thither, also, I expedited a Letter,[102] under | cover to the Duc de Luxembourg, Capitaine of the company to which M. d'Arblay belonged.

I lived now in a hurry of delight that scarcely allowed me breathing time; a delight that made me forget all my losses, my misfortunes—my Papers—Letters—Trinkets—Keepsakes—

[99] L. 852.

[100] The text of this letter to the dowager duchesse d'Ursel is given above in L. 856 n. 10.

[101] See v, pp. xliv; L. 510 n. 11; and vi *passim.*

[102] L. 854.

Valuables of various sorts, with our Goods, Cloaths, Money Bonds, & endless &c &cs, left, as I had reason to fear, to seizure & confiscation upon the entry of the Emperour in Paris—all, all was light, was NOTHING, in the scale of my Joy; & I wrote to my Alexander, & my dearest Friends, to rejoice in my joy, & that they had escaped my alarm.

Next Day, and again the next, came a Letter from M. d'Arblay himself[103] — — Ah!—what exquisite felicity!—past, past forever!—My Alexander will find these two precious Letters, Numbered 7. & 8, of the year 1815.[104] and he will understand ⏐ what must have been the excess of my Anguish, when he finds what are the contents of these Letters that procured me ever exquisite felicity! The first was from Ypres, & brought to me by M. de Carbonniere,[105] whose sweet pretty Wife, ci-devant Mlle de Bearnon, Alex will remember in our return to England by Dunkirk; the second was from Bruges,[106] & brought by the Post, as my beloved Correspondent was thus assured of my arrival at Brussels through the Duc de Luxembourg, à Ghistelle, near Ostende, which M. d'Arblay was slowly approaching, on Horse back, when he met the Carriage of Louis 18, as it stopt for a Relay of Horses—& where the Duc, espying him, descended from the second Carriage of the King's suite, to fly to & embrace him, with that lively friendliness he has ever manifested towards him. Thence they agreed that the plan of embarcation should be renounced, &, instead ⏐ of Ostende, M. d'Arblay turned his Horses' head towards Gand,[107] where he had a rendezvous with the Duc. BUT — — while thus much was good, the rest of the two Letters would have been heart-piercing to me at any other period, so melancholy was their tone, so deep were the misfortunes they related, & so agravated was every loss & evil by the shaken state of health & of NERVES in the hardly-tried sufferer — — And yet, such had

---

[103] This letter is missing.

[104] In the year 1823 FBA was evidently editing her husband's correspondence for the benefit of her son, who she fancied would one day read it at his 'Fire-side Rectory' (see i, p. xxxvi). The present number 857 she numbered at that time 8. Numbers 7 and 9 are now missing.

[105] Louis-Eugène de Carbonnière (vi, L. 603 n. 4), *dit* comte de Carbonnière, whose wife Henriette-Marie-Anne-Louise-Alexandrine *née* de Bournon (*c.* 1781–*post* 1812) had accompanied FBA and AA to England in 1812 (see Dunkirk Letters, vi, Ll. 600–31).

[106] L. 857 (numbered 8).

[107] At the court in exile Louis XVIII had decided to establish there.

been the horrour of my apprehensions, that these Letters, with all their touching devoloppment of calamity, filled me with thankfulness even to extacy — — for they assured me of his LIFE! Oh my Alex! destined as I am to survive him—I had then, in my fears, my first experience of the Void—the chasm between ME and HAPPINESS that, in this nether World, can never ı be filled up!—,[108] not even by Thee, my Alex,—for we possessed Thee together. Dear, therefore, as thou art to me above all things, thou canst only urge me to bear—not to forget, O never! my deprivation; for though my affection for Thee is encreased in being concentrated, in losing its sympathy it has lost its gaiety, though it must ever retain its tenderness. — — And not to Thee alone, albeit to Thee principally, do I owe a returning power that of late has pointed out to me the Duty, as well as Solace, of seeking comfort from every comfort that still remains;—my ever dear sisters—my nieces—

My Brothers Alas!—are gone![109]—and my few chosen excellent Friends—amongst whom some are even darlingly dear to me—all, and all along, have offered balm to my Wounds, which is now no longer poured into them in vain, but ı gently heals them, in reviving long deadened wishes of repaying their generous kindness by some reciprocation of pleasure.

From Gand reached me a Letter now daily, & a narration the most affecting of the dreadful passage from Bethune, where Mr le Duc de Berry had disbanded the Body Guard, from the inability of H.M. to retain it around him out of his own Kingdom, to the borders of Ostende, where the meeting took place with the Duc de Luxembourg, which changed the course of General d'Arblay from Ostende to Gand. There he remained, freshly to offer his services to his King, & there he was most peculiarly distinguished by M. le Duc de Feltre, (General Clark,)[110] who was still occupying the post assigned him on the restoration of Louis XVIII of Ministre de la Guerre.

Relieved now—or rather blest!—I was no longer deaf to the kindness of those who sought to enliven my Exile; I not only,

---

[108] i.e. in losing M. d'A through his death in 1818.

[109] CB Jr. had died in 1818, JB, in 1821.

[110] Clarke had in fact been removed from this ministry during the first Restoration and only resumed the post after Soult's disgrace and during Napoleon's advance on Paris (see L. 860 n. 2).

for ⎰ my own sake, saw Madame la Duchesse de Duras, but visited her also as a pleasant acquaintance: I cultivated the intercourse with the charming Madame de la Tour dupin, whom I was the more glad to find delightful from her being of English origin; a Mademoiselle Dillon, whose family was transplanted into France under James the Second, & who was descended from a Nobleman whose eminent accomplishments she inherited with his blood; the famous Lord Falkland, on whose tomb, in Westminster Abbey, is carved

Here lies The Friend of Sir Philip Sydney,[111]

Her sister, Miss Fanny Dillon, had been married, by Buonaparte, to General Bertrand;[112] & thus, while one of them was an Emigrant in following the fortunes of the Bourbons, the other was—soon after,—destined to accompany Buonaparte himself into Exile.—Le Colonel de Beaufort,[113] also, a warm early Friend of General d'Arblay, belonging to the Garison ⎰ of Metz, or of Toul, I forget which, had married a Lady of great wealth in La Belgique; a woman rather unhappy in her person, but possessed of a generously feeling & gentle heart: & this she instantly demonstrated, in seeking with ardour, & cultivating with delicacy, the acquaintance of the wandering Wife of the early *camarade* of her husbands. I found her so amiable, & so soothing in her commiseration during my distress, that I conceived a warm return in the marked, & almost tender partiality she delighted to shew me.

4 Days passed thus serenely, when, on the day that completed a Fortnights absence from my best Friend, I was present at a scene which I will not pass over in silence, on account of the great celebrity of one who bore in it a part.

Madame de Duras had invited to Tea, *à l'anglaise*, the Princesse d'Henin, Madame ⎰ de Maurville, a demoiselle de Mons,[114] & myself. The Duchess was now settled in l'hôtel Royale, sur la Place Royale, & with some appearance of the

---

[111] This would appear to be FBA's partial recollection of the epitaph of Fulke Greville (1554–1628), 1st Lord Brooke, for his tomb in St. Mary's Church, Warwick: 'Fulke Greville, servant to Queen Elizabeth, councillor to King James, and friend to Sir Philip Sidney. Trophæum Peccati' (*DNB*).

[112] For the marriage of Fanny Elizabeth Dillon (1777–1862) to General Bertrand, Napoleon's grand maréchal du palais, see L. 893 n. 13.

[113] See L. 872 nn. 3, 6.

[114] Possibly a sister or one of the aunts of Jean-Antoine-Claude-*Adrien* de Mun (1773–1843), several of whom were *religieuses* before the Revolution. He had

etiquette of her station, the Duc being with the King, Louis XVIII, at Gand, & having found means to put her more at her ease. Arrived at the Hotel, we mounted *au premier*, &, meeting no waiter in the way, & knowing that the Duchess had not any male Domestick, she would have opened the door of the great apartment in which we had all already been received; but a dreadful scream from within stopt her hand; we all stood in amaze & affright; when another scream induced Madame d'Henin to tap at the door. No answer was returned, but our Ears were presently terrified more & more by Groans deep & loud. Madame d'H. then tried to open the door, but found it locked. We were in the utmost ᴵ consternation; the sounds were indicative of bodily, not mental suffering, & we thought, therefore, that intrusion, far from being unseasonable, might perhaps be highly useful. Madame d'Henin, therefore, repeated her tapping with a vivacity belonging to her spirited & decided character, always zealous, & even nobly courageous where persuaded that exertion might do good, till her noise outsounded the dolorous cries from within. The Door was then unlocked, & the Duchess, holding it ajar, appeared, evidently in the greatest distress & disorder, & whispered us that her mother, Madame de Kersaint,[115] was taken violently ill. Madame d'Henin offered the soothings of friendship, Madame de Maurville proffered the services of attendance; the Duchess admitted them both; I would have retired, not being of sufficient intimacy to hope I could be useful; but Madame de Duras drew me into the room; & Mlle ᴵ de Mons accompanied me.[114] She made a motion to her Daughter, Mlle Clara de Duras, to conduct us to the Boudoir.

Softly & quickly as we crossed the spacious apartment which led to it, I could not avoid perceiving the Bed within the Alcove on which lay poor Madame de Kerseint, moaning, groaning, & uttering at times the most piercing shrieks. The Dinner was still on a large Table in the middle of the Room, & all spoke that the attack had been too terrible to allow time for any

---

married in 1805 Henriette-Amélie-Ferdinande d'Ursel (1772–1839), but a 'demoiselle' born of this marriage would have been too young presumably to join the ageing group above.

[115] Claire-Louise-Françoise de Coëtnempren *née* d'Alesso d'Éragny (*c.* 1755–1815), comtesse de Kersaint, originally from the French Antilles, where she was heiress to a large fortune.

arrangement. Madame d'Henin & Madame de Maurville remained by the Bed side with the Duchess; Mlle de Duras, in great grief & dismay, planted us in the Boudoir, & then joined her poor Grandmother, but speedily returned to us, though only to ı quit us nearly the same moment, when she had relieved her grief by a few tears & a little conversation. We learnt from her that the whole of this suffering had been the effect of a species of intemperance; not from any luxurious diet, or beverage, but simply from eating Cabbages! Mad^e de Kerseint had long been forbidden them, as particularly inimical to her health; but, as they were favourite food, & had long been denied, she found them so resistless at this hôtel, that the temptation beguiled her of forbearance, & she helped herself till she was taken suddenly so ill as to scream from convulsive pain which stopt as instantaneously as it came on, by a fit of apoplexy. From this she had just recovered as we arrived, but only recovered to ı the same sufferings. Another fit followed; & only such another recovery. A surgeon was sent for, by Madame de Maurville; a copious bleeding ensued — — but all was vain; & after two or three hours of dreadfully alternate insensibility and agony, poor Madame de Kersaint suddenly ceased to breathe.

This fatal catastrophe was announced to us by a terrible scream from the Duchess: while Mad^lle de Duras came to our Boudoir to sob aloud. I could not but rejoice that I had not known the poor Lady, thus abruptly called away — — & I earnestly wished I could have comforted Mad^e de Duras, who would not quit the Bed side, whence her sorrow was audible & violent. Madame de Maurville invited her to La Rue de la Montagne; but she refused to move; Madame d'Henin consoled her with an expression of sensibility ı always emanating from her heart on occasions of distress; but neither reasoning nor persuasion could prevail for a removal. Madame de Maurville then had recourse to the aid of M. de Chateaubriant,[116] for whom she sent, & who, obeying the summons, exerted his powerful & impressive eloquence with such energetic, yet gentle earnestness, that his harangue was not long fruitless, &, the Maids, & proper assistants, being called to take care of the poor

---

[116] Chateaubriand was more eloquent than observant. He later wrote of this episode that Mme de Duras 'eut la douleur d'y perdre sa nièce' (*Mémoires*, i. 929).

Remains, the Duchess was envellopped in a large shawl, & took the Bras of M. de Chateaubriant to be descend the stairs. Madame d'Henin took charge of Mlle de Duras; & Madame de Maurville, after giving, herself, all the necessary orders, with a usefulness of friendliness & presence of mind which ׀ mark her active & zealous character, went forward, to lead the way to her Apartments, whither Mlle de Mons & I followed in procession.

This was my last view of the celebrated M. de Chateaubriant in La Belgique: the Duc de Duras came the next day, I think, to convey his Wife to Gand, where he was himself in waiting upon Louis XVIII. & shortly afterwards, M. de Chateaubriant was made a privy Counsellor,[117] & settled there also. How little could I then foresee that my next intercourse with M. de Chateaubriant would be that of calling myself to his recollection in a little billet, 6 or 7 Years afterwards, written to him as Ambassadour to Great Britain; What a wonderful vicissitude! I wrote to beg his permission for forwarding in his *porte feuille* my Letters for my dear Madame de Maisonneuve. And my ׀ Letter, which recurred to his benevolent courtesy in conducting me to M. Le Duc de Viominil,[118] was answered with the extremest politeness, and a promise that he would call upon me, 'pour recevoir,' he says, 'vos ordres.'—&c I missed, however, the honour he thus kindly intended me, from the suddenness with which he was summoned back by his King, to attend the Congress at Vienna. Had we met, we might probably have been very good friends, from the interesting recollections of having begun our flight from Paris & Buonaparté on the same day, & on the same road.

But what is the vicissitude that can bear any comparison with that which I experienced, from the mournful cast of mind with which this shocking scene ׀ had sent me home, to that which chaced it for the highest happiness of which the human Heart is susceptible, within an hour or two after my return, when my door was opened by General d'Arblay! — — Oh how sweet was this meeting!—this blessed re-union!—how perfect—how

---

[117] Chateaubriand's appointment at Ghent was as 'ministre de l'intérieur par *intérim*', a portfolio whose absurdity he later described (*Mémoires*, i. 930). As such he was a member of the King's Council. He was privy Counsellor from the end of 1822 until 6 June 1824, when he was appointed French minister to the Congress of Verona, not Vienna as FBA says below.   [118] See L. 860 n. 13.

exquisite — — — Here I must be silent! — — The eternal—
Earthly eternal!—separation that has now dissevered us makes
the retrospection too Heart-piercing for communication even
to Thee, my Alexander—
  Perfect!—Exquisite!—Yes — — but short as perfect & exquisite! — — cares, fears, disturbances of every sort broke
into our felicity almost immediately after its attainment:—
a newspaper of England brought tidings of an infectious ı Fever
that was then raging at Cambridge![119] Oh my Alexander! what
a weight of horrour bowed down our spirits at this intelligence!
There, where so unwillingly I had left you—There, where Your
NOBLE Father, with such unexampled self-sacrifice, had consented to your ardent wish of remaining,—to know you by
yourself in the midst of contagion — —
  I wrote to every correspondent that could procure me information—for there was no quitting Brussels, where General
d'Arblay was only with me by the permission of the Duke de
Luxembourg, & liable to receive orders daily to return to Gand;
For I found—to my speechless dismay, yet resistless, though
agonized approbation, ı that General d'Arblay had made a
decision as noble as it was dangerous, to refuse no call, to
abstain from no effort, that might bring into movement his
loyalty to his King and his Cause, at this moment of calamity to
both. Yet such was the harrassed, or rather broken state of his
health, that his mental strength & unconquerable courage alone
preserved the poor shattered frame from sinking under fatigue
& pain into languor & inertion.
  Thus shaken—to know him in constant expectation of a summons to military duty—while both of us were equally trembling
for Thy safety, my Alexander — —
  O short, short, indeed, was the Felicity that terminated my
ten days of deplorable ignorance whether or not ı the Gates of
Earthly Happiness were shut upon me for ever—a suspence
that nearly distracted me—yet — — Oh that I could Now
renew it!—Suspence—that seemed, during its operation, the
Worst of evils, would be to me Now—in taking place of the
dread certainty that, since, has almost crushed me, the greatest
of welcomed Blessings! — —
  In the old memorandums from which I now write, I find

[119] See above L. 863 and L. 866.

these words on *April 12^h* 'The most suffering twelve months of my life concluded—I humbly hope!—This Day,—this anniversary of the loss of my beloved & honoured Father. Oh blessed be his Spirit!—in Heaven, in bliss eternal, be his Soul!—This Day,—we receive news, through my dear Sister Charlotte, that our Alexander has escaped the Fever, & is well.[119] ı

He had been compelled, nevertheless, to quit Cambridge, & he was passing his time we knew not where, & missing his studies in a manner pernicious to his advancement. With what dread astonishment did I find myself now again involved in a sort of series of apprehensions & sufferings that robbed me of the delight I had experienced by a re-union that I had sighed for as a Garantee from all future evil! but alas! the eternal expectation of a summons to M. d'Arblay for military operations,[120] while I saw him bowed down by indisposition & fatigue; with the cruel necessity of leaving Thee, my poor Alex, to thy inexperienced self, presented to me unceasingly such images of horrour or distress as kept me almost uninterruptedly in alarm & agitation.—Some ı Hours, indeed, were rescued from these pangs by tenderness and hope—but never with security, or serenity—the Cloud of impending mischief was always hovering—alas! alas! to sully the few days when a Union so sought was for so brief a term accorded!—

At this time, we boarded & lodged, by *pic-nic* contract, with the Princesse d'Henin; as did also M. de Lally, when he was not at Gand,[121] in attendance, as privy Counsellor, upon Louis 18. We exerted ourselves to visit, and Receive, my new pleasing Friend—such she sought to be—Madame de Beaufort, who was one of the richest dames of Brussels, & whose husband was passionately enraptured at meeting again with General d'Arblay, with whom he had been *Garrisoned*, during the youth of both, at Toul; & this lady, who gave him her hand & fortune, in his emigration,[122] enabled ı him to keep a splendid table, at

[120] A reference to his appointment as one of the 'commissaires royaux' (L. 867 and n. 1).

[121] Lally had been followed to Ghent by his mistress, Julie-Charles *née* Bouchard des Hérettes (1784–1817), a frail but ardent royalist. In 1816 she was to meet Lamartine, who loved her and celebrated her in his *Méditations*. She was to die of consumption in the following year.

[122] See L. 872 n. 3. Beaufort was never an *émigré*. He served throughout as an engineer officer and settled in Brussels after being directeur des fortifications there (L. 872 n. 6).

which our *couverts* were hospitably stationary. We reciprocated, also, morning visits with Madame de La Tour du Pin, & her young married Daughter, Madame de Liedekirke;[123] with the good & gay Madame de Maurville; & Madame de Merode, *ci devant* Mademoille de Grammont;[124] & we waited upon la Duchesse d'Ursel,[125] a woman of the highest manners & of very good discourse; & M. d'Arblay received M. de Carbonnière, & other Gentlemen; & I began an acquaintance with the family Boyd.[126]

About this time, I saw, also, the entry of the New King, William Frederick, of the new Kingdom of the Netherlands. Tapestry, or Branches of Trees, were hung out at all the Windows; or, in their failure, dirty carpets, old coats & cloaks, & even matts: a motley display of proud parade or vulgar poverty, that always, to me, made processions in such Countries on the Continent as I have seen their Ceremonies, appear burlesque; for ꟸ the Balconies & the Windows of all sort of mansions seem but encumbered with a medley mass of merchandise, spread out for Sale.

On *22ᵈ of April* opened a new source, though not an unexpected one, of tumultuous inquietude that preyed the more deeply upon my spirits & my happiness from the necessity it brought with itself of concealing its torments — — the military call for M. d'Arblay arrived from Gant — — Alas! from that moment I am not sure I ever tasted the delight of Peaceful Felicity!

The summons was from M. Le comte de Roch[127]

The immediate hope in which we indulged at this call, was that the Mission to which it alluded need not necessarily separate us, but that I might accompany my honoured husband, & remain at his quarters, without interfering in his occasionally quitting them, or in any performance of his duties: But alas! — — He set out instantly for Gand, whence he wrote me,[128] on the

---

[123] L. 872 n. 10.

[124] Rosalie (*c.* 1790–1823), a daughter of the marquis de Grammont (1746–90) and a niece of Mme de Lafayette, had married in 1809 comte Félix de Mérode (1791–1857) who, after her early death, went on to become a founder of Belgian independence.

[125] See L. 856 n. 10.   [126] L. 870 n. 2.

[127] The incompleted name is Rochechouart, chief of staff of the 'armée royale' at Ghent and Alost (L. 904 n. 1).

[128] L. 867, the text of which FBA then quotes.

instant he had had his audience of the Minister de la Guerre, Clark, Duc de Feltre,

> 'Nous nous sommes trompés, cruellement trompés — — ׀ ce qu'il y a de plus fâcheux c'est que Nous ne serons pas ensemble, car je ne crois ni prudent, ni même possible pour toi de me suivre sur l'extreme frontiere où l'on m'envoye. Cette mission, très delicate et en même tems très difficile, est encore plus embarassante puisque il ne s'agit de rien moins que d'agir avec les Prussiens, auquels il ne sera pas aisé de faire entendre raison, Et qui aurai-je à commander? des Gens qui jusqu'à prèsent sont à trouver,—des deserteurs, dans lesquels Je n'aurai aucune confiance — — — C'est bien à present qu'il faut rassembler tout nôtre courage! — — ׀

The next Day, April 23^d brought me a Letter much less dispirited:[128] the Mission was to Luxembourg. His Adjoint was the Colonel comte de Masancours;[129] his aide de Camp, M. de Premoral, & also that Gentleman's son. The plan was to collect, & examine, all the soldiers who were willing to return from the army of Buonaparté to that of Louis 18. Eleven other General officers were named to similar posts, all on frontier towns, for the better convenience of receiving the Volunteers.[130]

On the *24. April* M. d'Arblay again joined me—revived, by his natively martial spirit, & pleased to be employed: while he called upon me with a sweetness of tenderness unequaled, to aid his fortitude, upon this new & most precarious Mission, by my example — — the more, therefore, my heart suffered, the less I permitted it vent! — —

At the head of this Mission stood M. le General de Buornonville.[131]

The necessity of having Apartments to ourselves, with a Dining Room for the Adjoint & the aides de Camp, made us now relinquish our *pic-nic* with Madame d'Henin & M. de Lally, to go to a Dwelling, in the Marchés au Bois—[132]

April 26. We left La Rue de La Montagne, after, on my part, exactly a month's residence; of which I find in my pocket memorandum Book these words: 'I have passed here except

---

[129] Alexandre de Mazancourt (L. 868 n. 2).
[130] For the list of these officers see L. 896 n. 2. The circular list of early May, signed by Clarke and used by his staff to keep in touch with the various officers (Vincennes, C^{14} 60) includes fourteen names but fifteen numbers. The missing name is M. d'A's, which may help to explain why he was so often left without orders.
[131] L. 913 n. 18.   [132] L. 869 n. 17.

for Three separate days—a month of torture! ¹ from terrour the most tremendous for All my heart held most dear—but those Three days lifted up my Soul to a Happiness that seemed etheriel! The first of those blessed days was the sight of the first Letter from my adored husband,¹³³ which assured me of his life & safety; the second, was news from my dear Charlotte that Thou, my Alexander, had escaped the Cambridge Fever;¹³⁴ & the Third — — was, indeed, of Felicity unequaled! in my first meeting with your Father after our fearful sundrement—¹³⁵

Even yet, even Now, I can go back to those 3 Days with a feeling of re-animating Joy.

Our new apartments were *au premier*, & commodious & pleasant. One Drawing room was appropriated solely by M. d'Arblay, for his military friends, or military business. The other was mine

Here we spent together Seventeen Days. And not to harrass my recollections, I will ¹ simply copy what I find in my old memorandum Book, as it was written soon after those Days were no more.

'Seventeen Days I have passed with my best Friend—and alas, passed them chiefly in suspences terrific, and gnawing inquietude covered over with assumed composure; but they have terminated, Heaven be praised! with better views, with softer calms, and fairer hopes. Heaven realize them! I am much pleased with his Companions. M. Le Cᵗᵉ de Mazancourt, his Adjoint, is a gay, spirited, & *spirituel* young man, remarkably well bred, & gallantly fond of his profession. M. de Premorel, the aide de Camp, was interesting, though neither entertaining, instructive, nor instructed; but he is a man of solid worth & of delicate honour, and he is a descendant of Godefroy de Boulogne.¹³⁶ If he is not, ¹ therefore, on

---

¹³³ On 29 March FBA had received L. 852 from M. d'A, who addressed it to Mme de Maurville.
¹³⁴ On or about 12 April FBA learned from CBFB that AA was well and away from Cambridge.
¹³⁵ On 2 April FBA and M. d'A met in Brussels for the first time since 19 March.
¹³⁶ Godefroi IV de Boulogne (*c.* 1061–1100), known as Godefroy de Bouillon, duc de Basse-Lorraine, was famed as one of the first crusaders. After the city's fall in 1099 he was elected King of Jerusalem but chose instead to remain Protector of the Holy Sepulchre. He defeated the Egyptians at Askalon in 1100 but died soon after and passed into the world of heroic legend. Prémorel may possibly, or at least plausibly, have claimed descent, since the Durand de Prémorel family came from the area of Belgium and Luxembourg that had until recently been part of the duchy of Bouillon.

the first line with respect to intellect, he is certainly so with regard to Birth. To this must be added, that he is as poor as he is noble, & bears his penury with the Gentlemanly sentiment of feeling it distinct from disgrace.[137]

He is married, & has 10 or 11 Children; he resides, with a laborious and most deserving Wife, a woman, also, of family, on a small Farm, which he works at himself, & which repays him by its nourishment. For many days in the year, Potatoes, he told me, were the only food they could afford, for themselves or their offspring! But they eat them with the proud pleasure of independence & of Honour & Loyalty, such as befits their high origin, always to serve, or be served, out of the line of their legal Princes.[138] As soon as Louis ¹ 18 was established on his throne, M. de Premorel made himself known to the Duc de Luxembourg, who placed him in his own company in the Garde du Corps, & put his son upon the supernumerary list — — (as that kind Duc had done *our* son,—a distinction & promotion, my dear Alexander, that you declined, I trust, from a permanent persuasion of being better fitted for a different career.) This young man is really charming. He has a native *noblesse* of air & manner, with a suavity as well as steadiness of serene politeness, that announce the Godefroy blood flowing with conscious dignity & inborn courage through his youthful veins. He is very young, but tall & handsome, & speaks of all his Brothers & Sisters as if already he were ¹ *Chef de Famille*, & bound to sustain & protect them. I delighted to lead him to talk of them, & the conversation on that subject always brightened him into joy & loquacity. He named every one of them to me in particular, repeatedly, with a desire I should know them individually, & a warm hope I might one day verify his representations. (On my part, I equally desired his Acquaintance with Thee, Alex, both from his manners & his Character.)

This youth, Alphonse, & his Father dined with us daily at this period. I could not be glad — — but M. d'Arblay saw it

[137] The Prémorels were typical of the poor country gentlemen, known slightingly as 'hobereaux', who remained diehard royalists long after most of the higher and richer nobility had adjusted to the Napoleonic order.

[138] Others shared this view of Alphonse de Prémorel and his family situation. When his superior officer in the Maison du Roi recommended him for a captaincy in a line regiment, he too mentioned the eleven children and the impoverished *émigré* years of his father, 'un bon gentilhomme du département des Ardennes' (Personal dossier, Vincennes).

would be convenient to them, & therefore I tried not to be sorry. All the mornings were devoted to preparations for the ensuing expected Campaign; the General had no time to make any ¹ visits—save now & then an Evening and short call, arm in arm—on Madame d'Henin, Madame de la Tour du Pin, Madame de Maurville, the family Boyd, & Madame de Beaufort; whose sympathy in my approaching separation was very endearing.

When, however, all was prepared, & the Word of Command alone was waited for, from the Marschal Duc de Feltre, my dearest Friend indulged in one morning's recreation, which proved as agreeable as any thing, at such a period, could be to a mind oppressed like mine.

He determined that we should visit the Palais de Laken,¹³⁹ which had been the Dwelling assigned as the Palace for the Empress Josephine, by Buonaparte, at the time of his Divorce. My dearest Husband drove me in his Cabriolet, & the three Gentlemen, whom he invited to be ¹ of the party, accompanied us on Horse-back. The drive—the Day—the road—the Views— *our new Horses*—all were delightful, & procured me a short relaxation from the foresight of evil.

Ah! what would have been the contrast from comfort to agony, had I then been miserably gifted with anticipating the knowledge that This would be the Last time I should ever be driven by Him!—Never, after that refreshing excursion, were we again in a carriage that He had power to guide! — —

I must leave off copying, & write again from the mixture of memorandum & recollections, for the many events that have occurred since this Now regretted,—though Then so bewailed period, mingle themselves so forcibly with the sketch of narration committed to my pocket Book to help my memory for details always meant for Thee, ¹ my dear Alex, that to Copy without addition, change, or Comment, is not possible. To return to the Palace of Laken

It was, at this moment, wholly uninhabited, & shewn to us

---

¹³⁹ The château of Laeken or Laaken, then on the northern outskirts of Brussels and now a residential quarter within the city, was built in 1782–4 by Montoyer for Duke Albert of Saxe-Teschen. The editor has not found any evidence that it was intended for Joséphine (who stayed on at Malmaison), but it was used to welcome Marie-Louise to what had until recently been Austrian domains. See La Tour du Pin, p. 383.

by some common servant. It is situated in a delicious Park *à l'anglaise*, & with a taste, a polish, & an elegance, that parts it from the charge of frippery or Gaudiness, though its ornaments & embellishments are all of the liveliest gaiety. There is in some of the Apartments[140] some Gobelin Tapestry of the highest beauty, of which there are here and there parts & details so exquisitely worked, that I could have 'hung over them enamoured'[141] for several days following.

Previously to this reviving excursion, my dearest Friend had driven me, occasionally, in the famous *allée Verte*, which the Inhabitants of Brussels consider as the first *Promenade* [1] in the World; but it by no means answered to such praise in my Eyes; it is certainly very pretty; but too regular, too monotonous, & too flat to be eminently beautiful; though from some parts the most distant from the City there are views of cottages & hamlets that afford very great pleasure.

Our last Entertainment here was a Concert, in the great public & very fine Room appropriated for Musick or Dancing. The celebrated Madame Catalani had here a Benefit.[142] The Queen of the Netherlands was present: not, however, in State, though not incognita: and — — the King of Warriours, Marshall Lord Wellington, surrounded by his *Etat Major*, and all the officers and first persons here, whether Belgians, Prussians, Hanoverians, or English. I looked at him watchfully all Night, and was charmed with every turn of his countenance, with his noble and singular physiognomy, & his [1] Eagle Eye, and Aquiline, forcible Nose. He was gay even to sportiveness all the Evening, conversing with the officers around him on terms of intimacy and pleasantry. He never was seated, not even a moment, though I saw seats vacated to offer to him frequently. Whether this was an etiquette that he thought respectful for the presence of the Queen, to whose courteous inclination of the head he bowed with profound reverence; or whether it was simply from a determination to deny himself every species of personal indulgence, when he knew not how soon he might require an almost supernatural strength to endure the hardships of a Commander in chief during the great impending

---

[140] This was the Salle du Grand Concert in the rue Ducale (Romberg, p. 140).
[141] *Paradise Lost*, v. 13.
[142] See L. 877 n. 9.

Battle to which every thing looked forward, I cannot tell. But he seemed enthusiastically charmed with Catalana, [1] ardently applauding whatsoever she sang, — — except the Rule Britania: and there, with sagacious reserve, he listened in utter silence. Who ordered it I know not; but he felt it was injudicious, in every country but our own, to give out a Chorus of Rule, Brittania! Britannia, Rule the Waves!—And when an Encore was begun to be Vociferated from his officers, he instantly crushed it, by a commanding air of disapprobation; and thus offered me an opportunity of seeing how magnificently he could quit his convivial familiarity for imperious dominion, when occasion might call for the transformation. [1]

When the full order arrived from Gand, establishing the mission of M. d'Arblay at Luxembourg,[143] he decided upon demanding an audience of the Duke of Wellington, with whom he thought it necessary to concert his measures. The Duke received him without difficulty and they had a conference of some length, the result of which was that his Grace promised to prepare Blucher, the Great Prussian General, then actually at Luxembourg, for aiding the scheme.

M. d'Arblay himself also wrote to Blucher; but before any answer could be returned, a new ordonnance from the Duke de Feltre directed M. d'Arblay to hasten to his post without delay. [1]

13. May, 1815 — — My best Friend left me, to begin his Campaign; left me, by melancholy chance, upon his Birth Day.[144] What a Day to me! his shattered health, & fading Form for-ever before my Eyes, with the consciousness that a martial sense of duty, & an innately irrepressible bravery, would listen to no prudence, would yield to no pain, would be sensible to no danger, that would try to spare him from any risk, any exertion, or any difficulty, by pointing out his time of life, his enfeebled frame, or his harrassed nerves and Constitution. He would think only, I well knew, of what was Right to be Done, without any sort of reference to his sufferings in its performance.— [1]

I could not that day see a human Being; I could but consecrate it to thoughts of Him who had just left me—yet who

[143] See L. 871 n. 6.
[144] On this day, 61 years of age.

from Me never was—never can be mentally absent,—& of our poor Alexander, thus inevitably, yet severely cast upon himself.—

The next Day, the gentle & feeling Mad^e de Beaufort spent the morning with me, using the most engaging efforts to prevail with me to Dine constantly at her table, & to accompany her, in a short time, to her Villa. Without any charms personal or even intellectual to catch, or fascinate, she seemed to have so much goodness of character, joined to a most undeserved, but unbounded partiality for me, that I could not but resolve to try to attach myself to her, & to accept her kindness as the 'cordial drop'¹⁴⁵ to make the Cup of woe of my sad solitude ¹ go down. For Madame d'Henin, who to equal sensibility, joined the finest understanding, & who entertained for me the highest sentiments, was now so absorbed in politics, that she had no time for any expansion of sympathy; especially as in that predominant point in her turn of mind & taste, politics, our sympathy was by no means of the same blending sort that it always preserved—and now preserves,—in social feelings, opinions, and affections. She came, nevertheless, to see me in the Evening, & to endeavour to draw me again into human life! And her kind effort so far conquered me, that I called upon her the next Day, & met Madame de Vaudreuil,¹⁴⁶ for whom I had a still unexecuted commission from the Duchess Dowager of Buccleugh¹⁴⁷—upon whom I had waited at the request of

---

¹⁴⁵ FBA is recalling Rochester's lines on

> *Love*, the most gen'rous Passion of the Mind;
> The softest Refuge Innocence can find:
> The safe Director of unguided Youth:
> Fraught with kind Wishes, and secur'd by Truth:
> That Cordial drop Heav'n in our Cup has thrown,
> To make the nauseous draught of life go down:

'A Letter from Artemisa in the Town to Cloe in the Country', ll. 40–5

¹⁴⁶ The niece of the princesse d'Hénin, Pauline-Victoire de Riquet de Caraman (1764–1834), who had married in 1781 Jean-Louis Rigaud (1763–1814), vicomte de Vaudreuil. In writing of the early days of the Revolution, Chateaubriand observed that aristocratic taste and elegance could still be found 'aux soirées de mesdames de Poix, d'Hénin, de Simiane, de Vaudreuil . . .' (*Mémoires*, i. 183).

¹⁴⁷ Lady Elizabeth *née* Montagu (vi, L. 631 n. 29), to whom in 1812 FBA delivered a petition entrusted to her by the princesse de Chimay *formerly* Laure-Auguste Fitz-James (L. 845 n. 16). The petition was to be forwarded to the Prince Regent on behalf of Édouard, 4th duc de Fitz-James (L. 894 n. 8), her nephew, who was applying for the continuance of the pension formerly granted to his wife Élisabeth-Alexandrine *née* Le Vassor de la Touche, who had died in 1810 leaving two sons Jacques-Marie-Emmanuel (1799–1846) and Charles-François-Henri (1801–82).

the Princesse de Chimay, to entreat the interest of her Grace with the, then, Prince ¹ Regent, that the English Pension accorded to the just dead Duchess of St. James, might be continued to the Duke, her husband, who remained a ruined Widower, with several children.¹⁴⁷ I failed in my attempt, the natural answer being that there was no possibility of granting a Pension to a Foreigner who resided in his own Country, while that Country was at open War with the Land whence he aspired at its *obtention*—a word I make for my passing convenience. I reciprocated visits, also, with Madame de La Tour Du Pin, the truly elegant, accomplished, & high bred niece, by marriage, of Madame la Princesse d'Henin; & whom it was a fair pride to rejoice in knowing to be of English extraction— She was a Miss Dillon, & a descendant from the famed Lord Falkland.¹⁴⁸ Her Husband, M. de La Tour Du Pin, was at that time at Vienna, forming a part of the renowned Congress; by which he was sent to La Vendée, to announce ¹ there the resolution of the assembled Sovereigns to declare Buonaparté an outlaw, in consequence of his having broken the conditions of his accepted Abdication.¹⁴⁹

And I was discovered, & visited, by M. le Comte de Boursac,¹⁵⁰ one of the first officers of the Establishment of the Prince de Conde, with whom he was then at Brussels: a man of worth & cultivation, whom I was happy to again Encounter. At Paris he visited us so often, that he took up the name, at the Door, of 'Le Voisin', thinking it more safe to be so designated, than to pronounce too frequently the name of a known adherent to the Bourbons. The good Madame de Maurville I saw often, & the Family of the Boyds, with which my General had engaged me to quit Brussels, should Brussels become the seat of War.

The protestant Church was here open to me,¹⁵¹ & the King

---

¹⁴⁸ Mme de Latour du Pin (vi, L. 575 n. 2) was the daughter of the Hon. Arthur Dillon (1750–94) and his wife Lucy de Rothe (d. 1782), who was the granddaughter of Lucius Henry Cary (1687–1730), 6th Viscount Falkland (1694), and his wife Laura Dillon (1708–41).

FBA's interest in the Dillons in the 1820s, when at 11 Bolton Street she was writing the Waterloo and Trèves Journals, may have stemmed from her correspondence of these years with Lady Bedingfeld (*c* .1770–1854), whose mother Lady Jerningham, *formerly* the Hon. Frances Dillon (xi, L. 1250 n. 2), FBA was urged to visit as a near neighbour in Bolton Row.   ¹⁴⁹ See L. 872 n. 5.

¹⁵⁰ For the vicomte de Boursac, see L. 901 n. 7 *supra* and vi, L. 607 n. 2.

¹⁵¹ This was the royal chapel beside the Museum and between the rue Montagna

& Queen of the Netherlands[152] went to it themselves, with their family, but without the smallest State. ¹ They both look good, but too meek & unimportant to answer to the representative dignity of their high station, of which they inspire not an idea. The Prince hereditary was there also, & his air was rather more appropriate to his rank, though utterly unassuming. The Princess of Orange, also, the King's mother,[153] whose demeanour was perfectly in Character with her situation. She is sister to the King of Prussia,[154] & to the Duchess of York.[155] I had met her twice in the apartments of my English Princesses, & been Named to her both times, by my condescending Princess Augusta first, & next by my amiable & partial Princess Elizabeth, now Land Gravine of Hesse Hombourg. However the anxious, gnawing ¹

[*evidently an omission in making a fair copy*]

The Dutch ladies then in waiting were even comically fearful of making themselves of any consequence, & they ran skidding down the Aisle of the Chapel, tip tap, tip tap, like frightened Hares, making no sound in their progress, from apprehension of exciting notice, yet looking mean rather than timid; as their Royal Mistress looked humble, rather than grateful in bowing her way down the same Aisle. I thought of our Princess Charlotte, & how little her high spirit would accord with such obsequious gentleness.

I had no application to make for Tickets, or a Seat; whoever presented themselves ¹ at the Door, was admitted without difficulty, & took the best place vacant. There were no pews for the congregation at large, merely rows of Forms on each side of the unadorned Edifice, with room left between them for walking down to enter them, & to proceed to the Altar.

Brussels in general, nevertheless, was, then, inhabited by Catholics, & Catholic ceremonies were not infrequent. In particular, *le Fête Dieu*[156] was kept with much pomp, & a Pro-

de la Cour and the rue de Ruisbreek. In predominantly Catholic Brussels it provided Protestant services for the Royal Family and was often attended by foreign visitors.

[152] *Née* Wilhelmina (1774–1837), Princess of Prussia. See iv, L. 255 n. 24.
[153] Frederica Sophia Wilhelmina (1751–1820). See ibid.
[154] Friedrich Wilhelm III (1770–1840).
[155] *Née* Frederica (1767–1820), Princess Royal of Prussia (i, L. 11 n. 22).
[156] Otherwise known as the Fête du Saint-Sacrement or Corpus Christi, this

cession of Priests paraded the streets, accompanied by Images, Pictures, Paintings, Tapestry, & other *ensignia* for outward & visible worship; & the Windows were hung with Carpets & Rugs, & Mats, & almost with rags, to prove good will, at least, to what they deem a pious shew. Ludicrous circumstances without end interrupted, or marred the procession, from frequent hard showers, during which the Priests, decorated with splendid Robes, & Petticoats, & Ornaments the most gaudy, took sudden refuge at the doors of the houses by which they were passing, & great Cloths, Towels, or ¹ coarse Canvas, were flung over the consecrated Finery, and the Relics were swaddled up in Flannels, while dirt, splashes, running, scampering, & ludicrous Wrappings up, broke at once & disfigured the Procession.

Madame de Beaufort offered to take me to see all that was curious or beautiful in Brussels—but I had not sufficiently recovered from my consternation at this new separation before that kind new Friend was taken dangerously ill, of a pleurisy, which in a very short time deprived her of life. A hard blow I felt this—for she was not only amiable, powerful, & zealous, but she had conceived for me a friendship that was nearly enthusiastic. I lamented her loss in all directions—from that time I thought no more of examining this celebrated City; my spirits, already oppressed, were utterly sunk: & though I saw not unfrequently my dear Madame d'Henin, ¹ & also Madame La Tour du Pin & Madame Maurville, I only twice was induced to join in any social meeting at the houses of any of them. At Madame d'Henin's I saw the Marechal Marmont,¹⁵⁷ Duc de Ragusa; & M. Mounier,¹⁵⁸ whom I had known when he was private secretary to Buonaparte; M. Louis,¹⁵⁹ Ministre du

feast in honour of the Eucharist had been marked since its institution in 1264 by performances of plays and public processions. It fell on the Thursday following the octave of Pentecost or Whitsun. In 1815 Fête-Dieu was therefore on Thursday, 25 May.

¹⁵⁷ See vii, L. 793 n. 19 and L. 860 n. 11 above.
¹⁵⁸ L. 876 n. 27.
¹⁵⁹ Joseph-Dominique Louis (L. 918 n. 8), later Baron Louis, left the priesthood soon after the Revolution began, emigrated in 1791, and returned to France after Napoleon's seizure of power through the 18 Brumaire. He then began to make his name as a skilful administrator in the Imperial finance ministry, which led Louis XVIII to make him Minister at the first Restoration and reappoint him after the return from Ghent. Then Louis accomplished the triple feat of paying off the huge

Finance; & M. L'anglaise,[160] Pere of the Senate: as well as Hambert de La Tour du Pin,[161] & many others; but with no intimacy, for politics were then of so absorbing an ascendance, that save to be all on fire with those who were inflamed, or all in despair with those who were gloomy, there was not the smallest amity in any intercourse.

At Madame de la Tour du Pin I kept the Fête of Madame de Maurville, with a large & pleasant party; & I just missed meeting the famous Lady Caroline Lamb,[162] who had been there at Dinner, & whom I saw, however, crossing the Place Royale, from Madame de la Tour du Pin's to the grand Hotel: —dressed, or, rather, ¹ *not* dressed, so as to excite universal attention, & authorize every boldness of staring from the General to the lowest soldier, among the military Groups then constantly parading La Place,—for she had one shoulder, half her back, & all her throat & Neck, displayed as if at the call of some statuary for modelling a heathen Goddess. A slight scarf hung over the other shoulder, & the rest of the attire was of accordant lightness. As her Ladyship had not then written her *Glenarvon*, & was not, therefore, considered as one apart, from being known as an eccentric Authoress, this conduct & demeanour excited something beyond surprize; & Madame La Tour du Pin told me that such laxity of modesty in an English lady provoked censure, if not derision, upon the whole English

debts inherited from the Empire, negotiating settlements with the allies, and providing the fiscal base for renewed French prosperity. He withdrew from office during the reactionary period after 1820, but returned to the portfolio in 1831–2 after the July Revolution of Louis-Philippe and sat in the Chamber of Peers from 1832 until his death.

[160] Jules-Jean-Baptiste Anglès (1778–1828), comte Anglès, had become ministre de la Police générale in the provisional government of 1814 and was to be prefect of police under Louis XVIII from 1818 until 1821.

[161] L. 854 n. 9.

[162] Daughter of Lady Henrietta Frances *née* Spencer (i, L. 3 n. 103), Caroline Ponsonby (1785–1828) had married William Lamb (1779–1848), Lord Melbourne, but this marriage was increasingly troubled by her notorious liaison with Lord Byron, whom she was afterward to satirize in her novel *Glenarvon* (1816). In 1824 her mind was turned by a chance encounter with Byron's funeral procession and in 1825 she was permanently separated from her husband. FBA's 'missed meeting' must have been at least a month after the Fête-Dieu and the death of Mme de Beaufort, because Caroline Lamb did not come to Brussels until July, when she appeared to nurse her brother, who had been wounded at Waterloo, and to flirt with Wellington, whom she then followed to Paris. See Leslie A. Marchand, *Byron: A Biography* (6 vols., 1957–), ii. 536–7.

Nation. I could not hear this with indifference! & the less, as I had seen this lady, when a Child, at the house of her Grandmother, the virtuous & religious Lady ¹ Dowager Spencer,¹⁶³ where she was under the direction of the exemplary Miss Trimmer—who was Governess of her Cousins Lady Harriet & Lady Georgina Cavendish.¹⁶³

My time, at this suspensive interval, was almost wholly consigned to writing or reading Letters: my indulgent Husband commonly wrote to me thrice a Week—& kindly demanded a similar return—Ah Heaven Ah, how did my life hang upon these revivifying 3 Post Days! I gave the rest of my solitude to my dear English correspondents, & to reading the history of La Belgique by De W.¹⁶⁴ I strolled daily in the Park, or on the Place Royale, formed by very handsome white stone edifices. To the Botanic Garden¹⁶⁵ I went once with the good Boyds: but after Kew Garden it appeared a mere Doll's toy: on the Ramparts, whence the views are in some parts charming, I often walked while my best Friend rode—when he yet was with me—but I visited the *allée Verte* no more after my loss of Madame de Beaufort: ¹ though certainly I might have been tempted thither again, had I known in time the Day when the Duke of Wellington & Prince Blucher rode up & down there, amidst a concourse that included almost every inhabitant of Brussels but myself.

When Madame Duchesse d'Angouleme came over from England to commune with Louis 18 at Gand,¹⁶⁶ Mesdames d'Henin & La Tour du Pin went thither, to pay to her their devoirs; & they earnestly pressed me to join their party, as I had so recently been received at the Thuilleries by her *Altesse Royale*¹⁶⁷ with marked distinction: but I had no spirits for such an exertion.

Very soon after their return to Brussels, M. de Lally paid me

¹⁶³ Widow of the 1st Earl Spencer (i, L. 3 n. 100), Margaret Georgiana *née* Poyntz (1737–1814), at whose house in Bath in 1791 FBA had met among other members of the 'splendid race' Lady Spencer's granddaughter Lady Caroline, then aged six, along with her cousins the Cavendish daughters (then aged 8 and 6 years, respectively) and their governess 'Selina' Trimmer. See i. 37–50 and notes.
¹⁶⁴ Dewez (L. 890 n. 5).
¹⁶⁵ The botanical gardens mentioned here are not the later Jardin Botanique between the Porte de Laeken and the Porte de Schaerbeek, which was not completed until 1830, but rather the handsome Parc Public that faces the royal palace. This ancient garden was landscaped and replanted with many unusual shrubs and trees in 1774.   ¹⁶⁶ On 28 May (see L. 878 n. 2).
¹⁶⁷ On 24 February (see L. 845).

a long Visit, in which he read to me a Farewell to Public Life, addressed to Louis 18, in something between a Letter & a memorial. It was written with all the spirit, the nobleness, & the high sentiment belonging to his animated yet touching eloquence; yet ⎮ I sincerely regretted his resignation, which I saw was the effect of some disappointment; but which I had the great pleasure, not very long afterwards, to find relinquished— in consequence of which he became one of the most useful, as he was always the quite most exalted of the diplomatic Orators.

Another visit of an interest that came yet more home to my *business & bosom* I received from Monsieur le Duc de Luxembourg,[168] who came to inform me that he was on the point of negociating with the Duke of Wellington & Prince Blucher, upon raising a royal Corps to accompany their army into France, should the expected Battle lead to that result; & he desired me to prepare M. d'Arblay, should such be the case, for a recall from Treves, that he might resume his post in the body Guards belonging to the *Compagnie de* Luxembourg. He spoke of my Beloved in terms of such high consideration, and ⎮ with expressions so amiable of regard & esteem, that he won my heart. He could by no means, he said, be again under active military orders, & consent to lose so distinguished an officer from his Corps. I had formerly met the Duke in Paris, at Madame de Lavals, & he had honoured me with a visit *chez moi* immediately after my return from England: & in consequence of those meetings, & of his real friendship for M. d'Arblay, he now spoke to me with the unreserved trust due to a tried Confident in cases of peril & urgency. He stayed with me nearly two hours—for where once the heart ventured to open itself upon the circumstances & expectantions or apprehensions, of that eventful period, subjects, thoughts, opinions & feelings pressed forward with such eagerness for discussion, that those ⎮ who upon such conditions met, found nothing so difficult as to separate.

I wrote instantly to M. d'Arblay—but the Duke's plan proved abortive, as the Duke of Wellington & Prince Blucher refused all sanction to the junction of a French Army with that of the Allies. They thought, perhaps —— & perhaps justly,—that by

---

[168] See L. 882. The duc de Luxembourg had shortly before been appointed commissaire royal with Wellington's army.

entering France with Natives against Natives, they might excite a civil War, more difficult to conduct, than that of only Foreigners against Foreigners.

Suspence, during all this period, was frightfully mistress of the mind; nothing was known; every thing was imagined; Hope was constantly counterbalanced by Dread: the two great interests that were at War, the Bourbonites & Buonapartites, were divided & subdivided into Factions, or rather Fractions, without end, & all that was kept invariably & on both sides alive was Expectation. Wanderers, Deserters, or Captives, from France ¹ arrived daily at Brussels, all with varying News of the state of that Empire, & of the designs of Buonaparté. Amongst them, the Chevalier d'Argy made me a visit,[169] obtaining admission to my obscurity—generally impervious, but here willing, to deliver to me a Letter from M. de Premorel, for *M. Le General comte d'Arblay*. This Gentleman was just escaped from Sedan, in the disguise of a *Paysan*, & assisted by a *Paysanne*, belonging to his family. She conducted him through bye paths, & thick Forests, that she knew to be least frequented by the troops, Police, or Custom house officers of Buonaparté. He was going to offer his services to the King, Louis 18. He embarrassed me some what, by calling me, *à chaque mot, Madame la Comtesse*;[169] & I was on the point of begging his forbearance, till, considering the address on the Letter which he brought me, I restrained myself, from the fear I might not seem to be the Wife of my honoured ¹ General, if I disclaimed sharing his honours, but rather his house-keeper, or some sort of *complaisante*! I was forced, therefore, to submit to my momentary dignity with as good a Grace as I could assume. I had much interesting public news from M. d'Argy; but I pass bye all now except personal detail, as I write but for my nearest Friends: & all that was then known of public occurrence has long been stale.

About this time, I made myself some happiness in witnessing that of Madame de La Tour Du Pin & of Madame d'Henin, in the safe return of M. de La Tour Du Pin from his perilous undertaking in La Vendee,[170] of announcing the outlawry of Buonaparté. His life had been in the most eminent danger, &

---

[169] Argy (L. 881 n. 8) may already have known that Louis XVIII was about to make M. d'A a comte (see L. 840 n. 9).
[170] He actually arrived from Spain on 18 May (L. 876 n. 26).

he owed his escape from fearful captivity, at least, to the private good services of the famous General[171] Marechal Massena. [1]

During this melancholy period, when leisure, till now a delight, became a burthen to me, I could not call my faculties into any species of intellectual service; all that might else have resulted from mental exertion, was sunk, was lost, was annihilated in the overpowering predominance of anxiety for the coming event. I endured my suspence only by writing to or hearing from HIM who was its object. All my next dear connexions were well. I heard from them satisfactorily:—& I was also engaged in frequent correspondence with the Princess Elizabeth—Now Landgravine of Hesse Hombourg; whose Letters were—and are—charming, not only from their vivacity, their frankness & condescendsion, but from a peculiarity of manner, the result of having mixt little with the World, that, joined to great native fertility of fancy, give a [1] something so singular & so genuine to her style of Writing, as to render her Letters desireable & interesting, independent of the sincere & most meritted attachment which their gracious kindness warmly inspires.

I subscribed to the best Library,[172] & obtained some Books of amusement to endeavour to dissipate my lonely hours—but I had no success, save in a History of La Belgique, by Dewezt, & that, as it treated not only of *Brussels*, which I inhabited in Person, but of *Triers*, which I inhabited in Heart & imagination, drew me from my fearful reveries, & engaged me in making an abridgement from it, which I meant for my best Friend— but which I never looked over, nor [1] have even thought of till this moment, from the weight of cares, sorrows, & anxieties— occasionally chequered, indeed, by Heaven born Happiness— which from this time overwhelmingly absorbed my feelings & my faculties.

The abridgement, however, with all my Brussels Letters & memorandums, is now before me; but I find it a mere Content of Chapters, & of no value but to refresh memory.— [1]

I come now to busier scenes — — and to my sojourn at

---

[171] Masséna (L. 903 n. 19) was in command at Marseilles, where Latour du Pin had gone; and it may be that the marshal's two-faced policy included help to this emissary of the King.

[172] The Cabinet Littéraire, which was nearby in the Marché au bois (Romberg, pp. 176–7).

Brussels — — — my Letters to my General—all tenderly preserved!—& now before me, will want little more than copying for giving my promised account of the Brussels—or rather of my own sojourn there,—during the opening of one of the most famous Campaigns upon Record; & the Battle of Waterloo, upon which, in great measure, hung the fate of Europe

Yet upon reflexion, I will write no account of these great events, which have been detailed so many hundred times, & in so many hundred ways, as I have nothing new to offer upon them; I will simply write the narrative of my own history at that awful period, according to that sacred desire which at length— [1] puts my poor Pen again into my still reluctant hand —reluctant, except where it is to earn a return of communication from those yet—& for ever dear to me. THERE, its original vivacity holds—in great measure, at least, its place.

Thursday, 15th June, 1823,[173] I was awakened in the middle of the Night by confused noises in the house, & running up & down stairs. I listened attentively, but heard no sound of Voices, & soon all was quiet. I then concluded the persons who resided in the apartments on the second Floor, over my head, had returned home late, & I tried to again fall asleep.

I succeeded; but I was again awakened at about 5 o'clock, in the morning, Friday, *16th June,* by the sound of a [1] Bugle Horn in The Marché aux Bois; I started up, & passed into the Drawing room, & covered only with a long shawl, opened the Window. But I only perceived some straggling soldiers, hurrying in different directions, the Marchée aux Bois being open to several streets, & I saw Light, gleaming from some of the chambers in the Neighbourhood:—I hearkened attentively, to gather some information; but all again was soon still, & my own dwelling in profound silence, & therefore I concluded there had been some disturbance in exchanging sentinels at the various posts, which was already appeased; & I retired once more to my Pillow, & remained till [1] my usual hour, when I meant to enquire into the meaning of what had disturbed me.

I was finishing, however, a Letter for my best Friend when my Breakfast was brought in, at my then customary time of

---

[173] An inadvertence in dating, which betrays the year of composition.

8 o'clock; &, as mistakes & delays & miscarriages of Letters had caused me much unnecessary misery, I determined to put what I was then writing to the post myself, & set off with it the moment it was sealed. This I did, forgetting, in my haste to receive as well as forward a Letter, the questions I meant to ask; & which hung upon mere simple curiosity, since it was impossible for me to suggest that any public matter had occurred, of which neither my Host nor Hostess nor servant ¹ would give me any notice: since they All well knew the deep private interest in which every public occurrence was, for me, involved.

In my melancholy way back from the Post office, where I had failed in my hoped anticipation of the delivery of Letters, as Triers sent me none that Day—while slowly I passed into the Market Place, my Ears were alarmed by the sound of military music, & my Eyes equally struck with the sight of a Body of Troops marching to its measured time. As they were crossing over immediately in my direction, I begged leave to stand up at the door of a large shop till they should be gone by. This was accorded me with the usual Flemish ¹ Hospitality in silence. But I soon found that what I had supposed to be an occasionally passing troop, was a complete Corps; Infantry, Cavalry, Artillery, Bag & Baggage, with all its officers in full uniform—& that uniform was Black.[174]

This gloomy hue gave an air so mournful to the Procession, that, knowing its destination for Battle, I contemplated it with an aching heart.—On enquiry, I learned it was the Army of Brunswick. How much deeper yet had been my Heart-ach had I fore-known that nearly all those brave men, thus marching on in gallant though dark array, with their valiant Royal Chief at their head,—the Nephew of my own King, George ¹ the Third, —were amongst the First destined victims to this dreadful contest, & that neither the Chief, nor the greater part of his Warlike associates would—within a few short hours—breathe again the Vital air.

My interrogation was answered with brevity so concise, though not disrespectful, that I ventured not to make another; yet, anxious to gather, in any manner, any intelligence, I glided from this Grocer's shop to one of Porcelain. My success,

[174] The Brunswickers (see L. 891 n. 3).

however, was no better; & though, by every opportunity, I changed my quarters, I still met with no one more communicative or satisfactory. Yet Curiosity was all awake & all abroad; for the Procession lasted some Hours.— ˡ Not a door but was open; not a threshold but was crowded, & not a window of the many-windowed Gothic, modern, frightful, handsome, quaint, disfigured, fantastic or lofty mansions that diversify the large Market place of Brussels, but was occupied by lookers on. Placidly, indeed, they saw the Warriors pass; no kind greeting welcomed their arrival; no warm wishes followed them to Combat. Neither, on the other hand, was there the slightest symptom of dissatisfaction: yet even while standing thus in the midst of them, an unheeded, yet observant stranger, it was not possible for me to discern, with any solidity of conviction, whether the Belgians were, at heart, Bourbonites or Buonapartites: for my fears, in my helpless situation, of exciting hostility, did not more scrupulously ˡ ward off any positive investigation, than their own uncertainty of which might be the victor cased them in an appearance of impregnable neutrality. The Buonapartistes, however, were in general the most open, for the opinion on both sides, alike with Good Will & with Ill, was nearly universal that Buonaparté was invincible.

Still, I knew not, dreamt not, suspected not, that the Campaign was already opened: that Buonaparte had broken into *La Belgique* on the 15ᵗʰ & had taken Charleroi; though it's [news] was undoubtedly spread all over Brussels, except to my lonely self. My own disposition, at this period, to silence & retirement was too congenial with the constantly taciturn habits of my Hosts to be by them counteracted, & they suffered me, therefore, ˡ to return to my Home as I had quitted it, with a mere usual & civil salutation; while themselves & their house were evidently continuing their common avocations with their common composure. And, thus, at this great moment, big with the fate of Europe, I sent off a Letter to Treves from Brussels, on the 16ᵗʰ of June, 1815,¹⁷⁵ without the smallest intimation that Hostilities were begun! Surely, as my next Letter observed, to General d'Arblay, our coloquial use of the word PHLEGM must be derived from the character of the *FLEMINGS*.

¹⁷⁵ L. 890.

The important tidings now, however, burst upon me in sundry directions. The Princess d'Henin, Colonel de Beaufort, Madame de Maurville, the ¹ Boyd Family, All, with intelligence of the event, joined offers of service, & invitations that I would share their destinies in quitting my Home, to reside with them, during this momentous contest, should I prefer such protection to remaining alone at such a crisis.

Here, however, I could receive at once all Letters from Treves; & Necessity, therefore, only, could drive me from Brussels; especially just now, as my unfortunate ignorance of what was passing had prevented my making any provision for a change of direction.

I Now wrote with every precaution, & desired that my answers might be addressed to Madame de Burney, to avoid making known, in case Brussels should be surprized, that I belonged to an officer of Louis 18.'s body Guard. ¹

Part of the incoherent but impressive Letter that I next wrote to Treves I will Copy;¹⁷⁶ that Letter is now before me, but nearly worn out.

'What a Day of confusion & alarm did we All spend on the 17ᵗʰ — — In *my* Heart the whole time was Treves! Treves! Treves! That Day, & This, which is Now finishing, June 18ʰ I passed in hearing the Cannon! Good God! what indescribable horrour to be so near the Field of Slaughter!— such I call it, for the preparation to the Ear by the tremendous Sound of the Death-dispencing Balls of Fire, was soon followed by its fullest effect, in the view of the wounded, the maimed, the bleeding, groaning,—agonized martyrs to the formidable contention that was so soon to terminate the History of the War. And hardly less affecting was this ¹ disabled, debilitated return of the dislocated Votaries to the Onset of the Battle, than the sight of the continually pouring forth ready-armed & vigorous Victims that marched past my Windows to meet similar destruction — —'

I find I cannot copy—the risings of my memory so interlard every other sentence, that I shall take my Letters but as outlines, to be filled up by my recollections: still, nevertheless, literally copying where nothing new occurs, & merely marking what was written at the moment by inverted commas.

¹⁷⁶ L. 891.

Accounts from the Field of Battle arrived hourly; sometimes directly from the Duke of Wellington to Lady Charlotte Greville,[177] & to some other ladies who had near Relations in the combat; & which, by their means, were circulated ¹ in Brussels; & at other times from such as conveyed Those amongst the Wounded Belgians, whose misfortunes were inflicted nearly enough to the skirts of the spots of Action, to allow of their being dragged away by their hovering Country men, or other watching By-standers, to the City. The spots, I say, of Action, for the far-famed Battle of Waterloo was preceded by Three Days of partial engagements.

My disturbance, my uncertainties, my changes of plan during that period were of the most restless & suffering description. The immediate point of Buonaparté, all his hopes, his views, his preparations & his anticipations led to Brussels: & There, should my poor little person be included in its seizure, I ran the very risk I had fled Paris to avoid, of being shut up from all ¹ communication with my Friends, & of becoming a Prisoner who would be peculiarly watched & suspected, as the Wife of a General Officer then in active service for Louis 18; & of being, to boot, by Birth an Englishwoman.

Yet, in going thence with Those whose route I could only join, not command, I might be forced into some asylum which had no Post to & from Treves, except by Brussels, where, of course, all Letters would be intercepted.

From this dilemma, I spent my whole time in seeking intelligence, &, passing from House to House, of the associates of my perplexity—of my distress there could be none!—or of receiving them in mine. None, I say, because, whatever might be their feelings, they were as calm as a Rock is against Billows which, beating ¹ against a small vessel, threatens to shatter it to pieces.

Ten times, at least, I crossed over to Madame d'Henin, discussing plans & probabilities, & interchanging hopes & fears. I spent a considerable part of the morning with Madame de La Tour du Pin, who was now returned from Gand, where Louis 18 supported his suspence & his danger with a coolness &

---

[177] Daughter of the 3rd Duke of Portland, Lady Charlotte Cavendish-Bentinck (1775–1862), who had married on 31 Mar. 1793 Charles Greville (d. 1832), brother of Lady Crewe (vii, L. 642 n. 2). Among her 'near Relations' at Waterloo was Algernon Frederick Greville (1789–1864), one of Wellington's aides-de-camp.

equanimity which, when the eclat surrounding the Glory of his daring, & Great, Opponent shall no longer, by its over-powering resplendence, keep all around it in the shade, will carry him down to posterity as the Monarch precisely formed, by the patient good sense, the enlightened liberality, & the immoveable composure of his Character, to meet the perilous perplexities of his situation, &, if ¹ he could not combat them with the vigour & genius of a Hero, to sustain them at least with the dignity of a Gentleman.

Colonel de Beaufort came to me again with offers of service, sincere as well as polite, for he had belonged to the Regiment of Toul,¹⁷⁸ of which General d'Arblay had been the delight, & in which counted for an attached Friend every officer of which it was composed. And with Madame de Maurville & the Boyds I alternated visits from Morning to Night, as news of any sort reached either party.

Madame d'Henin & Madame de La Tour du Pin projected retreating to Gand, should the approach of the Enemy be unchecked; to avail themselves of such protection as might be obtained from ¹ seeking it under the Wing of Louis 18.   M. de La Tour du Pin had, I believe, remained there with his Majesty.

M. de Lally, & the Boyds inclined to Antwerp, where they might safely await the fate of Brussels, near enough to it for returning, should it Weather the storm, yet within reach of vessels innumerable to waft them to the British shores should it be lost.

Should this last be the fatal termination, I, of course, had agreed to join the party of the Voyage,—But O! with what torture could I project uniting in a scheme that must place the Sea between myself & my dearest tie, at an instant of defeat when if his Life were not sacrificed, it could only, his known valour assured me, be preserved by the medium of Wounds or of Captivity! ¹

All, however, was preferable to the risk of remaining a Prisoner, &, in imitation of all my Friends, I resolved to at least secure my Passport, that, while I waited to the extremity of danger, I might yet be prepared for a hasty retreat.

---

¹⁷⁸ Beaufort and M. d'A had after 1769 been officers together in the régiment d'artillerie de Toul.

Colonel Jones,[179] to whom the Duke of Wellington had deputed the military command of Brussels in his absence, was so unwilling to sanction an evacuation of Brussels which he still deemed premature, that he received all applications for Passports with an ill will bordering upon rudeness. I was anxious, therefore, for some respectable Companion in making the demand, though only from the fear of his ¹ Deputies, not of himself, to whom I was known, having met & been Named to him at the Princess d'Henin's, early after my arrival at Brussels; & having since been earnestly recommended to his protection by the tenderest of Husbands, in taking up his own Passport for Treves.

But my repugnance to depart had given time for every one I knew to be already provided, & I was compelled either to bear the brunt of the application alone, or to relinquish this security. The latter was impossible, & I went to the police office.

There arrived, I found it little mattered whether I were solitary, or one of many. The confusion was undiscribable. I could find no one to direct me to ¹ whom I should address myself nor which way I should turn. News was incessantly pouring in, now alarming, now encouraging, but so perpetually varying & contradictory, that Colonel Jones,[179] it is possible, was greatly distressed how to act, since by retaining his Countrymen, should they be captured, he cast upon himself a heavy responsibility; yet by aiding the migration, should the Allies be victorious, he would incur the high displeasure of the Duke, who would then be extremely offended that any doubts had been thrown upon his power to protect Brussels.

This embarrassment must be the apology for the roughness of the Colonel, who, ¹ not knowing how to satisfy himself, must easily be excused that he could not satisfy others. I tried to discover his Bureau;[180] but no one would venture to guide me to it: I sent to beg an audience; but I obtained no sort of answer; he would not delegate his signature to any Clerk, or under Officer; crowds, almost multitudes of persons were kept waiting in vain, in groups, in masses, or, like myself, in solitary singleness, through-out the various Rooms, Corridores, passages,

179 L. 901 n. 3.
180 The British commandant's office, which handled matters ordinarily dealt with by the police, was located during the Waterloo campaign at 25, rue de Louvain (*L'Oracle*, 6 July 1815).

nay, also, porticos & entrances of the Building—of which I forget the title, to which almost all of English now resorted, either for passports, intelligence, or counsel.

Patiently, or rather desperately, I still resolved to keep my Ground till I could ¹ obtain my suit; &, at length, called into this peopled scene by business of his own, Colonel Jones appeared, surrounded at once & followed by persons to whom he was giving directions, or from whom he was receiving notices.

Thus guarded, he might hope perhaps, to escape from new assailants: but this was not the nature either of his situation or of the times: he was immediately attacked, envellopped, entreated, reproached, or interrogated from all quarters; & his answers were so rough, his air was so boisterous, & his language was so harsh, that he shook off all who advanced affrighted or confounded, except such as, in preference to being repulsed, chose to abide the combat by ¹ rattling in his own Ears a similar artillery.

To penetrate through such a promiscuous swarm was as much out of the question as, so situated, to retreat: I saw but one resource; & that, I tried: I hastened to the principal Bureau, & There I made my stand, for There I concluded he must come. I was not mistaken; he soon made his way, to give some orders to the person who presided at it; & then, I requested my Passport.

He hastily answered that there was no occasion to depart; & turned from me to go on with his business.

I let him, perforce, finish his own affair, but presented myself so as to impede his walking off, &, when he made the attempt, I begged leave to represent that though I would stay if not driven away, I chose to hold myself in readiness for events.

His looks were all impatience, & his reply was severe: it was not, he said, for *us*, ¹ the English, to spread alarm, or prepare for an overthrow: he had not sent away his own Wife or Children, & he had no doubt but victory would repay his confidence.

I was silenced, but not convinced: The event was yet in the Womb of uncertainty, & my stake was, with respect to Earthly Happiness, my Existence. I suffered him to proceed to others, whom he rebuffed with yet less ceremony, but I could not abandon my privilege to be guided by occasion.

A compromise occurred to me, which, when again I could force his attention, suggested my dispensing with a new Passport, & one of his own, & content myself with obtaining his signature to my old one, accorded by M. le Cte de Jaucourt, by the aid of which I had reached Brussels from Paris. ¹

This therefore, I spread before him upon the Table. He could not refuse to sign it, which he did, nevertheless, with so ill a will, & so bad a grace, that it was evident he longed to rather trample it under foot. He wrote it, also, with so little care, & so coarsely, that it is more like a blot than hand-writing. Being examined, however, it appears to be Lt Col Jones & with equal alacrity to have done with each other, we then separated. I promised him, nevertheless, that I would remain to the last extremity. And I meant no other.

I was now better satisfied, though by no means at ease: what I wished at a period so nearly akin to Anarchy was a fresh passport, simply dated Brussels, & simply given to aid me in safety & Flight, should Buonaparté prove triumphant; ¹ not one announcing so undauntedly my principles, by beginning Par¹⁸¹

Yet I heartily forgive the motive of Colonel Jones, which was that all should yield to the glory of the British arms & the Duke of Wellington. And I had the less right to be surprised from the dreadful soldier's speech I had heard him utter when I first saw him, to the Princess d'Henin. Complaining of the length of time that was wasted in inaction, & of the inactivity & tameness of the Bourbons, he exclaimed 'We want blood, Madam! what we want is blood!—'

As this is no account of the public transactions of *the Hundred Days*, but merely a narration of my own little history during the close of that Epoch, I ought not to omit, & will not, therefore, ¹ omit, an anecdote which, though ludicrous to read when over, caused me very frightful apprehensions at the moment of its occurrence. It takes me back some days; to the 13th or 14th of June.

The brave High-Landers, who fought so nobly but fought to die! had passed about a week in Brussels, universally honoured & admired for their calm & gentle demeanour, & the modesty

181 The first word in the royal style that prefaced any passport issued during the reign of Louis XVIII.

& forbearance with which they accommodated themselves to whatever they found where they were quartered. They left the whole City their friends,—& soon after, alas! their Mourners. I had many conversations with Individuals amongst them, whom I casually encountered in my Walks. Their delight to hear the English Language where their Ears expected only the Dutch or the French, made them readily gratify me in answering, as far as they were able, my enquiries relative to what ¹ they publicly knew of their destination, or, from circumstances, foresaw of the time for opening hostilities. Of course, I only addressed Those whose countenances promised civility; for the Countenance, where Stranger meets Stranger, where no part is to be acted, & where no result that demands circumspection is foreseen, may very generally be trusted. For the Manners, I mean: I am well aware that for the Heart far deeper investigation is requisite; & the deepest, without the junction of Experience, may fail. But when I saw urbanity of disposition, whether through grave concentration or expansive hilarity of expression, I always sought, & always gathered, some intelligence or some anecdote to send to Treves. My earnestness to give that use to gave me courage to seek information by every ¹ means through which it might be obtained. My whole character, natively reserved, fearful, & retired, was conquered Now by a new sense of Duty animated by the most devoted affection.

My simple method of opening discourse was by asking them the way to some part of Brussels of which I was nearly certain they had never heard; & on their English 'I don't know;' I hailed them as Countrymen: I then gave them my good wishes, with an eulogium of the Duke of Wellington, & we were Friends immediately: & the little they could tell was communicated with pleasure.

I was sorry when these brave Sons of War were removed, though Those of equal bravery, the Hibernians, followed, for with them I attempted no intercourse, as, though they were much more easy of access, & perfectly good humoured, they are as prompt to familiarity as the Highlanders are to respect. ¹

I return now to having obtained the signature of Colonel Jones to my Paris Passport.

Notwithstanding all the encouraging assurances of Colonel

Jones, I found, upon again going my rounds for information that though news was arriving incessantly from the scene of action, & with details always varying, Buonaparté was not the less always advancing. All the people of Brussels lived in the streets. Doors seemed of no use, for they were never shut. The Individuals, when they re-entered their houses, only resided at the Windows: so that the whole population of the City seemed constantly in Public view. Not only Business as well as Society was annihilated, but even every species of occupation. All of which we seemed capable was to Enquire or to ¹ relate, to speak, or to hear. Yet no Clamour, no wrangling, nor even debate were intermixt with either question or answer; curiosity though incessant was serene; the Faces were all monotony, though the tidings were all Variety.

I could attribute this only to the length of time during which the Inhabitants had been habituated to Change both of Masters & Measures, & to their finding that, upon an average, they neither lost nor gained by such successive revolutions. And to this must strongly be joined their necessity of submitting, be it what it might, to the result. This mental consciousness, probably, kept their passions in order, & crushed all the impulses by which hope or fear are excited. No love of Liberty buoyed up resistance; no views of Independence brightened their imagination; & they bore even SUSPENCE, ¹ with all its piercing goadings & torturing contrarieties, with the calm of apparent philosophy, & an exteriour of placid indifference.

The first intelligence Madame d'Henin now gave me, was that the Austrian Minister extraordinary, M. le Cᵗᵉ de Vincent,¹⁸² had been wounded close by the side of the Duke of Wellington; & that he was just brought back in a litter to his Hotel. As she was much acquainted with him, she desired me to accompany her in making her personal enquiries. No one now sent servants, cards, or messages, where there was any serious interest in a research. There was too much eagerness to bear delay; & Ceremony & *Etiquette* always fly from distress & from business.

Le Comte de Vincent, we had the pleasure to hear, had been hurt only in the ¹ hand. Madᵉ d'Henin desired her name might

¹⁸² Vincent (L. 872 n. 13 and L. 891 n. 15) in time fully recovered from his wound and joked about it in a letter to Wellington (see L. 903 n. 14).

be entered in the Book of Enquiry, & was adding mine: asserting, with a partiality difficultly kept within the bounds of propriety, that it ought not to be omitted: but I had never seen him, & could not subscribe to such an assumption of importance. but this wound, as I heard afterwards, proved far more serious than at first was apprehended, threatening for many Weeks either gangrene or amputation.

News, however, far more fatal struck our Ears, soon after: the gallant Duke of Brunswick was killed![183] & by a shot close, also, to the Duke of Wellington!

The report now through-out Brussels was that the two mighty Chiefs, Buonaparté & Wellington, were almost constantly in view of each other! [1]

I went to the Boyds, Rue d'Assault, & found them panic-struck, & preparing to set off the next morning for Antwerp. I went back to Made d'Henin, for a last deliberation;—She was gone! So was M. de Lally; so was Made de La Tour du Pin! Too terrified now to any longer 'weather the storm,' I retraced my steps to la Rue d'Assault, & agreed to be of their party. We were to go by Water, in a Barge which Mr. Boyd had bespoke.

M. le Colonel de Beaufort, & Madame de Maurville, had each formed their resolutions to remain at their homes, whatsoever turn Fortune might take: though from reasons diametrically opposite, the first because too rich to risk his property by emigration; & the second, because so poor, that she thought herself no object for pillage [1] to either party.

Late at Night, accompanied by my Host, I went to la Rue d'Assault, to settle some mode of conveying my baggage; when, to my infinite satisfaction, I found they had just received some reviving intelligence from the Field, & had renounced their project of flight. Mine was most joyfully blown to the Winds, & I returned to my home, quieted & thankful.

BUT—what a Day was the next, *June 18th* The Greatest, perhaps, in its result in the annals of Great Britain; but, in its operation, & its conflicts, & its suspence, the most tremendous I ever, for my personal,—though not for my bosom feelings— experienced.—

My slumbers having been tranquilised by the close of the

[183] See L. 891 n. 14.

17ᵗʰ I was calmly ' reposing, when I was awakened by the sound of feet abruptly entering my Drawing Room. I started, & had but just time to see by my Watch that it was only Six o'clock, when a rapping at my Bed room door so quick as to announce as much trepidation as it excited, made me slip on a long kind of Domino, always, in those times, at hand, to keep me ready for encountering surprize, & demand what was the matter.

'Open your door! There is not a moment to lose!' was the answer, in the voice of Miss Ann Boyd. I obeyed, in great alarm, & saw that pretty & pleasing young woman, with her Mother, Mrs. Boyd,[184] who remembered having known & played with me when we were both Children, & who, in a singular manner, I had met with at Passy, after an elapse of more ' than Forty Years. They both eagerly told me that all their new hopes had been overthrown, by better authenticated news, & that I must be with them, Bag & Baggage, by 8 o'clock, to proceed to the wharf, & set sail for Antwerp, whence we must sail on for England, should the taking of Brussels by Buonaparté endanger Antwerp also.

To send off a few lines to the post, with my direction at Antwerp, to pack, & to pay, was all that I could attempt, or even desire; for I had not less time than appetite for thinking of Breakfast.

My Host & my Maid carried my small Package, & I arrived before 8 in the Rue d'Assault. We set off for the wharf on foot, not a fiacre or chaise being procurable. Mr. & Mrs. Boyd, 5 or 6 of their fine family, a Governess, &, I ' believe, some servants, with bearers of our luggage, made our party. Mr. Boyd took care of his Wife, & I walked with the amiable Miss Ann.

Though the distance was short, the Walk was long, because rugged, dirty, & melancholy. Now & then we heard a growling Noise, like distant Thunder; but far more dreadful was it to my imagination than any elemental Jar!

When we had got about a third part of the way, a heavy rumbling sound made us stop to listen. It was approaching nearer & nearer, & we soon found that we were followed by innumerable carriages, & a multitude of persons.

All was evidently military; but of so gloomy, taciturn, &

[184] See L. 870 n. 2, L. 878 n. 11, and vi. 795.

forbidding a description that, when we were overtaken, we |
had not courage to offer a question to any passer-by. Had we
been as certain that they belonged to the Enemy as we felt
convinced that, thus circumstanced, they must belong to our
own interests, we could not have been awed more effectually
into silent passiveness, so decisively repelling to enquiry was
every aspect. In truth, at that period, when every other hour
changed the current of Expectation, no one could be inquisitive without the risk of passing for a Spy, nor communicative,
without the hazard of being suspected as a traitor.

As, slowly, we now went on, we saw ourselves preceded, or
succeeded by Baggage Waggons, Artillery, carts filled with
women & children, & military | machines of all sorts & sizes.
Our ruminations & conjectures were, of course, as concentrated
& as mute as if we had been under the same martial discipline
as those by whom they were excited: for closeness & concealment is as contagious as frankness is healthful & diffusive.

Arrived at the wharf, Mr. Boyd pointed out to us our Barge,
which seemed manned, sailed, & fully ready for departure:
but the crowd already come & still coming, so incommoded us,
that Mr. Boyd desired we would enter a large Inn, & wait
till he could speak with the Master, & arrange our luggage &
places. We went, therefore, into a spacious room, & ordered
Breakfast: & I had just settled with Mrs. Boyd that I should
travel with her on this occasion upon | the same terms of a
mutual current Purse as had brought me from Paris to Brussels
with the Princesse d'Henin, when the room was entered by a
body of military men, of all sorts, &, I was going to say of all
ranks; but I can only describe them by saying of all *no* ranks;
for such, save some Corporals or Serjeants, who gave directions
& kept order, they seemed; & we could not appear to be more
surprized by their intrusion into these premises, than they
looked themselves at our pre-occupation. Mutual staring,
however, was mutually without speech, & we kept, & were
passively suffered to keep our ground till Mr. Boyd came to
inform us that we must all decamp!

Confounded, but without any interrogatory, we vacated |
the Apartment; & Mr. Boyd conducted us—not to the Barge,
not to the wharf, but to the road back to Brussels!

Mr. Boyd, who, with his excellent Wife & amiable Daughters,[184] thought that the safety of England & of Europe hung upon the overthrow of Buonaparté; & whose own peculiar interests ran in the same channel, had evidently suffered a rude shock, which, as soon as we were disencumbered of listeners or Observers, by finding ourselves nearly isolated in our retreat, he explained, by telling us, in an accent of depression, that he feared all was lost! that Buonaparté was advancing; that his point was decidedly Brussels, & that the Duke of Wellington had sent orders that all the Magazines, the Artillery, & the warlike | stores of every description, & all the Wounded, the maimed, & the Sick, should be immediately removed to Antwerp.[185] For this purpose, he had issued directions that every Barge, every Boat, every Vessel of every kind, should be seized for the use of the Army; & that every thing of value should be conveyed away, the Hospitals emptied, & Brussels evacuated.

If this intelligence filled us with the most fearful alarm, how much more affrighting still was the sound of Cannon, which next assailed our Ears!—The dread reverberation became louder & louder as we proceeded. Every shot tolled to our imaginations the Death of myriads: & the conviction that of the destruction & devastation so near us, with the probability that, if all attempt at escape should prove abortive we might be personally involved in the carnage, gave us sensations too awful for verbal expressions; | we could only gaze, & tremble; listen, & shudder.

Yet—strange to relate! on re-entering the City, all seemed quiet & tranquil as usual! & though it was in this imminent & immediate danger of being invested, & perhaps pilaged, I saw no outward mark of distress or disturbance, or even of hurry or curiosity.

Having re-lodged us in the Rue d'Assault, Mr. Boyd tried to find us some Land carriage for our removal. But not only every chaise had been taken, & every Diligence secured; the cabriolets, the caleches, nay, the Waggons & the carts, & every species of caravan, had been seized for military service. And,

---

[185] Wellington had indeed approved orders, given by his medical officers and by the mayor of Brussels, to requisition all transport—including barges—to evacuate the wounded to Antwerp (L. 891 n. 16). Although he never ordered any retreat from Brussels or wholesale removal of guns and equipment, he did advise English friends in Brussels to leave for Antwerp (L. 891 n. 5).

after the utmost efforts he could make, in every kind of way, he told us we must wait the chances of the Day, for that there was no possibility of escape from Brussels either by Land or Water. |

Remedy there was none; nor had we any other ressource: we were fain, therefore, quietly to submit. Mr. Boyd, however, assured me that, though no Land Carriage was likely to find Horses during this furious Contest, he had been promised the return of a Barge for the next morning, if he & his party would be at the wharf by Six o'clock.

We all, therefore agreed that, if we were spared any previous calamity, we would set out for the Wharf at 5 o'clock. And, as I had no means to arrive in the Rue d'Assault at such an hour, I accepted their invitation to be with them in the Evening, & spend the Night at their house.

We then separated; I was anxious to get home, to watch the post, & to write to Treves. |

My re-appearance produced no effect upon my Hosts: they saw my return with the same placid civility that they had seen my departure.

But even apathy—or equanimity,—which shall I call it?—like their's was now to be broken; I was seated at my Bureau & writing, when a loud 'Hurrah!' reached my Ears from some distance, while the Daughter of my Host, a Girl of about 18, gently opening my door, said the Fortune of the day had suddenly turned, & that Buonaparté was taken prisoner!

At the same time the 'Hurrah!' came nearer. I flew to the Window; my host & Hostess came also, crying: 'Buonaparté *est pris! le voilà! le voilà!*'

I then saw, on a noble War Horse in full equipment, a General in the full & splendid Uniform of France; but visibly disarmed, | &, to all appearance, tied to his Horse, or, at least, held on, so as to disable him from making any effort to gallop it off, & surrounded, preceded, & followed by a crew of roaring wretches, who seemed eager for the moment when he should be lodged where they had orders to conduct him, that they might unhorse, strip, pillage him, & divide the spoil.

This was the notion which the outward scene created. How far it was true or false I never knew. His high, feathered, glittering Helmet he had pressed down as low as he could on his forehead, & I could not discern his face; but I was instantly certain he was not Buonaparté, on finding the whole commotion produced by the rifling crew above-mentioned, which, though it might be guided, probably, by some [|] subaltern officer, who might have the captive in charge, had left the Field of Battle at a moment when none other could be spared, as all the attendant throng were evidently amongst the refuse of the Army followers.

The delusion was soon over. The pillagers & their prey were not a moment out of sight before all was as still as usual; while neither pleasure nor pain were sufficiently potent to excite any devellopment of what had passed.

I was afterwards informed that this unfortunate General was the Count Lobou,[186] so titled by Buonaparte for his exploits in the Battle of [Eckmühl] & known till then as General [Mouton]. He met with singular consideration during his captivity in the Low Countries, having thence *taken to himself a Wife*.[187] That [|] Wife I had met when last in Paris at a Ball[188] given by Madame la Princesse de Beauvau. She was quite young, & extremely pretty, & the gayest of the gay, laughing, chatting, sporting the whole Evening, chiefly with the fat & merry, the good-humoured, &, I believe amiable Duchesse de Feltre,[189] (Madame la Marechale Clarke) & her husband, high in office, in fame, & in favour, was then absent on some official duty, as I gathered, if I was not mistaken, by her answers to the civilities, of M. le Prince de Beauvau. What a reverse!—

The dearth of any expansion of positive News from the Field of Battle, even in the heart of Brussels, at this almost unequaled crisis, when every thing that was dear & valuable to either party was at stake, was at one instant nearly distracting in its [|] torturing suspence to the wrung nerves, & at another insensibly blunted them into a kind of amalgamation with the Belgic philosophy. At certain houses, as well as at public offices, news, I doubt not, arrived: but no means were taken to promulgate it: no Gazettes, as in London, no Bulletins, as in

---

186 Georges Mouton, comte de Lobau (L. 893 n. 14).
187 Félicité-Caroline-Honorine *née* d'Arberg (*c.* 1785–1860), who had married Mouton in 1809.
188 Probably the ball mentioned in L. 840 above.
189 This was Clarke's second wife, Marie-Françoise-Joséphine *née* Zaepffel (*c.* 1770–1838).

Paris, were cried about the streets, for support to sinking anxiety, or for nourishment to starving curiosity: we were all left at once to our conjectures & our destinies.

The delusion, as I have said, of victory instantly vanished into a merely passing advantage, as I gathered from the earnest researches into which it led me; & evil only met all ensuing investigation: Retreat & Defeat were the words in every mouth around me! The Prussians, it was asserted, were completely vanquished ⌐ on the 15ᵗʰ & the English on the 16ᵗʰ—while on the Day just passed, the 17ᵗʰ a Day of continual Fighting & Bloodshed, Drawn Battles on both sides left each party proclaiming what neither party could prove, success.

Lowered, disappointed, disheartened, I returned to my pen, with which alone I was able in pouring forth my fears to attract back my hopes, & in recording my miseries, to imbibe instinctively the sympathy which had the power, magnetic, to sooth them.

Not a quarter of an hour had I thus been engaged,

It was Sunday; but Church Service was out of the question, though never were prayers more frequent, more fervent; more supplicatory. Form, indeed, they could not have, nor Union; while constantly expecting the Enemy, with Fire & Sword at the Gates, who could enter a place of worship, at the risk of making ⌐ it a scene of slaughter? But who, also, in circumstances so awful, could require the exhortation of a Priest or the example of a congregation, to stimulate Devotion? no!—in those fearful exigences, where, in the full vigour of health, strength, & faculty, & all Life's freshest resources, we seem destined to abruptly quit this mortal Coil, & render an instantaneous account not only of our deeds & words, but of our Thoughts & Intentions, we need no spur; all is spontaneous; the Soul is unshackled from disguise, & either our Mediator irradiates us with Hope, or Infidelity deadens us to Annihilation.

And therefore, though not guided by Forms of service, nor impelled by an assemblage of fellow-petitioners, I have never more frequently addressed the Great Dispenser of All than during this dreadful Sabbath, 18. June, 1815. ⌐

Not above a quarter of an Hour had I been restored to my sole occupation of solace, before I was again interrupted & startled: but not as on the preceding occasion by riotous shouts:

the sound was a Howl, violent, loud, affrighting, & issuing from many voices. I ran to the Window, & saw the *Marchée aux Bois* suddenly filling with a rushing populace, pouring in from all its avenues, & hurrying on, rapidly, & yet in a scrambling manner, as if unconscious in what direction: while Women with Children in their arms, or clinging to their cloathes, ran screaming out of doors: & cries, though not a word was ejaculated, filled the air: and, from every house, I saw Windows closing, & Shutters fastening: — — all this, though long in writing, was presented to my Eyes in a single moment ⎮ and was followed in another by a burst into my Apartment, to announce that *the French were come*!

I know not even who made this declaration: my head was out of the Window, &, in drawing it in, I heard it; but the person who made it scarcely entered the room & was gone; leaving the door wide open, & running down stairs; or perhaps up; for my alarm was too great for observation; & a general sense of being struck with indecorum, or even hurry, for the first time in that house, encreased my conviction of danger.

How terrific was this moment! the most so, perhaps, for its immediate horrour, of my life—though not, alas, the most afflicting!—Oh no!—but while my Imagination rushed into Dungeons, Prisons, pillage, Insult, ⎮ bloodshed, mangled carcases, Fire, & murder, my recollection failed me not, & my perilous situation; if surprized in Apartments belonging to an Officer of the body Guard of Louis 18, then in active service for that Monarch, urged me to instant flight; &, without waiting to speak to the people of the house, I crammed my Letters, papers, & Money into a straw flat Basket, given me by my beloved Friend Mrs. Lock,[190] & throwing on a Shawl & Bonnet, I flew down stairs & out of doors.

My intention was to go to the Boyds, to partake, as I had engaged, their fate: but the crowd were all issuing from the way I must have turned to have gained the Rue d'Assault, & I thought, therefore, I might be safer with Made de Maurville, who, also, not being English, might be ⎮ less obnoxious to the Buonapartites. To la Rue de la Montagne I hurried, in consequence, my steps, crossing & crossed by an affrighted multitude; but I reached it in safety, & she received me with an

[190] See i, L. 1 n. 3.

hospitable welcome. I found her calm, & her good humour undisturbed. Inured to Revolutions, under which she had smarted so as she could smart no more, from the loss of all those who had been the first objects of her solicitude, a Husband & 3 Sons! she was now hardened in her feelings upon public events, though her excellent heart was still affectionate & zealous for the private misfortunes of the individuals whom she loved.

What a dreadful day did I pass! dreadful in the midst of its Glory! for it was not during those operations that sent details partially to our Ears that we could judge of the positive state of ¹ affairs, or build upon any permanency of success. Yet here I soon recovered from all alarm for personal safety, & lost the horrible apprehension of being in the midst of a City that was taken, Sword in hand, by an Enemy. An apprehension that, while it lasted, robbed me of breath, chilled my blood, & gave me a shuddering Ague that even now in fancy returns as I seek to commit it to paper.

The *Alerte* which had produced this effect I afterwards learnt—though not till the next day,—was utterly false; but whether it had been produced by mistake or by deceit I never knew. The French, indeed, were coming; but not triumphantly; they were Prisoners, surprised & taken suddenly, & brought in, being disarmed, by an escort; ¹ &, as they were numerous, & their French Uniform was discernable from afar, the almost universal belief at Brussels that Buonaparté was invincible, might perhaps, without any designed deception, have raised the report that they were advancing as Conquerors.

I attempt no description of this Day, the Grandeur of which was unknown, or unbelieved, in Brussels till it had taken its flight, & could only be named as Time past. The Duke of Wellington & Prince Blücher were too mightily engaged in meriting Fame to spare an instant for either claiming or proclaiming it; & the harrassed state of my mind led me to live, then, in such complete obscurity, that I had no chance to hear such relations as might be sent to the chosen few; or to public offices. ¹

I was fain, therefore, to content myself with such intelligence as reached Mad⁰ de Maurville fortuitously. The crowds in the streets, the turbulence, the inquietude, the bustle, the noise, the cries, the almost yells—though proceeding, I now believe, only from wanton Boys, mingling with disorderly females, or frightened mothers, kept up perpetual expectation of annoyance. The door was never opened, the stair Case was never ascended, but I felt myself pale & chill, with fear of some sanguinary attack, or military surprize. It is true that as Brussels was not fortified, & could, in itself, offer no resistance, it could neither be besieged nor taken by storm; but I felt certain that the Duke of Wellington would combat for it inch by inch, & that in a conflict between Life & Death, every means would be resorted to that could be ⎰ suggested by Desperation.

Even Now, therefore, in the cool reflection of succeeding years, I can neither marvel at nor blame the tremour of my Nerves, & the horrour of my thoughts at this crisis. The two greatest Captains of the Age, whose military prowess had mocked all rivalry, laid waste all opposition, & conquered, in their several martial careers, even opinion, alike in Friend & in Foe, of their brilliant supereminence to every thing living, as Warlike Chiefs, but each other, were now, in Battle & Bloody array, encountering upon the plains of WATERLOO. The lot of Millions was suspended while they fought, & Nations waited to know their masters from the Trumpet of the VICTOR. ⎰

In deep anxiety to learn whether the Boyds would now precipitate their retreat from this scene of actual terrour, &, perhaps, impending destruction, I wished to send a message to them of enquiry; but Madame de Maurville could not spare her servant, who was occupied in a thousand ways, to go forth so far. I glided therefore, down stairs, purposing to go to a shop where I was known, to find a carrier for a note: but my project was very short-lived; for though I had seized a moment that was particularly quiet, I found all egress & regress impracticable, from the hurried, busy, frightened, or boisterous, or curious comers & Goers, who elbowed themselves along, without care or consciousness whom they pushed, or hurt, or even overthrew; joined to obstacles yet more impenetrable in sturdy groups, formed of relaters ⎰ & listeners to passing news: to which were added occasional parties both of Infantry & Cavalry; & single Horse men, bearers of some Express from or to the Army, who gallopped on with a rapidity as resistless, & as dangerous to encounter, as that of a Race Horse in the last effort for winning.

This abortive [attempt] was soon, however, succeeded by a satisfaction the greatest such a period could produce. Mad^e de Maurville told me that an English Commissary was just arrived from the army, who had assured her that the tide of success was completely turned to the side of the Allies. She offered to conduct me to his apartment, which was in the same hôtel as her own, & in which he was writing, & transacting business; ǀ gravely assuring me, &, I really believe, herself, that he could not but be rejoiced to give me, in person, every particular I could wish to hear. I deemed it, however, but prudent not to put his politeness to a test so severe.

Urgent, nevertheless, to give me pleasure, & not easily set aside from following her own conceptions, she declared she would go down stairs, & inform Mr. Saumarez[191] that she had a Country woman of his in her Room whom he would be *charmé* to oblige. I tried vainly to stop her; Good humour, Vivacity, Sport, Curiosity, & Zeal were all against my efforts: & she went; &, to my great surprise, returned escorted by Mr. Saumarez himself: or — — with a formal invitation from me to descend; which I cannot now recollect; & have not mentioned in my memorandum. But his politeness, his readiness of communication, & his sparing time, at such ǀ a moment, to permit, or rather to anticipate my enquiries into the immediate state of Conquest or Defeat, I shall surely never forget. I regret having never seen him since to express my sense of his goodness to me. His narration was all triumphant, & his account of the Duke of Wellington might almost have seemed an exaggerated panygeric if it had painted some Warriour in a chivalresque Romance. He was every where, he said; the Eye could turn in no direction that it did not perceive him, either at hand, or at a distance; gallopping to charge the Enemy, or darting across the Field to issue, or to change some orders. Every Ball, also, he said, seemed Fired at him, & every Gun aimed at him; yet nothing touched him; he seemed as impervious for safety as he was dauntless for courage: while Danger all the time ǀ relentlessly envirroned him, and Wounds,

---

[191] Unidentified.

fractures, dislocations, loss of limbs, or Death continually robbed him of the services of some one of the bravest & the dearest of those who were nearest to him. But he suffered nothing to check, or appal, or engage him, that belonged to personal interest or feeling: his entire concentrated attention, exclusive aim, & intense thought were devoted impartially, impertubably, & grandly to the WHOLE, the ALL.

I could not but be proud of this account; &, pendant from its Glory, my revived Imagination hung the blessed Laurels of Peace.

But though Hope was all alive, Ease & Serenity were not her Companions: Mr. Saumarez,—who was just alighted from the scene of what he described, could ˡ not disguise that there was still much to do, & consequently to apprehend; & he had never, he said, amongst the many he had viewed, seen a Field of Battle in such excessive disorder. Military carriages of all sorts, & multitudes of Groups unemployed, occupied spaces that ought to have been left for manœvering, or observation, occasioned confusion unequalled; I attribute this to the various Nations who bore arms on that great day in their own manner; though the towering Generalissimo of All cleared the Ground, & dispersed what was unnecessary by every moment that was not absorbed by the Fight.

When the Night of this memorable Day arrived,[192] I took leave of Madᵉ de Maurville to join the Boyds, according to my engagement: for though all accounts confirmed the victory of the Duke of Wellington, we had so little idea of its result, that we still imagined the Four days already spent in the work of carnage, must be followed by as many more before the dreadful conflict could terminate.

Madame de Maurville lent me her servant, with whom I now made my way tolerably well, for though the crowd remained, it was no longer turbulent. A general knowledge of

192 As an aid in the writing of this journal, FBA jotted down the following notes on the events of the next few days:
Leave Mᵉ de Maurville for the Boyds & Antwerp. Sights of War & horrour, yet victory & Joy, by the way. I sat up all Night to be ready for Antwerp expedition but fuller confirmation of our success changes my plan, & I resolve to wait Events. The Boyds still fearing Bonaparte would rally his troops, & fight his way on to Brussels, went pursued their own flight, & I returned to la Marchee au Bois. Waterloo. Brussels. Prisoners. La Tour du Pin. Sick. Wounded. Pestilence feared. Madᵉ de Laval, Prince of Orange. Duke of Wellington. Protestant Chapel. Madame de Spagen. Capt. W. Burney   Charles Parr Burney, &c.

general success to the Allies was every where spread; curiosity therefore began to be satisfied, & Inquietude to be removed. The concourse were composedly—for no composure is like that of the Flemings—listening to details of the Day in tranquil Groups: ¹ & I had no interruption to my Walk but from my own anxiety to catch, as I could, some part of the relations. As all these have long since been published I omit them, though the interest with which I heard them was, at the moment, intense. Three or Four Shocking sights intervened during my passage, of officers of high rank, either English or Belge, & either dying or dead, extended upon Biers, carried by soldiers with relays, who, having fallen within reach of succour, were [being] convey[ed] to their friends, or their Apartments, for Nursing, or preparatory to Interment. The view of their gaily costly attire, with the conviction of their suffering, or fatal state, joined to the profound silence of their Bearers & Attendants, ¹ was truly saddening — — & if my reflections were morally dejecting—what—oh what were my personal feelings & fears, in my then utter uncertainty whether this victory were more than a passing triumph!

In one place, we were entirely stopt, by a group that had gathered round a Horse, of which a British soldier was examining one of the knees. The Animal was a tall War Horse, & one of the noblest of his species, in shape, size, colour & carriage. These are not, I know, Horse terms; but I have no Horse Dictionary; & I have still less its contents by rote. The soldier was enumerating to his hearers its high qualities, & exultingly acquainting them it was his own property, as he had taken it, if I understood him right, from the Field, from the side of his ¹ Master, who had fallen from him, shot dead. He produced also a very fine Ring, which was all he had taken of spoil, leaving the rest to others, while he secured the Horse, which he had walked gently to Brussels.

Yet this Man gravely added, that pillage had been forbidden by the Commander in Chief! & thought that those who took the purse, Watch, &c, would have to refund!—

I found the Boyds still firm for departure. The news of the victory of the Day, gained by the Duke of Wellington & Prince Blucher, had raised them to the highest delight; but further intelligence had just reached them, that the Enemy, since the great Battle, was working to turn the right Wing of the Duke of Wellington, who was in the most imminent danger; & that the | capture of Brussels was expected to take place the next morning, as everything indicated that Brussels was the point at which Buonaparté aimed, to retrieve his recent defeat. Mr. Boyd used every possible exertion to procure Chaises, or Diligence, or any sort of land conveyance, for Antwerp:[193] but every Horse [was] under military subjection, & held in requisition: even the Horses of the Farmers, of the Nobility & Gentry, & of Travellers, were then sequestered from private use. The hope of Water carriage was all that remained. We were to set off so early, that we agreed not to retire to rest.

A Gentleman, however, of their acquaintance, presently burst into the room, with assurances that better news was again arrived, & that the Enemy was | flying in all directions. This quieted the Boyds, who consented to seek some repose, though without undressing themselves. I endeavoured, on a sofa, to imitate their example: but in vain; my inquietude was too cruel; & I passed the Night in writing to Treves, alone, in the Parlour, & frequently alarmed by noises & outcries, from stragglers—that I always supposed to announce the sudden eruption of the Enemy! What a dreadful Night I spent, in defiance of the late intelligence. Confidence was out of the question where vicissitudes were so endless.

This better news, nevertheless, reanimated my courage for Brussels, & my trust in the Duke of Wellington; & when the Boyd Family summoned me, the next morning, at 4 or 5 o'clock, to set off with them for Antwerp, I | permitted my repugnance to quitting the only spot where I could receive Letters from Treves, to conquer every obstacle, & begged them to excuse my changed purpose. They wondered at my temerity, & probably blamed it; but there was no time for discussion, & we separated.

I remained in la Rue d'Assault till near 8 o'clock, not to parade the streets alone at an earlier hour: &, I had no one to accompany me.

My Hosts received me with their usual placidity, & I sent for my small baggage, & re-settled myself in my apartments.

I was now in a situation the most insulated, I might say

[193] See L. 891 above.

desolate, that can well be conceived. The Princesse d'Henin &
Mad^e de La Tour Du Pin, & M. de Lally, & the Boyds, had all
fled; Madame de Maurville, who alone remained, lived in
so populous a ᶦ part of the Town that I durst not, except when
stimulated by all inspiring Danger, venture to her house:
& she could not seek me herself, as she believed me at Antwerp.
Colonel de Beaufort also thought me departed; & cruelly
painful, indeed, were the Hours I thus spent in a sort of hopeless seclusion

It was not till Tuesday the 20th I had certain & satisfactory
assurances how complete was the victory. Unable any longer
to sustain my doubts, I then contrived to gain the house of
Madame de Maurville; & There I had, indeed, a fullness of
information that almost robbed me of breath—at least, that
made breathing labourirous & difficult to me, from the sudden
rush of conflicting sensations that mingled pity & Horrour with
the most excessive Joy — — for There I heard confirmed &
detailed the matchless ᶦ Triumph of the matchless Wellington
interspersed with descriptions of scenes of slaughter on the
Field of Battle, to freeze the blood, & tales of woe amongst
mourning survivors in Brussels, to rend the heart.

While listening with speechless avidity to these relations,
we were joined by M. de la Tour du Pin, who is a Cousin of
Madame de Maurville, & who was just come from the Duke
of Wellington, who had gallopped to Brussels from Wavre,
to see the Prince of Orange, & enquire in person after his
wounds.[194] Prince Blücher was in close pursuit of Buonaparté,
who was totally defeated, his Baggage all taken, even his
private equipage, & personals, & who was a fugitive himself,
& in disguise! The Duke considered the Battle to be so decisive
that, while Prince Blucher was posting after the remnant ᶦ
of the Buonapartian Army, he determined to follow himself,
as Convoy to Louis 18.—! and he told M. de la Tour du Pin,
& the Duke de FitzJames,[195] whom he met at the Palace of the
King of Holland, to acquaint their King with this his proposal,
& to beg his Majesty to set forward without delay, to join
him for its execution. The Duke de Fitzjames was gone already
to Gand with this commission.

How daring a plan was this, while the internal state of

[194] L. 895 n. 5.   [195] L. 894 n. 8.

France was so little known, while *les Places fortes* were all occupied, & while the Corps of Grouchy was still *intact*, & the hidden & possible resources of Buonaparté were unfathomed! The event, however, demonstrated that the Duke of Wellington had judged with as much quickness of perception as intrepidity of Valour.

'Twas to Tournay he had desired that the King of France would repair. ¹

The Duke now ordered that the Hospitals, Invalids, Magazines, &c &c should all be stationed at Brussels, which he regarded as saved from Invasion, & completely secure.

It is not near the scene of Battle that War, even with Victory, wears an aspect of Felicity! no, not even in the midst of its highest resplendence of Glory. A more terrific or afflicting sojourn than that of Brussels at this period can hardly be imagined. The Universal Voice declared that so bloody a Battle as that which was fought almost in its neighbourhood, & quite within its hearing, & which was afterwards called the Battle of Waterloo, never yet had spread the Plains with slaughter: and though Exultation cannot ever have been prouder, nor satisfaction more complete, in the ¹ brilliancy of success, all my senses were shocked in reviving the effects of its attainment. For more than a week from this time, I never approached my Window but to witness sights of wretchedness. Maimed, wounded, bleeding, mutilated, tortured victims of this exterminating contest, passed by every minute:—the fainting, the sick, the dying & the Dead, on Brancards, in Carts, in Waggons, succeeded one another without intermission. There seemed to be a whole, & a large Army of disabled—or lifeless soldiers!—All that was intermingled with them bore an aspect of still more poignant horrour, though not of such desolating suffering, for bosom affliction: for the Bonapartian prisoners, who were now poured into the City by Hundreds, had a mien of such ferocious desperation, ¹ where they were marched on, uninjured, from having been taken by surprize, or overpowered by Numbers; or faces of such agonized yet restrained anguish,— where they were drawn on in open vehicles, the helpless victims of gushing wounds or horrible dislocations; that to see them without commiseration for their direful sufferings, or admiration for the heroick, however misled enthusiasm to which they were martyrs, must have demanded an apathy dead to all feeling but what is personal, or a rancour too ungenerous to yield even to the view of Defeat. Both the one set & the other of these unhappy Warriours endured their calamities with a haughty forbearance of any species of complaint. The maimed & lacerated, while their ghastly visages spoke torture & | Death, bit their own Cloaths,—perhaps their Flesh!—to save the loud emission of their groans; while those of their Comrades who had escaped these corporeal inflictions, seemed to be smitten with something between Remorse & Madness,[196] that they had not forced themselves on to destruction ere thus, in full muscular vigour, their towering height, & martial Uniforms, were exhibited, in dreadful parade, through the streets of that City they had been sent forth to conquer. Their Countenances, grim & gloomy, depicted concentrated Vengeance & rage, as much against themselves that they yet lived, as against their Victors, that they were captured. OTHERS of these wretched prisoners had, to me, as I first saw them, the air of the lowest & most disgusting of Jacobins, in dirty tattered vestments, of all sorts & colours; or soiled Carter's Frocks: but disgust was soon turned to Pity, when I afterwards learnt that these shabby accoutrements had been cast over them by their | Conquerors, after despoiling them of their own!

Every body was wandering from home: all Brussels seemed living in the streets. The danger to the City, which had imprisoned all its inhabitants except the Rabble or the Military, once completely passed, the pride of feeling & shewing their freedom seemed to stimulate their curiosity & pleasure in seeking details on what had passed, & was passing. But neither the pride nor the joy of Victory was any where of an exulting Nature. London & Paris render all other places, that I, at least, have dwelt in, tame & insipid. Bulletins in a few shop Windows alone announced to the General Public that the Allies had vanquished, & Buonaparté was a fugitive.

I went myself to deliver a Letter for Her Royal Highness the Princess Elizabeth to the Secretary of the English Ambassadour, Sir Charles Stewart:[197] but the Secretary, & the Ambassa-

---

[196] The frenzied courage of Napoleon's troops, a recurrence of the *furia francese* of earlier days, was widely noticed throughout the Waterloo campaign and thought to have contributed to their defeat, in which hysterical bravery was outweighed by tactical blunders. [197] See L. 856 nn. 18, 19.

dour also had left Brussels, to repair to Gand, to join le Roi Louis 18. [1]

I met, however, with a courier, just setting out for England, who took charge of my Letter. And I met, also, at the Ambassade, an old English officer,[198] who gave me most interesting & curious information, assuring me that in the carriage of Buonaparte, which had been siezed, there were Proclamations ready Printed, & even Dated, From the Palace of Laken, announcing the downfall of the Allies, & the Triumph of Buonaparte! This officer, whom I never met with again, called himself Colonel Campbel.[198]

But no satisfaction could make me hear without deadly dismay & shuddering his description of the Field of Battle: Piles of Dead! Heaps, Masses, Hills of Dead, bestrewed the Plains!—

I met, also, Colonel Jones—so exulting in Success! so eager to remind me of his assurances that all was safe!—

And I was much interested in a naration made to me by a wounded soldier, who was seated in the Court Yard of the [1] Embassade. He had been taken Prisoner, after he was severely wounded, on the morning of the 18th & forced into a Wood, with many others, where he had been very roughly used, & stript of his Coat, waistcoat, & even his shoes, & of every thing that would not leave him utterly naked: but, as the fortune of the day began to turn, there was no one left to Watch him, & he crawled on all fours till he got out of the Wood, & was found by some of his roving Comrades.

The most common adventure of this sort, when heard at the moment of action, & from the Principal in what is narrated, has an interest beyond that of the most extraordinary event that is related by a Third person, or at a distance of time from the occurrence.

Thousands, I believe I may say without exaggeration, were employed voluntarily at this time, in Brussels, in dressing Wounds, & attending the Sick Beds of the [1] Massacred. Humanity could be carried no further, for not alone the Belgians & English were thus Nursed & assisted; nor yet the Allies, but all the Prisoners, also, who had suffered from the baleful

---

[198] Possibly Sir Neil Campbell (1776–1827), who had escorted Napoleon to Elba in 1814. He held the rank of colonel and had fought at Waterloo.

Instruments of War. The placid Belgians in this work of beneficence, might have braved the Nations the most renowned for
sensibility, to equal their useful & meritorious kindness. And
this, notwithstanding the greatest apprehensions [be]ing prevalent that the sufferers, from [th]eir multitude, would bring
Pestilence [in]to the heart of the City.

The immense quantity of English, [B]elgians, & Allies, who
were first, of course, [co]nveyed to the Hospitals[199] & prepared
houses [at] Brussels, required so much time for [ca]rriage &
placing, that although the [C]arts, Waggons, & every attain-
able, or seizable Vehicle, were unremittingly in motion, |
Now coming, Now returning to the Field of Battle for more,
it was nearly a Week—or at least 5 or 6 days, ere the unhappy
Wounded Prisoners, who were necessarily last served, could be
accommodated. And though I was assured that medical & sur-
gical aid were administered to them wherever it was possible
that it could be done, the blood that dried upon their skins
& their Garments, joined to the dreadful sores occasioned by
this corrosive neglect, produced an effect so pestiferous, that,
at every new entry, Eau de Cologne, or vinegar, were resorted to by every Inhabitant, even amongst the shop-keepers,
even amongst the commonest persons, for averting the menaced
contagion.

Even the Churches were turned into Hospitals. And every
house, I believe, & was told, in Brussels, was ordered to receive,
or find an asylum, for some of the Sick.

The Boyds were eminently good in | Nursing, dressing
wounds, making slops,[200] & administering comfort, amongst
the maimed, whether Friend or Foe. Madame d'Henin sent
her servants, & money, & cordials, to all the dislocated French
that came within her reach; Madame de la Tour Du Pin
was munificent in the same attentions; & Madame de Maurville never, I am persuaded, passed by an opportunity of
doing Good. M. de Beaufort, being far the richest of my friends
at this place, was not spared: he had officers, & others, quartered
upon him without mercy.

Meanwhile, to put a stop as much as possible to the most

---

[199] The most important of which were the Hospice des Ursulines in the rue du
Prévot and La Charité Romaine in the rue d'Orphan.
[200] Loose gowns or smocks to be worn by the wounded.

alarming putrid exhalations, Three Thousand Peasants were employed all at once, in burying the heaps, the piles, the Hills of Dead, on the plains!

This, at least, was the current account at Brussels |

It was not till June 26. that the blessed News reached me of the cessation of Hostilities. The extatic Felicity of That Day rose to its—Then—only Rival in superlative Joy;—buoyant, elevating, exalting, that I had yet experienced, and that after a misery which, in the same manner, had made the contrast indescribably brilliant. It was when the most deservedly loved of human Beings appeared before me, as a vision of Happiness, after the dark & deadly silent separation of the opening of the too famous 100 Days.[201] Not now, indeed, was he personally present to me, as on that exquisite Evening: but the view of Peace, besides its own genial charm, to ME anticipated a re-union that always seemed flying me, while depending upon | the perilous events of War.

Colonel Beaufort was the first who brought me this certain intelligence smiling kindly himself at the smiles he excited. Next came la Princesse d'Henin, escorted by my & *Her*—highly valued M. de Lally Tolendahl. With open arms that dear Princess reciprocated congratulations. Madame de Maurville next followed, always cordial where she could either give or behold happiness. The Boyds hurried to me in a body to wish & be wished joy. And last, but only in time, not in kindness, came Mad[e] la Viscomtesse de Laval, mother to the justly honoured Philanthropist, or, as others—but not I—call him Bigot, M. Mathieu de Montmorency, | [202] who at this moment is M. Le Duc de Montmorency. Madame de Laval had emigrated to England, at the breaking out of the Buonapartian eruption, & was now returned to the Continent, in the hope it was extinguished. We had interchanged Visits several times before this moment of general felicitation; for though there were reasons against my belonging to a society of which that lady was the *focus*,[203] she held a place in my personal gratitude that

[201] FBA earlier made this comparison between the news of peace and M. d'A's arrival in Brussels in L. 901, p. 258.

[202] L. 837 n. 16. Since FBA's early acquaintance with Mathieu de Montmorency-Laval, he had become a leader of the legitimist and Catholic reactionaries.

[203] For FBA's misgivings about Mme de Laval, whom she had in the past tried to avoid, see v, vi *passim*.

made me seize any opportunity of shewing it with eagerness. A faithful, zealous, earnest & most active Friend she had proved herself, upon every possible occasion, to M. d'Arblay. She loved, liked, & esteemed him with all her Heart; &, through Him, she had conceived so high an opinion of his Wife, that she always appeared to consider herself as receiving, not | conferring favour, in whatever intercourse at any time brought them together.

She had now, through her son, received the most authentic confirmation that All Fighting had ceased. Her son, except M. Le Viscount d'Agoût,[204] was the first Favourite of Madame, Duchesse d'Angoulême. This last, M. d'Agoût, was amongst the very most intimate Friends of M. d'Arblay.

Madame de Laval made me a visit of considerable length, & of yet more considerable Agreeability. Her conversation was peculiarly pleasing to me, & had there been no Lion in the way![205] I should gladly have met her almost enthusiastic advances to confidential friendship. Her manners were mild, high bred, & dignified. She had not the vehement vivacity *so* usual amongst les *Femmes d'Esprit* of France, | or, at least, it never burst forth when I was with her. But my acquaintance with her was not of a sort to make me sure whether,—like my dear Madame d'Henin, she was wholly unguarded, or whether, upon closer knowledge, similar sparks of Fire might not have been emitted from her Eyes & her speech, when encountering a difference of opinion. Her Understanding was good, nay penetrating, her observations were sagacious, & her satire, which was piquant, was too just to be ill-natured. She had a flow not alone of Words but of Ideas upon whatever topic conversation might turn. She was above all the hackneyed ressources for chat of the Weather, Public places, or even the News: for she was one of the very few who, in the language of my old Friend Sir William Pepys,[206] | could originate a discourse. With these talents, & a soul delighting in activity of service & cordiality of Friendship, it is not surprising that her

[204] L. 835 n. 7.
[205] An allusion to Proverbs xxvi. 13.
[206] Sir William Weller Pepys (1740/1–1825), a member of the 'Streatham set' of the 1780s (*DL*, i, ii *passim*), who in the years 1821–3 was to call on Madame d'Arblay in Bolton Street, giving, as she remarked in a letter of 29 Feb.–10 Mar. 1823, 'an Hour's social recollections of old time'. Her quoting Pepys in the Waterloo Journal helps to confirm the date of writing as 1823 (cf. headnote, p. 339).

house attracted an Evening society of the very first brilliancy—
M. d'Arblay told me—in Paris: & much appears in paliation,
if she had not always kept the straightest strict path, when we
weigh the general licence, during her Youth, of the high
Circles to which she belonged; & add that her husband was
worthless &, profligate, & *super*-add that—as I was informed
by Madame la Princesse de Poix,²⁰⁷ who generously spoke it
apologestically, that she had been *belle comme un Ange.* ˡ

It sooths me thus to trace the grateful remembrance I
retain of one who appreciated General d'Arblay with the
fullest sense of his excellence. And my dear Alexander will call
to mind, when he peruses these lines, the tenderly sorrowing
Letters she wrote to us Both on the bitterest calamity of our
lives.

Brussels, now, which had seemed for so many days, from the
unremitting passage of maimed, dying, or dead, a mere out-
doors Hospital, revived, or, rather, was invigorated to something above its native state; for from uninteresting tameness,
it became elevated to spirit, consequence, & vivacity.

On the following Sunday, I had the gratification of hearing,
at the Protestant ˡ Chapel, the Te Deum for the Grand Victory,
in presence of the King & Queen of the Low Countries—or
Holland,—& of the Dowager Princess of Orange, & the young
Warriour, her Grandson. This Prince looked so ill, so meager,
so weak, from his half cured Wounds, that to appear on this
occasion, seemed another, & perhaps not less dangerous
effort of heroism, to add to those which had so recently distinguished him in the field. What enthusiasm would such an
exertion, with his pallid appearance, have excited in London
or Paris! even here, a little gentle hurra, greeted him from his
carriage to the chapel; & for the same short passage, back
again. After which, he drove off as tranquilly as any common
Gentleman might have driven away, to return to his home
& his family dinner. ˡ

To the solemn, the even awful pleasure, of hearing, on such an
occasion, the Te Deum well sung, was added that of listening to
a pious hymn, warbled by three delightful voices, & in a manner
to melt me by its melody, thus harmoniously performed. The

²⁰⁷ See v, L. 513 n. 16 and *passim.*

453

Prince himself excited great interest by his modest, unassuming, & very sensible demeanour.

Every hour now, in July, brought some fresh intelligence of the security of the restoration of Louis 18, with details of the deepest interest. Madame de Maurville engaged me to walk about with her, *a News-Gathering*, & inveigled me one morning to call with her upon a Flemish lady of her peculiar acquaintance,[208] I use the word *inveigle*, because she knew well my backwardness in making new acquaintance, & my taste for solitude where I could not | coalesce with old ones. On this occasion, however, she had certainly a right to conquer my repugnance, as it was to a Name-sake, whom she believed to be a Relation,[209] that she wished to introduce me.

At the house of Madame la Baronne de Spagen there was quartered, at this time, Captain William Burney, a wounded young officer, who, hearing of my being at Brussels, earnestly desired this meeting.

I found him very young, yet entirely unpretending & modest, though full of that honest ambition to rise in his profession that marks zeal as well as bravery, & which manifested itself very naturally by his casting all his regret upon the subject of his wound to its having stopt his military career, without allowing even a phrase to its pain, or its danger, though both, as it was in his head, were very serious: and | though the Army surgeon had thought it so grave as to prohibit him from all study, or even reading, & had prognosticated that he would not be fit for service again within the space of 3 months. His head was bound round with bandages, but a muslin was twisted over them so as to give them the air, not unbecomingly, of a Turban.

Madame la Baronne de Spagen, his hostess, seemed a person of perfect goodness. Benevolence & urbanity were so prominently pourtrayed in her countenance & her manners that she won almost instantly my trust in her truth, & my reliance on her kindness, when she expressed, at once, her favourable sentiments towards me, & her warm wishes that she could prove them. Madame de Maurville had, doubtless, prepared her for this quick partiality; which I had so little, | however,

---

[208] Joséphine-Hortense de Spangen (L. 917 n. 8).
[209] William Burney (L. 917 n. 7).

expected, that I met it with as much surprize as pleasure. She was very plain, very dutch, & as much without Grace, or Air, as without youth or beauty; but the constant exercise of beneficence had marked every line of her face with so kind an expression, that I really liked, in a short time, to look at as much as to listen to her. The Eye — — I speak but, nevertheless, of a woman's Eye!—soon grows mental when the Imagination sets it to work upon devellopping virtues & good qualities from the lines of the face, be that face what it may, fair, or black, lovely, or deformed.

And, indeed, while I complain,—or rather while I own that I tired to death in the Netherlands, of that monotonous want of what we call Life in London & in Paris; and which, in those noble capitals, gives spirit, energy, animation, curiosity, & meaning to every thing that passes, I must not omit [|] mentioning that I found, in the Low Countries, one delightful perfection such as, in an equal proportion, it has not been my fortune to meet as commonly elsewhere: I mean—I speak here only of my own sex,—a native softness of voice & manner so feminine as to be touching.

I had the happiness to find also, in my own experience, amongst the female Flemish a warmth of disposition, & a tender cordiality to serve or to please, that their extreme placidity of air & manner was far from anticipating, & which, if it neither awakened nor met vivacity, excited something far higher in trust & gratitude.

I had found the same character, & had been equally engaged by it, upon sundry occasions during my six weeks residence at Dunkirk.[210]

The young Captain wished vehemently to make out that we were of one stock: we had no documents, however, to prove or to disprove; but certainly there is no family to which so gallant & civilized & amiable a [|] young officer would not be an ornament. I repeated my visit to the excellent Baronne, who returned it with eagerness: & Captain William Burney offered me his services on going to Paris, whither he was bound when recovered, for seeing after my affairs, & taking my Apartments, or Goods, or any thing of value, under his protection. I accepted his kind offer: but his wound proved more obstinate than he

[210] While waiting to cross to England in 1812 (v. 629 ff.).

expected & he was ordered to embark for England, with a Three months leave of absence, to recruit his health. He came to me, with La Baronne, to beg I would, at least, make use of him with my correspondents in our Native land. I joyfully complied with his obliging wish, & wrote copiously—to Thee, my Alexander,—& to all my Sisters & Brothers, alas!—Brothers Now have I none!—to 3 of my nieces, Maria Bourdois, Fanny Raper, & Charlotte Barrett,—& to Mrs. Lock—Mrs. Angerstein, Lady Keith, & Mrs. Waddington—Time only was wanting for more; the zeal | of my very pleasing Name sake would have engaged for carrying me a million.

At the good Baronne's, I met, also, two other English Youths,[211] who had been wounded in Battle, of the name of Stanley. They were almost Boys but, with eager courage, had forced themselves to bear arms.

About the middle of July—but I am not clear of the date —the News was assured, & confirmed of the brilliant rethronement of Louis 18 & that Buonaparté had surrendered to the English.

Brussels now became an Assemblage of all Nations, from the rapturous enthusiasm that pervaded All to view the Field of Battle, the famous Waterloo, & gather upon the spot details of the immortal victory of Wellington.

Amongst its visitors for this purpose, came Charles Par Burney, my nephew, & only child of my dear Brother Dr. Charles.[212] He discovered my abode, &, when he had visited the Seat of War, meant to go to Swizerland, & to pass through Treves, that he might pay his Respects to my General. I prepared him a Letter; but he was stopt by information that all the routes leading towards Treves, & Luxembourg, were encombered by Hordes of Fugitives, & *Traineurs*, & Banditti; |

---

[211] William and Godfrey Shenley (L. 917 n. 11).
[212] See L. 922 n. 13.

925   [Trèves], 19 July [1815

M. d'Arblay
To Madame d'Arblay

A.L. (Berg), 19 juillet
Single sheet 4to 1 p. *pmk* TRIER seal
Addressed: À Madame / Madame de Burney / A Bruxelles / *Marché au Bois*
Edited by FBA, p. 1, *annotated and dated*: ⋇· ⌐35⌐ (26) Triers. / a 19. Juillet / (1815) (NB These tender lines followed me also, to Treves.)

Je n'ai que le tems mon adorable amie de te dire que la meilleure de tes nouvelles est celle qui m'apprend que Larrey est au Brabant. Avant de partir pour venir ici,[1] pourrois tu le voir? Prends s'il le faut pour cela l'argent que nous avons chez le banquier ou une partie parce que en derniere analyse la perte, que nous ferions ne serait que de dix louis. Ô ma bonne et bien chere amie que j'ai besoin de pouvoir causer librement avec toi! arrive arrive!

Treves ce 19 Juillet

926   Trèves, 22 [July 1815]

M. d'Arblay
To Madame d'Arblay

A.L. (Berg), samedy 22
Single sheet 4to 1 p. *pmk* TRIER
Addressed: A Madame / Madame de Burney / à Bruxelles
Edited by FBA, p. 1, *annotated and dated*: ⌐36⌐ ⌐(25)⌐ (27) Juillet (1815.)
This letter, like its 3 predecessors,[1] followed me to Treves.

925. [1] This letter presupposes that FBA had already heard of M. d'A's accident and of his appeal to her to join him in Trèves. She in fact learned about them from the princesse d'Hénin and Colonel de Beaufort on 19 July, as the Trèves Journal explains (see pp. 476–8 below).

926. [1] The three earlier letters are 916, 921, and 925.

Treves
Ce Samedy 22

Au nom du Ciel, ma chere Fanny, arrive, arrive! — rejoindre et consoler ton malheureux ami. Arrive pour nous
occuper utilement des moyens d'assurer la ⟨semence⟩ de nos
choux aussitôt que je pourrai aller les planter ce qui ne peut
tarder. Ne sois pas trop inquiete et viens me joindre bien vite.
Je t'assure que tout va bien. Je viens d'ecrire à Mr Larrey
à Louvain ah s'il etait ici Tout en effet serait bientot bien Au
revoir mon adorable amie —!

927   London, 27 July 1815

From Alexander d'Arblay
To Madame d'Arblay

A. L. (Osborn), 27 July 1815
Two single sheets folio 4 pp. *pmk* 108 red seal
Addressed: A Madame / Madame d'Arblay / à Bruxelles /
Re-addressed: R^t Honb^l Lady / Alvanley / to the care of Colonel / Sir
Andrew Barnard / Commandant, &c &c à Paris
Docketed: July 27—1815—/ (July 27)
Annotated by Foreign Office [?]: Mr Burnie—Turnham Green *Mis sent to*
Lady Alvanly[1]

Turnham Green, July 27th 1815
Thursday Evening

Dearest Madre,
I came yesterday here, on a visit to dear Aunt Esther,[2] for
a week: and now, first of all, to essential business. Mrs Locke
has just written to my Aunt (tho' I think it very unnecessary to
trouble you about this, I must mention it) that Mr William
Locke 'earnestly wished to pay into Martin's hands the pur-

927. [1] Anne Dorothea Arden *née* Bootle (*c.* 1755–1825), widow of the 1st Baron
Alvanley (1744–1804), Lord Chief Justice of the Court of Common Pleas. Andrew
Francis Barnard (1773–1855), K.C.B. (1815) and later general (1851), a distinguished Peninsular veteran, was named by Wellington to command the British
troops occupying Paris.
[2] EBB (i, p. lxix), who is also 'my Aunt' in the following sentence and the 'Aunt
Hetty' mentioned below.

chase of the Cottage &c without waiting for M.H.[3]—compleat[s] the business, his Lawyer being ill, when to his great surprise M. M[artin] Burney explained that he was not empowered to receive the money, not having Mons[r] d'Arblay's power of attorney'[3]—I will walk to morrow to town, to see Martin upon this business, and try to get the money to be invested without waiting another fortnight at the least for your legal autorisation—And I shall not send off this Letter without writing to you the result of our conversation upon this matter—this is all I can do—it is a thousand pities that you did not leave a power of attorney behind you, before you left England. However, we must trust that '*Ce qui est différé, n'est pas pour cela perdu.*'

Mrs Locke 'shakes hands with me most cordially about the surrender of Boney': *you* will, no doubt, *join in* heart and soul: the thing is, now we have him, to keep him close; at St Helena, or Dumbarton Castle on the Clyde[4] (not in England—for the *tyrant* of the World should not be allowed to taint with his polluted breath the pure air of a *free* Country, or contaminate its soil with his unhallowed feet—especially as he has more friends and admirers in this Country than anywhere else, and that with his wonderful versatility of talent he might rouse a disturbance, or at least turn to his insidious ends the next riot about a *Corn Bill*, or a *Princess of W—s*, or any such non sense that the honest mob—John-Bull may chuse to *take up*, and to *run down*.[5] Nor is this merely a playful conjecture; for already the crew of the *Bellerophon*, (Capt[n] *Maitland*, on board of w[hich] he is *now* at *Torbay*) say that he is 'a devilish good fine fellow, and that they like him vastly'[6]—Nor does he spare any arts, any addresses, any flourishes, or addresses to their vanity, or appeals to their passions. |

When he arrived at Torbay—'*Enfin*', said he, 'le voilà ce beau päys! le noble sol de la Liberté! la voilà, cette Nation sans laquelle j'aurais été Empereur de l'Est et de l'Ouest!

---

[3] For the forced sale of Camilla Cottage, see vii *passim* and L. 863 n. 6. M.H. was apparently acting for Alexander Murray (L. 886 n. 10), Locke's solicitor.
[4] A fortress noted for its strong and picturesque site at the top of Dumbarton Rock. It seems to have been chosen by AA alone, but another Scottish stronghold, Fort St. George, was also mentioned as a place to imprison Napoleon (Houssaye, *1815*, iii. 520).
[5] Both London crowds and opposition spokesmen supported the estranged wife of the Prince Regent.
[6] On 24 July.

27 July 1815

C'est elle qui toujours florissante,—quoiqu'assaillie de toutes parts, a sans cesse déjoué par sa persévérance les projets du Génie; elle que j'ai voulu anéantir; elle qui du premier trône du Monde m'a deux fois replongé dans la Nuit; elle enfin qui toujours généreuse, offre seule un asyle à mon infortune— Eh quoi? Vous vous étonnez?—Ne sais je pas honorer mes ennemis?—C'est moi, c'est Napoléon qui loue aujourdhui les Anglais!—Voyez les coups du sort!—Eh bien! (shrugging his shoulders) la prospérité m'avait trop enivré—elle est passée— tant mieux—l'adversité me rend à moi même—je fus souvent petit dans le succès—mais vous me verrez grand dans les revers—je ne serai plus le souverain du Continent—je ne verrai plus les nations enchaînées à mon char—je ne pourrai plus élever ni abattre des Trônes mais n'importe—ce que j'ai fait est fait—l'histoire le Conservera—mon nom me reste— je suis Bonaparte!—et c'est assez!—' I do not say that these were his words, but that he spoke to that effect, in that rapid, restless, incoherent, but energetically and strikingly characteristic style. Another thing he said to Captn Maitland[7]— La force a rétabli les Bourbons—deux fois—l'Etranger est dans la Capitale—l'esprit de la Nation et de l'Armée est comprimé— mais c'est un volcan qui à leur départ éclatera sur lui—le choc sera électrique—la France fait ses droits—et mon fils, le fils des Césars, regnera!—Ils sont huit, je crois, ces Bourbons; 7 hommes et une femme—moralement, sept femmes et un homme! (meaning *that great man, the Duchesse d'Angoulême*.) In this I am afraid there may be more truth than we are willing to admit. The King is in the hands of the Jacobins—of his Brother's murderers—of Buoney's friends—of a set of ruffians—Fouché at the head—the crafty Talleyrand &c is it likely that such men should call such loyal subjects as my Father round the throne? And what honour to him *if he was asked* to mix with such people? such company? Why, he w[d] be quarrelling with them from morning to night, till they w[d] contrive to get him underhand removal secretly God knows where. What can we expect from a superannuated Monarch, an *Esclave couronné* ruling a demoralized nation with revolu-

[7] The welcome given to Napoleon by the crew of the *Bellerophon* and by her captain Sir Frederick Lewis Maitland (1777–1839), K.C.B. and rear-admiral (1830), was severely criticized in England, where the sailor's praises (slightly varied) were reported in *The Times* of 27 July.

tionary Ministers? Who, while they manage the State their own way, (and just give him permission to sign his name when his hand is not too tottering for even that), give him carefully and faithfully, I suppose, ⎪ some such things as a pill in the morning, a bit of plum pudding at noon, and a Clyster[8] at night, while he, poor soul!

> In spight of their most solemn declarations
> And of the plighted faith of Kings and Nations,
> On foreign arms borne from Batavia's plains,[9]
> Lolls thoughtless on his gouty throne, and REIGNS!!
> Reigns—as George Regent, when he goes to dance—
> Reigns—as the fainéant Kings of ancient France—
> Reigns—as Will. Fred. of Prussia mourns his wife,[10]
> In past regrets absorbing present life;—
> Heavens! how unlike his martial Sire of old,
> The brave, the gay,—the amiable—the bold—
> In battle, louder than the Cannon roaring—
> In peace, more placid than the shepherd snori[ng]
> While poor Fred leaning on his restless pillow,
> Or on a lonely bank beside a willow,
> Thinks ceaseless weeping is no peccadillo,
> While passengers, viewing the stupid drill—'*Oh!*
> Quantum,' they say, '*mutatus est ab illo!*'[11]

Which means, how different from his Sire! Virgil—n[œsis][12] —as ⟨Dʳ⟩ Pangloss wᵈ say.[13]—Aunt Hetty desires me to return you ⟨her⟩ thanks for a charming letter, which she wᵈ have answered before [this h]ad she not been afflicted with a lameness in her fingers, w[hich] is come she knows not how—the hand is for the present useless to her—she is having medical advice— and I hope it is getting better—but it will be a work of time —it occasions her many privations, and is at times very painful. —We are all equally anxious to hear of your Books and MSS. and greatly disappointed at my father's not being rewarded

---

8 A rectal injection, in this case to provide nourishment.
9 Wellington and Blücher entered France from the Lowlands.
10 Friedrich Wilhelm III (1770–1840) married in 1793 Princess Louisa of Mecklenburg-Strelitz (1776–1810), who proved to be a devoted and heroic consort during the early wars against Napoleon. The King's grief at her death and lengthy mourning were often noted in following years.
11 'Quantum mutatus ab illo Hectore' (*Aeneid*, ii. 274).
12 A transliteration of the Greek νοῦς, meaning mind or intellect.
13 The tutor in *Candide*.

as he ought. But I expected it all along. The Bourb. can neither discern hidden merit, nor have they spirit enough to foster it if they had the *nous* to *déterrer* it! My Aunt has passed some pleasant days at Norbury, where she had the pleasure of being when arrived your letter to Mrs Locke. Charles Parr's notice was too short,[14] for either Aunt H[etty] or Uncle J[ames] to write; w[hich] fretted them both. I am putting in French Verse at this moment Pope's Elegy to an Unf. Lady.[15] I shall write out my attempt for you at the first opportunity, tho' I believe it is more congenial to the spirit of Latin than of French. |

Since I wrote this, I have discovered that Martin had been on a tour to Margate—I therefore wrote to Mr Locke. — — I have finished my translation, and will send it by my next letter. I laboured hard at it, and it came off much better than I could expect. Aunt Hetty and Mr Burney were very much pleased with it.—I am very happy to see in to day's papers an act of vigour unexpectedly committed by the King[16]—but it w^d have been much better had the list of the proscribed appeared sooner—for now the most notorious have I fear escaped. I should likewise wish that *Fouché's name might appear a little higher up in the list than it does.*[17] I have no patience with that Scoundrel, tour à tour Minister of Buoney, and of Louis, tour à tour betrayer of both: who at the fall of the former took the reins of Government, *provisoirement,* with *Carnot:*[18] and now toad-eating the King the first thing he does is to sign, in the face of the world, the proscription of him who was his co-regulator of the State but a fortnight before; of *Carnot,* a much better man than himself, because, tho' his principles were often erroneous, he has always acted consistently; and I always feel some respect for a rogue who is uniformly faithful

[14] For CPB's travels, see L. 922, pp. 334–5.

[15] AA's translations took up much of his time during this period. He showed to his cousin CFBt's satisfaction that he had in fact memorized Pope's poem in the course of translating it (*HFB,* pp. 387–8).

[16] The ordonnance de proscription, promulgated by Louis XVIII, appearing on 23 July in the *Gazette Officielle* and on 26 July in the *Moniteur,* condemned fifty-seven of Napoleon's leading supporters.

[17] An ironic remark, since Fouché had signed and helped to draw up the list of those proscribed.

[18] See L. 856 n. 15. Carnot did in fact accept the interior ministry on 20 March; as a result of this proscription he spent the remaining years of his life in exile, dying in Prussia at Magdeburg in 1823.

to the same *species* of roguery. and he deserves as much to be honoured for surlily refusing the portfolio of Min[r] of the Interior, as for his consummate Genius, in the various characters of Statesman, Orator, Warrior and Mathematician.

By some mistake this letter, written a week ago, was not sent. I found it just now in my pocket; Aunt Hetty will forward it by the first opportunity.

928   Trèves, 9–20 August 1815

To Alexander d'Arblay

A.L. (Berg), 9–20 Aug. 1815
Double sheet 4to   4 pp.   *pmks*   60/P.P.   FOREIGN / 13 SE 1815   13 SP 1815   19 SE 1815   wafer
Addressed: ⌐Angleterre⌐ / Alexandre d'Arblay, Esqr, / ⌐at Mrs Broome's / or Henry Barrett's Esq, / Richmond, / Surry / *Angleterre.*⌐ To be forwarded : / if absent.
Re-addressed on folds in hand of CBFB: Alex[r] d'Arblay Esqr / *at* — — [Mr. Wa]ddington's Esqr / Lanover / near Abergavenny / Monmouthshire
Edited by CFBt. *See* Textual Notes.

Always—*Direct à Mad. d'Arblay, Post Restante, Bruxelles.*
August 9th 1815.[1]

I have waited, and not, I thank God! in vain, for THE MIEUX that might give me both Time & Courage to acquaint you with a new & terrible accident that I am thankful my dearest Alex has escaped hearing as I heard, with all the fearful misery of suspense as to its result. I will begin, therefore, with the End—since the End *vaut bien* the Beginning, by assuring you that the Danger is past, & that Recovery, though not yet at hand, is pronounced, I bless the Almighty! to be certain.

I will confine my first account to the Object of our tenderest solicitude, & speak afterwards of another for whom my poor Alex will soon become—*pour lui*—also anxious.

Sunday, the 9th of July—4 weeks from This Day—your

928.   [1] Note that this letter was finally posted on 20 August from Trèves.

beloved—unfortunate Father received, from a Horse he had recently purchased, & which he approached, inadvertently, while it was eating Oats, a kick upon 'la jambe droite, telle-ment violent que le crampon de son fer s'est entré dans cette jambe près du tibia, que le reste du fer a froissé d'une manière bien vigoureux—' These are the words written by M. de Premorul, to Brussels, 4 days afterwards. A wall behind him, prevented a fall; Henry, his Groom, was fortunately at hand, & helped him to reach his own, (Henry's,) Bed; which is in the stable, & then ran for M. de Mazancourt, the adjoint of your poor Father in his mission, who, in a Carriage, brought him gently to his apartment. A surgeon was recommended to him by the lady of the House, Made Nell, who immediately de-clared the accident to be immaterial, & dressed the wound slightly. Your Padre, therefore, conceived I might be spared its knowledge, & forced himself the next Day to write to me as usual. But the day after, from a most cruel mistake in the address which had been given to me, by himself, he missed, for a second post, receiving any Letter from me; & his imagination, playing [1] while suffering & confined, upon all the possible mischiefs that might have caused my supposed silence, so agitated his frame, that a fever was joined to his pain; & in this pitiable state, the surgeon closed the wound, & told him he might walk the next day. The next day, however, & the next night, his sufferings grew nearly insupportable, both bodily & mental; & his leg swelled to an enormous size, & the wound, & all the flesh around it, turned nearly black. He then himself had another surgeon called in, who called in a third. The wound was found in so bad a state, that it was forced to be opened, and 3 new ones were made, by incisions, deep & cut a cross, to give an issue to the bad blood caused by the premature shutting up of the evil: the First surgeon was then dismissed—& the 3d dismissed himself, for he was an inspector of the Prussian Hospitals, who only passed through la ville de Treves, to proceed to the army in France. The 2d a German, M. Tighe,[2] has remained ever since. on the 12th of July, your dearest Father was so ill, that he commissioned his aide de Camp, M. de

---

[2] Probably Lambert Bernard Theys (*fl.* 1802–27), a doctor of medicine and professor at Trier's midwifery school (Delamorre, p. 388), who lived at No. 931, Jakobgasse (now Jakobstrasse 11).

Premorel, to write an account of the cruel accident to Colonel Beaufort, at Brussels: with his desire that it might be broken to me: & that the Colonel would assist & counsel in what way I might undertake a Journey to Trèves. His dressings now were attended with acute anguish,[3] & which, with the inquietude of his mind, occasioned a nervous fever, that called for cordials & nourishing sustenance, & while the inflamatory condition of his leg demanded rigid abstinence & purifying medicines.

In this disastrous situation, on the 24th of July, 16 days after the terrible mischief, I found him!—With what joy, yet what acute sensations we met, after a separation of such suspensive misery, you may — — — perhaps, imagine; but I can never attempt to describe. ˡ

And how I arrived—through what dangers, what impediments, & what difficulties, I must reserve to relate in my future Letters.—I can bear to write now—& you can desire to read, exclusively of our beloved sufferer, again thus cruelly the victim of baleful accident.

The blackness, the violent swelling, & all that belong to danger, were, most happily, over just before my arrival;— but what had immediately preceded it was made most alarmingly clear to me, by the expression of almost every one, in a tone of felicitation, uttering *'Le Général est sauvé!'* My Alexʳ will conceive my feeling at those words! my shock—yet Gratitude. The *pansemens* were almost torture during the first fortnight, but the pain gradually diminished, & general amendment; though not without intermission, took place. All, slowly, slowly, but I trust surely, now prospers.

August 20th Your kind Father would not let me send off my Letter, nor any account of this new misfortune, till I could assure yo[u of h]is certain approach to complete recovery. He removes from [the Bed] to a sofa every day, & is wheeled to the Windo[w.] The dressings co[nt]inue Morning & Evening, & one of the wounds is n[ow] closed, & another is far advanced. Two still remain that demand more time; but the surgeon, M. Tighe,[2] has pronounced this Evening That the whole will be well enough for him to take leave in 14 days. He then advises the Waters of Aix la Chapelle, & the Baths; whether we shall try them or not is yet unfixed; but direct to me at

---

[3] Both the changing of bandages and the dressings themselves.

Brussels, whence my Letters will safely follow me, whether I am still here, or at Aix la Chapelle, or in Paris. Your Letter of *July the 7ᵗʰ* followed me hither.⁴ You never, my naughty Alexʳ, answer my enquiries relative to your Expences or your Studies or your Prospects. O yes, my dearest Alexʳ, I will surely do all that is in my power to accelerate our re-union. I desire it from the very bottom of my heart. Nothing less than the cruelly suspensive state in which I have been so long held with respect to your beloved Father could have made me endure so lingering a separation from his son. Do tell me quite sincerely your ultimate views & present pursuits. If you retain the admiration which your portrait makes so respectable, as well as natural,—do you think you can exert yourself ˡ to attain such a prize?⁵ It seems to me nothing less than desperate, if your efforts are regulated by what is useful as well as brilliant. The whole family love you—& write of you in such a style that our own favourite wish of little Julia by no means seems hopeless:⁶ for the same reason, therefore, the lovely Cecilia may, by the same exertions, prove attainable.⁵ My kind Mrs. L[ocke] actually calls you, in her Letters, *her Grandson!*—This, I know, means but maternity of kindness: nevertheless, it is an expression that announces a *species* of approbation the most flattering & encouraging. 'A *clever* and *amiable* companion' is, indeed, what we most earnestly wish for our dearest Alexʳ but we should *prefer* seeing him distinguish himself first, & by his conduct & talents procuring himself an independance that might save Prudence from being frightened away by his precipitance. You make me long to *know* & *see* the sweet Girl—& I am quite happy in the rectification of my mistake— for Prudence could NEVER sanction a choice in which BOTH parties would require an assistance & emulation that neither could give. I have entered into none of this interesting business with our best Friend. I fear, till he is more established, awakening an anxiety of so tender a kind. The two excellent Charlottes

⁴ This letter is missing.
⁵ At Norbury Park or at the home of the Angersteins, Alex was apparently smitten by the beauty of Georgina Cecilia Locke (1798–1867). This was an alliance that FBA could well have approved and a dream that Alex was to cherish for some years. Cecilia was to marry in 1822 the Hon. Robert Fulke Greville (1800–67). See further L. 930, pp. 471–2.
⁶ Mrs. Locke's granddaughter Elizabeth Julia Angerstein, now about ten years old.

love you equally, & equally desire your solid *good*, as well as your current happiness. How I grieve you use, already, the word *blazé*! Check, I beseech you, such early difficulty to be pleased. I *hope*, & *think*, we shall all be re-united soon—*My* thoughts, wishes, & struggles have all that object in constant view. But pray, *en attendant*, tell me what you *prepare* for, & what you *purpose*, & *hope*. Give my kind Love to all our dear Family; & if you are at Bradfield, include my valued old Friend Mr. Young.[7] My next Letter will be to my sweet Amine Try to thank my dearest Mrs. Lock for her last kind Lines— & your dear Aunt Hetty—& our amiable Fanny R[aper] Adieu —write as quickly [as] possible, & I will answer de même.

Treves 20 [Aug] 1815.

929   Trèves, 20 [August] 1815

To Viscountess Keith

L., copied in part by M. d'A (Barrett, Eg. 3699B, ff. 7–9b), 20 Apr. 1815 [Apr. *apparently a mistake in copying* August]

Pages 13–15 in the Letter Book *entitled*: The R. F^y / Mrs Beckersdorf. / L^y Keith . . . /   3 pp. (8·9 × 7″)

Treves ce 20 Avril 1815

In the midst of the almost continual evils or mischiefs that, of late, harass or afflict me, I feel not only a joy but a pride that it is the Partner the noble Partner of my dear & most loyal Lady Keith that gives, and in so lordly a manner gives the word of command to the late tyrant of Nations & Sovereign of Kings you would be pleased to see how Lord Keith is honoured on the continent, for not answering his letter, for declining to discuss his mock objections, & for refusing to accord him a private conference.[1] All here are quite indignant against those

---

7 Bradfield Hall near Bury in west Suffolk, the family house of Arthur Young (i, L. 14 n. 1). Alex had probably been invited by his cousins the Barretts (i, pp. lxxii–lxxiii), who in the summer and autumn of 1815 occupied a cottage on Young's estate (Gazley, pp. 663–4).

929. 1 A reference to Lord Keith's intransigence in dealing with Napoleon's attempts to negotiate the terms of his exile (L. 877 n. 15).

who treat him as a royal prisoner, not a perjured usurper. I wish excessively to know wether you saw him & How? Surely when curiosity seemed so universally awakened, you alone Lady of the Lord of the ascendant, have not been, of all Eve's daughters, the sole to disdain hereditary propensities?

I was called hither by a most melancholy accident that befal M^r d'Ay of a kick of a Horse upon the leg, that for the present, has wholly lamed him. The difficulties with which, & through which I got hither, should I ever be so happy as to be able to relate them to you in the dear tight little Island, will amuse as well as interest you. The surrounding Country was still infested with rambling Buonapartists & the Prussians, our dear Allies have conducted ^I themselves with such imperious presumption upon the rights of conquest that to pass through any town of Belgium or Germany in which they have a military commander, is nearly as difficult for their *bounden friends*, as for their *hostile enemies*; Hostile ennemies sounds a *platitude*; but how happy where it for society, had we as far as Hostile means warlike, no other! Yet though gay *now* to relate, my adventures as they *occured* were even tremendous, & I already look back to them with some surprise that I weathered the storm without more mischief. At one place, Liege,² I had omitted to prepare a passport, having in the hurry of fright with which I set out upon my expedition, totally forgotten to sollicit one from Bruselles. Nor will you marvell, when I inform you that the letter which acquainted me with the accident that had hapened to M^r d'Ay was only delivered to me ^I at about 3 o clock, & that I set out that very evening, between 6 & 7 and had every thing to prepare, bills to pay, appartements to resign, Banker to demand money of, whom I missed twice & Friends to take leave of, who thought me so mad for undertaking, so circumstanced, & at Such perilous moment, such a journey, that I was obliged to *hide* myself, literaly, to avoid their terrified importunity that I would relinquish my Theme.

² See the Trèves Journal, L. 932, pp. 485–8 below.

To Alexander d'Arblay

A.L. (Berg), 28 Aug.–30 Sept. 1815
Double sheet large 4to   4 pp. *pmks* PORT PAYE FOREIGN /
5 OC 1815   5 OC 18⟨ ⟩   13 OC .815   red seal
  Addressed: *Angleterre* / À / Alexander d'Arblay Esqr, / ᴦat Henry Barrets
Esq, / Richmond / Surrey¹ / London If not there / to be forwarded / else-
where / immediately
  Re-addressed: at—Waddington's Esqr— / Lanover, near Abergavenny /
Monmouthshire
[*on fold*:] Alexander D'Arblay Esqr / at—Waddington's Esqr / Lanover /
near Abergavenny / Monmouthshire / ᴦ⟨open⟩ to Richmond / T.P. C⟨ ⟩¹
  Edited by CFBt. *See* Textual Notes.

Treves, ce 28. août, 1815

My dear Alex's Letter, written in concert with his two
kind Cousins, has just reached me,¹ & I will begin an answer
immediately, however long I may be ere it is finished, for I have
very little time *de suite* at my own disposition, as you will easily
understand, when I tell you that I both Eat & sleep a full
quarter of a mile from the spot which contains all I have of
interest at Treves, & at which I spend every moment I can
snatch from those two vulgar, but inexorable instruments of
existence. This is a circumstance of constant annoyance, that
fatigues me inexpressibly, mentally as well as corporally: but
I stop my murmurs when I consider what I endured by being
separated not only by different houses, but different Towns,
nay, different Countries: for *CELUI* whose fate & fortune I
follow, spent more than 2 months in Germany while I continued in les pays bas.

But ere I treat more fully of myself, or even of my Boy,
let me give you, what I am sure you must most wish, a continuation of the account of our best Friend. The original
wounds are now fast healing, though they are still all open;
& the cruel incisions made by his most ignorant surgeons are
also in fair train: but the cure is perpetually delayed: the best

930   ¹ This letter is missing; the two cousins would appear to be CFBt and
Clement Francis.

artists are all in the towns, whether of France, Germany, or La Belgique, where the wounded have been conveyed from the bloody—though immortal Battle of Waterloo, & here we have no resource but a mad man of *all trades*, i.e. un accoucheur, Dentiste, medicin, et chirurgien:[2] & he tells us from Day to Day that 14 days will suffice to finish the business; but on the morrow it is still 14 days, & we can fix upon no term, even for our hopes, though all species of danger seems manifestly, thank Heaven, over. The poor Patient has not yet attempted to touch the ground: he is only rolled from his Bed to a sofa, & then from his alcove to the window. The sufferings, however, are considerably diminished, & the Dressings are now gone through with but little pain. How I would he were at Paris, under our medical oracle, Dr. Larrey![3] But he has not yet even received his orders for quitting Treves, though we hear that All his Collegues are at Paris. There is every reason to believe that our Letters are intercepted: you may form to yourself the inquietude of such an idea, with all its teeming concomitants. The Germans of this place are good sort of people, but the Prussians, to ¹ whom it has devolved by treaty, upon the first entrance of the allies into France, are dreaded for their power, & take no species of pains to soften that dread by any mixture of love or of esteem. The Minister at War is changed from the Duc de Feltre to Mar^al St. Cyr, to whom your Father is, unfortunately, unknown: & no orders arrive; but his mission, from its very nature, must now be over. He had sent to Paris his adjoint, M. le comte de Mazancourt,[4] before my arrival; but not a line comes from him; since, he has sent M. de Premorel, his aide de Camp—but with no better success.[5]

[a week later, Paris]

This Letter was begun an age ago—but stopt from being finished by a new alarm for your poor Padre, whose leg, which

² Dr. Theys (L. 928 n. 2).   ³ See L. 835 n. 6.
⁴ M. d'A had sent Mazancourt to Paris on 17 July, as he was to explain in a letter (France) of 20 August, addressed to the new minister of War, Gouvion-Saint-Cyr, after which, having had no reply, he was forced to send Prémorel on a similar request for orders of recall.
⁵ Prémorel had sent several letters back to Trèves in late August, but none apparently arrived. We know from a still later letter that he did carry out the d'Arblays' requests and saw both Mazancourt and the duc de Luxembourg (A.L.S., Vincennes, P.L.R.E. Durand de Prémorel to M. d'A, 7 September).

had seemed cured, became, by fresh mismanagement, of so alarming a colour & appearance, that we suddenly resolved upon travelling, at all risks, to Paris, for the purpose of consulting with Dr. Larrey. This we have done, & I now write, once more, from this celebrated—magnificent, oppressed & ruined capital!—Your dear Father is under the hands of Dr. Larrey—we have been here above a week—& in less than a fortnight, I hope & believe we shall set off for England—to embrace again our dearest Alexander. & spend there *at least* the ensuing Winter. He has demanded a *Congé* for that purpose, through the Duc de Luxembourg, which I cannot doubt will be granted, as he is at a time of life that puts him inevitably upon the *Retraite liste*, even were he well: but he is so far otherwise, that he can still scarcely put his foot to the Ground, & only creep about with crutches!—& now & then a Cane!

It is now, my Alex must immediately write me a *Sister's* Letter, to tell me his positive situation, with respect to his *studies*, his *preparations*, his *hopes*, his *expectations*, & his *views*; as well as the state of his *pecuniary affairs*.

If, as we must necessarily travel very slowly, you should be already at Cambridge ere we arrive, we shall be too eager to see you to wait for your vacation, & we mean BOTH of us to visit you at Cambridge, when the fatigues of our journey are past. Is there any choice of one part of a week in preference to another? ANY wish of selection that you may have, pray tell me without scruple. We are unfixed yet as to where we shall pass the winter: whether at Richmond, at our dear Charlottes, or near London, or at Bath. I shall write by to-morrow's post to entreat some documents œconomical from the 3 places, to decide us.

I am very impatient for some account of your Welsh expedition[6]—pray give me some *items* of it. I cannot imagine why you have not answered ¹ my very long Letter from Treves. I received the extremely interesting one you sent by Charles the day before I left Brussels. What you say there of my thinking you meant one 'too frivolous for you—' & for whom you were 'too thoughtful', makes me much desire to see & know the lovely Juliet[7] to whom you allude; for your description reminds

⁶ AA spent part of July with the Waddingtons at Llanover near Abergavenny.
⁷ Evidently Cecilia Locke (L. 928 n. 5).

me of your words in finishing the Wanderer, That if your Heart should dare be guided by your wishes, it was a Juliet that would completely enchain it. Pray give me a little word upon this subject. All the family love you: I was told you were *invited* to be of the party with this sweet syren at a play, with her sisters & mother! Has this idea induced you to spirited efforts for your return to College? By the way, some one has hinted to me that you *might* take your Degree as D.M.—let me hasten to inform you that your Padre would never consent to that; for reasons too long for detail, but that I am certain are insuperable. If, therefore, you cannot—alas—take a HIGH, you must content yourself with the LEAST LOW ONE you can take in Theology, as there is none other that can, even eventually, be useful to your future life. I hope, however, you have never yourself had the idea. How I regret your long separation from your Counsellor, & Confident—your *sister*, in short, at so interesting a period! Answer This Letter, I beg, quite immediately; that I may know both what to expect from *you*, & what your wishes are from *me*. Continue to write with the same *abondance de franchise* as in all your late Letters, letting your pen run on, without study or circumspection; *only* reading my queries; & not leaving me always in doubt whether or not my Letters reach you.

The history of my *travels in Germany* I now remit to our meeting. I am occupied so unceasingly in preparations for departure, & have so very much employment in examining & re-collecting our strayed or hidden Goods & Chattels, that I have scarcely a moment of rest *corporeal*, except at the expence of rest *intellectual*, for I only obtain it by the reception of visitors: & nothing is so rare as *half an hour* spent without them, at this instant, when your poor Padre, always confined, is known to [be] at home, & necessarily, according to the usage of this Chatty Country, visible, talkable, & —— —— sometimes, listenable. ¹

As Letters arrive now in 5 days regularly, & occasionally are delivered in 4, I can certainly hear from you before our Journey: but if any should come after our departure, they will be safe, as Made de Maisonneuve will keep them in charge, for the first safe opportunity to send them after us.

How shocked have I been by a Letter written only as an

anamuensis by your Cousin Fanny from my poor Sister Burney! & she tells me your worthy uncle James has had a severe fever! I know not yet where we shall lodge while we settle our Winter's habitation, but as I shall instantly seek my Brother James, to see how he is, ⟨our⟩ direction will be left there—& THENCE any thing you may have to tell me *AFTER* the 15ᵗʰ of October, may await me. But That must be only for any *SUPPLEMENT*—you will never let me stay so long for news of the points upon which I so anxiously enquire. I write by the Bedside of your dear Father, who is quite well except locally. We are both impatient to set out, as cold & damp were so mischievous to us last year, by making our Journey later: & any cold now fixing in his wounded leg, might fasten a Rheumatism there for life! France is in a state of distress, & disturbance past all description. But I reserve for talk what I have no more room to write. Be quick, my Alex—& give me all the satisfaction in your power to obviate disappointment & augment pleasure in our approaching ⟨junction⟩. I know not whether to direct—but continue as before.

Finished Paris—
Sepᵗʳ 30. 1815.

931   [*post* August 1815]

To M. d'Arblay

A.L. incomplete (Berg), *n.d.*¹
Double sheet 8vo   1 p.

Vous m'avez demandé, mon ami, avec tant d'instances, de vous donner par écrit l'histoire de mon petit voyage en allemagne, pour vous trouver à Treves, ou Triers, que je ne peux plus remettre l'execution de votre desir: mais, afin de me le rendre moins ennuyeux, je le ferai en des Thèmes, car comme cela, votre main se melera avec la mienne,¹

931.   ¹ This unfinished note, which seems to have been written soon after the departure of the d'Arblays from Trèves, proposed a sharing of the narrative—'en des Thémes'—alternating between FBA's account of her journey and M. d'A's tribulations as he waited for her arrival. The text of this note reappears in the Trèves Journal (p. 475 below).

JOURNEY TO TRÈVES, 1815

93²

A.J. (Diary MSS., 6422–[6597], re-paged 1–54, Berg), FBA [for AA], Journey from Brussels to Trèves and return to Paris, 19 July–[1 Oct.] 1815, written up Sept. 1824–19 July 1825, at 11 Bolton Street, London. The Journal comprises forty-four 8vos (7 × 4·4″), being 4to sheets folded and pinned and paged by FBA originally, later re-paged and also foliated. In all, 176 pages of text. For a detailed description of the physical components, *see* Textual Notes.

It had long been a favourite desire of the best beloved of my Heart that I should sketch upon in This Book, & upon This paper, presented to me for that purpose by Himself, the accounts I had related to Him of some peculiar events or scenes that had passed previously to our marriage or at periods when we had been separated: first, he said, that he might renew his interest in the recitals at his pleasure; &, next, that they might remain for his son; for whom his Paternal mind was ever at work to procure materials for improvement, or for innocent recreation. Alas!—he is Gone before any one of the little Narratives has been ¹ finished, though I have made Memoranda preparatory for almost all he had named: but sanguine—presumptuous Hope that *Time was in store*, occasioned a procrastination I now severely lament; & which, at least, shall be a lesson to me not to lose, by further delay, his wishes for his son also!—To that son I have been almost wholly devoted from the fatal period in which his Father,—our mutually best & dearest Friend upon Earth, has been torn from my Eyes — — From my Eyes alone could he be torn!—to my Thoughts, my Wishes, my fondest Hopes, my dearest Aspirations, he is ever Present! ever! ever!— ¹

I have long been embarrassed with which of the many little narrations HE enjoined me to write I should begin:— Naturally, I ought to go back to those of my early life—but my poor worn mind, & harrassed faculties, will not submit to be regulated by order, chronology, or any progressive considerations, Wise as I think them, & sound:—it is still too painful to me to Write, too great an effort, too wide from every pleasur-

able sensation that erst! made my Pen one of my greatest
delights —

———————

It is now Two years since I *began this beginning*!—but my
unhappiness so swells my breast, & so disorders my faculties,
when I try, when I even think of trying at [1] committing to
senseless paper those circumstances, anecdotes, or traits that,
to his finely discriminating mind, presented new ideas, or
varied combinations of characters or of casualties, that the
contrast of this dead Letter detail with the animating charm
of living discussion, dispirits every attempt, & casts me, with
augmented oppression of mind, into a species of inertness that
borders upon incapacity.

I speak, however, wholly of Writing, or Composition; I am
not—as yet!—sensible of any other decay of faculty. The
inability, however, now gradually diminishes;—& the thought
that it was HIS Request I should record these anecdotes, becomes more potent,—becomes, indeed, resistless. For His son,
—for Mine, I record them—& therefore, so to do may, perhaps, from an effort & a toil, grow into a fond occupation
& a pleasure. [1]

These following few words of opening compliance to the
Request I find in my destined Book—ah, with what endless
regret at the interruptions, or procrastinations, that impeded
the prosecution of my purpose, while yet He might have blest
it by the sanction of his kind acceptance!—

Vous m'avez demandé, mon Ami, avec tant d'instances,
de vous raconter encore les anecdotes, qui vous ont amusé;
et surtout de vous donner par ecrit l'histoire de mon petit
Voyage en Allemagne pour vous trouver à Treves, que je
ne peux plus remettre l'execution de votre désir; mais, afin
de me la rendre moins ennuyeuse, je la ferai, par des Thémes,
car, comme cela, votre écriture se mêlera avec la mienne, et
ce livre, que vous m'avez donné pour le consacrer à mes
souvenirs, deviendra[1]

So, in 1818!—had I begun a little Narration [1]
So had I begun a little Narration in happier days!—days
never to return, days such as few have known—& none—oh

932.   [1] This prefatory note is a near copy of L. 931.

NONE have more penetratingly, more gratefully appreciated —
— In This my deplorably Widowed state to do aught that was
suggested by Him—the lord & darling of my Heart—is All
for which I Now retain any voluntary spirit of Exertion, save
in what regards OUR Alexander, who occupies all that is left
me of life:—My adored Departed wished me to write This
Narration, with other anecdotes, First for his own perusal,
& next to ensure their future communication to our Son. The
former motive is ended—for-ever!—the latter still remains,
& that shall urge me to ¹ occupy, whenever I have the power,
some portion of my poor remnant Hours to the devellopment of
those events of my life of which He who rendered 25 Years of it
almost supremely happy desired me—enjoined me—to leave
some written trace.

I begin with that He most wished, my hazardous Journey to
join him at Treves.

On the 19. of July, 1815, during the ever memorable
Hundred Days, I was writing to my Heart's best Friend, at
our Apartments in the Marché aux Bois, at Brussels; whither
I had fled on the arrival of Buonaparte in Paris, & where my
honoured Husband had left me, on a Mission from his King,
Louis 18. to Treves; when I received a visit from la Princesse
d'Henin, & Colonel de Beaufort; who entered the room with
a sort of precipitancy & confusion that immediately ¹ struck me
as the effect of evil tidings which they came to communicate.
My ideas instantly flew to the expectation of new public disaster; for what was private, or personal, occurred not to me, as
I had no reason to imagine either of them likely to be informed
of any thing deeply interesting to me, but by myself. Madame
d'Henin had for very many years honoured me with her chosen
friendship, & given me proofs innumerable of her partiality
& esteem; but she was not in the way of my connexions, or
affairs, & knew of them but through my own information:
Colonel de Beaufort had been of the Regiment of Toul with
M. d'Arblay, &, in common with all its Officers, regarded
him rather as a Brother than a friend: but till public calamity
brought them together at Brussels, they had not met for so
many years, that they were totally ignorant of each other's
situation. I saw, therefore, their evident disturbance without
any reference to myself, ¹ though with much apprehension of

fresh commotion in France: & I waited with patience, though with pain, their own time & own method of explication. This silent attention only added to their embarrassment, & a general pause took place; during which I could not but observe that the Countenance of my dear Madame d'Henin became almost distorted from strong inward emotion, & that M. de Beaufort looked aghast. I was just imagining that Louis 18 was again dethroned, when Madame d'Henin faintly pronounced the name of M. d'Arblay—Alarmed, I started—certain that the evil, whatsoever it might be, was His!—I turned from one to the other, in speechless trepidation, dreading to ask, while dying to know what awaited me. Madame d'Henin then, in a husky ¹ voice, scarcely articulate, said that M. de Beaufort had received a Letter from M. d'Arblay.

This a little recovered me; yet, certain, by their distress, that some cruel tidings were impending, I became eager to learn them, that no time might be lost should there be any thing to do. I commanded myself, therefore, to assume sufficient composure to entreat for immediate & faithful intelligence.

Fearfully, then, one aiding the other, while I listened with subdued, yet encreasing terrour, they acquainted me that M. d'Arblay had received on the Calf of his leg from a wild Horse, a furious kick,² which had occasioned so bad a wound as to confine him to his Bed: ¹ & that he wished M. de Beaufort to procure me some travelling Guide, that I might join him as soon as it would be possible with safety & convenience.

I now started up, & with clasped hands, besought them to let me see the Letter at once.³ This they resisted, but their resistance only added torture to affright, & I became so urgent, so vehement, so over-powering, that they were forced to give way — — But oh Heaven!—What was my agony when I saw that the Letter was not in his own hand!—I conjured them to leave me, & let me read it alone—They offered, one to find me out a clever Femme de chambre, the other, to enquire a

---

² M. d'A's wound is described in some detail in the medical reports that accompanied his pension request. In A.L.S. (Vincennes), duc de Luxembourg to the ministère de la Guerre, 31 Oct. 1815, it is described as a 'Plaie contuse à la jambe droite . . . Cette blessure qui avait été accompagnée de la Contusion du Tibia, de la déchirure de son périoste, et de la destruction violente des ligamens articulaires a été suivie d'abcès considérable qu'il a fallu ouvrir avec l'instrument, tranchant de l'adhérence des cicatrices, d'une très Grande gène dans les mouvemens'.

³ This letter is missing.

Guide for me, to aid me to set out, if able, the next ⎮ day; but I rather know this from recollection, than from having understood them at the time: I only entreated their absence—&, having consented to their return in a few Hours, I forced them away.

No sooner were they gone, than, calming my spirits by earnest & devout prayer, which alone supports my mind, & even preserves my senses, in deep calamity, I ran over the Letter, & conceiving that the wound, from the entrance of the Iron hoof into so tender a part, which caused pain too acute to permit the poor sufferer even the use of his hand, must menace a gangrene, I called forth my utmost courage, & resolved to fly to him immediately.

What time, indeed, was there to lose, when the Letter, written by M. de Premorel, his aid. de Camp, was dated the 4th day after the Wound, & acknowledged ⎮ that 3 incisions had been made in the leg, unnecessarily, by an ignorant surgeon, which had so aggravated the danger, as well as the suffering, that he was now in Bed, not only from the pain of the lacerated limb, but also from a nervous fever! & that no hope was held out to him of quitting it in less than a fortnight, or 3 Weeks.

I determined not to wait, though the poor sufferer himself had charged that I should, either for the Femme de chambre of Mad[e] d'Henin, or the Guide of M. de Beaufort, which they could not quite promise even for the next day—& to me the next Hour seemed the delay of an Age.

Never was I blessed with such personal courage as at this crisis—The one object I had in view divested me of every fear & every feeling of personal ⎮ Danger, Prudence, Health, Strength, Expence, or Difficulty. To arrive in time to aid his recovery was my sole Thought—to know it was his ardent wish was my constant consolation.

I immediately announced to the people of the House my departure, & demanded their account. They did not speak, but their looks shewed concern.

I commissioned my little Brussels' maid[4] to collect my small Bills, & discharge them instantly.

My next attention was to money, as I had scarcely any: our

---

[4] Marie (L. 914 n. 9).

Banker, De Noots, lived almost next door to me. I hied to his house. — — —

It was past 3 o'clock, & the Banking house was closed!

Thunderstruck, at first, I remained | like a statue, but presently determined to state my case to him at his own home.

I went thither—he was out!—

He was not expected to return but at 5 o'clock, to dinner.

I know not whether this was a holy-day, or whether all business regularly ceases at 3 o'clock; but not even a clerk could I meet with! A good sort of servant, however, to whom I revealed my great distress, told me he doubted not but that his Master would take it into consideration. I fixed to return at 5.—& went home, & sent to order a Chaise at six, on the Road to Luxembourg.

The answer was that no Horses were to be had!

Almost distracted, I flew myself to the Inn that was recommended to me as the first for Travellers—but the answer was repeated! The route to Luxembourg the Book keepers told me, | was infested with straggling parties first from the wandering army of Grouchy,* now rendered pillagers from want of food; & next from the pursuing army of the Prussians, who made themselves Pillagers also, through the rights of Conquest—To travel in a Chaise would be impracticable, they assured me, without a Guard.

I had already heard—though now in the perturbation of my haste I had set the intelligence aside, that all the roads from Brussels to Treves were beset with desperate Banditti, the refuse of all the Armies: for my Nephew, Charles Parr Burney, had called upon me 2 Days previously, for Letters to my poor General at Triers, where he, Charles Parr, meant to wait upon him; but he had called again the preceding Evening, to tell me that he & his party had been forced to change their route, & content themselves | with visiting Antwerp & Amsterdam, as they were warned that they might else become spoil to the wandering hoards who were, on the one hand, escaping from slaughter or captivity, & on the other, ferociously existing as Banditti!

Constrained, thus, to give up going alone, or going immediately, I now resolved upon travelling in the Diligence: & desired to secure a place in that for Triers. (Treves.)

There was none to that City!—

'And what is the nearest town to Triers, whence I might go on in a chaise?' 'Luxembourg.'

I bespoke a place — — but was told that the Diligence had set off the very Day before, & that none other would go for 6 Days, as it only quitted Brussels once a Week.

The misery of this intelligence was almost equal to that which had been its origin. I quitted the Book keeper's office in agony indescribable, [|] [to] form some new plan, as staying another week was wholly out of the question.

At the Marché au Bois, I found M. de Beaufort, anxiously awaiting to see me, & say he would procure me both a travelling Femme de chambre & a Guide for the next Day.—

The next Day!—the next Hour seemed to me a Century, at an instant so critical. I thanked him tremulously but besought to be left alone—for I could not even speak without feeling near suffocation.

Sorrowing the kind Colonel retired: but I had not a moment to breathe ere Madame de Maurville forced herself into my Apartment.

I felt all her friendly zeal with gratitude, but could bear no intrusion, till she softened my torturing impatience by suggesting my going to my nephew, who had been ill, she had heard, & who perhaps might be yet in Brussels, & able to accompany me. [|]

On this hint, I flew with her to the Great Hotel de Flandre,[5] where he had lodged: but he was gone.—

I then supplicated poor good Madame de Maurville to leave me. I required to be wholly concentrated to one point, that I might form & execute at once some resolve.

When liberated, it occurred to me to call upon Madame la Baronne de Spaghan,[6] a lady of the Low Countries who had shewn me infinite kindness, & whom I wished to see before my departure.

She received me with a cordiality quite affecting, for she instantly perceived my distress. She pressed upon me offers of service, & besought earnestly to become my Banker in this emergency. I resisted her propositions, though with the most

[5] The Hotel de Flandre in the rue aux Draps (L. 858 n. 1).
[6] Mme de Spangen (L. 917 n. 8).

grateful acknowledgements; but I relied on meeting M. De Noots at 5 o'clock. She urgently endeavoured to dissuade me from a Journey she thought perilous, | in the existing state of things; but I supplicated her to spare me all exhortatio[n]. She then sought to help me on my own terms, & told me that, if travel I would, thus at all hazards, I had but to go by Leige,[7] which though not a direct, was the only safe road, that then she would put me under the protection of her Brother in Law, the Comte de Spaghan,[8] who was himself proceeding to that City by the ensuing Night Coach.

I heard, & accepted this kindness with rapture, embracing her with the warmth of an old Friend—she folded me to her breast, in return, with rolling tears of kindness & concern, expressing an attachment that she felt, she said, in her inmost heart. The Comte, she told me, had large landed property | about & beyond Liege, & to be accompanied by him so far on my route, would be security & ease to me for the whole way, as he would recommend me to powerful & useful persons for every stage. I went away blessing her — —

(And only last Night, from the time I am now writing this Narration, which has wiled on to this present 6th of September, 1824!—so often have I stopt in its course!—only last Night, I had a Letter from Madame de Maurville, in which she sends me the kindest Words from this excellent Baronè de Spaghan, who retains for me still her partial goodness, though I have never seen her since I parted from her on La Place Royale at the period of which I am relating the events.)

I flew myself to the Book Keeper I had so abruptly quitted, & instantly | secured myself a place in the Leige Diligence for Night.

Hence I passed to the House of Madame de La Tour Dupin, which was only next Door. Not only to take leave of herself did I spare this moment, but to Supplicate, through her means, the forgiveness of La Princesse d'Henin, that I should quit Brussels, not only wholly against her counsel, & exhortation, but without even saying to her farewell. I was truly grieved; but I knew the excessive difficulty of resisting her persuasions & remon-

---

[7] Liége.
[8] François Guillaume de Spangen (1768–1831), comte de Spangen and brother of the comte and baron de Spangen mentioned in L. 917 n. 8.

strances, yet knew I could not *live* if I took not the *first* moment that was in my power, to fly, through whatever obstacles, to my wounded & adored Husband

I found this highly accomplished & elegant lady at her frugal revolutionary repast with her two Daughters, Madame de Liedekirke & Mlle Cecile de La Tour du Pin[9] |

They were all truly grieved for my distress—Madame de Liedekirke even burst into tears: & Madame la Mere, as she told me afterwards at Paris, had sent herself to Charles Parr Burney, of whose arrival at Brussels she had accidentally heard, to enjoin him to accompany me to Treves: for Mad^e de La T. Dupin had been informed of my misery before its sufferance by her Aunt, the Princess d'Henin. But Charles, unfortunately, had with him some Pupils whom it was impossible for him to abandon.

Thence I proceeded to Messrs de Noots, the Banker's, for whom I had an unpresented Letter of Credit. — — But what was my consternation to be told they had all Dined abroad, & could not be followed, as they would not transact any further business that Day!— |

To Write, or attempt any representation, would employ a time that would make me inevitably too late for my place; blessing, therefore, my benevolent Madame de Spaghan, I resolved upon trusting to her kind recommendation, & borrowing money of the Comte her Brother in Law,[8] whom, after my arrival at Treves, I could pay by a Draft.

I was hurrying home, to pack & prepare — — but seeing from afar a figure upon the steps, I stopt, & looked with my Glass: I then perceived Madame d'Henin.—

I darted back like lightening—at 15 I had not more agility than that with which I was endowed at this sight, from the fear of her persuasion, the grief of resisting her, & the dread lest the conflict should make me too late. I loitered about at a distance till I saw the Coast clear, & that kind, anxious, really unhappy Friend sent | away.

I then entered my poor forlorn habitation, & set about my wretched packing. I had a very scanty Wardrobe, the remnant of my flight from Paris; but abundance of small matters difficult to arrange. I had not even a Trunk! nor power at such

[9] See L. 872 n. 10.

a moment to get one. I put all I had of value into a large flat hand Basket, made of straw by a French Prisoner, & which had been given to me by my dear Mrs Lock, & all else I thrust into Carpet Bags.

At a very late hour I sat down a moment to a little Dinner: Mr. Boyd visited me at that poor repast, & took my apologies to his family, & was much concerned & even alarmed at my expedition: but saw all advice or interference would be nugatory.

With difficulty & fatigue the most ˡ excessive, I had just settled the innumerable small but indispensable matters that hang upon *the Last*; where in cases of abrupt departure from places we have inhabited any time, & I was taking leave of my Hosts, a Brussells Fiacre being at the door, & laden with my little luggage, when I was told that Leroi, the confidential servant of Madame d'Henin, besought to speak a word to me from his Mistress.

Sick I felt at this intrusion, though always grateful for its kind & feeling motive: & I sent an earnest excuse, entreating not to be delayed.

The good Leroi retired unwillingly, & I then descended from my apartment, & was mounting into the Fiacre, when he came from some hiding place, & would be heard. He told me that the Princesse was quite miserable at my hazardous plan, which she had gathered from Mad^e de la Tour Dupin, ˡ & that she supplicated me to postpone only till the next day, when I should have some one of trust to accompany me.

I assured him that nothing now could make me risk procrastination, but begged him to still the fears of the excellent Princesse by acquainting her I should be under the protection of the comte de Spaghan.

He was obliged to be answered, though he said he knew not how to go home. Even the phlegm of my young Hostess & her Brother was softened by my threatened dangers, from the rumours of the disordered state of the route; & I left them in tears.

I arrived at the Inn — — after this last unprepared for impediment, 3 or 4 minutes too late!—

What was the fermentation of my mind at this News!— A whole Week I must wait for the next Diligence, ˡ & even then lose the aid & Countenance of le comte de Spaghan.

Leroi, who through some short cut of foot paths & alleys, had got to the Inn before me, earnestly pressed me, in the style of the true confidential old French servants of the Nobility, to go & compose myself *chez la Princesse.*

Even my Host & Hostess had pursued to wish me again good by, & now expressed their warm hopes I should return to them. But the Book Keeper[10] alone spoke a language to snatch me from despair, by saying my Fiacre might perhaps catch the Diligence 2 miles off, in the Allée Verte, where it commonly stopt for fresh passengers or parcels.

Eagerly I promised the Coachman a Reward if he could succeed, & off he drove.

My fear during this short route, which seemed to me of a length insupportable, were nearly distracting—but its ' termination—Oh! its termination was Heaven to me! The Diligence was at the appointed place; & that instant ready to proceed!

I rushed into it, with trepidation of hurry & of Joy extatic. I owe completely to the honesty of my worthy Dutch Coachman that I lost not all my luggage, for I completely forgot I had any belonging to me. My Basket was always in my hands, & from that I took my purse, to recompense his speed, & already we were on the Wing.

This escape from so dreadful a blow as had just menaced me gave me an entire new being: it raised in me such hopes, such confidence of joining my best beloved on Earth, that no dificulties, no trials afterwards, severely as I was put to the proof, had power to curb again the happy buoyancy of my restored spirits.

When these transporting feelings which first chaced such killing anguish ' first subsided, I recollected the Comte de Spaghan. I found I was seated in the last vacant place, & I looked about to try to recognize Him—rather disappointed that he himself did not immediately conceive that I must be his destined *Protegée.*

There were 4 Passengers.

A military man, of a high & haughty demeanour; a Dutch Gentlewoman, who seemed well bred & well educated; Her husband, an old man who was quiet & languid; & a middle-aged Gentleman who was muffled up so as to be hardly visible.

---

[10] Dispatcher of the diligence coaches.

Extreme was my eagerness to find out which of these might be the comte; but I dared risk no question. I sat wholly silent.

The others all entered into conversation on the late Great Event & immortal Battle. The plains of Waterloo would have been in sight had we ᴵ travelled by Day light. The discourse was all in German, which seemed to be the native language of every passenger but myself. And I was the more persuaded that not one was either French or English, by their not bestowing upon me the smallest attention: for I never yet saw a French person who let a female stranger pass utterly unnoticed; nor even an English one when meeting a Briton abroad; however silently phelgmatic is John Bull even to his own Countrymen when they are strangers to him at home. The Dutch, however, though slow from making acquaintance through instinctive good breeding, or native vivacity, like the French, seek not to pass by any occasion to serve: & where once conversation is incidentally opened, they are ready to cast aside their placid taciturnity, & become ᴵ kindly communicative.

When we stopt, in the middle of the Night, for some refreshment, at Tirlemont,[11] as I believe, I looked wistfully at each of the 3 men, & listened more attentively to their voices;— what, then, was my alarm to be convinced they were all Germans, & consequently that the comte de Spagen, a Belgian, was not amongst them! I know not how I should have supported this disappointment, had I not gathered, at the same *auberge*, that there were two Night Coaches from Brussels to Leige, & conceived, therefore, a hope that the comte was in the other, & had preceded, or would follow me.

We arrived at Leige at about 9 in the morning. I accompanied my fellow travellers to a Warehouse into which our luggage was conveyed, ᴵ earnestly looking around me, with the hope every instant of being accosted: All, however, but myself, had come to the end of their journey, the Leige Diligence going no further; they soon, therefore, settled their accounts, & departed.

I now advanced to the Book Keeper, & made enquiries about the comte de Spagn.

[11] Tirlemont, forty-five kilometres from Brussels on the main road to Liége. Coaches stopped in the Grote Markt of the town.

He had arrived in the earlier Coach: and — — was gone on in some other to his Estates.—

What then was my affright!—I had but 6 Napoleons left when my passage to Leige was paid. I remained in a sort of stupor that made the Book-Keeper[10] regard me with wonder, though, as I had mentioned the comte de Spaghan, without any air of suspicion or ill opinion.

The stare of the man brought back to me some presence of mind. I then ¹ resolved to keep my own counsel with regard to my poverty, lest I should be stopt, or affronted, & to go on as far as my 6 Napoleons would carry me, & when they were gone, to proceed by parting with my Gold Repeater, & some trinkets which I carried in my Basket.

As calmly as was in my power I then declared my purpose to go to Treves, & begged to be put on my Way.

I was come wrong, the Book Keeper answered: the road was by Luxembourg.

And how was I to get thither?

By Brussels, he said: & a week hence; the Diligence having set off the Day before.

Alas, I well knew that! & entreated some other means to forward me to Triers.

He replied that he knew of none from Liege; but that if I would go to Aix, I might there, perhaps, though it was out of the road, hear of some conveyance. ¹

How desperate a resource! Yet I could hear of no other: & for Aix, he told me a Diligence would set off in about an Hour.

I would now have secured a place; but he said I must first shew my Passport.

Passport? I repeated, I have none!

I could not, then, he dryly acquainted me, go on.

Astonished & affrighted, I pleaded my distress. I had not thought of a passport: none had been demanded for my quitting Brussels, & nothing of the kind had occurred to me: I had consulted no one; I had precipitated my flight to attend a sick Friend, & I besought the Book Keeper to let me proceed. ¹ It was utterly, he asserted, impossible. I could not leave Liege without a passport from the Prussian Police Office, where I should only & surely be detained if I had not one to shew from whence I came.

This, happily, reminded me of the one I had had from M. de Jaucourt in Paris,[12] & which was, fortunately, though accidentally, in my hand Basket. I begged, therefore, a Guide to the Prussian office.

There arrived, I was shewn to a room where two young officers received me very civilly; they were French, I believe; at least they spoke French well.

I told them my history, & gave them my Passport, signed by M. de Jaucourt[12] the 15th of March; & by Lieutenant Colonel Jones[12] at Brussels the 17th of June.—

They seemed quite satisfied, & carried the document to the next ˡ Appartment—but what was my consternation—when I heard a voice of thunder vociferate rude reproaches to them, & saw them return with my unsigned passport, to tell me the Commandant[13] refused his signature, & ordered me to depart from the office!

Brutality so unauthorized, however it shocked, I would not suffer to intimidate me. Where, I asked, was I to go? I had a claim to a passport, & if refused it here must be directed elsewhere.

The Commandant, hearing me, burst into the Room. He was a Prussian—but not like Prince Blücher, whom I had seen in England, & whose face, in private company, cast off all fiery hostility for pleased & pleasing benignity: this Mr. Kaufman[13] had an air the most ˡ ferocious, & seemed rather to be pouncing upon some prey, than coming forward to hear a reclamation of Justice; & in a tone & manner of revolting roughness, he said I had brought a stale old useless passport, with which he would have nothing to do.

He spoke in bad & broken French, & was going to leave me: but I dropt my indignant sensations in my terrour at this threatened failure, & eagerly represented that I had quitted Brussels too abruptly for seeking a new passport; but that this had been granted me at Paris in my flight from Buonaparte.

He cast his Eyes momentarily on the passport, & then, in an inquisitorial voice, said 'Vous êtes Francaise?—'

'Oui, Monsieur,' I readily answered, ˡ being such in right of my dear Husband, & conceiving that a recommendation, after having stated my escaping from Buonaparte. But he threw the

12 See J. 924, pp. 367, 429; L. 901 n. 3.   13 Unidentified.

Passport instantly back to me, with marks of disdain, & said it would not do.

Earnestly then I required to know what step I must take, what course I must pursue?

Go back, he harshly answered, & get another.

And then he stalked away to the inner Apartment.

Desperate from anguish, I followed him—I was travelling, I told him, to join a wounded General Officer, & should lose a whole Week by returning, which might be fatal to me;— he turned round, a little struck, yet as if amazed at my daring perseverance, & with undisguised contempt repeated ı 'Vous êtes Francaise?'

I then saw I had by no means made my court to him by my conjugal assumption, & that he was amongst that prejudiced mass that, confounding the Good with the Bad, made War against All the French. My affirmative, however, had been from a right I held too sacred to recall, & I again assented.

Taking up a News paper, he turned away from me, & walked towards a distant Window.

I was **then** reduced to making use of the most earnest supplication, & the two young officers looked ready to join me, from understanding me more perfectly, & evidently pitying my distress. But they had a tyrant to deal with whom it was clear they must implicitly obey.

At this deplorable moment, & when on the point of being compelled back to Brussels, I had the exquisite good ı fortune to recollect the Name of General Kleist, a Prussian Commander in Chief at Treves, who had distinguished M. d'Arblay in a manner the most flattering & even cordial: & no sooner had I mentioned this, & with circumstances of detail that demonstrated the authenticity of what I uttered, than M. Kauffman gave the Passport to the young officers, with leave to pass me on to Aix la Chappelle; There to present myself instantly to the commanding officer, to solicit permission *pour aller plus loin.*

Ungracious as this was, I received it with the highest joy, & hastened to the Book Keeper[10] to secure my place. This man, a German, whose compassion had now been awakened, saw my relief & delight with real satisfaction.

The Diligence for Aix la Chapelle ı was not to set out till

twelve: the Book-Keeper offered me a Boy to shew me the town: & I gladly took a little stroll, happy to escape ordering any repast,—for which my heart was too full, & my purse too empty!—

The stroll, however, was short & unsatisfactory, for a mizling rain came on that soon watered me back.

The entrance into this ancient City lies in a hollow almost surrounded by various small streams: & in fine Weather is a beautiful Valley, through which runs the Meuse,—a River of so much fame & frequent Name in History that I had raised expectations of it which were wholly disappointed, from the dinginess of its Colour, & from its want of any grandeur of width. The outside I saw of the antique Cathedral,¹⁴ ¹ looking so very old & so very brown, that it appeared, at a distance, like a weather-beaten Rock. The few streets, or rather Lanes, that I had opportunity of seeing, were ill built, narrow, intricate, hilly, & frightfully ill paved & dirty.—But perhaps in the sun shine they may be more commendable: or perhaps, in the sun shine of a happier state of mind, I might have seen them with more favourable Eyes. ¹

From Thursday, 20. July

It was not till past Twelve at Noon that the Diligence set out by which I was to arrive at Aix la Chapelle. I have lost my Memorandum of this part of my expedition; but I well recollect my joy at getting from the jurisdiction of the stormy, nay brutal M. Kauffman; even though I was only going in search of a Vehicle, & moving yet further from Treves. All, however, seemed preferable to being sent back, or kept stationary. A pleasing young female, with a Baby, & a gentle & respectful young man, were all my fellow travellers: They were Belgic, but as they concluded me to be French, they conversed together in English. This at some other time might have amused me; but I was not ¹ then amusable. I spared them, however, any indiscretion, by making known that I understood them. They looked simple, but were very courteous.

At Aix La Chapelle I lost them: for they arrived there to reside; not to travel further.

I now earnestly enquired for a conveyance to Treves: none

¹⁴ The Gothic cathedral of St. Paul in what is now the place Roi-Albert.

existed! nor could I hear of any at all, save a Diligence to Juliers,[15] which was to set out at 4 o'clock the next morning.

To lose thus a whole day, & even then to go only more North, instead of South, almost cast me into despair. But redress there was none! & I was forced to secure myself a place to Juliers, whence, I was told, I might get on.

At any more tranquil period I should have seized this interval for visiting the famous old Cathedral, [1] & the tomb of Charlemagne;[16]—but now, I thought not of them; I did not even recollect that Aix la Chapelle had been the Capital of that Emperor. I merely saw the town through a misty, mizzling rain, & that the road all around it was sandy & heavy—or that all was discoloured by my own disturbed view.

I laid down, in a scarcely furnished apartment, without undressing: but it was summer, & I caught no cold. I suffered no shutter or curtain to be closed, lest I should miss my vehicle: & such was my anxiety, that at Three o'clock, by my own Watch, I descended to enquire if we were not to set off. I wandered about by the twilight of a season that is never quite dark; but met no one. I returned to my Chamber: but, always in terror of being forgotten, I descended [1] again in a quarter of an Hour: though still without success. How dread was the impulse of impatient emotion that could raise a courage so little natural in a character that natively is so retiring & so fearful! but there is nothing—nothing in the World, of danger, difficulty, toil, pain, or enterprize I would not have encountered to have facilitated the meeting I was seeking.

An Hour, says Dr. Johnson, may be tedious, but it cannot be long:[17] 4 o'clock at last struck—& I ran into a vehicle then ready in the Court Yard of the Auberge.

[15] Or Jülich, north-east of Aix-la-Chapelle (or Aachen) and on the road to Trier by way of Bonn.

[16] A reader of history, and lately, for example, of Dewes (L. 890 n. 6), FBA knew that Aix (or Aachen) had been the favourite residence of the great King of the Franks and that, dying there in the year 814, he had been buried in what is now Aachen's cathedral, the Münsterkirche, fully dressed in his imperial regalia. The embellishment of his tomb began in the year 1000, when it was first put on public view, and continued after Charlemagne was declared blessed in 1166. In 1215 the Emperor Frederick II surrounded his sarcophagus with a gilded and ornamented tomb. See Heinrich Benrath, *Aachen, Burtscheid und ihre Umgebung* (Aachen, 1860), pp. 11–14. The opening of the original tomb by successive emperors and the reports of their marvellous findings form part of the Charlemagne legend.

[17] A remark, presumably remembered from the Streatham years 1778–84, when FB spent hours at a time with the lexicographer.

I found myself alone; which at first was a great relief to my mind, that was overburthened with care & apprehension, & glad of utter silence. Ere long, however, I found it fed my Melancholy, which it was my business ı rather to combat; & I was not, therefore, sorry when a poor woman with a Child was admitted from the outside, through the charity of the Coachman, as the rain grew heavier.

How my passport had been regulated I have totally forgotten; but I rather think it was merely directed on to Juliers, & that no Prussian Commandant had taken possession of Aix la Chapelle.

This was Friday, 21st July; The third day of my Journey: & still, from the time I left Liege, I was constantly but lengthening my distance from the Haven of my desires.

At about 10 miles from Aix La Chapelle some more passengers entered the Coach; & the poor woman returned to her more airy seat. The Weather, however, brightened, & the change was not material. ı

Of my new Companions I now made earnest enquiry relative to any route to Triers, expressing my unbounded eagerness to pass over to it by the cross road, if any carriage were obtainable. An elderly, but stout & robust German, who had appeared very ill disposed to every one, sarcastic, severe, & sneering, now suddenly cast off his malignancy, &, as if surprized into benevolence by my visible distress, offered to travel with & protect & direct me himself, if I could procure a vehicle.

Transported, I accepted this offer; but when we stopt, at some place of which I have forgotten the name, to change Horses, & take some refreshment, instead of demanding a chaise de poste, I felt myself assailed by Reflections that forced me to relinquish my design. ı I knew nothing of this man; he might be an adventurer, or something worse, who conceiving my Hand Basket, evidently heavy, to contain Money, or Jewels, or papers on some secret commission, might carry me what Road he pleased, to satisfy his curiosity, or disburthen me of my poor little Trinkets. I therefore thanked him, but declined his offer; & I neither spoke nor listened more till I arrived, at Noon, at Juliers, on Friday, 21st July.

We stopt at a rather large Inn, at the head of an immensely long Market Place. It was nearly, at that moment, empty, except where occupied by straggling Soldiers, poor lame or infirm Labourers, women & children. The universal War of the Continent left scarcely a man unmaimed to be seen, in civil life.

My fellow travellers, whoever they were, had ended their Journey, & repaired to their [1] homes; but while I was impatiently asking for some conveyance to Treves, a serjeant abruptly accosted me, & desired I would forthwith accompany him to the Police office.

Perforce, I obeyed: & here I had precisely the same scene to go through of gross authority & unfeeling harshness as that of Liege: the same peremtory demands of who & what I was; the same insolent contempt of my Passport; the same irascible menaces to send me back for one more recent & satisfactory. The only difference I remember is that the Commandant here seemed aware, by the words *laisser passée Madame d'Arblay, née Burney,* of my Country, for he said 'Vous êtes anglaise?' Hoping to fare better than I had done as being *francaise,* I readily answered 'Oui, Monsieur;—Je suis du paÿs du brave Wellington—' but I instantly saw my mistake, by the deepened scowl [1] that darkened his brow, & which was yet redoubled by my saying I was going to a General Officer who was confined to his Bed merely in consequence of aiding *la Cause commune Pish!*—he disdainfully uttered, in turning on his heel; &, enforcing all his arbitrary objections to letting me proceed, he was pronouncing a positive refusal, & making off from my remonstrances & petitions, when again I saved myself from so deadly a blow by naming General Kleist, & asserting his friendship for my husband. To this he seemed afraid to be deaf, however unwilling to listen; but my dauntless declaration that General Kleist would be extremely hurt if my Journey was impeded forced a signature of which I cannot read the handwriting to my Passport. But he would forward me no further than to Cologn, whither a Carriage was going from Juliers [1] almost immediately. I was fain to acquiesce, & returned to the Inn.

Of Juliers I can give no sort of account, save that it seemed small, but well fortified. The Women who met my Eyes were all fat, with very round & very brown faces. Most of them were bare footed, nay, bare legged, yet had on odd small Caps, very close round their visages. The better sort, I fancy, at that critical time, had hidden themselves, or fled the town.

Of the road & Journey from Juliers to Cologn I have not any memorandum,[18] or remembrance, save that I entered it through an avenue said to be 7 miles in length, of Lime Trees. [1] Though I rather think 'tis the Walls of Cologn, not the Avenue, I had then one only Companion, a woman who was silent & quiet, a German, who left me at least undisturbed to my uneasy reflections.

It was Evening, but very light, & Cologne had a striking appearance, from its general magnitude, & from its profusion of Steeples. It's Walls are 9 miles in circumference. It is one of the most ancient, & I believe largest Cities of Germany, founded by Agrippa[19]—& Rubens was Born in it.[20] But its streets are close built, narrow, & crooked; the houses are so high as to render them, also, dark, These have outside shutters from top to bottom, & Bars of Iron very generally to all the lower Windows. This has always an unpleasant, because a prison sort [1] of look. And I remember that when first I saw the general run of houses so guarded, in Walking through the streets of Calais,[21] I sighed in secret, under the persuasion I was continually passing by places of confinement. It was in the year 1802.

The better sort of houses were white, & looked neat, though in an old fashioned style, & elaborately ornamented. But, between the ravages of time, & of War, the greater part of them seemed crumbling away, if not tumbling down.

The few persons whom I encountered, or saw, looked kind & soft-mannered. I beheld the famed & venerable Cathedral, but without any means to visit or examine it, though the Diligence stopt at a part of its Cloisters;—stopt, or was stopt, I know not which, but while I expected to be driven on to [1] some *Auberge*, a police officer, in a Prussian uniform, came to the Coach door,

[18] This was the road that led from Lindenthal on the west into Cologne, where it became Lindenstrasse and ran to the Neumarkt in the centre of the city. FBA's afterthought in the next sentence may be a recollection of the Ringstrasse, the circular tree-lined boulevard that ran around the line of the city's ancient walls.

[19] Marcus Vipsanius Agrippa (63–12 B.C.), Roman statesman and general, founded the city when he transferred a settlement of the native Ubii from the right to the left bank of the Rhine, that is, to the present site of Cologne. Its Latin name Colonia Claudia Augusta Agrippinensium was given to it in A.D. 50 under the Emperor Claudius (10 B.C.–A.D. 54).

[20] Peter Paul Rubens (1577–1640) was actually born at Siegen in Westphalia but spent part of his childhood in Cologne.

[21] There is no mention of the 'guarded houses' in FBA's description of Calais (v. 228–33), which in 1802 struck her as 'a very clean & pretty Town' with 'an unexpected appearance of quiet order & civility'.

& demanded to look at our Passports. My Companion made herself known as a Native, & was let out directly. The officer, having cast his Eye over my Passport, put his head through the Window of the Carriage, &, in a low whisper, asked me whether I were French?

French, by marriage, though English by birth, I hardly knew which to call myself: I said, however, '*oui*.'

He then, in a voice yet more subdued, gave me to understand that he could serve me. I eagerly caught at his offer, & told him I earnestly desired to go straight to Treves, to a wounded Friend. I never, where I could escape its necessity, said *to my husband*, for the precipitance of my haste & my alarm had made me set out on my expedition in a ¹ mode so unbecoming his then high rank in actual service, that I knew he would never have consented to my scheme, though I was sure his best & tenderest feelings would gratulate its execution when it brought me the more quickly to his side — —

He would do for me what he could, he answered, for he was French himself, though employed by the Prussians.²² He would carry my Passport for me to the Magistrate of the place, & get it signed without my having any further trouble; though only, he feared, to Bonn, or, at farthest, to Coblentz, whence I might probably proceed unmolested. He knew, also, & could recommend me to a most respectable lady & Gentleman, both French, & under the Prussian hard gripe, where I might spend the Evening *en famille*, & be spared entering any *auberge*. ¹

This was delightful to me, after what I had suffered from the Prussian Police officers — — but, was there no imposition? no double dealing?—I was disturbed—but my real & great distress seemed to interest this new Voluntary friend, whose countenance voice & manner were all accordant with pity & good will—& therefore I left the Diligence, & put myself into his hands.

He conducted me, in utter silence, to a house not far distant, passing through the cloisters, & very retired in its appearance. Arrived at a door, at which he knocked, or rang, he still spoke not a word; but when an old man came to open it, in

---

²² The Prussians were busily promulgating and enforcing decrees that extended their control over the Rhineland. See, for example, the *Trierische Zeitung* for 1 June and 24 Aug. 1815.

a shabby dress, but with a good & lively face, he gave him some directions, in German, & in a whisper, & then—entrusted with my Passport, he bowed to me very respectfully, & hurried away.

There was something in this so singular, | that I should have been extremely apprehensive of some latent mischief at any common period: but Now—I had no fear that opposed action: my fears were all occupied mentally! & my whole altered Being was all courage for whatever, at any risk, could forward my Journey to the sole object of my anxiety & my wishes.

The old man, who I found seemed more ancient from his garb than from his speech & movements, led me to a very large room, with a very low ceiling, & very ill fitted up, & scarcely at all furnished. He pulled out of a Niche a sort of ebony arm chair, very tottering & worn, & said he would call Madame, for whom he also placed a *fauteuil*, at the head of an immense thick & clumsy table.

I remained alone about a quarter of an hour, ruminating in much solicitude about my Passport. I was then joined by an elderly Gentlewoman, who was led in, ceremoniously, by | [a] Gentleman still more elderly. The latter made me three profound obeysanses, which I returned with due imitation, while the lady approached me with gentleness, good breeding, & settled dejection, & begged me, by motions, to take my seat.

We all remained some time silent—The old man, then, who I found was their Domestic, served the Tea things.

I know not whether this was their general custom, or a compliment to a stranger. But when we had all taken a cup, they opened into a little conversation. It was I, indeed, who began, by apologising for my intrusion, & expressing, at the same time, my great relief in being spared going to an Auberge, alone as I was, & helpless. But I assured them that the Gentleman who had brought me to their dwelling had acted entirely by his own uninfluenced authority.

They smiled—or rather tried to smile, for melancholy was seated on | their countenances in its most fixed colours, & told me that that person was their best friend, & lost no opportunity to offer them succour or comfort. He had let them know my situation, by *un tel*, (I forget the name) & had desired they would welcome & cheer me. Welcome me, the lady added, in french, they did gladly, since I was in distress; but they had little power to cheer me, involved as they were themselves in the depths of sorrow.

Sympathy of compassion soon led to sympathy of confidence, & when they heard to whom I belonged, & the nature of my terrible haste, they related their own sad history. I recollect it but very imperfectly: I only know Death, Misfortune, & Oppression had all laid on them their Iron hands: they had lost their Sons, while, forcibly, fighting for a Usurpation which they abhorred; ¹ they had lost their property by emigration; & they had been treated with equal hardness by the Revolutionists because they were suspected of loyalty, & by the Royalists because their Children had served in the armies of the Revolutionist. They were now living nearly in penury, & owed their safety & peace solely to the protection of the officer who had brought me to them, who was French by birth, & French in heart & spirit, but who had served in Prussia & in Germany from his boyhood, & knew their languages as well as his own, & who was employed by both, as occasion offered, like a Native: but he seemed, they said, to covet occupation from them with no other view than that of acquiring means to serve his own unfortunate countrymen, to whom, wherever he resided, he always proved a blessing. And while ¹ to him they owed the peace of personal security, they owed all else they possessed of ease, comfort, & enjoyment to their excellent old Domestic, who served them for nothing but his board & dress, making mere offal suffice to his generous parsimony in the first, & contented with tattered garments that were nearly rags in the second: yet actively & effectively performing for them the offices of Butler, Footman, Cook, Housemaid, Valet & Femme de Chambre; & all with as much skill as zeal, for no soul shared his pains in any of these capacities.

With communications such as these reciprocated, time passed so little heavily, however sadly, that we were ill disposed to separate: & Eleven o'clock struck, as we sat over their œconomical, but well served & well cooked little supper, ere the idea of retiring was mentioned. They then begged me to go to rest, as I must be at the Diligence for ¹ Coblentz by 4 o'clock the next Morning

I was now, however, so extremely uneasy about my Passport that rest was out of all question: yet when I expressed my fears, my Host & Hostess, & their good Domestic, always in waiting, joined earnestly to assure me it was in most safe & honourable hands, & that I had nothing to apprehend. I entreated them, nevertheless, still to let me sit up & watch, but by no means to remain themselves. They would not listen to me; my encreasing apprehensions affected their kind hearts, & they stayed to encourage & to console me.

Midnight at length sounded—& no passport. I was now quite wretched, in the belief it would not arrive till next Day, when the Diligence would be gone, that would pass this way no more till the following Week. In expounding the cause of my exceeding pressure I touched them all, & the good Domestic, who was seated at the side board, suddenly came into the midst of ¹ us, & declared he would go in search of it, rather than see *Madame* suffer so, though it would be nearly to the further end of this long City.

I was in too dreadful affright to resist this humane proposal, & my kind Host consented. In misery quite irrepressible I spent the half hour of his absence; but his return brought me back to life & hope, for the admirable officer had secured my passport, without my personal attendance, & lodged it safely himself with the Book Keeper at the Auberge, & a charge to deliver it to this same good Domestic. It was only to Bonn; but he had written himself a note which would enable me to have it prolonged for Coblentz, without further difficulty. This he had given to the Coachman. It was all he could do, as at Coblentz he had no power or influence.²³

Delighted by this intelligence, I now agreed to go to my room, parting with my interesting & respectable Host & Hostess in loading them with ¹ acknowledgments, & in a warm interchange of good wishes.

To another large room, nearly empty except by the old high & narrow Bed, the Domestic now conducted me, promising

---

²³ After the victories of the *Befreiungskrieg* against Napoleon, and as compensation for great sacrifices, Prussia from 1803 until 1815 was allowed great parts of the Rhineland, including the cities and districts of Cologne, Aix-la-Chapelle, Düsseldorf, Coblenz, and Trèves—all of which were added to the old Prussian holdings of Cleve and Wesel. But the Prussians generally preserved the administrative divisions of the past, including the restrictions on the authority of the police referred to here.

to call me at half past 3 o'clock in the morning, & to attend me to the Diligence.

I did not dare undress; I tied my Watch, which was a small Repeater, round my wrist, & laid down in my cloaths, — — but to strike my Watch, & to pray for my beloved Invalid, & my safe restoration to him, filled up, without, I believe, 3 minutes of repose, the interval to my Conductor's return.

At half past 3 we set out—after I had safely deposited all I durst spare where my disinterested, but most poor Host would inevitably find my little offering, which if presented to him, he would probably have refused. I never heard his Name, which he seemed studious to hold back; ¹ but I have reason to think he was of the ancient provincial Noblesse—His manners, & those of his Wife, had an antique etiquette in them that can only accord with that idea.

The Walk was immensely long; it was through the scraggy & hilly streets I have mentioned, & I really thought it endless. The good Domestic carried my luggage. The height of the houses made the light merely not darkness; we met not a soul; &, the painful pavement, & Barred Windows, & fear of being too late, made the Walk still more dreary, lonely, & dread.

I was but just in time: the Diligence was already drawn out of the Inn yard, & some friends of some of the passengers were taking leave of one another. I eagerly secured my place;—& never so much regretted the paucity of my purse as in my inability to recompense as I wished the excellent Domestic whom I now quitted. ¹

I found myself now in much better society than I had yet been, consisting of two Gentlemen, evidently of good education, & a well bred lady, They were all German, & spoke only that language to one another, though they occasionally addressed me in French; by occasionally, I mean as often as my own absorption in my own ruminations gave any opening for their civility.

And this was soon the case, by my hearing them speak of the Rhine; my thoughts were so little Geographical that it had not occurred to me that Cologne was upon that River; I had not, therefore, looked for or perceived it the preceding Evening: but upon my now starting at the sound of its Name, & expressing my strong curiosity to behold it, they all began to watch for the first point upon which it became clearly visible, ׀ and all Five with one voice called out, presently after, '*Ah, la Voilà!*'

I bent towards the Coach Window, & they all most obligingly facilitated my sight. But Imagination had raised expectations that the Rhine, at this part of its stream, could by no means answer. It seemed neither so wide, nor so deep, nor so rapid, nor so grand as my mind had depicted it; nor yet were its Waters so white or so bright as to suit my ideas of its fame. Had I viewed it at [*blank*] where you, my dear Alexander, were so charmed with it,[24] I doubt not but it would have met all my notions of its celebrity.

Arrived at Bonn, the Garde, or directeur, called, I think, le Conducteur, took all the charge of my Passport, according to the promise of my French-Prussian. Bonn is a Fortress, & the residence of the ׀ *ci-devant* Prince Bishop of Cologne.[25] The Palace is said to be a quarter of a mile in length. How modest & moderate are the Palaces of England compared with those of even the minor Potentates of the Continent. I saw it not, however; I had not even any desire for the sight, nor for any other. We stopt at the Post office. The house was quite magnificent. But I only entered the Breakfast room, where I had the pain of hearing that we should remain at Bonn two Hours. My fellow travellers, gay & social, ordered a festive repast: I was so fearful of wasting any of my small remaining cash that I only took a Roll & a Dish of Coffee, at a table to which I stood, & then said I would wile away the time by walking in the Garden.

The Garden was of a tolerable size, & really pretty; but some Company from this vast Inn soon broke in upon my solitude, & I therefore stole off, resolving to take a view of the Town— ׀

I went out by a large Iron Gate, but could not venture to ask for a Guide, in a poverty where every shilling became important. The street was entirely without mark or interest, & nearly

---

[24] Perhaps at the *Rheinfall bei Schaffhausen* during AA's visit to Switzerland in 1821.

[25] Bonn had been fortified during the sixteenth and seventeenth centuries, and the baroque palace of the prince-bishop had been constructed from 1717 until 1730, in part from stone taken from the fortifications. Its façade was then 580 metres long.

without any inhabitants that were visible. The late absorbing War made that the case in every town I passed through. I walked strait on, till I came to a large market place.[26] It seemed to me, after the narrow & dim & empty street, very gay, busy, populous & alive. I think it was a sort of Fair.[27] As I saw numerous avenues to it, I stopt at the corner, to fix myself some mark for finding again my way back. And this was not difficult; for I soon observed an 'Unhappy Divinity stuck in a Nich';[28] & one as ludicrous as any mentioned [1] in her passage through Germany by Lady Mary Wortley Montagu.[29] It was a short, thick, squabby little personage, whose Wig, Hose, Sandals, Coat, Waistcoat, & trowsers were of all the colours—save those of the Rainbow—for, far from having the bright hues of that 'Radiant token,' the gaudy, but most dingy, muddy & vulgar full Blues, Reds, & yellows of each part of the Dress, & of the figure, seemed struggling with each other for which should be most obstrusively prominent—not graduating off into shades of evanescent softness. The Wig, I think, was blue; the Coat, Red; the Waistcoat, Yellow; the Sandals Green; the Trowsers, purple, & the Hose, pink. I am not certain, at this distance of time, that I give the right colours to their right places; I am only sure that the separate parts of the dress employed, separately, those colours, [1] and that what rendered them almost as prophane as they were risible, were some symbols—either of Golden rays round the Wig, or of a Crucifix at the back, shewed that this hideous little Statue was meant for a young Jesus.[30]

[26] The Posthaus, a fine eighteenth-century building in the Markt-Platz. See map in Joseph Dietz, *Topographie der Stadt Bonn vom Mittelalter bis zum Ende der kurfürstlichen Zeit* (Bonn, 1962–3).

[27] The Münster-Platz.

[28] Unidentified quotation.

[29] A reference to the gaudy statues commented on during her travels through Germany. See, for example, her description of one seen in a Catholic church in Nuremberg: 'not to be quite destitute of all finery, they have dress'd up an Image of our Saviour over the Altar in a fair full bottom'd wig very well powder'd'. See letter of 22 Aug. [1716] O.S. in *The Complete Letters of Lady Mary Wortley Montagu*, ed. Robert Halsband (Oxford, 3 vols., 1967), i. 253–4.

[30] What FBA saw was not in fact a statue of the Christ-child but rather a crude allegorical representation of the rainbow. This statue was placed in a niche on the wall of the house known by that name ('zum Regenbogen'), which stood at Sternstrasse 7 (No. 179 in the old system of numbering).

This has been explained in a letter to the editor from the Stadtarchiv und Wissenschaftliche Stadtbibliothek Bonn (10 May 1976): 'Die beschriebenen Kleidungsstücke "wig, waistcoat" etc sowie die geschmaklose figürliche als auch farbliche Gestaltung widersprechen zudem völlig den sonst üblichen Attributen bei

I now strolled about the vast market-place without fear of being lost. I observed, however, little besides Cattle, Toys, vegetables, crockary ware & cakes. There were Forms innumerable, & almost all covered by seated women, very clean & tidy, with profusion of odd shaped white caps, but not one of them with a hat. At other parts, there might perhaps be other merchandize. The whole was eminently orderly. Nothing like a quarrel, a dispute, or even any grouping for Gossipping. This is not, I imagine, a general picture of a German market-place; ¹ for Now could be general, as nothing was natural. The issue of the War, still to All uncertain, while the Army on the Loire, & the Corps of Grouchy had not submitted, appeared to all the common Inhabitants in the vicinity of France to await but some private project of Buonaparte for ending in his triumph. In all the few places I visited at this period I found this belief predominant, or, rather, Universal; & that alike from the fears of his foes, & the hopes of his Adherents. Constraint, therefore, as well as consternation operated, as if by mute consent, in keeping all things, & all persons, tame, taciturn, & secretly expectant.

When I had taken a general survey of all that was within sight without venturing from the sides of the houses amongst the people, I looked for my Guide in the Nich, & returned to the Inn. There I heard that, from some Cause I could not ¹ comprehend, the Diligence was still to remain two Hours longer. Unable to order any refreshment, I could not bring myself to enter any room for waiting so long a time. Again, therefore, I strolled out; &, having now seen all that led to the Right, I turned to the Left. I walked to the end of the street, without finding any thing to observe but common houses, without novelty, interest, or national peculiarity of any sort, & differing only from ours by having fewer windows, less regularity, & less chearfulness of aspect. In strolling leisurely back, I remarked, at the termination of a sort of lane, or outlet, some-

Darstellung des Christuskindes. Demnach sind die "golden rays around the wig" m. E. nicht als Heiligenschein zu interpretieren, sondern als Sonnenstrahlen, durch deren Lichtbrechung der Regenbogen in seinen typischen Farben für uns sichtbar wird.' ('The clothing described ... as well as the tasteless appearance and colouring of the representation contradict utterly the usual attributes of the infant Jesus. The "golden rays around the wig" are therefore not to be interpreted as a halo, but as the sunbeams that through reflection make the rainbow appear to us in its typical colours.')

thing that looked like Ruins.[31] I eagerly advanced towards them, & found myself on the skirts of a plain over laid with the devastations of half consumed & still crumbling fortifications. I mounted some old ǀ broken steps, protuberating here & there through masses of dust, mortar, & heaped old half-burnt bricks; but the view that presented itself was only terrible, from shewing the havock of War, without including any remains that were noble, elegant, or curious in architecture, or that mixed any emotions of admiration with those of compassion that necessarily are awakened by the sight of dilapidations, whether owing to the hostility of Time or of War.

When I had remained here till I was tired of my own meditations rather than investigation, for there was nothing to investigate, I descended my steps, to return to the Inn. But I then perceived two narrow streets, or lanes, so exactly resembling each other, that I could not discern any difference that might lead me to ascertain ǀ by which I had arrived: & I had turned in so many directions while surveying the Ruins, that, not having noticed a second street[32] before I mounted them, I now knew not which way to turn.

Startled, I resolved to hasten down one of them at a venture, & then, if that should fail, to try the other.

This I did, & found myself in a long street, that might well be that which I sought, but I could espie in it no jutting Iron Gate: I therefore hurried back, & made the same experiment down the other lane. This, however, led me on to some other street that I was sure I had not seen.

With yet greater speed I regained my Ruins: but here a new difficulty arose. I saw a third strait passage, which had no more mark or ǀ likelihood than the two first. It might be, nevertheless, that this which had escaped me, was the Right; & I essayed it directly. The same failure ensued, & I remounted it.

Vainly I looked around me for help—Dirty & ragged little Children, of the lowest class, were playing about, & chattering in German, but, though I attempted to speak to them repeatedly, they could not understand a word I uttered, & ran, some laughing, others frightened, away.

---

[31] FBA's directions suggest that these may have been the ruins of the barracks at the Sternenthor, on the western side of Bonn. See Gebhard Aders, *Bonn als Festung* . . . (Bonn, 1973), pp. 127–30.
[32] Running between the ruins at Sternenthor and the Viehmarkt.

Yet these poor little ones were all I met with in these lanes; which, as they lead only to a barren plain over run with Ruins, were unfrequented.

I was now dreadfully alarmed, lest I should miss the Diligence: & I speeded again to the long street in search ⟨ of any one who could give me some succour.

I espied a good looking man, who was lame, at some distance. I was with him in an instant, & entreated him to direct me to the Hotel de la Diligence.

He seemed good naturedly sorry for the great perturbation in which I spoke, but shook his head, & shrugged his shoulders, in sign that he could not understand me.

I then saw a poor Woman—& made the same request; but with equal ill success.

Next I saw a Boy—the same story!—Then a Beggar—still the same!

From side to side, strait-forward & retrograding, I ran up to every soul I saw—speaking first in French, next in English, but meeting only with the lowest & most common Germans, ⟨ who, like all other common Natives know only their vernacular tongue.

I could now only resolve to return to my Ruins, & in making them my rallying point, to start from them, & back again, till I had perambulated every street whatsoever that was in their neighbourhood.

But oh good Heaven! what now was my consternation! I had started up & down in so desultory & precipitate a manner that I could no longer find my way back to the Ruins! I had wandered, I have no knowledge how, from their immediate vicinity, & could not discover any one of the 3 avenues by which I had reached them. Turn which way I would, I met no possible informant; all the Men were in the various Armies; the higher sort of Women were ⟨ fled from Bonn, or remained in their houses; & the lower sort were all, with the whole of the general population, in the market-place. At least so it was in the streets I patrolled, for nothing did I behold but the maimed, or Beggars, or Children. Most of those above probably would have known a few words of French. And some of these poor souls, when I addressed them, seemed very kindly concerned at my evident distress; yet with a calm, a composure that was wide from even striving to devize means for understanding or aiding me: & their enquiries, in their own dialect, were so insupportably slow & placid, that the moment I found my French not intelligible to them, I flew from their speech as I would have fled from pestilence. ᴵ

If I should be too late for the Diligence, I too well knew not another would pass for a Week: & even if I could here meet with a separate conveyance, the tales now hourly recounted of marauders, straggling Pillagers, & military Banditti, with the immense Forests, & unknown roads through which I must pass, made me tremble —— as I now do, even now, 9 years after—at looking back to my position at this fearful moment.

Oh! this was, indeed, nearly, the most tortured crisis of misery I ever experienced! one only has been yet more terrible! —nay, a thousand & ten thousand—ten million of times more terrible, because—Alas! irretrievable! This, however, was a herald to my affrighted soul of what the other inflicted—To know my Heart's ᴵ Partner wounded—ill—confined—attended only by strangers;—to know, also, that if here detained, I could receive no news of him; for the Diligence in which I travelled was the Mail:—to know the dread anxiety, & astonishment that would consume his peace, & corrode all means of recovery, when Day succeeding Day neither brought me to his side, nor yet produced any tidings why I was absent— Oh gracious Heaven! in what a distracting state was my Soul!—In a strange Country—without Money, without a Servant—without a Friend—& without Language! Oh never— never shall I forget my almost frantic agony! Neither can I ever lose the remembrance of the sudden transport by which it was succeeded when, in pacing wildly to & fro', I was suddenly struck by the sight I have already ᴵ described of the Unhappy Divinity stuck in a Nic[he.]

What rapture at that moment took place of anguish little short of Despair!—I now knew my way, & was at the Hotel with a swiftness resembling flight. And There—what a confirmation I received of the timely blessing of my arrival, when I saw that the Coach was just departing! The Horses harnessed, every passenger entered, & the Drivers with their whips in hand extended!—Oh my God! what an escape! & what thankful Joy & Gratitude I experienced!

Now then, at last, my heart became better tuned. A terror so dreadful averted, just when so near its consummation, opened me to feelings akin to happiness. I was now on my right road; no longer travelling Zig Zag, & as I could procure any means to get on, but in the strait road, by Coblentz, to the City which contained the Object of all my best ¹ hopes—solicitude—& impatience.

And Now it was that my Eyes opened to the beauties of Nature;³³ now it was that the far famed Rhine found justice in these poor little Eyes, which, hitherto, from mental pre-occupation, or from Expectations too high raised, had refused a cordial tribute to its eminent merit; unless, indeed, its Banks, till after Bonn, are of inferiour loveliness. Certain it is, that from this time, till my arrival at Coblentz I thought myself in Regions of enchantment.

The Rhine from hence flows so continually through lofty Mountains, & winds in such endless varieties, that it frequently appears to be terminating in a Lake; & those who sail upon it must often believe themselves inevitably destined to land, as the turnings are so rounded, that no prolongation of the River is apparent. And scarcely is there a ¹ Reach that does not exhibit some freshly charming View. Mountains, Towers, Castles, Fortifications half demolished; interspersed with Trees, Hills, valleys, plains, elevations covered with vineyards, thick Woods of Lime Trees, country seats, new plantations, & pictoresque villages. The Houses were highly ornamental to the prospect, being mostly white, covered with blue slate; looking brilliant, however diminutive, because saved from all soil by the purity of the surrounding air.

At first, we had constantly *The Seven Mountains*³⁴ to form a noble repose for our Eyes as the boundary of the principal prospect: afterwards, we passed through such stupendous mountains on each side, that the Rhine & its Banks, which constituted our Road, made the whole of the valley; while stately ¹ Rocks, of striking forms, & hanging woods, of exquisite beauty, invited, on one side, our gaze & admiration; & prospects eternally diversifying varied our delighted atten-

³³ This impression of the Rhine is especially strong between Unkel and Andernach and during the last ten kilometres of FBA's journey to Coblenz.
³⁴ The famous peaks, including the Drachenfels, between Königswinter and Honnef on the right bank of the Rhine.

tion on the other. Now, mounting some steep ascent, we saw this fine River winding perpendicularly beneath us; now descending again, the Rocks & Woods again seemed to embower us. Almost every eminence was crowned with an ancient Castle or Fortress, whose falling Turrets & scattered fragments, moss grown, & widely spread around, gave as much interest & as great a charm to the scene, as they caused, on the other hand, sorrow, resentment: & even horror to the reflections: for these Ruins were not the indispensable effect of all conquering, irresistible Time, to which we All bow, or, rather, are bowed down, but of wanton, aggressive, invading War, & of ┃ insatiable ambition.

I am assured that this charming River becomes yet finer after Coblentz: & I am aware that whoever has visited the Alps & the Apenines will call my lofty Mountains little Hills: However — — I write only for Thee, my dear Alex—& all I say is True: though, had I proceeded farther, I might have saved some of my terms for an enchantment yet greater — — for—

What can we Reason but from what we know?[35]

Absorbed as I was within by my own fearful ruminations, & occupied as I was without by my enraptured view of Nature's prodigies of perfection, nothing else of my passage from Bonn to Coblentz remains in my memory, save our being abruptly joined on the way ┃ by a stranger whose air & appearance could not pass unnoticed.

He was on foot, & alone, but he hailed the Coachman with a voice of authority that gave him immediate admission to our Vehicle. His luggage, I imagine, had been sent on before, or was to follow, as he was wholly unincumbered, & remarkably well equipped. He was a fine looking man, hale, florid, embellished with the *embonpoint* of health, & the sprightly Eyes of high animal spirits. He was in the prime of life, & seemed in that of Fortune, prosperity, courage for any enterprize, & a sense of pleasure for any enjoyment. I soon discovered that he was English. And I doubt not that the discovery was as soon reciprocated, for he gave me—though I was far the *least, youthful* personage of the party, ┃ by far the greatest portion of his

[35] Pope's *An Essay of Man*, Ep. i. 17.

attention & discourse, mingling it with courtesies the most distinguishing, &, whenever I spoke—which indeed was never but by necessity—with looks of investigation that seemed earnest to develop whom or what I might be. Where Natives meet unexpectedly in a foreign Country an interest is almost always excited, even though the same place of Nativity is its exclusive spur:

He was going to Switzerland, &, I fancy, upon some important project.

At Dinner—I forget where—he did the honours of the table; & did them most handsomely; calling for whatever was best & most costly, & claiming, from that reason, the right of paying the *Aubergiste*. This was smiled at, but not disputed, by the company,—till it came to my turn, | when, though sorry to mortify his magnificent spirit, I positively insisted upon being my own purveyor. He was evidently much disappointed; but too much a Man of the World, & a Gentleman, to be officiously pertinacious. How much more would his spirited nature have been hurt, had he known that, by aggravating thus undesignedly my Charges, he reduced me, as we quitted this Dinner-auberge, to less than my last Napoleon!—And truly it is astonishing that I had proceeded already thus far, without having been reduced to present & to pledge my dear—& yet sacred Gold Repeater! But travelling here was remarkably cheap, & I was penuriously circumspect in avoiding all extra-expences. |

We did not reach Coblentz till past 10 o'clock at night. The Weather, for the last 2 or 3 Hours, had entirely changed. The sky was overcharged with black Clouds; a misty Rain ensued; all our prospects were intercepted, & the spirit & pleasure of the day's Journey was compleatly finished.

I became myself so comfortless, so filled with apprehensions how I might fare in my moneyless state, & what perplexities might again await me concerning my Passport, that I no longer saw or knew any thing of my companions: I merely have a general idea that the English man who had joined us last was claimed instantly by some expectant Friends. At all events, he alone came not, like the rest, to the Warehouse of the Book-Keeper, as he had no luggage. I was sorry he was gone; for I felt convinced that, should any | pecuniary disturbance ensue, he would have sprung forward to offer me assistance—which, in that case, I should thankfully have accepted, in making known my name, & demanding his, for restitution.

My other comrades adjusted their business, one by one, with the Book-Keeper; & I found they were all at the end of their journey, while I stood aloof, close to my small luggage, & almost over powered by my fears of what might follow.

Each of the passengers addressed me with leave-taking civility in departing. I could only return a little bow of the head. I had no voice at command.

When, however, all were gone, & some Waiter, taking up my baggage, asked where I would have it carried, I called all my faculties to order, and advanced ǀ with all the firmness I could assume, to the Book-Keeper, to enquire for the first & swiftest conveyance to Treves.

A Diligence was to set off the next morning, by 4 o'clock.

I desired him to secure me a place.

He asked me for my passport.

I produced it; begging that, without delay, I might go on.

It was too late, he answered, to get me a place for the next Diligence, as my passport must be twice visited[36] before I could proceed.

When, then, may I set out?

Not till that day Week, all the Diligences in that part of the World travelling only once a Week at that time.

In an agony I could not express, I besought him to tell me to whom I could apply for permission to continue my route the next morning. ǀ To the usual Town police, he replied, & to the new Prussian authorities.

I entreated him to send some one to him with my passport & request.

Impossible! he cried; no business could be done so late, & he durst not make the application.

At what hour might they be broken in upon in the morning?

Certainly not in time to save the Diligence.

O give me, then, I cried, a Guide, & let me go to them directly myself.

The Book-Keeper was a German, but both spoke & understood French assured me I should not be admitted, as the old

---

[36] FBA here wrote 'visited' for 'visaed'.

officers, who were only here because too infirm to join the Army, would be gone to Bed; & the young ones, who only remained because not yet of an Age to serve, were power-less.

I was now in such misery that the Book-Keeper, whose countenance I was natively benevolent, looked full of concern. I then told him that procrastination was destruction to me, & implored his compassionate succour. He feared, he said, all attempt would be vain to induce the authorities to act, or even see me, so late at night when they were probably gone to rest; but if I wished to make the experiment, & could bear the Rain & the dark, & the bad walking, he could not refuse me a Guide to the Police office.

It was not with dry Eyes I could thank him, & he sent for a youth who was intelligent, he said, & well brought up.

A Boy who seemed about 13 or 14 years of Age then was summoned. He was yawning, &, I fancy, was, at least, pre-paring for Bed: but he was very civil & good-humoured, & I made acquaintance with him I very briskly.

The Night was the most gloomy; a small but continual mist damped, without absolutely wetting my apparel, & made the ill-paved & ill lighted streets through which we passed, slippery, darksome, & dangerous. The Town seemed all gone to repose, or all empty, & never had I taken a walk so lonely & so dreary:[37] yet with what alacrity was it made, what buoyant hope from the result!

Arrived at the office, all was shut up. We knocked gently & fearfully. But without notice. Again, then, more boldly, we repeated the charge. Still in vain! I then re-iterated the attempt with the loudness of desperation.

The Door now opened, & an ill favoured man, more asleep than awake, appeared at it.

But no sooner had I put forth my paper, & named my Passport, than he rudely shut the door in my face, I drawing back without uttering a Word.

Horror struck—the waning night darkling before me—& the fatal delay menacing a Week's durance in this distant—unknown—unfriending—City—I scarcely kept my feet; I

[37] FBA seems to have crossed Coblenz from east to west, from Clemensplatz to the police office in Löhrstrasse.

tottered, & held by something, I know not what, that I caught at in the Portico.

The good Boy, whom my kind Book-Keeper had chosen from his knowledge of French, bid me *ne rien craindre*, but offer the Porter a *franc* or two; & then he knocked again.

This ceremony was again twice repeated before it succeeded. The surly porter then re-appeared, convinced that I was determined, at least, not to be dismissed unheard.

He was beginning, in a voice of brutality, to order me off, when, urged again by my sensible young Interpreter, I slipt 2 francs into his hands, while the Boy said I wanted only a signature ⎸ to my passport.

He grumbled, but took the passport, & went off with it — — But — — he shut us out, in the Street, & in the Rain, while he repaired to his masters!

He returned in about 10 minutes, & told the Guide, in gruff German, that it was too late to come upon business, & that if it were earlier, the police now signed nothing, & passed nothing, without the previous authorisation of the Prussian Command-ant.

I took my rejected passport, & begged my conductor to lead me instantly to the dwelling of the Commandant.

He chearfully complied, being now not only wide awake from sleep, but really wide awake to a desire to aid me in a distress he began to pity, without waiting to comprehend.

Another dismal walk, through Rain, mud, dirt, & sharp pointed stones, brought us to the Prussian Guard house. ⎸

It was at least clear that no apprehension existed here of revolt or mischief, for all was shut up, & I observed not a sentinel.

We knocked—The Door was speedily opened, & by a smart young officer in full uniform.

I advanced, & eagerly told him I had brought a passport—

He interrupted me, but in a voice & manner perfectly polite, & said I must trouble myself to come again in the MORNING, as no business was transacted so late.

I rapidly told him that I was travelling on an affair of life & death; that to lose to night would lose me a Week, & that I demanded & supplicated an immediate signature.

He instantly invited me into a large apartment; &, quickly

comprehending my sad necessity, sent up a messenger to the Commandant with my petition, remaining himself in conversation with me, & proving ¹ amiable, obliging, & humane. I was glad to see such a Prussian, after samples so different as I had encountered of his Nation.

A rough answer, harshly conveyed by its messenger, came from the Commandant, to desire I would be gone, & return at a more proper hour.

I now, as briefly as I could, in so disturbed a state, poured forth my whole story to my attentive young officer, told my Name, & my Husband's Rank, & that I was travelling through every difficulty & obstacle to arrive at him with speed, as he was confined to his Bed by a Wound & a fever, at Triers, where he had been detained by this accident while on a mission from his KING, Louis 18.

The officer, without staying to answer me, brought a *fauteuil* for my accommodation, & taking my passport, ran up stairs to plead for me. ¹

How I trembled during his absence! It was not short—but his re-entrance was triumphant. He held forth to me the Passport with an extended arm, & an air of exulting congratulation, & told me he had prevailed on M. le Commandant to grant my request.

I thanked him with rapture, though mingled with acute apprehensions of obtaining a similar favour from the German Police.

My truly admirable new young Friend hastily flew out of the Room, & came back with his Hat & cane, &, offering me *le bras*, said he would accompany me himself, & force me an entrance.

What goodness! what benevolence of heart!—We were not a moment in arriving, his youth & my eagerness giving Wings to our feet. The Porter let us in, & shewed us to [a] large apartment; but said his Master was in Bed.

My young officer sent up stairs to him ¹ in his own name.

A kind of House-Keeper descended, & said her Master was sound asleep, & that he was infirm & unwell, & she did not dare awaken him.

My terror & despair now so touched my new Friend, that he darted up stairs himself, & I heard him rap at the door, & call out aloud in German.

Involuntarily & irresistably I followed; the Housekeeper, a quaint, muffled up old German, keeping, all amazed, by my side.

The officer whispered me that the Master must either pretend to be asleep, in order to avoid rising, or be as deaf as a post.

Encouraged by this sally, I ventured to rap at the door myself, calling out that I came from an intimate friend of General Kleist.

I had no sooner pronounced this name, than my new associate, giving me, gaily, a nod, siezed my passport, &, opening the door without waiting for leave, carried it to the Bed side, & called ¹ out aloud General Kleist. — —

Immediate permission was given for carrying a pen & Ink to the Bed side, & again, in a few minutes, my benevolent new friend came to me with his triumphant success.

I blest him! though I could hardly speak—but he saw that he had blest me, & I doubt not but he left me with feelings nearly as pleased as my own.

My good Boy guided me to the Auberge, heartily partaking, also, in the relief—the even gaiety he now witnessed succeeding to a state so forlorn.

It was not till I re-entered the Warehouse that I recollected having a difficulty remaining—but suddenly, then, flashed back upon me my nearly pennyless state. With what fear & inward anguish did I approach the Book-Keeper, lest again I should be retarded! I thanked him most ¹ gratefully for his assistance, & paying my good-humoured Guide, I desired to have my place secured for Treves: but, laying upon the Desk my last half Napoleon, I acknowledged my Cash to be exhausted, & related the abruptness & haste of my quitting Brussels, without power to meet with M. De Noots, my Banker: & then, saying I was going to General d'Arblay, who was acting in concord with General Kleist, I put down my Gold Repeater, & entreated to be trusted for redeeming it as soon as I arrived at Treves; but implored him not to impede my saving the morning's Diligence, as such a delay would break my heart.

Never can I forget the benevolent look of my Book-Keeper, while, calmly & silently, but instantly, he entered my ¹ Name for a place from Coblentz to Treves; nor the kind countenance with which he gave me back my Watch, & refused even my demi Napoleon, as I might need it on my way. And, while I was pouring forth my acknowledgements, he added that he would take care himself, as the Diligence would be once more changed, & I must sleep upon the road, that the Coachman should make no demand upon me till my arrival at Triers.

Excellent, feeling, benignant German! What amends did this make me for the austerity by which I had nearly been blasted in my perilous route!

In leaving him I seemed in Heaven![38] |

Soon after 4 o'clock the next morning, [23] July, I had the joy of mounting my vehicle. The little I saw of Coblentz in quitting it had quite a new air; it looked clean, neat & white. Whether the part through which we drove was really of another cast than what I had so painfully patrolled the preceding Evening; or whether the Night & the Rain had given a dreary & murky semblance that was only passingly disadvantageous; or whether new hopes & new views rising with a new sun painted all in fresher, gayer, more pleasing colours, I cannot now tell: but my nocturnal & my matinal memory are widely different with regard to Coblentz. I had not time— & far less had I any disposition—to visit the City; but the immense Castle, with Fort above Fort, on a high Rock, is a noble object,[39] which I caught a | view of merely by a Glance through some opening as we drove away. Nor did I see, till the morning that Coblentz is situated on the confluence of the Rhine with the Mozelle.

From Coblentz to Treves I was 2 Days travelling,[40] though it might with ease have been accomplished in less than half that time. But from Sunday [23] July at 4 o'clock in the morning, till late on Monday Evening, I was kept in a convulsive agony of fruitless impatience by the cruel slowness of our proceeding: not through the sluggish motion of the Horses, but through the unconscionable length of time bestowed upon *les auberges*.[41]

We no longer journied in any Diligence that may be com-

[38] FBA left Coblenz on the morning of 23 July (see Memorandum, p. 553).
[39] The fortress of Ehrenbreitstein across the Rhine from Coblenz.
[40] The distance by the winding road FBA followed along the Moselle was roughly 190 kilometres.
[41] Later travellers along the Moselle were struck by these same delays and by the slow service at the inns. See Octavius Rooke, *The Life of the Moselle* (1858), pp. 148–9.

pared with one of France or of England, but in a true & queer German carriage, ¹ resembling something mixed of coach, a chaise, & a cart. My passengers were only a young man & young woman, both German, & speaking no other language. They are civil, modest, & well behaved, apparently not yet Man & Wife, but on the open road so to become.

Where we dined I know not. The Postilions like the passengers were German, & I could gain no information. I had time now to regret that I had not studied that language when opportunity was given, & aid offered me, during my abode in The Queen's Establishment—where Her Majesty, to encourage me, deigned herself to write out for me the German alphabet, in large Characters & in small.⁴² I have always with gratitude & deep respect preserved the little document & it is not here I shall dilate upon the circumstances that withheld me from availing my self of this goodness of my Royal Mistress. ¹

We stopt for the *Night*, to my great misery, in the middle of the *afternoon* Oh what I suffered from such harrasing detention, where I could make no remonstrance, nor request any reason for such lethargic slowth!

The Name of the place I know not; it was a small wet Village, comfortless, dirty, &, save of women & children, un-inhabited.

A young Prussian officer seemed to have the superintendence & command at the House at which we stopt. He spoke French well, & was intelligent & civil. Eager for information himself, in the then precarious state of things, from any body who arrived from Coblentz, he was politely communicative in return. The Conversation this occasioned between us a little lightened my tedious sojourn—which was of Ten endless Hours on this uninteresting spot, in a ¹ mansion extremely ancient, but ill built, dilapidated, large, straggling, & weather beaten, & to which every Avenue, & every sort of approach was all mud & filth, in the middle of July!

I was so truly wretched at such procrastination, that I should surely have gone on on foot, had I known my way, or been able to demand it as I went along.

I can give no further details—the rest of this day, & all of Monday, my perturbation was so extreme from the un-

⁴² In the hand based upon *Frakturschrift* or German type.

certainty of my fate—from torturing Anxiety, quickened rather than mitigated by the most exquisite sensations of trembling Hope —— Ah—those who assert that with added years are coupled blunted feelings, can never have been called to the proof by such a Husband—& such a Friend as General d'Arblay & Susanna Phillips!—43 For common & current things, & for ¹ passing & ordinary attachments, the assertion may be just: indeed, I am conscious of its truth myself: but for sympathies such as Those two almost perfect Beings could inspire there can be no extinction but with Memory.—concentrated Recollections—acute regrets and fervant Aspirations Live unremittingly in the Breast of which they have taken possession.

One general remembrance alone occurs to my unobservant passage on my route for these two last days; namely, that my Eyes, though almost mechanically, were unavoidably struck by the beauty of the Moselle, & its Banks & prospects; & that my mind was frequently & revoltingly moved by the view, at every place where we stopt, whether for repast or for Horses, by the oppressive brutality with which the Prussian subaltern officers behaved to the poor subdued Inhabitants; ¹ swearing, storming, throwing about, with wanton violence, every thing they did not want, &, siezing without mercy every thing that was to their taste. Though this part of the country was not a prey to Victory, as there had been no army, or force there for attempting resistance, the Prussians, or others, who took possession of it, for safety to the advanced troops of the allied Army, treated all the Dwellers of the Land as a Conquered people.—

[TRÈVES]

At Treves, at length, on Monday Evening, the 24ᵗʰ of July, 1815, I arrived: after travelling one whole Night, & from 3 o'clock one morning, & from 4 o'clock 4 other mornings.

I was set down with the other passengers at some Inn⁴⁴—in a tremor of Joy & terror indiscribable.

I stood by the side of my little property till All else were

---

⁴³ SBP, like M. d'A, suffered at a distance, which FBA tried to overcome through her letters and offers of help. For SBP's unhappy marriage and life in Ireland, see L. 864 n. 7 and iv *passim*.
⁴⁴ Coaches came and went from an inn at No. 767 in the Kornmarkt.

departed—though ⏐ dying to hasten to the loved object of all this exertion; But my first care was to avoid hazarding any mischief from surprize; & my first measure was to obtain some intelligence for myself previously to risking an interview. It was now 6 Days since any tidings had reached me!—My own last act in leaving Brussels had been to write a few lines to M. de Premorel, my General's Aid de Camp, to announce my journey, & prepare him for my arrival.

I now demanded pen & Ink & Paper, & I wrote, in French, a few lines to the valet of M. d'Arblay, *Francois*, a *Colognese*,[45] whom I had known, & myself recommended to his place at Brussels. I merely desired he would come Instantly to the Inn, for, the Baggages of Madame d'Arblay, who was then on the road; & that he would bring money from the General to pay for its carriage. ⏐

Having sent this off, breathless I waited for its answer. I had no timidity here, though I had paid nothing since I had quitted Coblentz: but I was now near my noble Protector,[46] whose Name & Rank at Treves, where he was on active service for his King, was generally known.

Hardly 5 minutes elapsed ere Francois, running like a Race Horse, though in himself a staid & soberly composed German, appeared before me.

How I shook at his sight!—with terrific suspence!—The good creature relieved me instantly—though with a relief that struck at my heart with a pang of agony—for he said that the Danger was over—& that both the Surgeons said so.

He was safe, I thanked God!—but Danger, positive Danger had existed! Faint I felt, though in a tumult of grateful ⏐ sensations, I took his arm; for my tottering feet would hardly support me, & made him a motion—for I was speechless—to lead me on.

He proposed going for the General's Calesh, which was hardby, with his Groom: but I only shook my head, & forgetting both my Debt & my luggage, I bent forward.

I recovered myself as we proceeded, & then demanded all

---

[45] See L. 887 n. 2.

[46] M. d'A lodged with the Nells (L. 879 n. 11) at No. 1003 Simeonstrasse, a short distance away beyond Trier's main square, the Hauptmarkt. The Nells also owned a large warehouse next door at No. 1004. See *Trierische Taschen-Kalender für das Jahr 1810* (Trier, 1810), p. 32.

sort of details. Francois had delivered my Note to his Master—
who instantly divined that I was already arrived—Ah! could
he think me so little like himself as to know him ill, & suffer
any obstacle, that was surmountable, to keep me from him,—
— Ah! how different had then been our Union from that which
for so many years made me the happiest of Wives—& of
Women!—

M. de Premoral, hastening to meet me at the street door,
told me that the General had decidedly declared he was ¹
certain I was already at Treves:—I therefore permitted myself
to enter his apartment at once — — Oh Alexander! What a
meeting of exquisite felicity!—to BOTH—

Yet, when he heard how I had travelled—with what risks,
& through what difficulties—which I poured forth to him in a
torrent of delighted exultation that I had conquered them,—he
almost fainted!—though he learnt them from myself, & saw me
not only in safety, but in gaiety of spirits unbounded!

I grieved at the precipitance of my Joy—but had far, far
more reason to grieve at the weakened state of altered nerves
that made

'pleasure thus to pain refine—'!—⁴⁷

So exquisite was grown his sensibility beyond his fortitude,
that the same effect was nearly produced, through feelings of
overpowering tenderness, when I recounted to him, 2 or 3
years afterwards, my very ¹ singular, nay, tremendous adventure, occurring during his absence in France, of being
surrounded by the Sea on a lonely Rock;⁴⁸ yet then,—already
at Bath for his health, I was aware of the shock that his strength,
& his vivacity of disposition, had alike sustained from the
accumulating sufferings of insidious, yet unknown disease, &
cautiously, therefore, I came to the point of the danger I had

---

⁴⁷ FBA identifies this line in her own note, numbered (2), as a quotation from
'Mrs. Greville's Ode to Indifference'. Frances Greville *née* Macartney (*c.* 1725–89)
first published this poem in *The Edinburgh Chronicle* (19 Apr. 1759). The passage in
which it appears emphasizes the torments of acute sensibility:

> Take then this treacherous sense of mine,
> Which dooms me still to smart;
> Which pleasure can to pain refine,
> To pain new pangs impart.
>
> (*Oxford Book of Eighteenth-Century Verse*, No. 276)

⁴⁸ FBA's dangerous adventure at Ilfracombe in the summer of 1817, when she
was trapped by a rising tide and, as she thought, narrowly escaped drowning (*HFB*,
pp. 399–401) and x, A.J. 1126.

surmounted by the gentlest gradations of narratory detail.—
But his whole mind was disordered by the bare idea being
presented to it, that there had ever been a moment that
threatened our Earthly separation—Ah! who can, rationally,
wonder at the permanence or the acuteness of Grief intailed
upon the survivor of a Life's Companion whose attachment was
so transcendent!—Blamed I know I am—but it is surely by
those only who conceive not the changed condition that
wretchedly succeeds to the happiness of so rare a lot!— ⏐

A few pages more will finish the little Narrative of this
excusion. Dreadfully suffering, but always mentally occupied
by the duties of his Profession, I found Your noble Father, my
dear Alex. Three wounds had been inflicted on his leg by the
kick of a wild Horse, which he had bought at Treves, wth
intent to train to military service. As he was felled by them to
the ground, if he had not, with never-failing courage, darted, in
the first pang of acute pain, forwards out of his reach, another
blow, & higher up, had inevitably been fatal! — — For this
escape, at least, I know I ought to be thankful — — and I
am!—Yet—alas from the instant of this infliction I am not
sure I can date one hour of perfect health & enjoyment of
Life! — — Yet, had he been skilfully attended, he might
completely have been cured! But all the best ⏐ surgeons,
throughout every district within reach, had been seized upon
for the Armies: & the ignorant hands into which he fell,
aggravated the evil, by incisions, hazardous, unnecessary,
& torturing, in a manner that still harrows up my soul with
deadly grief & horror to recollect — — —

The terrible Operator who had performed this barbarous
mistake had already been detected, by a successor, who,
though a better anatomist, was wholly unequal to the urgency
of the case; & a Gangrene was mortally menaced, when the
Prussian General officer who was in command at Treves,[49]

[49] August Wilhelm von Massow (1778–1851). In Mazancourt's personal dossier
at Vincennes there is a notarial document that gives the name of his father-in-law
as 'de Masson', which appears elsewhere as a French approximation to the name
of the Prussian noble family of von Massow. Further research has shown that both
brother and sister came from a Silesian branch of the family that has since died out.
August Wilhelm entered the Prussian army as a cornet of dragoons in 1793 and
after numerous campaigns became in 1811 a staff captain and in 1813, adjutant to
Generallieutenant von Zieten.* Promoted to *Rittmeister* (captain of cavalry) in 1814, he
was given on 14 May 1815 command of the 3rd Rheinisch Landwehr-Kavallerie-
Regiment. This was clearly a recent and mediocre unit based in Trier, and Mas-

sent for an army surgeon quartered many miles off, to dress the Wounds—5 in Number!—& give directions for the treatment! It was at this period that my martyrized General made M. de Premorel write for me through the medium of Colonel de Beaufort. ¹ This Army Surgeon had remained at Treves till he could pronounce that the Danger to Life was past.

Twice a day—every Morning & every Evening,—these wounds were probed & dressed—& with sufferings so severe, so cruel,—that still I see the convulsive agony that was produced! —Ah Heaven! could relief have been allowed him through participation, how had all his pains been mitigated!

The Prussian General officer I have mentioned, but whose name I have forgotten, was Brother in Law to the Adjoint of M. d'Arblay, M. le Comte de Mazancourt, who at this moment had been sent to Paris, by M. d'Arblay, to demand Leave & passports for returning to France, the Battle & Peace of Waterloo having ended the ¹ purpose for which he had been appointed, by Louis 18 himself, through the orders of the Marshal duc de Feltre, Clarke, Minister at War, to raise recruits from the Faithful who wished to quit the Usurper.

I saw this Prussian officer from time to time, & found him very Gentleman like & agreeable: &, his sister, la comtesse de Mazancourt,⁵⁰ who, some time afterwards, was brought by her husband to see me in Paris, was a peculiarly pleasing, amiable, & engaging young person: And the only Prussian lady with whom I ever conversed—except her Royal Highness the Duchess of York,⁵¹ to whom I had once the high honour, at Windsor Lodge, to be presented by Her Majesty Queen Charlotte, at the time I waited upon Her ¹ Majesty to present a Copy of Camilla.

sow was obliged to advertise in the local newspaper for recruits (*Trierische Zeitung*, 24 Aug. 1815). He transferred in 1816 into a hussar regiment, was put on half-pay in 1825, and retired as a major in 1833. A Knight of the Order of the Iron Cross (*Ritter des Eisernen Kreuzes*), he settled in Berlin in 1842 and died there nine years later. See Paul Hermann Adolph von Massow, *Nachrichten über das Geschlecht derer von Massow* (Berlin, 1878), p. 298.

⁵⁰ Charlotte Wilhelmine *née* von Massow (1781–1824) married Mazancourt (L. 868 n. 2) in 1802, when he was a lieutenant in the Prussian regiment of Graf von Wartensleben. She appears to have become increasingly estranged from her husband after 1817, finally leaving him altogether and returning to Prussia, where she died at Breslau (now Wroclaw) in 1824. See *Nachrichten . . .*, p. 295.

⁵¹ For the Duchess of York, who was also the Princess Royal of Prussia, see iii. 191–2, where FBA describes their meeting and conversation.

My poor sufferer had been quartered upon Mr. Nell, a Gentleman of Treves, who, with his family, gave him such entertainment as accorded with his Rank. Messrs de Mazancourt & de Premorel were, I believe, quartered elsewhere: M. de Premorel had with him his son, named Godfroy, from Godefroy of Boulogne, from whom the family de Premorel was descended. Godefroy was a truly noble youth, & worthy his high & chivalresque birth.

There was no room for me at Mr. Nell's, & I was obliged— most reluctantly—to be conducted by the de Premorels to an Hotel at some distance; for the night. But the next day M. d'Arblay entered into an agreement with Madame de La Grange,[52] a lady of condition who resided at Treves, to admit me to ¹ eat & lodge at her house, upon the pic nic plan, of paying the over plus of that expence I should cause her, with a proper consideration, not mentioned, but added by my dear General, for my apartment, & incidental matters. This sort of plan, since their ruin by the Revolution, had become so common as to be called fashionable amongst the Aristocratic Noblesse, who were quite too much impoverished to receive their Friends under their roofs but by *community* of fortune during their junction.

Madame de La Grange was a chearful, sensible, clever & pleasant Woman, & agreeably handsome. Her husband, who married her for her birth & beauty, was a far less bred person, but good-humoured, active, & lively. They had sundry Children:[52] & an old habitation of vast size,[53] in which it was more easy to be lost than found, for the stair-cases were many, & there were ¹ such endless short openings, with two or three steps, for leading into separate & detached rooms, that I was always obliged to have one of the Children for a Guide, or sure to go astray, & find myself in some dark, dreary chamber, with one thick casement in a corner, & neither paper, tapistry, picture or Print or painting on the Walls to be seen, or aught

---

[52] Scholastica Thiaut (1777–*post* 1816), who had married *c.* 1795 Louis-Pierre Lagrange (1762–*post* 1816), a commissaire des guerres at Trier from 1800 until 1815. See 'État de population de la mairie de Trèves pour l'an X', Stadt-bibliotek Trier, MS./FZ/694. Of their children, Charles was born in 1797, Elizabeth in 1799

[53] In the old system of numbering this rambling house was No. 902 in Diederichsgasse (now Dietrichstrasse 40), a seventeenth-century mansion built around a central courtyard. It now belongs to the Jesuit order and retains many of the features that help to explain FBA's Gothic description.

else but dun wainscoat, or oaken pannels, & a look of desertion if not of a place for secret captivity. The whole house was so ancient & dilapidated it seemed hardly tenable. The Gates of entrance were of an enormous height, & of a breadth proportionate. What this mansion had been, or to whom appertaining, in its origin, I could not learn. Whether it was any remnant of a Palace or public building from the time of the Romans, I to whom Triers was, at times, a seat of Empire, the La Grange's, but lately its possessors, could not tell, & did not care: & I could gain no information, though I continued to repast & to lodge during my whole stay at Treves in this large, roomy, gloomy, straggling, spacious, old built, old fashioned, curious & dismal fabrick.

The squeakings, whinings, murmurings & squally sounds that found their way into these time-beaten apartments at Night, through crevices, broken panes, loose boards, & immensely open chimneys, must have made a residence there in the Winter seem inhabiting so many Dens of Ghosts & restless spectres.

The Garden was vast & wild, growing all sort of Fruits & Vegetables & plants & ever Greens, all mixed together, without cultivation or care, but with a luxuriance & abundance I that mocked neglect.

Every night I was driven in my General's Calesh, by Henry, his Groom, to this old place, which was at the end of so dark & dingy a street,[54] that I never turned into it without fear of accident, though at the other end it opened into a far more spacious situation: & every morning, after Breakfast, one of the Family conducted me back to Mr. Nell's: where I remained till the hour of Dinner, when M. Godefroy de Premorel commonly gave me *le bras* for returning, & Francois watched for me at the end of the Repast. This was to me a cruel arrangement, forcing my so frequent absences: but I had no choice! The Nell family were of worthy people, evidently, but by no means gifted with minute attentions to the comforts or indulgencies of others. I No people in the World do that with the vivacity & obligingness of the Really high bred French.

[54] Dietrichstrasse, which runs in a north-westerly direction to the edge of the old city, remains a narrow street with some forbidding structures—one of which is the Frankenturm, a medieval fortified tower. At one end, however, it opens into the Hauptmarkt, and at the other into a view toward the Moselle.

In my flight from Paris to Brussels I had carried so small a Wardrobe, that now, in my Second Flight, from Brussels to Treves, I was so little overladen with Drapery, that I was forced to immediately have recourse to the friendly Madame de La Grange to accompany me to the proper shops for the purchase of two Robes, & such other small geer. These were remarkably well made up by a little hump-backed German mantua-maker, who, though famous, & highly employed, as Mad^e de la Grange told me, lived up 2 or 3 pair of short, crooked, winding & dark stairs. How unlike the elegant dwellings of such sort of Mistresses of Attire in England & France! She could only speak German, though, ¹ to make me understand her, when she turned from her Interpreter, Madame de La Grange, to address me, she always said *Madama la Generalé*: & such was her direction to my Bill, of which every word was German, & in German Characters.

Slow was the progress, fearfully slow, to all amendment in my dear—Oh too dear Invalid!—When the morning came, it was to have his wounds dressed,—& with pain indiscribable, & nearly intolerable! To dress his person was, next, another, however less keen, torment, as every movement was difficult. He had always a regular Nurse on these occasions, aiding his own two domestics. The Nurse also sate up every night. When attired, he was lifted from the Bed to a sofa placed close to its edge, & then wheeled away towards the Window. ¹ There he remained all day, the poor tortured Leg always lifted up, & immoveable, & the whole person in a state of cruel constraint from apprehension of any motion that might cause a fresh shock. What terrible—terrible—yet ever dear, ever sacred recollections hang upon this period! I must draw myself away from its excruciating fascinations, & confine myself to little matters of Fact.

Madame Le Clerc,⁵⁵ the widow of a General officer formerly much known to M. d'Arblay, was now resident at Treves, in

---

⁵⁵ Mme Leclerc, who later wrote a letter to FBA signed with her maiden name (Host), does not appear in any of the Trèves records the editors have thus far examined. Her husband, whom FBA identifies as a general and whose papers survive in the Berg Collection, does not appear in any of the dossiers of generals kept in the Vincennes archive. FBA had the habit of promoting people (Massow, also called a general, was in fact far below that rank) and it may even be that Leclerc's service and career were in the service of one of the German states rather than in France after the Revolution and during his period in emigration.

deep grief at the recent loss of her husband, a man of Letters as well as of arms, but—I believe, an Emigrant, & on half pay; applied to my General for counsel & assistance in her distress. He dressed up for her Memorials & petitions, & admitted her often to his sick room for consultation. She brought ᴵ to him many Manuscripts of her late husband,—& to look these over was the chief occupation of my ever mind-employed Invalid—ever! to his last hour, when not impeded by sufferings insupportable!—

These writings were very voluminous, & very diversified, as well as very clever, but wearisomely long, & unarranged. M. d'Arblay set about making abstracts, extracts, annotations, & re-writing whole pages; &, as they were chiefly, I believe, upon statistic subjects, & general views of Government, they required so much thought to adjust & clear, that he had always some work at hand for when his pains abated, & his devoted Companion was forced to relinquish his sight.

And this, to my infinite ill will, ᴵ was not only for Table & repose, but, from time to time, for airings & excursions, to which, in his too great anxiety for my health, my generous, ever self-sacrificing Invalid, occasionally forced my consent. Yet to me the separation was always too great a pain to make its result a service. With the attentive & intelligent & faithful Francois I was never, indeed, uneasy in leaving him; but —— even had I foreseen I was so soon to lose for-ever the society & sight I most prized, I could scarcely have forgone a moment of them more reluctantly.

His Groom, Henry, well acquainted with the whole country, had the charge to drive me in the Calesh to every beautiful or curious spot in the vicinity of this ancient City. ᴵ

All, however, that was visual was gratified by the view of the Country encompassing Triers—it was beautiful, grand, romantic, varied, NOBLE. The Moselle is the most enchanting River I have ever beheld, for genuine, unfabricated, picturesque effects. It has not, indeed, the splendour beaming from high historical imagery of the Rhine, where every reach mingles a moral lesson with its magnificent scenery: but there is a charm in its meandering loveliness, its verdant winding banks, now shaded by smiling Woods, now opening to glowing Meadows & rich pasturage, that makes it as innocently gay, & inviting to enjoyment, as the Rhine is beautifully sublime, & impressively urges to meditation. The one gave me a constant idea of natural Felicity from unadulterated & unsophisticated ꟾ rural objects; the other awakened an enlarged, but thoughtful sensation blending admiration of the Works of the Creator, with awe at the vicissitudes of humanity.

The Roads were superb,[56] & in as fine order as if the Roman Emperors who so often visited, & sometimes held the Seat of Government at Treves, were still lording it imperiously over the humbled World, & expected, with all their pomp & all their legions, to survey the adjacent territories. Their spaciousness was magnificent; their firmness, evenness, the cleanliness & clearness of their colour, & their air of durability, made me imagine they are chiefly cut through Rocks, as there was no occasion for any foot path, so rarely did any rut, or roughness, render the mid way inconvenient. Nor did I ever observe any laborers employed in any reparation. ꟾ

The Forests on each side, were, occasionally of the most striking & golden luxuriance, & all of a gay & smiling description—& the paths, made by passengers, or sheep, for none seemed enough frequented to denote the work of hands, were delicious in boundless variety of open prospect & seclusion. I alighted often to take a short view —— but I had no dear Companion—& I always remained reluctantly away from him, even for a moment.

I was driven also, along the banks of the Moselle, to see the confluence of the Saar with that River,[57] at a spot of the wildest & most fertile scenery.—

Another course was to visit some yet remaining antique Roman Baths,[58] about 2 miles from the City. They were curious from their origin only, not from their excellence. ꟾ Here I went repeatedly, the weather & the convenience making Bathing delightful. But the climate of Treves is delicious; the air, pure, clear, odoriferous, balsamic.

I do not mean this praise for the City itself, but for its

[56] There were two major and at least four minor Roman roads that passed through Trier. See Edith Mary Wightman, *Roman Trier and the Treveri* (1970), map, pp. 136–7 and 205–6.
[57] The two rivers meet at Konz, south-south-west of Trier.
[58] Of the two Roman baths at Trier, FBA here gives a description of the Barbara-thermen near the banks of the Moselle.

outside: for in the City I saw little to admire. No great buildings remain, except in such a state of transformation to merely useful, but ignoble offices, as to have been degraded from all power to charm the Eye by any air of former grandeur. Many things & places were curious from their antiquity in detail; but nothing — — at least nothing that I came in the way of — was striking as a whole, or in a mass: The market place, in which Mr. Nell resided,[59] though large was not handsome; the streets were dreadfully ill paved, without any side Walk, and very ¹ miserably ill lighted up at Night. I never returned to Madame de La Grange, whether on foot or in our Carriage, but in fear of some accident, from the dismal darkness of the streets.

Once, indeed, they were brightened, when the authorities of magistracy ordered a general illumination for the victory of Wellington & Blücher. My dear Invalid made me be driven all over the town, round & round, in & out, up & down, to visit the display of Joy, whether sincere or artificial. But the exhibition was necessarily faint & poor to one who had witnessed such manifestations in London & in Paris.

The same remark I must repeat upon the shops; though they were really neat & pretty in themselves.

I was much disappointed in being taken to see the Theatre,[60] where no vestige was discoverable of Roman times. It was simply small & mean. ¹

I aired occasionally to the Garden of Mr. Nell, which was at some distance from Treves, which was luxuriant in Fruits, Flowers, & Vegetables — — but producing no effect of art that could bear the least comparison with the noble works of Nature in its vicinity.

Anxious—too anxious!—to procure for me all of entertainment this Abode could offer, my Invalid made me accept an invitation of the La Grange's to keep some Birth Day in a rural excursion. Mr. & Mad^lle La Grange, & the eldest son & myself sailed in a pretty small Boat up the Moselle, while Madame de La Grange went in our Calesh, with her younger Children;[61] & we met at the place appointed for a little repast,

---

[59] See n. 46 *supra*.
[60] Most of the Amphitheatre, which was constructed in A.D. 100, had not yet been excavated when FBA saw it. Her impression may also have been caused by its unusual and undramatic siting, which is dug into a slope on a hillside south-east of the city.   [61] The two older children are probably those named in n. 52.

525

carried by their Domestic, consisting of Cakes, Honey, & Fruits, to which were added, from ᴵ a Cottage, rich cream, fresh churned Butter, & Brown Bread, & new laid Eggs. This we partook of in a native arbour, of the most romantic beauty, looking up to a lofty wood, & looking down upon the beautiful Moselle, with a boundary of high & superb mountains at a distance. They were all so happy, & the Children so frolicsome & joyous, that I tried to find some pleasure—but I sighed for the reciprocating companion who had so often rendered such scenes epocks of the purest felicity!—sighed—not alone at his absence, but at his sufferings. Had He been well, I should have surely have enjoyed such natural recreation, & have been cheered all the time with the idea of its recital.

Another day Mademoiselle La Grange was my obliging *Cicerone* to visit an antique Church called [*blank*]⁶² ᴵ

In This Edifice, still in good repair, there is much remain of the former splendour of the Roman Catholic Religion, grand, antique, sacerdotal & venerable. I imagine it to have been built in the early times of the Christian Emperors; but not sooner, as I saw no appearance of any Pagan dedication or Ornament. There were several very old & very curious tombs, & funereal emblems & embellishments in subterraneous small cloisters, or lengthened arched vaults, into which some grated Windows, just above the Ground, admitted literally 'Darkness visible.'⁶³

We were stopt, once, at the massy Gates⁶⁴ still subsisting at one of the entrances into the City, by a Procession⁶⁵ in honour of some saint: ᴵ it seemed rather funereal than of Thanksgiving, & consisted chiefly of Priests & Children. They sung from time to time, & then marched onward, slowly & dismally, in profound silence, & with such cautious softness of step, that they made not the smallest sound. Again then they chaunted, in gloomy tones, & entirely without any Instrument. All the words were German, & I could not collect their import; but the procession

---

⁶² FBA's description and contemporary paintings make it plain that this was the Dom or Cathedral, whose construction was begun under Constantine and continued in Romanesque, Gothic, and Baroque styles.

⁶³ *Paradise Lost*, i. 62.

⁶⁴ The monumental Roman fortified gate, the Porta Nigra, at the northern end of Simeonstrasse, was constructed during the last third of the second century.

⁶⁵ The religious feast of the Assumption (or *Himmelfahrt*) on 15 August, which was marked by lengthy processions.

was very long, & I was utterly amazed how a City, now so nearly abandoned, & so completely in decay from all its former Imperial magnificence, without any retribution through commerce or the arts, & inhabited so thinly that most of the streets had the air of being evacuated, should still possess so extraordinary a body of the Priesthood. I could not but conjecture that many of them were Emigrants from the recent persecutions in France, who had stayed here for ¹ safety till they had no Friends or patrimony to which they could return, or no means remaining to try whether any such were yet to be found.

A branch of the family of de Serre,⁶⁶ with whose former Chief my beloved Partner had been intimately connected, came to visit me as soon as my arrival at Treves was known. It was the youngest Brother of that Chief,⁶⁷ an extremely amiable man, with his Wife, & his Sister in Law, Wife of the eldest remaining Brother. These two ladies were of the loveliest, the most innocently attractive, & the softest & gentlest mannered females I ever saw in France, or, in truth, in England. It was impossible to see & speak with them, & not love them. They brought two of their beautiful Baby Children, & made a visit that gave nearly as much pleasure to Me as to my Husband. But a little they lessened my share in it, by their urgency that I would pass a day with them, at their Villa, some miles off,⁶⁸ which M. d'Arblay told me was in a high style of completely ¹ elegant comfort, with munificent prosperity. He joined earnestly in their desire—but to absent myself for so long a time when I

⁶⁶ Pierre-François-*Hercule* de Serre (1776–1824), comte de Serre, although short and slight, which led his contemporaries to joke about the name by which he was known, entered the army in 1789 and made it his career. An artillery cadet in 1790, he emigrated to join the Armée de Condé and did not return to France until 1802. He then switched to the law and rose to become president of the imperial court at Hamburg in 1811. He welcomed the Restoration, followed the King to Ghent, and became a liberal member of the ministry formed after the Second Restoration. In 1822 he was appointed ambassador to Naples, where he died in 1824.

⁶⁷ Roch-*Hyacinthe*-Louis-Pierre-Fourier de Serre (1779–1846) entered the army young and followed his brother in emigrating, apparently to fight in Germany. He returned to France in 1801, joined the navy, and was taken prisoner in 1803. He was sent to England and lived there until 1814, marrying a woman identified in Serre family records only as 'une Anglaise' and begetting a large family of daughters, one of whom, born in July 1814, may be referred to here. Like the d'Arblays, he wavered between living in England or returning to France, and decided the matter by entering the French consular service, in which he served until his death in Edinburgh in 1846.

⁶⁸ At Le Quint.

knew him in so pitiable a state, would have made me quite miserable. I could not consent. The elder Brother yet living, M. de Serre, has since acted a considerable & most nobly honourable part in public life. He has been a great Speaker in the Senate, & a faithful & zealous Patriot Minister to Louis 18: But—while still in the very prime of his life, he has fallen into a Decline—& is Dead, within a Week or two of the Date at which I am now writing, September, 1824, to the desolation of his tender Wife, while Ambassadour at Naples. —to which place he was probably sent with hope of restoration! [1]

I have nothing more, my dear Alex, to add of Treves: all else was illness—pain—Torture!—save what moments were rescued from such sufferings for goodness & indulgent tenderness quite, I believe, unexampled in the history of such acute bodily infliction! — —

It was not till after reiterated applications, by Letter, & by Mess[rs] de Mazancourt & de Premorel in person, that My poor General could obtain his Letters of recall, though the reestablishment of Louis 18 on his Throne made the mission on the Frontiers null; & though the hapless & helpless state of the health of M. d'Arblay would have rendered him incapable of continuing to fulfil its duties if any yet were left to perform. The mighty change of affairs so completely occupied men's minds & bosoms, as well as their hands & interests, that they could work only for themselves & the [1] PRESENT: the Absent were utterly forgotten. The Duke de Luxembourg, however, at length, interfered, & procured Passports, with the ceremonies of Recal. The Duke loved, almost revered M. d'Arblay, & had consulted with him frequently in points of delicacy & perplexity during the first dawn, & all the progress, of the counter revolution that placed Louis 18 on the Throne of his Ancestors. He was Capitaine of the Garde de Corps of the King to which M. d'Arblay belonged; & when the orders of the King, through his Majesty's Minister at War, the Duc de Feltre, removed M. d'A. to the troops of the line, the Duc wrote a most flattering Letter of regret, mixed with congratulation. So did he in sending to M. d'Arblay the Brevet of his promotion to being a Lieutenant-General, of *Les Armées du Roi*, blending there his regret that only accompanied ˡ the poor Lieutenant-General's *Retraite*, with warm congratulations that it was bestowed, avowedly, by the King, as a mark of high esteem for past services.

On the morning of our departure from Treves, all the Families Nell & La Grange, filled the Court-yard, & surrounded the little carriage in which we set out. Poor Madame Le Cler also joined the friendly groups, with others unknown by me, but acquainted with the General, & lamenting to lose sight of him— as who that ever knew him failed doing? M. de Mazincourt & the De Premorels had preceded us.

In the General's own Calesh we travelled, & with his own Horses, driven by Henry; while Francois rode & led two others. Various circumstances, military, had necessitated his keeping at least 4 during his whole mission. ˡ

The difficulty of placing the poor wounded Leg was great & grievous, as our luggage, or rather, the General's, was considerable: an arrangement was made, however, at last, by stretching the Leather Apron[69] of the Calesh to its utmost extent, so as to give full scope to the movements of the poor Limb; while the Baggage was so placed as to keep the Leather hollow, that nothing might press upon the tender part.

Our journey was any thing but gay; the cure, alas, was so much worse than incomplete! the spirits of the poor worn Invalid were sunk, &, like his bodily strengh, exhausted. It was so new to him to be helpless, & so melancholy! After being always the most active, the most enterprizing; the most ingenious in difficulty & mischance; & the most vivacious in conquering evils, & combatting accidents; to find himself thus suddenly ˡ bereft not only of his useful, pleasing, delightful powers to serve & oblige all around him, but even of all means of aiding & sufficing to himself, was profoundly dejecting to his high & vigourous spirit. Nor, to his Patriot-Heart, was this all; far otherwise! We re-entered France by the permission of Foreigners; & could only re-enter it at all by Passports of All the Allies! It seemed as if All Europe had freer egress to it than its Natives!

Yet no one more rejoiced in the victory of Waterloo; no one was more elated by the prospect of its glorious results: for the

[69] The covering for the legs in such an open carriage.

Restoration of the Monarchy he was most willing to shed the last drop of his blood. But not such was the manner in which he had hoped to see it take place; ¹ he had hoped it would have been more spontaneous, & the work of the French themselves to overthrow the Usurpation. He felt, therefore, severely shocked, when, at the Gates of Thionville, upon demanding admittance by giving his name, his military rank, & his personal passport, he was disregarded & unheard, by a Prussian sub-officer—a Prussian to repulse a French General, in the immediate service of his King, from entering France! His cholor rose, in defiance of sickness & infirmity—but neither indignation nor representation were of any avail, till he was forced to condescend to search his port-feuille for a Passport of All the Allies, which the Duc de Luxembourg had wisely forwarded to Treves, joined to that of the Minister at War. ¹ Yet the Prussian was not to blame: save for his uncourteous manners: the King of France was only such, at that moment, through Blücher & Wellington.

One feeling of a softer & compensating sort my poor Traveller was indulged with, however, almost the next minute—he was suddenly recognized by a favourite old Friend, M. de Serre,⁷⁰ Eldest of the House of which I have spoken at Treves: this Gentleman came to the Apartment of which we took possession for rest,—& a most affecting yet delightful meeting took place. They had not encountered each other since the Revolution, & though only brought together by accident, they knew not how to separate, such fullness of matter occurred to Both, equally in past events & future prospects. M. de Serre was one of the ¹ most pleasing, the best bred, & most amiable of men: & his esteem & admiration of M. d'Arblay, with the affectionate pleasure he manifested in again embracing him, won all my heart, & made me truly rejoice in the elevated places he soon after held in the Administration, to which he was raised alike from his Talents, conduct, character, & class in society. He was long Keeper of the Seals; but he fell into an early decline from over application to business, & excess of anxiety at every disturbance; & he finished his early career at Naples, whither he

---

⁷⁰ See n. 66. Serre became Garde des Sceaux in the ministry formed by Decazes in 1818 and held that post until 1820, when he became Richelieu's minister of justice.

was sent as Ambassadour.—Alas—he had meant to shew a
last tribute of attachment to his Friend by shewing one of
Respect—perhaps I should say Justice—to his Afflicted
survivors; for he [1] was one of an honorable Self-created committee which was formed by some of the Friends in power, to
demand the customary offering made to the married survivor
of a General officer.[71] The suggestion was by our dearest &
warmest Friend, General Victor de La Tour Maubourg, when
he was Ambassadour in England:[72] it was seconded by M.
le Marquis de Lally Tolendahl, one of the Privy Council; &
supported by M. de Lauriston,[73]—my dearest Departed's
early collegue at the Garrison at Toul, & then Lord Steward, I
think, of the King's Household, & M. de Serre, Keeper of the
Seals: & the proposition was abetted & presented to the King
by the Duc de Caze,[74] & the Marechal S[t] Cyr:[75] it was all
done without my knowledge, & conducted with the extremest
delicacy. The King instantly consented, [1] pronouncing himself
the *Eloge* of General d'Arblay, & recollecting & reciting the
various efforts of loyalty & bravery by which the General was
entitled to all of remuneration & of Honour that his family
could claim — — yet the project failed—I never knew how;
&, as I never had applied personally, nor ever could have borne
so to do, for a mark of so melancholy a Nature, I have no
means to discover where nor in whom the fault lies, as the
King positively gave orders that there should be no delay in the
acquittal of what he regarded as a Just Debt.

In my collection of peculiar papers, I have now the Letters
that passed on This subject between my excellent Friends
Victor de Maubourg & Mr. de Lally, with M. le Duc de Caze.
They have been Copied for me by my kind Madame de
Maisonneuve. Of M. de Lally I have the original Epistle

[71] Nothing, apparently, came of this. See the study of M. d'A's finances, x,
Appendix. [72] In the year 1819 (see x *passim*).
[73] Lauriston (L. 862 n. 9) was to become minister of the Maison du Roi in 1820.
[74] Elie Decazes (1780–1860), comte (1816) and duc (1820), began his career as
lawyer and judge under Napoleon. His political rise dates from his ardent royalism
during the Hundred Days, after which the King rewarded him by making him
Prefect of Police in Paris. Becoming a favourite and trusted minister of Louis XVIII,
he headed the ministry formed after Richelieu's resignation in 1818, but was
forced to resign in 1820. He became ambassador to London, then returned to busy
himself as a peer, landowner, and ironmaster. Although he continued in public life
and supported the July Monarchy, his political importance waned quickly and he
returned to private life after the Revolution of 1848.
[75] See L. 918 n. 6.

in his own Hand. | I am glad of seizing every opportunity that occurs to impress you, my Alexander, with the true & high sense which the Friends of your noble Father had of his worth; as well as to acquaint you, thus appropriately, with the depth of respect they proved for him by the Great & constant goodness & kindness with which they distinguished, while yet he lived! the Partner of his choice, & with which they have honoured her for his memory's sake, since he has been no more. Not, indeed for his memory's sake *alone*, as many had conceived, as well as inspired, a true personal friendship for but what she owes to His Remembrance is a thousand times more touchingly dear to her than any partiality that is simply her own. |

AT METZ my poor Invalid had again the soothing comfort of meeting one of the Friends of his early Youth, M. de [*blank*]76 a man of great but modest merit, who had been pining under the ruins of his race & expectations in life, with unresisting resignation, from the æra of the Revolution. He had been spirited, gay, convivial & happy,—but disappointment & misfortune had now settled into a melancholy placidity that the present change of aspect in affairs, though meeting all his sentiments, came too late to dispel. Three or four days, I think, we passed at Metz, where the General put himself into the hands of a surgeon of eminence, who did what was now to be done to rectify the gross mismanagement at Treves. In this | time, I saw all that was most worth remark in the old & famous City of Metz, M. d'Arblay insisting upon my leaving him, to be conducted by his Friend to a survey; but so entirely was my attention left behind, that I merely recollect visiting the antique & venerable Cathedral,77 the Artillery Ground,78 some great works for Warlike purposes, the Ramparts, & the Market place—& public Walks. But all looked dreary & abandoned: as every where during my Journey. Nothing was yet restored, for confidence was wanting in the state of things. Blücher & Wellington, the Lords of the Ascendant, seemed alone gifted

---

76 Unidentified.

77 A Gothic cruciform structure begun in the thirteenth century, with three naves and architectural features that resemble those of Rheims cathedral.

78 The old artillery school on the north-eastern side of the city faced the arsenal de génie across a large artillery park and training ground. Metz was one of the great fortresses along France's eastern borders and as such was well known to M. d'A and his fellow officers.

with the power of fore-seeing, as they had been, instrumentally, of regulating Events. [1]

Not long after, I forget exactly where, we came under New, yet still Foreign Masters; The Russians;[79] who kept posts, like sentinels, along the high Road, at stated distances. They were gentle & well behaved in a manner, & to a degree, that was really almost edifying. On the Plains of Chalon there was a grand Russian Encampment.[80]— We stopt at some small place for rest half a Day in its neighbourhood; & I walked about, guarded by the good François, to view it. But—on surveying a large old House, which attracted my notice by a Group of Russian officers that I observed near its entrance, how was I struck on being told, by François, that the Emperor of all the Russias was at that moment its [1] inhabitant! I approached a slight palisading that formed a sort of yard to this very common looking, though not small house, & looked up at the Windows. The house was insulated & appeared to belong to some respectable Farmer. At the entrance of the little Gate that opened this palisade, stood a *Lady*[81] with two or three Gentlemen, who were fashionably dressed, & apparently of a quite upper class, but in the civil, not military line. The lady was rather handsome, & very elegant.

There was no crowd, & no party of Guards, nor any sign of caution, or parade of Grandeur, around this so royally honoured Dwelling. And, in a few minutes, the door was quietly opened, & the Emperor came out, in an undress uniform, wearing no stars nor orders, or none visible, & with an air of [1] gay good humour, & unassuming ease & liveliness. He seemed in blyth & flourishing health, & replete with happiness, internal & demonstrative. But there was something in his whole appearance of hilarity, freedom, youthfulness, & total absence of all thought of state & power, that would have led me much sooner to suppose him a jocund young Lubin,[82] or Country Esquire, than an Emperor, a Warrior, or a Statesman.

[79] The Czar's army, most of which arrived in France after Waterloo, crossed the Rhine near Mainz and moved westward into Champagne.

[80] Near Châlons-sur-Marne at Vertus, where on 11 September Czar Alexander staged a huge military review before the other allied sovereigns and commanders.

[81] Possibly Barbara Juliane von Krüdener (1764–1824), the mystic visionary who had so much influence upon the Czar's policies and personal attitudes at this time, and who travelled with his entourage into France.

[82] Molière's rambunctious peasant in *Georges Dandin*.

The lady courtsied low, & her Gentlemen bowed profoundly as he reached, in the quarter of a second, that Group: He instantly recognized them, & seemed enchanted at their sight. A sprightly conversation ensued, in which he addressed himself chiefly to the lady, who seemed accustomed to his notice, yet to receive it with a species of rapture. The Gentlemen, also, had the easy address of conscious welcome to inspirit them, and I | never followed up a Conversation I could not hear with more certainty of its being agreeable to all parties. They all spoke French, & I was restrained only by my own sense of propriety from advancing within hearing of every word; for no sentinel, nor Guard of any kind interfered to keep the few lookers on at a distance.

This discourse over, he gallantly touched his hat, & leapt into his open Carriage, accompanied by a Russian officer, & was out of sight in a moment.

How far more happy, disengaged, & to his advantage, was this view of his Imperial Majesty, than that which I had had the year before in England,[83] where the crowds that surrounded, & the pressure of unrestrained Curiosity, & forwardness, certainly embarrassed, if they did not actually alarm him. |

At *Meaux* I left again my Captive companion for a quarter of an hour, to visit the Cathedral of the sublimely eloquent Bossuet.[84] In happier moments, I should not have rested without discovering & tracing the house, the chamber, the Library, the study, the Garden which had been, as it were, sanctified by his Virtues, his piety, his learning & his Genius—& Oh how eagerly, if *not* a Captive, would my noble-minded companion, have been my conductor!

Alas! ——

A new change again of Military controul soon followed, at which I grieved for my beloved Companion—I almost felt ashamed to look at him, though my heart involuntarily, irresistibly palpitated with emotions which had little, indeed, in unison with either Grief or Shame; for the Sentinels, the Guards, the Camps, became English. |

All converse between us now stopt; involuntarily, & as if by

---

[83] On 8 June 1814. See vii, L. 790, p. 366.

[84] Jacques-Bénigne Bossuet (1627–1704), the famous orator and churchman, was buried in the cathedral at Meaux, where he had been bishop from 1681 until his death.

tacit agreement. M. d'Arblay was too sincere a Loyalist to be sorry; yet too high spirited a Freeman to be satisfied. I could devize nothing to say that might not cause some painful discussion or afflicting retrospection, & we travelled many miles in pensive silence—Each, nevertheless, intensely observant of the astonishing NEW SCENE presented to our view, on re-entering the Capital of France, to see the vision of Henry V revived, & Paris in the Hands of The English!—

I must not omit to mention that, notwithstanding this complete victory over Buonaparte, the whole of the Peasantry & common people, converse with them when or where or How I might during our route, so long, lingering & slow, with one accord avowed themselves utterly incredulous of his Defeat. They all believed he had only given way to come forward with new forces, to extirpate all opposers, & exalt himself on their ashes to permanent Dominion.[85]

The little I can recollect of This my terminating residence in France, I will now commit at once to paper, till I bring my dear Alex to our restoration to one another on our return to England.

I have no memorandums—& can only put down Names & things as they occur.

The first person to seek us was my dear—tender—faithful— most endearing & most beloved Madame de Maisonneuve; & her amiable, admirable Brother, the General Victor de la Tour Maubourg, came over to me—for we were near neighbours, with eager vivacity & kindness, not only to greet our return, & rejoice in our safety, & sympathize in the wounds & pains of his chosen *ami*, my honoured Partner, but also, with a curiosity ardently alive to hear the history of my extraordinary Journey to Treves;—alone—without even a passport; without the language of the Country, & nearly without Money! When I related my adventure to my dear Madame d'Henin, she declared it was a *devouement* such as she had scarcely

[85] Other contemporary witnesses support FBA's comments on the strong support for Napoleon in these eastern regions, marked often by loud opposition to the Bourbons.

conceived. Ah! thought I, it was not more rare than its Exciter! These dear persons, & the excellent *two* Mesdames de La Tour Maubourg,[86] & Madame de Tracey,[87] were those we chiefly saw, during our short residence at Paris. My incomparable Baron Larrey came to dress the Wounds of my poor sufferer, & enable us to depart. M. de LaFayette paid us a truly affectionate visit. All Politics, & all Military apart, he loved M. d'Arblay with even fervant affection; & to his Wife & his Son he took a fancy almost enthusiastic. Whatever may be the Character of M. de LaFayette as a Statesman & Politician, his Character is one of the most loyal, according to the French acceptation of that word, that exists; & he is a man of ¦ the most amiable manners, the greatest suavity of disposition, the most zealous & indefatigable worker of acts of friendship, & the most lenient Judge of his neighbours, I have ever known.

Madame d'Henin & Madame de Maurville had not yet forgiven my escape from them at Brussels — — but came to me with unfading kindness: The good & highly mentally accomplished M. Le Noir[88] almost lived with us during our stay; & the charming—in all ways, external & internal, Madame de Grandmaison came to us frequently,—as did M. de la Jaqueminiere, our worthy cousin.[89]—But that which was our greatest consolation, nay, delight, was the sudden appearance of our dearly cherished uncle, M. Bazile, with his deserving Daughter, Madame Meignen, & her Children.[90] To our utter, but delicious astonishment, they arrived the very day before our departure. I saw, & received the blessing of that beloved, that parental Uncle, with a gratitude & a Joy that quite melted me with pleasure. He was turned of EIGHTY ¦ when he made this great exertion, to bestow, & receive a delight of half an hour. He was a man who, in native sagacity, acute penetration, knowledge of the World, benevolence of heart, & strength of intellect with the most arch gaiety of Fancy, resembled my earliest & ever doated on old Friend, Mr. Crisp,[91] beyond any other person I ever knew: though he

[86] See v, L. 446 n. 12 and vi, L. 557 n. 7.
[87] See L. 845 n. 23.   [88] See L. 840 n. 24.
[89] See v, L. 448 n. 10.
[90] See genealogical table, vi, *facing* p. 476. For a similar journey to Paris, see v, p. xlix. Gabriel Bazille, M. d'A's maternal uncle, had died in 1817, six years before FBA composed this elegy.
[91] For Samuel or 'Daddy' Crisp, see *HFB*, pp. 16–18, Plate I, and *passim*.

did not super add to these excellencies a knowledge & acquirements in all the polite arts, & a classical taste & skill in literature, such as, also, distinguished that honoured Friend.

On the Eve of setting out, I made a round to all I could reach of my intimate acquaintance, to make—as it has proved—a last farewell! La Princesse de Poix[92] was still brilliant in animation, elegance, understanding, high breeding & quickness, though sickness & sorrows had attacked her as well as years! M. de Poix, though inferior to his charming Wife in every thing, except Rank, was uniformly kind to M. d'A. & to me almost to enthusiasm. ⎮ I found at home, also, the Princesse de Craon,[93] mother to the Prince de Beauvau, & a most spirited & entertaining woman, with her adopted Daughter, Mlle d'Alpy,[93] & saw them with very great pleasure. Also that most zealous & exemplary of Friends—though not, alas! of *Women,* the *spirituelle* & engaging Mad^e la Vic^sse de La Val—& Mad^e Chastel & her Daughters,[94] & Madame de La Tour Dupin— that accomplished & high mannered descendant of the Dillons,[95] &, erst, of Lord Falkland:[96]— & some others.

We set out with much embarrassment, from the poor always suffering Leg, & travelled still in our own Calesh. The kind Dr. Esparron[97] was with us to the last: M. Le Noir was indisposed, or would never have failed us; but my dear—dear invaluable Madame de Maisonneuve[98] hovered over us to the latest minute, with an affectionate sensibility that cost me a flood of tears as I drove from the Court-yard in which I left her musing, melancholy, & afflicted. How ⎮ little did either of us foresee the misery that was to rob me of all Joy even in our meeting! or the Grandeur in the turn of affairs that was to bring her to my Country as sister the French Ambassadour,[98]—for such was our next interview, when she came to me, in London, in the superb Carriage of her Brother, his

[92] See v, L. 513 n. 16.
[93] Louise-Étiennette (*c.* 1747–1831), princesse de Craon, and her adopted daughter Bonne-Jeanne d'Alpy (1777/8–1839). See also in FBA's lists of visits, vi. 77–95 *passim.*
[94] See L. 842 n. 8. [95] See vi, L. 575 n. 2.
[96] See L. 924 n. 148.
[97] M. d'A's physician (L. 885 n. 12).
[98] Mme de Maisonneuve (v, vi *passim*) was to accompany her brother Victor de Latour-Maubourg and his wife to London in 1819, when for a few months he acted as Ambassador to the Court of St. James. For FBA the pleasure of the visits was mixed with misery because of d'Arblay's recent death. See xi *passim.*

Excellency the Marquis de La Tour Maubourg. Yet Then, as before, she had all the same winning charm of genuine simplicity, & unaffected modesty, that had ever enhanced the value of her solid understanding, & innumerably pleasing qualities.

I have omitted to mention, that the renowned M. de Talleyrand Perigord, ci-devant Eveque d'Autun, & *ci-apres* Prince of Benevento, came in to Madame de Laval's Drawing Room during my visit of Leave-taking. He was named upon entering; but there is no chance he could recollect me, as I had not seen him since the first month or two after my Marriage, when he ¹ accompanied M. de Narbonne & M. de Beaumetz on a Wedding congratulation to our cottage at Bookham.⁹⁹ The West Hamble Hermitage was not then built. I could not forbear whispering to Madame de Laval, next to whom I was seated, How many *souvenirs* his sight awakened!—not *then*, of my own lost happiness —for M. d'Arblay was in La Rue de Miromenil,—but M. de Narbonne was gone,¹⁰⁰ who made so much of our social felicity during the period of our former acquaintance; & Mr. Lock was gone, who made its highest intellectual delight; & Madame de Staël,¹⁰⁰ who gave it a zest of wit, deep thinking, & light speaking, of almost unexampled entertainment. — — & my beloved Sister Phillips, whose sweetness, intelligence, Grace & Sensibility, won every heart, & engaged universal approbation—All these were gone,¹⁰⁰ who all, during the sprightly period in which I was known to M. de Talleyrand, had almost ¹ always made our society—joined to my honoured Partner, the amiable & exemplary Mrs. Lock, & her charming Daughters, now Lady Martin & Mrs. Angerstein. Ah! What parties were those! how delectable, how select, how refined though sportive, how investigatingly sagacious, though invariably well bred!

Madame de Laval sighed deeply, without answering me, for her secret ruminations were on M. de Narbonne: but I left M. de Talleyrand to Madame Duchess de Luynes, & a sister,

⁹⁹ Though not mentioned at the time, Talleyrand's visit must have taken place in December of 1793, when Beaumetz after his second escape from France (iii, L. 131 nn. 2, 12), visited the d'Arblays in Great Bookham. Soon after this both men were deported.

¹⁰⁰ The comte de Narbonne had died on 17 Nov. 1813 (vii, L. 731 n. 2); William Locke of Norbury Park, on 5 Oct. 1810 (vi, L. 594 n. 2); Mme de Staël (i, ii, v, vii *passim*), on 14 July 1817; and Mrs. Phillips, on 6 Jan. 1800.

whose name I have forgotten, of M. Le Duc de Luxembourg,[101] & another lady or two, while I engaged my truly amiable Hostess, till I rose to depart: & then, in passing by the Chair of M. de Talleyrand, who gravely & silently, but politely, rose & bowed, I said 'M. de Talleyrand m'a oublié: mais on n'oublie pas M. de Talleyrand.—' I left the room with quickness, but saw a movement of surprize by no means unpleasant ᴵ break over the habitual placidity, of the nearly imperturbable composure of his general—& certainly *made up* countenance. O what Days were those of conversational perfection! of Wit, ingenuity, gaiety, repartee, information, badinage, & eloquence!—

The charming Family de Beauvaux—M. le Prince, the delightful Mad^e la Princesse—Natalie the lovely, Gabrielle la belle,—Charles le Noble, et Edmond le spirituel,[102] were all absent from Paris at our return. I believe they were at their Terre of Harcourt.

Of M. de Lally, whom I so warmly love as well as admire, I saw nearly nothing, from my incessant occupations, & the gnawing anxiety of my MIND for my dear companion; joined to his own almost exclusive seizure by new scenes of politics & patriotism.

But the Male & the Female the most *spirituel*—the most admirably eminent for Wit parts, & the highest powers of Conversation, M. de Narbonne & Mad^e la Comt^sse de Tessé[103] —were Gone!—We left not Them! but by Them had been left. ᴵ

Our Journey was eventless, yet sad,—sad, not alone, though chiefly, from the continued sufferings of my wounded Companion, but sad, also, that I quitted so many dear Friends, who had wrought themselves, by innumerable kindnesses, into my affections, & who knew not—for we could not bring ourselves to utter Words that must have reciprocated so much pain,—that our intended future fixed Residence was England.

101 Guyonne-Élisabeth-Josèphe *née* de Montmorency-Laval (1775–1830), sister-in-law of Mme de Laval (*supra*) and widow of Louis-Joseph-Charles-Amable d'Albert (1747–1807), duc de Luynes (see v, L. 469 n. 8). The duc de Luxembourg's sister would have been Bonne-Charlotte-Renée-Adélaïde (1773–1840), who had married her kinsman Anne-Adrien-Pierre de Montmorency-Laval (1768–1837), prince, duc de Laval.
102 For the Beauvau family, see v, L. 513 n. 2 and *supra* Ll. 840 n. 19, 924 n. 12. Their estate was in Normandy.   103 See v, L. 510 n. 11 and pp. xliv–xlv.

The most tender & most supremely generous of Fathers had taken this difficult resolution for the sake of his Son, whose decided & most earnest wish, petition & prayer had been repeatedly expressed for permission to establish himself in the land of his Birth. That My wishes led to the same point, there could be no doubt, & powerfully did they weigh with the most disinterested & most indulgent of husbands. All that could be suggested to compromize what was jarring in our feelings, so as to save All parties from murmuring or regret, was the plan of a yearly journey to France |

Our passage home was in full & terrible unison with our jarred & unstrung feelings: there was a continued storm of the loudest Winds, & roughest Waves. I resolved, however, to try staying this time upon the Deck: & my poor weakened, but ever noble Partner, seated me so as to support me during my sea sufferings, in despight of all difficulties, & all pains of his own! Towards the end of the Voyage, however, the fury of the Elements occasioned such disturbance, that to manage the tackle it was necessary to clear the Deck. We descended into the Cabin—We then both became equally ill, & equally unable to aid the other: a dreadful scene followed; when we were anchored, & a Boat came for the Passengers, M. d'A. was, with much danger from his wounds, obliged to be carried into it, calling out to the Captain to take me in charge himself. This the Captain would have done; but I was in a state of exhaustion that threatened me with fainting, & utterly incapable to move, or to listen to any representations. I have only since learnt that any were made, for I was nearly senseless; & I have still no recollection | how I was conveyed on shore; but my poor, harrassed, tender & affrighted Partner has told me that they were going to row him off without me, & that the despair with which he was seized, & his state of helplessness, made him even scream with impatient horrour as he adjured them, by any reward they could name, to bring me to the Boat.—

Here I stop.—we came to town in our own easy Calesh— We stopt at Deptford, to see my dear Brother Charles whom— alas, alas! I never saw more![104] for our next—and Last! 3 years were spent at Bath, whither he never came—And from

---

[104] Charles Burney, the Greek scholar, died on 17 Dec. 1817.

Deptford we went to Greenwich, to see Charles Parr & his Wife & fine Children[105]—& thence to La Sablonière Hotel in Leicester Square, where we again were re-united—with our dearest Alexander—brought to us from the hospitable mansion of my excellent Brother James, by that dear Brother himself.[106] Oh my dear Charles! how little—I thank Heaven!—did I then conceive I saw your affectionate Face for the last Time on Earth:!— |

933   Paris
                          27 September–3 October 1815

To Mrs. Barrett

A.L.S. (Berg), 27 Sept.–3 Oct. 1815
Double sheet 4to 4 pp. *pmks* PORT PAYE FOREIGN/7 OC
1815 7 OC .815 red seal
Addressed: Angleterre / Mrs. Barrett / at Arthur Youngs, Esqr / Bradfield Hall / near Bury—Suffolk / *ANGLETERRE.*

Rue de Miromenil
fᵍ Sᵗ Honore
Paris
le 27ⁿ Septembre 1815

My first dear Charlotte[1] will, I well know, pardon me that I give to my second the body of this Letter, leaving only for herself a limb to be amputated at the extremity. Where to address either of you I know not—& I am myself so literal a

---

[105] For CPB's family see i, p. lxxii.
[106] As an aid to memory in concluding the journal FBA jotted down the following memoranda:
    'Madame de Maisonneuve, Gˡ Victor de La Tour Maubourg. Mesdames de Maubourg—Madame d'Henin.—Baron de Larrey M. de La Fayette—Madᵉ de Maurville M. Le Noir. Madᵉ de Grandmaison. M. de La Jaqueminiere. M. Bazile—Mᵈᵉ Meignen. Pˢˢᵉ de Poix—Pˢˢᵉ de Craon Mˡˡᵉ d'Alpy. Maᵈᵉ & M. de La Tour Dupin Madᵉ Chastel.—Madᵉ de Laval. M. de Talyrand Prince de Benevento, Les de Beauvaux. M. de Lally.
    'Grievous quitting Paris! terrible Voyage—but blest re-joinder with our Alex & view of my two dear Brothers.'
For an itinerary of the Journey to Trèves, see Memoranda, p. 553.

933. [1] CBFB.

Wanderer, that my Letters follow me—not from Town to Town, but from Country to Country. They are always, however, safe, for, in every flight, or Excursion, public or clandestine, my never-abating eagerness for news of those I leave, & love, makes way, through every disturbance, & every precipitance, to put me upon my guard for the safety of my Correspondence. Your last Letter, directed to me in Les Pays bas, came to me in Germany, & I now answer it in France.

I am so sensible, my very dear Charlotte, of the effort it must have cost you to develope with some sincerity the character & conduct of my poor excentric Alexander,[2] that it will make me hold you nearer than ever to my heart, not only with esteem, but a confidence of the solidity of your affection that doubles its value. *Some* sincerity I say! for I am well aware your gentle repugnance to give me pain has modified, & molified, all that Truth did not exact for doing good in your delineation.

It would be useless, & therefore cruel to talk to you of my disappointment; I will pay your exertion better, by assuring you it would have been doubled had I returned to England in my ignorance. I do, of course, all that is in my power to soften to my Partner this blow; but it falls upon him the heavier, from his having still, nay far more than myself cherished higher expectations. He has not so long seen & studied as I have done, because they have been ┃ critically parted, the cruel perversity of pursuit that is always meandering out of the way in search of Flowers, instead of digging, sewing, & Cultivating for the

---

[2] This is FBA's acknowledgement of CFBt's letters of *n.d.* [1815] and 8–10 July (Eg. 3702A, ff. 11–14b), evidently sent in reply to her aunt's request for a report on young d'Arblay and his application to his studies. Alexander was not 'absolutely idle' but lacking the 'plodding industry' of his cousins CPB and CF, he had left his 'mathematical books' at Cambridge, she felt forced to say. 'He does not read' but plays chess and plays 'by himself when we resist his challenges'.

I really do not much think our dear Alexander will ever plod in the Cambridge way—he is disgusted, very reasonably, with the bad style of mathematics there, & he now tells me that it is too late for him to *read for a high degree*, for he has been so long idle while his opponents were working hard, that he says he could not now, by any application, be enabled to take a high degree. . . . for *distinction* he must look to his future achievements in the world, rather than to these college studies, which he half despises & entirely dislikes.—I hope I shall not have grieved you too cruelly my dearest Aunt, by this very unvarnished tale bearing — . . . I cannot doubt that he will rise to eminence in any employment hereafter which may accord with his taste & feelings. . . .

Alexander was to graduate 10th wrangler from Christ's College, Cambridge, in 1818, but not without his mother's driving supervision. There was much to do, see ix, x *passim*.

production of Fruits. yet Alex sees all his errours, & avows & blames them with the candour & simplicity he might discuss those of a third person: but he is blind, alas, to the greatest of his faults, that of detailing & bewailing what he should start from & amend. His understanding, however, when not counter acted by his eccentricities, is good, & will lead him, I trust, in time, from the zig-zags of his fancies to the straighter line of common sense. How bright would be his prospect, even yet, could he drudge through the mire & the thorns that obstruct its true point of view! But his Imagination is too ardent for his judgment, & we must be content, alas, to wait for the correction of Experience! He is not aware how severe a master that will prove! he would spare himself, else, such lessons, by listening to the warnings of advice.

I thank you truly, my dear Girl, for your really sisterly solicitude in his favour; &, with all his imperfections, he merits it, for he appreciates you completely; & his heart—when he happens to consult it—is so good, & his meaning is always so pure, that I have often flattered myself he is free from any species of vice. And then, I own, in the midst of all my regrets for his neglect of worldly advantages, & so due prosperity, I bless Heaven that his foibles are not of a deeper tint, & only hope his own philosophy hereafter may not embitter his resolute want of it at present. Where is he now? I have 3 Letters written to him from 3 Countries, La Belgique, Germany, & France unanswered!³ |

We are coming, however, to England—I am sure these are words that will not be read unmoved: my poor *Boiteux* is preparing for the journey. You have certainly heard the history of his second deplorable accident, & our approaching re-union deters me from writing either the history of his Mission, or of my perilous expedition to join him, at Treves, when I heard of his misfortune. I can scarcely myself now conceive how I found courage to combat the obstacles I continually encountered. But I was so absorbed by an anxiety that had nothing to do with myself, or my situation, that both were nearly driven from my thoughts & my calculations, & how to arrive, in defiance of every impediment, at Treves, alone interested, occupied, & impelled me. Yet once, when, by accident, I

³ This and the other letters mentioned are missing.

543

was alone in a City of Germany, Bonn, sur le Rhin, when I knew not my way to the post office, of which I had inadvertently lost sight, & whence I was to proceed in my Journey, when all my enquiries were fruitless, because I could not make myself comprehended, nor understand one word that was said to me, for both English & French were as unintelligible to all whom I addressed, as German was to me;—then, indeed, I was dreadfully frightened; not only because I had very little money, & no protection; as little use of speech as if I had been dumb, & not even my PASSPORT—which had been taken from me upon my arrival—to save me from passing for some Emissary, Impostor, or spy—*BUT*,—beyond all that, which though tremendous, must be transitory, I knew that to be too late by a single moment at the post office, was to miss a vehicle that was to convey me onwards, & which, setting out but once a week, would leave me 8 days in a Town, a Country, rather, in which I was utterly unknown, desolate, forlorn—Deaf & MUTE!—*AND* without any possible tidings of [1] my Invalid, who must remain, mean time, wholly ignorant what was become of me. A quarter of an hour so spent, appears, even to my remembrance, to have been at least a day; but, while roving up & down, backwards & forwards, to recover the hôtel des postes, I was relieved, at length, by the delightful sight of a deformed little shapeless wooden pigmy, a blue wig painted upon its head, & gilt carved waistcoat, patched with red spots, reaching its knees, & large silver Buckles projecting from bright blue shoes—for top and bottom were in exact harmony of colouring. This figure, stuck in a nich, on the corner of a street, I had already remarked, & could not easily forget,—it was designed for the holy Infant![4]—this Image might in me, nevertheless, excite devotion, for it was my guide out of a labyrinth of terrific perplexity, that teemed with mischief incalculable.—

Oct[r] 3[d]—yesterday morning my dear sister Broome's Letter from Bradfield, with a most kind note from her beloved Charlotte, reached me from Bruxelles, with a Letter from dear Fanny Raper, &—alas—another from Mrs. W[addingto]ⁿ telling me Alexander was not quite well—To the affright thus raised, all considerations yield, & we have already begun preparations the most active for our return to England—We

4 See L. 932 n. 30.

shall set out *the INSTANT* it is possible—but do not let Alex know his health hurries us; he is so imaginative, he will believe We are told he is in danger. He has never got the better of Dr. Thomas's[5] injudicious acknowledgment that he was hypochondriac.[6] Thank & embrace my dearest Sister for her Letter —I will write to her when I arrive immediately. Our purpose is to winter in Bath. We know nothing more yet even of our possibilities. How my heart aches every way for my Alex[2d] while still ill at ease for Alex[1st] I need not say. Our affairs will detain us about 10 days in London.—We were already decided to winter in England—but meant first to go to Joigny. I fear we have little chance to see you, my dearest Charlottes— accept, BOTH, my tenderest love, & most fervant thanks for all your kindness & exquisite attentions to my Alex—& join Mr. Barrett in our acknowledgments—for I have heard of his zeal & goodness with infinite pleasure—my kind love to dear Marianne, to whom I have not a moment now to write—& to Dolph—& when you see him, to Clement & my very affectionate remembrances to my valued old friend Mr. Young.[7] I am uneasy about my poor sister Burney, & my brother James! When may we, publicly or privately, be tranquil! All here is the very reverse — — !!! adieu, sweet Charlottes both—Love always as you have shewn you Love now.

Your truly affec[te].

F.B. d'Arblay.

The Archdeacon, Cordelia, Mrs. Baker—[8]

I write to Alex—but am at a loss whither to direct.— All my Letters have been directed to Richmond—but he seems not to have rec[d] them—All that is kind from M. d'A.— & embrace for us both the dear children. We earnestly entreat my dear sister to pay Herself & all others whatever is owing for Alex—fr[m] M[ssrs] Hoare—

5 JB's physician Honoratus Leigh Thomas (vii, L. 676 n. 2) of Leicester Fields.
6 This medical term here seems to have its older meaning of one who suffers from an actual ailment marked by depression and melancholy (*OED*).
7 See L. 838 n. 7.
8 See L. 843 nn. 5, 6.

934 Dover, 18 October 1815

To Mrs. Locke
and Mrs. Angerstein

L., incomplete copy in the hand of CFBᵗ (Diary MSS. viii. 6676–[77], Berg), 18 Oct. 1815
Single sheet 4to   2 pp.   foliated 291

Dover. Oct. 18. 1815.

To Mʳˢ Lock and
Mʳˢ Angerstein.[1]

Last night, my ever dear Friends, we arrived once more in Old England.

I write this to send the moment I land in London. I cannot boast of our health—our looks—our strength—but I hope we may recover a part of all when our direful fatigues, mental & corporeal, cease to utterly weigh upon & wear us.

We shall winter in Bath. The waters of Plombières have been recommended to my poor *Boiteux*, but he has obtained a *Congé* that allows this change. Besides his present utter incapacity for military service, he is now, unavoidably on the *Retraite* list, & the King of France permits his coming over, not alone without difficulty, but with wishing him a good journey, through the Duc de Luxembourg, his Captain in the *Gardes du Corps*.

Adieu dearest *BOTH*! almost I embrace you in dating from Dover. ' Had you my letter from Treves? I suspect *NOT*—for my melancholy new history would have brought me your kind condolence: or, otherwise, *that* missed *me*. Our letters were almost all intercepted ' by the Prussians while we were there. Not *one answer* arrived to us from Paris, save by private hands—

My kindest love to my dear Lady Martin.[2] I waited a happy moment to write her my congratulations—alas!—I have been persecuted by disaster almost from the time I left England.— Flights—illness—terrors—& grievous accidents have followed, or met me at every step.— '

934.   [1] By reaching Dover FBA has come almost close enough to her old friends to embrace them,   [2] Mrs. Locke's daughter Mary Augusta (L. 900 n. 2).

546

NOTEBOOKS, MEMORANDA, DIARIES

for the years 1814–1815

Diary Entries (Berg), Nov. 1814–7 Feb. 1815

Written on 6 leaves (4·6 × 3″) torn (or subsequently torn) from an English Pocket Diary or Memorandum Book ruled and lettered for the year 1802. 9 pp.

Novr 1814
In Novr came M^e de *Maisonneuve*
M. de *Larrey*—La Princesse *d'Henin*
Mad^e de *Tracy*—M. de *La Fayette*
Mad^e G. de *La Fayette*—M. *Lajard*—
Le G^l *Victor de Maubourg*—Me Ahmuty
Me G^l *Victor de Maubourg*—*M^e d'Auch*
Edmond de *Beauvau*—M^e de *Chastel*—
Le Prince de *Beauvau*—M^e de *Cadignan*
La Princesse de *Beauvau*—M. *Le Noir*
Charles de *Beauvau*—M. *Norry*
M^e de *Germinez*—*Maxime de* Maisonneuve
Me *Felicité de Germinez*: M. *de Lally*—
M^e de L'*Asterye*
Mlle de *Bourzac*
M. de *Bourzac*—M. *Esparron*—
M. de *Chavagnac*
M^e de *Chavagnac*
Le G^l *Gassendi*
M^e de *Gassendi*

S[unday] 1 January [1815].
The good M. *Le Noir* calls

M[onday] 2 January
M. *Esparron*—
My dear G^l Victor de Maubourg—& his Brother Charles—

1815

F[riday] 6 January

Oh Day—for ever dreaded—yet for-ever loved! That Gave & took away my Angel Sister!—

S[unday] 8 January

Mad^e de Grandmaison—

M[onday] 9 January

Mad^e de L'aubepin—elegant & *bien elevée*

T[uesday] 10 January

Ma chère Me de Maisonneuve

W[ednesday] 11 January

M^e de *Grandmaison* makes me a most chearful & cheering visit.—

My dearest Princess d'Henin sits with me an Hour—

T[hursday] 12 January

Mr. *Bartlet* calls, with intelligence that I should write to E. by Mr. Rolston—&c

My kind M^e de *Maisonneuve* brings me my constant Friend & Favourite, *Florimond*

[Friday] 13 January

Me George de *la Fayette* calls—sensible, informed, modest, & full of merit

And mon cher excellent—admirable et amical M. *de Lally*—

S[aturday] 14 January

Florimond, Marq^s de Maubourg called, & his dear Aunt *Marie*

S[unday] 15 January

I had to day a delightful visit from M. *Gallois*—full of instruction, his mind as fraght with ideas of his own, as his memory with those of others.

M[onday] 16 January

Make 1st round of visits on recovery—

To *Mad^e d'Henin*, my honoured & loved & most invariable

Friend; to *Mad^e d'Auch*, digne Daughter of my valued M. de Lally; to Me de Tracy, all amiability, vivacity, feeling, & politeness—to Me *Victor de Maubourg*, always natural, friendly, sensible & unpretending; to—[*blank*]

Also—but without finding them, to Mme la P^{sse} *de Beauvau* & to Mme de *Chastel.*

T[uesday] 17 January

We went to day to M^e de *Gassendi*—ever unaffected, & unpretending, with real good sense, but we missed her original & worthy Husband, my Friend.

W[ednesday] 18 January

Charles *de Cadignan* calls. Leaves little to observe—neither the seduisante aimabilité ni la finesse de sa mere:—but I hope he is good though maussade

T[hursday] 19 January

By appointment came to day *Cornelia* de Boinville, now *Mrs. Turner*—the loss of her poor unhappy Father—frozen in Russia, made, to me, the meeting painful—My Alex occupied much of our discourse—she recollects all your frolics together.

F[riday] 20 January

My constant & affectionate Adrienne Chavagnac *de la Bretonière* flew into my arms this morning with the kind vivacity of all her juvenile fondness. She seems happily married to a pleasing young man. I reproached her for infidelity to my dear Alex—her early promised husband—but she rejected the fault on Thee, my Boy, for absenting thyself—

S[aturday] 21 January

Mes 2 meilleures amies hors de mon Pays charmed me with their society this morning—When the melancholy tribute of funeral rites was at length, accorded to the murdered King & Queen of France—

S[unday] 22 January

My dear Genl Victor de Maubourg spent a most pleasant hour with us—

M[onday] 23 January

M. de Bourzac, enquired much after my Alex—who is remembered here with very general kindness—

T[uesday] 24 January

The lovely & amiable P^{ss} *de Beauvau* made us an interesting little visit

T[hursday] 26 January

Mad^e de Maubourg, just arrived from sa Terre, agreeably surprised me with a visit.

F[riday] 27 January

Ma chere *Marie de Maisonneuve* gave me 2 hours—& informed me that Stephanie *d'Andreossi* was arrived from Constantinople—

S[unday] 29 January

M. de La Gallissoniere called upon me—& S.A.R. Mme d'Angouleme told M. d'A., at court, that she was reading, & with pleasure, my last ouvrage—but helas in French! & it is so miserably translated

M[onday] 30 January

I returned or made, guided by mon ami visits to the obliging *Mme Larrey*—to Mme *de Meulan* & *Mme Guizot: Me de Grandmaison Mme de La Tour du Pin*—*Mme de Montagu*—Mme de Germanie—Mme de Beauv[au]—& *Mme de Laval*—all of whom we found chez eux—& left Cards for the *D^{ss} de* Cadore; Mme *de* L'asteyre—*Mrs Ahmuty*—*Mme Allart Mme de Craon* & Mlle *d'Alpy*—*Mrs Solvyns* Mme. *de Simiane* & *Mme de Poix*—Mme *de Cadignan:* Mme *de Maubourg*—

Chez *Mme de Laval* I saw the Princess T[yszkiewic]z—soeur of the Prince Poniatousky—a woman of great intellectual merit—who was actively useful in bringing forward the new state of things. & M. le *Duc de Luxembourg*, nephew to Me de Laval, came in while we were there, & most politely began an acquaintance, which he has desired beginning from my arrival—& il *m'a comble* de *politesses*—he is truly a high bred nobleman.

With Mme de Montagu—that pattern of virtue & charity—I lamented my dear lost incomparable Mad^e de Tessé—that most highly accomplished, deeply cultivated & expansively generous of women: peace to her Manes!

W[ednesday] 1 February

I made nearly the rest of my visits—
To Ma^de *d'Astorg, Cornelia*—Me *Pinkney*—Me *de Souza*—

T[hursday] 2 February

Me *G. de La Fayette*—M^e *de l'Aubepin* All out: To Me *de Tracey*, who I had the pleasure to find & chat with—the most respectable Me *Dupont* de Nemours, in Bed from a Fall—as was her admirable husband in another apartment—but both happy in the highest degree on the restoration—Me *Charles de Maubourg*, I found also, modest & humble, & with a bent down head, as if still in one of the Prisons

S[unday] 5 February

Le *Viscount d'Agoult*, the old & faithful Friend of my Chevalier, made me a very kind & pleasant visit, & heard the history of my intended presentation, to M^e La D^ss d'A. & undertook to guide & aid for me a private Audience.

M[onday] 6 February

Mad^e Solvyns called—she is established at Anvers, très bien, with her mari, & only here for an excursion. Toujours gaie et de bon humeur. *Me Bazille* also called—

T[uesday] 7 February

I accompanied My & Thy best Friend, my Alex, a tour through la Rue St. Honoré et les Boulvards to keep Mardi Gras. I have often seen more & better masks, but never more voitures or more *monde*, or a better appearance of being pleased

Memoranda (Berg), Paris, *pre* March 1815

Written on 5 leaves (6 × 3·6″) torn (or subsequently torn) from an English Pocket Diary or Memorandum Book ruled and lettered for the year 1798. Four pages show entries in the hand of Dr. Burney (CB), evidently the original owner of the book. A heading 'A.P.d'A' indicates that Madame d'Arblay intended the journals (when completed) for her son. 5 pp.

progress from
Sunday
France previous to 19. mars

Ball Beauvaus—
D^{ss} Wellington
⟨G^t⟩ Hat
Ly. Templetown &c
Mme D'Auch
Humbert
Mme. de Praslin—
Cornelia you don't remember
How is Mr Alexander—
My Comp^{ts} to Mr. Alexander
Mlle d'Alpy
Miss Lati⟨er⟩
Rather see her than Mme de Staël
Lady Kinaird—sister of L^y [*blank*] Henry
Lord Kinaird.

France till 19. mars 1815.

Mme de Maisonneuve
Victor de Mau[bourg]
Mme victor.
Mme d'Henin
Me de Grandmaison
M. de la Gallissoniere
Mme Chastel
⟨dead—⟩
Mme de Tesse Gone!
M. de Narbonne Gone!
Mme de Simiane
M. de La Fayette
M. d'Esparron
M. Le Noir.
Mme de Poix

France till 19.[*blank*] 1815
_____

Rencontre. M. de Poix chez p^{sse} d'Henin
Congrat. hearty on charge of affairs—
Le Roi—
Famille Royale &c

France till 19. mars 1815
_____

M. La Fayette to visit my loved & ever Adored!
Meets M. Esparron
I introduce them He relates hist^{ry} of the
⟨Bona.⟩ in 100;
Clears himself
Ends greatly

France till 19. mars 1815
_____

Simiane & La Fayettes at d Henin's

Notes (Berg) for the Trèves Journal

Written on a torn scrap of paper (8 × 2·7 to 3·3″), 1 p.

Wednesday, 19th July 1815. Left *Brussels*
Thursday 20. *Liege*
— — *Aix la Chapelle*
     sleep.
21 *Friday* early to Juliers
     noon   sleep at cologn
22 *Sat^y* early to Bonn. noon   sleep at Coblentz
23 *Sunday* sleep on road
24 *Monday* Night *Treves.* Ah!!
      Sleep
Tuesday   Brussels
Wednesday Liege road
Thursday   Aix la Chapelle
Friday   Cologne
Sat^y   Coblentz
Sunday   —
Monday   Treves!—
Englishman

INDEX

to Volume viii

Members of the British nobility are listed under family names with cross-references to titles.

Members of the French and European nobility are listed under the name and title by which they are best known, with cross-references to other names or titles.

Women are listed under their married names, with cross-references to maiden names and earlier married names.

In listing members of family groups the alphabet is normally disregarded in order to clarify family relationships.

Short biographies or concentrations of biographical information are marked by numbers in bold face.

Index

Index

V. Works written or in progress;
editorial work.

I. CHIEF EVENTS OF HER LIFE
(ANNUAL OUTLINES)

1814: In Richmond stores effects
from Camilla Cottage and in
November sets out with her husband for Paris. On the way to
Dover calls on her nephew Charles
Parr Burney at Greenwich and her
brother Charles at Deptford.
Suffers sea sickness and at Calais,
the shock of the injury sustained
by M. d'A. At Paris slowly recovers
from the physical and mental
strains of the year.

1815: In Paris social life, including
visits from friends and her presentation at the Tuileries to the
duchesse d'Angoulême, is disrupted, like that of all Paris, by the
return of Napoleon from Elba.
She joins the princesse d'Hénin in
an adventurous flight to Brussels,
is received by a former *émigrée*
known to her in England, shares
for a time an apartment with the
princesse. On the arrival of her
husband, who had fled with his
company of the Garde du Corps
to Ghent, she settles at 1358
Marché au bois. Determined to
remain on the Continent as long
as her husband was on military
duty and in danger (see pp. 108–9,
145, 223, 250, **321**), she remains
in Brussels. There in June she hears
the guns at Waterloo and witnesses
in the streets some of the prelimi-
nary scenes and the ghastly
aftermath of battle.

Learning in July of an injury
sustained by her husband at
Tréves she sets out alone by
public conveyance across France
and through the Prussian Rhineland to join him. When he is
sufficiently recovered they traverse
occupied France to Paris, say farewell to friends and embark for
England with the view of aiding his
recovery at Bath.

Index

Index

Beauvau, Nathalie-Henriette-Victur-nienne de, *née* de Rochechouart de Mortemart (1774–1854), princesse de Beauvau-Craon, wife of the preceding, **31 n.**;
beauty, manners, lineage of, 345; dame du palais de l'impératrice, 31 n., 343–5;
Napoleonic favours, 150 n.;
reciprocated visits, ball, 149, 437, 547, 549, 552.

Beauvau, François-Victurnien-*Charles*-Just de (1793–1864), 4th prince de Beauvau-Craon, son of the above, 24, 343, 346–7, 539, 547.

Beauvau, Lucie-Virginie, *née* de Choi-seul-Praslin (1795–1834), princesse de, wife of the preceding, 24, 346 n., 347.

Beauvau, Edmond-Henri-Étienne-Victurnien de (1795–1861), brother of the 4th prince (*supra*), 24, 343, 346–7, 539, 547.

Beauvau, Henriette-*Gabrielle*-Apolline de, sister of the preceding. *See* Talon, vicomtesse de.

Beauvau, Nathalie-Irène-Marie-Victurnienne de, sister of the pre-ceding. *See* Le Lièvre, Nathalie.

Beauvillier, Emma-Victurienne-Nathalie de, *née* de Rochechouart (1790–1824), duchesse de Saint-Aignan, 385.

Bedingfeld, Charlotte Georgiana, *née* Jerningham (*c.* 1770–1834), 413 n.

BELGIANS, the:
apathy, characteristic placidity of, 212, 254–5, 283, 393, 423, 425, 431, 436, 455;
customs, manners, 405, 455, 485;
humanity, hospitality of, 273, 422, 450;
political uncertainties, divided loyalties, 59 n., 67 n., 76 n., **283–4**, 384;
history of, works by Louis Dewez and Edmund Wheatley (q.v.).

BELGIUM
I. as refuge, flights to. *See* Brussels and Antwerp.
II. *Districts, cities, fortresses, towns, traversed or mentioned*:
Alost (q.v.); Antwerp (q.v.); Arlon,

244 n.; Atot (Ath or AAth), 224 n., 389; Bertrix, 187; Breda, 76 n.; Bruges, 77, 78, 80 n., 81, 90 n., 116, 397; Brussels (q.v.); Chapelle-Saint-Lambert, 323 n.; Charleroi (q.v.); Chimay, 154; Courtray, 231; Furnes, 230 n., 231; Gembloux, 216 n.; Ghent (q.v.); Ghistelles, 79, 98, 397; Grammont, 152 n., 224 n.; Jemappes (q.v.); Liege (q.v.); Louvain, 330 n., 335, 338, 458; Malines (or Mechlin), 212; Mechlin lace, 261 n.; Menin, 75, 82 n., 116; Mons (q.v.); Namur (q.v.); Nivelles, 237 n.; Ostend (q.v.); Paliseul, 232; Quatre Bras (q.v.); Roeselare, 118 n.; Termonde, 127 n.; Tirlemont, 485; Tournay (q.v.); Waterloo (q.v.); Wavre, 216, 237, 446; Ypres (q.v.).

Bellerophen, H.M.S., the, 459.

Bell's Weekly Messenger, 223 n., 253 n.

Benfield, Paul (*c.* 1740–1810), banker, 121 n.

Benrath, Heinrich, *Aachen, Burtscheid . . .*, 490 n.

Berry, Charles-Ferdinand d'Artois (1778–1820), duc de, 117, 242;
military action, 56 n., 57 n., 95 n., 96, 106, 118, 250, 354 n.;
defection of his forces, 55 n.;
flight, route of, 61 n., 80 n., 87 n., 88, 89 n., 90 n., 117;
disbands the Maison du Roi, 118, 395, 398;
débâcle at Béthune (q.v.);
mentioned, 40 n., 55 n., 356, 395 n.

Berthier, Louis-Alexandre (1753–1815), prince de Wagram, prince de Neu-châtel, maréchal de France, 87, 117, 243.

Bertier de Sauvigny, Anne-Ferdinand-Louis de (1782–1864), comte de, *commissaire*, 230 n., 231.

Bertrand, Fanny Elizabeth, *née* Dillon (1777–1862), wife of the following, 221 n., 399.

Bertrand, Henri-Gratien (1773–1844), comte, grand maréchal du palais, follows Napoleon into exile, 221, 399.

Index

Burney, the Revd. Charles Parr (*cont.*):
arrives in Brussels, 334, 337–9, 456,
462, 471, 479, 482.

Burney, Frances Bentley, *née* Young (*c.*
1792–1878), wife of the preceding,
36, **37 n.**, 105;

Burney, Frances Anne, daughter of the
above. *See* Wood, Frances Anne.

Burney, Rosetta d'Arblay, sister of the
preceding. *See* Wood, Rosetta.

Burney, the Revd. Charles Edward
(1815–1907), brother of the preceding, Archdeacon of Middlesex, birth
of, 335.

BURNEY, Charles Rousseau (1747–
1819), musician and music teacher,
FBA's cousin and brother-in-law,
at Turnham Green, 15, 17, 106, 203,
279, 335, 458, 462.

Burney, Esther, *née* Burney (1748–
1832), wife of the preceding,
FBA's sister [EBB], 28, 32–3, 35,
64, 66 n., 122, 124, 235, 456, 462,
467;
Letters to, Nos. 838, 865, 907;
with FBA, residuary legatee of CB's
estate, 41 n., 155, 203, 279–80,
335;
and arthritic hand, 461, 473;
and AA, 15, 458, 462–3.

Burney, Hannah Maria, daughter of the
above. *See* Bourdois, Hannah Maria.

Burney, the Revd. Richard Allen
(1773–1836), brother of the preceding, Rector of Rimpton, with
Brightwell, 281.

Burney, Frances (1776–1808), sister of
the preceding, 16, 106, 193.

Burney, Sophia Elizabeth (1777–1856),
sister of the preceding, 16, 106, 288.

Burney, Cecilia Charlotte Esther
(1788–1821), sister of the preceding,
16, **17**, 106, 282.

Burney, Amelia Maria (1792–1868),
sister of the preceding, 16, 106.

BURNEY, James (1750–1821), F.R.S.,
Rear-Admiral, FBA's brother, of
26 James Street, Buckingham
Gate [JB], 12, 16–17, 23, 63, 93,
101, 107–8, 121, 123, 130, 203,
233 n., 234, 236 n., 398, 456, 462,
473, 545;

Letters to, Nos. 842, 853, 863, 918;
characteristic hospitality, 231, 541;
entertains AA, 115, 117, 119, 123,
155, 193, 213, 236, 281, 287, 304,
312, 316, 324, 329, 541;
resents Hazlitt's review of *The
Wanderer*, 317;
writes to, **317 n.**;
'History of the Buccaneers of
America', part of *A Chronological
History of the Voyages and Discoveries in the South Sea or Pacific
Ocean*, 29;
intro. to, Barnes, Malcolm, 29 n.

Burney, Sarah, *née* Payne (1758–1832),
wife of the preceding, 16, 29, 31, 64,
102, 233 n., 234.

Burney Martin Charles (1788–1852),
attorney, son of the above, 16–17,
29, 31, 64, 102, 281, 294, 321, 462;
acts for FBA and EBB, 63, 102, 130,
155, 192–3, 203, 236, 281, 334,
458–9.

Burney, Sarah, sister of the preceding.
See Payne, Sarah.

BURNEY, Sarah Harriet (1772–1844),
novelist, FBA's half-sister [SHB],
17, 23, 64, 125, 235, 290.

Burney, Susanna Elizabeth. *See* Phillips,
Susanna Elizabeth.

Burney, Edward Francis (1760–
1848), artist, FBA's cousin, 16, 290.

Burney, Ann, sister of the preceding.
See Hawkins, Ann.

Burney, Elizabeth Warren *called* 'Blue'
(1755–1832), sister of the preceding,
17.

Burney, Rebecca, sister of the preceding. *See* Sandford, Rebecca.

BURNEY, William (1793–1878), Captain of the 44th Regiment of Foot,
at Brussels, 314–15, 320, 443 n.,
454–6.

Butler, Samuel (1612–80), poet, *Hudibras*, 277, 323.

Byron, George Gordon (1788–1824),
sixth Lord:
and Caroline Lamb (q.v.), 416 n.;
reads *The Wanderer*, 317;
Childe Harold's Pilgrimage, 226 n.
biography of, by Leslie A. Marchand
(q.v.).

Index

Chambers, Sarah. *See* Haggit, Sarah.

'Chant françois' in *Chansonnier royal, ou Passetems des bon Français*, 131–2.

Chapman, the Revd. Benedict (1770–1852), tutor, Caius College, Cambridge, 20, 21–2, 25, 114.

Charlemagne, Charles the Great, or Charles I (742–814), King of the Franks, tomb of, 490.

Charleroi, Napoleon reaches, 212 n., 216 n., 239, 423.

Charles X (1757–1836), King of the French (1824–30), as comte d'Artois, 6, 130 n.;
establishment of, 6 n., 303;
military and diplomatic activity, 24 n., 55 n., 61 n., 64 n., 70 n., 80 n., 87 n., 89 n., 90 n., 117–18, 217 n., 240 n., 250, 266 n., 268 n., 272, 370;
incidental mention, 39 n., 57 n., 96 n., 230 n.

Charlotte Augusta, Princess (1796–1817), daughter of George IV of England, 145.

Charlotte Augusta Matilda, H.R.H. Princess Royal of England. *See* Würtemberg, Queen of.

Charlotte Sophia, H.R.H. (1744–1818), Queen of England:
as 'the Magnolia', 11, 150, 219–20;
manners, presence, 414;
birthday of, 9–10;
and Princess Elizabeth: visits her cottage at Old Windsor, 201 n., 219–20;
and the duchesse d'Angoulême, 144;
and FBA (q.v.), kindnesses to:
grants audience to, 3 n.;
offers lessons in German, 514;
arranges presentation to the duchesse d'Angoulême, 9, 38–9, 52;
continues pension, 288 n.;
presents with a watch, 69 n.;
approves correspondence with H.R.H. the Princess Elizabeth 3, 7 n., 52;
mentioned, 1 n., 9, 208 n.

Charlotte, Queen, daughters of. *See* Princesses of England.

Chastel, Catherine-Françoise, *née* Garaudé (b. *c.* 1763), 552.

Chastel de Boinville, Cornelia, daughter of the following. *See* Turner, Cornelia.

Chastel de Boinville, Harriet, *née* Collins (*c.* 1773–1847), wife of the following, 144;
and Shelley at Bracknell, 30 n.

Chastel de Boinville, Jean-Baptiste (1756–1813), 30 n., 144 n.

Chastel de Boinville, Alexandre (1785–*post* 1849) *dit* de Fresne (or Dufresne), natural son of the preceding, 144, 173–4, 210, 240, 249, 260, 284, 304, 327.

Chastel d'Oriocourt, Anne-Félicité, *née* Canot (b. *c.* 1770), wife of the following, 350, 537, 541 n., 547, 549.

Chastel d'Oriocourt, Antoine-Louis-Benjamin (1761–*post* 1831), 350 n.

Chastel d'Oriocourt, Nicole-Augustine-Angélique, daughter of the above. *See* Nettancourt, Nicole-Augustine-Angélique.

Chastel d'Oriocourt, Catherine-Louise-Félicité, sister of the preceding. *See* Luchaise, Catherine-Louise-Félicité.

Chastelien du Mesnil, Denis-Victoire. *See* Germigney, Denis-Victoire.

Chateaubriand, Céleste de, *née* Buisson la Vigne (1774–1847), wife of the following, 388–90, 392, 395.

Chateaubriand, François-René (1768–1848), vicome de, 387;
and Napoleon, 391–2;
at Tournai, Ath, and Brussels, 59 n., 74 n., 387–92, 395, 401–2;
political alignments, activities, and appointments, 80 n., 143 n., 160 n., 360 n., 388 n., 402.
Works:
Atala . . ., 388 n., 389, 391;
Essai historique . . ., 390 n.;
Le Génie du Christianisme . . ., 389 n., 390;
Itinéraire de Paris à Jérusalem . . ., 389 n.;
Les Martyrs . . ., 391;
Mémoires d'Outre Tombe, 74 n., 388 n., 391 n., 402 n.;
Rapport sur l'état de la France . . . (1815), 140 n.

Index

Courtown, Earl and Countess of. *See* Stopford, James and Lady Mary.
Crewe, Frances Anne, *née* Greville (1748–1818), Lady, 38 n., 232, 336, 425 n.;
friend of CB, 37;
Crewe Hall, 37 n.
Crisp, Samuel 'Daddy' (*c.* 1707–83), FB's early friend and mentor, compared to Gabriel Bazille (q.v.), 536–7.
Croy-Havre, Josephe-Anne-Auguste-Maximilien de (1744–1839), duc d'Havre, prince de Saint-Empire, 98, 117, 150, 369.
Cunchy, Alphonse (*fl.* 1821), comte de, 130 n.
Cunchy, Ermelina, comtesse de, *née* Liedekerke-Beaufort (1791–1871), wife of the preceding, 130 n.

Dalmatie, duc de. *See* Soult, Nicolas-Jean.
Damas d'Antigny, Diane-Adélaïde de. *See* Simiane, comtesse de.
Damas-Crux, Anne-*Simonne*-Félicité, *née* de Serent (1772–1848), duchesse de, wife of the following, 11 n., 42 n.
Damas-Crux, Étienne-Charles (1751–1846), duc de, 42 n.
Danby, Mary. *See* Harcourt, Countess of.
Danoots, Daniel, & Son, bankers in Brussels, 63 n., 169, 205–6, 213, 259, 275, 307, 457, 468, 479, 481, 512.
'Darby and Joan' or 'The Joys of Love never forgot. A Song', 29.
Davout, Louis-Nicolas (1770–1823), duc d'Auerstadt, prince d'Eckmühl, maréchal de France, 76, 221, 297, 304, 307 n.
Davy, Martin (1763–1839), D.D., Master of Caius College, 22.
Day, Benedicta, *née* Ramus (d. 20 May 1811), wife of the following, 208 n.
Day, Sir John (d. 1808), of Bengal, Advocate, 208 n.
Decazes, Elie (1780–1860), duc, lawyer, ironmaster, diplomat, 530 n., 531.
de Fresne. *See* Chastel de Boinville, Alexandre.
Delamorre, Charles Henri, *Annuaire topographique et politique du department*

de la Sarre pour l'an 1810, 159 n., 168 n., 464 n.
Denmark, 319 n.;
commitment to war, 183, 191.
Deprez, M., M. d'A's groom, 54–5, 349–50, 352, 355–6.
Deprez, Mme., (?)wife of the preceding, 'femme de charge' of d'Arblay's apartments, Paris, 65–70 *passim*, 143, 303, 328, 338, 358, 362.
Deptford, Kent, 35;
as CB Jr.'s living, 115, 192, 540.
Desandrouin, Julie-Caroline. *See* Liedekerke-Beaufort, Julie-Caroline.
Desmier d'Archiac de Saint-Simon, Louis-Étiennette. *See* Beauvau, Louise-Étiennette, princesse de Craon.
Dessein, M. (*fl.* 1764) and Mme, hoteliers at Calais, 3, 4, 13.
DESTUTT de Tracy, Antoine-Louis-Claude (1754–1836), marquis de Tracy, 47 n.
Destutt de Tracy, Émilie-Pérette-Antoinie, *née* de Durfort de Civrac (1754–1824), wife of the preceding, 47, 536, 547, 549, 551.
Destutt de Tracy, Françoise-*Émilie*, daughter of the above. *See* Lafayette, Françoise-*Émilie* de.
Destutt de Tracy, Augustine-Émilie, sister of the preceding. *See* Laubespin, comtesse de.
Dewez, Louis-Dieudonné-Joseph (1760–1834), *Histoire générale de la Belgique . . .*, 207, 417, 420, 490 n.
Dibdin, Thomas John (1771–1841), *The British Raft* (1797), phrases or epithets from, cited, 10, 22, 30, 35, 40, 152, 214, 219, 238, 261, 292, 334, 468.
Dibich-Zabalkansky, Ivan Ivanovich (1785–1831). *See* Diebitsch, Johannes (*below*).
Dictionnaire du département de la Moselle, 291 n.
Dictionary of the Vulgar Tongue, 333 n.
Diebitsch, Johannes Karl Friedrich Anton (1785–1831), Russian field-marshal, 270.
Dietz, Joseph, *Topographie der Stadt Bonn . . .*, 500 n.

Index

FRANCE
I. characteristics, manners, customs, ways of life, 367, 370, 376; compared to England, 8 n., 16 n., 45 n., 348; political alignments. *See sub* Louis XVIII, Napoleon I, and, Orléans, duc de. occupation of, 479, 504, 529, 533–5; *Travels in*, ed. Maxwell, Constantia, 14 n.

II. *Cities, towns, villages, departments, traversed or mentioned*: Abbeville, 59 n., 86, 87 n., 92; Alsace, 338; Amiens (q.v.); Ardennes, 408 n.; Arras (q.v.); Auxerre, 57 n.; Auxonne, 158 n.; Bavay, 239 n.; Bayonne, 10 n.; Beauvais, 58 n., 59 n., 61 n., 74 n., 87, 341 n.; Besançon, 149; Béthune (q.v.); Bordeaux (q.v.); Boulogne, 34; Bressuires, 175; Brittany, 48 n.; Calais (q.v.); Cambrai (q.v.); Cateau-Cambresis, 237 n., 258; Cette or Sète, 72 n.; Châlons-sur-Marne, 533 n.; Champagne, 553 n.; Châtillon-sur-Seine, 181 n.; Chaumont, 86 n.; Cherbourg, 48; Chimay, 154; Compiègne, 271, 357; Douai, 59 n., 379; Doullens, 59 n.; Dunkirk, 57 n., 198, 230 n., 397, 455; Estaire, 61 n.; Fontainebleau (q.v.); Gonesse, 295 n.; Guienne, 94; Haguenau (q.v.); Haute-Loire, 143 n.; Havre, Le, 272; Hayange, 158 n., 197 n.; Issy or Issy-les-Moulineaux, 306 n.; Joigny (q.v.); Languedoc, 72 n.; Laon, 221 n.; Lens, Pas-de-Calais, 373 n.; Lille (q.v.); Loire, or Haute-Loire, 143, 338, Army of, 297 n.; Lons-le-Saunier, 80 n.; Louvres, 295 n.; Lyons, 55 n., 97 n., 342, 348; Malplaquet, 264 n.; Marseilles, 135 n., 250 n., 268 n., 420 n.; Maubeuge, 175 n., 251, 263; Mayenne, 143; Meaux, 341 n., 534; Melun, 56 n., **116**, 117 n., 341 n., 354; Metz (q.v.);

Mouchy, 365 n., 370; Nancy, 271, 295 n.; Neufchâteau, 187, 232; Nîmes, 71 n.; Nivernais, 230 n.; Noailles, 61 n., 370; Normandy, 202 n., 391 n., 539 n.; Orchies (q.v.); Paris (q.v.); Parthenay, 175; Pas-de-Calais, 74 n., 87 n.; Péronne, 263; Picquigny or Pécquigny, 130 n.; Plombières-les-Bains, 327 n., 546; Poix, 59 n., 61 n., 370; 'Pont-des-Mathis', 175 n.; Pont-sur-Yonne, 85 n.; Provence, 72 n., 97 n.; Puiseaux, 61 n.; Rambouillet, 169 n.; Rochefort, 272 n., 295 n., 297 n.; Rochelle, La, 55 n.; Rocroi, 74 n.; Rodemack, 291; Roye, 59 n., 92, 267 n., 277 n., 284, 304, 370; Saint-Cyr (q.v.); Saint-Just, 370; Saint-Pierre-des-Echaubrognes, 181 n.; Saint-Pol, 61 n., 95; Sarreguemines or Saarqemünd, 245; Sedan, 167–8, 419; Seine-et-Marne, 143 n.; Senlis (q.v.); Solre-le-Château, 250; Somme, the, 74 n., 130 n.; Thionville, **157**, 269, 291 n., **530**; Toul (q.v.); Toulon, 135 n., 210 n.; Toulouse (q.v.); Tours, Touraine, 14, 28; Trèves or Trier (q.v.); Valenciennes, 251, 263, 297; Vendée, the (q.v.); Verdun, the fortress, 121 n.; Vertus, 533 n.; Villejuif, 7 n., 56 n.; Vizille, 267 n.; Yeu, Île d', 97 n.; Yonne, 328 n.

FRANCIS, Charlotte, daughter of the following, FBA's niece [CFBt]. *See* Barrett, Charlotte.

Francis, Charlotte Ann, *née* Burney, FBA's sister, wife of the following. *See* Broome, Charlotte Ann.

Francis, Clement (*c.* 1744–92), surgeon at Aylsham, Norfolk, 16 n., 23 n.; his will, 415 n.

Francis, the Revd. Clement Robert (1792–1829), son of the above, FBA's nephew [CF], 15, 16, 25, 32–3, 115, 545;

575

Index

Index

and Lally-Tolendal, comte de (q.v.);
shares ménage, 72 n., 364–6;
flight, Paris to Brussels, 2 (map
showing route), 57, 62, **72**, 78–9,
85–8, 91–2, 94, 98, 280, 351,
353–92 *passim*, 434;
in Brussels: shares residence, **66–7**,
83, 121, 134–5, **394**, 404, 409, 427;
political interests and activity, 145 n.,
199–200, 345, **348, 412**, **417**;
waits on the duchesse d'Angoulême
(q.v.) at Ghent, 417.
Orléanist leanings, 145 n., 291–3;
flight, Brussels to Antwerp, 212, 240,
254, 426, 432, 446;
and FBA (q.v.);
mention, 42–553 *passim*.
Henri IV (1553–1610), King of France,
132, 271, 304.
Henri or 'Henry', M. d'A's stable-boy
at Trèves, 145, 194, 232, 464, 516,
521, 523, 529.
Henry, Lady Emily Elizabeth, *née*
Fitzgerald (1778–1856), 552.
Henry V (1387–1422), King of England,
in France, 535.
Héricourt, Achmet-Marie de Servin,
comte d' (1819–1871) and Alexandre
Godin, *Les Rues d'Arras*, 375 n.
Hesse-Cassel, 157, 158 n., 160;
commitment to war, 182, 191.
See also under commanders, Friedrich
Wilhelm I, Engelhardt and Müller.
Elector of. *See* Friedrich Wilhelm I.
Fulda, 130 n.
See also sub Losch.
Hesse-Darmstadt: Mayence (Mainz),
244.
Hesse Homburg, Landgravine of. *See*
Elizabeth, H.R.H. Princess of
England.
Hickey, William (1746–1809), *Memoirs
of . . .*, 208 n.
Hill, Rowland (1772–1842), Viscount,
general, **xv**, 64 n.
Hill, Sir Thomas Noel (1784–1832),
K.C.B., **xv**, 64 n.
Hill, Constance, *Fanny Burney at the
Court of Queen Charlotte*, 131 n.
Hoare, Messrs., bankers, Fleet Street,
15–16, 36, 63, 104, 115, 124, 213,
290, 334, 545.

Hobhouse, John Cam (1786–1869),
Baron Broughton, *xx*;
Recollections . . ., and *Substance of
some Letters . . .*, 143 n.–4 n.,
187 n.
Hohenzollern:
Benrath, château of, 204–5 n., 227;
Prague, 157 n., 160 n.
Holland, Lord. *See* Fox, Henry Richard
Vassall.
Holland, 76 n., 155 n., 228 n.;
Utrecht, 359 n.
See Netherlands, the Kingdom of the.
Homer, 34 n., 145.
Hope, Lady Jane. *See* Wallace, Lady
Jane (Dundas).
Horace, Quintus Horatius Flaccus
(65–8 B.C.), Roman poet, 253 n.
Host, Mlle. *See* Leclerc, Mme.
Houx, Joseph-Hyacinthe-Charles du
(1734–1827), marquis de Vioménil,
royalist, 88, 97 n.;
raises Infantry volunteers, 86 n., 349,
387;
at Tournai, 59 n., 387–8.
Howard, Lady Georgiana Dorothy,
née Cavendish (1783–1858), Countess
of Carlisle, as a child at Bath,
417.
Hugo, Joseph-Léopold-*Sigisbert* (1773–
1828), général, 157 n.
Hugo, Victor-Marie (1802–85), author,
son of the preceding, 157 n.
Humphrey, Duke, proverbial, 231.
Hunter, Catherine, *See* Cadignan,
comtesse de.
Hurst. *See* Ursel.

Ilfracombe, Devonshire, FBA's ad-
ventures (of 1817) at, 517 n.
India, Bengal Establishment, 64 n.,
208 n.
Ireland:
Burney antecedents in, 315;
'the Irish business' (CB's mortgage
on the farm of Belcotton, co.
Louth), **102**, 106, 155, 203, 281;
see also sub Phillips, Molesworth.
Hiberians characterized, 430.
ITALY:
Austrian forces in, 48 n., 182, 190,
208 n;

579

Index

Index

Index

Humbert-Frédéric-Arthur (1790–1816), son of the above, **67**, 369, 385, 416, 552.

La Tour du Pin de Gouvernet, Marie-Charlotte-Alix, sister of the preceding. *See* Liedekerke-Beaufort, comtesse de.

La Tour du Pin de Gouvernet, Cécile-Élisabeth-Charlotte (1800–17), sister of the preceding, 254, 482.

LATOUR-Maubourg, Marie-Charles-*César*-Florimond de Fay de (1758–1831), marquis de, 24 n.; serves under Napoleon, 48, 285 n.; pair des Cent-Jours, 49 n., 210, 258, 285 n., 303, 329, 351, 362; family history, by Joseph du Teil (q.v.).

Latour-Maubourg, Marie-Charlotte-Hippolyte de Fay de, *née* Pinault de Thenelles (d. 1837), wife of the preceding, 541 n., 550.

Latour-Maubourg, Just-Pons-*Florimond* de Fay de (1781–1837), baron, marquis de, eldest son of the above, diplomat, 24, 548.

Latour-Maubourg, Éléonor-Marie-Florimonde de Fay de, sister of the preceding. *See* Pinckney-Horry, Éléonor.

Latour-Maubourg, Marie-*Victor* Nicolas de Fay de (1768–1850), marquis de, général, brother of César (*supra*), royalist, 24, **24 n.–5 n.**, 49 n., 57 n.–8 n., 58, 85–6, 91, 258, 285, 303, 351, 360, 387; wounded at Leipsic, 360; waits on Louis XVIII, 86; raises volunteers, 86 n.; Ambassador to England, 531, 537–8; and the d'Arblays, 531, 535, 541 n., 547, 549, 552.

Latour-Maubourg, Petronella-Jacoba de Fay de, *née* van Rijssel (1772–1844), wife of the preceding: at the approach of Napoleon, 359–60; visits the d'Arblays, 547, 549, 552.

Latour-Maubourg, Jules-*Charles*-César de Fay de (1775–1846), comte de, brother of César (*supra*), **57**, 58 n., 351; delivers M. d'A's note, 72, 86, 91, 117, 359–61.

Latour-Maubourg, Anastasie-Louise-Pauline de Fay de, *née* du Motier de Lafayette (1777–1863), wife of the preceding, 361, 551.

Latour-Maubourg, Célestine-Louise-Henriette, daughter of the preceding. *See* Brigode, baronne de.

Latour-Maubourg, Louise, sister of the preceding. *See* Perron de Saint-Martin, baronne de.

Latour-Maubourg, Marie-Françoise Élisabeth de Fay de, sister of César (*supra*). *See* Maisonneuve, Marie Bidault de.

Laubespin, Augustine-Émilie-Victorine de Battefort, *née* Destutt de Tracy (1787–1850), comtesse de, 548, 551.

Lauragais de Saint-Poulet, comte de. *See* La Tour d'Auvergne, Joseph-Denis-Édouard-Bernard de.

Lauriston, marquis de. *See* Law, Jacques-Alexandre-Bernard.

Laval. *See* Montmorency-Laval.

Law, Jacques-Alexandre-Bernard (1768–1828), marquis de Lauriston, 61 n., 89 n., **96 n.**

Léautaud-Donnine, Louis-Auguste-Marie-Xavier de (1766–1830), comte de, maréchal de camp, 248.

Leclerc, Mme, *née* Host (*fl.* 1815), of Tréves, 522–3.

Leclerc, M., (?)général, 522 n.

⟨Legendre⟩, M., of Lille, 326;

Leigh and Sotheby, auctioneers, 16, 36, 106.

Le Lièvre, Auguste-François-Joseph (1780–1826), chevalier de Lagrange et de l'Empire, 346 n., 347.

Le Lièvre, Nathalie-Irène-Marie-Victurnienne, *née* de Beauvau (c. 1798–1852), 346–7, 539.

Lemierre d'Argy, A. J., co-translator of *The Wanderer*, 11 n.

Lemprière, John, D.D., *Bibliotheca Classica* . . ., 27 n.–8 n.

Lennox, Charles (1764–1819), 4th Duke of Richmond and Lennox, 226 n.

Lennox, Lady Charlotte, *née* Gordon (1768–1842), wife of the preceding, gives ball at Brussels, 226, 324.

583

Index

LOUIS XVIII (*cont.*):
   progress towards Paris, entry, 267 n., 268, 274, **277 n.**, 284, 287, 296, 298, 304 n., 307, 319; new ministry, 319, 327–8, 415–16, 460, 531 n.;
   decrees, 297 n.;
   proclamations, 258, 307;
   and the d'Arblays:
   FBA's presentation to, 49–50; receives M. d'A, 147 (*see also sub* M. d'A).

Louis, Joseph-Dominique (1755–1837), laicized abbé, diplomat, ministre des Finances, 319, 327, **415–16.**

Louise, Auguste-Wilhelmina-Amalie, *née* Princess of Mecklenberg-Strelitz (1766–1810), Queen of Prussia, 461.

Louis-Marie-Thérèse, *née* d'Orléans (1812–50), Queen of Belgium, 55.

Lubrez-Pachonski, Jan, *Legiony Polskie, 1794–1807* . . ., 47 n.–8 n.

Lucan, Earl of. *See* Bingham, Sir Charles.

Luchaise, Catherine-Louise-Félicité, *née* Chastel d'Oriocourt (1802–*post* 1829), 350.

Luxembourg, the duke of. *See* Montmorency-Luxembourg.

Luxemburg, the duchy of, 232–3.

Luxemburg, fortified city:
   Prussian military base, 111, 112, 126, 127 n., 137 n., 148, 187 n., 231, 243 n., 245, 284, 291 n., 298, 337, 406, 411, 456, 479–80, 486; *commissaire* at, *see sub* M. d'A.

Luynes, Guyonne-Élisabeth-Joséphine d'Albert, duchesse de, *née* de Montmorency-Laval (1755–1830), 538.

Lys, the river, 61 n., 80 n.

Macartney, Frances. *See* Greville, Frances.

Macdonald, Étienne-Jacques-Joseph-Alexandre (1765–1840), duc de Tarente, général, 55 n., **87**, 117 n., 243.

Macirone, Francis (1780–*post* 1823), soldier of fortune, aide-de-camp to Murat (q.v.), 297.

Mackintosh, Sir James (1765–1832),

Scottish philosopher, politician, and lawyer, reads *The Wanderer*, 317.

Mainwaring-Ellerker, Elizabeth (1751–1831), of Richmond, 109.

Mainwaring-Ellerker, Harriet (1759–1842), sister of the preceding, 109 n.

Maison, Nicolas-Joseph (1771–1840), maréchal de France, 86 n., 117 n.

MAISON DU ROI, **23 n.**, 57, 58 n.;
   companies or units of, **75 n.**, 78 n., **87 n.**, 95 n., 98 n., **117**, 118 n., 137 n., 167 n., 175 n., 304, 341 n., 343, 368–9;
   review of, 56, 58 n., 63, 72, 84, 91, 117;
   postings of, **75 n.**, 341 n., 343, 351, 354 n., 360 n., 361, 368–9;
   loyalty of, 75 n., 95 n.;
   flight from Paris, **56 n., 58 n., 59 n., 61**, 71–3, **87 n.**, 88, **89 n.**, 95 n., 104, 106, 117, 118, **229–30**, 250, 280, 351, 355, 368–9, 394;
   at Béthune, 95 n., 106, 118, 377 n., 398;
   partially disbanded, **61 n., 89**, 97, 118, 229–30, 310, 395;
   in Belgium, Alost, Ghent, Brussels, Ypres, **61**, 101, 224–5, 227, 239, 250, 260, 265, 396;
   return, with King, to Paris, 228, 250, 260, 265, 314;
   members of, mentioned, 113 n.;
   future status, 310.
   See also under military career of M. d'A.

MAISONNEUVE, Gérard-Joseph Bidault de (*fl.* 1770–1800), 19 n.

Maisonneuve, Marie-Françoise-Élisabeth Bidault de, *née* de Fay de Latour-Maubourg (1770–1850), wife of the preceding, FBA's friend, **19**, 24, 85, 285, 303, 348, 351, 358–62, 402, 472, 531, **535, 537,** 541 n., 547–8, 550, 552;

Maisonneuve, Frédéric-Gérard-Bénoni-César, 'Maxime' Bidault de (1797–1869), son of the above, **24**, 85, 359 547.

Maitland, Sir Frederick Lewis (1777–1839), R.N., captain of H.M.S. *Bellerophon* (q.v.), 459–60.

Index

Index

Index

Index

Index